UK, EU AND GLOBAL ADMINISTRATIVE LAW

Paul Craig's analysis of UK, EU and global administrative law examines the challenges facing each system and reveals the commonalities in and differences between their foundational assumptions. The challenges which they face may be particular to that legal order, endemic to any legal system of administrative law or the result of interaction between the three systems. The inter-relationship between the three levels is important. The legal and practical reality is that developments at one level can have an impact on the other two. Legal doctrine fashioned at the national level may therefore inform developments in EU and global administrative law. The doctrine thus created may then function symbiotically, shaping developments within a domestic legal order. The inter-relationship is equally marked from the regulatory perspective, since many such provisions originate at the global or EU level.

PAUL CRAIG is Professor of English Law at the University of Oxford and a Fellow of St John's College. He specialises in administrative and EU law, and has authored leading works in these areas.

UK, EU AND GLOBAL ADMINISTRATIVE LAW

Foundations and Challenges

PAUL CRAIG

CAMBRIDGE
UNIVERSITY PRESS

CAMBRIDGE
UNIVERSITY PRESS

University Printing House, Cambridge CB2 8BS, United Kingdom

Cambridge University Press is part of the University of Cambridge.

It furthers the University's mission by disseminating knowledge in the pursuit of education, learning and research at the highest international levels of excellence.

www.cambridge.org
Information on this title: www.cambridge.org/9781107125124

First published 2015

A catalogue record for this publication is available from the British Library

Library of Congress Cataloguing in Publication data
Craig, P. P. (Paul P.), author.
UK, EU and global administrative law : foundations and challenges / Paul Craig.
pages cm
Partially based on the Hamlyn Lectures, 2014. – ECIP galley.
Includes index.
ISBN 978-1-107-12512-4 (Hardback) – ISBN 978-1-107-56308-7 (Paperback)
1. Administrative law. 2. Administrative law–Great Britain. 3. Administrative law–European Union countries. 4. International agencies–Law and legislation.
I. Title.
K3400.C73 2015
342′.06–dc23 2015020011

ISBN 978-1-107-12512-4 Hardback
ISBN 978-1-107-56308-7 Paperback

CONTENTS

The Hamlyn Trust

The Hamlyn Trust owes its existence today to the will of the late Miss Emma Warburton Hamlyn of Torquay, who died in 1941 at the age of eighty. She came of an old and well-known Devon family. Her father, William Bussell Hamlyn, practised in Torquay as a solicitor and JP for many years, and it seems likely that Miss Hamlyn founded the trust in his memory. Emma Hamlyn was a woman of strong character, intelligent and cultured; well-versed in literature, music and art; and a lover of her country. She travelled extensively in Europe and Egypt, and apparently took considerable interest in the law and ethnology of the countries and cultures that she visited. An account of Miss Hamlyn by Professor Chantal Stebbings of the University of Exeter may be found, under the title 'The Hamlyn Legacy', in Volume 42 of the published lectures.

Miss Hamlyn bequeathed the residue of her estate on trust in terms which, it seems, were her own. The wording was thought to be vague, and the will was taken to the Chancery Division of the High Court, which in November 1948 approved a Scheme for the administration of the trust. Paragraph 3 of the Scheme, which follows Miss Hamlyn's own wording, is as follows:

> The object of the charity is the furtherance by lectures or otherwise among the Common People of the United Kingdom of Great Britain and Northern Ireland of the

> knowledge of the Comparative Jurisprudence and Ethnology of the Chief European countries including the United Kingdom, and the circumstances of the growth of such jurisprudence to the Intent that the Common People of the United Kingdom may realise the privileges which in law and custom they enjoy in comparison with other European Peoples and realising and appreciating such privileges may recognise the responsibilities and obligations attaching to them.

The Trustees are to include the vice-chancellor of the University of Exeter; representatives of the Universities of London, Leeds, Glasgow, Belfast and Wales; and persons co-opted. At present there are eight Trustees:

From the outset it was decided that the objects of the Trust could be best achieved by means of an annual course of public lectures of outstanding interest and quality by eminent lecturers, and by their subsequent publication and distribution to a wider audience. The first of the Lectures were delivered by the Rt Hon. Lord Justice Denning (as he then was) in 1949. Since then there has been an unbroken series of annual

Lectures published until 2005 by Sweet & Maxwell and from 2006 by Cambridge University Press. A complete list of the Lectures may be found on pages ix to xiii. In 2005 the Trustees decided to supplement the Lectures with an annual Hamlyn Seminar, normally held at the Institute of Advanced Legal Studies in the University of London, to mark the publication of the Lectures in printed book form. The Trustees have also, from time to time, provided financial support for a variety of projects which, in various ways, have disseminated knowledge or have promoted to a wider public understanding of the law.

This, the sixty-sixth series of lectures, was delivered by Paul Craig at the University of Oxford, the Queen's University of Belfast and Gray's Inn Hall, London. The Board of Trustees would like to record its appreciation to Paul Craig and also the three venues which generously hosted these Lectures.

AVROM SHERR
Chair of the Trustees

The Hamlyn Lectures

1949	Freedom under the Law by the Rt Hon. Lord Denning
1950	The Inheritance of the Common Law by Richard O'Sullivan
1951	The Rational Strength of English Law by Professor F.H. Lawson
1952	English Law and the Moral Law by Professor A.L. Goodhart
1953	The Queen's Peace by Sir Carleton Kemp Allen
1954	Executive Discretion and Judicial Control by Professor C.J. Hamson
1955	The Proof of Guilt by Professor Glanville Williams
1956	Trial by Jury by the Rt Hon. Lord Devlin
1957	Protection from Power under English Law by the Rt Hon. Lord MacDermott
1958	The Sanctity of Contracts in English Law by Professor Sir David Hughes Parry
1959	Judge and Jurist in the Reign of Victoria by C.H.S. Fifoot
1960	The Common Law in India by M.C. Setalvad
1961	British Justice: The Scottish Contribution by Professor Sir Thomas Smith
1962	Lawyer and Litigant in England by the Rt Hon. Sir Robert Megarry

1963	Crime and the Criminal Law by the Baroness Wootton of Abinger
1964	Law and Lawyers in the United States by Dean Erwin N. Griswold
1965	New Law for a New World? by the Rt Hon. Lord Tangley
1966	Other People's Law by the Rt Hon. Lord Kilbrandon
1967	The Contribution of English Law to South African Law: And the Rule of Law in South Africa by the Hon. O.D. Schreiner
1968	Justice in the Welfare State by Professor H. Street
1969	The British Tradition in Canadian Law by the Hon. Bora Laskin
1970	The English Judge by Henry Cecil
1971	Punishment, Prison and the Public by Professor Sir Rupert Cross
1972	Labour and the Law by Professor Sir Otto Kahn-Freund
1973	Maladministration and Its Remedies by Sir Kenneth Wheare
1974	English Law: The New Dimension by the Rt Hon. Lord Scarman
1975	The Land and the Development; or, The Turmoil and the Torment by Sir Desmond Heap
1976	The National Insurance Commissioners by Sir Robert Micklethwait
1977	The European Communities and the Rule of Law by Lord Mackenzie Stuart

1978 Liberty, Law and Justice by Professor Sir Norman Anderson
1979 Social History and Law Reform by Professor Lord McGregor of Durris
1980 Constitutional Fundamentals by Professor Sir William Wade
1981 Intolerable Inquisition? Reflections on the Law of Tax by Hubert Monroe
1982 The Quest for Security: Employees, Tenants, Wives by Professor Tony Honoré
1983 Hamlyn Revisited: The British Legal System Today by Lord Hailsham of St Marylebone
1984 The Development of Consumer Law and Policy: Bold Spirits and Timorous Souls by Sir Gordon Borrie
1985 Law and Order by Professor Ralf Dahrendorf
1986 The Fabric of English Civil Justice by Sir Jack Jacob
1987 Pragmatism and Theory in English Law by Professor P.S. Atiyah
1988 Justification and Excuse in the Criminal Law by Professor J.C. Smith
1989 Protection of the Public: A New Challenge by the Rt Hon. Lord Justice Woolf
1990 The United Kingdom and Human Rights by Dr Claire Palley
1991 Introducing a European Legal Order by Gordon Slynn
1992 Speech and Respect by Professor Richard Abel

2007 The Prisoners' Dilemma by Professor Nicola Lacey
2008 Judging Civil Justice by Dame Hazel Genn
2009 Widening Horizons: The Influence of Comparative Law and International Law on Domestic Law by Lord Bingham
2010 Lawyers and the Public Good: Democracy in Action? by Alan Paterson
2011 The Rule of Law and the Measure of Property by Jeremy Waldron
2012 Aspects of Law Reform: An Insider's Perspective by Jack Straw
2013 The Common Law Constitution by Sir John Laws

Introduction

I had the honour of delivering the Hamlyn Lectures in 2014. The three lectures that comprise the Hamlyn series were delivered in November–December 2014 and dealt with the following topics: 'Foundations of UK Administrative Law: The Common Law Method, Values and Contestation'; 'Foundations of EU Administrative Law: Treaty Foundations, Judicial Creativity and the Hierarchy of Norms'; and 'Foundations of Global Administrative Law: Governance, Regulatory Power beyond the State and Administrative Legality'.

A unifying theme running through the three lectures was therefore that they dealt with aspects of the foundations of UK, EU and global administrative law respectively. The word 'aspects' should be emphasized in this context, because this book is not simply the product of the three lectures duly polished for publication. The reality was that the lectures covered only part of the material concerning the foundations of administrative law in the three legal systems, on average circa 25–30 per cent, and did not touch the analysis of the challenges faced by each system.

The book seeks to do what it says 'on the tin', viz. address the foundations and challenges of administrative law in and between these three systems. It is not a literature review. It does not seek systematically to expound the state of the art in relation to all issues discussed. It does explicate the background to the discussion, providing sufficient information for the reader to understand what follows, as exemplified by the treatment of the foundational material on global administrative law, with which many readers will be less familiar. The book also examines the views of particular scholars where that is pertinent to the inquiry. The overall objective is nonetheless to advance the debate on contentious issues, not to provide some potted version of the status quo. The choice of the three legal orders is reflective of the fact that administrative law functions at the national, regional and global level.

It is axiomatic that there is a developed regime of administrative law in the UK and in the EU. The reality is that there is also a growing body of administrative law at the global level. This material is less well known and less well understood than that in the UK and the EU, but it exists and not just as an aspiration, or a matter of academic speculation. There is already a considerable body of administrative law developed by, for example, the adjudicative organs of the World Trade Organization (WTO), and bodies such as the IMF Administrative Tribunal. The extent to which such precepts currently exist does, however, vary between different international and transnational bodies, and there is considerable academic discourse as to the desirability of expanding these principles further.

It is also axiomatic that there is much 'vertical interaction' between the national, the regional and the global that impacts on the subject matter of administrative law broadly conceived, including the doctrines of judicial review, regulatory competence and individual decisions. EU law is the foundation for much regulatory activity that affects the UK, in areas ranging from the environment to telecommunications, from energy to consumer protection and from competition to intellectual property. The UK is bound by the general principles of EU law when it acts within the sphere covered by the EU, and these principles embody the precepts of judicial review, such as proportionality, legitimate expectations, fundamental rights, equality, legal certainty and the like. There is, however, also 'vertical interaction' between the global level and the regional and national levels. This includes high-profile individual cases such as the *Kadi* litigation, but the interaction is far more extensive than this. It is exemplified by the activities of a diverse range of international and transnational bodies such as the World Trade Organization, the International Organization for Standardization, the International Accounting Standards Board, the World Health Organization, the Codex Alimentarius Commission and the Basel Committee on Banking Supervision. These bodies are merely the tip of the iceberg in terms of numbers, which have been estimated to be in the order of 2,000 international and transnational regulatory regimes. The reality is that many regulatory choices that bind the EU and the UK emanate de jure or de facto from the global level, although the extent of this impact perforce varies.

The sense of 'foundations' used in the three relevant chapters is broad. It includes the conceptual, judicial, theoretical, administrative and regulatory foundations of UK, EU and global administrative law, although the relevance of each perforce varies. The literature used reflects this breadth. This is a law book, but the analysis is nonetheless informed by a broad range of primary and secondary sources in addition to classic legal materials. The sources include material from history, economics, political science, international political economy, legal theory and political theory.

While there is, of course, discussion concerning the foundations of administrative law in the three systems, there is nonetheless much that is imperfectly understood. There is indeed an inverse relationship between the longevity of the legal orders considered in this book and our understanding of their respective foundations. We understand least about the foundations of UK administrative law, notwithstanding its being the oldest of the systems studied by approximately 400 years; we know rather more about the foundations for EU administrative law although there is much that has not been unpacked; and we know the most about the foundations for global administrative law notwithstanding its relative novelty and notwithstanding the fact that it may be contentious. A word is necessary by way of explanation for this paradox.

The study of global administrative law began in earnest towards the end of the millennium. It was undertaken by scholars who investigated the challenges posed by global regulation and the role that precepts of administrative law could play in addressing them. There was an intense burst of scholarly activity, fuelled in part by the recognition that the foundations for global administrative law were not self-evident and had therefore to be explicated. The result was a considerable body of high-quality literature, although there are, as will be seen in Chapter 5, a number of key foundational issues that require further inquiry.

The study of EU administrative law dates back to the 1970s. It has attracted considerably more scholarly attention since the new millennium, although the amount of scholarship relative to some other aspects of EU law is still relatively small. The foundations of EU administrative law nonetheless remain imperfectly understood, in part at least because much of the scholarly attention has been directed towards particular problems of the here and now, rather than its formal, substantive and regulatory foundations. The challenges of the present must assuredly be addressed, although so too must the very foundations of the subject. There is, as will be seen in Chapter 3, much room for further inquiry as to the formal, substantive and regulatory foundations of the subject, and their interaction. Nor are the issues that require further inquiry minor or interstitial. To the contrary, they go to the very heart of EU administrative law and are of significance more generally for EU law. This is exemplified by the category of general principles of law, which constitutes the foundation for core precepts of EU administrative law, and shapes many substantive areas of EU law. There is, as will be seen, much concerning the textual and juridical foundations for such principles that has not been comprehended, and this story forms part of Chapter 3.

The foundations of UK administrative law date from the mid-sixteenth century. There is challenging scholarship on modern UK administrative law, but this is not matched by understanding of its conceptual, judicial or administrative foundations. Indeed the more that I study the subject, the more do I realize the limits of our understanding. The limitations in this respect relate to central dimensions of the subject, not matters that are peripheral or secondary. Thus many presuppose that there was 'not much' judicial review judged quantitatively, and that the range of doctrinal grounds for such review was very limited. It is often assumed that the quantitative limits on judicial review were reflective of the fact that there was 'not much' regulatory or administrative activity in the sixteenth through to the nineteenth centuries. There is a further presupposition that when courts did engage in such review it was underpinned by the need to hem in 'dangerous' manifestations of the administrative state. None of these assumptions reflects the historical reality in judicial or administrative terms. The story is, as will be seen in Chapter 1, much richer and more interesting. Mistaken presuppositions as to the judicial, regulatory and administrative foundations of administrative law in turn shape, explicitly and implicitly, theoretical constructs that inform the subject.

The three chapters on foundations are matched by three chapters dealing with the challenges faced by the respective systems. A challenge in writing these chapters has been to choose what to cover and what to leave out. That is my choice and it will be for others to judge the wisdom thereof, or not, as the case may be. What I would emphasize is that each chapter seeks to address a range of issues that cuts across administrative law broadly conceived, including practical challenges of caseload, central issues in procedural and substantive review, and issues of regulatory design. The challenges thus addressed are both 'horizontal', in the sense of internal to that legal order, and 'vertical', in the sense of how national, regional and global legal orders interact in the sphere of administrative law.

The horizontal challenges are eclectic. They are in part temporally contingent, as exemplified by the problems posed for all three legal orders by the need to respond to post-9/11 legislation or executive action that has serious implications for process rights. They are also in part endemic to any legal order, such as the intensity of substantive review, which raises perennial concerns as to the proper balance between judicial supervision and freedom of political choice. This issue features prominently in all three legal orders. There is extensive judicial and academic commentary on it in the UK, it is the subject of scholarship in the EU, and it features also in the case law of bodies such as the WTO and the commentary thereon. While the issue is endemic, its resolution is shaped by an admixture of normative and practical considerations that may be particular to that legal order. Thus the common law approach to substantive review is informed by background precepts concerning the legitimate boundaries of judicial intervention that are not necessarily accepted to the same degree by those schooled in a civil law tradition. The way in which the issue plays out at the global level may be different yet again, in part because the body being supervised will normally not have democratic credentials.

The horizontal challenges may also be more specific to a particular legal order, and that is especially so when we think about administrative law at the global level. Thus while there may be good foundational justification for arguing that principles of administrative law should inform the global level, that still leaves a plethora of issues as to the way in which we transpose principles designed within a statal or regional framework to the different institutional reality that prevails at the global level. These issues are still relatively underexplored, and are addressed in Chapter 6.

The vertical challenges between legal orders are manifest in various ways. Such challenges can arise at the regulatory level, the most obvious manifestation being where regulatory competence to enact measures for one legal order is exercised de jure or de facto by another legal order. This can generate a plethora of problems, including the difficulties of ensuring regulatory efficacy and the dangers that administrative law safeguards valued by a legal order may be undermined or bypassed when the relevant norms are made by another legal order.

Vertical challenges can, however, also assume a more overtly judicial dimension. The courts are not the sole architects of the terms on which a legal order will engage with other legal orders. The legislature may well have something to say on the matter, but the courts are nonetheless principal players in this respect. They determine the conditions for legitimate interchange, more especially when what is at stake is the acceptance of norms made elsewhere, which include not merely substantive regulatory norms, but doctrinal public law precepts and rival interpretations of rights. It is the courts that act as the prime gatekeepers. They shape the relative autonomy of the legal order, and in doing so protect what they conceive as its important autochthonous values. The conception of autonomy and autochthony may be relatively thin or relatively thick, and the choice will have a marked impact on the legal system's willingness to be open to norms made elsewhere. Autochthony can be juridically manifest in three different ways, which I term status, source and substantive autochthony, the meanings of which are explicated in Chapter 2. There is, moreover, increasing evidence of this, especially within the UK and the EU jurisprudence. This is not fortuitous. It is the increased vertical interaction between the national, EU and global levels that prompts courts to react and think hard about the terms on which they are willing to accept 'external' norms. To be sure, there is a sense in which courts have been doing this for hundreds of years, as attested to by the developed jurisprudence concerning the relationship between national and international law. There is nonetheless little doubt that sensibilities have been heightened by the creation of the EU and the ECHR, both of which demand of contracting states a degree of acceptance over and beyond what is demanded by most international treaties. There is equally little doubt that the tensions have become more acute because of increased globalization, which has the consequence that many rules that bind at national level de jure or de facto emanate from international and transnational bodies.

The vertical challenge is addressed within each of the relevant Chapters, viz. 2, 4 and 6. It is not hived off for discussion within a single separate chapter. This choice was driven by a number of related considerations. There is, as will be seen, an interplay between horizontal and vertical challenges that would be lost if the latter were dealt with in a wholly separate chapter. A separate chapter would also risk losing important insights about how a particular legal system conceives of its relationship with a variety of other legal orders, as exemplified by the discussion in Chapter 2, which analyses the sense of autochthony that informs the UK courts' conception of the relationship between national law, EU law, the ECHR, and international and transnational law. There are therefore three different 'takes' on the vertical challenge as perceived from the perspective of UK, EU and global administrative law.

I have learned a great deal in writing this book, and it has generated more new research ideas than I can realistically complete. I hope that it will be found useful by others, whether they are interested to learn more about one of the legal orders considered in this book; whether they are interested by the interaction between the national, EU and global level; or whether they are just interested.

For the sake of clarity it should be noted that there are some differences in administrative law as it pertains in Scotland, and to a lesser extent in Wales and Northern Ireland. Exigencies of space preclude detailed treatment of these. There is nonetheless very considerable commonality in the procedural and substantive principles of administrative law across the UK, more especially in the light of the Human Rights Act 1998. Moreover, judges from both Scotland and Northern Ireland have made notable contributions to the development of such principles in the House of Lords and Supreme Court. The concept of UK administrative law as used in this work connotes the general principles of administrative law that prevail across the UK, without thereby diminishing distinctive legal features that are present within a particular part of the UK.

1

UK administrative law

Foundations

1 Introduction

This chapter explores the foundations of administrative law in the UK. It advances a model of common law constitutionalism that is more moderate than that presented by some other writers, but which best captures the historical provenance of the subject, is consonant with constitutional principle and coheres with legal practice. The argument proceeds in the following stages.

It begins with discussion of how administrative law evolved, which is analysed from three related perspectives, conceptual, judicial and administrative. The conceptual strand considers the different levels at which doctrine develops and the values that inform this. There is then consideration of the evolution of administrative law from a judicial perspective, through the principal case law developments in the seventeenth, eighteenth and nineteenth centuries. The focus then shifts to the administrative perspective, in order to understand the nature of administration, the powers wielded and the types of body that commonly came before the courts on judicial review.

This is followed by analysis of the relationship between theory, values and fact within public law discourse. Contestation as to the theoretical underpinnings of administrative law is inevitable, although no more or less than analogous debates that prevail in private law as to the normative foundations of contract, tort, property or restitution. In the public law realm the contestation will often reflect, at one stage removed, assumptions drawn from different political and legal theories, since the former will provide insight as to matters such as the nature of rights, conceptions of justice, the relationship between justice and other virtues, and the extent to which the state should seek to prescribe behaviour for its citizens, while the latter will furnish guidance as to the role of the courts when adjudicating on such issues. There are important general issues concerning the relationship between theory, value and fact, which are considered within this part of the chapter. While different perspectives on the values that underpin public law are inevitable this still leaves open whether there are fundamental binary divides that might provide the key to such differences. It has been argued that the distinctions between normativism and functionalism, and between the internal and external perspective, perform this role, and these claims are subjected to critical scrutiny.

The focus then shifts to the relation between common law and legislative intent when considering the foundations of judicial review. There was a lively debate on these issues a decade ago, the details of which will not be repeated here. It will, however, be argued that the debate is fundamental for the foundations of judicial review, since it has major implications for the role of courts and legislature in the development and application of legal norms, the consequences of which are relevant for any area where courts seek to apply common law precepts to statute, irrespective of whether it concerns judicial review, contract, tort or property. This section is therefore designed to clear the ground by rebutting two prominent objections to the relevance of the debate, viz. that it has no doctrinal significance and that it has no normative significance.

The final section of the chapter then addresses the arguments that have been put as to why legislative intent must be regarded as central. There are three such arguments that must be disaggregated: the analytical, the empirical and the normative. There is much that is wanting in relation to each argument. The claim that legislative intent is required in order to prevent a strong challenge to sovereignty is based on an analytical foundation that is not sustainable, combined with mistaken normative assumptions about the meaning of parliamentary sovereignty and the relationship between courts and legislature.

2 The evolution of administrative law: the conceptual perspective

We begin with the evolution of administrative law from a conceptual perspective, the focus being on the different levels at which this occurs, their interaction and the relationship between values and doctrine within this development. The inquiry is conceptual, but consistent with the historical trajectory. Three such levels can be discerned, exemplified initially in relation to private law, and then administrative law.

The first level is the imperative for judicial involvement to deal with a problem, which might be specific, such as the infliction of intentional harm; it might be more wide-ranging, as exemplified by the need for rules to cover non-intentional harm to a spectrum of interests; it might be broader yet again, such as the requirement for doctrine to deal with delictual harm in general, the regulation of consensual relations and the like. The very idea that there is an 'area' covered by the legal rules was itself an evolving one. The reality was that initial judicial involvement was often premised on resolution of a particular problem, as was the case with early deployment of the prerogative writs.[1] The idea that there was a doctrinal area that embraced more discrete rules, or that such rules could be regarded as exhibiting features that lent themselves to inclusion within such an area, whether that be tort, contract, trust, quasi-contract, or property, was a later development, with the boundaries between such areas changing over time.[2] The label ascribed to the doctrinal area would often be the result of emerging judicial doctrine, facilitated by analogical judicial reasoning, coupled with academic commentary that sought to bring order to individual judicial decisions. The objectives served by the particular rule, or by the body of rules that comprised a doctrinal area, were often eclectic, and could alter over time. The search for a single value that informs a doctrinal area is often illusory, or dependent on deployment of a single value at such a high

[1] E.G. Henderson, *Foundations of English Administrative Law* (Cambridge, MA: Harvard University Press, 1963).

[2] S.F.C Milsom, *Historical Foundations of the Common Law* (Oxford: Oxford University Press, 2nd ed., 1981); D.J. Ibbetson, *A Historical Introduction to the Law of Obligations* (Oxford: Oxford University Press, 1999); J.H. Baker, *An Introduction to English Legal History* (Oxford: Oxford University Press, 4th ed., 2002).

level of abstraction that in reality it embodies a plethora of more particular values.

The second level is the fashioning of particular categories of legal doctrine for the salient area, such as mistake, misrepresentation and illegality in contract, or trespass, negligence, nuisance and defamation in tort. These legal doctrines shaped and were shaped by the doctrinal area of which they formed the component parts. Thus, for example, the courts decided that one category of emerging tortious liability was a cause of action to protect property rights from physical incursions, or from non-physical unreasonable uses of land by neighbours. The importance attached to property rights was legally evident in the fact that if a user of land was unreasonable in relation to a neighbour, it was no defence for the creator of a nuisance to claim that all reasonable care was taken when engaging in the impugned activity. By way of contrast, the courts increasingly determined that tort liability should in general be predicated on fault, not cause, with the consequence that the risk of losses caused by the defendant where fault could not be proven lay with the plaintiff. By way of contrast yet again, the values that informed the emerging law of economic torts exhibited a delicate blend in which the desire to allow competition to operate was balanced against what the courts perceived as the limits of legitimate competition. This was exemplified by the doctrinal conclusion that inducement to breach of contract was not to be regarded as a legitimate instance of financial incentive to break a contract through a more lucrative offer, but rather the illegitimate breach of a contract obligation between the plaintiff and a third party. In all these instances, the doctrine is perforce based on assumptions about the important values within that legal sphere, whatsoever those might be. In that sense the values embodied within legal doctrine will be regarded as fundamental, when viewed in the light of the principles and objectives served by that body of law.

The third level concerns the more detailed meaning of the doctrines established. Thus there will be further questions as to the nature of liability for nuisance, the type of defences that should be available, and the like. Resolution of these issues will necessarily involve an admixture of normative and practical considerations, with assumptions being made concerning the type of conduct that should give rise to legal responsibility, and the considerations that provide the foundation for an excuse or defence. Thus courts will, for example, make more detailed doctrinal decisions as to what account, if any, should be taken of the fact that the defendant in a negligence action had limited physical or mental capacity. They will decide on the application of negligence liability when the defendant is exercising a particular skill, such as a surgeon, or when faced with difficult discretionary determinations, as is often the case with public bodies. It will be for the courts to determine the scope of defences such as contributory negligence, and *volenti non fit iniuria*, and the conclusions will necessarily embody assumptions as to the normative justification for reducing or removing the defendant's prima facie liability. They will shape the contours of statutory liability, as in the case of damages liability under the Human Rights Act 1998 (HRA), where the courts fashioned the criteria for liability under section 8 on assumptions concerning the relationship between the HRA and the

European Convention on Human Rights, and assumptions as to the relationship between damages and other remedies under the HRA as ways of vindicating rights-based claims.

There are certain noteworthy features of this development. Thus it is incremental and analogical. This is true not only for case law, but also for the doctrines that inform the levels adumbrated above. These do not emerge 'perfect' and 'fully formed'. They are fashioned, refashioned, developed, altered and changed over time. The courts may well proceed relatively cautiously in this respect.[3]

The relationship between the three levels is symbiotic, with developments at one level impacting on the others. Thus articulation of categories of legal doctrine at the second level may well prompt reconsideration of the overarching values to be served by that body of law as a whole. Or more detailed consideration of particular legal doctrine at the third level may be the catalyst for rethinking the very division between the categories that comprise the subject.

The content of the three levels will, moreover, evolve; it is not static. The very values that underpin a body of the law change over time. So too will the categories of legal doctrine that comprise the second level, or their more detailed meaning, the third level. The changes may come from within the common law itself, or they may result from legislative intervention.

[3] C. Sunstein, *One Case at a Time: Judicial Minimalism on the Supreme Court* (Cambridge, MA: Harvard University Press, 1999); C. Sunstein, 'Incompletely Theorized Agreements in Constitutional Law', Chicago, Public Law and Legal Theory Working Paper No 147.

The preceding framework facilitates understanding of the emergence of judicial review, and its legitimacy. When viewed from a historical perspective, the background objective and value at the first level was the need to render public power broadly conceived accountable, which connoted the twin ideas that an institution complied with conditions laid down in the enabling grant of power, and with certain precepts of good governance, thereby enhancing legitimacy.[4] This was the imperative for judicial involvement and the most basic rationale for judicial review. The development of what we now term 'administrative law' was doctrinally incremental and driven largely through remedial expansion. It might be argued by those opposed to judicial review that this rationale for judicial intervention is unconvincing. This requires argumentation, and would be a daunting task, given that a very similar rationale is found in pretty much all developed legal systems. While 'is' does not make 'ought', it reinforces the conclusion that the basic normative premise for judicial review in the UK is plausibly grounded. Thus if political constitutionalists wish to challenge the legal status quo then it must be at the second and third levels, concerning the doctrinal implications drawn from the basic premise.

[4] S.A. de Smith, 'The Prerogative Writs' [1951] *Cambridge Law Journal* 40; S.A. de Smith, 'Wrongs and Remedies in Administrative Law' (1952) 15 *Modern Law Review* 189; L. Jaffe and E. Henderson, 'Judicial Review and the Rule of Law: Historical Origins' (1956) 72 *Law Quarterly Review* 345; Henderson, *Foundations of English Administrative Law*; A. Rubinstein, *Jurisdiction and Illegality* (Oxford: Oxford University Press, 1975); P. Craig, '*Ultra Vires* and the Foundations of Judicial Review' [1998] *Cambridge Law Journal* 63.

Subsequent development of judicial review refined the background objectives through development at the second and third levels. It is common for criticism to be voiced against legal constitutionalism on the ground that the doctrine is only justified through recourse to abstract concepts such as natural law, public reason or fundamental values. I shall have more to say about the nature of values in public law in a later section. Suffice it to say for the present that the historical development of doctrine rests on more specific and discrete foundations than is commonly acknowledged. This does not mean that the doctrinal categories are value-free, nor does it mean that they are premised on some universal theory of value. What it does mean is that the existence of these categories, and their more specific meaning, levels two and three, are the result of reasoned analysis that draws on, and gives more concrete expression to, the foundational ideas that underlie judicial review explicated above. Such doctrinal development is incremental and symbiotic in the manner described above and thus may well lead to refinement or modification of the foundational precepts that underlie this body of law. The nature of the connection between the three levels can be briefly exemplified.

Consider in this respect certain core doctrines of judicial review that constitute what was termed the second level. It is axiomatic that if the courts are to render public power accountable then there must be legal doctrine that serves to keep the relevant body within its assigned sphere of power. It is equally axiomatic that there must be controls to determine whether the power has been used for an improper purpose. Such legal doctrine is fundamental in the sense that if we are to have any body of law to check public power, then there must be doctrinal categories of this kind. This is equally true for the law dealing with the consequences of invalidity, which is grounded on the fundamental precept that where a public body makes an invalid decision, it should, in principle, be retrospectively void. It is therefore unsurprising that these doctrinal categories have existed from the seventeenth century, and have been refined since then. This still leaves a plethora of issues at the third level, concerning the more detailed content of these doctrinal categories, as exemplified by the debates concerning the criterion for jurisdictional review, the test for misuse of power where the public body pursues multiple purposes, or the qualifications that should be made to retrospective nullity. Resolution of these issues will perforce entail normative assumptions, and commentators may disagree about the 'best solution'. Analogous debates occur in all areas to which the common law applies.

Consider also in this respect the fact that the courts developed from the outset principles of legality that took account of moral precepts and were designed to enhance good governance. A prime instance is natural justice. It was central to the objective of rendering public power accountable: in instrumental terms, decisions were more likely to be correct if people were heard before the decision was taken; in non-instrumental terms, it was part of what it means to be a person to be heard before the state took action against the individual.[5] Natural justice was therefore reflective of the twin

[5] J. Mashaw, *Due Process in the Administrative State* (New Haven: Yale University Press, 1985); D. Galligan, *Due Process and Fair Procedures:*

precepts underlying judicial review identified above. It helped to ensure that public bodies remained within their assigned area, since a correct decision was more likely if a person was heard before it was taken, and it also functioned as a principle of legitimate good governance, as reflected in the non-instrumental rationale for natural justice. Another less well-known principle of legality is that public or quasi-public bodies with monopoly power could charge no more than a reasonable price.[6] The principled reasoning in the seminal cases was posited on grounds that were part economic, and part concerned with precepts of good governance that should be demanded from bodies 'imbued with a public interest', given their de facto or de jure monopoly power. The fact that such doctrinal categories were shaped by normative and moral considerations is neither surprising nor illegitimate, and the same occurs when categories are forged in private law. It does not mean that we should simply accept any such judicial evaluation. The justification for the relevant category must rest on the strength of the normative argument, viewed against the objectives and values of the overall area.

Consider in this respect a third example concerning discretionary power. The courts recognized that the primary decision-maker had been given discretionary power by Parliament and therefore that they should not substitute judgment on the merits. They recognized also that public authorities

A Study of Administrative Procedures (Oxford: Oxford University Press, 1996).

6 *Allnutt* v. *Inglis* (1810) 12 East 527; P. Craig, 'Constitutions, Property and Regulation' [1991] *Public Law* 538.

such as ministers and local authorities had some democratic mandate. Legal intervention was nonetheless deemed warranted because of the twin precepts that underpin judicial review identified above: the imperative of checking that discretionary power was exercised in accord with the enabling legislation, plus the belief that good governance demanded some judicial oversight over choices made by the administration. The result was limited-reasonableness review, and, as will be seen below, review cast in terms of what seventeenth-, eighteenth- and nineteenth-century courts termed proportionability. There is no doubt that this accords the judiciary a measure of interpretive choice, that the meaning ascribed to the relevant terms has altered over time, and that there is debate as to the meaning that the terms ought to bear.[7] These debates, which include the choice between reasonableness and proportionality, exemplify the discourse that commonly occurs about any area of law at the third level, viz. the more particular meaning to be accorded to a doctrinal category. The reality is nonetheless that if some control over discretionary power is warranted for the preceding reasons, then it will perforce be undertaken through criteria such as reasonableness or proportionability/proportionality, which allow for differences of interpretation.

The common law model of judicial review is therefore based on the premise that the principles of judicial review, and their application, are created by the courts. It is the courts that have fashioned these principles in accord with

[7] *R* v. *Chief Constable of Sussex, ex p International Trader's Ferry Ltd* [1999] 2 AC 418, 452; *R* v. *Secretary of State for the Home Department, ex p Daly* [2001] 2 AC 532, 549.

the principles of justice and the rule of law in the manner explicated above. They will therefore decide on the appropriate procedural and substantive principles of judicial review which should apply to statutory and some non-statutory bodies alike. Action which infringes these principles will be unlawful. Advocates of the common law model have nothing against the idea of legislative intent. Thus if Parliament manifests an intent as to the grounds of review the courts will obey this, in just the same way as they will obey such intent in other areas where the primary obligations themselves are the creation of the common law. There is nothing unusual about a set of principles derived from the common law, which are then supplemented by legislative intent if and when this is to be found. Parliament and the courts can perfectly well share in the development of the principles of review. Adherents of the common law model contend, however, that it is not necessary for the principles of judicial review to be cloaked with such intent in order to avoid a strong challenge to sovereignty, or to guard against unchecked judicial supremacism.

It is equally important to be clear at this juncture what the common law model of judicial review does not entail, since much confusion is generated in this regard. There is nothing within moderate legal constitutionalism, or within legal constitutionalism more generally, that denies the significance of non-judicial methods of accountability, or recourse to settlement outside the courts.[8] Legal constitutionalists

[8] H. Arthurs, *'Without the Law': Administrative Justice and Legal Pluralism in Nineteenth-Century England* (Toronto: University of Toronto Press, 1985).

recognize and analyse forms of accountability and legitimacy other than judicial review, as will be seen in this chapter and the next. There is nothing in legal constitutionalism to suggest that the courts always get it right, and that the political process gets it wrong, nor is it premised on some 'Whig version' of legal history. There is, moreover, nothing within legal constitutionalism that denies the important contribution made by the political process to fundamental values or valuable societal reform. It is not predicated on the assumption that the common law is the primary repository of fundamental values of the political community insofar as that connotes exclusivity. The common law will play a role in this regard, but this will be in conjunction with the political branch of government, not to the exclusion thereof. Their respective contributions will vary, more especially when considered over a lengthy temporal frame, during which the responsibilities of central government changed markedly. It is readily apparent, as political constitutionalists have rightly emphasized, that Parliament has made many positive contributions to the development of fundamental societal values, as you would expect in a democratic society. Parliament will thereby shape the more particular meaning accorded to concepts such as liberty, security, equality, autonomy and the like. This will sometimes be done by Parliament; on other occasions it will emerge from a symbiotic relationship with the courts, more especially when Parliament has assigned them such a role, as it has under the Human Rights Act 1998, or in the interpretation of other rights-based statutes. The nature of their respective contributions will be considered later in this and the subsequent chapter.

3 The evolution of administrative law: the judicial perspective

It is not possible in this chapter to relate the history of judicial review as it developed over four centuries. That would require a book in itself. It is nonetheless important to convey some principal strands of this legal development.[9] A word by way of introduction is necessary before embarking on this analysis. It is not uncommon to see statements to the effect that the UK did not possess a system of administrative law until the 1960s or thereabouts. The precise meaning of such statements is unclear.

The emphasis might be on the word 'system', connoting the idea that the earlier administrative law was in some sense 'unsystematic'. The sense in which this was so is, however, never explained, and the argument is not readily sustainable. The statement might, alternatively, be intended to connote the fact that the range of administrative law, judged in terms of the doctrines thereby covered, had expanded considerably by the 1960s from the period hitherto. There may be some truth in this, but the reality as judged by what the courts were actually doing for 400 years is that the difference between 'then' and 'now' is exaggerated.

The statement might carry a different meaning yet again, being used to capture important decisions from the

[9] Henderson, *Foundations of English Administrative Law*; Rubinstein, *Jurisdiction and Illegality*; de Smith, 'The Prerogative Writs'; de Smith, 'Wrongs and Remedies in Administrative Law'; Jaffe and Henderson, 'Judicial Review and the Rule of Law'.

1960s in which the House of Lords expanded the reach of procedural fairness and review for error of law, while limiting the remit of public-interest immunity. The premise, viz. the significance of these decisions, does not, however, justify the conclusion that there was no system of administrative law hitherto, more especially given that some of the impediments thereby removed were grafted onto administrative law doctrine in the twentieth century and had not existed before then. The rationale for such statements might more simply be a legacy of the Diceyan heritage that we have no system of administrative law of the kind that existed in Continental Europe, to which the response is that Dicey not only misunderstood the Continental regime, but also ignored the body of UK case law dealing with the subject.

It may well be true that 'administrative law' as an organizing concept for teaching and text writing is a relatively recent phenomenon, but this should be kept firmly in perspective. The legal reality is that we have had a body of legal rules concerned directly with the legal constraints that should be placed on the administration broadly conceived for at least 400 years, and many of the core concepts that we use today would be recognized by our judicial forebears such as Coke, Holt, Hale, Abbott, Blackstone, Mansfield and Kenyon because they created them. The rules were part of relations between individual and state, thereby forming the foundations for classic administrative law review, and were central also to relations between the arms of government, thereby operating as a form of structural constitutional review.

Some 'crude' figures may help to put matters in perspective. A search of the prerogative writs reveals the following. Between 1220 and 1867 there were 6,637 separate citations to certiorari, 5,563 to prohibition and 7,111 to mandamus. The very great majority of this judicial activity occurred from the late sixteenth century onward.[10] There were, in addition, 2,512 citations to quo warranto, which was the action used to challenge the entitlement of a person to hold office. These figures are crude,[11] and I have not yet had three lifetimes in which to check whether the claimant won or lost, or the relevance of the action, although it will be my next project.

The figures do not cover collateral challenges, where the claimant used an action in, for example, tort to challenge an illegality. These challenges were often used even after the birth of the prerogative writs, because the plaintiff wished to secure a monetary remedy, or because there might be a no-certiorari clause in the statute. Some figures concerning just two of the principal administrative authorities that were active during this time, commissioners and justices of the peace, can help put matters in perspective.[12] The figures for cases involving commissioners are: trespass, 3,200; trover, 1,942; action on the case, 1,138; and replevin, 1,001. The figures for cases involving justices of the peace are: trespass, 1,308;

[10] There were, for example, 1,169 cases involving poor law guardians, 1,028 cases involving turnpike trustees, and 408 involving inspectors.

[11] This is in part because there can be more than one digital citation of the same case, the consequence of their being more than one report, and in part because the same passage can on occasion be cited more than once.

[12] A further caveat in addition to that mentioned in the previous note is that the case citations in these figures can sometimes inadvertently run together mention of, for example, 'trespass' in one case and 'commissioners' in another.

trover, 534; action on the case, 470; and replevin, 392. These latter figures are almost certainly too low, since in many cases the citation is simply to 'justices' rather than 'justices of the peace', but a search framed in terms of 'justices' can also bring in citations to judges, and therefore be too high. It is nonetheless interesting for the record to note that the search couched in terms of 'justices' reveals the following figures: trespass, 7,605; trover, 2,883; action on the case, 1,964; and replevin, 2,498.

These figures do not touch the many collateral challenges to other administrative authorities, such as tortious actions against municipal corporations for illegality and abuse of power. The preceding figures also do not touch the number of unreported cases. Law reporting was private, and did not cover all cases. There might have been no reporter at a particular case, or it might be that the case was felt to raise no new legal point and therefore did not warrant a report, although such cases would still be important for an overall picture of the incidence of judicial review.

When reflecting on the historical incidence of judicial review compared to now it is noteworthy that the population at the turn of the seventeenth century was circa 4.8 million, 6 million at the beginning of the eighteenth century, and 16.3 million by the nineteenth century. It is not therefore self-evident that judicial review was less used then than now, more especially if one removes the very large number of immigration/asylum cases from current figures,[13] and if one

[13] In 1974 there were 160 applications for judicial review. This had risen to circa 11,000 in 2011, but 75 per cent concerned asylum and immigration. Judicial Review: Proposals for Reform, Cm 8515, 2012, paras. 28–9.

takes account of the fact that the preceding figures were for decided cases, since leave was not required until 1933.[14] It is, moreover, important to bear in mind the limited number of judges. King's Bench was staffed by the Chief Justice and three other justices, the number rising to five in the nineteenth century. The numbers of judges in Common Pleas and Court of Exchequer were similarly limited.[15] This limited number of judges would, moreover, be dealing with a whole range of legal business in addition to judicial review.

The preceding figures concerning the incidence of judicial review, crude though they may be, are a corrective to the view that we never had any administrative law before the 1960s, since 'we' clearly were doing quite a lot of this activity that supposedly barely existed. It also means that what follows in this section and the next is just scratching the surface.

(a) Grounds: jurisdiction and error

There is a continuity running throughout administrative law, which is the centrality accorded to the concept of jurisdiction as the foundation for judicial intervention. The malleability of this concept within modern law is well recognized, and this was equally true in earlier years. The concept of jurisdiction

[14] Administration of Justice (Miscellaneous Provisions) Act 1993, s 5. The number of cases decided at a substantive hearing in 2011 was circa 400. Judicial Review: Proposals for Reform, para. 30.

[15] J. Sainty, *The Judges of England, 1272–1990: A List of Judges of the Superior Courts* (London: Selden Society, 1993).

was the touchstone through which King's Bench controlled the inferior bodies it bought within its purview. Its precise meaning was, however, difficult to pin down, and there is scant indication of any general theory of jurisdiction in the work of Coke, Blackstone or Hale.[16]

It was left to individual courts to reach decisions which they felt expressed the appropriate standard to be imposed pursuant to the common law power of judicial review. Not surprisingly, views differed on this, in much the same manner as they do in the modern day. Some, such as Heath J in *Commins*,[17] expressly acknowledged that the court could intervene to examine jurisdiction and not justice, but then so applied jurisdiction as to embrace in effect any error of law. Others, such as those who gave judgment in *Woodsterton*,[18] construed the concept of jurisdiction more narrowly.

We can, nonetheless, make progress in identifying the different types of error that were reviewable, and thereby construct a picture of administrative law as it unfolded. Care must be taken in this regard. The case law does not always come with clear labels denoting the rationale for review. This may only be discerned by a close reading of the case, the facts therein and the reasoning used. It is also important to take due account of cases of collateral attack, as well as those concerning direct challenge. With these caveats, we can convey some impression of the legal doctrine relating to: review for law and fact, process-based review,

[16] Henderson, *Foundations of English Administrative Law*, pp. 126–7.

[17] (1643) March N.C. 196. [18] (1733) 2 Barnard K.B. 207.

review of discretion, and rights-based review. These will be considered in turn.

It is fitting to begin with review for law and fact, which is central to any regime of administrative law. This category of review was acknowledged early in the courts' jurisprudence, although its application could be difficult to predict. This was in part because there were two rival theories evident in the courts' jurisprudence.

The commencement theory of jurisdiction was predicated on the claimant showing an error relating to the nature of the case that the relevant body was authorized to consider at the outset of the inquiry. It was exemplified by *Bolton*,[19] where Lord Denman CJ held that where the charge laid before the magistrate did not constitute the offence over which the statute gave him jurisdiction, affidavit evidence could be introduced to show want of jurisdiction. However, where the charge had been well laid before the magistrate, on its face bringing itself within his jurisdiction, any error would be only an error within jurisdiction. The question of jurisdiction depended not on the truth or falsehood of the charge, but upon its nature, and was determinable at the commencement, not at the conclusion, of the inquiry.

[19] *R* v. *Bolton* (1841) 1 Q.B. 66, at 72–4; *Brittain* v. *Kinnaird* (1819) 1 B. & B. 432, at 442; *Ackerley* v. *Parkinson* (1815) 3 M. & S. 411; *Wilson* v. *Weller* (1819) 1 B. & B. 57; *Fawcett* v. *Fowlis* (1827) 7 B. & C. 396; *R* v. *Justices of Cheshire* (1838) 8 Ad. & E. 398; *Re Baines* (1840) Cr & Ph 31; *Cave* v. *Mountain* (1840) 1 M. & G. 257; *Mould* v. *Williams* (1844) 5 Q.B. 469; *Allen* v. *Sharp* (1848) 2 Ex. 352; *R.* v. *Wood* (1855) 5 El. & Bl. 49; *Revell* v. *Blake* (1872) 7 C.P. 300.

The dominant theory was, however, the collateral or jurisdictional fact doctrine, which, notwithstanding its appellation, was applicable to law and fact. It too was predicated on a distinction between the nature of the case that the public body was to inquire into and the truth of the inquiry thus made, but the former was interpreted more broadly than in the commencement theory and thus generated more searching review. Certain facts were required to be proven to the satisfaction of the reviewing court before the magistrate or tribunal could go right or wrong. It was this theory that informed Chief Baron Hale's reasoning in *Terry* that an error relating to person, place or subject matter could justify judicial review.[20] It was used in the early decision in *Nichols*,[21] where the plaintiff who lived in Totteridge brought a trespass action against the assessors for the poor rates of Hatfield, and succeeded on the ground that their remit did not cover Totteridge. It was Coleridge J who produced the oft-cited general principle underlying the collateral fact doctrine, in a case where the defendant denied his liability for debt for non-payment of tithes on the ground that he was exempt. The existence of land legally subject to a tithe was held to be a collateral fact for the purposes of judicial review, and was thus reviewable:

[20] (1668) Hardres 480.

[21] *Nichols* v. *Walker* (1632–3) Cro. Car. 394; *Milward* v. *Caffin* (1778) 2 Black. W 1330; *Lord Amherst* v. *Lord Somers* (1788) 2 T.R. 372; *Weaver* v. *Price* (1832) 3 B. & Ad. 409; *Governors of Bristol Poor* v. *Wait* (1834) 1 A. & E. 264; *Fernley* v. *Worthington* (1840) 1 Man. & G. 491.

> Now it is a general rule, that no court of limited jurisdiction can give itself jurisdiction by a wrong decision on a point collateral to the merits of the case upon which the limit to its jurisdiction depends; and however its decision may be final on all particulars, making up together that subject-matter which, if true, is within its jurisdiction, and, however necessary in many cases it may be for it to make a preliminary inquiry, whether some collateral matter be or be not within the limits, yet, upon this preliminary question, its decision must always be open to inquiry in the superior Court.[22]

The outcome of the court's jurisprudence was difficult to predict even when it was clear that the court used the collateral or jurisdictional fact doctrine. It was difficult to forecast *ex ante* whether a particular condition in the enabling statute would be regarded as jurisdictional, and equally difficult to produce coherent rationalization of similar cases that had been decided differently in this respect. This was because all the requirements in the enabling statute could be said to condition jurisdiction, which rendered the choice between them invidious. If a statute provided that an employee who is injured at work shall receive compensation there was no ready way to say why any of the three conditions – the existence of an employee, an injury and the fact that it

[22] *Bunbury* v. *Fuller* (1853) 9 Ex. 111, at 140. See also *Dale* v. *Pollard* (1847) 10 Q.B. 505; *Thompson* v. *Ingham* (1850) 14 Q.B. 710; *Chew* v. *Holroyd* (1852) 8 Ex. 249; *R* v. *Badger* (1856) 6 El. & Bl. 138; *R* v. *Stimpson* (1863) 4 B. & S. 301; *Ex p Vaughan* (1866) L.R. 2 Q.B. 114; *Elston* v. *Rose* (1868) L.R. 4 Q.B. 4; *Ex p Bradlaugh* (1878) 3 Q.B.D. 509.

occurred at the workplace – should be any more 'jurisdictional' than any other.[23] Erudite judicial attempts to resolve this by harking back to the distinction between the nature of the case that the public body was intended to inquire into and the truth of the inquiry thus made were unavailing.[24] This explains the academic critique of the doctrine[25] and its judicial replacement with a test for review based on error of law.[26]

We should nonetheless pause before concluding that the collateral fact jurisprudence was based on a misguided judicial assumption that judicial intervention had to be limited in this manner. This is wrong. It is clear from a reading of the case law that the courts did not feel that they were bound by some a priori logic to employ either of the now discredited theories. They acknowledged the possibilities open to them when devising the tests for jurisdictional control. The truth is that they adopted the collateral fact doctrine or the commencement theory because they believed that these best captured the appropriate balance between judicial control and the autonomy of the bodies being reviewed.[27] The courts did not believe that that they should be substituting

[23] P. Craig, *Administrative Law* (London: Sweet & Maxwell, 7th ed., 2012), pp. 477–8.

[24] *Anisminic Ltd* v. *Foreign Compensation Commission* [1968] 2 QB 862, at 887–905.

[25] D. Gordon, 'The Relation of Facts to Jurisdiction' (1929) 45 *Law Quarterly Review* 459; D. Gordon, 'Observance of Law as a Condition of Jurisdiction' (1931) 47 *Law Quarterly Review* 386, 557.

[26] *R* v. *Hull University Visitor, ex p Page* [1993] AC 682.

[27] P. Craig, 'Jurisdiction, Judicial Control and Agency Autonomy', in I. Loveland (ed.), *A Special Relationship: American Influences on Public Law in the UK* (Oxford: Oxford University Press, 1995), Ch. 7.

judgment on every issue of law since this would emasculate autonomy over issues that had been assigned to the body by Parliament. They realized also that some judicial control was required. The collateral fact doctrine and the commencement theory were the tools used to preserve control, while giving some leeway to the public body. The tests were defective, but this should not lead us to forget the rationale for adopting them.

Substantive review pursuant to the collateral fact doctrine was complemented by process review protective of hearing rights. *Bagg*'s case, so central to the development of mandamus, was also of seminal significance for process rights. Coke CJ in adjudicating on the removal of Bagg from office reasoned from first principle. He concluded that it appeared that the corporation had proceeded against Bagg without 'hearing him answer to what was objected', and 'that he was not reasonably warned'. The removal was therefore void, being against 'justice and right' and in breach of the *audi alteram partem* principle.[28] The same principle was evident in *Bonaker*,[29] where a bishop had ordered the profits due to a vicar to be sequestered by the Consistory Court because the vicar had not resided in the parish. Nothing daunted, the vicar brought a restitutionary action for money had and received against the sequestrator. He succeeded on the ground that the sequestration had issued without notice given

[28] (1615) 11 Co. Rep. 93b, at 99a; *Brownlow* v. *Cox and Mitchell* (1615) 3 Bulstrode 32; *Hesketh* v. *Braddock* (1779) 1 Dougl 119; *The King* v. *The Company of Fishermen of Faversham* (1799) 8 T.R. 352.

[29] *Bonaker* v. *Evans* (1850) 16 QB 163.

to the vicar as to why it should not issue, and the Court of Exchequer Chamber held that this was essential before the sequestration could proceed. *Dr Bonham*'s case is most often cited for Coke's dictum as to the court's power to declare void statutes that offended against common right or reason, or that were morally repugnant.[30] This dictum did not fall on fertile soil, and subsequent UK courts have not exercised that power of constitutional review. They did adopt the other central limb of process rights, the *nemo iudex* principle. It was forcefully expressed in the instant case. Thus in determining whether the College of Physicians had the power to fine and imprison Dr Bonham, Coke held that censors could not at one and the same time be judges, ministers and parties: 'judges to give sentence or judgment; ministers to make summons; and parties to have the moiety of the forfeiture', since this would offend the *nemo iudex* principle.[31]

Process-based review was therefore well established in addition to substantive review for law and fact. This did not exhaust the grounds of challenge, for the courts also reviewed the exercise of discretion. This specific 'head of review' was not articulated with the same degree of particularity as in modern case law, but it was nonetheless clearly discernible from the courts' reasoning. Thus, for example, controls cast in terms of purpose were evident in a number of cases, so too were those framed in terms of reasonableness or proportionability.

This is exemplified by the seminal decision in *Rooke*'s case, given in the twilight of the Elizabethan age five years

[30] (1609) 8 Co. Rep. 113b. [31] (1609) 8 Co. Rep. 113b, at 118a.

before James I took the throne.[32] Commissioners of Sewers levied charges on one person for the repair of river banks, notwithstanding that numerous landowners benefited from the work. This was held to be unlawful, since the 'commissioners ought to tax all who are in danger of being damaged by the not repairing equally, and not him who has the land next adjoining to the river only'.[33] The reasoning strikes a remarkably modern chord. If the charge could be levied solely on the owner with land nearest the river, this might defeat the purpose of the statute, 'for perhaps the rage and force of the water might be so great, that the value of the land adjoining will not serve to make the banks',[34] and it thus followed that he who derived the benefit should share the burden.[35] The statute required equality which 'well agrees with the rule of equity'.[36] The court had this to say about the discretion accorded to the commissioners:

> notwithstanding the words of the commission give authority to the commissioners to do according to their discretions, yet their proceedings ought to be limited and bound with the rule of reason and law . . . For . . . discretion is a science or understanding to discern between falsity and truth, between wrong and right, between shadows and substance, between equity and colourable glosses and pretences, and not to do according to their wills and private affections.[37]

[32] (1598) 5 Co. Rep. 99b. [33] (1598) 5 Co. Rep. 99b.

[34] (1598) 5 Co. Rep. 99b, at 100a.

[35] *Qui sentit commodum sentire debet* & *onus*.

[36] (1598) 5 Co. Rep. 99b, at 100a. [37] (1598) 5 Co. Rep. 99b, at 100a.

The case was followed in *Hetley*,[38] where the Commissioners of Sewers had satisfied a levy on a town by ordering the seizure and sale of the plaintiff's cattle, and had then ordered his imprisonment when he complained of this. Chief Justice Coke had no hesitation in ordering certiorari against the commissioners, since their action was in direct conflict with the ruling in *Rooke's* case. He reiterated that 'the commissioners of sewers cannot tax a whole township, but it ought to be done severally and proportionably to every inhabitant to himself',[39] and that discretion was framed through law to attain justice. The same principle was applied to Commissioners for Paving in *Leader*,[40] where the plaintiff complained that the ground floor of his houses had been blocked as a result of the repaving of the street, thereby rendering them valueless. It was argued that the matter lay within the discretion of the commissioners and could only be appealed to Quarter Sessions. The court disagreed, concluding that the plaintiff could properly bring an action on the case. It held that the discretion must be limited by 'reason and law', and that had Parliament meant that certain houses could be sacrificed for the benefit of others it would have so specified and provided compensation as a result.[41]

[38] *Hetley* v. *Boyer* (1614) Cro. Jac. 336. See also *Keighley's Case* (1610–11) 10 Co. Rep. 139a; *The Case of the Isle of Ely* (1610–11) 10 Co. Rep. 141a; *R.* v. *Peters* (1758) 1 Burr. 568, at 570; *Kerrison* v. *Sparrow* (1815) 2 Ves. Jun. Supp. 587; *R.* v. *Commissioners of Sewers for Tower Hamlets Tower* (1829) 9 B. & C. 517, at 521; *Soady* v. *Wilson* (1829) 3 Ad. & E. 248.

[39] (1614) Cro. Jac. 336.

[40] *Leader* v. *Moxon* (1773) 2 Black. W. 924.

[41] (1773) 2 Black. W. 924, at 926.

Analogous reasoning is apparent in other cases. Thus in *Customs, Subsidies and Impositions* the court held that the king could not at his pleasure place any imposition on merchandise imported or exported, unless it was for advancement of trade.[42] While it was open to the king to prohibit a person with some commodities to leave the realm, this was only where the end sought was public rather than private. The king could also impose tolls for the repair of highways and bridges for the benefit of the subjects, but 'the sum imposed ought to be proportionable to the benefit'.[43] *R* v. *Page* concerned the legality of a toll for navigation on a river. Lord Kenyon CJ stated that the ground on which his opinion proceeded was that 'where a person has a valuable interest in any parish or township, he ought to contribute towards the relief of the poor in that parish in proportion to such valuable interest'.[44] In *Godfrey*'s case it was held that justices could adjudicate on the reasonableness of a fine imposed by a lord on a copyholder, and so too could the court in an action for replevin.[45] In *R.* v. *Young and Pitts* a criminal prosecution was brought against justices of the peace for wilfully and unreasonably refusing to grant a licence to run an inn.[46] The case failed on its facts, but Lord Mansfield responded in the following terms to the argument that the legislature had made the justices sole judges over such matters:

[42] (1607) 12 Co. Rep. 33. [43] (1607) 12 Co. Rep. 33.
[44] *R.* v. *Page* (1792) 4 T.R. 544, at 547. [45] (1605) 11 Co. Rep. 42a.
[46] (1758) 1 Burr. 557.

> But yet if they have no reasonable objection to the man, they ought to licence him: and if they have any reason, they ought to give it. For though they have, it is true, a discretion in these cases, yet, it must not be permitted to them to exercise an arbitrary and uncontrolled power over the rights of other people, and in cases where their livelihoods are so essentially concerned.[47]

The courts' willingness to engage in substantive review of discretion was further evident in the case law concerning price regulation where the property owner possessed monopoly power. In *Allnutt* v. *Inglis* the issue was whether the London Dock Company, which by licence from Parliament possessed a monopoly to receive certain wines, could lawfully exclude from the docks a cargo owner who had refused to pay their schedule of charges.[48] Lord Ellenborough reasoned that while a man could fix his own price for the use of his own property, he could not do so where the public have a right to resort to the premises and to make use of them. Where a person had the benefit of a monopoly, this entailed a correlative responsibility with the consequence that he could charge no more than a reasonable price for the service offered. The monopoly could be 'legal', the result of grant of an exclusive licence from Parliament, or 'factual', where the

[47] (1758) 1 Burr. 557, at 559.

[48] (1810) 12 East 527; *Bolt* v. *Stennett* (1800) 8 T.R. 606; *Corporation of Stamford* v. *Pawlett* (1830) 1 C. & J. 57; *Gard* v. *Callard* (1817) 6 M. & S. 69; *Wright* v. *Bruister* (1832) 4 B. & Ald. 116; *Gann* v. *Free Fishers of Whitstable* (1865) 11 E.R. 1305; *Att.-Gen.* v. *Horner* (1912) 107; LT 547; *Duke of Newcastle* v. *Worksop Urban District Council* [1902] 2 Ch. 145, at 161; *Nyali* v. *Att.-Gen.* [1956] 1 QB 1, at 13–14, [1957] AC 253, at 265–6, 273.

service provider controlled all space for warehousing the goods. The statute which required that the goods be warehoused in the company's premises was not passed solely for the benefit of the company, but also for the benefit of the public and trade, which would be defeated if the dock company were at liberty to charge any price it chose. Lord Ellenborough drew on the work of Hale, who reasoned from first principle to the effect that private property could, in the circumstances set out above, be vested with a public interest.[49]

We should, moreover, when considering substantive review of discretion, not forget collateral challenge. This was, as we shall see, central to the remedial schema as it unfolded from the sixteenth century. The actions for replevin, trover, trespass and the like were the foundation for contesting the legality of the public body's action, enabling the plaintiff to argue, for example, that the action was illegal for jurisdictional error, or for failure to accord a hearing. Collateral challenge through negligence gave added impetus, because the very structure of the tort encouraged the plaintiff to contend that the negligent exercise of a statutory power gave rise to liability, requiring the courts to pass judgment on the reasonableness of the way in which the power had been exercised. The courts equivocated in this regard,[50] but a duty to take reasonable care to ensure that no unnecessary damage

[49] Craig, 'Constitutions, Property and Regulation', 540.

[50] P. Craig, 'Negligence in the Exercise of a Statutory Power' (1978) 94 *Law Quarterly Review* 428, at 429–31; T. Hickman, 'The Reasonableness Principle: Re-assessing Its Place in the Public Sphere' [2004] *Cambridge Law Journal* 166.

was done pursuant to exercise of such powers was established by the mid-nineteenth century,[51] and there were earlier cases on point.[52] The application of negligence liability to public bodies has generated much case law and academic comment, which is beyond the scope of the current inquiry. It does not, however, alter the point being made here, which is that exercise of power could be contested collaterally through a damages action, as well as in a direct action for a prerogative writ, and that in doing so the courts would adjudicate on the reasonableness of the way in which the power was exercised.

The most significant difference between the earlier system of review and the current regime is in relation to rights-based review. We have grown rapidly accustomed to the Human Rights Act 1998, and the way in which it has altered judicial review by giving greater weight to rights, more especially so since the Convention rights brought into UK law accord the status of rights to some interests that would not have been so regarded in the seventeenth or eighteenth centuries. Insofar as interests such as free speech and the like were protected, it was in the form of negative residual liberties, as exemplified by the Blackstonian view that the liberty of the press consisted in the absence of prior restraint on publication, and not in freedom from censure when the matter was published. Thus while every freeman had an undoubted right to lay what sentiments he pleased before

[51] *Mersey Docks and Harbour Board Trustees* v. *Gibbs* (1864–6) 11 H.L.C. 686; *Geddis* v. *Proprietors of Bann Resevoir* (1878) 3 App. Cas. 430.

[52] See, e.g., *Sutton* v. *Clarke* (1815) 6 Taunt. 29; *Boulton* v. *Crothier* (1824) 2 B. & C. 703.

the public, 'if he publishes what is improper, mischievous, or illegal, he must take the consequence of his own temerity'.[53] This was echoed judicially by Lord Coleridge, who noted that free speech was in the public interest, and should be exercised without impediment, 'so long as no wrongful act is done'.[54]

There were, nonetheless, elements within the earlier jurisprudence that strike a chord with more modern case law. Certain interests were conceptualized as rights and protected as such, both directly and collaterally through tort actions, the principal examples being interests in property and bodily security. Thus the reasoning concerning the legality of the Secretary of State's action in searching the plaintiff's property in *Entick* v. *Carrington* was predicated on the assumption that

> our law holds the property of every man so sacred, that no man can set his foot upon his neighbour's close without his leave; if he does he is a trespasser, though he does no damage at all; if he will tread upon his neighbour's ground, he must justify it by law.[55]

There were, moreover, instances where the court's reasoning encapsulated a precept analogous to the legality principle as enunciated in *Simms*,[56] as in *Dr Bonham*'s case, where it was held that the 'Act giving a power to imprison until he be delivered by the president and censors, or their

[53] Sir W. Blackstone, *Commentaries on the Law of England* (London: Butterworths, 16th ed., 1825), Vol. 4, p. 151.

[54] *Bonnard* v. *Perryman* [1891] 2 Ch 269, at 284.

[55] (1765) 2 Wils. K.B. 275, at 291. See also *Leach* v. *Money* (1765) 3 Burr. 1692.

[56] *R* v. *Secretary of State for the Home Department, ex p Simms & O'Brien* [2000] 2 AC 115.

successors, shall be taken strictly, or otherwise the liberty of the subject is at their pleasure'.[57]

(b) Subject matter: statute and prerogative

The discussion thus far has concentrated on the way in which judicial review was fashioned through decisions concerning the grounds of review. The subject matter in such actions was commonly statute, but the courts were also willing to review the prerogative and in doing so established principles that were central to constitutional architecture. The seminal decisions were both the work of Coke: *Prohibitions del Roy*[58] and the *Case of Proclamations.*[59]

The first of these cases established limits to the prerogative insofar as it threatened to impinge on judicial power. It arose as a result of uncertainty as to the limits of authority of ecclesiastical judges, and uncertainty also as to the meaning of statutes to be applied by such judges. The king was advised by the Archbishop of Canterbury that 'the King may decide it in his Royal person', and moreover that the judges were but delegates of the king, with the consequence that he could take 'what causes he shall please to determine, from the determination of the judges and determine them himself'.[60]

Coke was unmoved and duly defended judicial autonomy. He responded, having secured the agreement of 'all the judges of England, and Barons of the Exchequer', by saying that the 'king in his own person cannot adjudge any

[57] *Dr Bonham's Case* (1609) 8 Co. Rep. 113b. [58] (1607) 12 Co. Rep. 63.
[59] (1611) 12 Co. Rep. 74. [60] (1607) 12 Co. Rep. 63.

case, either criminal, as treason, felony etc., or betwixt party and party, concerning his inheritance, chattels or goods etc., but this ought to be determined in some Court of Justice, according to the law and custom of England'.[61] When the king was moved to inquire whether the law was founded upon reason, and that if this was so, he too had reason as well as the judges, Coke countered in terms which have become famous:

> that true it was, that God had endowed His Majesty with excellent science, and great endowments of nature; but his Majesty was not learned in the laws of his realm of England, and causes which concern the life, or inheritance, or goods, or fortunes of his subjects, are not to be decided by natural reason but by the artificial reason and judgment of law, which law is an act which requires long study and experience, before that a man can attain to the cognizance of it: that the law was the golden met-wand and measure to try the causes of the subjects; and which protected His Majesty in safety and peace: with which the King was greatly offended, and said, that then he should be under the law, which was treason to affirm, as he said; to which I said, that Bracton saith, *quod Rex non debet esse sub homine, sed sub Deo et lege.*[62]

What *Prohibitions del Roy* achieved for the divide between executive and judicial power, the *Case of Proclamations* did for the division between executive and legislative competence. The case concerned the legality of two proclamations made

[61] (1607) 12 Co. Rep. 63, at 64.

[62] (1607) 12 Co. Rep. 63, at 65. 'That the King ought not to be subject to man, but under God and the law'.

by the king, which prohibited new buildings in and about London, and the making of starch from wheat. Coke was in no doubt as to the importance of the issues raised by the case, stating that they 'concerned the answer of the King to the body, viz. to the Commons of the House of Parliament'.[63] The Lord Chancellor, pressing the king's case, was untroubled by the absence of precedent, arguing that 'every precedent had first a commencement',[64] and that where there was no precedent the matter should be left to the king to decide in accordance with his wisdom, for otherwise 'the King would be no more than the Duke of Venice'.[65] Coke's response was that where precedent was wanting there was a need of great consideration 'before that any thing of novelty shall be established'.[66]

The judgment went against the King. It was held that the king cannot by his proclamation change any part of the common law, statute law or custom. Nor could the king create any new offence by way of proclamation, for that would be to change the law. Indictments could conclude in the form *contra leges et statuta*, but no indictment had ever been known to conclude *contra regiam proclamationem.* The king, therefore, 'hath no prerogative, but that which the law of the land allows him'.[67]

The case established that the prerogative was bounded, and the boundaries were to be delineated through the courts, which would determine the existence and extent of

[63] (1611) 12 Co. Rep. 74.
[64] (1611) 12 Co. Rep. 74.
[65] (1611) 12 Co. Rep. 74.
[66] (1611) 12 Co. Rep. 74, at 75.
[67] (1611) 12 Co. Rep. 74, at 76.

prerogative powers.[68] The decision became central for relations between the executive and the legislature, since it denied the king a general, free-standing regulatory power, with the consequence that if he wished to attain certain ends these could only be achieved by the passage of statutes, and hence the assent of Parliament. This point was captured by Christopher Hill,[69] who noted that 'this was a crucial period in which legal decisions contributed very substantially to preventing the Crown establishing a control over the economic life of the country similar to that which the French monarchy enjoyed'. Coke was, moreover, against what he regarded as unwarranted fetters on free trade: 'Coke's unspoken assumption that men have a right to do what they will with their own persons and skills represents the thread of continuity running through all his decisions. It explains his campaign for economic liberalism'.[70]

This did not mean that the Crown always lost important legal battles concerning the prerogative in the seventeenth century. It did not. The preceding decisions were nonetheless of central importance for the scope of executive power in relation to the courts and legislature respectively and remain so to the present. For the Crown to succeed it had to be shown that the power claimed really fell within an established head of the prerogative.

[68] There are, however, issues as to when the report of the case was known and its immediate impact. E. Cope, 'Sir Edward Coke and Proclamations, 1610' (1971) 15 *American Journal of Legal History* 215.

[69] C. Hill, *Intellectual Origins of the English Revolution* (Oxford: Clarendon, 1965), p. 234.

[70] Hill, *Intellectual Origins of the English Revolution*, pp. 236–7.

This is exemplified by *Bate's Case*.[71] John Bate, a merchant, refused to pay a levy of five shillings per hundredweight on imported currants imposed by James I by letters patent under the great seal, in addition to the statutory poundage of two shillings and sixpence. It seems, although it is not entirely clear, as if Bate refused payment on the ground that it amounted to indirect taxation without the consent of Parliament, in breach of statute. While the judgments of Fleming C.B. and Clarke B. contain broad statements as to the general reach of prerogative power, the main thrust of the decision in the Crown's favour was more narrowly framed. In essence the levy was held to be justified as an incident of the Crown's power to regulate foreign affairs. Given that the Crown could prohibit the import of certain goods, so too could it allow such products into the country on condition that duties be paid.

The *Case of Ship-Money* was likewise concerned with the scope of prerogative power in the all-important field of revenue.[72] In 1634 Charles I needed a navy to protect English trade, but was unwilling to call a Parliament to raise the necessary funds. He therefore issued a writ requiring seaports to provide ships that were fully equipped, and to raise the funds required. The judges were asked their opinion as to the legality of these writs and answered in favour of the king, who then repeated his demands for money in the years which followed. Not surprisingly, these repeated demands were met with increasing resistance, so Charles I went back to the courts to confirm the legality of his actions. The court again

[71] (1606) 2 St. Tr. 371. [72] *R.* v. *Hampden* (1637) 3 St. Tr. 825.

found in his favour, stating that the king was the guardian of the country's safety, that this empowered him to raise money for the defence of the kingdom, and that the king was also the sole judge as to the best manner of providing for such defence. John Hampden refused to pay the sum levied upon him.

The arguments proffered on behalf of both parties were lengthy and complex.[73] The essence of Hampden's contention was that while the king was indisputably the defender of the realm, and therefore must have the financial means to carry out this task, this had to be done through Parliament: the king, 'though he is the fountain of justice, can administer justice only with the assistance of his judges, so he can take away the property of the subject only in Parliament',[74] which would authorize just demands. The argument for the king rested ultimately upon the claim that he possessed certain absolute powers in his capacity as ruler, including those relating to war and peace. In these areas it was contended that he had no need of Parliament.

The majority of the judges found for the king. They reasoned that the king had sole responsibility for the defence of the realm; that he must therefore have revenue for this purpose; that the most equitable manner of obtaining this money was by a charge on his subjects; that while generally taxation required the consent of Parliament, the defence of the realm could require the king to act without Parliament; that any attempt by Parliament to fetter the exercise of the

[73] D. Keir, 'The Case of Ship-Money' (1936) 52 *Law Quarterly Review* 546.
[74] *R.* v. *Hampden* (1637) 3 St. Tr. 825, at 828.

undoubted prerogative power to defend the realm would be void, and so too would be any attempt to impose limits on the way in which the king acquired the revenue to fulfil this prerogative power.

While the Crown was victorious the victory was premised on finding that the power could be properly regarded as within the bounds of the prerogative. What divided the two sides was a radical difference of opinion on what these boundaries actually were. The result was not necessarily wrong at the time,[75] but the litigation cast into sharp relief the lines between monarchical and parliamentary authority. Where these lines were to be drawn was inherently contestable and the division of power altered across time, with Parliament ultimately being victorious. Keir and Lawson offer a salutary perspective:

> The struggle in *Darnel's Case*[76] and *Hampden's Case* was really the same. The prize was the debatable ground between *property* and *government* . . . Taxation as a general rule belonged to the former. But if, in the one case, the King could imprison anybody who refused to contribute to a forced loan, or, in the other, could levy direct taxation by Prerogative whenever he chose to allege the existence of a state of emergency, it was clear that he could dispense with parliaments altogether. Property would have been swallowed up by government. If on the other hand he failed, then in the long run Parliament could, by its control of the purse strings, control the government of the country. The theory of

[75] Keir, 'The Case of Ship-Money'. [76] (1627) 3 St. Tr. 1.

> the Tudor constitution had been that the King should govern, but Parliament should tax. The system for several reasons proved unworkable under the Stuarts, and both parties tried to encroach on the other's preserves. Both found an opportunity because they held certain territory in common, and each looked upon the other as a usurper, as indeed he was. The mere fact that Parliament won should not blind us to the fact that in strict law it had no better case than the King. If it was no part of the Tudor theory of government that emergency powers should be used for the raising of revenue, neither was it a bona fide use of the power of the purse to attempt to remove foreign policy or the defence of the realm from the hands of the Crown.[77]

(c) Remedies: direct and collateral attack

The history of judicial review is inextricably bound up with the elaboration of remedies. The amplification of grounds for review took place within, and was framed by, the evolution of adjectival law. Direct and collateral challenge were the vehicles for this development, the former through the prerogative writs, the latter primarily, albeit not exclusively, through tort actions.

Mandamus was the earliest of the prerogative writs to be transformed into a more general-purpose tool for the remedying of administrative error. *Bagg*'s case[78] was the

[77] Sir D.L. Keir and F. H. Lawson, *Cases in Constitutional Law* (Oxford: Oxford University Press, 5th ed., 1967), p. 95. Italics in the original.

[78] (1615) 11 Co. Rep. 93b.

seminal judgment in this respect. Edith Henderson captured the importance and novelty of the decision.[79] A 'writ of restitution' existed prior to *Bagg*'s case. Its primary focus was, however, to protect the privilege of a claimant who had been deprived of an office, so as to ensure that he could consult with a King's Bench counsel. If such a person was arrested while attempting to exercise this right a writ would be sought to command the prison to release the person thus detained. By 1613–15 the writ had been transformed and *Bagg*'s case was of central importance in this respect. The colourful case concerned the disenfranchisement of James Bagg, who had been a burgess of Plymouth. He had made a succession of abusive comments about the mayor and other burgesses. Coke CJ in the King's Bench found for Bagg, concluding that the offensive words were an insufficient cause for disenfranchisement from a freehold office. This factual conclusion was buttressed by a more important finding as to the jurisdiction of King's Bench. It was held that this court had the authority

> not only to correct errors in judicial proceedings, but other errors and misdemeanors extra-judicial, tending to the breach of the peace, or oppression of the subjects, or to the raising of faction, controversy, debate or to any manner of misgovernment; so that no wrong or injury, either public or private, can be done but that it shall be (here) reformed or punished by due course of law.[80]

[79] Henderson, *Foundations of English Administrative Law*, pp. 46–58.
[80] (1615) 11 Co. Rep. 93b, at 98a.

The decision was of far-reaching importance for expansion of the remedy, more especially given the types of error that were now said to be reviewable. Henderson captures the point well:

> by 1613–15 a new writ had appeared with a definite though potentially very flexible form. Moreover, by this writ King's Bench did something quite different from its traditional activities. It was not addressed to the sheriff or any other law enforcement official ... Nor was it directed to other judicial authority like the writs of prohibition, error ... and some of the medieval forms of certiorari. By this new writ a public official *outside* the normal law enforcement system was required to do something ... All this was a very far-reaching departure from tradition. Yet as may be seen, the writ as it was now worded said nothing to explain why King's Bench could do this, beyond the bare generality that an injustice had been done and that it ought to be set right.[81]

The significance of the latter point, the scope of errors which King's Bench could address, was not lost on those who read the judgment. Thus in the *Observations on the Lord Coke's Reports*, Lord Ellesmere,[82] having noted that the case was simply concerned with the legality of removal from an office, had this to say about the broader dicta concerning the scope of the King's Bench power:

[81] Henderson, *Foundations of English Administrative Law*, pp. 61–2. Italics in the original.

[82] The observations are attributed to Lord Ellesmere, although Henderson, *Foundations of English Administrative Law*, p. 70, questions whether he was indeed the author.

> Herein (giving excess of authority to K.B.) he hath as much as insinuated that this Court is all-sufficient in itself to manage the State; for if the King's Bench may reform any manner of misgovernment (as the words are) it seemeth that there is little or no use either of the King's Royal care and authority exercised in his person, and by his proclamations, ordinances, and immediate directions, nor of the council table, which under the King is the chief watch tower for all points of government . . . and besides the words do import as if the King's Bench had a superintendency over the government itself, and to judge wherein any of them do misgovern.[83]

Theoretical justification for the expansive power arrogated by King's Bench was not immediately forthcoming. There was no attempt to legitimate this exercise of judicial power by reference to ultra vires in the sense of legislative intent, howsoever it might be defined. There is no such indication in the judgment of *Bagg*'s case, and this conclusion is reinforced by the fact that Parliament was not at that time the fount of all authority. Power was divided between the king and Parliament, and it was to take a civil war and consequent settlement before it became meaningful to begin to think of Parliament with a truly sovereign capacity in the modern sense of the term. Yet one suspects that even if Parliament had attained this status at the time of *Bagg*'s case it would not have suited Coke's temperament and intellectual leanings to rest judicial review on the foundation of legislative intent. He was a supporter of Parliament in its struggles with the

[83] The quotation can be found in (1615) 11 Co. Rep. 93b, at 98a fn B.

king, as manifested in the seminal decisions concerning the prerogative considered above. Yet his enduring belief was in the power of the common law itself. Given that this was so it is very doubtful if Coke would have been content to rest judicial intervention on the vindication of Parliamentary intent in the sense used in modern academic debate.

One hundred and fifty years later the 'parties' had changed, but the story remained the same. Parliament's position had improved considerably during this time, although the monarch still exercised real power. The leading judicial decisions declined, nonetheless, to rest review powers on ideas of legislative intent. What was true of Coke in this respect was true also of Lord Mansfield, who stated in relation to mandamus that 'there is no doubt that where a party, who has a right, has no other specific legal remedy, the Court will assist him by issuing this prerogative writ in order to his obtaining such right'.[84] This echoed his earlier rationalization of mandamus in *R. v. Barker*:

> The original nature of the writ, and the end for which it was framed, direct upon what occasions it should be used. It was introduced, to prevent disorder from a failure of justice, and defect of police. Therefore it ought to be used upon all occasions where the law has established no specific remedy, and where in justice and good government there ought to be one.[85]

A number of possible justifications for the newly created judicial power were advanced. Coke sought to rest it in part

[84] *R.* v. *Askew* (1768) 4 Burr. 2186, at 2188. [85] (1762) 3 Burr. 1265, at 1267.

upon Magna Carta and the protections for freehold offices derived therefrom, although, as Henderson has pointed out, it was by no means self-evident that a municipal alderman possessed such a freehold in his office.[86] More generally, Coke advanced a theory of delegation, whereby the king was taken to have committed all his judicial power to the courts, including in this respect the power to do justice.[87] This theory is equally applicable to all areas of the law; there is no basis for distinguishing between public and private law. There are, however, empirical and conceptual difficulties with this explanation.[88] In truth, we would do well to pay attention to the language used by both Coke and Mansfield, and to acknowledge that both jurists based their conclusions on the capacity of the common law to control governmental power. Indeed, as Jaffe and Henderson aptly remark, Coke's doctrine of irrevocable delegation was in truth but a corollary of 'his boldest and most spacious notion', the autonomy of the common law.[89]

The evolution of certiorari into a generalized remedy capable of catching a variety of governmental errors was to postdate the developments in mandamus charted above. While there was therefore a temporal difference in the elaboration of the remedies, the conceptual foundation for the

[86] Henderson, *Foundations of English Administrative Law*, pp. 77–8.

[87] Coke, *The Fourth Part of the Institutes of the Laws of England* (1648), p. 71, cited by Henderson, *Foundations of English Administrative Law*, pp. 70–1.

[88] Henderson, *Foundations of English Administrative Law*, pp. 71–2.

[89] Jaffe and Henderson, 'Judicial Review and the Rule of Law', 362.

expansion in the remit of certiorari paralleled that which we have identified in the context of mandamus.

Certiorari existed during the medieval period, and was used for many purposes, most notably as a means for calling up the record on a particular matter. Certiorari to quash emerged later. The judgment in *Commins* v. *Massam* was of central importance.[90] It arose out of a decision by the Commissioners of Sewers to charge the cost of repairs to a sea wall to the lessee of the land. The court was divided as to whether certiorari would lie or not. Mallett J was of the view that it would not, but Heath J and Bramston CJ held to the contrary. Heath J was firmly of the opinion that certiorari would lie since there was no court which could not be corrected by King's Bench.[91] It seems that this newly created remedy of certiorari to quash was originally only available against courts of record.[92]

It was Holt CJ who built on these foundations to fashion a remedy of more wide-ranging application. In the *Cardiffe Bridge* case orders by justices of the peace for the payment of money to repair the bridge were contested.[93] It was argued that certiorari would not lie, because it was a new jurisdiction created by an Act of Parliament, the execution of which 'reposed' in the justices. The consequence, so it was argued, was that if the justices proceeded according to the statute, then there would be no reason to remove their orders, and if they did not then the orders would be *coram non judice*,

[90] (1643) March N.C. 196. [91] (1643) March N.C. 196, at 197.

[92] Henderson, *Foundations of English Administrative Law*, p. 112.

[93] (1700) 1 Ld. Raym. 580.

and void, with legality being contested collaterally via a tort action. Holt CJ was unconvinced by this limit on the jurisdiction of the King's Bench to intervene via certiorari:

> For this Court will examine the proceedings of all jurisdictions erected by Act of Parliament. And if they, under pretence of such Act, proceed to incroach jurisdiction to themselves greater than the Act warrants, this Court will send certiorari to them, to have their proceedings returned here; to the end that this Court may see, that they keep themselves within their jurisdiction: and if they exceed it, to restrain them. And the examination of such matters is more proper for this Court. As in the case in question; whether the Act of Queen Elizabeth empowers the justices to raise money to mend wears, and to determine the doubt upon the Act.[94]

The same theme was developed by Holt CJ in *Groenvelt* v. *Burwell*.[95] The College of Physicians regulated doctors in London and within a radius of seven miles. It fined and imprisoned Dr Groenvelt for administering '*insalubres pillulas & noxia medicamenta*'. The issue before the court was whether certiorari was available to contest such a decision. The Chief Justice framed the court's power in broad terms, stating that wherever a power was given to examine, hear and punish, it was a judicial power, such that those who possessed it acted as judges. Moreover, whenever there was

[94] (1700) 1 Ld. Raym. 580. See also *Colonial Bank of Australasia* v. *Willan* (1874) LR 5 PC 440; *R* v. *Cripps, ex p Muldoon* [1984] QB 68, at 87; *R (Cart)* v. *Upper Tribunal* [2011] QB 120, at [69].

[95] (1700) 1 Salkeld 200.

a jurisdiction erected with power to fine and imprison, the body was a court of record,[96] and where any court 'is erected by statute, a certiorari lies to it; so that if they perform not their duty, the King's Bench will grant a mandamus'.[97] It was therefore a consequence of all jurisdictions to have their proceedings examined by King's Bench. Moreover, although the statute did not 'give authority to this Court to grant a certiorari', this was not conclusive since 'it is by the common law that this Court will examine if other Courts exceed their jurisdictions'.[98]

The discussion thus far focused on the judicial creativity evident in development of direct challenge through the prerogative writs. This operated in tandem with collateral attack, which constituted the early method of challenging decisions. It pre-dated the expanded application of the prerogative writs,[99] and was much used even after the seminal decisions explicated above. Collateral attack embodied the very interaction between private and public law that characterized the common law. It was through actions in trover, replevin, conversion, false imprisonment, nuisance, trespass, case, negligence, and money had and received that plaintiffs sought to press their claims against public bodies. The legality of the contested decision would be the central issue in the success or failure of such claims.

Collateral attack was used by the ordinary courts to keep in check specialist judicial authorities. This is

[96] (1700) 1 Salkeld 200. [97] (1700) 1 Ld. Raym. 454, at 469.

[98] (1700) 1 Ld. Raym. 454, at 469.

[99] Rubinstein, *Jurisdiction and Illegality*, Ch. 4.

exemplified by the *Case of the Marshalsea* where the plaintiff brought an action for trespass and false imprisonment, claiming that the Marshalsea Court possessed no jurisdiction over him as he was not of the King's House.[100] The court held that an action would lie where the challenged authority had no jurisdiction over the case, the entire proceedings being *coram non judice*. No such action would lie where the error was one within jurisdiction.

Collateral challenge was also commonly deployed against administrative authorities. Thus in *Terry* v. *Huntington* the plaintiff brought an action for trover and conversion against the Commissioners of Excise on the ground that they had judged 'low wines to be strong wines perfectly made' and thus exceeded their jurisdiction.[101] Chief Baron Hale held that the matter could be examined, since the commissioners had a 'stinted, limited jurisdiction',[102] which implied that they could not proceed in other cases. If they made an error within their jurisdiction it would not be examinable, but matters were other otherwise if they exceeded their jurisdiction with respect to place, person or subject matter, since then the decision would be void and *coram non judice*, and the excise officers would be open to an action in trover and conversion. The same approach is evident in *Doswell* v. *Impey*,[103] where the plaintiff brought an action for trespass and false imprisonment against the Commissioners of Bankrupts.

[100] (1612) 10 Co Rep 68b. [101] (1668) Hardres 480.

[102] (1668) Hardres 480, at 484. See also *Fullers* v. *Fotch* (1695) Carthew 346; *Miller* v. *Seare* (1777) 2 Black. W. 1141.

[103] (1823) 1 B. & C. 163.

The commissioners suspected that he was concealing the property of the bankrupt, questioned the plaintiff, were dissatisfied with his answers, and thus imprisoned him. He contested this via an action for trespass and false imprisonment. Abbott CJ held that such an action would lie against persons with limited authority, such as the Commissioners of Bankrupts, if they acted beyond the limit of their authority, but if the act was done within the limits of that authority there would be no such action, notwithstanding that the decision was erroneous. The judgment contains an astute insight into the difficulty of applying this distinction, and the rationale for the choice thus made.

While tort actions constituted the principal method of collateral challenge, there were many other ways in which this could occur.[104] An accuser's guilt might be dependent on the validity of a ministerial order. If the order was ultra vires then the accused could be exonerated.[105] A ratepayer could resist a demand for rates or charges by claiming that the demand was invalid.[106]

The general principle from the seventeenth century onwards was that the claimant in a collateral challenge could assert any illegality that went to jurisdiction that could be pleaded in a direct action. There are exceptions to this principle,[107] but the general principle was reaffirmed in

[104] Rubinstein, *Jurisdiction and Illegality*, pp. 39–46.

[105] *DPP* v. *Head* [1959] AC 83.

[106] *Daymond* v. *Plymouth City Council* [1976] AC 609.

[107] Craig, *Administrative Law*, Ch. 24.

Boddington.[108] Boddington was convicted by a stipendiary magistrate for smoking in a railway carriage, contrary to a by-law of the British Railways Board. The House of Lords held that it was open to a defendant in criminal proceedings to challenge subordinate legislation, or an administrative decision made thereunder, where the prosecution was premised on its validity, unless there was a clear legislative intent to the contrary. It was, said their Lordships, unacceptable in a democracy based on the rule of law for a magistrate to be able to convict a person who would be precluded from relying on a defence that he might otherwise have had. A direct action for judicial review was an inadequate safeguard in the instant case: the defendant might be out of time before becoming aware of the by-law, he might not have the resources for such a challenge, leave might be refused, or a remedy might be denied pursuant to the court's discretionary power over such matters.

(d) Regulatory efficacy: the Janus nature of judicial review

The preceding sketch will hopefully assist in understanding the judicial evolution of administrative law. It nonetheless provides an incomplete picture of the reality of judicial review and the gap is important since it has ramifications over and beyond the historical analysis. Indeed it is not going

[108] *Boddington* v. *British Transport Police* [1999] 2 AC 143; *EN (Serbia)* v. *Secretary of State for the Home Department* [2010] QB 633, at [86]–[87].

too far to suggest that the gap is responsible for imperfect understandings of administrative law and theory to the modern day.

The nature of the gap is remarkably simple. Judicial review has always possessed a Janus-like quality. It is the mechanism through which the preceding doctrines are used when an individual contests the legality of a decision or regulatory norm made by a public or quasi-public body. This is the face that we perceive. Judicial review is, however, also the legal mechanism through which the courts commonly effectuate the regulatory schema challenged before them. The claimant challenges the legality of a decision and loses, because the court does not agree that there is such an illegality judged by the terms and purposes of the legislation. In reaching this conclusion the courts interpret the statute to attain the specified objectives, and often fill gaps to render the legislation more efficacious. This face is not hidden, but is largely ignored in our evaluation of what administrative law is 'about'.

This skews our perception of the nature and effect of judicial review. The debate concerning, for example, 'red-light' and 'green-light' theories of administrative law is not solely about the role of the courts, but it is predicated on assumptions about what courts do and what they should do when engaging in judicial review.[109] The assumption integral to red-light theory is that the administration is to be

[109] The distinction was initially advanced by C. Harlow and R. Rawlings, *Law and Administration* (London: Weidenfeld and Nicolson, 1984), Chs. 1–2.

distrusted, with the consequence that the purpose of review is primarily to control this dangerous entity, which hypothesis is then challenged by green-light theorists who point to the social value of the regulatory schemes, with the consequence that they should be interpreted positively. The line betwixt the two has been softened in subsequent debate, with varying degrees of 'amber', but that is not apposite to the point being made here. What is relevant is the fact that these opposing perspectives presuppose that there is only one face to judicial review, with rival interpretations being proffered as to how it should be interpreted.

This misses the significance of the other face of judicial review, which has important consequences for how the debate is framed at its very inception. This is particularly apparent when judicial review is perceived from a historical perspective. The reality was that in many subject matter areas the judicial decisions exhibited attachment to both dimensions of judicial review. The case law over four centuries revealed the courts' desire to forge the principles of review adumbrated above, but an understanding of that case law also shows judicial concern to ensure the efficacy of the regulatory schema litigated before them. The courts did not ignore the social value of these administrative regimes, nor did they generally approach the subject matter from a red-light perspective. This duality continues to be reflected in current law.

The previous point must be kept in perspective. Courts have interpreted statutory regimes in a manner that undermines the desired objective, and have been prejudicial to, for example, worker interests at certain periods in history.[110] They may, moreover, not always be correct in their assessment of what a particular statutory regime demands. This can be readily acknowledged, but does not undermine the force of the preceding argument. It just means that courts, like any other institution, are imperfect, but as stated above I am not writing Whig legal history wherein courts can do no wrong. The imperfection inheres also in political institutions, and more specifically in the mechanisms of political accountability. The blend of the two dimensions of judicial review is exemplified in the section that follows, when discussing the principal administrative institutions making the decisions that were challenged before courts.

4 The evolution of administrative law: the administrative perspective

(a) Introduction

This section considers the evolution of administrative law from an administrative perspective and thus complements discussion in the preceding two sections. A few words by way of introduction are in order.

First, this section is not designed to provide a history of administration over four centuries, which would clearly be far beyond the scope of this work. It is intended to convey an idea of some of the principal bodies exercising administrative

[110] See, e.g., C. Gearty and K. Ewing, *The Struggle for Civil Liberties: Political Freedom and the Rule of Law in Britain, 1914–45* (Oxford: Oxford University Press, 2000).

power from the fifteenth century to the nineteenth. This is important in and of itself, since there is something very odd about a historical analysis of administrative law that pays scant regard to the bodies subject to review. It is also important since it enables us to understand the duality of judicial review adumbrated at the end of the previous section, and the interaction between judicial, political and administrative mechanisms of accountability in the relevant areas.

Second, it is important to understand that there was, put simply, a lot to administer. We commonly think of government before the twentieth century as having limited responsibility, as doing a whole lot less than now. There is some truth in this, but misapprehension nonetheless exceeds veracity. It is important to distinguish between centralization of state authority and decentralization of administration. England was highly centralized compared to its Continental neighbours, more especially from the Tudors onwards. Social and economic legislation occupied a great deal of time in Elizabethan parliaments,[111] and 'was considered, after the granting of taxation, to be the primary function of the House of Commons'.[112] Adam Smith's free-market ideas were two centuries away, and there was statutory regulation of diverse

[111] For social legislation see, e.g., P. Slack, *Poverty and Policy in Tudor and Stuart England* (London: Longman, 1988); for Elizabethan parliaments see G.R. Elton, *The Parliament of England 1559–1581* (Cambridge: Cambridge University Press, 1986). See also D. Smith, *The Stuart Parliaments 1603–1689* (London: Arnold, 1999).

[112] R. Sgroi, 'Elizabethan Social and Economic Legislation', www.historyofparliamentonline.org/periods/tudors/elizabethan-social-and-economic-legislation.

matters, including trades such as leather, alcohol, iron and cloth; wages; poverty, unemployment and vagrancy; land use; and morality. There was, in addition, much legislation pertaining to police powers broadly conceived, and to tax and flood defences. The fact that these measures were enacted by Parliament did not mean that they were necessarily initiated by central government departments. The later advent of free-market principles led to some diminution in trade regulation, but there was also increased regulation in areas such as factories, health and the like, which is the backdrop to continuing historical debates as to whether the nineteenth century really ever was an era of laissez-faire.[113]

Third, while the legislation was enacted from the centre, the general pattern of administration was decentralized. Central departments of government with generalized administrative responsibility as understood in the twentieth century were not the norm in earlier centuries. A catalyst for their development was the growth of the fiscal–military state towards the end of the seventeenth century, which prompted increased departmentalization in central government.[114] Administrative responsibilities were nonetheless commonly assigned to a wide range of bodies, with justices of the peace and commissioners performing prominent roles. Their remit will be explicated below.

[113] See, e.g., A. Taylor, *Laissez-Faire and State Intervention in Nineteenth-Century Britain* (London: Macmillan, 1972).

[114] J. Brewer, *The Sinews of Power: War, Money and the English State 1688–1783* (Cambridge, MA: Harvard University Press, 1988); J. Innes, 'Governing Diverse Societies', in P. Langford (ed.), *The Eighteenth Century* (Oxford: Oxford University Press, 2002), pp. 119–20.

Justices had judicial, administrative and regulatory responsibilities, so too did commissioners, which were the forerunners of modern agencies, with adjudicatory, decisional and rule-making powers. Many such bodies were later incorporated into either central or local government in the nineteenth century,[115] in large part because Parliament desired a greater degree of control than was possible when the activity was undertaken by a board, commission or agency. The late twentieth century saw the tide moving in the opposite direction, with central departments being slimmed down, and activities 'hived off' to agencies. Tribunals came to assume increased importance in the nineteenth century,[116] and have remained central to the administrative landscape since then.

Fourth, while the challenges to securing administrative accountability perforce varied across time, there were also endemic problems. Our political and legal forebears might not have captured these challenges in the language of principal/agent, but they would nonetheless have understood full well their import. The ensuing discussion is designed to reveal the interplay between political, administrative and legal mechanisms to ensure such accountability. It is not predicated on the assumption that the courts were

[115] D. Roberts, *Victorian Origins of the British Welfare State* (New Haven: Yale University Press, 1960); H. Parris, *Constitutional Bureaucracy: The Development of British Central Administration since the Eighteenth Century* (London: Allen & Unwin, 1968); Sir D.N. Chester, *The English Administrative System 1780–1870* (Oxford: Oxford University Press, 1981).

[116] C. Stebbings, *Legal Foundations of Tribunals in Nineteenth-Century England* (Cambridge: Cambridge University Press, 2006).

all-important in this respect, but they did play a significant role, which varied depending on, inter alia, the existence and efficacy of political and administrative modes of accountability. The following discussion is not, moreover, premised on the assumption that administrators, or the schemes they administered, were to be approached with some inherent suspicion. The regulatory schemes were enacted to attain valuable social purposes broadly conceived, even if some were contestable, and courts, while seeking to ensure legal accountability, also strove to attain regulatory efficacy, much as they do today.

(b) Justices of the peace

Justices of the peace were crucial to the administration of statute. The office evolved over time, its origins lying in the appointment of knights of the shire to undertake police work. The 'conservators' of the peace were transformed into justices of the peace during the reign of Edward III, the key statute being the Justices of the Peace Act 1361, which provided as follows:

> That in every county of England shall be assigned for the keeping of the peace, one Lord, and with him three or four of the most worthy in the County, with some learned in the Law, and they shall have power to restrain the offenders, rioters, and all other barators, and to pursue, arrest, take, and chastise them according their trespass or offence; and to cause them to be imprisoned and duly punished according to the law and customs of the realm, and according to that which to them shall seem best to

> do by their discretions and good advisement; and also to inform them, and to inquire of all those that have been pillors or robbers in parts beyond the sea and be now come again and go wandering and will not labor as they were wont in times past; and to take and arrest all those that they may find by indictment, or by suspicion, and to put them in Prison; and to take of all them that be [not] of good fame, where they shall be found, sufficient surety and mainprise of their good behaviour towards the King and his people, and the other duly to punish; to the intent that the people be not by such rioters or rebels troubled nor endamaged, nor the peace blemished, nor merchants nor other passing by the highways of the Realm disturbed, nor [put in the peril which may happen] of such offenders; and also to hear and determine at the King's suit all manner of felonies and trespasses done in the same county according the laws and customs as aforesaid; and that writs of oyer and determiner be granted according to the statutes made, and that the justices which shall be thereto assigned be named by the court and not by the party.[117]

The authority of justices of the peace increased with the decline of the Norman police system. Thus, as Joanna Innes writes, 'from the later middle ages, justices of the peace rose to ascendancy as county authorities, marginalizing sheriffs'.[118] This is exemplified by Richard II's statute of 1388 according justices a supervisory jurisdiction over other local officials. The justices were to inquire

[117] 34 Edward III., c. 1.

[118] Innes, 'Governing Diverse Societies', p. 103.

> if the said mayors, bailiffs, stewards, constables and gaolers have duly done execution of the said ordinances [and statutes] of servants and labourers, beggars and vagabonds, and shall punish them that be punishable by the same pain of an hundred shillings by the same pain; and they that be found in default and which be not punishable by the same pain shall be punished at their discretion.[119]

The justices became pivotal to administration touching diverse subject matter. It was the justices that administered the growing body of legislation dealing with police control broadly construed, ranging from riot to sea defences, from disturbance of the peace to livery and maintenance, and from felony to the regulation of activities allowed only to people of a certain rank, the latter including regulation prohibiting servants and labourers playing football, tennis, coits and other such 'importune games'.[120] It was, moreover, the justices that enforced the social and economic regulatory legislation, and there was much of it. This included far-reaching wage and labour regulation, and the statutory oversight of guilds. There was, in addition, much general trade regulation, as Charles Beard reveals:

> They adjusted the profits which victuallers were to receive; they punished regrators of wool and other merchandise of the Staple; they supervised the shipment and exportation of wool and the details of the manufacture of woolen cloth. They enforced the statutes regulating

[119] 12 Ric. II., c. 10. [120] 12 Ric. II., c. 6.

> the preparation of leather, the manufacture of arrowheads, tuns, barrels, and hogsheads, wax candles and images and tiles.[121]

The extensive subject matter jurisdiction of the justices of the peace continued during the Tudor period and beyond,[122] confirming their centrality to administration. Indeed, the commission issued by Chancery from which justices acquired their powers had grown to such an extent by statutory additions that the senior judges revised it, deleting obsolete material to render the commission more intelligible.

The justices served the needs of the centralizing Tudor state well: 'appointed by the crown, forced to hold office unless excused by letters patent, serving during pleasure and liable to heavy penalties for negligence, the justices exactly met the requirements of the central autocracy'.[123] They possessed the virtue of local knowledge, but were subject at the same time 'to the ever watchful scrutiny of the centre' and thus 'never secured enough corporate independence to endanger the cohesion of the national system'.[124]

It is clear, nonetheless, that the system was not free from what we would, in modern parlance, term principal/agent problems. Thus, as Innes notes, while appointment as a justice of the peace might have been gratifying in

[121] C.A. Beard, *The Office of Justice of the Peace in England in Its Origin and Development* (New York: Columbia University Press, 1904), pp. 63–4.

[122] Beard, *The Office of Justice of the Peace in England*, pp. 78–113, 130–8.

[123] Beard, *The Office of Justice of the Peace in England*, p. 71.

[124] Beard, *The Office of Justice of the Peace in England*, p. 71.

symbolic terms, it involved considerable work, with the consequence that 'intelligibly, if frustratingly, men were least eager to serve where the workload promised to be heaviest',[125] more especially because the ordinary justice of the peace received no pay. The problems were addressed, as might be expected, in a number of different ways. Statutes were enacted to deal with negligence, corruption by justices or laxness in the enforcement of the regulatory legislation. There was statutory provision whereby a person aggrieved by a decision from a justice of the peace could complain to another justice nearby, or, if that proved to no avail, there was the possibility of taking the case to the Justices of Assize.[126]

There were, in addition, more structural methods for maintaining control over the large body of justices. The Privy Council played a central role in this respect. It owed its loyalty to the Crown, composed as it was of royal advisers, and therefore sought to ensure that 'justices of the peace were orthodox on the prevailing ecclesiastical policy and loyal to the government',[127] this being facilitated by the termination of the commissions of justices on the death of the sovereign, thereby freeing the successor to appoint those who would adhere to the new policy, whatsoever that might be. The commission was, moreover, open to 'more or less radical tinkering in between [sovereigns] as central authorities saw fit'.[128]

[125] Innes, 'Governing Diverse Societies', 105. [126] 4 Henry VII., c. 12.
[127] Beard, *The Office of Justice of the Peace in England*, p. 118.
[128] Innes, 'Governing Diverse Societies', 104.

It was the Privy Council that devised a system to oversee enforcement of the laws by the justices, as well as to deal with individual complaints against them.[129] This did not mean that all such laws were efficaciously enforced, as attested to by Beard's conclusion that 'it cannot be doubted that the execution of the law was lax when viewed in the light of modern administration'.[130] While central government thus exercised both disciplinary and supervisory control, much of the correction of justices of the peace was done by the ordinary courts of law, which included well-developed use of certiorari.[131] Indeed, as Innes states, institutions of local government had traditionally been overseen by three forms of central body – 'privy councils, parliaments, and courts – and, with modifications, this pattern persisted throughout into the nineteenth century'.[132]

It is to the judicial control that we now turn. The centrality of justices of the peace to administration between the fifteenth and nineteenth centuries is reflected in the 4,237 case citations making reference to them during this period, although this figure must be read subject to the caveats noted earlier.[133] This jurisprudence reveals both dimensions of judicial review, the classic face whereby courts deployed such precepts to render administrative power accountable, and the less recognized facet of review whereby such actions were the medium through which courts advanced regulatory efficacy.

[129] Beard, *The Office of Justice of the Peace in England*, pp. 121–2.
[130] Beard, *The Office of Justice of the Peace in England*, p. 124.
[131] Beard, *The Office of Justice of the Peace in England*, pp. 151, 154.
[132] Innes, 'Governing Diverse Societies', p. 118. [133] See above, p. 27.

The classic use of review in relation to justices is evident in the *Cardiffe Bridge* case,[134] discussed above, whereby Holt CJ powerfully affirmed the jurisdiction of the King's Bench to intervene via certiorari.[135] It was Holt CJ once again who showed his intolerance of abuse of power in *Caly* v. *Hardy*.[136] The town magistrates procured a forcible entry to remove the clerk of the market from his office, and unsurprisingly would not inquire into the occurrence. Holt CJ's response was double-edged: if the town magistrates would not inquire, then it was incumbent on the county justices to do so; and mandamus was issued to the town magistrates jointly and severally to inquire into the use of force, 'for the Court would otherwise suppose them all guilty'. The judicial approach to discretion was exemplified by *R.* v. *Justice of the Peace for Nottingham*, where Ryder CJ acknowledged that justices had very considerable discretion over alcohol licensing, and the court should therefore be wary of issuing mandamus. He qualified this, however, by stating that the 'abuse of discretionary power should be more severely punished than the abuse of power that was not discretionary', and concluded somewhat drolly that there had been an abuse in the instant case, since 'it is not probable

[134] (1700) 1 Ld. Raym. 580.

[135] See also, e.g., *Inter the Inhabitants of the Parish of Chittinston and Penhurst* (1795) 2 Salk. 475; *Inter Inhabitan. King's Norton in Wigorn* (1795) 2 Salk. 481; *The King* v. *Sir Edmund Elwell* (1790) 2 Ld. Raym. 1514; *The Queen* v. *The Justices of Worcestershire* (1839) 11 Ad. & E. 57; *The Queen* v. *The Mayor, Aldermen and Citizens of New Sarum* (1853) 2 El. & Bl. 653.

[136] (1794) 6 Mod. 164.

that the occupiers of twenty publick houses should all have so misbehaved at the same time, so as to make it improper to grant them licenses'.[137] In *Beaudry* v. *Montreal* the court held that justices had erred in concluding that a party claiming compensation for land taken by the corporation was not entitled to produce witnesses as to its value, Pollock C.B. opining that 'any manifest failure of observing the fundamental forms and principles of the administration of justice would vitiate the proceeding before the Justices, and render it null and void'.[138]

There are, by way of counterpoise, many instances where the courts, in rejecting claims, promoted the effectiveness of the particular regulatory regime.[139] In *The King* v. *The Justices of Essex* the issue was whether justices who might be affected by the setting of a poor rate for the area could determine the matter.[140] Lord Ellenborough CJ warned that the courts should avoid interpreting the relevant statutes so as to disable a great many justices from acting in execution of the poor laws, since this would undermine policy in this area. In *Dominus Rex* v. *Randall* justices at quarter sessions had overturned an alehouse license issued by two other justices, the rationale being that there were sufficient alehouses in the town already.[141] Holt CJ quashed this determination, since the

[137] (1755) Sayer 216, at 217. [138] (1858) 11 Moore 399, at 426.

[139] See also, e.g., *The King* v. *Commings* (1696) 5 Mod. 179; *Dr Sand's Case* (1700) 1 Salk. 145; *The King* v. *The Inhabitants of Woolstanton* (1760) Sess. Cas. 59; *Rex* v. *Inhabitants of the Borough of Stamford* (1766) Cun. 102; *The King* v. *Talbot* (1796) 11 Mod. 415; *Rex* v. *Fairfax* (1794) Comb. 164; *The Queen* v. *Ashburton* (1846) 8 Q.B. 871.

[140] (1816) 5 M. & S. 513. [141] (1795) 2 Salk. 470.

clear legislative policy was that the initial decision by two justices could only be overturned at quarter sessions if the alehouse was disorderly. In *Regina* v. *Gouch* the court was willing to uphold an order by justices compelling the master to pay wages, even though they only had jurisdiction to do so for servants in husbandry who were bound by statute so to work.[142] The court construed the statute liberally and was willing to assume that the work had been done for husbandry.

(c) Commissioners

If justices of the peace were central to the administration of statute, so too were commissioners. They were integral to policy delivery in a plethora of areas. There were Commissioners of Sewers, Excise, Inclosure, Tithes, Improvement, Bankruptcy and Railways, to name but the principal examples, and that is without mention of bodies such as turnpike trustees, which undertook analogous functions in relation to roads; the guardians of the poor, who oversaw the poor law; and factory inspectors. Commissioners bestrode the land. They were the chosen medium for administration across diverse areas, they made decisions and regulations that impacted directly on the citizen, and they were therefore not surprisingly the subject of judicial review, direct and collateral.

It is important at the outset to dispel any assumption that commissioners were organized according to some homogeneous institutional format. To the contrary, they were

[142] (1790) 2 Ld. Raym. 820.

marked by institutional heterogeneity, although there were common features. The concept of commission captured the idea of an authority and duty granted by the Crown, the terms of which could vary significantly. It is not possible within the scope of this work to deal with all types of commissioner, nor would that be profitable given the purpose of this inquiry. It is, however, important to understand the centrality of commissioners to the historical–administrative landscape. It will be seen that most commissioners were in reality akin to what we would now regard as administrative agencies, functioning outside the established departments of government. The discussion begins, however, with the commissioners of excise, who operated centrally and became the prototype for the modern central government department.

(i) Commissioners of Excise: the embryonic modern department

Money matters and it mattered a great deal to successive sovereigns in the Tudor and Stuart periods. It mattered even more when a king was minded to go to war. There is much in sixteenth- and seventeenth-century history that turns on Crown finances and the king's need for recourse to Parliament for revenue. Thus, as Keith Brown notes:

> Without regular taxation, the Crown's political manoeuvrability was extremely limited, hence the many successful attempts to maximize those income streams that were available to the king. Under James VI and I the use of impositions, the selling of monopolies and titles, searching out old debts, and the revival of feudal rights were all exploited. Nevertheless, by 1617, even before the

> full effect of Buckingham's impact on royal finances had been felt, and at a time when England was still at peace, the debt stood at £726,000, approaching a doubling of the Tudor legacy.[143]

The problems of finance were exacerbated during war, as became evident after 1688. James II had fled to France, to be replaced by William of Orange, whose reign was marked by military commitment on the Continent. This led to frequent summons of Parliament, in order to vote subsidies. It led also to the regime of deficit financing, which originated in the last decade of the seventeenth century and continued thereafter.[144] It entailed the floating of public loans on the security of future taxes, and the issue of government stock in the Bank of England established in 1694, thus heralding the birth of the national debt.[145] Herein lies the connection between deficit financing, the excise and the professionalization of the administrators responsible for its collection. The regime of deficit financing was crucially dependent on an assured flow of future tax, since without this the investors would have lacked the confidence to proffer the loans. Much early eighteenth-century bureaucracy was relatively ramshackle and inefficient

143 K. Brown, 'Monarchy and Government in Britain, 1603–1637', in J. Wormald (ed.), *The Seventeenth Century* (Oxford: Oxford University Press, 2008), pp. 35–6.

144 P. Dickson, *The Financial Revolution in England: A Study in the Development of Public Credit, 1688–1756* (London: Macmillan, 1967).

145 D. Hayton, 'Contested Kingdoms, 1688–1756', in P. Langford (ed.), *The Eighteenth Century* (Oxford: Oxford University Press, 2002), pp. 39–40.

as judged by modern standards,[146] but the need to secure the requisite flow of tax provided the spur to organizational reform, in which the Commissioners of Excise played the central role.

The excise grew more than fourfold between 1690 and 1782, and 'from the 1720s more men worked for the Excise than for all the other revenue departments taken together'.[147] Excise was an indirect tax levied on goods either when produced or when distributed. The range of goods thus taxed expanded over time. It was initially imposed on alcohol, but under the pressure of financial exigency it was expanded to cover goods such as soap, salt, leather and candles. The excise became the largest source of tax revenue for the Crown, and this required an administrative organization that was fit for purpose. In the words of John Brewer, 'excises became the largest category of taxes, excisemen the biggest body of officials, and the Excise Office a byword for administrative efficiency'.[148]

The Commissioners of Excise were at the apex of this administrative regime. The provinces were divided into collections, which corresponded approximately to the English counties, presided over by a collector who toured his area circa eight times per annum, receiving the money from traders that had been assessed by his officers, this being then sent on to London. The number of such officers ranged from 1,000 in 1690 to 2,800 in 1780. There was an analogous system

[146] Hayton, 'Contested Kingdoms, 1688–1756', p. 42.

[147] Brewer, *The Sinews of Power*, p. 67.

[148] Brewer, *The Sinews of Power*, p. 68.

for towns.[149] Excise officers were required to pass an exam plus a practical test, the work being complex and technical, involving long hours, as attested to by the fact that a 'foot-walk' surveyed each day by an officer was normally between 12 and 16 miles, while an 'out ride' could often be 40–50 miles.[150] Excise officers were therefore a visible manifestation of central power, with authority to tax.

> The exciseman was a ubiquitous presence in eighteenth century England, for he worked not merely in the ports and on the coast, like the customs officer, but in every small town and hamlet where beer and ale were brewed or tea sold over the counter. He was a state official, an executive rather than judicial officer, working under a system of statutory administrative law. As such, he was the symbol of a new form of government. He was also a sign of the state's determination to extract sufficient revenues from the public to ensure that England secured its place as a major international power.[151]

There is little doubt that an assessment by the excise officer was difficult to resist or challenge, although whether there is much difference between then and now is contestable. An initial determination as to fraud or evasion was made by the Commissioners of Excise in London, or by two or more justices where cases were heard in the counties. The jurisdiction of the ordinary courts was limited by the presence of a no-certiorari clause in some excise statutes.

[149] Brewer, *The Sinews of Power*, pp. 102–4.
[150] Brewer, *The Sinews of Power*, p. 105.
[151] Brewer, *The Sinews of Power*, p. 114.

The ordinary courts did not, however, view with equanimity the denial of their jurisdiction, any more than they do now.[152] They continued to exercise supervisory control, the form of which varied depending on whether a preclusive clause existed, and its precise wording. Thus where the clause precluded resort to certiorari, the courts could use mandamus or prohibition instead; where it was worded in more omnibus fashion to prevent all use of the prerogative writs, the plaintiff could proceed via collateral attack in a tort action; and if it was formulated in yet more general terms so as to bar all challenge, courts could interpret this so as not to prevent judicial oversight in cases involving jurisdictional invalidity. Whether courts chose to exercise this degree of activist oversight would depend, inter alia, on the character of the particular judges hearing the case and the nature of the alleged error.

The judicial determination to exercise control over the commissioners is exemplified by *Terry* v. *Huntington*,[153] the relevance of which for the emergent law on jurisdictional error was considered above. It is Chief Baron Hale's reasoning concerning the authority of the ordinary courts that is of interest here. Hale acknowledged that the statute created a special court 'for the more speedy recovery of the duty', but held that this did not 'leave all parties concerned to the arbitrary power of the commissioners, and to deliver all up to their will and pleasure'.[154] It was for the commissioners to

[152] See, e.g., *The King* v. *Smith and Others Commissioners of Sewers* (1682) 1 Lev. 288.

[153] (1655) Hardres 480.

[154] (1655) Hardres 480, at 483.

inquire into the matter initially, but it was for the common law to ensure that they had not exceeded their jurisdiction. The hearing before the commissioners did not, moreover, privilege any person from being subject to an action. The decision exemplified the classic face of judicial review, with the courts policing directly and collaterally the boundaries of power.[155]

There were, however, many decisions exemplifying the other face of judicial review, whereby the plaintiff failed and the court reinforced the regulatory schema.[156] *Cooper* v. *Booth* provides a fitting example.[157] The issue was whether an action for damages in trespass could lie against an excise officer who had obtained a warrant from the commissioners to search for tea, having reasonable suspicion that it was concealed on the premises, when it transpired that no such tea was actually found. The plaintiff was much displeased that the excise officers had 'burst' his locks and 'rummaged' his goods, which were 'thrown all about'. In an earlier case, *Bostock* v. *Saunders*,[158] it had been held that such an action would lie, Blackstone J reasoning to the effect that even if

[155] See also, e.g., *Collett* v. *Young* (1695) 1 Keb. 634; *Warwick* v. *White* (1722) Bunb. 106; *Fuller* v. *Fotch* (1741) Carth. 346; 5; *Bredon* v. *Gill* (1795) 2 Salk. 555; *Miller* v. *Seare* (1777) 2 Black. W. 1141; *Austin* v. *Whitehead* (1795) 6 T.R. 436; *Attlee* v. *Backhouse* (1838) 3 M.& W. 633; *R* v. *Excise Commissioners* (1845) 6 Q.B. 97.

[156] See also, e.g., *The King* v. *The Commissioners of Excise* (1788) 2 TR 381; *R.* v. *Surrey JJ* (1788) 2 T.R. 505; *Christie* v. *A-G.* (1796) 6 Bro. P.C. 520; *R.* v. *Steventon* (1802) 2 East 362; *Attlee* v. *Backhouse* (1838) 3 M.& W. 633; *Regina* v. *Speller* (1847) 1 Exch. 401.

[157] (1785) 3 Esp. 135;. [158] (1746) 2 Black. W. 913.

the suspicion was plausible, the officer was liable in trespass if it transpired that there were no concealed goods. Lord Mansfield in *Cooper* acknowledged the 'great authority' of the judges that had decided *Bostock*, but concluded nonetheless that it should be overruled. Lord Mansfield adverted to the purpose of the statute, which was to prevent fraud on the excise by concealing taxable goods. The excise officer who suspected such concealment had a duty to put this before the commissioners or the justices, with the consequence that the warrant was lawful when issued. Lord Mansfield responded to the argument that the absence of concealed goods should render the officer liable in trespass by saying that this would defeat the purpose of the statute; it 'repeals the Act of Parliament', which is 'entirely adapted to probable circumstances', whereas the plaintiff's argument would 'require positive certainty'.[159]

(ii) Commissioners of Sewers: the embryonic modern agency

Sidney and Beatrice Webb begin their account of the Court of Sewers by noting the difficulty faced by the twentieth-century observer in appreciating just how much of England had been composed of vast fens and marshes.[160] Therein lies the explanation for the early attention given to drainage and defences against the sea, culminating in the Statute of Sewers 1531,[161] which gave statutory foundation for the

[159] (1785) 3 Esp. 135, at 145.

[160] S. Webb and B. Webb, *English Local Government: Statutory Authorities for Special Purposes* (London: Longmans, 1922), p. 13.

[161] 23 Henry VIII, c. 5.

Commissioners of Sewers and the Courts of Sewers. They resembled in many respects justices of the peace for the counties, albeit with a specialized jurisdiction over rivers, sewers, ditches, bridges, locks, weirs, sea defences and the like. Their jurisdiction resembled in many respects that of a modern environmental agency. This analogy can be pressed further, insofar as the Commissioners of Sewers 'combined in themselves, judicial, executive and even legislative powers'.[162] They could, in modern parlance, adjudicate, make rules and execute the specified precepts, and their powers were in certain respects more extensive than those of their modern successors. The analogy to the modern agency is, however, subject to the important qualification that the Commissioners of Sewers operated in distinct geographical areas, and there could often be tension between different groups of commissioners.

The commissioners had extensive judicial authority. They were statutorily empowered to hold a Court of Sewers within their assigned area, and the sheriff was required to provide juries of honest and lawful men. It was a court of record and gave rulings in accord with jury decisions. This judicial status meant that the commissioners had judicial discretion to fine or imprison those who committed offences wilfully and *vi et armis*, while those who were guilty of neglect of matters for which they were responsible, such as maintenance of a riverbank, could be made to bear the cost of repair, or have their goods distrained if they failed to do so.

[162] Webb and Webb, *English Local Government*, p. 21.

The commissioners also had broad decision-making discretion, being statutorily charged to survey the rivers, bridges, banks and streams that fell within their jurisdiction, and cause them to be made or repaired according to their 'wisdom and discretion'. This primary decision-making power was reinforced by grant of secondary power to appoint surveyors, bailiffs and the like, to hire or impress into service labourers, and to acquire, compulsorily if need be, the requisite materials, such as timber.

The commissioners' rule-making authority was equally impressive. They had power to make statutes, ordinances and provisions as might be required for the safeguard, conservation and redress of the constructs that fell within their jurisdiction. They could, to this end, use the laws and customs of Romney Marsh as a boilerplate, or devise provisions according to their own discretion. This rule-making capacity was reinforced by the fact that the rules thus made could be binding even after the expiry of the commissioners' term of authority, provided that certain conditions were met, leading the Webbs to comment that 'truly, the Parliaments of Henry the Eighth and Elizabeth weighed out powers to the King's commissioners with no niggard hand'.[163]

There were, however, as with the case of the Commissioners of Excise, problems that we would describe in principal/agent terms, which was unsurprising given the breadth of their powers. These problems were particularly marked in the growing urban centres. The commissioners' discretionary power over expenditure was always a temptation

[163] Webb and Webb, *English Local Government*, p. 24.

to corruption, with the consequence that the 'naïve and petty jobbery of the earlier years of the eighteenth century was replaced by collusion between some of the commissioners and the contractors, who were allowed to go on charging the same prices year after year, without competitive tendering'.[164] There were, in addition, problems of neglect, with the Webbs revealing their moral disdain for the 'inexcusable' behaviour of the Westminster Commissioners, who failed to exercise their considerable discretion, with the consequence that they had no accurate plans of existing sewers and took few steps to construct new ones.[165] Growing urbanization led to difficulties of a more structural nature, as commissioners initially created to deal primarily with rural flooding and the like struggled to cope with the demands of growing urbanization, with the attendant problems of transporting water and urban waste underground. There were, moreover, structural difficulties in the way that commissioners functioned, becoming 'in effect close bodies, homogenous in class, renewing themselves by co-option', with the commissioners' judicial process replaced increasingly by 'standing administrative committees meeting behind closed doors, unchecked by public reports or open discussions, and acting through salaried officials', while being plagued by 'gangs of self-seeking building speculators, architects, surveyors and others who could make a profit out of them'.[166]

164 Webb and Webb, *English Local Government*, p. 79, referring to practice of the Westminster Commission.
165 Webb and Webb, *English Local Government*, p. 83.
166 Webb and Webb, *English Local Government*, p. 103.

There were perforce limits as to how far courts could redress problems of this kind. Commissioners of Sewers nonetheless often featured in judicial review actions, and the case law reveals the same duality as in the other areas discussed above, with both faces of judicial review being evident.

Thus there were cases where the courts applied the emerging precepts of review and invalidated Commission action, as exemplified by the seminal decisions in *Rooke*'s case,[167] and in *Hetley*,[168] discussed earlier.[169] They were the forerunner to many similar decisions. The courts carefully policed the statutory remit accorded to commissioners, as in *The Queen* v. *Inhabitants of Westham in Essex*,[170] where an order made by the commissioners who had charged the inhabitants for erecting a lock and tumbling bay was quashed, because the commissioners had no power to charge for what was in the circumstances found to be a private benefit flowing from the river improvement. The courts further refined their controls over discretion, as in

167 (1598) 5 Co. Rep. 99b.

168 *Hetley* v. *Boyer* (1614) Cro. Jac. 336.

169 See also, e.g., *The Case of the Isle of Ely* (1610–11) 10 Co. Rep. 141a; *Farr* v. *Crisp* (1733) 2 Barn. K.B. 321; *The King* v. *The Commissioners of Sewers in the County of York* (1760) Sess. Cas. 91; *The King* v. *The Commissioners of Sewers in Nottinghamshire* (1760) Sess. Cas. 51; *Ex parte Owst* (1821) 9 Price 117; *Stracey* v. *Nelson* (1844) 12 M. & W. 535; *The Queen* v. *Ingham* (1863) 4 B. & S. 205; *The Saint Katherine Dock Company* v. *Higgs* (1845) 10 Q.B. 641; *Pettiward* v. *The Metropolitan Board of Works* (1865) 19 C.B. (N.S.) 489; D. Chan Smith, *Sir Edward Coke and the Reformation of the Laws: Religion, Politics and Jurisprudence, 1578–1616* (Cambridge: Cambridge University Press, 2014), Ch. 3.

170 (1795) 10 Mod. 159.

Keighley's Case,[171] in which they subtly gradated the obligations incumbent on those charged with river defences. Thus if a person was bound by prescription to repair a wall against the sea, which was broken though no fault of his by sudden and unusual flow of water, the Commissioners of Sewers should tax all according to the quantity of their land. If, however, the person charged with repair was at fault and the danger was not inevitable, the commissioners could charge him to repair it. If the reality was that the danger became inevitable through his fault, those who suffered loss could have an action on the case against him. The courts were, moreover, willing to develop the commissioners' tortious liability, as exemplified by *Jones* v. *Bird*,[172] where the commissioners were liable for the neglect of their contractors that resulted in property damage, and the court imposed a duty on the commissioners to warn neighbouring landowners of specific dangers, a general warning being insufficient in this respect.

There are, however, as with justices of the peace and Commissioners of Excise, numerous cases where the courts rejected claims and strengthened the regulatory scheme.[173]

[171] (1610–11) 10 Co. Rep. 139a. Compare, however, *The Queen* v. *Leigh* (1840) 10 Ad. & E. 398.

[172] (1822) 5 B. & Ald. 837.

[173] See also, e.g., *The Case of Chester Mill on the River of Dee* (1572–1616) 10 Co. Rep. 137b; *Custodes* v. *The Inhabitants of Owtwell, Tyd, Newton* (1649) Style 178; *The King* v. *The Commissioners of Sewers for the Levels of Tendring, Lexden and Winstree* (1790) 2 Ld. Raym. 1479; *The King* v. *The Commissioners of Sewers for the Levels of Pagham* (1828) 8 B. & C. 355; *The Queen* v. *The Commissioners of Sewers of Tower Hamlets*,

Thus in *Saunders* v. *Taylor* it was held that a collector of sewer rates was bound to pay the commissioners sums collected by virtue of a rate made by commissioners acting under a commission that expired before the execution of the bond under which payment was due.[174] Lord Tenterden CJ construed the bond in the light of the commissioners' role, which was 'to discharge a public trust for the public benefit'.[175] The trust and the benefit were permanent, even though the personal authority of the commissioners was temporary, with the consequence that acts begun under one commission are continued under another. A similar approach is evident in *The King* v. *The Commissioners of Sewers for Tower Hamlets*,[176] where claimants sought certiorari on the grounds that the rate was in part to defray the expenses of works already done, that it was to cover the legal expenses of the commissioners, and because the rate was framed in terms of work done 'or' to be done. Lord Tenterden CJ robustly rejected all three parts of the claim: the very nature of the Commission's role meant that it would be called on to repair past flood damage that could not be foreseen; the commissioners had an incidental authority to pay legal expenses in discharge of their duty, since 'if it were otherwise, it would be impossible for the country to obtain the services of any gentlemen in that office';[177] and the disjunctive

excluding St. Katherine's and Blackwall Marsh (1842) 3 Q.B. 670; *Pew* v. *Metropolitan Board of Works* (1865) 6 B. & S. 235.

174 (1829) 9 B. and C. 35.

175 (1829) 9 B. and C. 35, at 41.

176 (1830) 1 B. & Ad. 232.

177 (1830) 1 B. & Ad. 232, at 239.

wording of the rate should be read conjunctively, since it made sense to do so.

A comparable awareness of political and regulatory reality is evident in *The Queen* v. *The Commissioners of Sewers for the County of Norfolk*,[178] where the court held that it fell within the commissioners' power to expend money, and recover it thereafter via a rate, in order to oppose a bill in Parliament that would have damaged drainage in their area. Lord Campbell CJ was willing to interpret the phrase 'litigation and controversy' in the commissioners' powers as covering such parliamentary opposition, noting that while opposing a drainage bill before Parliament was not litigation 'in the proper sense', Parliament was the 'forum for such disputes', it was there that the 'battles between levels must be fought' and if 'the battle is not fought the level may be ruined'.[179] A more general cognizance of the importance of the commissioners' work is evident in *The King* v. *The Commissioners for the Western Division of Somerset*,[180] where Lord Kenyon CJ opined in the context of a case concerning repair of sea defences that courts were reluctant to issue certiorari against a poor rate 'lest the poor starve in the meantime', and that there was an analogous rationale for being wary of issuing an order in this type of case 'lest in the meantime the whole country be inundated'.

There were also cases the correctness of which could be questioned in terms of the regulatory objectives. The basic principle underlying the law in this area was that the costs of

[178] (1850) 15 Q.B. 549. [179] (1850) 15 Q.B. 549, at 566.
[180] (1799) 8 T.R. 312, at 314.

the work were apportioned among those who took the benefit. The definition of 'benefit' could be controversial, more especially when considering whether attachment to an urban sewer was a sine qua non for being regarded as benefiting therefrom. It has been argued that some judicial decisions in the early nineteenth century hampered the commissioners' efforts to improve the provision of sewerage by taking too narrow a definition of benefit.[181] The optimal interpretation of legislative criteria of this kind is, however, often inherently controversial, and it is therefore unsurprising that this should have been so in earlier centuries. To be balanced against this is the fact that courts made decisions that facilitated discharge of the commissioners' task in assigning the costs of work done.[182]

(d) Towns

Towns exercised wide-ranging administrative power. Their organizational form varied considerably. Some towns were corporations, although relatively few, somewhere between a quarter and a third.[183] Corporations were normally composed of a mayor or other chief magistrate, one or more councils, and in some instances a body of freemen. A corporate officer

[181] J. Hanley, 'The Metropolitan Commissioners of Sewers and the Law, 1812–1847' (2006) 33 *Urban History* 350; e.g., *Masters* v. *Scroggs* (1815) 3 M. & S. 447.

[182] See, e.g., *Bow* v. *Smith* 9 Mod. 94; *Dore* v. *Gray* (1788) 2 T.R. 358; *Warren* v. *Dix* (1805) 3 Car. & P. 71.

[183] J. Innes and N. Rogers, 'Politics and Government 1700–1840', in P. Clark (ed.), *The Cambridge Urban History of Britain*, Vol. 2, *1540–1840* (Cambridge: Cambridge University Press, 2000), p. 530.

was normally ex officio a justice of the peace. Joanna Innes neatly summarizes the powers of the corporation.

> The traditional corporation operated in four main capacities. It was first a property-owning entity, managing certain forms of property as public facilities – market buildings, harbours, prisons – and others as a source of corporate revenue. It was secondly a regulatory body: regulating, or overseeing the regulation of, (among other things) commerce and industrial production, street lighting, cleansing and policing. It was thirdly a court-maintaining body: providing convenient civil and criminal tribunals. It was fourthly guardian of the town's interests within the realm.[184]

Where there was no corporation some of these functions would be undertaken by manorial institutions. Where this did not suffice the functions could be exercised by the county magistracy or by parish or voluntary societies, or through improvement commissioners,[185] the powers of these last being sanctioned through statute.[186]

It is little surprise that the courts became involved in reviewing different aspects of the corporation's powers. This is evident from the seminal decision in *Bagg*'s case relating to due process and membership of the corporation.[187] This was

[184] Innes, 'Governing Diverse Societies', p. 111.

[185] Innes and Rogers, 'Politics and Government 1700–1840', pp. 532–6.

[186] Webb and Webb, *English Local Government*, Ch. IV.

[187] (1615) 11 Co. Rep. 93b, at 99a; *Brownlow* v. *Cox and Mitchell* (1615) 3 Bulstrode 32; *The King* v. *The Company of Fishermen of Faversham* (1799) 8 T.R. 352.

the issue yet again in *Rex* v. *Cutbush*,[188] where Lord Mansfield held that a by-law inconsistent with the voting rights laid down in a corporation charter was invalid. The writ of quo warranto was frequently used in such actions to test by what authority a person exercised certain power,[189] and it became a potent weapon in factional disputes concerning corporation membership.

There was also judicial intervention relating to the corporation's regulatory power.[190] Thus in *The King* v. *Tappenden* the court struck down a corporation by-law,[191] Lord Kenyon CJ opining that while reasonable restraints on trade could be imposed through by-laws, the contested by-law was bad because it altered the qualifications of those to be taken as apprentices, which went beyond the purpose of the power to make by-laws. The corporation's regulatory powers were in issue once again in *Cocksedge* v. *Fanshaw*, the issue in this instance being entitlement to receipt of a toll levied by the Corporation of London. Lord Mansfield concluded that freemen who sold corn could retain that part of the toll that pertained to their goods, since this accorded with usage as understood by both sides and 'we cannot suppose, that, during that time, one half of the city were fools, and the other knaves'.[192]

188 (1768) 4 Burr. 2204.

189 See, e.g., *The King* v. *Blunt* (1738) Andrews 293; *Dominus Rex* v. *The Mayor and Aldermen of Hertford* (1795) 1 Salk. 374; *The King* v. *Grout* (1830) 1 B.& Ad. 104.

190 See also, e.g., *Mayor of London* v. *Mayor of Lynn* (1796) 7 Brown 120.

191 (1802) 3 East 187.

192 (1779) 1 Dougl. 119, at 123.

Lord Mansfield was in full cry in *Hesketh* v. *Braddock*,[193] a case that combined due process and regulatory monopoly, arising out of a fine imposed by Chester Corporation on the defendant for breaching a by-law that precluded anyone who was not a freemen from operating a shop. The by-law was void as an illegal restraint on the common right of the subject unless there was a custom to support it, but the adjudication of such a custom had occurred in the local court where only freemen could act as jurors. Lord Mansfield was singularly unimpressed by attempts to convince him that this involved no violation of due process, responding that 'the law has so watchful an eye to the pure and unbiased administration of justice, that it will never trust the passions of mankind in the decision of any matter of right',[194] and thus would not trust the freemen as jurors. While Lord Mansfield was against the substantive restraint of trade in the instant case, the judicial approach to such by-laws differed over the years.[195]

5 Administrative law development: theory, values and fact

The preceding discussion has touched on the role played by values in administrative law as it developed over 400 years. It is, however, important to address three more general issues concerning public law and theory.

193 (1766) 3 Burr. 1847. 194 (1766) 3 Burr. 1847, at 1856.

195 See, e.g., *Clark* v. *Denton* (1830) 1 B. & Ad. 92; *Shaw* v. *Poynter* (1834) 2 Ad. & E. 312; *The Queen* v. *Edmonds* (1855) 4 El. & Bl. 993.

(a) Theory and fact

It is fitting to begin with the relationship between theory and fact. The factual corpus of public law is constituted by an admixture of judicial decisions; legislation; and executive and administrative action, including decisions and rule making by ministers, central bureaucracy, local government, agencies, and the like. The relationship between the facts, theory and values depends on the nature of the inquiry.

Thus the inquiry might be as to whether a constitution had a particular theoretical underpinning, which entails factual investigation as to whether, for example, the US Constitution was informed by republican or liberal theory.[196] It might by way of contrast be contended that a particular doctrinal rule or body of law ought to reflect certain liberal, socialist or republican values, there being no ready assumption that it presently does. It might conversely be maintained that the existence of certain doctrinal precepts reflects attachment to a particular political or democratic theory. These are all fruitful and valuable lines of inquiry, in which the relationship between theory and fact differs.

It is, however, important that we do not blur the line between 'ought' and 'is', or 'ought' and 'was', and that we are clear as to the 'facts' that are said to sustain the perceived

[196] See, e.g., L. Hartz, *The Liberal Tradition in America: An Interpretation of American Political Thought since the Revolution* (New York: Harcourt Brace, 1955); B. Bailyn, *The Ideological Origins of the American Revolution* (Cambridge, MA: Harvard University Press, 1967); G. Wood, *The Creation of the American Republic, 1776–1787* (Chapel Hill: University of North Carolina Press, 1969).

status quo. The reality is that the relationship between our theoretical discourse and the facts of public law often assumes the form of a play within a play, where the facts in terms of judicial decisions, legislation, executive action and the like shade into the background, to be replaced by battles waged between theorists that are often disconnected from those facts.

A literary analogy can be found in Tom Stoppard's brilliant play *The Real Inspector Hound*. It is a classic whodunit that takes place in a country house. The murder mystery is intertwined with commentary from two theatre critics that sit at the edge of the stage. They provide insights on the unfolding play, and on the nature of their craft, on which they differ markedly. They also allude sardonically to the plight of Puckeridge, an aspiring critic who never gets a look in because of the dominance of the established duo. As the play unfolds the phone rings onstage, which prompts one of the dramatis personae to turn to a critic and say 'it's for you'. Gradually both critics get drawn into the whodunit, and their discourse dominates the unfolding drama. Both are eventually murdered, the villain being the third-string critic who was out to eliminate his rivals, the play ending with the immortal death throw line, 'Puckeridge, you cunning bastard'.

Reflect for a moment on the pattern of our theoretical discourse. Consider how we conduct such debates. Thus for Carol Harlow and Richard Rawlings the main characters in the red-light–green-light discourse are commentators, principally academics, with Wade and Dicey exemplifying the red-light approach and Robson, Jennings and Griffith fulfilling this role for the green-light school of thought.[197] For Martin Loughlin the conservative vision of public law is epitomized by Oakeshott, Dicey and Wade; the liberal by Hayek, Dworkin, Allan and Jowell; the functionalist by Griffith, Mitchell and Robson.[198] For Tom Poole the meaning of common law constitutionalism is scripted from Allan, Laws, Craig, Jowell and Oliver; while the tenets of political constitutionalism are drawn from Loughlin, Tomkins and Poole himself.[199]

This is fine. Debate about the nature of public law is central to our subject, in the same way that it is in private law. We must nonetheless take care not to confuse the 'ought' with the 'is', or with the 'was', by assuming that there is some ready connection between such debates and the reality of current public law, or what constituted public law as it unfolded over the first 400 years of its existence. We are in danger of doing just this. The line between representation of factual reality and that which is desired becomes blurred in the preceding accounts. This is in part because writers commonly take only partial account of the facts of public law when developing their own vision. It is in part because the conclusions from such writers are

[197] Harlow and Rawlings, *Law and Administration*. See also C. Harlow and R. Rawlings, *Law and Administration* (Cambridge: Cambridge University Press, 3rd edn, 2009), Ch. 1, for a modified version of the theory.

[198] M. Loughlin, *Public Law and Political Theory* (Oxford: Clarendon Press, 1992).

[199] T. Poole, 'Back to the Future? Unearthing the Theory of Common Law Constitutionalism' (2003) 23 *Oxford Journal of Legal Studies* 453; T. Poole, 'Questioning Common Law Constitutionalism' (2005) 25 *Legal Studies* 142; T. Poole, 'Legitimacy, Rights and Judicial Review' (2005) 25 *Oxford Journal of Legal Studies* 697.

used by later writers with little regard for their reasoning or the facts that underpinned them. It is in part because we make all manner of implicit assumptions, often untested, about the fit between the theoretical construct and the facts.

Consider by way of example the red-light–green-light distinction, as rival depictions of what public law is and ought to be. It is the commentators who are placed centre stage in this debate. They are, however, not in reality the principal dramatis personae in this particular play, nor does their script capture what was actually going on for 400 years. A rival script focusing on the principal players might read as follows. Parliament over four centuries enacted a very great deal of social and economic legislation that was regarded as valuable, subject to normal political contestation as to the desirable direction of policy. It readily used a plethora of institutions to discharge policy, there being no general animadversion to any particular administrative form. Those charged with administration would normally discharge their task with care, but things could and did go wrong, hence the need for mechanisms of accountability, which were an admixture of the political, the administrative and the legal. The legal contribution was predicated on the normative assumption that constraints were warranted to control such public power. There was, however, nothing specific about public law in this respect, since control was also central to many rules of private law. The legal contribution was not premised on the assumption that administration was something dangerous in the manner conveyed by red-light theory, nor does the evidence support the conclusion that courts generally ignored the social value of the regulatory legislation that they were interpreting. To the contrary, they were mindful of this, and sought to effectuate it in the manner adumbrated above. The courts could, of course, err, being an imperfect institution like all others.[200] It is true that some judges evinced a preference for the common law over legislation, but this was in relation to areas that had been developed by the common law. The courts did not, by way of contrast, feel that they should be devising broad regulatory schemes relating to the poor, land use, trade regulation, tax and the like. Nor did the courts regard such regulatory legislation in terms akin to being engulfed by some unnatural administrative leviathan. To the contrary, this was the ordinary nature of things in the world they inhabited, the existence of such measures being the norm from the fifteenth century onwards, although their incidence would perforce vary over time.

Consider, by way of further example, the dangers if we take such theoretical labels and map them onto the facts of administrative law as it unfolded over 400 years. There is a temptation to regard early judicial review as 'conservative' by way of contrast to more extensive modern doctrine. This should be resisted. The idea that those such as Coke, Holt, Hale, Blackstone, Kenyon and Mansfield, laying the foundations of modern administrative law, should be regarded as conservative does not withstand scrutiny, given their path-breaking jurisprudence and willingness to craft doctrine from first principle. The idea that the reach of administrative law

[200] There is, as stated earlier, nothing said here that should be taken to excuse restrictive and erroneous judicial interpretation of, for example, labour legislation, or of some aspects of nineteenth-century factory legislation dealing with the relay system.

was very much narrower than now is overstated, given that many of the core precepts of review were well established. The idea, moreover, that one can take precepts of 'conservatism' in twentieth-century philosophical thought and apply them to the seventeenth or eighteenth century is deeply problematic. So too is the idea that there was any necessary connection, let alone correlation, between conservative thought that prevailed in those centuries and the facts of administrative law during that period. The same caution is warranted when we move closer to the present. Thus the fact that Dicey and Wade might, for the sake of argument, be depicted as 'conservative normativists' tells one nothing about the nature of administrative law as it existed at the relevant times.

Consider a third example drawn from Tom Poole's depiction of common law constitutionalism.[201] He discerns a number of related propositions that constitute common law constitutionalism. These are: that a political community is ordered according to a set of fundamental values; that political decision making is or ought to be a matter of discovering what fundamental values require in particular cases; that the common law is the primary repository of the fundamental values of the political community; that ordinary politics does not necessarily connect with fundamental values; that public law therefore consists of a set of higher-order principles and rights; and that decision making in judicial review is or ought to be value-oriented. This thesis is derived from the views of writers including Allan, Laws, Oliver, Jowell and Craig.

201 Poole, 'Back to the Future?'; Poole, 'Questioning Common Law Constitutionalism'; Poole, 'Legitimacy, Rights and Judicial Review'.

The dangers of eliding 'is', 'was' and 'ought' are evident in this analysis. There is some reference to history within Poole's analysis, but not much, and that analysis does not capture or reflect what the courts were doing over 400 years. The very meaning of common law constitutionalism shades into the common law theory about the foundations of judicial review, such that it is assumed that adherence to the latter means subscription to all tenets of the former as set out by Poole. This is not so. The common law theory of judicial review embodied a vision of common law constitutionalism, but it was more nuanced, more moderate and less dramatic than is apparent from Poole's propositions.

Thus it is indeed central to the common law model that the courts could develop administrative law doctrine to control public power broadly conceived and that this was not dependent on showing legislative intent. This undeniably involved judgement by the courts as to the values that should be served through legal doctrine. This is, however, inevitable whenever legal doctrine is developed in any branch of the law. The development of administrative law was no different in this respect. Thus when the courts developed the common law of crime, contract, tort, and restitution they did so by articulating doctrine that was premised on assumptions about the important values within such areas. They made choices within the law of tort that were reflective of commitment to corrective or distributive justice; they developed doctrine within criminal law that was premised on conceptions of moral responsibility and justifiable excuse; and they moulded contract law by considerations relating to matters such as consent, autonomy, bargain and the like. Doctrine could not be developed without resort to such considerations, and this was just as true of the emerging administrative law as it was of private law doctrine.[202]

It was, by way of contrast, not central to the common law model, or the constitutionalism that it embodied, that the rights or interests regarded as important were incontrovertible, nor that the courts had a monopoly on their identification. To the contrary, contestability in this regard was acknowledged, but this too was endemic to all areas of the law. This is attested to by the vibrant debates in contract, tort, restitution and crime, where courts and commentators discuss the values that underpin the respective subjects, and the more discrete doctrinal components thereof. Public law values are not wholly self-evident, and even if there is agreement on abstract concepts such as liberty, equality, property, security, citizenship and the like, there are different conceptions of such values in particular contexts. Nor was it central to the common law model that the courts should be able to invalidate primary legislation. To the contrary, notwithstanding the oft-quoted statements from Coke, the courts for four centuries continually eschewed power to declare primary legislation invalid in the manner exercised by constitutional courts in other countries.

(b) Normativist and functional

Martin Loughlin championed what became an influential distinction between what he terms normativist and functionalist

[202] See above, pp. 13–17.

approaches to public law theory. The nomenclature of 'functionalist' public law theory was coined by Loughlin, who used it in contrast to what he termed 'normativist' theories, whether of a liberal or a conservative persuasion.[203]

For Loughlin, normativist theories are said to be grounded in ideas about the separation of powers, the rule of law and the need to subject government to law, with the emphasis on adjudicative and control functions, coupled with an idea of the autonomy of law. Law is said to precede legislation, and rights to precede the state, the latter being conceived of in largely negative terms.[204]

Loughlin contrasts such theories with those of a functional nature, which embrace more sociological conceptions of law.[205] Law is said to be viewed as part of the apparatus of government, with the focus on an active role for the state and law's regulatory and facilitative functions. Legislation is said to be the highest embodiment of law, freedom is perceived in positive not merely negative terms, and the relationship between citizen and state is conceived in more organic and less atomistic terms. On this view, public law should be used for the purpose of promoting human improvement, a healthy body politic and social solidarity. Government is the subject of duties, and public law is concerned with their substantive realization. Public law must, on

[203] Loughlin, *Public Law and Political Theory*; M. Loughlin, 'The Functionalist Style in Public Law' (2005) 55 *University of Toronto Law Journal* 361.

[204] Loughlin, *Public Law and Political Theory*, pp. 60–1.

[205] Loughlin, *Public Law and Political Theory*, pp. 60–1; Loughlin, 'Functionalist Style', 363–4.

this view, be interpreted purposively, in the sense of having regard to its function. Rights are regarded as claims 'that are recognized and enforced only insofar as their recognition promotes the common good'.[206]

Martin Loughlin has shed valuable light on the constituent elements of what he terms the functional approach to public law, and on its philosophical foundations. The dichotomy between normativist and functionalist theory is nonetheless doubly problematic. It aggregates theories under the label 'normativist' that are very different. It disaggregates those theories from others that are regarded as 'functional' when the reality is that all theories of public law are irreducibly both normative and functional, and that is so irrespective of whether they are grounded on conservative, liberal or more collectivist/socialist foundations.

Consider first the normative perspective. The approaches to public law that Loughlin identifies are explicitly predicated on certain political theories. That is self-evidently so in relation to what he terms conservative and liberal normativism. It is, however, equally true in relation to what he terms functionalism, since, as Loughlin readily acknowledges, many, albeit not all,[207] of the principal proponents had a socialist or left-of-centre political philosophy.[208] Political

206 Loughlin, 'Functionalist Style', 363.

207 J.N. Figgis, *Churches in the Modern State* (London: Longmans, 1913).

208 See, e.g., H.J. Laski, *Studies in the Problem of Sovereignty* (New Haven: Yale University Press, 1917); H.J. Laski, *Authority in the Modern State* (New Haven: Yale University Press, 1919); G.D.H. Cole, *Social Theory* (London: Methuen, 1920); G.D.H. Cole, *Guild Socialism Restated* (London: Parsons, 1920).

theories address a variety of issues, which include the nature of rights, conceptions of justice, the relationship between justice and other virtues, and the extent to which the state should seek to prescribe behaviour for its citizens. Political theories such as liberalism, conservatism, republicanism, communitarianism and socialism give different answers to such issues. Indeed, it is these very differences that render them distinct political theories. All such theories are normative, as that term is commonly used. They all seek to provide convincing arguments as to why certain answers ought to be given to the preceding issues, based on certain factual assumptions.

This is equally true for those Loughlin regards as coming within the functionalist school, as for those of a more liberal or conservative persuasion. Thus when, for example, Fabians or New Liberals argued for greater protection of social and economic interests this was clearly premised on normative arguments as to why such interests should be protected in the manner argued for. This was equally true for those who argued in terms of social interdependence or social solidarity.[209] Proponents of these theories also had strong views about the separation of powers and the rule of law, albeit different from those propounded by adherents of other political theories. It is precisely because all such theories are normative that classic or current works on liberalism, conservatism, republicanism, socialism and

209 See, e.g., L. Duguit, *Law in the Modern State*, trans. by F. and H. Laski (London: Allen & Unwin, 1921).

the like discuss such concepts without any addition of the word 'normativism'.

It is, moreover, equally important to take care when arguing that certain visions of public law are wedded to particular normative precepts. Loughlin's running together of all liberal theories is especially problematic. Thus repeated assertions that liberals conceive of liberty in negative terms as the absence of external restraint, coupled with the idea that liberals regard government as repressive, conceal far more than they reveal.[210] The statement may be true in relation to the liberalism of Hayek or Nozick,[211] but it is not so in relation to that of Rawls, Dworkin or Raz.[212] Similar difficulties attend broad assertions that normativists regard rights as preceding the state, whereas functionalists regard rights as emanating from legislation.[213] Political theories clearly differ concerning the way in which rights are conceptualized. This is a central normative issue for all political theories, but the answer provided by functionalists is not necessarily so different from that

210 Loughlin, *Public Law and Political Theory*, pp. 60, 61, 96.

211 F. Hayek, *The Constitution of Liberty* (London: Routledge and Kegan Paul, 1960); F. Hayek, *Law, Legislation and Liberty: A New Statement of the Liberal Principles of Justice and Political Economy* (London: Routledge and Kegan Paul, 1973–9). R. Nozick, *Anarchy, State, and Utopia* (New York: Basic Books, 1974).

212 J. Rawls, *A Theory of Justice* (Oxford: Oxford University Press, 1973). R. Dworkin, *Sovereign Virtue: The Theory and Practice of Equality* (Cambridge, MA: Harvard University Press, 2000); R. Dworkin, *Freedom's Law: The Moral Reading of the American Constitution* (Oxford: Oxford University Press, 1996). J. Raz, *The Morality of Freedom* (Oxford: Clarendon Press, 1986).

213 Loughlin, *Public Law and Political Theory*, p. 60.

given by, for example, liberal theories. Thus Laski regarded society as preceding the state and believed that individuals came to the state with rights that the state had a duty to protect.[214] This is without prejudice to a second-order issue, which is whether to protect such rights through courts, legislation or an admixture of the two.

Consider now the functional dimension. The reality is that all political theories have a functional as well as a normative dimension. There is no reason why the term 'functional' should be reserved for those theories that are more collective or socialist in orientation. Loughlin uses the term 'functional' in a variety of ways, but none warrant the conclusion that only collectivist-type theories have this dimension, or that it is lacking from liberal or conservative theories.

The term is used by Loughlin in part to capture the idea that those who subscribe to functionalist theories argue for legal norms and governmental action that will effectuate the desired ends. They seek ways to ensure that the machinery of the state attains these particular goals. This is, however, equally true in relation to all political theories. Thus, for example, libertarian or public-choice theorists are also functional in this sense. They too wish to ensure that the relevant constitutional, legal and political machinery of the state is configured so as to attain the functions that they believe the state should be performing. They too believe that public law should be used to support a healthy body politic. They go to

[214] H.J. Laski, *The Foundations of Sovereignty and Other Essays* (London: George Allen & Unwin, 1921); H.J. Laski, *Liberty in the Modern State* (London: George Allen & Unwin, 1948).

very considerable lengths to specify what this entails.[215] They can and do regard law as part of the machinery of government. They too focus on law's regulatory and facilitative function. They just adopt a radically different view of what that is compared to those of a more socialist persuasion.

The term 'functionalism' is also used by Loughlin in a different sense. He contends that liberal normativists are committed to law being non-purposive, in the sense that the state is meant to be neutral between differing conceptions of the good. Functionalists are, by way of contrast, said not to be troubled by this attachment to neutrality, with the consequence that they can perceive of law as functionally serving broader societal and governmental goals.[216] It is certainly true that deontological liberal theory of the kind posited by Rawls is premised on the assumption that the state should be neutral between conceptions of the good, in the sense that it is not for the state to make choices between the value of a life reading philosophy or one playing sport.[217] Liberals of this persuasion are not, however, neutral about the principles of justice. Nor are they neutral about legislation or adjudication that affects

[215] See, e.g., J.M. Buchanan and G. Tullock, *The Calculus of Consent: Logical Foundations of Constitutional Democracy* (Ann Arbor: University of Michigan Press, 1962); J.M. Buchanan, *The Limits of Liberty: Between Anarchy and Leviathan* (Chicago: The University of Chicago Press, 1975); J.M. Buchanan, *Freedom in Constitutional Contract: Perspectives of a Political Economist* (College Station: Texas A & M Press, 1977); G. Brennan and J.M. Buchanan, *The Reason of Rules* (Cambridge: Cambridge University Press, 1985).

[216] Loughlin, *Public Law and Political Theory*, pp. 60, 93, 96, 102.

[217] Rawls, *A Theory of Justice*. Compare the perfectionist liberal approach in Raz, *The Morality of Freedom*.

these principles. To the contrary, they demand legislative, executive and judicial action that is purposive insofar as it relates to such principles of justice, including in this respect protection for civil and political liberties, and including also, under a Rawlsian theory, action to alleviate the plight of the socially and economically disadvantaged. Liberals regard law as purposive and functional to attain these ends. It is no answer to contend that some might prefer, for example, more extensive social rights or greater economic redistribution. This might well be so, but it has nothing to do with whether public law is purposive or functional. It simply reflects disagreement as to the background political theory that underpins public law.

There is, moreover, a third sense of the term 'functional' that appears in Martin Loughlin's work, although it is less evident than the preceding two. Thus the term is sometimes used to capture the positive or descriptive dimension of a desired approach. There is a meaningful distinction between positive/descriptive aspects of political science and more normative political theory, although values permeate the former as well as the latter. The relevant point for present purposes is that the distinction between positive/descriptive political science and normative political theory is equally applicable to all types of political belief. Thus one might ask how far a society exhibits the features of republicanism, and then proceed to advocate their further development, because it is felt to be the best way to order society. The same might equally be true in relation to liberalism, socialism, conservatism and communitarianism. The argumentation might take a different form, whereby the observer concludes in descriptive terms that the pattern of societal ordering conforms to a liberal stereotype, and then argues that a more socialist society would be preferable. All this is standard fare, and reflects much of the to and fro of political discourse. It offers no basis, however, for any distinction between normative and functionalist theories, precisely because the descriptive and normative dimensions are applicable to all types of political belief, whether they be conservative, liberal, socialist or idealist.

(c) External and internal

Trevor Allan's recent work has been driven by the distinction between an internal and and external approach to public law,[218] and he strongly favours the former over the latter. There are, however, difficulties with this dichotomy and how it is applied.

(i) The meaning of the distinction

The distinction between the external and the internal is not clear, notwithstanding the fact that it is Allan's central organizing thesis.[219] Put more accurately, he proffers a number of different meanings of the external/internal distinction. Thus, following Allan's introductory narrative, at least four senses of this divide can be discerned.

In one sense it is used to capture the existence or not of law on a particular topic: we are told that from an external

[218] T.R.S. Allan, *The Sovereignty of Law, Freedom, Constitution and Common Law* (Oxford: Oxford University Press, 2014).

[219] Allan's appendix on methodology does not clarify the issues addressed above.

perspective the absence of settled law as laid down by courts means that that there is no answer as a matter of strict law, and hence only academic discourse external to the law, whereas from an internal perspective the answer can still be discerned by recourse to normative judgement based on moral and political theory.[220] A related but distinct sense of the divide is that the external is equated with the descriptive, the internal with the normative/evaluative, such that the answer, for example, to the issue of whether there are limits to parliamentary sovereignty cannot be discerned merely on the basis of what judges or senior officials say, which is deemed to be the external perspective, but must be determined by recourse to arguments of principle, an internal perspective.[221] A third meaning is that external is said to connote a descriptive stance commonly used by the political scientist, whereas the internal is that found in interpretive legal reasoning,[222] while a fourth is that the external perspective is detached, while the internal is committed.[223]

It would have been helpful if Allan had provided a clear definition at the outset, and helpful also if the rationale for the distinction had been explicated, since it is not self-evident. Insofar as there is a unifying theme that underlies these diverse meanings it is Allan's adherence to a non-positivist approach to legal theory, drawing in particular on Dworkin's work, in preference to the positivism associated with Hart and Raz.

[220] Allan, *Sovereignty of Law*, p. 5.

[221] Allan, *Sovereignty of Law*, pp. 10, 14.

[222] Allan, *Sovereignty of Law*, p. 11.

[223] Allan, *Sovereignty of Law*, p. 13.

(ii) Positivism: contestable conclusions

The conclusions said to flow from positivist accounts are, however, contestable and exaggerated. Trevor Allan is perfectly entitled to prefer a non-positivist view of law. I share this perspective.[224] The conclusions must nonetheless be carefully evaluated. The meaning of positivism, and its implications for the way in which we think about public law, are captured throughout the book by repeated recourse to language such as 'detached', 'descriptive' or 'non-normative', drawn from the range of meanings used to describe the external perspective, as if these accurately capture the meaning of positivist legal theory. This is mistaken.

The positivist thesis does not maintain that the 'law's merits are unintelligible, unimportant, or peripheral to the philosophy of law', but that they 'do not determine whether laws or legal systems exist'.[225] The existence of laws depends on what social standards are recognized as authoritative, such as legislative enactments, judicial decisions, or social customs. However, as Leslie Green makes clear, 'it is no part of the positivist claim that the rule of recognition tells us how to decide cases, or even tells us all the relevant reasons for decision', and it follows that 'positivists accept that moral, political or economic considerations are properly operative in some legal decisions, just as linguistic or logical ones are'.[226]

[224] Craig, *Administrative Law*, Ch. 1.

[225] L. Green, 'Legal Positivism', *Stanford Encyclopaedia of Jurisprudence*, available at http://plato.stanford.edu/entries/legal-positivism, 1.

[226] Green, 'Legal Positivism', 9.

Allan repeatedly assumes that because an academic is a positivist it must therefore mean that their argument can be cast in the language of the external, connoting descriptive, detached and non-normative. This is a non sequitur, and an important one, since it enables Allan to dismiss contending arguments by repeated resort to such labels without engaging with them. Belief in positivism means acceptance of the proposition that the existence of a law does not depend on certain moral precepts. It does not mean that, when engaging in academic debate about the content of a particular rule, the positivist reasons merely as the descriptive political scientist, recording for the empirical record what is out there. It does not mean that such an academic is detached or non-normative.

It is an accepted tenet within positivism that legal rules will be informed by values and reasons. Legal positivists regard the rule and the values that underpin it as formally distinct, in part at least because that allows a rule to exist, notwithstanding that there may be a plethora of competing values that inform it. While the tenability of this distinction can be questioned, the salient point for present purposes is that adherents of legal positivism do not rest content with description of the legal rule's existence in the manner of the political scientist. They do not simply identify and catalogue as if that thereby exhausted the inquiry. To the contrary, they inquire into the background values that underpin the rule in order to determine its scope and assess its desirability. This is true for secondary and primary rules.

It is evident in relation to, for example, the secondary rule of recognition. Allan is dismissive of the concept, regarding it as a prime instance of external fact stripped of underlying justification. This misconceives the rule of recognition. Hart had his own well-developed internal normative perspective, which was 'manifested in the criticism of others and demands for conformity made upon others when deviation is actual or threatened, and in the acknowledgement of the legitimacy of such criticism and demands when received from others'.[227] For Hart this was especially important for the rule of recognition, which, 'if it is to exist at all, must be regarded from the internal point of view as a public, common standard of correct judicial decision, and not as something which each judge merely obeys for his part only'.[228] It is equally, if not more, important for present purposes to recognize that constitutional writers such as Coke, Blackstone and Dicey who extolled the supremacy of Parliament did not ground this proposition solely on 'external fact'. To the contrary, each had a clear normative argument as to why Parliament should be thus regarded, even if this was contestable. For Coke it was a particular conjunction of monarchical and parliamentary authority, for Blackstone the normative precept was balanced constitutionalism, while for Dicey it was a conception of self-correcting majoritarian democracy.[229] They did not approach the subject as if the answer was to be found through detached and non-committed observation. This is readily apparent once again in the modern debate

[227] H.L.A. Hart, *The Concept of Law* (Oxford: Clarendon, 1961), p. 56.

[228] Hart, *The Concept of Law*, p. 112.

[229] P. Craig, 'Public Law, Political Theory and Legal Theory' [2000] *Public Law* 211.

about parliamentary sovereignty between Trevor Allan and Jeffrey Goldsworthy.[230] Goldsworthy is a positivist whose argument rests in part on the sources thesis and the rule of recognition. But it is also based squarely on normative argumentation as to the respective claims of courts and legislature to have the final word on contentious moral issues.[231] On this normative topic Goldsworthy is just as 'committed' as Allan, and so too are other writers opposed to constitutional review.

The same point is equally evident in relation to the primary norms that constitute public law. I do not know how many public law academics are positivist as opposed to non-positivist, how many subscribe to some other version of legal theory, or indeed how many do not care too much one way or another.[232] Let us assume that some public law academics are indeed broadly positivist, or that they do not subscribe to Dworkinian non-positivism. Allan's view that the positivists will be external in the sense of descriptive, detached and non-normative does not cohere with reality. It is just such engagement that characterizes public law scholarship, whether it relates to analysis of case law, legislation, or new directions that the law should take.[233] Consider, by way of example,

[230] Allan, *Sovereignty of Law*, pp. 154–8.

[231] J. Goldsworthy, *Parliamentary Sovereignty: Contemporary Debates* (Cambridge: Cambridge University Press, 2010).

[232] There are certainly more positivists than not among legal theorists, but that breakdown may not be replicated within public law.

[233] Take just one *ad hominem* example. Sir William Wade was a positivist and yet wrote with verve, commitment and conviction throughout his academic career, addressing what he believed to be the pressing

the way in which we approach reasonableness or legitimate expectations. A positivist does not merely catalogue and describe the doctrinal rule from some purely external perspective. To the contrary, the relevant case law is analysed against the backdrop of values that are felt to inform that doctrinal precept. The academic debates are marked by exchanges in which such values are identified and assessed. There is discourse as to the meaning to be accorded to reasonableness in the light of background values such as the separation of powers. There are rival positions taken as to what is the best justification for legitimate expectations, and what this should tell us about the ambit of this doctrine.

This is even more apparent when moral or merit considerations are unavoidably part of the source-based rule, whether derived from legislation or from case law.[234] There are many instances in law where sources, whether derived from statute or from the common law, demand moral reasoning in adjudication. This is particularly relevant in public law. It finds expression not only in rights recognized at common law and under the Human Rights Act 1998, but also in many other common law principles concerning procedural and substantive judicial review. There is therefore no reason why a positivist, when interpreting such legal

normative issues underpinning the public law developments of his day. Whether others agree with his views is not relevant for present purposes. It is the nature of the inquiry.

234 J. Coleman, 'Negative and Positive Positivism' (1982) 11 *Journal of Legal Studies* 139; W.J. Waluchow, *Inclusive Legal Positivism* (Oxford: Clarendon Press, 1994); P. Soper, 'Legal Theory and the Obligation of a Judge: The Hart/Dworkin Dispute' (1977) 75 *Michigan Law Review* 473.

precepts, will take a descriptive, detached and non-normative approach to this exercise. It is, indeed, difficult to know precisely what this would mean. To the contrary, in cases where the meaning of a particular right is contested, or where the scope of application of natural justice is at stake, a positivist will have recourse to relevant moral precepts in deciding what the meaning of the law actually is, not just what it ought to be.

While there are undoubted theoretical differences between positivist and non-positivist legal theory, they do not play out in the contrast between the external and the internal that Allan draws within public law. Nor does adherence to a non-positivist perspective necessarily give one some crucial 'edge' in resolving the key issues within public law, and I say this as a non-positivist. Thus while the Dworkinian non-positivist maintains that, subject to issues of fit, justice is central to the determination of the existing law, this still leaves for resolution the conclusions to be drawn as to the existence, scope and application of particular legal precepts. This is equally true in relation to Allan's very broad concept of the rule of law based on liberty. It does not change the kinds of value that inform our debates about reasonableness, legitimate expectations, proportionality and the like, nor does it provide some magic resolution of them.

Consider, in this respect, Allan's discussion of law and convention.[235] He is against any hard and fast distinction between law and convention. He strongly criticizes a range of writers, including Nick Barber, Mark Elliott and

[235] Allan, *Sovereignty of Law*, Ch. 2.

Joseph Jaconelli,[236] who adopt a different perspective, the error being said to stem from the fact that they took an external perspective. Allan's assumption that academics of a positivist persuasion remain in the descriptive and detached dark, by way of contrast to those of a non-positivist persuasion who bask in the committed and normative light, allowing them to perceive the true relation between law and convention, conceals more than it reveals. The reality is that all participants in this particular debate take into account a range of factors, descriptive and normative, in reaching their conclusions as to whether law and convention should be regarded as similar or distinct. To be more accurate, everyone recognizes that there are some differences between law and convention, and some similarities. The issue, then, is whether you believe that the former outweigh the latter, or vice versa. I do not have hard and fast feelings on this one way or another, and nor do I think that the internal perspective sheds some light hidden to others. The differences of view reside in the weight that particular scholars attach to different variables – such as the degree of enforceability, the nature of the subject matter regulated, and suitability for judicial oversight – when reaching their conclusion.

[236] N. Barber, *The Constitutional State* (Oxford: Oxford University Press, 2010). M. Elliott, 'Parliamentary Sovereignty and the New Constitutional Order: Legislative Freedom, Political Reality and Convention' (2002) 22 *Legal Studies* 340. J. Jaconelli, 'The Nature of Constitutional Convention' (1999) 19 *Legal Studies* 24; J. Jaconelli, 'Do Constitutional Conventions Bind?' [2005] *Cambridge Law Journal* 149.

(iii) Non-positivism: contestable conclusions

It is also interesting to reflect on Trevor Allan's thesis from his own internal perspective, to see what light this sheds on resolution of core issues relating to supremacy and the rule of law.

A central issue is whether legislative supremacy should be limited by constitutional review. Trevor Allan favours such review, which is not only to be used in extremis to cope with bills of attainder, statutes demanding that all blue-eyed babies should be killed, or legislation abolishing the entirety of judicial review. Allan rejects such limits, and argues to the contrary that constitutional review should be available whenever there is an infringement of the rule of law, in the wide sense that he postulates. He also rejects distinctions between hard and softer forms of constitutional review. That is fine. Allan is perfectly entitled to take this view, but that increases the need to engage with the contending literature.

There is a veritable mountain of literature concerning the legitimacy of constitutional review, more especially the 'hard-edged' variant whereby courts actually invalidate statute for breach of rights-based norms. Jeremy Waldron[237] and Richard Bellamy[238] are leading opponents of rights-based

[237] J. Waldron, *Law and Disagreement* (Oxford: Oxford University Press, 1999); J. Waldron, 'The Core Case against Judicial Review' (2006) 115 *Yale Law Journal* 1346.

[238] R. Bellamy, *Political Constitutionalism: A Republican Defence of the Constitutionality of Democracy* (Cambridge: Cambridge University Press, 2007).

constitutional review of statute.[239] Waldron is a court-sceptic, but not a rights-sceptic. Bellamy's position is more complex. He is certainly a court-sceptic, and is also more sceptical about rights.[240] There is, nonetheless, much common ground in the reasons for their court-scepticism. Thus the premise central to Waldron and Bellamy's argument is the prevalence of disagreement concerning the rights that should be included within any Bill of Rights and their interpretation, which pervades the very foundational ideas of justice on which society is grounded. They maintain, therefore, that whether viewed in terms of process or outcome it is preferable for such matters to be decided ultimately by the political and not the legal process.

There may well be responses to these arguments, but although Allan addresses them his internal perspective does not produce the insights that win the day. It is no response to claim that democracy is more than majoritarianism, entailing also commitment to rights, since Waldron is not a rights-sceptic, the key issue being who should have the ultimate say as to the interpretation of such rights.[241] Nor is

239 See also M. Tushnet, *Taking the Constitution away from the Courts* (Princeton: Princeton University Press, 1999); L. Kramer, *The People Themselves: Popular Constitutionalism and Judicial Review* (Oxford: Oxford University Press, 2004).

240 R. Bellamy, 'Constitutive Citizenship versus Constitutional Rights: Republican Reflections on the EU Charter and the Human Rights Act', in T. Campbell, K. Ewing and A. Tomkins (eds.), *Sceptical Essays on Human Rights* (Oxford: Oxford University Press, 2001), p. 15.

241 Waldron, *Law and Disagreement*; Waldron, 'The Core Case against Judicial Review'; J. Waldron, 'A Rights-Based Critique of Constitutional Review' (1993) 13 *Oxford Journal of Legal Studies* 18.

it any response to point to the possibility that absolute legislative supremacy will lead to the 'let-us-kill-all-blue-eyed-babies scenario', because Allan expressly rejects limiting constitutional review to such instances. Nor can it be claimed that the internal perspective in itself demands such review, since this begs the very question in issue.

It is also no answer to maintain that concerns about constitutional review can be sidestepped on the ground that 'the common law constitution escapes the opposition between legislative supremacy and judicial review that Waldron postulates', because it 'envisages a division of functions between the enactment and application of law, distributing responsibility between Parliament and judiciary according to context and circumstance',[242] since so much depends on the meaning accorded to this ambiguous formulation. Allan's answer in essence is that courts should exercise constitutional review in protection of fundamental rights, acknowledging that there might be 'uncertainty or disagreement about the nature or scope of those rights in all the circumstances', it being 'the court's constitutional role to settle such doubts and disagreements as they arise on the facts of the particular cases'.[243] This does not, however, meet the concerns of those opposed to constitutional review; it reinforces them. It is true that for Allan the judicial interpretive exercise is to be conducted while giving the elected representatives some range of judgement to accommodate reasonable disagreement,[244] but there

[242] Allan, *Sovereignty of Law*, p. 326.
[243] Allan, *Sovereignty of Law*, p. 326.
[244] Allan, *Sovereignty of Law*, p. 328.

are different statements throughout the work as to how much space should be given to the legislature in this regard. They are also equivocal. Thus Allan concludes with the stricture limiting legislative choice, stating that 'reasonable disagreements must divide positions equally consistent with the root ideas of human dignity and independence that undergird a liberal polity',[245] which provides little guidance for court or legislature as to the ambit of their respective roles.

This is especially important given the intimate connection between Allan's vision of constitutional review and his conception of the rule of law, since it is breach of the latter that triggers the former. Allan gives a resolutely substantive meaning to the rule of law, which is held to connote the 'sovereignty of the principle of liberty', thereby upholding 'the freedom and dignity of those independent citizens who comprise the political community'.[246] Allan had previously contended that this conception of the rule of law was compatible with various liberalisms, that it did not therefore involve commitment to a particular conception of justice, and that it did not embrace all rights commonly protected in a constitutional document, but only those that he felt were significant for the preservation of autonomy, consent and dignity, such as freedom of speech, freedom of association and the like.[247] He continues to adhere to the first tenet, but

[245] Allan, *Sovereignty of Law*, p. 326.

[246] Allan, *Sovereignty of Law*, p. 91.

[247] T.R.S. Allan, 'The Rule of Law as the Rule of Reason: Consent and Constitutionalism' (1999) 115 *Law Quarterly Review* 221; T.R.S. Allan, *Constitutional Justice: A Liberal Theory of the Rule of Law* (Oxford: Oxford University Press, 2001).

now appears to accept that a broader range of rights may come within 'liberty' for the purposes of his conception of the rule of law, although his position is not clear.[248]

This point is crucial and cannot be avoided. The reality is that while a substantive conception of the rule of law can be consistent with more than one conception of justice, it is not and cannot be independent of the particular theory of justice, or vision of liberty, which constitutes the content of the rule of law thus conceived at any point in time, and that is so irrespective of whether the conception of justice draws on differing intellectual traditions, as opposed to some pure theory.

If one regards only selected fundamental rights as coming within the substantive conception of the rule of law, this will perforce involve choices as to which rights are more constitutive of liberty. Nor can this point be avoided by recourse to background precepts of autonomy or consent that might underpin liberty and dignity, since these merely push the inquiry one stage further back.[249] Thus some might regard basic civil and political rights as most constitutive of liberty and dignity, and conceive of autonomy and consent in these terms. Others might contend that social and economic rights are integral in this respect. Yet others might believe that constitutionalization of property rights entailing limits to the state's redistributive power is equally or more important.[250]

[248] Allan, *Sovereignty of Law*, pp. 338–9.

[249] P. Craig, 'Constitutional Foundations, the Rule of Law and Supremacy' [2003] *Public Law* 92.

[250] See, e.g., G. Brennan and J.M. Buchanan, *The Reason of Rules* (Cambridge: Cambridge University Press, 1985).

If, by way of contrast, one regards all fundamental rights as coming within the rule of law thus defined, it is still necessary to make choices between them. Thus it may be decided, explicitly or implicitly, that property rights will not be given the elevated status desired by public-choice theorists. It may also be assumed, explicitly or implicitly, that social and economic rights will have less purchase than civil and political rights, thereby rejecting conceptions of liberty of those who differ with this assessment. In making such choices, particular conceptions of justice are thereby excluded when applying the substantive conception of the rule of law conceived in terms of liberty.

6 Common law doctrine and legislative intent: clearing the ground

Discourse concerning the foundations of UK administrative law cannot avoid analysis of the relationship between common law doctrine and legislative intent, whatsoever one's view about that might be. The debate burned fiercely at the turn of the new millennium. The effluxion of time has not led to change in my view, but it has lent perspective on the central issues in this discourse. The core contentious issue is unaltered. It is the claim that the precepts of judicial review must be based on legislative intent, since if this were not so such review would constitute a strong challenge to the sovereignty of Parliament.

A word should be said at the outset concerning legislative intent. There is a lively theoretical debate concerning the more general nature of such intent, focusing on whether it is meaningful to consider a collective body such as the legislature as having an intention. This has been doubted by Ronald Dworkin and Jeremy Waldron, but Richard Ekins has more recently put the opposing case.[251] The debate raises complex philosophical issues that cannot be explored here. Suffice it to say the following. While there is much that is of value in Richard Ekins's work, I have reservations as to what precisely is added by the idea of group intention, since it is, according to Ekins, the content of the proposal for legislative action as embodied in the bill placed before Parliament, and thus coterminous with the plan of what the legislature seeks to attain.[252] This means that the legislature intends to regulate, for example, anti-terrorist activity when introducing a bill to that effect, in accord with its proposed content. I am unclear as to what the intent adds to the proposed plan, other perhaps than to convey the idea that the plan was not coerced by any external force.

This tells us little as to how we should resolve contestable issues of statutory interpretation of the kinds that regularly confront the courts. Now to be sure, Richard Ekins provides further criteria in this respect, such as that the legislation should be interpreted purposively and not literally so as to best attain its objectives, but these criteria are

[251] R. Dworkin, *Law's Empire* (London: Fontana, 1986), pp. 313–54. J. Waldron, *Law and Disagreement* (Oxford: Oxford University Press, 1999), pp. 199–246. R. Ekins, 'The Intention of Parliament' [2010] *Public Law* 709; R. Ekins, *The Nature of Legislative Intent* (Oxford: Oxford University Press, 2012).

[252] Ekins, 'The Intention of Parliament', 714, 716, 726; Ekins, *The Nature of Legislative Intent*, pp. 12–13, 224, 230–1, 242–3.

generally acknowledged as tools of statutory interpretation. It is not clear what we gain regarding their legitimate use by linkage with the sense of intent as coterminous with the legislative proposal, more especially given that it is contestation as to the meaning of the enacted legislation that is the live issue before the court.

The live issue for the purposes of the present analysis, however, is not whether such group intent might exist, but, assuming that it does, its content, and whether such intent is necessary for the constitutional legitimacy of the doctrines that comprise judicial review. The arguments why this is said to be so will be considered in the next section, but before doing so we should clear the ground.

(a) 'It makes no doctrinal difference'

It is important to address the jibe that the debate between proponents of the common law model of judicial review, and those who insist that legislative intent is vital in order to avoid a strong challenge to Parliamentary sovereignty, has no doctrinal consequences.[253] The conclusion is right, the reason is wrong and the error is important. The critique assumes that the reason why there are scant, if any, such consequences is because the resulting doctrine is somehow an admixture of the common law combined with legislative intent.

[253] T.R.S. Allan, 'The Constitutional Foundations of Judicial Review: Conceptual Conundrum or Interpretative Inquiry' [2002] *Cambridge Law Journal* 87.

This might indeed be true if the model in issue were that of specific legislative intent. The shift from specific to general legislative intent is, however, much more profound than the mere adjectival change would indicate.[254] The specific-intent model was predicated on the assumption that Parliament had such intent as to the meaning and application of review in a particular instance, and in that sense could validly be said to be part author of the resulting doctrine.

The general-intent model is entirely different, and is in reality a modified common law doctrine, rather than a modified ultra vires doctrine. On the general-intent model, Parliament is taken to intend that its legislation conform to the basic principles of fairness and justice which operate in a constitutional democracy.[255] However, because Parliament itself cannot realistically work out the precise ramifications of this general idea, it leaves,[256] or delegates,[257] power to the

[254] M. Elliott, 'The Demise of Parliamentary Sovereignty? The Implications for Justifying Judicial Review' (1999) 115 *Law Quarterly Review* 119.

[255] M. Elliott, *The Constitutional Foundations of Judicial Review* (Oxford: Hart, 2001), pp. 110–12.

[256] See, e.g., Elliott, *Constitutional Foundations*, pp. 109–10: 'However the task of transforming this general intention – that the executive should respect the rule of law – into detailed, legally enforceable rules of fairness and rationality is clearly a matter for the courts, through the incremental methodology of the forensic process. Parliament thus leaves it to the judges to set the precise limits of administrative competence.'

[257] See, e.g., M. Elliott, 'The Ultra Vires Doctrine in a Constitutional Setting: Still the Central Principle of Administrative Law' [1999] *Cambridge Law Journal* 129, at 143, 144, 145, where the language used is delegation.

courts, which then fashion the more particular application of this idea in accordance with the rule of law.

The real reason why the modified ultra vires doctrine does not lead to different consequences from the common law model is that the former has no content other than that provided by the latter. The legislative intent is merely a key to unlocking the door to allow the courts to decide on the ambit of judicial review in accord with the rule of law. It has no specific content, this being determined by the courts in accord with whatsoever they choose to include within it pursuant to the ideal of the rule of law. Indeed, the very precepts that form the general constitutional desiderata are taken from those developed by the courts over the previous centuries. The reality is that the modified ultra vires model functions merely as a renvoi back to the common law. In the history of judicial review there is no doctrine that owes its origin to general legislative intent.[258] It is no answer to contend that the specific statute might contain indications as to the nature or incidence of review. It might, and if it does then proponents of the common law model have always accepted that this will be taken into account. The modified ultra vires model has in any event nothing further to add in this respect, since by definition the general legislative intent will be insufficiently specific to discern the contours of judicial review in a particular statute.

[258] There have, of course, been important pieces of legislation that have contributed to the content of judicial review, but that is a different matter and is expressly acknowledged within the common law model.

This is equally true of the other adjectival shift advanced in the literature, which is the move from specific legislative intent to constructive legislative intent. Thus Trevor Allan acknowledges that it will be for the court to decide on the appropriate restrictions on administrative discretion, and that they draw on a range of constitutional values.[259] However, the values that inform constructive legislative intent are synonymous with the rule of law. Constructive legislative intent performs no function in relation to the identification of those values. It simply expresses the conclusion about the choice thus made. It serves no independent normative function, and has no independent content.[260]

Allan's assertion that the common law model entails a specious distinction between the grounds of review, attributed to the common law, and their application to particular instances, where 'the importance of legislative intent can scarcely be coherently denied', is unfounded.[261] Nor is it correct to assert that the categories of administrative law, such as illegality, procedural impropriety and the like, are 'futile and self-serving',[262] with no identifiable content except in relation to the exercise of particular powers in particular instances.

This misrepresents the principles of judicial review. We do not, for example, simply have a head of review called

[259] T.R.S. Allan, 'Constitutional Dialogue and the Justification of Judicial Review' (2003) 23 *Oxford Journal of Legal Studies* 563, at 570.

[260] Allan, *Sovereignty of Law*, Chs. 3 and 6.

[261] Allan, 'Constitutional Dialogue', 567.

[262] Allan, 'The Constitutional Foundations of Judicial Review', 99–100.

procedural propriety. We have a detailed set of principles, dealing with matters such as notice, the type of hearing, when representation should be required, the giving of reasons, the nature of the evidentiary requirements and the like. The same is true in relation to the heads of review that comprise illegality, including error of law, fact, relevancy, propriety of purpose, equality, human rights and the like, given that each specific head of review will have a plethora of more detailed doctrinal rules developed by the courts. The normative arguments that justify these detailed principles have force independently of the particular context in which they are applied. Thus the instrumental arguments for a duty to give reasons include the connection between reason-giving and the correctness of the final outcome, and the way in which reason-giving facilitates substantive review. The non-instrumental arguments focus on the connection between reason-giving and dignity. These arguments frame the application of the reason-giving requirement in a particular area.

The argument also misconceives the relationship between review, application and legislative intent. The common law model draws no distinction between the grounds of review and their application. Nor is it entailed in any way by the theory. They are treated in precisely the same manner. If legislative intent can be found in relation to either it will be applied. The error in the argument is to reason from the premise that judicial review will be applied in a particular context by the courts to the conclusion that there must therefore be some species of legislative intent as to the issue being adjudicated by the courts. The premise is correct: courts apply judicial review in particular contexts. The conclusion is wrong, since it does not follow that there is any discernible legislative intent as to that issue. This is precisely why no one subscribes to the specific-legislative-intent model, and it is also why the general-legislative-intent model cannot, because of its very generality, furnish the answer, merely acting as a renvoi back to the common law courts. Thus the fact that the courts might properly take account of the 'context' being social welfare rather than licensing, tax rather than planning, tells one nothing as to whether there is any cognizable legislative intent as to how the principles of judicial review should play out in that 'context'. This intent may exist, in which case it will be taken into account or indeed be determinative. To assert that there must, or necessarily will be, such intent, merely because the courts are considering review in a particular context, is a non sequitur. The courts will perforce take into account the nature of the statute, and its purpose, when engaged on this inquiry. This is, however, to say no more than the self-evident proposition that courts interpret statutes to achieve their overall purpose when deciding on the application of particular principles of judicial review.

The preceding argument can be tested in relation to other types of legal doctrine. Thus the judicially created principles of contract, tort, restitution, property and trusts are set at a certain level of generality and then applied to particular contexts. They are no more or less detailed than the principles that comprise judicial review. No one claims that these principles are therefore 'futile and self-serving'; no one claims that their application to particular contexts, including statutory, means that Parliament must be regarded as having some specific intent as to how such principles play out in that context. The courts will naturally apply the common law created principles so as to achieve the relevant statutory purpose. If, however, this suffices to sustain the argument that a body of law is based on legislative intent then we would have to say that all bodies of law are grounded in legislative intent, at least insofar as they interpret statutory provisions that pertain to that area.

(b) 'It makes no normative difference'

The ground must also be cleared in normative terms. It is common to see argument to the effect that the debate concerning the foundations of judicial review does not really matter; it is conceptualism using that term in a derogatory manner, which conceals the 'real normative issues' or those matters that are 'fundamental' for any regime of public law. This argument is evident in the work of, for example, Tom Poole and Trevor Allan.[263]

The argument that there is no doctrinal difference is right for the wrong reason. The argument that there is no normative difference, or that the normative issue is unimportant, is simply wrong. The requirement of legislative intent, whether specific, general or constructive, means that it is not constitutionally legitimate for courts to apply common law doctrine to a statute in the absence of such intent, and thus they do not have autonomous power.[264] While those who subscribe to the modified ultra vires model acknowledge that

[263] Poole, 'Back to the Future'; Allan, 'Constitutional Dialogue'.

[264] This may also be so even in the absence of a statute; see below, pp. 149–50.

the 'existence' of the principles of judicial review is derived from normative precepts such as the rule of law, it is integral to their thesis that 'application' of the principles must be grounded in some legislative intent since it is thought that this would otherwise entail a strong challenge to sovereignty.[265] Legislative intent thus conceived is the condition precedent for judicial review, in the sense of an operative set of principles used by courts to decide real cases. In the absence of such intent the principles may 'exist' in abstract, but are inapplicable to real statutes in the real world, which provide the foundation for circa 90 per cent of public law authority. It follows that the courts cannot legitimately apply such principles in the absence of such intent. It follows also that because the intent is couched at a general level Parliament is said to delegate/leave/authorize the courts to develop and apply the principles of judicial review. The courts do not therefore have autonomous legal power. This limits, as will be seen below, the application of any common law precept to a statute, irrespective of whether it concerns public law, private law or criminal law.

You may think that this is uncontentious and orthodox. You may think that it is contestable and heterodox. The importance of the proposition one way or the other cannot, however, be denied. It is fundamental and foundational to our legal order. It is not conceptual formalism, and it is not a side issue. It is central and underpins much else. It is substantive and principled, and would be so regarded in any legal system, civil or common law. It speaks to the respective powers of

[265] Elliott, *Constitutional Foundations*, pp. 115–16.

courts and legislature in a constitutional democracy. It reflects contending views as to the autonomy of courts when developing judicial review. It encapsulates differing views about the relationship between the rule of law and Parliament. To argue to the contrary is untenable, and to feign indifference is to fudge the normative issue.

Consider in this respect Tom Poole's summation of common law constitutionalism set out above. You cannot adhere to the constituent elements of this theory while at the same time expressing indifference as to the normative proposition adumbrated above. You cannot at one and the same time maintain, in accord with this theory, that a political community is ordered according to a set of fundamental values, the primary repository of which is the common law as articulated by the courts; that ordinary politics do not necessarily connect with fundamental values; and that public law consists of a set of higher-order principles and rights; *and* at the same time maintain that it is illegitimate for the courts to apply such principles to statute without legislative intent. This is neither normatively nor conceptually coherent. The respective parts of this formulation can only co-exist by radically reinterpreting one or undermining the other. If the former part is taken seriously there is no normative foundation for the latter; if the latter part is taken seriously it denudes the former of substance.

Consider in this respect also Trevor Allan's alleged indifference as to whether public law doctrine is grounded on the common law or legislative intent, coupled with the iteration that the relationship should best be conceived in terms of sharing between common law and legislative intent.

The reality is that, as the modern scholar that best exemplifies Tom Poole's articulation of common law constitutionalism, he cannot be indifferent to the normative premise that underpins the legislative-intent model. Nor is such indifference compatible with Allan's theory of the rule of law. If he were really indifferent then he would be content to premise his analysis on the assumption that the application/existence of the principles that constitute the rule of law is dependent on legislative intent.[266] He would be content to accept that the principles comprising the rule of law could equally be regarded as being dependent on legislative intent, or not, as the case may be, without this affecting the normative centrality of the concept. The discussion is not, however, conducted in this vein, since Allan does not accept that the normative force of the rule of law is dependent on this linkage with legislative intent.

Nor, moreover, can the normative issue be resolved through invocation of the verb 'to share', as if this had some magic property. There is no theory of public law that could not describe itself through recourse to the motif of sharing. This is true for the common law model, the specific-legislative-intent model, the general-legislative-intent model, the constructive-legislative-intent model, and different variants of political constitutionalism. They all embody some vision of the appropriate role to be accorded to courts and legislature in the development of public law. The concept

[266] P. Craig and N. Bamforth, 'Constitutional Analysis, Constitutional Principle and Judicial Review' [2001] *Public Law* 763, at 773–5.

of sharing merely expresses a conclusion, by capturing the desired balance as articulated by advocates of any one theory. It cannot provide anything remotely akin to a 'tie-break' or 'resolution' between the theories.

This is perfectly exemplified by Allan's own work. He presses the idea of sharing as between common law and legislative intent, but it is given a very specific connotation. Thus he regards the common law as the source of the foundational values that constitute the rule of law; he contends that Parliament is not able even expressly and unequivocally to depart from a particular precept that constitutes the rule of law in a particular instance; and he believes that courts should undertake review for non-compliance with the rule of law thus broadly defined.[267] You may well agree with this or not as the case may, but do not pretend that the answer one way or another is advanced by recourse to the concept of 'sharing', and do not pretend that the answer is premised on indifference as to the normative issue examined here.

7 Common law doctrine and legislative intent: the analytical, the empirical and the normative

The normative significance of the legislative-intent thesis cannot, therefore, be denied. This necessarily invites reflection as to its foundations. There are three arguments that are relevant in this respect.

[267] Allan, *Sovereignty of Law*, Chs. 3, 6, 8.

(a) The analytical dimension

Analytical arguments have a cutting edge. They have power and force. The desired goal is reached through logical argumentation the force of which cannot be denied. The result of the analysis may or may not be desirable, depending on the content of the argument said to be proven. It is the analytic logic that imbues the resulting conclusion with its strength.

There is, however, a flip side to this coin, a double price that has to be paid. If you rest your thesis on an analytical argument then you had better make sure that it really works. You should also ensure that it does not lead you in directions that you do not wish to go in. An analytical argument has its own integrity, which must be followed through to its logical conclusion, even where this creates problems that the author would rather ignore or deny. Academic life being what it is, and academics being human, the normal response is a bit of both. If you see the problem then there is a temptation to ignore it, hoping that others will not notice. If you have not seen the problem and it is pointed out then the temptation is to deny, or distinguish the situations to preserve the force of the argument. This strategy is inherently precarious. Ignoring and hoping that no one will notice is simply giving hostage to fortune, because sooner or later someone will. Denying and distinguishing is equally problematic, because it can only be adjudged a success if it fits with the integrity and logic of the analytical claim. All of which is as it should be. Those who seek to live by the analytic sword must recognize that its power is indifferent to authorial parentage.

The analytic argument was at the forefront of the claim that legislative intent was crucial for the legitimacy of judicial review. It was indeed the hare that set the whole debate about the foundations of judicial review running. It was initially articulated by Christopher Forsyth,[268] who contended that in the absence of such intent judicial review would constitute a strong challenge to parliamentary sovereignty. He maintained that what an all-powerful Parliament did not prohibit, it must be taken to authorize either expressly or impliedly. From this it was said to follow that all elements of judicial review must be cloaked with legislative intent, since if this were not so the assumption would be that Parliament did not intend the constraints on statutory power to exist, with the consequence that the judicial imposition of such limits would amount to a strong challenge to parliamentary sovereignty. The analytical argument is, however, problematic on both counts adumbrated above; it does not work and it leads in directions that its supporters would rather not go.

The difficulties with the argument were noted by Sir John Laws, who pointed out that there may be circumstances where we do not have any intent about an issue one way or another.[269] This argument was never developed and was treated dismissively by adherents of the legislative-intent model. This was unwise, for Sir John Laws was right, and

[268] C. Forsyth, 'Of Fig Leaves and Fairy Tales: The Ultra Vires Doctrine, the Sovereignty of Parliament and Judicial Review' [1996] *Cambridge Law Journal* 122.

[269] Sir John Laws, 'Illegality: The Problem of Jurisdiction', in M. Supperstone and J. Goudie (eds.), *Judicial Review* (London: Butterworths, 2nd ed., 1997), 4.17–18.

the argument has been developed in greater detail by Timothy Endicott.[270] It has far-reaching implications. We wish to inquire, for example, of the legislature's intent in relation to error of law. There are numerous options as to the test for such review: administrators should be subject to some control for error of law; courts should be able to substitute judgment on all errors of law; courts should be able to substitute judgment on jurisdictional errors of law; courts should substitute judgment on some issues and exercise rationality review on others; they should show greater deference to legal determinations made by tribunals, but not to other administrative bodies; the intensity of review should be based on functional considerations; or that there should be no distinction made between review for law and for fact.

The legislature might have an intention in relation to the first option, viz. that administration should be subject to some control for error of law. In relation to all the other options the legislature would likely have no intent one way or the other, and the choice between them is the real doctrinal issue, since the first option is, in reality, not a meaningful test for review at all.[271] There is nothing special about this example of review for error of law. The same exercise could be undertaken for pretty much all heads of review. This reveals a deeper problem with the analytical argument.

[270] T. Endicott, 'Constitutional Logic' (2003) 53 *University of Toronto Law Journal* 201.

[271] Whether it is possible to have 'an intent' on an issue that you do not understand, and what sense of 'intent' would thereby be entailed, is a matter that I leave for those expert in philosophy.

If its force is restricted to very abstract determinations about which Parliament might have an intention, viz. that there should be some control over errors of law, with the more detailed doctrinal specification delegated to the courts, then there is very unlikely ever to be a clash between the courts and parliamentary sovereignty, since Parliament will likely express an affirmative answer to the question posed at this level of abstraction, but the affirmation of Parliament's sovereignty is purely formal since the courts make the real decisions through choice among the options listed above.

If, by way of contrast, the analytic argument is tested against the real options concerning error of law, or any other doctrinal issue, which the courts choose between, it cannot be contended that legislative intent is necessary to prevent a strong challenge to parliamentary sovereignty, since that argument is premised on the assumption that Parliament has a definite intent on the particular doctrinal issue one way or another. If it does not then the courts could choose between any of the available options listed above without fear of infringing sovereignty. If it is felt that judicial power must nonetheless be predicated on such a delegation then this must in reality rest on a normative claim, which will be unpacked below.

The analytical argument does not, therefore, provide the foundation for the legislative-intent hypothesis. Let us, however, presume that it is correct, in order to see where it leads us. The logic dictates that legislative intent must equally be regarded as the foundation for all bodies of law, including contract, tort, trusts, property, restitution and the like, where the common law principles are read into legislation.

The reason is readily apparent. Legislation will be read subject to these common law principles, unless there is something to indicate the contrary. Thus tortious-liability rules will be deemed applicable to all statutory contexts, irrespective of whether the statute concerns public or private bodies, unless there is some statutory rationale to modify or deny their application. The same is true for contractual, proprietary and restitutionary rules. If the analytic argument is correct then we must equally cloak the application of such common law principles to statutes with legislative intent in all areas of the law. If positive legislative intent is necessary to cloak judicially created precepts of public law with legitimacy when applied to a statute, then the same must also be true in relation to judicially created principles of contract, tort, trusts, property and restitution.

The analytical claim is an argument about parliamentary sovereignty, which specifies when it is legitimate to read common law principles into legislation. It can make no difference whether the legislation relates to public law, private law, criminal law or international law. The core precept underlying the analytic claim as to why legislative intent is deemed necessary does not magically change because the common law principle is derived from tort as opposed to public law, nor because the legislation deals with private parties as opposed to public bodies. It can equally make no difference whether the common law principle read into the legislation empowers, constrains or structures the powers of the relevant parties, since common law principles in all areas are an admixture of the three. Those who subscribe to the analytical argument, then, have a choice.

They might accept the force of the preceding argument, and contend that legislative intent must therefore be regarded as a condition precedent in all areas, whenever common law principles are applied to legislation. This view is unlikely to be shared by scholars in private law, criminal law and international law, who do not conceive of their subject in this manner.

They might alternatively seek to deny and distinguish. This is the more likely strategy, but its plausibility depends on advancing an argument that preserves the application of the analytical claim in the public law context, while successfully denying its applicability to other legal areas. This is no small task and I have yet to see an argument that comes close to doing so. Thus there are hints in the literature to the effect that private law is different because, for example, private parties require no authorization before making a contract, whereas public bodies have to point to some such authorization to enable them to act. There may well be some truth in this, but it is wholly irrelevant to the present argument. It is, indeed, looking down the wrong end of the telescope. The issue is not whether private parties can make contracts without any prior authorization, which they can. The issue is whether the common law rules devised to regulate those contracts require legitimation through legislative intent when they are read into legislation, and this is the issue irrespective of whether it relates to public or private parties. The former proposition does not touch the latter, nor does it furnish any reason for distinguishing the application of the analytical argument to all areas of the law. A variant of this form of argumentation is that public law and private law are distinct in certain respects, performing different functions.[272] This may well be so, although there is considerable debate as to the nature of such differences. Whatsoever one's view on this it is irrelevant here. The relevant issue is whether the analytical argument that underpins the claim that legislative intent is required when common law precepts are read into a statute is any less applicable if those precepts are derived from property, trusts, tort, restitution or contract, as opposed to public law. The extent to which public law is or is not different from private law provides no basis for a differential answer to that specific inquiry, nor has any suggested reason been given.

The difficulty of any such distinguishing exercise is thrown into sharp relief when one considers the implications for interpretation of a particular statute. Many statutes are applicable to public bodies and private individuals. Many deal with issues that cross legal subject-matter boundaries. The distinguishing exercise whereby the analytical argument is held applicable to public law principles read into the statute, but not to common law principles from other legal areas, does not withstand examination. It entails the firm affirmation that legislative intent must be found when public law principles are read into the statute in order thereby to safeguard parliamentary sovereignty, coupled with the equally firm affirmation that this is unnecessary when the relevant principle is derived from contract, tort, trust or restitution. This would in turn generate 'nice' doctrinal contestation as to whether a particular precept was properly to be regarded as coming

[272] Allan, *Sovereignty of Law*, pp. 232–3.

within 'public law', thereby requiring the legislative-intent trigger, or whether it should properly be viewed as an aspect of private law, in which case it could be waived through the system without it. It also generates 'nice' inquiries as to what should happen when the same common law principle, for example fault or restitutionary liability, is applied in a statutory context to both public bodies and private parties. There would assuredly be room for an academic symposium with papers arguing rival positions as to whether legislative intent was required when such liability was applied in a statutory context to the private party as well as the public body. The reality is that the distinguishing exercise is untenable, leading to distinctions that would make the debates that beset medieval scholasticism look positively principled.

(b) The empirical dimension

Empirical arguments have an intuitive appeal based on their factual foundation. An argument derives succour and support from its attachment to practical reality. It is therefore unsurprising that this dimension has assumed greater prominence, more especially with the adjectival shift from specific to general legislative intent. The former was subject to the critique that it was empirically unrealistic to assume that Parliament had a specific legislative intent as to the application of judicial review in a particular statute. The latter was said to be justified because Parliament could realistically be regarded as having a general intent that administration should be subject to general precepts of substantive and procedural legality, the details of which would then be worked out by the courts acting pursuant to authority accorded or left to the courts by Parliament.[273]

The empirical argument comes with an 'edge'. It is proffered with a latent, or indeed not so latent, challenge, which at its most basic takes the form of 'deny that if you can'. This is a jibe uttered in many contexts, from youth to old age. It may be an integral part of human nature. Its present application in the context of intellectual controversy does not alter the essential character of the argument, or the intuitive appeal of making it. Yet all 'good things' come with attendant dangers. There are three problems with this argument.

First, there are some who seem to maintain that the empirical claim resolves the debate between the common law and the modified ultra vires models in favour of the latter. The impression is given that all you have to do is to sustain the factual foundation for the empirical claim, which then 'proves' the triumph of the latter model over the former.[274] This is untenable, because 'is' does not imply 'ought'. The fact that such intent might, for the sake of argument, exist furnishes no normative reason for concluding that it is necessary for the legitimacy of judicial review.

Second, the argument elides 'approval' with 'creation'. Empirically grounded abstract or general legislative intent could doubtless be posited for all manner of things, including an end to child poverty, international conflict and economic

[273] See, however, Endicott, 'Constitutional Logic', 206–8, on this aspect of the argument.

[274] Sir P. Sales, 'Rationality, Proportionality and the Development of the Law' (2013) 129 *Law Quarterly Review* 223.

recession. It could equally be posited for liberty, equality and human happiness. This does not mean that anything done by Parliament necessarily had a causative impact on ending any of the former, nor does it mean that its general approval was a necessary condition for the existence of any of the latter. In the same vein, empirical proof of general legislative intent provides no evidence that the legislature had any role in the creation of the principles of judicial review.

Third, if it is felt that mere approval in the preceding sense suffices for general legislative intent to be regarded as the foundation for judicial review, even if it played no part in doctrinal creation, the same must equally be true for all areas of the law. There is no more or less reason to say that the legislature believes in basic precepts of justice in contract, as mediated through concepts such as autonomy, consent, responsibility and the like, the details of which will be worked out by the common law courts through a delegation of power by the legislature, which is unable to make detailed provision for such matters itself. There is equally no more or less reason to say that the legislature exhibits a general intent that tortious liability should be fair and reflect some appropriate balance between corrective and distributive justice, and fault and non-fault liability, the details being once again worked out by the common law courts pursuant to legislative authorization of power. The same exercise could be applied to all areas of private law, and indeed to criminal law. If the empirical argument as to general legislative intent suffices for the conclusion that such intent is foundational for public law, then the same must be true for all areas of the law where statute exists.

(c) The normative dimension

Normative argumentation is central to public law, as it is to other legal disciplines. It is often assumed by adherents to the ultra vires model that it 'wins' in normative terms, because it coheres with the constitutional orthodoxy of parliamentary sovereignty. Indeed the very sanctity of parliamentary sovereignty protected through the cloak of legislative intent is presumed to give this model its normative superiority.

There is a paradox here, because the normative claim is untested. It is asseverated, it is assumed to be self-evidently true, and it is portrayed as axiomatic. The argument has, however, never been 'unpacked', and the reality is that constitutional orthodoxy over 400 years does not conform to that postulated by those who support the ultra vires model. This misreading of constitutional orthodoxy is the consequence of mistaken assumptions about the meaning of parliamentary sovereignty, combined with equally mistaken assumptions about the relationship between courts and legislature.

There are in reality three different models of sovereignty in play and the distinction between them is central to the normative dimension. They embody very different assumptions about the relationship between courts and legislature in a constitutional democracy. The live issue is which model best reflects and coheres with UK constitutional tradition, and the answer is the first.

The 'classic continuing-sovereignty model' embodies the idea of legislative omnipotence in the sense of ability to change. This is reflected in its central tenets: there are no substantive limits on Parliament's power, such that it can in theory legislate on any subject matter, and no procedural limits, such that it can do so by simple majority, uninhibited by any manner and form of conditions laid down by an earlier Parliament. The centrality of capacity to change is reflected in the traditional precept that Parliament is not bound by any other organ and can therefore overrule earlier Parliaments and judicial decisions. The consequence of this view is that the judicially created controls apply unless Parliament has indicated otherwise in pursuance of its continuing sovereignty.

The 'statutory-monopoly model' demands in addition that an integral aspect of sovereignty is that any legal norm that impacts on legislation can only be legitimate if it has the imprimatur of the legislature through some showing of legislative intent. This model of sovereignty therefore demands that Parliament must give prior approval to any limit or term read into legislation as a condition of constitutional legitimacy, with the consequence that judicial power is contingent on finding such consent. It does not suffice on this model that Parliament can change, reject or modify any conditions imposed by courts.

The 'parliamentary-monopoly model' is more far-reaching yet again. On this view all judicial authority must be traced back to, and receive the imprimatur of, Parliament in order to secure constitutional legitimacy. Common law judicial rulings, even in the absence of legislation, would then be rationalized on the ground that Parliament intends general precepts of justice relevant to contract, tort, property, crime and public law, and leaves/delegates to the courts the task of defining their doctrinal content, the legitimacy of the judicial rulings being dependent on this connection with legislative will.[275]

The distinction between the first model and the other two was recognized by Sir John Laws. He rejected the claim that judicial review without legislative intent entailed a strong challenge to sovereignty, noting that the argument was 'vitiated by an implicit mistake: the mistake of assuming that because Parliament can authorise anything, all authorities and prohibitions must come from Parliament'.[276] Sir John Laws rightly regarded this as a non sequitur. Trevor Allan contends that John Laws missed the point, since all common law rules are vulnerable to legislative abrogation. To the contrary, it is Allan that has missed the point. John Laws's insight captures the distinction between the models of sovereignty set out above, which Allan simply elides.

Forsyth's analytical argument is predicated on the assumption that sovereignty 'means' the statutory-monopoly model, as defined above. John Laws's insight was to recognize that being all-powerful in the sense of the continuing-sovereignty model did not logically entail the conclusion that

[275] The meaning of parliamentary monopoly articulated here is distinct from the Diceyan idea that all governmental power should be channelled through Parliament for legitimation and oversight, especially by the House of Commons. This latter sense of parliamentary monopoly provided the foundation for the ultra vires principle conceived in terms of specific legislative intent. The connection is explored in Craig, *Administrative Law*, Ch. 1, as are the deficiencies of this model, which is no longer regarded as a plausible explanation for judicial review.

[276] Laws, 'Illegality', 4.17–18.

all constraints on legislation must necessarily be authorized by Parliament *ex ante* in order to be constitutionally legitimate. The fact that the common law rules remain 'vulnerable to legislative abrogation' is indubitably true and is central to the classic model of continuing sovereignty, which has at its core Parliament's ability to amend, repeal and change. The analytic claim that legislative intent is required to prevent judicial review from being constitutionally illegitimate is, however, premised on the assumption that the statutory-monopoly model is true. A legal system might choose this model, but it is nonetheless different from the classic model of continuing sovereignty. The reality is that the classic model of continuing sovereignty best coheres with our constitutional tradition as judged by three criteria: constitutional scholarship, the status of judicial decisions as sources of law and judicial practice.

First, in terms of constitutional scholarship, it is noteworthy that prior to the debates about the foundations of judicial review there was no indication that such doctrine entailed a strong challenge to sovereignty in the absence of legislative intent. This is not fortuitous. It is reflective of the fact that sovereignty as enumerated by the classic writers such as Blackstone, Dicey and Wade[277] embodied the continuing-sovereignty model. Their formulations are framed in terms of sovereignty as parliamentary capacity to change prevailing

[277] Sir W. Blackstone, *Commentaries on the Law of England* (Philadelphia: R.H. Small, 16th. ed., 1825), Vol. 1, Bk 2; A.V. Dicey, *The Law of the Constitution* (ed. J.W. Allison) (Oxford: Oxford University Press, 2013), p. 27; H.W.R. Wade, 'The Basis of Legal Sovereignty' [1955] *Cambridge Law Journal* 172, at 174.

rules or create new rules afresh. There is no hint in these classic formulations that sovereignty also entailed statutory or parliamentary monopoly coupled with prior authorization in the sense adumbrated above.[278] There is no difference in this respect if one subscribes to a conception of sovereignty that allows Parliament to impose manner and form limits on its authority.[279]

Second, it is axiomatic in our constitutional system that judicial rulings are sources of law, and this is supported, albeit in different ways, by both positivist and non-positivist legal theory. It is chapter and verse in first-year law courses. Legislation is a source of law, so too are common law judicial decisions. The latter are sources of law and constitutionally legitimate, subject to the fact that they can be overruled by the former, this being an integral part of continuing sovereignty. This standard reading of our constitutional system must be significantly revised if we subscribe to the statutory-monopoly model. It means that common law rulings cannot be regarded as constitutionally legitimate when applied in the context of legislation unless they are cloaked with the imprimatur of the legislature, signalled through specific or general intent. They are not regarded as a valid source of law unless such consent can be located, because they are said to entail a strong

[278] See also Sir Stephen Sedley, 'Human Rights: A Twenty-First Century Agenda' [1995] *Public Law* 386.

[279] R.F.V. Heuston, *Essays in Constitutional Law* (London: Stevens, 2nd ed., 1964), Ch. 1; Sir I. Jennings, *The Law and the Constitution* (London: University of London Press, 5th ed., 1967), Ch. 4; G. Marshall, *Constitutional Theory* (Oxford: Oxford University Press 1971), Ch. 3.

challenge to sovereignty as embodied in this model. This stricture is applicable to all common law doctrine read into all legislation, not just that concerning judicial review.

Third, the continuing-sovereignty model coheres with judicial practice, as exemplified by the legality principle developed in cases such as *Witham*[280] and *Simms*.[281] The common law recognized certain fundamental rights, and it was for the courts to determine their meaning and ambit, subject to Parliament's ability to change, alter or repeal what had been done at common law. The courts policed the conditions on which this could take effect, demanding express words or necessary implication to limit such rights. The orthodox position is exemplified once again by Lord Reed in the *BBC* case, where he stated that, 'since the principle of open justice is a constitutional principle to be found in the common law, it follows that it is for the courts to determine its ambit and its requirements, subject to any statutory provision', with the consequence that 'the courts therefore have an inherent jurisdiction to determine how the principle should be applied'.[282] There are many other judicial statements to like effect.[283]

280 *R* v. *Lord Chancellor, ex p Witham* [1998] QB 575, at 585–6.

281 *R* v. *Secretary of State for the Home Department, ex p Simms & O'Brien* [2000] 2 AC 115; *R (Morgan Grenfell & Co. Ltd)* v. *Special Commissioner of Income Tax* [2003] 1 AC 563; *R (Anufrijeva)* v. *Secretary of State for the Home Department* [2004] 1 AC 604; *A* v. *HM Treasury* [2010] 2 AC 534.

282 *A* v. *BBC* [2014] UKSC 25, at para. 27.

283 See, e.g., *R* v. *Secretary of State for the Home Department, ex p. Daly* [2001] 2 AC 532, at para. 30.

8 Conclusion

There will be no attempt to summarize the entirety of the preceding argument. Suffice it to say the following. The common law of judicial review developed as a body of law no differently from other common law doctrine, such as contract, tort, property or restitution. While the doctrinal content in these areas perforce differed, the common law's evolution followed the same general conceptual structure. This was unsurprising, given that courts did not make firm doctrinal distinctions between public and private law. The emerging doctrine was necessarily based on assumptions about the important values within the particular legal sphere, whatsoever it might be. These values were in that sense regarded as fundamental, when viewed in the light of the principles and objectives served by that body of law.

In all areas of the common law there is contestation as to the background theory that best explains the nature of the subject, and this is evident in the vibrant debates concerning the theory that underpins contract, tort and property, no less than it does public law and judicial review. In the public law sphere this debate is shaped by political and legal theory. Conceptions of rights, justice, the role of the state and the relationship between courts and legislature will differ depending, explicitly or implicitly, on the background theory that frames such issues. There is, nonetheless, danger in the lure of binary divides that are said to provide the key to such differences. The distinctions between normativism and functionalism, and between the internal and external perspective, are problematic for the reasons given above.

The respective roles of court and legislature remain central to the foundations of judicial review. The requirement of legislative intent means that it is not constitutionally legitimate for courts to apply common law doctrine to a statute in the absence of such intent. The courts do not in that sense have autonomous legal power. This limits the application of any common law precept to a statute, irrespective of whether it concerns public law, private law or criminal law. This is not correct, nor does it capture the relationship between courts and Parliament that is our constitutional heritage. For those who take the contrary view, the magic wand of general legislative intent will have to be waved to sanction each area of legal doctrine when the precepts are read into legislation. Or perhaps we might just take a lesson from Chicago efficiency. We could simply issue one 'general card' to the effect that Parliament leaves/delegates to the common law courts the power to construct just rules for all forms of legal relations, combined with the correlative assumption that Parliament can be taken to intend to comply with them whenever it legislates in the relevant area. Just be mindful that if this step is taken it should be done with eyes wide open. This is not constitutional orthodoxy as we have known it for 400 years. It does not reflect our existing conception of sovereignty.

2

UK administrative law

Challenges

1 Introduction

The previous chapter considered the foundations of UK administrative law; this chapter looks at the challenges it faces. There is an inevitable subjective dimension as to what should be counted as a challenge for these purposes, and there are doubtless other issues that could be raised. The topics considered are, however, central.

The discussion begins with caseload and the impact that recent government reforms have had on the availability of judicial review. This is important since the reforms will shape access to review in the forthcoming years. While there are understandable governmental concerns about the number of applications for judicial review, the reforms are nonetheless problematic.

This is followed by discussion of the political constitutionalist challenge to legal constitutionalism, which has been the subject of lively exchanges. The foundational dimensions to this challenge are examined, followed by the historical and the normative dimensions. The difficulties with these aspects of the political constitutionalist argument are revealed. So too are the problems with the proposals advanced by political constitutionalists as to their preferred conceptual foundation of administrative law and their vision of its legitimate doctrinal reach.

The focus then shifts to the challenges faced by UK administrative law in terms of procedural and substantive judicial review. The discussion concerning process focuses primarily on the difficult determinations that the courts have had to make flowing from legislation enacted in the post-9/11 world. Much judicial and academic commentary focuses on the appropriate limits to substantive judicial review given the fact that courts may be required to make difficult determinations balancing incommensurable variables, or complex normative assessments. The assumption is that the judicial role in public law is different in this respect from that in private law. This is, however, far from self-evident, as the subsequent discussion will show. The analysis then turns to the standard of substantive review, and engages with the vibrant debate concerning the deference/respect/weight that courts ought to accord to primary decision makers.

The final two sections of the chapter address vertical challenges faced by UK administrative law as it interacts with other legal systems at the regional and international levels. The first of these sections addresses the judicial relationship between UK law, EU law, the ECHR and international law. The interaction between the UK and these legal orders is considered in terms of autochthony, capturing thereby the sense in which the UK courts seek, through a series of juridical techniques, to protect what they regard as important values within the national legal order. The juridical techniques address what I term status, source and substantive dimensions of autochthony. The final section of the chapter then examines the interaction between the UK, the EU, and international and transnational organizations from a regulatory perspective, with particular attention focused on issues of regulatory competence, design, efficacy and control.

2 Caseload

The challenges facing any regime of judicial review vary, as is evident from the subsequent discussion. It is, however, fitting to begin with issues concerning caseload and the government's response thereto, since this can have a marked impact on a claimant's ability to make use of judicial review at all.

The back story to the recent changes to judicial review is the government's concern over the steep rise in applications for judicial review, which had risen from 160 in 1974 to 4,250 by the turn of the millennium and to in excess of 11,000 by 2011, although 75 per cent of the latter number concerned asylum and immigration.[1] This was the trigger for two rounds of reform,[2] the proposals for which were strongly opposed by many who responded to the consultations.[3] The government made some concessions in the light of the consultations, but not many, and pressed ahead with its principal desired changes. While the 'burden of judicial review' was the avowed purpose of the exercise,

[1] Judicial Review: Proposals for Reform, Cm 8515, 2012, paras. 28–30.

[2] See https://consult.justice.gov.uk/digital-communications/judicial-review;https://consult.justice.gov.uk/digital-communications/judicial-review-reform.

[3] Reform of Judicial Review: The Government Response, Cm 8611, 2013; Judicial Review: Proposals for Further Reform, Cm 8703; Judicial Review: Proposals for Further Reform: The Government's Response, Cm 8811, 2014.

Banquo's ghost hovering in the background was the government's irritation with the impediments that review could place on pursuit of its desired policy. The result of the two-stage exercise has been to circumscribe judicial review in different ways.

(a) Substantive constraints: likelihood of substantially different outcome for the applicant

Important changes are enshrined in the Criminal Justice and Courts Act 2015 (hereafter the CJCA), Part 4, which imposes substantive constraints on courts and the Upper Tribunal when exercising judicial review. The CJCA, section 84, amends the Senior Courts Act, section 31, the latter statute containing the principal framework for judicial review in primary legislation. It does so by limiting the circumstances in which permission to proceed and the award of relief at the substantive hearing can be given.

In deciding whether to grant leave/permission the High Court is now empowered to consider of its own motion whether the outcome for the applicant would have been substantially different if the conduct complained of had not occurred, and it must consider that question if the defendant asks it to do so.[4] If it appears to the High Court to be highly likely that the outcome would not have been substantially different, the court must refuse to grant leave,[5] subject to the

[4] Senior Courts Act 1981, s. 31(3)(C).

[5] Senior Courts Act 1981, s. 31(3)(D).

caveat that the court can disregard the preceding requirement if it considers that it is appropriate to do so for reasons of exceptional public interest, but must certify that it is making use of this proviso.[6] There are analogous conditions limiting the award of relief if the case proceeds to the substantive hearing, the court being instructed to refuse relief and/or a monetary award if it appears to be highly likely that the outcome for the applicant would not have been substantially different if the conduct complained of had not occurred, subject to the proviso concerning exceptional public interest.[7] The same provisions are rendered applicable to the Upper Tribunal when it exercises its judicial review powers.[8] It remains to be seen how these provisions are interpreted by the courts and Upper Tribunal respectively. There are, however, two causes for concern.

First, it requires the court or Upper Tribunal to make a difficult estimation as to the likelihood that the outcome would have been substantially different had the error complained of not occurred. It brings to the forefront of judicial review something that the courts have hitherto largely resisted, which is consideration of causation. The courts' wariness in this respect is warranted. Where review is based upon procedural grounds the applicability of such protection should not be placed in jeopardy by the court second-guessing whether a hearing would have made a difference, and the

[6] Senior Courts Act 1981, s. 31(3)(E),(F).

[7] Senior Courts Act 1981, s. 31(2)(A)-(C).

[8] Tribunals, Courts and Enforcement Act 2007, ss. 15(5)(A)–(B), 16(3)(C)–(G).

weight of authority is against this being a material consideration.[9] The path of the law is, as Megarry J stated,[10] strewn with examples of unanswerable charges that were completely answered. A generation later the same sentiment was powerfully voiced by Sedley LJ, who opined that you could never be sure of anything until all the evidence had been heard, and that even then you might be wrong, the consequence being that you could never know what difference disclosure of evidence might have made in a particular case.[11] The wariness concerning causation is, moreover, not confined to process-based review. It is apposite in the context of substantive review, more especially when it is based on grounds such as relevancy, legitimate expectations, and factual error.

Second, the preceding concerns are compounded by the fact that the limits on judicial review introduced by the CJCA 2015 bite at the permission stage as well as at the substantive hearing. The court will perforce have limited material to hand when it makes its determination about permission, and limited time in which to make the assessment

[9] See, e.g., *General Medical Council* v. *Spackman* [1943] AC 627, at 644; *Annamunthodo* v. *Oilfield Workers' Trade Union* [1961] AC 945, at 956; *Ridge* v. *Baldwin* [1964] AC 40; *R* v. *Thames Magistrates' Court, ex p Polemis* [1974] 1 WLR 1371, at 1375; *R* v. *Board of Visitors of Hull Prison, ex p St Germain (No 2)* [1979] 1 WLR 1401, at 1411–12; *R* v. *Secretary of State for the Environment, ex p Brent London Borough Council* [1982] QB 593, at 645–6; *R* v. *Chief Constable of the Thames Valley Police Forces, ex p Cotton* [1990] IRLR 344; *Secretary of State for the Home Department* v. *AF (No 3)* [2009] 2 WLR 423, at [113].

[10] *John* v. *Rees* [1970] Ch 345, at 402.

[11] *Secretary of State for the Home Department* v. *AF (No 3)* [2009] 2 WLR 423, at [113].

demanded by the CJCA. There will almost inevitably be slippage between the permission stage and the substantive hearing, since possible invocation of the new criteria at the former stage will spur the claimant's counsel to introduce more detailed material in order to rebut the suggestion that the outcome would not have been substantially different if the alleged error had not occurred. This is, moreover, likely to increase the 'lottery' that prevails at the permission stage. It will exacerbate the differential success rates between judges attested to in the literature,[12] the danger being that they will interpret the new powers in different ways, and evince differing readiness to use them.

(b) Financial constraints: assets, costs and actions

There is more than one way to limit judicial review, if one is inclined to do so. Litigation is dependent on money, public or private. So if you are minded to limit review, you increase the possible financial liabilities for those involved, and reduce the likelihood of financial aid. It does not take a Nobel Prize-winning economist to predict that this will stem the tide of applications, as the financial risks of actions increase. The government was clearly rather taken with this approach,

[12] A. le Sueur and M. Sunkin, 'Applications for Judicial Review: the Requirement of Leave' [1992] *Public Law* 102; V. Bondy and M. Sunkin, 'Accessing Judicial Review' [2008] *Public Law* 647; V . Bondy and M. Sunkin, 'The Dynamics of Judicial Review Litigation: The Resolution of Public Law Challenges before Final Hearing', Public Law Project, 2009.

which informs its entire strategy. Thus earlier governmental consideration of limiting standing rights was dropped in the face of opposition, but this 'concession' was accompanied by the following:

> The Government is clear that the current approach to judicial review allows for misuse, but is not of the view that amending standing is the best way to limit the potential for mischief. Rather, the Government's view is that the better way to deliver its policy aim is through a strong package of financial reforms to limit the pursuit of weak claims and by reforming the way the court deals with judicial reviews based on procedural defects.[13]

True to its word, the strong package was duly forthcoming. There are different dimensions to this new financial armoury, which, put crudely, can be characterized as 'you risk more and receive less'. The increased risk is evident in a number of new provisions. Thus one strand of the 'new financial order' is amendment to section 31(3) of the Senior Courts Act 1981, which adds an extra condition to be satisfied by applicants for judicial review, viz. the provision to the court, specified in rules of court made for these purposes, of any information about the financing of the application. This includes information about the source, nature and extent of financial resources available, or likely to be available, to the applicant to meet liabilities arising in connection with the application.[14]

[13] Judicial Review: Proposals for Further Reform: The Government's Response, para. 35.

[14] Senior Courts Act 1981, s. 31(3)(A).

There are analogous provisions for the Upper Tribunal. The information can be used to determine by whom and to what extent costs of, or incidental to, judicial review proceedings are to be paid, and the court or tribunal hearing the action has a duty to consider whether to order costs to be paid by a person other than a party to the proceedings.[15]

The increased financial risk is also apparent in the new provisions about interveners. In this context the attack is double-edged. A relevant party to the proceedings cannot, save for exceptional circumstances, be ordered to pay the costs of the intervener.[16] A relevant party, which in practice will normally be the defendant in the action, can, however, apply to the court for an order that an intervener should pay costs incurred by the relevant party as a result of the intervener's involvement in that stage of the proceedings.[17] The court must make such an order, save for exceptional circumstances, provided that any of the following conditions are met: the intervener is in substance the sole or principal applicant, defendant, appellant or respondent; the intervener's evidence and representations, taken as a whole, have not been of significant assistance to the court; a significant part of the intervener's evidence and representations relates to matters that it is not necessary for the court to consider to resolve the issues; or the intervener behaved unreasonably.[18]

[15] Criminal Justice and Courts Act 2015, s. 86.

[16] Criminal Justice and Courts Act 2015, s. 87(3)–(4).

[17] Criminal Justice and Courts Act 2015, s. 87(5).

[18] Criminal Justice and Courts Act 2015, s. 87(6).

The flip side of the financial coin is that 'you receive less'. This too is manifest in various ways in the new schema. Thus the basic premise moving forward is that legal aid will not be available for cases that fail at the permission stage, with the permission test thus becoming the basic threshold for payment, subject to some discretion being accorded to the Legal Aid Agency to pay in meritorious cases that conclude prior to permission.[19]

A further change limits the availability of orders capping costs. These are orders that limit the liability of a party to pay the costs of another party. They are regarded as important in judicial review actions because of the relative disparity in the parties' resources, such that if the claimant was liable for the costs of the defendant it could well dissuade her from bringing the claim. The availability of such orders has been limited by the CJCA. They cannot be given prior to leave. An application for such an order requires the applicant to provide information as to resources. The court can then only make such an order if it is satisfied that:[20] the proceedings are public-interest proceedings,[21] that in the absence of the order the applicant would withdraw the application for judicial review or cease to participate in the proceedings, and that it would be reasonable for the applicant for judicial review to do so. In deciding whether to make such an order a court must have regard to a range of factors, including the

[19] Judicial Review: Proposals for Further Reform: The Government's Response, paras. 45–6, Annex B.

[20] Criminal Justice and Courts Act 2015, s. 88(6).

[21] Criminal Justice and Courts Act 2015, s. 88(7)–(8).

financial resources of the parties to the proceedings; the extent to which the applicant for the order is likely to benefit if relief is granted to the applicant for judicial review; the extent to which any person who has provided, or may provide, the applicant with financial support is likely to benefit if relief is granted to the applicant for review; whether the applicant's legal representatives are acting free of charge; and whether the applicant for the order is an appropriate person to represent the interests of other persons or the public interest generally.[22]

The practical consequences of the reforms remain to be seen. There is, however, no doubt that life will be more difficult for claimants. That indeed is the government's intent. The substantive and the financial constraints will, moreover, operate severally and in tandem to limit review. What is equally concerning is that if they do not achieve the government's desired purpose, it will not accept this with equanimity, but is likely to return with an even more 'robust package', assuming that the government is still the government.

3 Legal and political constitutionalism

It is important to address the general critique of legal constitutionalism advanced by those who argue from a political constitutionalist frame. While there is a very considerable literature on political constitutionalism and constitutional

[22] Criminal Justice and Courts Act 2015, s. 89(1).

review of primary statute,[23] there has been less consideration of its implications for administrative law. It has, however, been developed in the UK most notably by Adam Tomkins and Tom Poole.[24] We need, for the sake of analytical clarity, to disaggregate different dimensions to the political constitutionalist argument.

(a) The foundational dimension: I

It is important to be clear at the outset as to the foundational assumptions of political constitutionalist thought, since this frames the critique of legal constitutionalism. The precise content varies from writer to writer, but Adam Tomkins's six tenets of legal constitutionalism encapsulate ideas that are also voiced by others.[25]

[23] See, e.g., J. Waldron, *Law Disagreement* (Oxford: Oxford University Press, 1999); J. Waldron, 'The Core Case against Judicial Review' (2006) 115 *Yale Law Journal* 1346; M. Tushnet, *Taking the Constitution Away from the Courts* (Princeton: Princeton University Press, 1999); R. Bellamy, *Political Constitutionalism, A Republican Defence of the Constitutionality of Democracy* (Cambridge: Cambridge University Press, 2007); L. Kramer, *The People Themselves: Popular Constitutionalism and Judicial Review* (Oxford: Oxford University Press, 2004).

[24] A. Tomkins, *Our Republican Constitution* (Oxford: Hart, 2005); A. Tomkins, 'The Role of the Courts in the Political Constitution' (2010) 60 *University of Toronto Law Journal* 1; T. Poole, 'Back to the Future? Unearthing the Theory of Common Law Constitutionalism' (2003) 23 *Oxford Journal of Legal Studies* 453; T. Poole, 'Questioning Common Law Constitutionalism' (2005) 25 *Legal Studies* 142, T. Poole, 'Legitimacy, Rights and Judicial Review' (2005) 25 *Oxford Journal of Legal Studies* 697.

[25] Tomkins, *Our Republican Constitution*, pp. 10–25. See also, e.g., Poole, 'Back to the Future?'.

The first is that law is an activity that is not only distinct from, but also superior to, politics. The soundness of the first part of this claim involves complex considerations that are barely touched upon by Tomkins. He perceives the common law as just as much a political enterprise as parliamentary law-making, but the rationale for this conclusion is never made apparent. The assumption might be any of the following: that public law adjudication entails balancing of values; that legal reasoning is not distinct from political reasoning; that it deals with matters that might be or have been considered in the political process; that legal decisions have political implications; that judges have inherent 'political' biases; or that all law is political. This is not the place to analyse these criteria for the law/politics divide, save to say that each of these possible meanings raises complex empirical and normative issues. The second part of this 'tenet' presents equally complex considerations: it might mean that some law is superior to some politics within a particular legal order, as manifest in the susceptibility of, for example, ministerial decisions to judicial review; that law is superior even to primary statute when and to the extent mandated by a constitution or another primary statute; that legal reasoning is in some way inherently superior to political reasoning; or that law can trump statute even without formal provision in a constitution or another primary statute providing for this. The soundness or not of these arguments raises once again complicated considerations, on which there is a mountain of literature. Suffice it to say for the present that there is nothing within legal constitutionalism that requires acceptance of the more far-reaching options adumbrated above, and that is so notwithstanding the fact that a particular legal constitutionalist might favour such an option. The moderate legal constitutionalism espoused in this and the preceding chapter is not premised on the assumption that 'politics is bad, law is good'; this does not underpin the primary legal material, nor does it follow therefrom.

Nor is legal constitutionalism premised on the assumption that the courts are the only institution for the regulation of public power, Tomkins's second 'tenet' of legal constitutionalism. Legal constitutionalism is premised on the assumption that courts are important for legal accountability, while recognizing, as pretty much all legal constitutionalists do, that there are other ways of promoting accountability quite independently of judicial review. There is nothing within moderate legal constitutionalism, or within legal constitutionalism more generally, that denies the significance of non-judicial methods of accountability. Legal constitutionalists deal with issues of accountability and legitimacy quite independently of judicial review.[26] There is no sense in which they think that courts are the only relevant players when

[26] See, e.g., J. Jowell, *Law and Bureaucracy: Administrative Discretion and the Limits of Legal Action* (New York: Dunellen, 1975); J. Jowell and D. Oliver (eds.), *The Changing Constitution* (Oxford: Oxford University Press, 7th ed., 2011); D. Oliver, *Government in the United Kingdom: The Search for Accountability, Effectiveness and Citizenship* (Milton Keynes: Open University Press, 1991); D. Oliver, *Constitutional Reform in the UK* (Oxford: Oxford University Press, 2003); D. Oliver and G. Drewry, *Public Service Reforms: Issues of Accountability and Public Law* (London: Pinter, 1996); P. Craig, *Administrative Law* (London: Sweet & Maxwell, 7th ed., 2012), Chs. 2–11; P. Craig, *EU Administrative Law* (Oxford: Oxford University Press, 2nd ed., 2012), Chs. 1–7.

thinking about constitutionalism. Nor is there any inconsistency in maintaining that judicial review is one component in the search for accountability and legitimacy, while being aware of the importance of institutional design, political controls, internal agency organization and the plethora of other matters that these and other authors have written about. This is not a zero-sum game whereby focus on judicial review implies a lack of concern with other mechanisms for accountability and legitimacy.

Nor, yet again, is moderate legal constitutionalism, or legal constitutionalism more generally, premised on the assumption that individuals should, as far as possible, remain free from constraint. This is Tomkins's third tenet, which he labels liberalism. Many legal constitutionalists subscribe to liberalism, as evidenced by the secondary literature. Liberalism is not, however, captured by Tomkins's third tenet. There are, as is well known, significant differences within liberalism, ranging from welfarist Rawlsian conceptions to more libertarian conceptions, with a plethora of variants in between, with differing consequences for the role of the state. Commitment to liberalism does not, therefore, necessarily connote the desirability of a minimal state, nor does the fact that legal constitutionalists speak in terms of autonomy or human dignity. The contingent fact that a particular legal constitutionalist might subscribe to a libertarian view of liberalism,[27] or interpret concepts such as autonomy and human dignity in that manner, does not entail the conclusion that the precepts

[27] None of the writers commonly associated with legal constitutionalism in the UK subscribe to this view of liberalism.

of legal constitutionalism developed by the courts are 'wired' to that version of liberalism, or indeed any particular version thereof. It is therefore perfectly possible, for example, to support republicanism, favour legal oversight within administrative law, and orient the basic precepts of judicial review so as best to effectuate the goals of that theory.[28]

Tomkins's fourth tenet of legal constitutionalism is that where government interference is unavoidable it should be justified by reason. This assumption is indeed part of all versions of legal constitutionalism, but it is surely defensible on any plausible thesis of accountable government, irrespective of the particular political theory that underpins it. It is difficult to imagine how one would normatively defend the contrary proposition, to the effect that governmental interference does not have to be justified by reason. This is more especially so given the instrumental and non-instrumental justifications proffered for reasoned decision making.[29] Provision of reasons can assist the courts in performing their substantive supervisory function and help to ensure that the

[28] See, e.g., C. Sunstein, 'Interest Groups in American Public Law' (1985) 38 *Stanford Law Review* 29; C. Sunstein, 'Beyond the Republican Revival' (1988) 97 *Yale Law Journal* 1539; F. Michelman, 'Foreword: Traces of Self-Government' (1986) 100 *Harvard Law Review* 4.

[29] See, e.g., G. Richardson, 'The Duty to Give Reasons: Potential and Practice' [1986] *Public Law* 437; P. Craig, 'The Common Law, Reasons and Administrative Justice' [1994] *Cambridge Law Journal* 282; Sir Patrick Neil, 'The Duty to Give Reasons: The Openness of Decision-Making', in C. Forsyth and I. Hare (eds.), *The Golden Metwand and the Crooked Cord: Essays in Honour of Sir William Wade* (Oxford: Oxford University Press, 1998), pp. 161–84; M. Elliott, 'Has the Common Law Duty to Give Reasons Come of Age Yet?' [2011] *Public Law* 56.

decision has been thought through by the agency. It can counter arbitrariness, one facet of which is to have one's status redefined without an adequate explanation of the reasons for the action, and increase the legitimacy of the administrative process by enhancing public confidence.

Adam Tomkins's fifth and sixth tenets of legal constitutionalism can be conveniently considered together. They are respectively that the extent of and justification for government interference is a matter for the courts, and that the law should control government through the enforcement of specific rules and general principles of legality. His critique of both propositions is grounded in an admixture of reasons that underlie his opposition to judicial review: there is no legitimate foundation for such principles, they entail too much balancing, and they intrude on issues that are legitimately the preserve of the political process. The foundational legitimacy of such principles was considered in the previous chapter.[30] The difficulties with this aspect of the critique will be considered below. It will be seen that evaluative judgement and balancing are evident in all areas of law, public and private. It will also be seen that Tomkins's criterion as to what should be regarded as part of the judicial and political process is not tenable.

(b) The foundational dimension: II

There is a related but distinct version of the political constitutionalist critique advanced by Tom Poole. His depiction of

[30] See above, pp. 18–65.

common law constitutionalism accords in many respects with that of Adam Tomkins.[31] Poole does not directly question the legitimacy of non-constitutional review, but contends, rather, that it does not fit with the vision of legal constitutionalists. Thus he maintains that participation in adjudication is ill-adapted to consideration of a range of competing views; that judicial review is ill-suited for polycentric disputes; that the arguments in judicial review cases are relatively spartan when compared to political debate; and that judicial review in cases concerned with rights does not typically address fundamental values, but is more commonly concerned with second-order considerations such as the intensity of review. It is right and proper that legal constitutionalism should be subject to close scrutiny in terms of whether it lives up to its 'billing'. By parity of reasoning the same is true for critiques thereof.

Consider Poole's critique that judicial review is essentially adjudicative and bipolar, is ill-adapted to consideration of competing points of view and cannot therefore be a forum for deliberating about fundamental values, and cannot match the republican model of active citizenship. Most legal constitutionalists do not claim that judicial review presently

[31] See, e.g., Poole, 'Back to the Future?'. He depicts legal constitutionalism in the following terms: a political community is ordered according to a set of fundamental values; political decision making is or ought to be a matter of discovering what fundamental values require in particular cases; the common law is the primary repository of the fundamental values of the political community; ordinary politics does not necessarily connect with fundamental values; public law therefore consists of a set of higher-order principles and rights; and decision making in judicial review is or ought to be value-oriented.

comports with a model of republican discourse, although some, including the present author, contend that broadened participatory rights before the initial decision maker, combined with relatively liberal standing and intervention rights before the courts, will enhance the deliberative, republican aspects of decision making, albeit within the parameters imposed by being within a judicial forum. Poole's argument is, in any event, predicated on how decisions are made within the political forum, this being full consideration of competing views on which the decision is made. A full debate on primary legislation with detailed consideration of competing values cannot be matched elsewhere,[32] and legal constitutionalists would laud this process. It is equally clear that much primary legislation does not receive this considered analysis: Parliament may not be cognizant of all rights-based issues raised by the legislation; time constraints may mean that any consideration is brief; and the views of the Joint Committee on Human Rights may not be adequately taken into account.[33] The problems are far greater for statutory instruments.[34] They become more difficult yet again when we consider decision making by agencies, ministers, prison governors, health boards and the like, which can rarely take account of a full range of competing considerations because of practical, epistemic and political constraints.

[32] J. Waldron, *The Dignity of Legislation* (Cambridge: Cambridge University Press, 1999).

[33] D. Feldman, 'Parliamentary Scrutiny of Legislation and Human Rights' [2002] *Public Law* 323.

[34] Craig, *Administrative Law*, Ch. 15.

Consider the critique that judicial review is unsuited to polycentric disputes, which Poole argues are better considered in political terms. Legal constitutionalists accept that courts are limited in their capacity to deal with polycentric issues, and this has been recognized by the courts.[35] Polycentricity is, however, as Jeff King has shown,[36] pervasive in many legal areas, private as well as public. If the fact that a dispute was polycentric were to signal that it should be a no-go area for the courts, then law would be emasculated, although the polycentric nature of the issue may affect the intensity of review.[37] It should not, moreover, be assumed that the political process will conform to some perfect deliberative ideal when polycentric matters are in play, since there will often be pragmatic, political and epistemic constraints when decisions are made in that forum.

Consider further the critique that the argumentation in judicial review is relatively spartan compared to the richness of political debate. Legal constitutionalists, whether positivist or non-positivist, accept that there are differences between judicial review and political argument. Legal

[35] See, e.g., *R* v. *Cambridge Health Authority, ex p B* [1995] 2 All ER 129; *R (Walker)* v. *Parole Board, R (Wells)* v. *Parole Board* [2007] EWHC 1835.

[36] J. King, 'The Pervasiveness of Polycentricity' [2008] *Public Law* 101.

[37] See, e.g., J. King, 'The Justiciability of Resource Allocation' (2007) 70 *Modern Law Review* 197; A. Pillay, 'Courts, Variable Standards of Review and Resource Allocation: Developing a Model for the Enforcement of Social and Economic Rights' [2007] *European Human Rights Law Review* 616; J. King, *Judging Social Rights* (Cambridge: Cambridge University Press, 2012).

argument must be fitted into one of the established heads of review, which are premised on assumptions about the relationship between courts and primary decision makers, such as the injunction against substitution of judgement on matters of discretion assigned to the latter. This does not, however, mean that judicial consideration of an issue will necessarily be less rich than in the political process, since there may well have been scant consideration as to whether a particular provision conflicts with public law precepts when legislation is enacted, and this is true a fortiori when decisions are made by the plethora of other bodies that constitute the administrative state.[38] Insofar as the matter has been thought through rigorously by the primary decision maker, this will properly affect the incidence of judicial review.[39]

Consider, finally, Tom Poole's contention that judges decide cases, even those concerned with rights, not by reflecting on what fundamental values require, but by focusing on second-order considerations relating to the standard of judicial review, the assumption being that this constitutes a diminution of the precepts of legal constitutionalism. This argument is misconceived. Legal constitutionalists take different views as to when, for example, deference/respect should

[38] Jeremy Waldron's argument concerning the relative capacity of courts and legislatures to engage in moral reasoning is predicated on a normative ideal as to how the legislature acting at its best might approach moral matters, and he accepts that in many instances this is not matched by actual performance. J. Waldron, 'Judges as Moral Reasoners' (2009) 7 *International Journal of Constitutional Law* 2.

[39] See, e.g., *R (Animal Defenders International)* v. *Secretary of State for Culture, Media and Sport* [2008] 1 AC 1312.

be accorded, but this does not mean that consideration of the standard of review is problematic for legal constitutionalism.[40] It is, to the contrary, natural for courts to focus on it, as well as on the meaning of the contested right, since the former may be a condition precedent to determination of the latter. The standard of review encapsulates important values concerning the relationship between courts and the initial decision maker, which have always been central to legal constitutionalist thought. There is therefore nothing contradictory about taking account of such considerations in a rights-based approach to adjudication. It is clear, moreover, that there are many instances where the courts substitute judgment on the meaning of speech, assembly, deprivation of liberty or the like, where the focus will be squarely on the meaning of the contested right.

(c) The historical dimension

Tomkins's analysis of modern judicial review is premised on what he regards as the failure of legal constitutionalism from a historical perspective. He writes engagingly and with verve about the seventeenth century, which is the exclusive focus of his analysis, and which he labels the failure of the

[40] See, e.g., *R (International Transport Roth GmbH)* v. *Secretary of State for the Home Department* [2003] QB 728; J. Jowell, 'Judicial Deference and Human Rights: A Question of Competence', in P. Craig and R. Rawlings (eds.), *Law and Administration in Europe: Essays in Honour of Carol Harlow* (Oxford: Oxford University Press, 2003), Ch. 4.

common law constitution.[41] There are, however, very real difficulties with this analysis.[42]

His conclusion concerning the failure of legal constitutionalism is based exclusively on the seventeenth-century case law on the prerogative, and his interpretation is contestable, to say the very least. He downplays the significance of the seminal decisions in *Prohibitions del Roy*[43] and the *Case of Proclamations*,[44] for reasons that are not convincing.[45] Whatsoever the broader motivations behind the decisions might have been, they are authority respectively for the propositions that the monarch did not have autonomous judicial power, nor any general regulatory power that could be exercised independently of Parliament. These decisions were of real significance for our legal and political order. The fact that the 'clock' is stopped at the end of the seventeenth century means, moreover, that we get a distorted picture of the efficacy of legal control over the prerogative. We hear nothing about the seminal decision in the *De Keyser* case,[46] which established that where Parliament had legislated the executive could not use prerogative power which might touch the same

[41] Tomkins, *Our Republican Constitution*, pp. 69–87.

[42] P. Craig, 'Political Constitutionalism and Judicial Review', in C. Forsyth, M. Elliott, S. Jhaveri, A. Scully-Hill and M. Ramsden (eds.), *Effective Judicial Review: A Cornerstone of Good Governance* (Oxford: Oxford University Press, 2010), Ch. 3.

[43] (1607) 12 Co. Rep. 63. [44] (1611) 12 Co. Rep. 74.

[45] P. Craig, 'Prerogative, Precedent and Power', in Forsyth and Hare, *The Golden Metwand and the Crooked Cord*, pp. 65–89; T. Hickman, 'In Defence of the Legal Constitution' (2005) 55 *University of Toronto Law Journal* 981, at 1013.

[46] *Attorney General* v. *De Keyser's Royal Hotel* [1920] AC 508.

subject matter. The executive had to follow the statutory conditions, and could not seek a more advantageous result by reliance on a prerogative power. We hear nothing either about the seminal *GCHQ* case,[47] which held that the courts could, subject to certain limitations, control the manner of exercise of an admitted prerogative, such that where the executive exercised prerogative power it should in principle be subject to the same controls as for statutory powers.

This leads to a further difficulty with Tomkins's historical thesis, which is more serious, viz. that there is no mention of the general law on judicial review, whereby the courts exercised control over statutory power. To test the history of common law constitutionalism with limited reference only to judicial control over the prerogative is unbalanced to say the least, more especially given that the case law on review of statutory power outnumbered that on the prerogative by a very significant factor, my guess would be in the order of a minimum of 250–1. The activities performed directly by the state were limited in the seventeenth and eighteenth centuries, and even in the nineteenth century many functions were undertaken by boards, commissions, inspectors and the like. Judicial review of bodies ranging from tithe commissioners to inclosure commissioners, from tax commissioners to local justices, and from poor law boards to local authorities, constituted an important element of accountability in the administrative state. It can be accepted that certain legal decisions were open to criticism. This must,

[47] *Council of Civil Service Unions* v. *Minister for the Civil Service* [1985] AC 374.

however, be kept in perspective given that the political controls over the plethora of bodies that constituted the administrative state were not well developed, and that the direct democratic mandate was limited.[48] Prior to the 1832 Reform Act only approximately 5–10 per cent of the population were enfranchised with any direct 'political voice', and women were not fully enfranchised until 1928. The more egalitarian demands of the Levellers eloquently put by Lilburne and Rainsborough in the seventeenth century were not to be fulfilled for nearly 300 years.

(d) The normative dimension

The general thrust of political constitutionalist thought has been to limit legal constitutionalism in the form of judicial review and to extol in its place political oversight. There are, however, four challenges facing a political constitutionalist minded to limit judicial review of the kind practised in administrative law.[49]

(i) Disagreement

The first challenge is to advance a convincing normative justification for this limitation. The critics commonly reason by analogy from the literature on constitutional review, especially strong constitutional review, where the focus is on disagreement about the meaning and content of rights.

[48] See, e.g., C. Stebbings, *Legal Foundations of Tribunals in Nineteenth-Century England* (Cambridge: Cambridge University Press, 2006).

[49] P. Craig, 'Political Constitutionalism and the Judicial Role: A Response' (2011) 9 *International Journal of Constitutional Law* 112, at 113–17.

Little thought is, however, given to the transferability of this argument to the terrain of judicial review within administrative law. This argument cannot, however, per se provide the desired justification, since it proves too much. If the premise against judicial review is that courts should not be involved in cases where there are contentious value assumptions or difficult balancing exercises, then the premise is unsustainable, since it would destroy adjudication across private as well as public law. We shall return to this point in more detail below.[50] Suffice it to say for the present that the disagreement endemic within plural democratic societies concerning the more particular meaning to be ascribed to abstract concepts such as liberty, equality and security in public law is matched by analogous disagreement in private law on these and related issues.

This is attested to by the debates about theory and doctrine in, for example, contract, tort, restitution and crime, where commentators discuss the values that should underpin the subjects. Courts in private law routinely develop doctrine that is reflective of defensible, albeit contestable, normative assumptions and will often balance competing values. Judicial doctrine within criminal law is premised on conceptions of moral responsibility and justifiable excuse. Contract law is shaped by considerations relating to matters such as consent, autonomy, bargain and the like. Tort theorists debate as to whether the law should be informed by corrective or distributive justice, or some admixture of the two, and if so what precisely that mix should be.

[50] See below, pp. 209–36.

Similar academic debates and judicial discourse are apparent in areas as diverse as restitution and trusts.

(ii) Disagreement plus democratic status

It might then be contended that the normative justification for limiting administrative law judicial review is to be found in the combination of disagreement concerning matters such as rights, combined with the democratic status of the primary decision maker. The analogy with the argument against strong constitutional review is evident from this formulation. The analogy, however, conceals more than it reveals. It is problematic for three reasons.

First, the extent to which primary decision makers in administrative law have democratic credentials varies very considerably. Political constitutionalist argument assumes that the initial decision will be made by the legislature, or a member of the executive with some direct democratic credentials, the paradigm being a government minister. The tapestry of administration in the modern state is, however, far more complex. The initial determination will often be made by bodies such as local authorities, local agencies, central agencies, prison governors, school governors, health boards and bodies to whom power has been contracted out. The extent of their democratic credentials varies considerably. There is clearly a distinction between the existence of democratic legitimacy that inheres by virtue of the vote, and the authority given by a democratically elected body to an agency or institution that is not itself democratically elected.

Second, the courts already take cognizance of democratic status at numerous points within the fabric of traditional judicial review doctrine. It is built on certain assumptions concerning the relationship between the legal and political branches of government, as exemplified by the generally accepted proscription on judicial substitution of judgement for that of the administration in relation to the merits of discretionary power. It is apparent once again in the judicial recognition of some degree of deference, discretionary area of judgement or respect to be accorded to the initial decision maker under the Human Rights Act 1998, the extent of which will vary depending, in part, on the nature and extent of the initial decision maker's democratic credentials.[51] There is considerable judicial and academic debate as to the extent to which such deference should be afforded, which will be considered in detail below.[52] This discourse does not, however, alter the point being made here, which is that traditional judicial review does not ignore the relationship between the political and the legal.

Third, any radical limitation on judicial review must, moreover, be squared with the realization that even in relation to initial decision makers who possess some democratic legitimacy, such as ministers, there is the commonly accepted need for judicial oversight to ensure that they do not transgress the limits laid down by their democratic parent, the legislature. The transmission-belt theory no longer provides a convincing explanation for the entirety of administrative law. This can be accepted, while acknowledging that controls

[51] See, e.g., *R (International Transport Roth GmbH)* v. *Secretary of State for the Home Department* [2003] QB 728.

[52] See below, pp. 236–71.

to ensure that the initial decision maker does not stray beyond the sphere accorded by the legislature are to be found in all regimes of administrative law. Thus political constitutionalists could not without self-contradiction so transform judicial review as to destroy this species of judicial oversight.

(iii) Doctrine

The third challenge facing the political constitutionalist minded to curtail judicial review is to identify the parts of judicial doctrine that are to be axed or constrained, and to justify the choice thus made by providing some normatively convincing explanation to differentiate such doctrine from that which remains. A target for political constitutionalists minded to challenge judicial review in administrative law is adjudication in rights-based cases, and some political constitutionalists wish to axe or radically curtail other parts of administrative law doctrine, such as rationality/proportionality review. This nonetheless leaves open two challenges for any political constitutionalist minded to restrict judicial review, the first being analytical, the second conceptual.

The analytical challenge is to justify why certain parts of administrative law doctrine are to be axed or curtailed, while others are allowed to remain. The rationale normally given is that the former covers those aspects of judicial review that involve complex balancing or weighing of values. The idea that the courts should be barred from such cases is itself contestable. The apposite point for present purposes is, however, that even if one subscribes to this thesis its application is far more difficult than its proponents would have us believe. The idea that the terrain in which judicial review is allowed to operate by political constitutionalists can be regarded as free from the very 'infirmities' that lead them to curtail it in other areas does not withstand examination.

The conceptual challenge is, if anything more problematic, albeit less obvious. The rationale given by some political constitutionalists for limiting judicial review is that legal rights-based claims of the kind typically grounded on the European Convention on Human Rights and the Human Rights Act 1998 are merely political statements of political conflict pretending to be resolutions of it. The contestability of this assertion is not apposite for the present analysis. The consistency of the reasoning of those who subscribe to this thesis is, however, directly relevant. If a commentator believes that the courts are to be barred from rights-based adjudication on the ground that such cases really are political claims dressed up in legal garb, then this premise must be consistently maintained throughout. The reality is, however, that this conceptual assumption is frequently contradicted by other parts of their analysis.

(iv) Consequence

The final challenge facing a political constitutionalist minded to limit significantly the scope of judicial review is to advert to the consequences for individuals aggrieved by governmental action who can no longer resort to the courts. It can be acknowledged that the courts are not the only means of obtaining relief. This is readily accepted by legal constitutionalists, who also consider, as we have seen above, other means of securing redress. Political constitutionalists who advocate limitation of the judicial role must by parity of reasoning explicate how diminution of judicial protection is to be compensated by increase in non-legal protection. Political constitutionalists are mindful of this challenge, but their response thus far has been partial and the conclusions contestable. This is so for two related reasons.

First, their focus on the compensating political quid pro quo for the reduction in legal protection has been almost exclusively on the extent to which Parliament exercises meaningful control over the executive and the ways in which this might be enhanced. Thus political constitutionalists such as Tomkins and Bellamy try to show that Parliament can exert real control over legislation and the executive.[53] Their assessment of the status quo is, however, contestable. The fact that Parliament has managed to exert some control over some parts of legislation in some limited instances falls short of sustaining their case. The executive continues to exert significant control over the legislature, notwithstanding the fact that backbench MPs have flexed their muscles more recently.[54] Such interventions may well improve legislation, but Select Committee reports dating from after the Second World War to the first decade of the new millennium do not sustain a vision of Parliament as the site of republican virtue of the kind desired by Tomkins and Bellamy.[55]

[53] Bellamy, *Political Constitutionalism*, Ch. 6; Tomkins, *Our Republican Constitution*, pp. 124–31.

[54] P. Cowley, *How Blair Mislaid His Majority* (London: Politico's Publishing, 2005).

[55] The principal Select Committee reports are cited and discussed in Craig, *Administrative Law*, Chs. 3, 22.

Second, there is scant attention given to the impact of diminution of judicial control insofar as this affects the rest of the administrative state, independently of Parliament and the executive. If judicial review is curtailed then the impact on those affected by decisions of agencies, prison governors, school governors, health boards and local authorities must surely be considered. If they cannot press their case through legal means then it is incumbent on the political constitutionalist to explain how non-judicial controls through the Ombudsman, complaints machinery, institutional design and the like will avail such individuals. It does not suffice in this respect to talk in abstract terms about the availability of such controls. It is incumbent on those minded to limit judicial review to explain more precisely just how these mechanisms can fill the gap left by the absence of legal relief. This must, moreover, be done without contradiction. Thus while, for example, the Ombudsman is mentioned in this context, there is no thought given to the fit between empowering this figure while disempowering the courts. If the objection to judicial intervention is premised on the undesirability of courts balancing different values, it is not apparent why this should be acceptable when the same exercise is done by the Ombudsman.

(e) The positive dimension

Academics are terrific critics. It is part of their genetic make up to test arguments for their weaknesses, real or apparent. Part of the 'academic deal' is, however, to take responsibility, which means proposing something to replace the status quo.

Hence the rationale for the title of this section: the responsibility to proffer some positive suggestion for how the subject should be conceived, the only caveat being where the critique is so far-reaching that it destroys the very subject matter, thereby absolving the critic of the duty to say how it should be reconfigured. Political constitutionalists do not, however, believe that administrative law should cease to exist, and they cannot therefore be absolved from the attendant duty. This perforce raises the interesting inquiry as to the intellectual sustainability of the alternative vision. It means also subjecting it to searching scrutiny, given that academics are, as noted above, adept critics. All of which just goes to show that what goes around comes around. It is to the credit of Tom Poole and Adam Tomkins that they do not seek to avoid their positive obligations. The difficulties of constructing the alternative vision are, however, formidable. It demands articulation of a different foundation for legal intervention, and requires also identification of the doctrinal differences of their preferred regime. These difficulties can be exemplified in turn by focusing on suggestions made by Poole and Tomkins.

(i) Alternative conceptual foundations

The problem of constructing a conceptual foundation for administrative law that is distinct from that of legal constitutionalists is evident in Tom Poole's work.[56] His preferred vision focuses on legitimacy. In instrumental terms, this is said to connote the idea that judicial review is justified

[56] Poole, 'Legitimacy, Rights and Judicial Review'.

because of the fallibility in government decision making. In non-instrumental terms, it is said to capture the idea of trust in government. Legitimacy is important, but it is not distinct from more traditional approaches to judicial review, nor is it distinct from legal constitutionalism.

Values and legitimacy are intimately linked, which is why legitimacy has always been a feature of legal constitutionalism and properly so. There is nothing new in this respect, nor is there anything antithetical between the role of values as explicated in the previous chapter and legitimacy.[57] The very idea of legitimate government is predicated on assumptions about fundamental values that inform our considered judgement as to whether a polity is legitimate. This is equally true in relation to specific public law precepts. Thus the conclusion that deciding without a hearing is illegitimate is grounded on assumptions about the instrumental and non-instrumental values served by natural justice. Legitimacy is expressive of conclusions based on values regarded as normatively relevant to the inquiry. This is the causality of the relationship between values and legitimacy in this context. This intimate connection between legitimacy and values is readily apparent in relation to process, output and institutional legitimacy.

Thus process legitimacy will reflect certain normative values as to, for example, 'process writ large': electoral representation, constituency boundaries and the like; and 'process writ small': who should be entitled to be heard, or participate in agency rule making. Conclusions as to output legitimacy

[57] See above, pp. 95–125.

will reflect certain values concerning, for example, the distributive justice entailed in a tax regime, whether the burdens placed on an individual by an executive decision are proportionate, or whether limitations of a right are warranted. Institutional legitimacy captures the idea that courts are reviewing governmental decisions, which is reflected in the injunction against judicial substitution of judgement of discretionary power, and in the case law on deference under the HRA.

The difficulty of disaggregating values and legitimacy is further apparent in relation to rights. Rights can be seen as enhancing legitimate government. This is standard fare within legal constitutionalism, and exemplifies the connection between values and legitimacy adumbrated above. Poole wishes to ground rights in terms of legitimacy, without the interposition of fundamental values cast in terms of autonomy, dignity and the like, preferring to base rights on empirical generalizations founded ultimately in mistrust. This is, however, untenable, since it becomes apparent that the precepts of autonomy, dignity, liberty and the like that have been purportedly excluded from the analysis nonetheless re-enter and inform any conclusion by the 'side door'. Thus, to take but one example, whether governmental action leads to 'intolerable results' cannot be answered without consideration, explicitly or implicitly, of the concepts of liberty, equality or autonomy that are relevant to the particular case.[58]

[58] Poole, 'Legitimacy, Rights and Judicial Review', 722.

(ii) Alternative doctrinal precepts

The critique of legal constitutionalism means that it is incumbent on a political constitutionalist to articulate some alternative vision of judicial review. It can, of course, be different from the status quo, but the legal consequences of subscribing to it must be thought through and it must be coherent in its own terms. This is no easy task, and Adam Tomkins deserves credit for undertaking it.[59] He and I chased each other around the law reviews on this issue, and the discourse is, inter alia, mixed with claims that I misunderstood the content and import of the arguments. The reality is that I accurately represented the text that I was commenting on at the time, and the resulting vision was untenable.[60] The reality concerning Adam Tomkins's later offering is more prosaic, and exemplifies a temptation to which all academics can succumb when the infirmities of earlier work have been revealed, viz. to change its substance while purporting to adhere to the principal tenets of the initial thesis.[61] Tomkins's later offering is in reality very different from that proffered earlier, as attested to by the fact that it is akin to much that is on offer in mainstream legal constitutionalism. The subsequent discussion thus begins with Adam Tomkins's general thesis concerning the role of courts in the political constitution, coupled with my response, followed by the shift in position evident in his later work.

[59] Tomkins, 'The Role of the Courts in the Political Constitution'.

[60] Craig, 'Political Constitutionalism and the Judicial Role: A Response'.

[61] A. Tomkins, 'What's Left of the Political Constitution?' (2013) 14 *German Law Journal* 2275.

Tomkins's thesis as advanced in 2010 was as follows. He believed that the role of the courts should be to nourish the political constitution. He believed also in rights, but followed Griffith in regarding a rights-based claim of the kind typically found in the ECHR as being a political statement of political conflict pretending to be resolution of it, with the consequence that it should be resolved through the political process.

> I agree with John Griffith's statement that provisions of the European Convention on Human Rights (ECHR) (and other like instruments) such as ECHR art. 10 are statements of political conflict pretending to be resolutions of it. For a political constitutionalist, the appropriate forum for the resolution of political conflicts is a political forum and cannot be the courtroom. The liberty-enhancing aim of modern human rights law is laudable, to be sure, but some of the means it adopts necessarily, inevitably, *and vastly* increase judicial power. For a political constitutionalist, this is too high a price to pay; an alternative means of protecting liberty has to be found.[62]

The nature of qualified rights is said to render them ill-suited to judicial resolution. Thus he stated that 'my argument attacks not the judicial enforcement of rights as such, but the structure of rights and, in particular, of substantive rights, as they are set out in human rights instruments such as the ECHR':[63]

[62] Tomkins, 'The Role of the Courts in the Political Constitution', 4. Italics in the original. J.A.G. Griffith, 'The Political Constitution' (1979) 42 *Modern Law Review* 1, at 14.

[63] Tomkins, 'The Role of the Courts in the Political Constitution', 5.

> Judicially enforceable substantive rights may be deemed compatible with political constitutionalism when they are narrowly defined and absolute. An absolute ban on torture, for example, is a rule that can and ought to be a rule of law enforceable by the courts. It is those qualified political claims that are elevated to the status of substantive rights that are problematic. Where and how to draw the lines between acceptable and unacceptable expression is quintessentially a political question, which, under a political constitution, ought to be addressed and resolved politically.[64]

Tomkins advocated judicial review in cases where the government had no legal authority for its action, and this was to be undertaken against a strong presumption in favour of individual liberty. He was, however, opposed to rationality or proportionality review because such concepts were too open-textured, and could be applied with differing degrees of intensity. He had earlier lambasted the courts for developing general principles of legality such as reasonableness review, viewing them as giving rise to 'untrammelled judicial discretion',[65] and was similarly critical of the recognition of constitutional rights.[66] This view of such juridical doctrines was maintained in the 2010 article. Tomkins was unequivocal, and his sentiment in this respect is captured vividly in the following extract:

64 Tomkins, 'The Role of the Courts in the Political Constitution', 5.

65 Tomkins, *Our Republican Constitution*, p. 22.

66 Tomkins, *Our Republican Constitution*, pp. 23–4.

> in the vast majority of art. 10 cases, as in the vast majority of cases concerning privacy or freedom of religion, it is on the matter of proportionality that all else hinges. As it happens, the British courts have by and large shown considerable wisdom and caution in their rulings on proportionality in the post-Human Rights Act era. I have no quibble with the decisions reached by the House of Lords in any of *Denbigh High School, Miss Behavin'*, or *Animal Defenders*, for example. My argument is not that the courts are reaching the wrong decisions, but that they are ruling on matters which, properly understood, are not their business.[67]

Tomkins did not, however, reveal the legal consequences of embracing this view, which would be far-reaching. The UK would have to exit the ECHR, since if he was unwilling to countenance national courts engaging in judicial review of qualified rights, then he must by parity of reasoning be unwilling to accept adjudication on the same issues by the Strasbourg Court. The nature of the adjudicative issues does not alter depending on whether they are dealt with at home or overseas. The UK would, in any event, on Tomkins's thesis, be in fundamental breach of the ECHR, flowing from the denial of direct adjudication by national courts over qualified rights, and from the rejection of proportionality review. There may well be room for debate, as we shall see below,[68] as to the relationship between the Strasbourg Court and national courts. This does not alter the fact that Tomkins's argument

[67] Tomkins, 'The Role of the Courts in the Political Constitution', 4.
[68] See below, pp. 280–5.

against legal adjudication of qualified rights by national courts cannot be reconciled with membership of the ECHR. Adam Tomkins's thesis would also lead to the demise of the Human Rights Act 1998, since the great majority of rights contained therein would on Tomkins's taxonomy be regarded as qualified rights.

There were, in addition, very real difficulties with the consistency and coherence of Tomkins's argument. It was central to Tomkins's thesis that the courts should engage in judicial review in order to determine whether the government had legal authority for its action. Public lawyers would agree that this is a central component of judicial review, but would also acknowledge that the phrase 'legal authority to act' is indeterminate as to the range of doctrinal rules that are thereby brought within judicial review. It could connote legal authority in a narrow sense, whereby the government must be able to point to some statute or prerogative power enabling it to act. It could at the other end of the spectrum mean that governmental action will only be lawful if it complies with principles of legality, including rationality/proportionality, legitimate expectations, equality, due process, and respect for established rights. There are numerous intermediate possibilities. The meaning of the phrase 'legal authority to act' is not therefore self-defining. It is not a mantra the mere incantation of which will magically resolve the proper limits of judicial review.

Tomkins provided no indication of the more particular meaning that he accorded to this phrase. It might be felt that he would incline to a narrow view, but this did not square with his repeated injunction that the limits of governmental authority to act included a very strong presumption in favour of fundamental rights. This raised the question as to why testing governmental action against fundamental rights was justified, while the judicial creation of other principles of legality or good governance was not. It also raised a deeper question concerning the coherence of the argument. Thus while Tomkins argued stridently that rights-based protection should be limited to absolute rights and process rights, to the exclusion of qualified rights, he argued equally stridently that the government's legal authority to act must be read against a strong presumption of non-interference with rights more generally. The difficult issues of interpretation in rights cases arise, however, in the latter type of case, just as much as in the former. The strictures against direct judicial review of qualified rights were premised on contestability as to their interpretation, coupled with dislike of the judicial balancing attendant upon application of proportionality. Yet the same type of inquiry is demanded in relation to process rights, and is also required through his preferred route of judicially policed determination of the limits to executive power, coupled with a strong presumption in favour of rights.

Similar tensions were apparent in other parts of the thesis. Thus Tomkins disliked rationality/proportionality, because such doctrines were open-textured, required judicial balancing and hence left too much discretion to the courts. It followed that the principal doctrinal foundations for ensuring that the executive remained within the proper limits of its authority to act had to be grounded in the controls of purpose and relevancy. The conceptual divide between purpose/relevancy and rationality/proportionality is, however, inherently uncertain, and assessment of value and balancing often occurs when applying the former, thereby diminishing the difference between the judicial reasoning in such cases and that which applies in cases of rationality/proportionality.[69] The preference for resting all control over discretion on controls of purpose/relevancy was, moreover, paradoxical for a political constitutionalist, since the judiciary substitute judgement on such issues, by way of comparison with the lesser forms of intervention that flow from reasonableness and proportionality review.

The message from the later work is markedly different.[70] We are now told that qualified rights can be subject to judicial review, and that Adam Tomkins never meant to deny this, notwithstanding clear statements to the contrary adumbrated above. We are now also told that there was never any intent to exclude proportionality or rationality review, notwithstanding the unequivocal statements set out above, to the effect that even if the courts had reached sound decisions in particular cases, they were nonetheless ruling on matters that were not their business, thereby echoing the same strident sentiment voiced in his earlier work.[71] Adam Tomkins now believes that such review should be countenanced, subject to the stricture that courts should properly take into account factors such as the extent to which Parliament had considered

[69] See, e.g., *R. (Bancoult)* v. *Secretary of State for Foreign and Commonwealth Affairs* [2009] 1 AC 453; *R. (Corner House Research)* v. *Director of the Serious Fraud Office* [2009] 1 AC 756.

[70] Tomkins, 'What's Left of the Political Constitution?'

[71] Tomkins, *Our Republican Constitution*, pp. 20–4.

the relevant issues in reaching their conclusion, and the nature of the public body that made the decision.

It is fine for people to change their mind, which is what Adam Tomkins has done, but it is preferable if this is done openly, rather than pretend that there is continuity with past thought that belies the reality. His present position is pretty mainstream, as exemplified by the factors that he believes to be relevant in the application of proportionality review, which are precisely considerations of the sort that inform the general debates about the degree of deference or respect that should be taken into account in judicial review.

To put the same point another way, if Tomkins's current view really reflects continuity of thought with past work, then it raises an important question, which is what precisely was the purpose of the earlier work, characterized as it was by the sound and fury of the attack on legal constitutionalism? If you are going to lead the troops up the hill with clarion calls as to the infirmities of legal constitutionalism and the ills of judicial review, then when they reach the summit they are going to expect some equally radical vision of the proper role of judicial review going forward. This is precisely what Tomkins delivered in the 2010 offering, although it was not tenable for the reasons set out above and developed in greater detail elsewhere.[72] If he truly always believed in the ambit of judicial review that he now espouses, which is broadly reflective of the legal status quo, then the troops would raise justified queries as to the purpose of the intellectual enterprise. The mixed constitution has always

[72] Craig, 'Political Constitutionalism and the Judicial Role: A Response'.

been a reality. Legal constitutionalism does not deny the significance of non-judicial methods of accountability, or the importance of the democratic mandate, nor does it deny the important contribution made by the political process to fundamental values or valuable societal reform.

4 Process and security

(a) Strains on process: security and closed-material procedures

The post-9/11 world is one in which security is firmly back on the mainstream agenda, although, truth to tell, it was of concern hitherto from diverse threats, including that flowing from the situation in Ireland. Nonetheless, 9/11 generated a plethora of legislative and executive responses that in turn led to a rich literature exploring the tensions between liberty and security in modern polities.[73] The issues thereby raised go considerably beyond the confines of this book, and the subsequent discussion is perforce limited to the impact on procedural fairness in the form of natural justice.

[73] See, e.g., M. Ignatieff, *The Lesser Evil: Political Ethics in An Age of Terror* (Princeton: Princeton University Press 2004); D. Dyzenhaus, *The Constitution of Law: Legality in a Time of Emergency* (Cambridge: Cambridge University Press, 2006); E. Posner and A. Vermeule, *Terror in the Balance: Security, Liberty, and the Courts* (New York: Oxford University Press, 2007); K. Moss, *Balancing Liberty and Security: Human Rights, Human Wrongs* (Basingstoke: Palgrave Macmillan, 2011); C. Gearty, *Liberty and Security* (Cambridge: Polity Press 2013).

The right to be heard and freedom from bias were central precepts in the law of judicial review forged in the seventeenth century.[74] They have remained central ever since, and this is so notwithstanding the low period in the early twentieth century, when the previously expansive jurisprudence was limited by unwarranted judicial constructs that were later swept away.

The post-9/11 world has, however, seen increased recourse to procedures that modify the normal hearing process. A closed-material procedure (CMP) involving special advocates is the procedure whereby relevant material, the disclosure of which would harm the public interest ('closed material'), can still be considered in the proceedings rather than being excluded as with public-interest immunity, the aim being to provide individuals with 'a substantial measure of procedural justice in the difficult circumstances where, in the public interest, material cannot be disclosed to them'.[75] The proceedings have both 'open' and 'closed' elements, with all material relied on by the government being laid before the court and the special advocate.[76] The individual and his legal representative are present at the open hearings, and have access to the open material. They cannot be present at the closed parts of the proceedings, or see the closed material.

[74] See above, pp. 35–6.

[75] Justice and Security Green Paper, Cm 8194 (2011), p. 52.

[76] J. Ip,'The Rise and Spread of the Special Advocate' [2008] *Public Law* 717; M. Chamberlain, 'Special Advocates and Procedural Fairness in Closed Proceedings' (2009) 28 *Civil Justice Quarterly* 314; C. Murphy, 'Counter-terrorism and the Culture of Legality: The Case of Special Advocates' (2013) 24 *King's Law Journal* 19.

A special advocate is appointed who attends all parts of the proceedings, and sees all the material, including the closed material not disclosed to the individual. He is able to take instructions from the individual before he reads the closed material, and written instructions after he has seen the closed material. A special advocate can also communicate with the individual after he has seen the material, subject to permission from the court. Special advocates are security-cleared barristers/advocates, who are given special training for this role. They act for the individual's interests in relation to closed material and closed hearings, but the individual is not their client. They ensure that the closed material is subject to independent scrutiny and adversarial challenge, and they can make submissions in closed session as to whether or not the closed material should be disclosed to the individual. It is for the court, not the Secretary of State, to decide whether material should be withheld.

The closed-material procedure was initially introduced in the context of immigration deportation decisions, with the stimulus coming from the European Court of Human Rights.[77] The CMP has subsequently been used by the Special Immigration Appeals Commission, by the Proscribed Organisations Appeal Commission, in Employment Tribunal cases concerning national security, in control order cases under the Prevention of Terrorism Act 2005, in financial restrictions proceedings under the Counter-Terrorism Act 2008, in orders made under the Justice and Security

[77] *Chahal* v. *United Kingdom* (1996) 23 EHRR 413.

Act 2013, and by the Sentence Review Commission and Parole Commission in Northern Ireland.

(b) Closed-material procedures: the courts and natural justice

The compatibility of the CMP with natural justice was, not surprisingly, challenged before the courts. In *AF* the appellant was subject to a non-derogating control order made pursuant to the Prevention of Terrorism Act 2005, section 2, (PTA), because the Secretary of State had reasonable grounds for suspecting that the appellant was, or had been, involved in terrorism-related activity, and that he considered it necessary to make such an order to protect the public from a risk of terrorism.[78] It was not necessary to prove that the person subject to the control order had actually committed any further offence. The PTA and Civil Procedure Rules made provision for a CMP and for special advocates.[79] The issue was whether the procedure for the making of a control order complied with Article 6 ECHR and hence with the Human Rights Act 1998.

The House of Lords held that there was a core minimum of procedural justice and that this could not be overridden by arguments that the procedural rights would not

78 *Secretary of State for the Home Department* v. *AF* [2010] 2 AC 269; P. Craig, 'Perspectives on Process: Common Law, Statutory and Political' [2010] *Public Law* 275; A. Kavanagh, 'Special Advocates, Control Orders and the Right to a Fair Trial' (2010) 73 *Modern Law Review* 836.

79 CPR 76.

have made any difference. The consequence was that the relevant provisions of the PTA 2005 were read down so as to be compatible with Convention rights. Their Lordships were influenced by the decision of the ECtHR in *A* v. *United Kingdom*,[80] which held that non-disclosure could not deny a party knowledge of the essence of the case against him, in cases where the consequences were of the kind that flowed from a control order. The regime of special advocates could alleviate but not cure the problems caused by non-disclosure of closed material to the affected party.

The House of Lords accepted the ECtHR decision, stating that it established that the person subject to the control order must be given sufficient information about the allegations against him to enable him to give effective instructions in relation to those allegations. Provided that this requirement was satisfied there could be a fair trial notwithstanding that the person was not provided with the detail or the sources of the evidence forming the basis of the allegations. Where, however, the open material consisted purely of general assertions and the case against that person was based solely or to a decisive degree on closed materials, the requirements of a fair trial would not be satisfied, however cogent the case based on the closed materials might be.[81]

The argument from case law was reinforced by that from principle. Lord Phillips adduced instrumental and non-instrumental reasons that underlie natural justice to support

[80] Application No 3455/05, 19 February 2009.

[81] *AF* [2010] 2 AC 269, at [59], [81], [85], [96], [101], [108], [114].

the preceding conclusion.[82] Thus in instrumental terms Lord Phillips noted that there were strong policy considerations to support a rule that a trial procedure could never be considered fair if a party was kept in ignorance of the case against him, since there would be many cases where it would be impossible for the court to be confident that disclosure would make no difference. This conclusion was reinforced by non-instrumental or dignitarian considerations, since resentment would undoubtedly be felt by the controlee and the family where there was no proper explanation for the control order: they and the wider public 'need to be able to see that justice is done rather than being asked to take it on trust'.[83] The decision in *AF* was welcome, but the CMP regime was nonetheless inherently problematic.

Later courts were forced to adjudicate on the difficult line as to whether the claimant had received sufficient information about the essence of the allegations to be able to defend himself,[84] and on whether the closed-material procedure could be used to submit evidence on behalf of the claimant, subject to strict duties of non-disclosure of the evidence where it might endanger the witness.[85] There were problematic issues that could arise when a case in which a

[82] *AF* [2010] 2 AC 269, at [56], [58], [60]–[66].

[83] *AF* [2010] 2 AC 269, at [63], [83].

[84] *AH* v. *Secretary of State for the Home Department* [2011] EWCA Civ 787; *Secretary of State for the Home Department* v. *CD* [2011] EWHC 2087; A. Tomkins, 'National Security and the Role of the Court: A Changed Landscape?' (2010) 126 *Law Quarterly Review* 543.

[85] *W (Algeria) (FC)* v. *Secretary of State for the Home Department* [2012] UKSC 8.

closed-material procedure was used was appealed, and the Supreme Court furnished guidance as to best practice in this regard.[86]

Later courts were also required to decide the types of case when the individual could demand to be told the essence or gist of the case against him. This too was problematic, as was evident from *Tariq*,[87] where the claimant who was employed by the Home Office as an immigration officer had his security clearance withdrawn after the arrest of his brother and cousin during an investigation into a suspected terrorist plot, even though there was no information that Tariq was involved with the plot. The claimant contended that he should be able to know the essence of the case against him. The Supreme Court disagreed. It held that 'gisting' was not required in every context in which Article 6 ECHR was engaged and that it was not necessary in the instant case of security vetting, more especially because the case concerned employment rather than loss of liberty,[88] although there were uncertainties as to what constituted loss of liberty for these purposes.

Later courts, moreover, placed limits on use of the closed-material procedure as in *Al Rawi*.[89] The majority of the

[86] *Bank Mellat* v. *Her Majesty's Treasury (No 1)* [2013] UKSC 38, at [68]–[74].

[87] *Tariq* v. *Home Office* [2011] UKSC 35.

[88] *Tariq* [2011] UKSC 35, at [67]–[69], [81]–[83], [86]–[92], [138], [143]–[147], [158].

[89] *Al Rawi* v. *Security Service (Justice and Others intervening)* [2011] UKSC 34; A. Zuckerman, 'Closed Material Procedure – Denial of Natural Justice: Al Rawi v Security Service' (2011) 30 *Civil Justice Quarterly* 345.

Supreme Court held that a closed-material procedure could only be introduced by statute, and that the courts could not do so pursuant to their power to regulate their own procedure. They held that the principles of open and natural justice whereby proceedings generally take place and judgments are delivered in public and parties know and can respond to the cases against them, calling witnesses and cross-examining opposing witnesses, were fundamental features of a common law trial. While the court had inherent power to regulate its own procedures, it could not, in doing so, deny parties' rights to participate in litigation in accordance with those principles. These limits were, however, qualified in *Bank Mellat (No. 1)*,[90] where the Supreme Court held that even though it had no express statutory authority to conduct a CMP, it had power to do so. This power could be exercised in an appeal where the lower court's judgment was wholly or partially closed, since there would be a serious risk of not doing justice if the court could not consider the closed material, and it could only do so if it adopted a closed-material procedure.

(c) Closed-material procedures: Justice and Security Act 2013

The Government was unhappy with the position as it had unfolded in the case law, more especially the uncertainties as to when a CMP could be used consequent on the *Al Rawi* case. It therefore proposed legislation to make CMPs available

[90] [2013] UKSC 38.

wherever necessary in civil proceedings.[91] Most worrying was the proposal to vest the decision whether to use a CMP in the Secretary of State on the ground that he is 'best placed to assess the harm that may be caused by disclosing sensitive information'.[92] It was accepted that this decision could be judicially reviewed, but it would be difficult for the claimant to succeed, since in most instances the court would be asked to review the exercise of ministerial discretion and this would be subject to limited rationality review.

The Justice and Security Act 2013 did not retain this feature. It is for the court to make a declaration allowing a CMP procedure in civil proceedings. The application may be made by the Secretary of State,[93] or any party to the proceedings, or it may be made of the court's own motion.[94] Two conditions must be satisfied before the court issues such a declaration. The first condition is that in the course of the proceedings a party to the proceedings would be required to disclose sensitive material to another person, or that a party to the proceedings would be required to make such a disclosure were it not for one or more circumstances specified in the Act. The second condition is that it is in the interests of the fair and effective administration of justice in the proceedings to

[91] Justice and Security Green Paper, Cm 8194, at [2.5].

[92] Justice and Security Green Paper, Cm 8194, at [2.6].

[93] The court must not consider an application by the Secretary of State unless it is satisfied that the Secretary of State has, before making the application, considered whether to make, or advise another person to make, a claim for public-interest immunity in relation to the material on which the application is based. Justice and Security Act 2013, s. 6(7).

[94] Justice and Security Act 2013, s. 6(1)–(2).

make a declaration. Sensitive material is defined to be material the disclosure of which would be damaging to national security.[95] The court has a duty to keep the CMP under review, and may revoke it at any time if it considers that it is no longer in the interests of the fair and effective administration of justice in the proceedings.[96] Special advocates are part of the CMP regime.[97]

Adam Tomkins is assuredly right that the Justice and Security Act 2013 benefited from close scrutiny by the House of Lords, which secured a number of valuable amendments during the legislative process.[98] There is also little doubt that there are tensions integral to the closed-material procedure, and that its generalized availability through the 2013 legislation exacerbates those tensions. The difficulties experienced by special advocates will likely continue. There is, moreover, the point forcefully expressed by Lord Kerr, who questioned the premise underlying the CMP, which is that placing before a judge all relevant material is preferable to having to withhold potentially pivotal evidence. Lord Kerr acknowledged the deceptive attraction of this proposition, but argued that it was nonetheless fallacious:

> The central fallacy of the argument, however, lies in the unspoken assumption that, because the judge sees everything, he is bound to be in a better position to reach

[95] Justice and Security Act 2013, s. 6(11).
[96] Justice and Security Act 2013, s. 7(2).
[97] Justice and Security Act 2013, s. 9.
[98] A. Tomkins, 'Justice and Security in the United Kingdom' (2014) 47 *Israel Law Review* 305.

> a fair result. That assumption is misplaced. To be truly valuable, evidence must be capable of withstanding challenge. I go further. Evidence which has been insulated from challenge may positively mislead. It is precisely because of this that the right to know the case that one's opponent makes and to have the opportunity to challenge it occupies such a central place in the concept of a fair trial. However astute and assiduous the judge, the proposed procedure hands over to one party considerable control over the production of relevant material and the manner in which it is to be presented. The peril that such a procedure presents to the fair trial of contentious litigation is both obvious and undeniable.[99]

5 Substance: normative judgement and balancing

There are a number of enduring themes relating to substantive judicial review, including its intensity, the legal form through which this should be expressed, and the extent to which the courts should show deference, respect or appropriate weight to the views of the initial decision maker. These will be considered in the section that follows. There are, however, related inquiries concerning the limits of law.[100] These concerns vary, but include the difficult normative assessments that courts may be required to make even where the issue is

[99] *Al Rawi* [2011] UKSC 34, at [93].

[100] See, e.g., Lord Sumption, 'The Limits of Law', 27th Sultan Azlan Shah Lecture, Kuala Lumpur, 20 November 2013, available at http://supremecourt.uk/news/speeches.html.

not incommensurable; the capacity of courts to undertake the kind of assessment required of them, given that they may be required to balance incommensurable considerations; the difficulties posed by polycentricity; and the relationship between courts and legislature in the resolution of such issues. These are important questions, and they should not be ducked.

It is, however, noteworthy that much of the soul-searching undertaken in this regard by public lawyers is set exclusively within a public law frame. We the public law fraternity pose the preceding questions focusing on the standard fare of constitutional and administrative law. This may be because we have made a considered judgement that public law issues are so distinctive as to render any comparison with private law otiose. It may be for more prosaic and contingent reasons, viz. that increased specialization within academia has meant that scholars simply do not know enough about private law to test their assumptions about the limits of law as determined from a public law perspective.

Whatsoever the answer to that empirical inquiry, it is axiomatic that the conclusion we reach on the preceding issues as judged from a public law perspective must be consistent with any judgment that we might make about private law. This is so irrespective of the fact that the underlying purposes of public law and private law may well be different. If the principal rationales for disquiet concerning public law adjudication relate to matters such as the making of complex normative assessments that are felt to be beyond the judicial role or the balancing of incommensurables, then we must surely test whether such problems are also to be found in the private law context.

(a) Private law: normative judgement and balancing

This inquiry concerns both the making of complex normative assessments, and the balancing of values that are felt to be incommensurable to some degree. The focus will, for exigencies of space, be on the law of torts.

There is very considerable normative contestation as to the background object or purpose that is to be served by tort law. It plays out most dramatically in the debates between those who conceive of it as being concerned with economic efficiency, and those who adopt a corrective-justice perspective. This is just the tip of the iceberg, because there is considerable normative contestation as to what corrective justice means,[101] which can in turn lead to very different concrete implications for particular doctrines within tort law. The identification of the nature of the interests that should be protected through the law of torts; whether the standard of liability should be conceived in terms of fault, intent or strict liability; and the more particular meaning accorded to these standards are all fiercely debated in the academic literature. The normative complexity and contestability raised by

[101] See, e.g, E. Weinrib, *The Idea of Private Law* (Oxford: Oxford University Press, 2012); J. Gardner, 'The Purity and Priority of Private Law' (1996) 46 *University of Toronto Law Journal* 459; J. Gardner, 'What Is Tort Law For? Part 1: The Place of Corrective Justice' (2011) 30 *Law and Philosophy* 1; R. Stevens, *Torts and Rights* (Oxford: Oxford University Press, 2007); J. Oberdiek (ed.), *Philosophical Foundations of the Law of Torts* (Oxford: Oxford University Press, 2015); H. Hurd, 'The Innocence of Negligence', at http://ssrn.com/abstract=2612084.

these issues matches anything that is found in public law, and what is salient for present purposes is that the courts make the relevant determinations through development of tort doctrine and we accept with equanimity that this is a legitimate part of the judicial role.

The prevalence of complex normative judgement and balancing of incommensurables is further apparent when we move from theory to concrete case law. They are present throughout tort law.[102] The test for negligence as judicially interpreted requires courts to balance a range of incommensurable considerations in deciding whether a duty of

[102] There are numerous instances of incommensurability embedded on the face of the 'legal rule', as exemplified by the fair-/honest-comment rule in defamation cases, whereby the common law courts have decided that free speech is sufficiently important that there can be a defence for defamation even where the critic is extreme or unbalanced, provided only that he is not malicious. The rule is premised on a balance between the value of free speech manifest in the very great freedom accorded to the critic, and the interest of the individual whose life may be destroyed by the captious and excessive critique. *Merivale* v. *Carson* (1888) 20 QBD 275, at 281; *Slim* v. *Daily Telegraph Ltd* [1968] 2 QB 157, at 170; *Reynolds* v. *Times Newspapers* [2001] 2 AC 127, at 193; B. Markesinis and S. Deakin, *Tort Law* (Oxford: Oxford University Press, 7th ed., 2013), pp. 664–9. The rule in nuisance, such that a person who 'comes to' a nuisance will not be able to complain of smell, noise or the like, but can still claim if there is some physical incursion into the property that constitutes an unreasonable use of land by the neighbour, encapsulates a balance between the interests of the property owner and the public interest, the rationale being that industrialization should not be impeded by private complaint of noise, smoke and the like within the relevant area. *Sturges* v. *Bridgman* (1879) 11 Ch D 852, at 865; Markesinis and Deakin, *Tort Law*, pp. 428–9.

care exists.[103] Historically there were doubts raised as to the necessity of duty as a separate juridical concept.[104] These doubts were predicated on the assumption that the test for duty was cast simply in terms of reasonable foresight, the argument being that this led to duplication of inquiry, given that the same issue would be considered to determine whether there had been a breach of the duty on the facts of the case. We do not require proof of an antecedent duty in other torts. We simply state that failure to comply with the legal rules that pertain to nuisance, assault, economic torts and the like is an actionable wrong. The role of duty within negligence may, however, be defended on certain grounds.[105]

It is nonetheless the case that duty is the medium through which policy considerations are taken cognizance of by the courts in order to decide whether liability should be imposed, even assuming that the defendant has been careless and caused the loss. Current orthodoxy is for a three-stage test to decide whether a duty of care exists: reasonable

[103] J. Fleming, 'Remoteness and Duty: The Control Devices in Liability for Negligence' (1953) 31 *Canadian Bar Review* 471; F. Lawson, 'Duty of Care: A Comparative Study' (1947) 22 *Tulane Law Review* 111; Markesinis and Deakin, *Tort Law*, p. 102; B. Markesinis and S. Deakin, 'The Random Element of Their Lordships' Infallible Judgment: An Economic and Comparative Analysis of the Tort of Negligence from *Anns* to *Murphy*' (1992) 55 *Modern Law Review* 619.

[104] P. Winfield, 'Duty in Tortious Negligence' (1932) 32 *Columbia Law Review* 41, at 66; W. Buckland, 'The Duty to Take Care' (1935) 51 *Law Quarterly Review* 637.

[105] See, e.g., J. Goldberg and B. Zipursky, 'Tort Law and Responsibility', in Oberdiek, *Philosophical Foundations of the Law of Torts*, Ch. 1; and S. Perry, 'Torts, Rights and Risk', in ibid., Ch. 2.

foresight; a relationship of proximity between plaintiff and defendant; and whether it would be fair, just and reasonable to impose a duty of care.[106] Duty of care thus conceived has been used as the vehicle through which the courts have denied liability in relation to types of loss, types of defendant and types of act.[107] The considerations that inform the determination whether it is fair, just and reasonable to impose a duty of care will often vary and require balancing inter se.[108] This determination may also turn on complex normative judgements as to what justifies the imposition of liability, as exemplified by the distinctions drawn between acts and omissions, and bodily harm as compared to psychiatric harm.

Balancing may also be required in order to decide whether there has been a breach of the duty of care. This was given voice most famously by Learned Hand and become known eponymously as the Learned Hand formula.

> The degree of care demanded of a person by an occasion is the resultant of three factors: the likelihood that his conduct will injure others, taken with the seriousness of the injury if it happens, and balanced against the interest that he must sacrifice to avoid the risk. All these are practically not susceptible of any quantitative estimate,

[106] *Caparo Industries plc* v. *Dickman* [1990] 2 AC 605; *Governors of the Peabody Donation Fund* v. *Sir Lindsay Parkinson and Co. Ltd* [1985] AC 210, at 241, 245; *Investors in Industry Commercial Properties Ltd* v. *South Bedfordshire District Council* [1986] QB 1034; *Murphy* v. *Brentwood District Council* [1991] 1 AC 398.

[107] Markesinis and Deakin, *Tort Law*, pp. 102–4.

[108] See, e.g., *X (Minors)* v. *Bedfordshire CC* [1995] 2 AC 633; *MacFarlane* v. *Tayside Health Board* [2000] AC 59.

> and the second two are not so, even theoretically. For this reason a solution always involves some preference, or choice between incommensurables, and it is thought most likely to accord with commonly accepted standards, real or fancied.[109]

For advocates of law and economics this was a quintessential example of the common law fashioning a rule to enhance economic efficiency, since an accident is deemed to be legally negligent only if the cost of avoiding it is less than the losses incurred by the injured party, discounted by the chance that the injury will actually occur.[110] It is important, however, not to forget the language used by Learned Hand J, since this is a corrective to any idea that it is a simple economic calculus, reducible to precise monetary amounts. It is more debatable how far English courts take cognizance of the costs of precautions when adjudicating on breach,[111] but it is in any event generally accepted that there can be considerable practical and normative difficulty in ascertaining what constitutes an unreasonable risk for the purposes of negligence liability.[112]

There are also numerous instances that require courts to make contestable normative judgements within negligence, over and beyond any issues of balance per se, as exemplified by the test for remoteness. The House of Lords settled the

[109] *Conway* v. *O'Brien* 111 F. 2d 611, at 612 (1940).

[110] R. Posner, 'A Theory of Negligence' (1972) 1 *Journal of Legal Studies* 29.

[111] See, e.g., *Bolton* v. *Stone* [1951] AC 850; *Latimer* v. *AEC Ltd* [1953] AC 634; *Wagon Mound (No 2)* [1967] 1 AC 617; *Smith* v. *Littlewoods Ltd* [1987] AC 241; *Tomlinson* v. *Congleton* [2004] 1 AC 46.

[112] Markesinis and Deakin, *Tort Law*, pp. 209–14.

matter in the *Wagon Mound (No 1)*, stating authoritatively that the test was to be cast in terms of foreseeability, castigating the alternative causal criterion as illogical and unjust.[113] Herbert Hart and Tony Honore revealed the questionable assumptions underlying this conclusion, noting that foresight was not self-evidently more consistent, simpler or more just than a test framed in terms of cause.[114] Thus, to take but one example, in their response to the argument that it is unfair to burden the defendant with large losses beyond what could have been contemplated, they noted that 'if the liability is out of all proportion to the defendant's fault it can be no less out of proportion to the plaintiff's innocence'.[115] This has been countered by those such as Weinrib,[116] who argue that corrective justice demands the linkage between culpability and compensation forged in the *Wagon Mound (No 1)*, but the reasoning is contestable. The salient point for present purposes is that courts routinely make choices in private law based on considerations of justice and fairness, which are contestable on normative grounds.

This contestability is equally apparent when we consider judicial choices as to standards of liability and the implications of those choices. The premise of negligence liability is that to justify the shifting of loss from plaintiff to defendant the former must show fault caused by the latter.

[113] *Overseas Tankship (U.K.) Ltd* v. *Morts Dock & Engineering Co. (The Wagon Mound)* [1961] AC 388, at 424.

[114] H.L.A. Hart and Tony Honoré, *Causation in the Law* (Oxford: Clarendon Press, 2nd ed., 1985), pp. 259–75.

[115] Hart and Honoré, *Causation in the Law*, pp. 267–8.

[116] Weinrib, *The Idea of Private Law*, Ch. 6.

This has significant distributive consequences, since it means that the risk of non-fault accidents lies with the plaintiff rather than with the defendant, even where the defendant caused the loss. The normative premise is that the defendant was not at fault and thus should not be required to pay the plaintiff. The obvious rejoinder is that nor was the plaintiff at fault, yet she is required to shoulder the loss even where it is unequivocally clear that this was caused by the defendant. The legal status quo has been defended on the ground that it comports with corrective justice,[117] but this argument is controversial in various respects. The argument is not that negligence liability is therefore 'wrong', but rather that it embodies contestable normative assumptions, chosen by the courts as the standard of liability. Matters were not always so. There were prominent areas where liability was based on cause.[118]

The significance of judicial choice as to the standard of liability is apparent yet again in judicial limitation of the *Rylands* principle.[119] Strict liability was regarded as something alien and unnatural, to be confined to the narrowest possible circumstances. Non-natural user was defined in *Rickards* as

[117] Weinrib, *The Idea of Private Law*, Ch. 6.

[118] See D. Ibbetson, *A Historical Introduction to the Law of Obligations* (Oxford: Oxford University Press, 1999), Ch. 4, for a balanced assessment of the cause of action for trespass to the plaintiff's person, goods or land, and the extent to which elements of fault in a medieval sense intruded on the action grounded in causation.

[119] (1865) 3 H. & C. 774; (1866) LR 1 Ex 265; (1868) LR 3 HL 330; A. Simpson, 'Legal Liability for Bursting Reservoirs: the Historical Context of *Rylands* v. *Fletcher*' (1984) 13 *Journal of Law and Society* 209; R. Bagshaw, '*Rylands* Confined' (2004) 120 *Law Quarterly Review* 388.

'some special use bringing with it increased danger to others, and must not merely be the ordinary use of the land or such a use as is proper for the general benefit of the community'.[120] Strict liability was reserved for socially unusual or abnormal activities, not ordinary uses of land.[121] No judgment did more to block the development of *Rylands* as a modern principle of strict liability that could be applicable precisely where the activity was normal, and yet entailed an inevitable number of accidents where it was difficult to prove fault, such as the running of utilities.[122] The idea that the burden of such losses should be spread among those who take the benefit of the activity, rather than being left to lie on the person fortuitously injured, is an attractive one, but was precluded by the courts' jurisprudence. The possibility of using *Rylands* in such instances was further limited by questionable decisions concerning the impact of statutory authority on such liability.[123] The same message was evident in the House of Lords decision in *Read*.[124] The ratio that escape was necessary for *Rylands* liability was predicated on unwillingness to recognize any distinct rule for dangerous activities, and a desire to prevent the tort encroaching on what was felt to be the natural domain of negligence liability.[125] None of the

[120] *Rickards* v. *Lothian* [1913] AC 263, at 280.

[121] For doubt as to the utility of the concept of 'general benefit to the community', see *Transco* v. *Stockport MBC* [2004] 2 AC 1.

[122] See, e.g., *Transco* v. *Stockport MBC* [2004] 2 AC 1; *British Celanese* v. *A.H. Hunt* [1969] 1 WLR 959.

[123] See, e.g., *Smeaton* v. *Ilford Corporation* [1954] Ch. 450; Craig, *Administrative Law*, pp. 939–41.

[124] *Read* v. *J. Lyons and Co. Ltd* [1947] AC 156.

foregoing was preordained; nor was it value-free. It was the result of contestable normative judgements, which in the words of Markesinis and Deakin 'progressively emasculated' the *Rylands* principle of its potential.[126]

The significance of judicial choice is also apparent in other areas, such as economic torts. The courts determine the extent to which tort law should impose limits on free competition. It is axiomatic that such competition can impose economic loss on other parties, and this may indeed be the intent or inevitable outcome of a person's action, as exemplified by price competition, the legitimacy of which is a foundational value in this area.[127] It is, however, qualified by values that serve to define what the judiciary believes to be the legitimate limits to that competition. The precise contours of these competing values are, however, contestable, more especially given that the judicial criteria have often been enumerated in trade disputes between employer and employee. This is readily apparent from the three areas that constitute economic torts: inducement to breach of contract, interference with trade by unlawful means, and conspiracy. There are tensions as to the foundational assumptions between these areas, and within each of them.

The fundamental tension between these areas is whether the courts will decide directly what should be the

[125] J. Fleming, *The Law of Torts* (Sydney: Law Book Co., 9th ed., 1998), p. 383.

[126] Markesinis and Deakin, *Tort Law*, p. 518.

[127] *Mogul Steamship Co. Ltd* v. *McGregor, Gow & Co. Ltd* (1889) LR 23 QBD 598, [1892] AC 25; *Allen* v. *Flood* [1898] AC 1.

limits of free competition, and make judgements as to the legitimacy thereof. The general assumption in the case law concerning interference with trade by unlawful means is that this is not the correct province for the judiciary, with the consequence that the boundary of legitimate competition is defined by proof of independent illegality. This obviates the courts from making free-standing judgments in this respect, but at the cost of making liability turn on parasitic concepts of illegality, the presence or absence of which may be fortuitous and of questionable relevance for establishment of liability.[128] This approach is, moreover, in tension with that concerning inducement to breach of contract, where liability is not predicated on the existence of some independent illegality, such as breach of statutory duty, a crime or committal of another independent tort. The fundamental assumption underlying inducement to breach of contract is that the value of free competition is bounded by the value of the claimant's contractual right to the services of the person induced to break their contract by the defendant.[129] There is no a priori reason why this should be so. The court might have decided that the plaintiff should be left to pursue any contractual claim against the person breaking their contract, without any independent recourse in tort against the person who offered the inducement. This might well be regarded as the optimal solution in terms of efficient breach viewed from a law and economics perspective. The choice to regard the contract as generating rights actionable against third parties in tort was not therefore

[128] J.D. Heydon, *Economic Torts* (London: Sweet & Maxwell, 2nd ed., 1978).
[129] *Lumley* v. *Gye* (1853) 2 E & B 216.

preordained, but was reflective of what the judiciary regarded as a legitimate limit on free competition. In true compromise style, the two limbs of the law relating to conspiracy reflect respectively the two preceding approaches, the one predicated on the existence of unlawful means, the other not.

There are, moreover, tensions within each of the three areas. The subsequent case law on inducement to breach of contract revealed contestation within the judiciary as to how far they were willing to press this competing value that embodied the limit on free competition. There was classic incremental case law development whereby the courts expanded the cause of action to include indirect interference with the contract[130] and hindering of the contract,[131] followed by judicial retrenchment disapproving these developments.[132] Analogous tensions are apparent in the case law on interference with trade by unlawful means. It was suggested with good reason, in the light of the expanded case law on inducement to breach of contract, combined with the case law on intimidation,[133] that UK law should develop from a series of nominate economic torts to an innominate tort cast in terms of interference with trade by means of action that the defendant was not at liberty to commit.[134] The time seemed ripe for an Atkin-type judgment in this area. It never happened

[130] *D.C. Thomson Ltd* v. *Deakin* [1994] EMLR 44.

[131] *Torquay Hotel Co. Ltd* v. *Cousins* [1969] Ch 106; *Merkur Island Shipping Corp.* v. *Laughton* [1983] 2 AC 570.

[132] *OBG Ltd* v. *Allan* [2008] AC 1.

[133] *Rookes* v. *Barnard* [1964] AC 1129, at 1168–9.

[134] T. Weir, 'Chaos or Cosmos: *Rookes*, *Stratford* and the Economic Torts' [1964] *Cambridge law Journal* 225.

and the courts once again pulled back, through a more constrained definition of what constitutes unlawful means and increased focus on intent to inflict economic damage.[135] The case law throws into sharp relief the real choices that have to be made as to what constitutes unlawful means for these purposes, both in terms of the nature of the illegality that should qualify in this regard and in terms of its causal connection to the harm suffered.

(b) Public law: normative judgement and balancing

Normative judgement and balancing are endemic within public law, and the appropriate limits to judicial intervention will be analysed in due course. Before doing so I wish to take a step back, and consider two issues that frame this inquiry: the relationship between controls relating to purpose/relevancy and reasonableness/proportionality, and the extent to which value judgements and balance pervade both levels of inquiry.

Controls over the way in which discretion is exercised commonly operate at two levels.[136] The initial inquiry is whether the public body used the discretion for a proper purpose and based on relevant considerations, followed by

[135] *OBG Ltd* v. *Allan* [2008] AC 1.

[136] Lord Woolf, J. Jowell and A. Le Sueur, *De Smith's Judicial Review* (London: Sweet & Maxwell, 6th ed., 2007), Chs. 5, 11; Craig, *Administrative Law*, Chs. 19, 21; H. Wilburg, 'Deference on Relevance and Purpose? Wrestling with the Law/Discretion Divide', in H. Wilburg and M. Elliott (eds.), *The Scope and Intensity of Substantive Review* (Oxford: Hart, 2015), Ch. 11.

analysis cast in terms of reasonableness/proportionality.[137] Control framed in terms of purpose and relevancy is central to the very idea of judicial review. It would be logically possible to stop there and make this the only species of control over discretionary power. The fact that pretty much all legal systems use a further method of control is, however, readily explicable. Legal constraints framed in terms of purpose/relevancy are relatively blunt tools, and the courts substitute judgement on these matters, treating them as a matter of statutory interpretation. Legal constraints framed in terms of reasonableness/proportionality allow the court to review in circumstances where it is not self-evident that the purpose was wholly improper or the consideration was wholly irrelevant, enabling the court to weigh such matters and to do so in accord with a less exacting standard than substitution of judgement.

Judicial statements that relevancy and reasonableness can shade into each other commonly capture the situation where courts are unsure whether to treat a consideration as wholly irrelevant, and hence take it into account and weigh it when undertaking reasonableness review.[138] This may in part be for interpretive reasons, viz. that it is unclear from the statutory remit whether the consideration should be deemed wholly irrelevant. It may also be in part for more conceptual

[137] *Associated Picture Houses Ltd* v. *Wednesbury Corporation* [1948] 1 KB 223, at 228–31, 233–4; *Council of Civil Service Unions* v. *Minister for the Civil Service* [1985] AC 374, at 410; *R* v. *Lord Saville of Newdigate, ex p A* [1999] 4 All ER 860, at [32]–[33].

[138] *Wednesbury Corporation* [1948] 1 KB 223, at 228–31.

reasons. Courts will necessarily have to decide on the level of abstraction or specificity with which to pose the inquiry. The broader or more abstract the inquiry at the level of purpose/relevancy, the more likely that the challenged action will satisfy those precepts, the corollary being that the case will be decided through reasonableness/proportionality. By way of contrast, the narrower the initial inquiry at the level of purpose/relevancy, the more likely that the case will be resolved at that level, the corollary being that less remains to be done through reasonableness review. Thus in the *Wednesbury* case the hypothetical of the teacher being dismissed for the colour of her hair was tested for conformity with reasonableness, the assumption being that dismissal on such grounds satisfied the tests of purpose/relevancy.[139] This could only be so if the issue was posed in relatively broad terms, viz. that 'physical characteristics could be relevant in hiring or dismissing a teacher'. If, however, the issue was framed in more specific terms, viz. that 'the natural colour of a person's hair could never be a relevant consideration in hiring or firing a teacher', then the case would have been resolved without recourse to reasonableness review.

It is, moreover, clear that value judgements and balance pervade both levels of inquiry. The pure theory underlying review for purpose/relevancy is that the courts are simply demarcating the four corners of the relevant statutory power. This may be so in some straightforward cases, but in many it will not. The decision as to allowable purpose, and the determination of relevant considerations, will frequently

[139] *Wednesbury Corporation* [1948] 1 KB 223.

require judicial assessment of values, and application of background principles, as is readily apparent from consideration of any of the leading decisions.[140]

The fact that value judgements and balance are prominent in reasonableness/proportionality is acknowledged, but it is nonetheless worth dwelling for a moment on the variability of such review in cases of rights even prior to the HRA, since it raises more general issues concerning the bounds of judicial legitimacy. The existence of rights increased the intensity of reasonableness review,[141] legislation was interpreted with a strong presumption that it was not intended to interfere with rights,[142] and the courts held that Convention rights were embedded in the common law.[143] These developments were regarded as controversial by some political constitutionalists.[144] They were court-sceptic and opposed to expansion of judicial review; some were also rights-sceptics, and they regarded balancing in such cases as

[140] See, e.g., *Roberts* v. *Hopwood* [1925] AC 579; *Council of Civil Service Unions* v. *Minister for the Civil Service* [1985] AC 374; *Secretary of State for Education and Science* v. *Tameside Metropolitan Borough Council* [1977] AC 1014; *Hazell* v. *Hammersmith and Fulham London Borough Council* [1992] 2 AC 1; *Bromley London Borough Council* v. *Greater London Council* [1983] 1 AC 768; *R. (Corner House Research)* v. *Director of the Serious Fraud Office* [2009] 1 AC 756.

[141] *R* v. *Secretary of State for the Home Department, ex p Brind* [1991] 1 AC 696; *R* v. *Ministry of Defence, ex p Smith* [1996] QB 517.

[142] *R* v. *Secretary of State for the Home Department, ex p Simms & O'Brien* [2000] 2 AC 115; *R* v. *Lord Chancellor, ex p Witham* [1998] QB 575.

[143] *Derbyshire County Council* v. *Times Newspapers Ltd* [1993] AC 534.

[144] Tomkins, *Our Republican Constitution*, pp. 18–25; J.A.G. Griffith, 'The Brave New World of Sir John Laws' (2000) 63 *Modern Law Review* 159.

problematic. The judicial decision to recognize rights in the preceding ways was not value-free, but the reality is that there is no neutrality to be had. Thus the political constitutionalists' objections grounded in either court-scepticism and/or rights-scepticism are every bit as value-laden as the opposing views.

If the courts apply reasonableness review to control discretionary power, there is good reason for varying its intensity depending on the affected interest. It makes no sense in normative terms to assume that a relatively trivial interest is of the same import as an interest that is objectively more significant, indeed the very statement is a contradiction in terms. It was therefore perfectly defensible for the courts to vary the intensity of such review. This requires evaluation of the importance of the interest, and whether it should be recognized as a right, in the manner explicated by, for example, MacCormick and Raz.[145] The proposition that statute will be read so as not to interfere with rights unless Parliament made clear its intent for it to be so is normatively sound because of the importance of the interest denominated as a right, and for the reasons powerfully expressed by Lord Hoffmann, viz. that Parliament should be mindful of such incursions and accept the political cost of doing so by making its intent explicit.[146] The development signalled in *Derbyshire* that Convention rights were to be regarded as embedded in

[145] D.N. MacCormick, 'Rights in Legislation', in P. Hacker and J. Raz (eds.), *Law, Morality and Society, Essays in Honour of H.L.A. Hart* (Oxford: Clarendon Press, 1977), Ch. 11; J. Raz, *The Morality of Freedom* (Oxford: Clarendon Press, 1986).

[146] *Simms* [2000] 2 AC 115.

the common law was potentially the most far-reaching.[147] While much development in administrative law was remedy-driven, the courts nonetheless had explicit regard for some rights, such as the right to vote, and most notably property rights. Rights-talk was not therefore absent from our legal heritage, but became obscured by the Diceyan formulation of negative residual liberties. There was, however, always a tension in this characterization. It carried a descriptive connotation, that the scope of, for example, your freedom of speech was the result of the aggregate limits placed thereon by statute or common law. It nonetheless also embodied the normative recognition that the relevant interests were indeed liberties. The real importance of the change to talking openly of rights was that it signified both that duties could flow from the rights and that any limitations of the rights would not simply be acknowledged, but be rigorously scrutinized.

(c) Normative judgement and balancing: reflections

Before proceeding to consider some of the more detailed public law issues, such as the appropriate degree of respect or weight to be given to the views of the primary decision maker, it is worth dwelling for a few moments on what we might learn more broadly about the nature and limits of the judicial role from the preceding analysis.[148]

[147] *Derbyshire County Council* [1993] AC 534.

[148] See more generally, C. Sunstein, 'Incommensurability and Valuation in Law' (1993–4) 92 *Michigan Law Review* 779; Symposium on Law and

(i) Polycentricity, private law and social policy

An oft-voiced element in the discourse concerning the limits of what the courts should do is the stricture that the courts should be wary about adjudicating on social policy, more particularly given the fact that judicial decisions may well resonate more broadly where the problem is polycentric in nature. Such concerns have been raised by Lord Sumption.[149] The extent to which polycentricity should be regarded as problematic in this regard has properly been questioned by Jeff King, who revealed its pervasiveness and the judicial techniques that could be used to deal with it short of judicial abstention.[150] It is interesting that those who express concern about polycentricity normally do so from within the frame of public law. It is public law broadly conceived that is felt to be problematic in this respect.

This does not, however, withstand examination. Reflect for a moment on the foregoing analysis of private law. It has profound social implications in two senses: it embodies social-policy choice and has far-reaching consequences for such choices made by the legislature. It would be reductionist to claim that all instances of private law adjudication embody social-policy choice, but it would be equally blinkered to deny the linkage. Tort law sets the

Incommensurability (1998) 146 *University of Pennsylvania Law Review* 1169.

149 Lord Sumption, 'The Limits of Law', pp. 15–16.

150 J. King, The Pervasiveness of Polycentricity' [2008] *Public Law* 1; J. King, 'The Justiciability of Resource Allocation' (2007) 70 *Modern Law Review* 19.

boundaries for private responsibility in relations between individuals that are primarily non-consensual. It expresses a social-policy choice that is not preordained as to when a person should bear the costs of loss caused to another, and the social dimension to that choice is not magically resolved by being cast in terms of corrective justice. The courts make the value judgements, they modify them and amend them over time.

The choice thus made then has far-reaching implications for social policy in the second sense. It will determine the respective areas in which losses are borne by a private party and those where they are borne by the state in terms of social-welfare payments and the like, as is evident from the seminal literature on accidents, compensation and the law.[151] If there are concerns as to the limits of law flowing from polycentricity in a public law context, then they are more than matched by the realization that defining the boundaries of private responsibility has far-reaching implications for the general social-welfare budget. Indeed, the systemic nature of this impact casts many polycentric problems posed in public law into the shadow.

(ii) Normative choice, balancing, and private and public law

There is a temptation to think that issues of normative choice are less problematic if balancing is not involved. There is a

[151] P. Atiyah, *Accidents, Compensation and the Law* (London: Weidenfeld & Nicolson, 1970); P. Cane, *Atiyah's Accidents, Compensation and the Law* (Cambridge: Cambridge University Press, 8th ed., 2013).

further temptation to think that issues of normative choice and balancing are more common and complex in public as opposed to private law, thus fuelling conclusions that we should conceive of the limits of law through adjudication differentially in this regard. There is a kindred temptation to think that the ways of dealing with such issues are somehow more tractable in the realm of private as opposed to public law, thereby lending further fuel to the same conclusion. All three temptations should be resisted.

There is no sound foundation for the belief that issues of normative choice that do not entail balancing are less problematic than those that do. A normative choice may express the result, explicitly or implicitly, of a range of incommensurable values. This choice may, by way of contrast, simply be between two or more foundational theories. There is, moreover, no a priori reason why a normative choice that does not involve the balancing of incommensurables will be less contestable than one that does. It may; it may not. There can be straight normative choices between rival theories that are fundamental to the relevant area, even where there is no balancing entailed, such as that between fault and strict liability, or between different conceptions of property that affect the constitutionality of regulation. There can, by way of contrast, be matters involving the balancing of incommensurables that are, in the grand scheme of things, relatively trivial. It is, in any event, the case that issues of normative choice pervade many rules in private as well as in public law, most certainly those of any significance. This is evident in the very determination whether the tortious standard of liability should be based on fault, strict liability or intent, and how far this should differ depending on the nature of the interest infringed.

There is, moreover, no sound foundation for claims that issues of normative choice and balancing are more common in public as opposed to private law. Nor is there any reason to conclude a priori that the issues are necessarily more complex, as judged by any dimension that the word might bear, in public law as opposed to private law. We can all think of morally foundational issues that arise in the context of judicial review that can affect the life or liberty of particular individuals,[152] which will receive considerable media coverage, but there are also many cases that do not raise concerns of this nature. We can, however, readily consider issues of analogous importance that arise in areas such as crime and tort, while recognizing that they also regulate matters of less significance.

The idea that such issues can be resolved in a more tractable manner in private as opposed to public law should also be resisted. There are, doubtless, different ways in which courts can address the balancing of, for example, incommensurable vales, but these differences do not pan out neatly on a private–public law divide; nor, more importantly, is one such technique unequivocally 'better' than another. The choice of techniques includes: ad hoc balancing of the relevant factors in each case, as exemplified by the duty concept in negligence and by the determination of the particular hearing rights that should be accorded to the claimant; a modified version of this approach whereby the balancing is undertaken with

[152] See, e.g., *R (Nicklinson)* v. *Ministry of Justice* [2014] UKSC 38.

different intensity for different kinds of case, as epitomized by proportionality review; formulation of a doctrinal rule that embodies the chosen result of the balancing, as in the context of the rules for nuisance, defamation or restitutionary relief for mistake of law; or the division of the specified area so that its component parts represent the outcome of the balancing differentially judged, as illustrated by the subdivisions within economic torts. These are different juridical techniques that cut across the public–private divide, and they each have different merits and demerits.

It might be felt that it is better in terms of legal certainty for the result of the balancing to become part of the rule, which can then be applied evenly thereafter. This is, however, dependent on the issue, whatsoever it might be, being amenable to embodiment in a rule-like format, which will not be the case if the number of variables is too broad or too fact-specific. Even where this is not so, there can be other, less obvious, disadvantages with rule-type formulations. Thus where the balancing is not readily apparent on the face of the rule it is common for it to take on a canonical nature and for the balancing that underpins it to be forgotten, such that it is not reassessed, which is in effect what happened in relation to the rule concerning restitutionary relief for mistake of law prior to recent judicial reforms, and is also what has occurred in relation to the remoteness rules in tort since the 1960s.

(iii) Statute, private and public law

It might be felt that, while private law is reflective of normative choice, and while it might entail balancing of incommensurables, it is nonetheless distinctive from public law in a crucial respect, this being that the former will be largely confined to the terrain of adjudication between private parties, while the latter will be primarily applicable in the context of power exercised pursuant to a statute. The normative choices and balancing exercises at common law nonetheless impact on legislative choice in two senses. There are many statutes dealing solely and directly with private law relationships, and the general principles of contract, tort, restitution and the like will be read into the statute, unless there is some clear indication therein to the contrary. The results of the common law choices will, in addition, inform statutes that deal with public law issues. This is readily apparent from the case law on negligence and public bodies, where the precepts of negligence have been used to shape the confines of such liability, whether through the definition of duty[153] or at the level of breach.[154] It is readily apparent yet again in the way that foundational common law assumptions, such as opposition to strict liability, have been used to limit radically the extent to which such statutes will be read as leading to the imposition of such liability.[155]

153 See, e.g., *X (Minors)* v. *Bedfordshire CC* [1995] 2 AC 633; *Stovin* v. *Wise* [1996] AC 923; *Curran* v. *Northern Ireland Co-ownership Housing Association Ltd* [1987] AC 718.

154 See, e.g., *Barrett* v. *Enfield LBC* [2001] 2 AC 550; *Phelps* v. *Hillingdon LBC* [2001] 2 AC 619.

155 See, e.g., *O'Rourke* v. *Camden LBC* [1998] AC 188; *Hammersmith Ry Co.* v. *Brand* (1869) LR 4 HL 171; *Manchester Corporation* v. *Farnworth* [1930] AC 171; *Allen* v. *Gulf Oil Refining Ltd* [1981] AC 1001; *Dunne* v. *North Western Gas Board* [1964] 2 QB 806; *Smeaton* v. *Ilford Corporation* [1954] Ch 450.

It might also be felt that it is more difficult for Parliament to overturn a public law decision. The HRA 1998 was, however, a conscious choice made by Parliament, and it can be amended or repealed. While it remains in force Parliament has the last word, and that is so notwithstanding constraints on how it exercises that power. The common law judicial reaction to repeal of the HRA is a related but distinct issue.

(iv) Statute, courts and respect

The centrality of normative choice and balancing of incommensurables to both private and public law does not mean that courts should ride roughshod over legislative choice, nor does it mean that they should fail to accord respect to it. The parameters will be fleshed out in more detail below, but they should be framed by the following two considerations.

We have always taken cognizance of democratic status within the fabric of judicial review. It is built on assumptions concerning the relationship between the legal and political branches of government, as exemplified by the generally accepted proscription on judicial substitution of judgement for that of the administration in relation to the merits of discretionary power. The extent to which primary decision makers have democratic credentials varies very considerably. The strongest case for such respect is in relation to primary legislation, which embodies the result of legislative choice expressly made after due consideration, although there may, by way of contrast, be rights-based issues that the legislature was unaware of, more especially in long, complex legislation. The initial determination may be made by bodies such as local authorities, agencies, prison governors, school governors, health boards and bodies to whom power has been contracted out. The extent of their democratic credentials varies considerably. There is clearly a distinction between the existence of democratic legitimacy that inheres by virtue of the vote, and the authority given by a democratically elected body to an agency or institution that is not itself democratically elected.

The second consideration should be regarded as a counterpoise to the first. The Human Rights Act 1998 is not the source of the problem in the manner that some conceive it to be. It is not just that its amendment or repeal might trigger judicial recourse to the common law jurisprudence that predated it. It is more fundamentally because the very recognition of such rights at common law, justified for the reasons set out above, necessarily requires inquiry as to the scope of the right and possible justifications for limitations thereof, thereby raising the same issues that currently require resolution. The only way to avoid such a conclusion is either through some form of rights-scepticism whereby the very denomination of certain interests as rights is felt to be misconceived, or through some fairly extreme form of court-scepticism, which would connote not merely the need for respect calibrated according to the nature of the primary decision maker, but something more akin to judicial abstention. Nor should it be thought that the difficulties of such review at common law or pursuant to the HRA will be obviated or overcome if reasonableness/proportionality control were to be radically limited or even cast aside. Courts would engage in analogous value judgements in the context of purpose/relevancy, and for those concerned about the limits of legitimate judicial intervention the position would be worse insofar as courts substitute judgement on these heads of review.

6 Substance: judicial review and deference/respect/weight

The preceding discussion of statute, courts and respect serves as a neat bridge to the more specialist discourse concerning the precise contours of such deference/respect within judicial review, on which there is a complex literature.[156] Neither this

[156] See, e.g., R. Edwards, 'Judicial Deference and the Human Rights Act' (2002) 65 *Modern Law Review* 859; J. Jowell, 'Judicial Deference and Human Rights: A Question of Competence', in Craig and Rawlings, *Law and Administration in Europe*, Ch. 4; J. Jowell, 'Judicial Deference: Servility, Civility or Institutional Capacity' [2003] *Public Law* 592; M. Hunt, 'Sovereignty's Blight: Why Contemporary Public Law Needs the Concept of "Due Deference"', in N. Bamforth and P. Leyland (eds.), *Public Law in a Multi-layered Constitution* (Oxford: Oxford University Press, 2003), Ch. 13; Lord Steyn, 'Deference: A Tangled Story' [2005] *Public Law* 346; T.R.S. Allan, 'Human Rights and Judicial Review: A Critique of "Due Deference"' [2006] *Cambridge Law Journal* 671; Lord Justice Dyson, 'Some Thoughts on Judicial Deference' [2006] *Judicial Review* 103; R. Clayton, 'Principles for Judicial Deference' [2006] *Judicial Review* 109; J. King, 'Institutional Approaches to Judicial Restraint' (2008) 28 *Oxford Journal of Legal Studies* 409; A. Young, 'In Defence of Due Deference' (2009) 72 *Modern Law Review* 554; A. Kavanagh, 'Defending Deference in Public Law and Constitutional Theory' (2010) 126 *Law Quarterly Review* 222; T. Hickman, *Public Law after the Human Rights Act* (Oxford: Hart, 2010), Ch. 5; T.R.S. Allan, 'Judicial Deference and Judicial Review: Legal Doctrine and Legal Theory' (2011) 127 *Law Quarterly Review* 96; A. Brady, *Proportionality and Deference under the Human Rights Act 1998: An Institutionally*

book, nor this chapter, is a literature review, and there will therefore be no attempt to survey all shades of opinion, although some of the main contours thereof will be considered in the ensuing analysis. It is helpful for the sake of analytic clarity to disaggregate five such issues that arise in this context.

(a) Nomenclature: deference, respect and weight

There have been differences of judicial view as to the label that best captures the courts' approach under the HRA. The label 'deference' has been used by a number of courts. So too has the phrase 'discretionary area of judgement'.[157] Lord Hoffmann in *ProLife* was, by way of contrast, unhappy about the language of deference, since he believed that it had overtones of servility.[158] It was, said Lord Hoffmann, necessary in a society based on the rule of law and the separation of powers to decide which branch of government

Sensitive Approach (Cambridge: Cambridge University Press, 2012); P. Daly, *A Theory of Deference in Administrative Law: Basis, Application and Scope* (Cambridge: Cambridge University Press, 2012); A. Young, 'Will You, Won't You, Will You Join the Deference Dance? (2014) 34 *Oxford Journal of Legal Studies* 1. M. Elliott, 'From Bifurcation to Calibration: Twin-Track Deference and the Culture of Justification', University of Cambridge Legal Studies Research Paper Series, No 27/2015.

[157] *R (P and Q and QB)* v. *Secretary of State for the Home Department* [2001] 1 WLR 2002; *Samaroo* v. *Secretary of State for the Home Department* [2001] UKHRR 1150; *R (Farrakhan)* v. *Secretary of State for the Home Department* [2002] QB 139.

[158] *R (ProLife Alliance)* v. *BBC* [2004] 1 AC 185, at [75]–[76].

had decision-making power and what the legal limits of that power were. That was a question of law to be decided by the courts. The inevitable consequence was that the courts themselves would often have to decide the limits of their own decision-making power:

> But it does not mean that their allocation of decision-making power to the other branches of government is a matter of courtesy or deference. The principles upon which decision-making powers are allocated are principles of law. The courts are the independent branch of government and the legislature and executive are, directly and indirectly respectively, the elected branches of government. Independence makes the courts more suited to deciding some kinds of questions and being elected makes the legislature or executive more suited to deciding others. The allocation of these decision-making responsibilities is based upon recognised principles. The principle that the independence of the courts is necessary for a proper decision of disputed legal rights or claims of violation of human rights is a legal principle. It is reflected in article 6 of the Convention. On the other hand, the principle that majority approval is necessary for a proper decision on policy or allocation of resources is also a legal principle. Likewise, when a court decides that a decision is within the proper competence of the legislature or executive, it is not showing deference. It is deciding the law.[159]

[159] *R (ProLife Alliance)* v. *BBC* [2004] 1 AC 185, at [76].

Lord Bingham expressed impatience with prolonged discussion about due deference, discretionary area of judgement, democratic accountability, relative institutional capacity and the like.[160] He stated that giving weight to factors legitimately taken into consideration by the initial decision maker was not properly described as deference. It was rather 'performance of the ordinary judicial task of weighing up the competing considerations on each side and according appropriate weight to the judgment of a person with responsibility for a given subject matter and access to special sources of knowledge and advice', which was 'how any rational judicial decision-maker is likely to proceed'.[161]

Different judges and indeed commentators may well have preferences as to the language that should be used when the courts undertake review under the HRA. It is, however, doubtful whether anything follows from the choice of this terminology, at least insofar as judicial practice is concerned. Thus the mere fact that a particular court chooses to use the language of deference does not in itself indicate that it is likely to leave more leeway to Parliament or the executive than if it had adopted the approach of Lord Hoffmann or Lord Bingham, since much depends on how it weighs the factors that incline in favour of or against deference on the facts of the case. This will be apparent from the subsequent analysis. My own preference is to use respect or weight, but in

[160] *Huang* v. *Secretary of State for the Home Department* [2007] 2 AC 167, at [14].

[161] *Huang* v. *Secretary of State for the Home Department* [2007] 2 AC 167, at [16].

the subsequent discussion these terms will be used interchangeably with deference, not least because it is the terminology used by some other scholars, and it would therefore be inappropriate to alter that language.

(b) Conceptual contestation: special doctrine or part of ordinary judicial review

While most academics would probably agree with the preceding conclusion, viz. that nothing per se turns on the choice of nomenclature, there is very considerable academic dispute as to how one should conceptualize what the courts are and should be doing. It is, indeed, the defining consideration in the fierce debates that have waged in this area. Matters are rendered more complex because terminology has been used somewhat differently by different writers. With these caveats the principal fault lines are nonetheless as follows.

There are some writers, notably Trevor Allan and Tom Hickman, who object to the articulation of any distinct doctrine of deference as such. They do not object to the idea that the courts should show some restraint when reviewing the exercise of discretionary power in a rights-based or non-rights-based context, although they may differ as to what those factors should be and the weight accorded to them, as will be seen below. They nonetheless share the view that there is no need for any special doctrine of deference, since the factors that the courts take into account when showing judicial restraint are properly taken into account through application of the normal processes of judicial review. They are, moreover, both sceptical as to the utility of generalizations about such factors, since they regard them as too abstract to be of use when it comes to the specifics of a particular case. For Allan, any doctrine of deference is thus either empty in merely repeating what is currently done within standard judicial review doctrine, or it is pernicious if it accords any latitude over and beyond this, since this is unwarranted and leads to the vice of double counting, whereby weight is given to considerations such as administrative expertise twice over.[162] Thus Trevor Allan states,

> It is important, however, to be clear at the outset that I am not rejecting the idea of judicial deference, if all that is meant is that judges should acknowledge the legitimate sphere of judgment or discretion that normally belongs to the political branches. There are considerations of jurisdiction and expertise or competence that courts must respect: they inform and shape established constitutional principle, defining the nature and scope of the judicial role in public law. My objection was to the notion of a special *doctrine* of deference, which would occupy a distinctive place in our theory and practice of judicial review – independent of the various standards of review or of the principles defining the content of specific constitutional rights. No such doctrine is necessary, in my view, and its general acceptance would be damaging to the coherence and effectiveness of our public law.[163]

Tom Hickman expresses analogous concerns, opining that it is the pervasive and fact-sensitive nature of weight

[162] Allan, 'Human Rights and Judicial Review', 675–6.

[163] Allan, 'Judicial Deference and Judicial Review', 97. Italics in the original.

'which makes it unsuitable for crystallization into a formal set of prescriptive categories'.[164] There should be no special doctrine of deference because it would 'require the reasons for affording weight to the assessments made by the primary decision-makers to be crystallized into rules or principles which would then prescribe a certain test or judicial approach', which would be of limited utility because the reasons could only be given at a high level of abstraction.[165] For Hickman this difficulty is compounded by the fact that even if one could generalize about the circumstances in which weight should be afforded by the court, that would tell one little about the result, since it would provide little by way of indication of the effect of the weight on the contested decision.[166]

There are other writers, notably Aileen Kavanagh, Alison Young and Jeff King, who contend that there is more to be said in favour of articulating the factors that do and should play into judicial restraint. We need to tread carefully here, because Kavanagh, Young and King's respective positions have been defined in this debate in part by their opponents, without too close consideration of whether that coheres with their actual approaches. Thus Allan would regard these writers as articulating the view he opposes, viz. the idea that deference should be given some formal status as a separate doctrine, and that the alleged infirmities of their theories 'prove' that there is no point to any such exercise. The reality

[164] Hickman, *Public Law after the Human Rights Act*, p. 137.
[165] Hickman, *Public Law after the Human Rights Act*, pp. 137–8.
[166] Hickman, *Public Law after the Human Rights Act*, p. 138.

is rather different. Thus when Kavanagh wrote her principal contribution it was not clear from Allan's initial foray into the field that he favoured much by way of judicial restraint, operating even within the confines of ordinary judicial review,[167] and his asseveration in later work that he only opposed a doctrine of deference and not restraint per se might reflect his current view,[168] but is not the impression that most readers took from the earlier work. This should be borne in mind when reading Kavanagh's contribution, which makes the case for the existence of such restraint and articulates the kinds of reason, cast in institutional and democratic terms, as to why it should be afforded. While the phrase 'doctrine of deference' features in her work it simply captures the results of Kavanagh's view as to the more particular considerations that should be taken cognizance of when deciding on the appropriate degree of restraint that a court should give to the primary decision maker, while making clear that this does not amount to a call for judicial abstention or non-justiciability. Young's view concerning the precise role to be played by deference is not the same as Kavanagh's, but she shares the assumption that it will refine the way in which judicial review operates, and denies that it will lead to double counting or some independent doctrine unrelated to the existing confines of judicial review.[169] A similar point is apposite in relation to King's work. It would be wrong to portray this as seeking some wholly separate doctrine of deference of

[167] Allan, 'Human Rights and Judicial Review'.

[168] Allan, 'Judicial Deference and Judicial Review'.

[169] Young, 'In Defence of Due Deference'.

the kind that Allan deprecates. His work seeks rather to flesh out factors of the type that should inform our considered view as to when it is fitting for courts to show restraint. He is, moreover, against the creation or utility of abstract categories in this respect, as is apparent from the following quotation:

> This article seeks to explain, justify and elaborate what I call institutional approaches to judicial restraint. Institutional approaches focus on the comparative merits and drawbacks of the judicial process as an institutional mechanism for solving problems. On my account, institutional approaches to restraint put emphasis on the problem of uncertainty and judicial fallibility, on the systemic impact of judging and on rights as prima facie claims subject to balancing rather than as trumps over collective welfare. For precisely these reasons, institutional approaches advocate a somewhat modest, case-by-case and incrementalist role for courts in public law adjudication. To understand the reasons why institutional approaches have these features, however, it is necessary to see the faults of their two principal alternatives: non-doctrinal approaches and formalist approaches. Non-doctrinal approaches suggest that we ought to trust judges to use their good sense of restraint on a case-by-case basis rather than employ any conceptual framework. Formalists believe that judges should apply abstract categories such as 'law', 'politics', 'policy' and 'non-justiciable' that they believe properly allocate decision-making functions between different branches of government.[170]

[170] King, 'Institutional Approaches to Judicial Restraint', 410.

My view on the robust exchanges generated by the conceptual dimension of the deference debate is that deference or restraint must be located within the standard fabric of judicial review. It is not and cannot be a free-standing concept in its own right. This is not simply because we work within certain perceived heads of judicial review concerning law, fact, discretion and the like, since it is perfectly possible for the courts to add to the existing armoury of review, as they have done in the past. The reason is, rather, that deference, respect or weight are not in and of themselves tests for review at all, and this is so whatever their content. They are by their very nature considerations that inform the way in which some other tests for review, such as reasonableness or proportionality, should be applied. It would therefore be meaningless to conclude that considerable weight should be accorded to the primary decision maker without posing the inquiry in the context of a test for review, since no answer could logically be forthcoming. Deference and respect modulate application of, for example, proportionality. They are not in themselves tests for review.

While Allan is assuredly correct in this respect, the issue is a red herring given that no one argues to the contrary. Kavanagh, Young and King may differ as to the rationale for deference and the parameters thereof, but none advocates that it should be perceived as independent of the existing fabric of judicial review. They are, therefore, not guilty of the charge of being pernicious by fostering some latitude to be accorded to the legislature or executive over and beyond what would result from application of the ordinary principles of review. They are, by way of contrast, determining what that ought to be, more particularly in a post-HRA world.

This leaves the allegation that deference, respect or weight are empty vessels that add nothing to the normal application of the principles of judicial review. This is the nub of Allan's other critique. It is founded on the twin assumptions that the ordinary fabric of judicial review already incorporates ideas of respect for the legislature and executive, and that nothing in the deference literature adds significantly to this, given that any guidance provided will be set at too high a level of generality to be of any utility. These twin assumptions are themselves contestable.

The contention that the existing tools of judicial review give us all that we need to determine the meaning of a right, or to shape the application of reasonableness/proportionality, is far from self-evident. There are, to be sure, strictures that courts should not substitute judgement on the merits for that of the primary decision maker, reflecting thereby an important precept of the separation of powers. There are also well-established principles concerning the variability of reasonableness review in cases dealing with rights, or where socio-economic choices are made by the legislature. The idea that this is the best that we can do does not readily withstand examination. It is clear in the post-HRA world that the simple division between rights-based and non-rights-based cases does not capture the fact that not all rights are of equal importance, and not all cases concerned with the same right raise equally pressing issues.

This has consequential implications for the application of judicial review. Properly understood, the literature on deference seeks to refine and flesh out the factors that should affect this, whether they arise in the definition of the initial right, or in the context of proportionality review. This is crucial precisely because we can disagree as to what these factors should be. It is far better to have this debate openly, rather than pretend that the matter is already resolved by bare application of the existing principles of review, or profess that the issue can be avoided by general invocation of ideas of weight, since the very ascription of weight may itself be based on contestable assumptions that are hidden from view. Factors would be accorded weight or not as the case may be within the fabric of judicial review, without too ready an inquiry as to the rationale for this choice. This danger is reflected in Allan's claim that deference adds nothing to the existing fabric of judicial review, while at the same time describing the precepts of such review so as to incorporate a selective input of the very factors that he deprecates examination of by others.[171]

The related assumption is that deference is empty since it is set at too high a level of abstraction to be of use. There is, on this view, nothing meaningful to be said betwixt and between the abstract statement of a principle, to the effect that legislatures have democratic legitimacy, and the resolution of a particular case where the weight to be accorded to that principle is of little value in deciding the outcome. No one maintains that institutional, epistemic or constitutional considerations that play into deference or respect will determine the outcome in a push-button mechanistic fashion. It is nonetheless mistaken to conclude that there is nothing of

[171] Allan, 'Human Rights and Judicial Review', 692; Allan, 'Judicial Deference', 97.

juridical value between the abstract general and the singular detail. The preceding considerations can help to inform outcomes even if they do not determine them. Thus the abstract statement of, for example, democratic legitimacy inhering in legislatures is important, and can be rendered more refined so as to shape the judicial determination in a particular case.

This can be exemplified by Lord Bingham's reasoning in *Animal Defenders*.[172] It is clear from the ruling that considerations central to debates about deference and respect are not excluded by framing the inquiry in terms of what constitutes giving 'appropriate weight' to the judgement of the initial decision maker. It is clear also that the considerations shaping the appropriate degree of weight in the instant case are capable of informing judgements in other cases. Thus in deciding that a blanket ban on political advertising was compatible with Convention rights, Lord Bingham held that significant weight should be accorded to Parliament's judgement because it was reasonable to expect that democratically elected politicians would be sensitive to measures necessary to safeguard the integrity of our democracy; Parliament had resolved that the prohibition of political advertising on television might infringe Article 10 ECHR, but nonetheless decided to proceed with the legislation, and Parliament's judgement on this issue should not be lightly overridden. Legislation had to lay down general rules, which meant that a line must be drawn, and it was for Parliament to decide where.

[172] *R (Animal Defenders International)* v. *Secretary of State for Culture, Media and Sport* [2008] 1 AC 1312.

(c) Normative contestation: the relevant factors

The difficulty of navigating this terrain is exacerbated by the fact that the preceding conceptual discourse is intertwined with a more overtly normative debate as to the kinds of factor that courts should take into account when exercising judicial review. Framing the conceptual debate in terms of weight provides no short cut in this respect. It can express the conclusion of the normative inquiry, but it cannot be a substitute for it, since the very determination of weight will be based on some prior normative assumption that this feature of the primary decision maker is worthy of the weight afforded to it. The difficulties are further compounded by the fact that commentators do not always ascribe the same meanings to the same terms. There is, nonetheless, greater commonality of view than might be apparent at first sight.

We might afford weight or respect to the view of the primary decision maker within the fabric of judicial review for three reasons: epistemic, institutional or constitutional. The primary decision maker might have knowledge of the relevant matter that is greater than could be matched by any reviewing court; it might, independent of epistemic considerations, have a deeper understanding of the contested issue by reason of its institutional place within the fabric of government; the legislature might express a considered view as to the meaning of a right in legislation in circumstances where it has no particular epistemic or institutional advantage over courts.

Commentators generally agree that it is legitimate for epistemic and institutional considerations to be taken into account by courts when applying the precepts of judicial review, either when defining an aspect of the relevant right, or in the context of proportionality review. There may be some taxonomic divergence as to which category is most appropriate in a particular case, but this is not that significant for present purposes. There may also be differences of view as to the degree of weight to be accorded, but this too should be kept in perspective since the great majority of commentators rightly agree that the final determination is still to be made by the court. The courts give respect to the primary decision maker in accordance with the epistemic or institutional considerations. They do not abjure judgement on the matter, which remains in the hands of the court.[173]

Commentators disagree to a greater extent as to whether deference, respect or weight should be given on constitutional grounds. The paradigm instance of this dispute is whether such weight or respect ought to be given to the legislature, by reason of its democratic pedigree. It is important to disaggregate two dimensions of this disagreement that are related but distinct.

There is the issue of whether it is deserving of such respect per se because of its democratic status, as exemplified by Aileen Kavanagh's concept of minimal deference being accorded to the legislature qua legislature.[174] This has been opposed by writers such as Tom Hickman, who contend that constitutional deference conceived in this way would be

[173] See, e.g., *R (Lord Carlile of Berriew QC)* v. *Secretary of State for the Home Department* [2014] UKSC 60.

[174] Kavanagh, 'Defending Deference in Public Law and Constitutional Theory'.

contrary to the HRA, which contains nothing to suggest that 'individual rights should be less secure against interferences for which the public officials are accountable to the electorate',[175] and that it would, moreover, run counter to the fact that Parliament conferred a duty on the court to determine whether the legislation was compatible with the rights protected by the HRA.[176] There is, indeed, room for legitimate disagreement on this issue, but it should nonetheless be kept within perspective. Kavanagh's argument is for minimal deference, not judicial abstention. Whether one favours such minimal deference or not, Hickman's counterarguments are not as compelling as he would have us believe, since they could equally be used against epistemic or institutional deference, given that there is nothing express in the HRA to suggest that such factors should influence judicial determination of the compatibility of legislation or decisions with the HRA.

There is the related but distinct issue as to whether weight or respect should be accorded to the legislature when it has made a considered judgement about the meaning and applicability of a constitutional right that is then challenged before the courts. We can, for the sake of argument, presuppose that there are no independent epistemic or institutional reasons to give weight to the legislature's determination. If any such weight is to be given, then it must be on constitutional grounds by virtue of its democratic pedigree. There are differences on this issue too, but less so than on the related

[175] Hickman, *Public Law after the Human Rights Act*, p. 160.
[176] Hickman, *Public Law after the Human Rights Act*, p. 160.

issue considered in the preceding paragraph. The rationale for affording weight to the legislative choice resides ultimately in the fact that there is room for legitimate disagreement as to the meaning and application of constitutional rights. The courts do not have a monopoly of wisdom in this respect, and judges not infrequently disagree among themselves as to what is demanded by a particular right in particular circumstances. A considered legislative choice is therefore deserving of respect as embodying its reflective view as to what the right means in a particular legislative context. It deserves this respect on constitutional grounds as the elected legislature charged with making such choices. To afford such respect is not inconsistent with the HRA, its wording or the principles underlying it. The argument is not for the courts to abstain or capitulate, but to take cognizance of the legislative choice when making its own final determination.

This is in reality what Lord Bingham did in *Animal Defenders*.[177] We see the same theme in Lord Sumption's judgment in *Carlile*, where he stated that 'even in the context of Convention rights, there remain areas which although not immune from scrutiny require a qualified respect for the constitutional functions of decision-makers who are democratically accountable',[178] examples being decisions involving important policy choices, broad questions

[177] *R (Animal Defenders International)* v. *Secretary of State for Culture, Media and Sport* [2008] 1 AC 1312. See also *R (Nicklinson)* v. *Ministry of Justice* [2014] UKSC 38.

[178] *R (Lord Carlile of Berriew QC)* v. *Secretary of State for the Home Department* [2014] UKSC 60, at [28].

of economic and social policy, or issues involving the allocation of finite resources.

The approach is evident in *Carson*,[179] where the House of Lords adopted the US distinction between strict scrutiny for discrimination on grounds of race, gender, sexual orientation and the like, with rationality review being applicable to other forms of differential treatment. The instant case was held to fall into the latter category, with the result that where differences of treatment were made on grounds such as ability, occupation, wealth or education the courts would demand some rational justification. These differences in treatment were, said Lord Hoffmann, normally dependent on considerations of the public interest, which were 'very much a matter for the democratically elected branches of government'.[180] *Hooper* is equally interesting for present purposes, since it reveals judicial acceptance of legislative justification for discrimination cast in terms of remedying past disadvantages.[181] The extent to which such measures are consistent with equality has long been debated in the academic literature. The claimants were widowers, who alleged discrimination contrary to Articles 14 and 8 ECHR on the ground that if they had been widows they would have been entitled to certain benefits that were denied to them as widowers. The House of Lords acknowledged that the discrimination was

179 *R (Carson)* v. *Secretary of State for Work and Pensions* [2006] 1 AC 173.

180 *R (Carson)* v. *Secretary of State for Work and Pensions* [2006] 1 AC 173, at [16], [55].

181 *R (Hooper)* v. *Secretary of State for Work and Pensions* [2005] 1 WLR 1681.

based on gender and therefore subject to strict scrutiny. It nonetheless upheld the legislative scheme. Lord Hoffmann surveyed the legislative rationale for, and the history of, such pensions. He concluded that differential treatment between men and women was justified given that older widows as a class were likely to be needier than older widowers as a class, more especially given that for much of the last century it was unusual for married women to work. He concluded, moreover, that the comparative disadvantage of women in the labour market had not disappeared. It was for Parliament to decide when the special treatment for women with respect to this particular benefit was no longer required.

The approach in the preceding cases exemplifies the way in which the constitutional justification for respect or weight can operate. In none of these decisions did the court abstain from adjudication, or merely accept the legislative choice as conclusive. In all four cases the court might have simply decided the rights-based issue for itself as a matter of first impression, and substituted judgment, without any particular consideration of the imperatives driving the legislative or executive choice. In all four cases it did not do so, but rather considered the choice concerning rights against the backdrop of the problem that the legislation sought to resolve, giving due weight to the reasons for that choice.

This was surely the correct approach, and its application will perforce depend on the extent to which there is evidence that the legislature has addressed the salient issue. There will, by way of contrast, be rights-based claims made in relation to legislation where the legislature was not aware in advance that a particular legislative provision was problematic, since the issue only became apparent when the legislation became live.

While there will therefore necessarily be variation in the extent to which according weight to legislative choice is warranted, Allan's distinction between matters that are 'internal' to the determination of the right and those that are 'external' is an imperfect guide, in relation to epistemic, institutional or constitutional rationales for restraint. It presupposes a neat two-step inquiry in which the meaning of the right is elaborated – the internal inquiry – and there is then a further determination as to whether that might be modified through taking cognizance of epistemic, institutional or constitutional considerations – the external inquiry. The preceding discussion reveals the difficulty with this distinction.

The House of Lords in the preceding cases did not make an abstract determination of whether freedom of speech was violated by the legislative constraint in *Animal Defenders*, and then consider any possible legislative excuse. To the contrary, the legislative rationale for placing this constraint was crucial to the judicial inquiry as to whether the right had been violated at all. The same is true for the mode of judicial inquiry in most cases where epistemic or institutional considerations are taken into account in deciding whether a limitation of a right was proportionate or not, such factors being part of the initial legal determination on this issue, not something undertaken as an external inquiry after an internal assessment has been made.[182]

[182] See, e.g., *Samaroo* v. *Secretary of State for the Home Department* [2001] UKHRR 1150; *R (Bloggs 61)* v. *Secretary of State for the Home*

(d) *Doctrinal contestation: reasonableness and proportionality*

The penultimate dimension to this debate is doctrinal in nature, with the principal inquiry being whether proportionality should become a general head of review of discretion that can be used in all cases irrespective of whether they involve EU law or the HRA, or whether reasonableness review should be retained outside the areas where proportionality is currently applied. There has been vibrant debate on this issue.[183] My position is well known, viz. that I favour

Department [2003] 1 WLR 2724; *R (Begum)* v. *Denbigh High School Governors* [2007] 1 AC 100.

183 M. Taggart, 'Proportionality, Deference, Wednesbury' [2008] *New Zealand Law Review* 423; M. Hunt, 'Against Bifurcation', in D. Dyzenhaus, M. Hunt and G. Huscroft (eds.), *A Simple Common Lawyer: Essays in Honour of Michael Taggart* (Oxford: Hart, 2009), Ch. 6; P. Craig, 'Proportionality, Rationality and Review' [2010] *New Zealand Law Review* 265; M. Elliott, 'Proportionality and Deference: The Importance of a Structured Approach', in C. Forsyth, M. Elliott, S. Jhaveri, M. Ramsden and A. Scully Hill (eds.), *Effective Judicial Review: A Cornerstone of Good Governance* (Oxford: Oxford University Press, 2010), Ch. 16; T. Hickman, 'Problems for Proportionality' [2010] *New Zealand Law Review* 303; J. King, 'Proportionality: A Halfway House' [2010] *New Zealand Law Review* 327; J. Goodwin, 'The Last Defence of Wednesbury' [2012] *Public Law* 445; T. Endicott, 'Proportionality and Incommensurability' Oxford University Legal Research Paper Series, No 40/2012; C. Chan, 'Proportionality and Invariable Baseline Intensity of Review' (2013) 33 *Legal Studies* 1; Sir P. Sales, 'Rationality, Proportionality and the Development of the Law' (2013) 129 *Law Quarterly Review* 223; P. Craig, 'The Nature of Reasonableness Review' [2013] *Current Legal Problems* 1; Lord Carnwath, 'From Rationality to Proportionality in the Modern Law' (2014) 44 *Hong Kong Law Journal* 1; M. Arden, *Human*

proportionality becoming a generalized head of review. I do not intend to rehearse all the arguments back and forth on this issue. Suffice it for present purposes to say the following.

First, courts have an obligation to say what they do and do what they say. This is more especially so in the context of administrative law, where judicial review is designed, in part at least, to ensure that the administration complies with this precept. The same must be true a fortiori for courts. The standard formulations of reasonableness review, derived from Lord Greene in *Wednesbury*[184] and Lord Diplock in *GCHQ*,[185] would, if taken seriously, mean that no claimant would ever win. It is difficult, if not impossible, to think of a real as opposed to hypothetical case where the alleged error could be described as coming within these judicial tests. Nor is it self-evident in normative terms why this should be regarded as the default position. Concerns as to the separation of powers require judicial restraint. They do not demand a default test that sets the bar so high that litigants in non-rights cases can never surmount it. The reasonableness test only survived because some courts were willing to apply it even where the alleged error did not match the level of egregiousness required by Lord Greene and Lord Diplock, or where the case was expressly recharacterized in terms of anxious scrutiny review. Judicial recognition of the variability

Rights and European Law, Building New Legal Orders (Oxford: Oxford University Press, 2015), Ch. 4.

[184] *Associated Picture Houses Ltd* v. *Wednesbury Corporation* [1948] 1 KB 223.

[185] *Council of Civil Service Unions* v. *Minister for the Civil Service* [1985] AC 374.

of reasonableness review is to be welcomed, although it does not alter the fact that the default baseline still seems set in the terms specified by Lord Greene and Lord Diplock.

Second, the debate between reasonableness and proportionality is commonly predicated, explicitly or implicitly, on the assumption that the latter concept is a foreign import, and thus alien to common law review of discretion. This is wrong. It is certainly true that data searches of the older case law framed in terms of proportionality will reveal no hits, but that is because it is the wrong search term. The legal terminology from the mid-fifteenth century was 'proportionable' or 'proportionably', and this was a recognized component of review in cases of direct and collateral challenge.[186] The debate between reasonableness and proportionality is also premised on the assumption that the latter concept is suspect because it entails balancing, which is said to be absent from reasonableness review. This is untenable. It is common to see jibes directed at proportionality to the effect that it contains little guidance as to how the balancing should be conducted. A condition precedent to reasoned deliberation as to how balancing should be conducted is open and honest recognition that it is being undertaken. Balancing is integral to reasonableness review, ever more so as we move away from the very low-intensity review of Lord Greene and Lord Diplock.[187] A more liberal approach to reasonableness

[186] See above, pp. 36–9.

[187] Craig, 'The Nature of Reasonableness Review'; *Kennedy* v. *Charity Commission* [2014] UKSC 20, at [54]; *Pham* v. *Secretary of State for the Home Department* [2015] UKSC 19, at [60], [95], [109], [114].

review is far more defensible in terms of the court–administration boundary. It does, however, lead to the same kinds of question being posed as in the context of proportionality, albeit less clearly, in a less structured manner and with less recourse to evidentiary resources essential for informed oversight.

Third, the three-part proportionality inquiry structures and facilitates reasoned evaluation. It focuses the attention of the agency being reviewed, and the court undertaking the review. The agency has to justify its behaviour in the terms demanded by this inquiry. It has to explain why it thought that the challenged action was necessary and suitable to reach the desired end, and why the action did not impose an excessive burden on the applicant. If the reviewing court is minded to overturn the agency choice, it too will have to do so in a manner consonant with the proportionality inquiry. The three-part inquiry means that cases may be resolved at the first two stages, thereby obviating the need for recourse to the third stage. It also means that if a case is determined via proportionality *stricto sensu*, the issue posed will commonly be more fine-tuned because of the prior adjudication concerning necessity and suitability.

Finally, there is no one who argues for 'unification' insofar as this connotes the same test of review being applied in the same way in all types of case. This is not even a straw man. My argument in favour of proportionality becoming a general head of review has always been expressly predicated on its variable application. This variation pertains not only between rights-based and non-rights-based cases, but also within the former category. Not all rights are of equal importance.[188] There can, moreover, be significant variance in the importance of the claim when the same right is pleaded, as exemplified by the fact that freedom of speech may be pleaded to protect political speech, and the ability to run a sex shop. The courts take account of these differences in a number of ways, inter alia through varying the intensity of proportionality review.[189]

(e) Structural contestation: rights and non-rights cases

It is fitting to conclude this section by consideration of the divide between rights and non-rights-based cases, and the implications that this has for substantive review. Jason Varuhas has argued that this divide is central to public law.[190] He contends that human rights law is directed towards the protection of individual rights, and that the remainder of public law is concerned with the vindication of the public interest, with the consequence that attempts at 'unification' of administrative law are to be deprecated, so too are efforts to apply tools such as proportionality review to cases that do not involve rights.

[188] See, e.g., *R (Lord Carlile of Berriew QC)* v. *Secretary of State for the Home Department* [2014] UKSC 60, at [13].

[189] See, e.g., *Bank Mellat* v. *Her Majesty's Treasury (No 2)* [2014] AC 700, at [69]–[70]; *R (Lord Carlile of Berriew QC)* v. *Secretary of State for the Home Department* [2014] UKSC 60, at [20], [34].

[190] J. Varuhas, 'Against Unification', University of Cambridge, Legal Studies Research Paper Series, Paper No 28/2015.

The academic reality is that no one claims that rights-based and non-rights-based cases should be treated in exactly the same way. There is no claim to unification in that sense. It is a red herring and does not accurately capture academic scholarship. The salient issue has always been the more particular differences that do and should persist between the two types of case. Space precludes detailed consideration of Varuhas's thesis. Suffice it to say the following.

(i) Rights and non-rights cases in historical perspective

The rigid bifurcation articulated by Varuhas is misconceived. All statutes that accord power to ministers, agencies and local authorities are designed to serve the public interest. Administrative law is concerned in part with the limits that should be placed on the way in which such power is exercised, and these have from the very inception of review 400 hundred years ago been designed to protect the interests of individuals as well as to foster the public interest. The idea that administrative law is grounded on a strict dichotomy between judicial review cases directed towards protection of the public interest, and those directed towards protection of individual rights, does not reflect reality. The protection of the individual's interest was always central to judicial review, irrespective of whether it would be regarded as a right *stricto sensu*. When the common law courts began to accord more protection to rights prior to the Human Rights Act 1998 they did so explicitly on the assumption that the more important the interest, the more searching should be the judicial scrutiny. They did not proceed on the basis that interests falling short of rights *stricto sensu* should be regarded in the bifurcated manner articulated by Varuhas.

(ii) The central thesis and the 'principal public interest'

Varuhas's central thesis is that the purpose of public law in non-rights cases is to advance the public interest, prevent abuse of power and ensure that the law is public-regarding, with the consequence that he regards protection of the individual as 'subsidiary' or 'secondary'. This is juxtaposed to rights-based cases, which are seen as individual-regarding, with the focus on the interests of private individuals in the face of administrative action motivated by concern for the public interest.[191]

Varuhas uses the term 'public interest' in a plethora of ways when seeking to differentiate rights-based and non-rights-based cases, without realizing their different meanings. It is necessary to disaggregate them to assess the soundness of the argument. The central thesis concerning ordinary judicial review is wrong when viewed from the perspective of what is the 'principal public interest', viz. the effectuation of the aims of the legislation.

Consider the linkage between this sense of the public interest and core doctrinal concepts of ordinary judicial review, such as error of law or propriety of purpose. They are designed, respectively, to ensure that the legal criteria in the legislation as to the scope of the public body's authority are correctly applied, and that the discretion accorded to it is

[191] Varuhas, 'Against Unification', p. 11.

used for proper purposes. Press further, consider why this is important, and what is the public interest thereby entailed? The answer is assuredly that if these errors occur, the interests of individuals that the legislation is designed to serve will not be fulfilled: a licence will be rejected on improper grounds, an asylum application will be wrongly decided, and a disability claimant will be denied a benefit. It is to prevent this that we have these doctrinal concepts. The idea that protection of the individual interest is somehow separate from, or subsidiary to, the public interest thus conceived is incoherent.

Such errors will perforce be revealed in legal claims, the great majority of which, circa 95 per cent, are brought by the affected individual. The individuals are not subsidiary within the schema of administrative law; they are not a second-order consideration; and they are not merely the means to attain some other, independent collective good, whatsoever that might be. Abuse of power is not something that exists in the abstract. It is manifest in its very impact on the affected individuals who seek judicial review. The consequence of a failure of due process is first and foremost harm to the affected individual; the result of an error of fact is that the particular claimant has been wrongly treated; and proof of unreasonableness impacts on the affected individual. It is proof of such errors that constitutes harm to the individual that the legislature has protected.

In deciding whether such an error has occurred, the court will take account of the aims of the legislation, and seek to fulfil its objective, in the manner analysed in the previous chapter. A claimant's assertion of a violation does not therefore mean that there has been an infringement of the interest protected by the legislation. This is, however, equally true for rights-based claims, which may fail at the outset because the court does not accept that there has been an infringement judged in the light of the nature of the particular right. It does not alter the point being made here, which is that the principal public interest underlying the legislation is not severable from the interests of the individuals, whether welfare claimants, asylum seekers or license applicants, that the legislation is intended to serve, and it is these interests that are protected through doctrines such as error of law, and improper purposes.

The ground of judicial review proven in a particular case, such as error of law, will necessarily have implications for analogous cases, by making clear that the administration has exceeded the bounds of its authority. This is true for much common law adjudication. It is equally true in rights-based cases, where the finding of a violation will not only vindicate the claimant's right, but also signal the public-interest message that the administration cannot attain its chosen ends in this particular manner in an analogous situation. This public interest is further manifest in mainstreaming human rights within public decision making. It is expressive of the public interest that good governance requires respect for such rights, this being regarded non-instrumentally as a good in itself, and instrumentally as rendering it less likely that there will be a violation of rights in the future.

(iii) The central thesis and the 'secondary public interest'

It is important to distinguish the primary sense of public interest adumbrated above from the way in which the public interest may be used in a secondary manner, to qualify the interest or right of the individual. There is certainly evidence of this in non-rights-based cases, where the existence of, for example, discretion as to the grant of remedies, and procedural constraints on the bringing of judicial review actions, are explicable on this ground. However, human rights cases are also shot through with considerations of the public interest. The majority of human rights cases are brought by way of judicial review, and will have to surmount the same hurdles concerning permission and time as those for ordinary judicial review actions. The public interest is manifest most markedly in the fact that many Convention rights are qualified. These qualifications are expressly designed to serve the public interest, through according legitimacy to limitations on rights where necessary to secure public health, public order, public security and the like. The public interest may, moreover, be evident when courts decide on the ambit of the right.[192]

Secondary conceptions of the public interest may alternatively be used to expand the range of those who can invoke the relevant ground of review. This is most evident in the liberal rules of standing that are applicable in ordinary judicial review actions. The rationale is that illegality should be brought to light, more especially because there may be situations in which there is no specific individual affected. To suggest, as Varuhas does, that this proves that the affected individual is secondary or subsidiary within ordinary judicial review cases is, however, a non sequitur. The reality is that

[192] See, e.g., *R. (Gillan)* v. *Commissioner of Police of the Metropolis* [2006] 2 AC 307.

circa 95 per cent of cases are brought by the affected individual. There is no live issue of standing, which is accepted without argument, precisely because the harm to the claimant constitutes the required sufficiency of interest and is the central focus of the judicial review. The fact that the legal system makes provision for others to bring actions in circa 5 per cent of cases is perfectly sensible for the preceding reason, and the court will regard such standing as discretionary.

(iv) The central thesis and doctrinal differentiation

Varuhas's attempt to sustain the central thesis and draw a stark line between the principles of ordinary judicial review and human rights adjudication by focusing on doctrinal differences is equally problematic. Detailed analysis takes us beyond the scope of the present work, but the following will suffice for present purposes.

Some evidence for the doctrinal divide is wrong. Varuhas contends that the claimant has the burden of proof in ordinary judicial review cases, whereas the contrary is said to be so in relation to human rights cases. The legal reality is that the claimant has the initial burden of proof in both types of case. It is for the claimant to show a violation of human rights. If he cannot do so, the case ends there. If he surmounts this hurdle, the burden then shifts to the defendant to prove any defence. This is no different from a case of, for example, legitimate expectations, where it will be for the claimant to prove the existence and breach of such an expectation, with the onus then shifting to the government to prove a possible public-interest defence.

Some evidence is inconsequential, because there is little difference between the doctrinal rules that prevail in the two areas. Varuhas places considerable emphasis on the proposition that judicial review is supervisory and not appellate, which is undoubtedly correct in principle, but it does not lead to differences as to the circumstances in which courts will substitute judgement. Thus it is certainly true that courts will decide on the legal meaning of Convention rights, substituting judgment on this issue for any determination made by a public body. It is, however, equally true that courts in ordinary judicial review actions substitute judgement on issues of law, subject to recent exceptions concerning tribunals, and they also do so in relation to matters such as propriety of purpose and relevancy. Whether they should so is a matter of academic debate, but the salient point for present purposes is that they have not felt constrained in this respect by the fact that their jurisdiction is supervisory.

Some evidence for the divide is overstated, as is the case in relation to judicial review of discretion. There are differences in this respect, since it is accepted that courts should in general exercise more searching review in rights-based than in non-rights-based cases. The distinction is nonetheless overplayed. We are told that courts make the determination concerning proportionality in rights-based cases, which is said to stand in stark contrast to the more limited oversight in ordinary judicial review cases, the latter reflecting the injunction that courts should not substitute judgement on the merits. Courts do indubitably make the ultimate determination concerning proportionality in rights-based cases, but this does not mean that they substitute judgement for that of the initial decision maker. The court will make the determination, according whatever degree of deference/respect/weight is felt to be appropriate, as evidenced by the vibrant debate on this issue considered above. The fact that the courts' jurisdiction in ordinary judicial review is supervisory provides, moreover, no certain guide as to how searching such review should be, as attested to by the debates surrounding this issue.

(v) The central thesis and rationality/proportionality

It is, as noted above, generally accepted that rights-based cases should be treated differently to some degree from cases that do not involve rights. I share this view, and believe that varying intensity of review is warranted even within rights-based cases. The key issue has always been what differences are normatively warranted, not whether any such differences are warranted at all.

This can be exemplified by the reasonableness/proportionality debate. Varuhas's argument against proportionality is predicated on the twin claims that because such cases are concerned with the 'public interest', this naturally legitimates the very limited reasonableness review of Lord Greene and Lord Diplock and that the application of proportionality would entail the 'privatization' of public law, with private interests trumping the public good. Both aspects of this argument are wrong.

Administrative law has, as stated above, always been concerned with the protection of the individual interest, and not merely vindication of the public interest. It is readily acknowledged that courts should limit their intrusion into the discretionary choices made by public bodies, but Varuhas furnishes no normative argument as to why the separation of powers demands a default test for review that is so exiguous as to be meaningless. The contestable nature of this assumption is cast into sharp relief by the fact that it was certainly not shared by the judicial founders of UK public law, who applied a broader concept of reasonableness and also a concept of proportionability 250 years before it became a twinkling in a Germanic judicial eye. This contestability is exemplified yet again by the fact that modern judges, such as Lord Cooke, regard the default test of unreasonableness as regressive and unwarranted by concerns of separation of powers.

The claim that proportionality entails the 'privatization' of public law is equally unfounded. It is reductionist, since any qualification to the exercise of discretionary power framed in terms of its impact on the individual could be so regarded. The claim is groundless, in that it is predicated on the unsustainable proposition that ordinary judicial review is designed to serve the public interest in some manner distinct from the individual interest. The claim does not withstand scrutiny, in that it is premised on untenable assumptions as to what the public interest itself connotes, since it assumes that this is served by upholding the exercise of discretionary power that may be unnecessary or unsuitable to attain the end in question, or which imposes excessive burdens on individuals. The claim is, finally, based on mistaken assumptions about what is entailed by proportionality. It is a structured test for assessing the exercise of discretionary power. The intensity with which it is applied is decided by the courts and will vary between different types of case. There is, contrary to what Varuhas appears to believe, no particular intensity of review built a priori into the test. This is evident from the application of proportionality in German law and EU law.[193] The latter jurisprudence powerfully demonstrates that variable-intensity proportionality review can be used without any of the consequences that Varuhas believes flow from attachment to this standard of review.

It is instructive to reflect on the particular interests that can be affected by administrative action in ordinary judicial review cases. There is no plausible normative ground for treating the interests in all such cases in the same way, irrespective of the nature and importance of the interest affected. This has been recognized by courts, which either have manipulated the language of reasonableness, implicitly or explicitly, to engage in more searching inquiry, or have used anxious scrutiny. The latter was used not merely for rights-based claims prior to the HRA, but also for non-rights-based cases that courts felt were deserving of closer scrutiny, as exemplified by many of the asylum cases.[194] When the courts undertake such review they do not substitute judgement for that of the administration. They do, however, engage in balancing, but it is less clear and less structured than in proportionality.[195] Varuhas might deny that this has

[193] G. Lubbe-Wolff, 'The Principle of Proportionality in the Case Law of the German Federal Constitutional Court' (2014) 39 *Human Rights Law Journal* 12; Craig, *EU Administrative Law*, Chs. 19–20.

[194] P. Craig, 'Judicial Review and Anxious Scrutiny: Foundations, Evolution and Application' [2015] *Public Law* 60.

[195] Craig, 'The Nature of Reasonableness Review'.

occurred as a matter of positive law, which runs into a brick wall of the evidence. He might, alternatively, accept that it has occurred, and is legitimate, but contend that the type of review is fundamentally different from lower-intensity proportionality review, which is untenable in conceptual terms.

It is equally instructive to reflect on assumptions concerning the relative importance of rights-based and non-rights-based claims. Varuhas's thesis is predicated on the assumption that all the former are necessarily more important than all the latter, by very reason of their connection with a protected right. Reflect for a moment. Consider whether the intelligent bystander would think it self-evident that there should be far more searching judicial review for invocation of speech rights in order to open a shop selling pornography, as compared to non-rights-based claims concerning the exercise of discretion brought by an asylum seeker, a disability claimant, or a person whose livelihood is at stake in a licence case. Varuhas has a stark choice. He might seek to defend the divide, which is very contentious in normative terms and unlikely to persuade the intelligent bystander. He might alternatively accept that the divide has to be qualified, which throws his central thesis into freefall.

7 Interaction between legal orders: autochthony and its limits

An enduring challenge for national legal orders is how they respond to the legal interaction flowing from membership in international organizations, and more generally from being part of a world where regulatory norms are increasingly globalized. This issue has featured prominently in legal and extra-legal discourse, primarily in relation to the legal consequences of UK membership of the ECHR and EU. There are various dimensions to the jurisprudence, but there is nonetheless a discernible theme, which is the judicial desire to assert some degree of independence in the relations between the UK and other legal orders, consistent with our obligations as signatories of the respective treaties.

This is the intent behind the heading, framed as it is in terms of autochthony. The etymological foundations are Greek, connoting the idea of springing from the land, or being grown from the soil. There are diverse interpretations of the term, but a prominent strand embodies the descriptive and normative ideal of attachment to indigenous or native values.[196] It stands in counterpoise to themes of globalization, expressive of the desire to maintain some degree of national control. The ensuing discussion considers different manifestations of this in legal thought, and evaluates how far such an ideal can or should be pressed in the administrative law context.

(a) UK and ECHR: status, source and substantive autochthony

There has been considerable discourse concerning the relationship between the UK and the ECHR, judicial and

[196] V. Rosivach, 'Autochthony and the Athenians' (1987) *Classical Quarterly* 294; P. Geschiere, *The Perils of Belonging: Autochthony, Citizenship, and Exclusion in Africa & Europe* (Chicago: The University of Chicago Press, 2009), Ch. 1.

extra-judicial. Three senses of autochthony can be discerned within this discourse, which are related but distinct.

(i) Autochthony and status

There has been considerable judicial and academic discourse as to the status of ECtHR judgments, and the extent to which UK courts should feel free to develop their own indigenous conception of human rights. The HRA strategy in section 2 is that national courts must take account of ECtHR judgments, although they are not formally bound by them.[197] The more precise interpretation of section 2 has nonetheless been contentious.[198]

On Lord Bingham's 'mirror principle' in *Ullah* it was the duty of the national courts 'to keep pace with the Strasbourg jurisprudence as it evolves over time: no more, but certainly no less'.[199] The idea that Strasbourg case law

[197] *Kay* v. *Lambeth LBC* [2006] 2 AC 465; *Leeds City Council* v. *Price* [2005] 1 WLR 1825.

[198] R. Masterman, 'Section 2(1) of the Human Rights Act 1998: Binding Domestic Courts to Strasbourg?' [2004] *Public Law* 725; R. Masterman, 'Taking the Strasbourg Jurisprudence into Account: Developing a "Municipal Law of Human Rights" under the Human Rights Act' (2005) 54 *International and Comparative Law Quarterly* 907; F. Klug and H. Wildbore, 'Follow or Lead? The Human Rights Act and the European Court of Human Rights' [2010] *European Human Rights Law Review* 621; J. Wright, 'Interpreting Section 2 of the Human Rights Act: Towards an Indigenous Jurisprudence of Human Rights' [2009] *Public Law* 595; R. Clayton, 'Smoke and Mirrors: The Human Rights Act and the Impact of the Strasbourg Case Law' [2012] *Public Law* 639; E. Bjorge, 'The Courts and the ECHR: A Principled Approach to the Strasbourg Jurisprudence' (2013) 72 *Cambridge Law Journal* 289.

[199] *R (Ullah)* v. *Special Adjudicator* [2004] 2 AC 323, at [20]; *R (Quark Fishing)* v. *Secretary of State for Foreign and Commonwealth Affairs*

provides a floor, a minimum below which the national courts should not fall, is sound in terms of principle, subject to exceptional cases where the UK courts believe that the ECHR has misunderstood a feature of UK law,[200] or some other such circumstance. The idea that Strasbourg case law should operate as a ceiling to human rights protection has been more controversial. It has been argued that UK courts should feel able to accord more extensive protection than that given by Strasbourg where it is felt appropriate, and should be able to apply Convention rights in the way suited to national traditions and values.[201]

Thus in *Re P* the claimants, an unmarried heterosexual couple, were prevented from adopting a child by statutory regulations in Northern Ireland.[202] The Strasbourg Court had not yet pronounced on the issue. The House of Lords nonetheless found that the fixed rule precluding adoption was disproportionate. The majority held that, given its developing jurisprudence, it was likely that the ECtHR would hold that

[2006] 1 AC 529, at [34]; *R (Al-Skeini)* v. *Secretary of State for Defence* [2008] 1 AC 153, at [90], [106]; *R (Smith)* v. *Oxfordshire Assistant Deputy Coroner* [2011] 1 AC 1, at [60], [93], [147]; *McGowan (Procurator Fiscal, Edinburgh)* v. *B (Scotland)* [2011] UKSC 54; *Ambrose* v. *Harris (Procurator Fiscal, Oban)* [2011] UKSC 43, at [20].

200 *R* v. *Horncastle* [2010] 2 AC 373; *Al-Khawaja and Tahery* v. *the United Kingdom* [2011] ECHR 2127.

201 *Begum* v. *Tower Hamlets LBC* [2002] HRLR 24, at [17]; *R (ProLife Alliance)* v. *British Broadcasting Corporation* [2002] 3 WLR 1080, at [33]–[34].

202 *In re P (Adoption: Unmarried Couple)* [2008] 3 WLR 76; *Rabone* v. *Pennine NHS Care Foundation Trust* [2012] UKSC, at 112; *Sugar* v. *BBC* [2012] UKSC 4, at [59].

the challenged provision was discriminatory and that the House should not be inhibited from going further than the ECtHR, since the margin of appreciation available to Member States in delicate areas of social policy was not automatically appropriated by the legislature. It held, moreover, that Convention rights under the HRA were domestic rights, not international rights, and that the House was therefore free to give what it considered to be a principled interpretation to the concept of discrimination on grounds of marital status.

Lord Kerr has been notable for willingness to question this dimension of the mirror principle. He held that it was not open to our courts 'to adopt an attitude of agnosticism and refrain from recognising such a right simply because Strasbourg has not spoken'.[203] The Strasbourg Court would not, said Lord Kerr, resolve all issues concerning the meaning of Convention rights, many of which would be determined by national courts without formal guidance from the ECtHR. It remained the duty of the Supreme Court to consider those issues when they arose, even if the existing Strasbourg case law was unclear, and this duty was reinforced by section 6 HRA.[204]

Richard Clayton and Eirik Bjorge have argued convincingly that this principled approach to the ECHR is preferable to strict adherence to *Ullah*, and that it coheres well with common law tradition.[205] It respects the floor provided by the ECHR in terms of minimum rights protection, while

[203] *Ambrose* v. *Harris (Procurator Fiscal, Oban)* [2011] UKSC 43, at [128].
[204] *Ambrose* v. *Harris (Procurator Fiscal, Oban)* [2011] UKSC 43, at [129].
[205] Clayton, 'Smoke and Mirrors'; Bjorge, 'The Courts and the ECHR'.

giving legitimate space for development of conceptions of rights that are more extensive and cohere with national values. It resonates, moreover, with the legislative objectives of the HRA, which would enable our courts to make a 'distinctively British contribution to the development of the jurisprudence of human rights in Europe'.[206]

(ii) Autochthony and source

The ECHR imposes obligations on signatory states to comply with the rights therein. The Supreme Court has, in recent judgments, emphasized that the common law should be regarded as the first source in assessing how the demands of membership should be met in a particular case.

This was evident in *Osborn*,[207] where the Supreme Court considered whether the Parole Board had breached the ECHR by not providing an oral hearing to three prisoners whose sentences it reviewed. Lord Reed gave judgment for the Supreme Court. He held that protection of human rights was not a distinct area of the law, based solely on the jurisprudence of the ECtHR, but permeated the domestic legal system. Compliance with the ECHR should initially be determined through relevant rules of domestic law. This was more especially so given that the ECHR rights were set out at a high level of generality. It followed that 'the values underlying both the Convention and our own constitution require that Convention rights should be protected primarily by a detailed

[206] Rights Brought Home: The Human Rights Bill, Cm 3782, at paras. 1.14–1.15.

[207] *Osborn* v. *Parole Board* [2013] UKSC 61.

body of domestic law'.[208] The courts could, pursuant to the Human Rights Act 1998, take account of ECHR obligations in the development of the common law and in the interpretation of legislation. While the importance of the HRA was unquestionable, it did not 'however supersede the protection of human rights under the common law or statute, or create a discrete body of law based on the judgments of the European court', with the consequence that 'human rights continue to be protected by our domestic law, interpreted and developed in accordance with the Act when appropriate'.[209] Lord Reed then proceeded to decide when an oral hearing should be required, taking into account the instrumental and dignitarian justifications for process rights.

The same approach was evident in the *BBC* case,[210] where the Supreme Court considered, inter alia, whether UK courts retained any power at common law to protect the anonymity of a party whose Convention rights were engaged, and the relationship between such a power and Convention rights. It was Lord Reed once again who gave judgment for the Supreme Court. He held that it was a general principle of constitutional law that justice should be administered in public and be open to public scrutiny, this being an aspect of the rule of law in a democracy. The court

[208] *Osborn* v. *Parole Board* [2013] UKSC 61, at [56].

[209] *Osborn* v. *Parole Board* [2013] UKSC 61, at [57], citing *R (Daly)* v. *Secretary of State for the Home Department* [2001] 2 AC 532 and *R (West)* v. *Parole Board* [2005] 1 WLR 350 as examples of this juridical technique.

[210] *A* v. *BBC* [2014] UKSC 25.

could, therefore, decide to depart from the principle where appropriate, and to permit the identity of a party or a witness to be withheld where necessary in the interests of justice:

> Since the principle of open justice is a constitutional principle to be found in the common law, it follows that it is for the courts to determine its ambit and its requirements, subject to any statutory provision. The courts therefore have an inherent jurisdiction to determine how the principle should be applied.[211]

While the principle of open justice was recognized in Article 6(1) ECHR, it was not absolute, and the exceptions broadly reflected those at common law. Lord Reed, however, rejected the argument that where Convention rights were engaged the court's power to prevent disclosure came solely from the Convention. To the contrary, the starting point was the domestic principle of open justice,[212] with its qualifications under both common law and statute, which would normally cohere with Convention requirements, given that the courts had power to develop the common law in line with Convention obligations. If there was a conflict between the common law and the Convention then effect would be given to the latter in accord with the HRA.[213]

There is much to be said in favour of Lord Reed's approach, from the perspective of both practicality and

[211] *A* v. *BBC* [2014] UKSC 25, at [27].
[212] *A* v. *BBC* [2014] UKSC 25, at [55–7].
[213] *A* v. *BBC* [2014] UKSC 25, at [57].

principle. It enables the court to draw on the resources of the common law, which may well have more detailed jurisprudence on the meaning of a particular Convention right than is evident in the ECtHR's case law. What is equally apposite is that even where there is more plentiful Strasbourg jurisprudence, this will, by definition, have been honed in relation to cases arising from very diverse jurisdictions. Lord Reed's approach, drawing on the resources of the common law, coheres with the legitimate desire for subsidiarity in application of Convention precepts. It enables UK courts to fashion a solution that is consistent with the ECHR, and consistent also with common law traditions in the UK, which, as we saw in the previous chapter, date back to the mid-sixteenth century. Lord Reed acknowledges that if at the end of the day there is an inconsistency between the demands of the ECHR and received common law wisdom then the latter will have to give way, in accord with the dictates of the HRA. This does not, however, undermine the value of the methodology in the preceding cases. This is because in most instances the common law will cohere with Convention demands, or can be adapted to do so, and because the Convention requirements can be met in more than one way in accord with ECHR conceptions of subsidiarity.

The reasoning in the preceding cases strengthens in certain respects the place of the ECHR within the UK. Thus while the judgments accord centrality to the common law as a resource for protecting common law rights, they also emphasize repeatedly that the ECHR should not be perceived as wholly distinct, but rather as a body of principle that permeates all UK law.

(iii) Autochthony and substance

There is a more radical strain of autochthony evident in the literature, the implications of which are more far-reaching for the relationship between the UK and the ECHR. Thus there have been voices raised extra-judicially against ECtHR decisions that are perceived to be ill-advised, or are felt to press the claims of Strasbourg too far in relation to signatory states.[214] Lord Judge, speaking in the context of the charged debate over prisoner voting rights, contended that the Strasbourg Court was claiming too much power for a body of unelected judges through its espousal of the 'living-instrument doctrine', more especially since its decisions could not effectively be overturned by an elected legislature.[215] In a similar vein Lord Sumption, while acknowledging the importance of Convention rights, criticized the Strasbourg Court for being 'the international flag-bearer for judge-made fundamental law extending well beyond the text which it is charged with applying', the driving force being the 'living-instrument' doctrine, which 'transformed the Convention from the safeguard against despotism which was intended by its draftsmen, into a template for many aspects of the domestic legal order'.[216]

The ECHR regime has also been criticized in more systemic terms by Lord Hoffmann,[217] who contends that

[214] K. Ziegler, E. Wicks and L. Hodson (eds.), *The UK and European Human Rights: A Strained Relationship?* (Oxford: Hart Publishing, 2015).

[215] 'A View from London', *Counsel* magazine, October 2014.

[216] Lord Sumption, 'The Limits of Law', 7.

[217] Lord Hoffmann, 'The Universality of Human Rights', Judicial Studies Board, Annual Lecture 2009.

human rights are universal in abstraction, but national in application, with the consequence that an international court could not properly decide individual cases, more especially when the number of signatory states to the ECHR had more than quadrupled in later years. The right to a fair trial did not, said Lord Hoffmann, demand the same trial procedure in all countries, and he was unconvinced that the margin of appreciation alleviated the difficulty. The message was unequivocal: if rights-based review was to happen it should be done at home.[218]

A judicial counterpoise to the preceding arguments is to be found in the work of Sir Philip Sales, who has lauded the ECHR for being supportive of democracy.[219] He argues that the principles underlying the ECHR reflect democratic principles and a substantive view of what a democratic society should be, and include also the accepted imperative to balance the rights of the individual and the general interest of the community. This balancing is conducted such that 'weight is to be given to the democratic process as the process which often best captures in concrete form in a given setting a considered view of what the general interest of the community might be'.[220] The ECHR should not in his view be seen simply as a constraint on 'otherwise unrestrained democratic political processes', but as a mechanism whereby protection

[218] Lord Hoffmann, 'The Universality of Human Rights', 26.

[219] Sir P. Sales, 'Law and Democracy in a Human Rights Framework', in D. Feldman (ed.), *Law in Politics, Politics in Law* (Oxford: Hart, 2013), Ch. 15.

[220] Sir P. Sales, 'Law and Democracy in a Human Rights Framework', p. 225.

of fundamental rights is 'increasingly important in itself for viable democracies to be maintained'.[221]

The preceding differences of view are deep-seated, and will not be resolved here. They raise difficult normative issues which have political consequences, as attested to by the proposal that the UK should have a British Bill of Rights, a quintessential manifestation of autochthony. While there are differences of view as to whether this would necessitate leaving the ECHR, the legal answer is that it would. The protagonists of such a move could not achieve what they desire while the UK remains within the ECHR, and the ECHR would not accept a state as signatory that sought to condition its membership in the manner desired by these protagonists for change. A few points by way of reflection on this dimension to autochthony are nonetheless relevant here.

First, the UK is bound by the ECHR because the government of the day decided to sign the Treaty, this being duly ratified by Parliament. The HRA 1998 is a statute enacted by Parliament that brought Convention rights into UK law. Lord Sumption would say that not everything done by a democratically elected Parliament enhances democracy.[222] He is right as a matter of abstract principle. This argument is, however, fraught with danger. It can be wielded too easily by supporters of democratic choice who wish nonetheless to deprecate a particular exercise of that choice of which they disapprove. The bottom line is that there may be all manner

[221] Sir P. Sales, 'Law and Democracy in a Human Rights Framework', p. 237.

[222] Lord Sumption, 'The Limits of Law'.

of reasons why a Parliament might wish to place constraints on itself, even if the temptations to be avoided are not directly analogous to Ulysses and the Sirens. The fact that a particular commentator believes that this is not sensible is no reason to deny the democratic legitimacy of that choice, unless, paradoxically, we presuppose that the onlooker is elevated to a Platonic guardian, sitting over and above the democratic forum that he avowedly espouses.

Second, notwithstanding all the storm and thunder about the Strasbourg Court making decisions that some believe to be ill-advised in particular cases, such as prisoner voting, it is clear that in most cases the ECtHR has either dismissed actions against the UK, or found in its favour at the substantive hearing, and that in most cases when it has decided against the UK the general consensus is that it was right to do so.

Third, there is a real issue as to the legitimate bounds of Treaty interpretation. The debate has focused on the ECtHR's 'living-instrument' approach to the founding Treaty, which has been opposed by those of an originalist persuasion. Space precludes detailed analysis. Suffice it to say the following. In theoretical terms I can understand the meaning of some 'pure' form of originalism, whereby judicial choice is bounded by the framers' intent strictly conceived. This is, however, dependent empirically on agreement as to what the framers really intended, and the evidence must be sufficiently specific as to be able to set the limits of particular Treaty provisions. It is dependent also on normative argumentation as to why that choice should necessarily bind us now in circumstances where the relevant language, such as 'due process', could also bear a different meaning. These twin conditions are difficult to satisfy, as attested to by the fact that originalists commonly disagree about the empirical dimension, and disagree also as to the normative argument.[223] The reality is, moreover, that much that passes as originalism is less 'pure', according some latitude to constitutional or Treaty interpretation over and beyond anything that could be justified in strict originalist terms. This allows authors to present their desired vision of the constitutional order under the pretence that it is demanded by original intent, and deny that they are foisting their normative choice on others, whereas the reality is that original intent is used as a cloak to hide the creative normative inquiry being undertaken. The consequence is critics wishing to have it both ways, recognizing the need for some latitude to Treaty interpretation over and beyond anything that could be justified in originalist terms, yet strongly criticizing the ECtHR for transgressing a boundary that they are unwilling or unable define.

Fourth and finally, we should recognize the very duality that underpins autochthony. It embodies the positive desire for indigenous values, and encapsulates the natural yearning for culture locally framed. It also has a darker side, manifest in distrust of the 'other', whomsoever that might be, whether the foreign court, the foreign person or the minority living in one's own land. It is thus not surprising that

[223] S. Smith, M. Rappaport, W. Baude and S. Sachs, 'The New and Old Originalism: A Discussion', University of San Diego, School of Law, Research Paper No 15-178, 2015; H. Hurd, 'Why Would Anyone Care about Original Intent?', available at http://ssrn.com/abstract=2612115.

conceptions of autochthony have proved attractive to far-right groups, eager to exclude those who are felt not to 'belong'.[224] This duality recurs, as we shall see, in the discussion of autochthony in relation to the EU, to which we now turn.

(b) The UK and the EU: status, source and substantive autochthony

There has also been considerable discussion concerning the relationship between the UK and the ECHR, judicial and extra-judicial. It is helpful to consider this within the frame of the three senses of autochthony discussed above.

(i) Autochthony and status

The decision in *HS2* makes clear that the constitutional status of EU law within the UK is to be determined by UK law.[225] While the European Court of Justice (ECJ) held from the outset that EU law has supremacy over national law, it is for each Member State to decide whether it accepts this supremacy, and whether to ground its acceptance in the ECJ's *communautaire* reasoning, or in domestic constitutional principle, or in some admixture of the two.[226] The reality is

[224] Geschiere, *The Perils of Belonging*, Ch. 1.

[225] *R (HS2 Action Alliance Ltd)* v. *Secretary of State for Transport* [2014] UKSC 3; P. Craig, Constitutionalizing Constitutional Law: HS2' [2014] *Public Law* 373.

[226] P. Craig and G. de Búrca, *EU Law: Text, Cases and Materials* (Oxford: Oxford University Press, 6th ed., 2015), Ch. 9.

that the great majority of Member States base acceptance of the supremacy of EU law on national constitutional law.

Lord Bridge's reasoning concerning supremacy in *Factortame* contained elements of both approaches.[227] His Lordship acknowledged the functional argument advanced by the ECJ, viz. that the supremacy of Community law could be regarded as inherent given the Treaty objectives, and noted also the contractarian line of reasoning, to the effect that supremacy was well established when the UK joined the Community and therefore we knew the terms of the agreement. These arguments cohered with those used by the ECJ and were reinforced by national legal foundations, notably the European Communities Act 1972.

It was, however, the domestic acceptance of supremacy that was emphasized in *Thoburn*.[228] Laws LJ held that the constitutional relationship between the UK and the EU was not to be decided by the ECJ's jurisprudence, which could not itself entrench EU law within national law, but by the common law in the light of any domestic statutes. This approach was reinforced in *HS2*. The Supreme Court considered whether Article 9 of the Bill of Rights 1689 concerning the limits of judicial intervention in the parliamentary process might be said to have been implicitly qualified by the European Communities Act 1972. The argument was that if the Court of Justice of the European Union (CJEU) were to hold that national courts were obliged to scrutinize the

[227] *R* v. *Secretary of State for Transport, ex p Factortame Ltd (No 2)* [1991] 1 AC 603, at 658.

[228] *Thoburn v. Sunderland City Council* [2003] QB 151.

parliamentary process to comply with EU environmental directives then the UK courts would be bound to accept this result. This was because the UK had accepted the supremacy of EU law, with the consequence that the European Communities Act 1972 would be regarded as qualifying the force of Article 9 of the Bill of Rights 1689. Lord Reed in *HS2* rejected the argument:

> Contrary to the submission made on behalf of the appellants, that question cannot be resolved simply by applying the doctrine developed by the Court of Justice of the supremacy of EU law, since the application of that doctrine in our law itself depends upon the 1972 Act. If there is a conflict between a constitutional principle, such as that embodied in article 9 of the Bill of Rights, and EU law, that conflict has to be resolved by our courts as an issue arising under the constitutional law of the United Kingdom. Nor can the issue be resolved, as was also suggested, by following the decision in *R* v. *Secretary of State for Transport, Ex p Factortame Ltd (No 2)* [1991] 1 AC 603, since that case was not concerned with the compatibility with EU law of the process by which legislation is enacted in Parliament.[229]

It can be accepted that the status of EU law in the UK resides in the European Communities Act 1972, and that it is for UK constitutional law to determine the impact of EU membership on sovereignty in the light of existing domestic legislation. It follows that any conflict between the European Communities Act 1972 and other statutes such as

[229] *R (HS2 Action Alliance Ltd)* [2014] UKSC 3, at [79]. See also [203]–[205].

the Bill of Rights 1689 is to be resolved as a matter of UK constitutional law by the UK courts.

This does not, however, mean that in determining the impact of EU membership on UK sovereignty the arguments used by the CJEU should be irrelevant. The contractarian, egalitarian, functional and analytical arguments used by the CJEU can properly be regarded as having force when deciding, as a matter of UK constitutional law, on the effect of EU membership on sovereignty.[230] This does not mean that the UK courts must reach the same conclusion as the CJEU, to the effect that any norm of EU law is supreme over any norm of national law. Most national courts place some qualifications on the extent to which the supremacy of EU law will be accepted within their legal system. This does not, however, alter the preceding point, which is that the CJEU's normative arguments can properly be regarded as relevant when determining the outcome of a conflict between EU and national law. They should be regarded as having normative force in terms of their ability to persuade, as opposed to being accepted merely by virtue of their authority as stemming from the CJEU.

It should not, moreover, be forgotten in this respect that the European Union Act 2011 is a powerful legislative affirmation of its determination to reinforce the UK's control over Treaty amendments that accord new power to the EU. The Act is problematic in many respects,[231] but that does not deny the force of the referendum lock that it embodies.

[230] Craig and de Búrca, *EU Law*, Ch. 9.

[231] P. Craig, 'The European Union Act 2011: Locks, Limits and Legality' (2011) 48 *Common Market Law Review* 1881.

(ii) Autochthony and source

There is a contrast between the way in which autochthony plays out in relation to the ECHR and the EU, although not as great as might initially be imagined. UK courts have accepted with equanimity the fact that general principles of EU law bind the UK whenever it acts within the scope of EU law. There is, as will be seen in Chapter 4, continuing discourse as to what the scope of EU law connotes for these purposes, but this does not alter the point being made here.

Thus while the UK may have a reputation as being politically problematic in the EU, UK courts have caused fewer difficulties for the EU legal order than those from many other Member States. They have accepted that EU administrative law precepts, such as proportionality and legitimate expectations, must be applied by UK courts in challenges via judicial review that involve EU law. They have applied EU principles of damages liability and had little difficulty in accommodating this new cause of action alongside the armoury of other available forms of claim.

They have, moreover, been willing to consider whether such precepts should be applied in cases where there is no EU dimension to the case, thereby adding to the corpus of domestic administrative law principle. In this respect, the demands placed by EU law can be the catalyst for legal spillover, causing the UK courts to rethink and alter pre-existing precepts, as exemplified by the law relating to interim relief against the Crown.[232] All of this is in accord with the

[232] *R* v. *Secretary of State for Transport, ex p Factortame Ltd (No 2)* [1991] 1 AC 603; *M* v. *Home Office* [1994] 1 AC 377.

fact that the UK is in general open as a legal system to external influence, a ready importer of ideas as well as an exporter.[233]

The willingness to accept such influences is not in itself antithetical to autochthony, since all cultures will be fashioned by a plethora of influences, some of which will inevitably emanate from outside. In legal contexts, it is who controls the recognition and application of such precepts that is more significant for autochthony. UK courts recognize that EU membership means that the basic choice of administrative law norms will be for the CJEU, and they accept also the logic that such norms should then be applicable to Member States acting in the scope of EU law. In this sense they readily acknowledge the limits that such membership places on autochthony, although this does not have to mean uniform EU principles that allow no room for national differentiation.

There is, nonetheless, some 'pushback' evident at various points of the system so far as administrative law is concerned, as exemplified by national reaction to a proposed set of EU rules of administrative procedure.[234] Member States are already bound by EU requirements of procedural fairness, but the applicable rules remain those in national law, supplemented if necessary to comply with EU norms concerning process as articulated by the CJEU and the General Court (GC). If the model rules were applicable to Member States

[233] C. Harlow, 'Export, Import: The Ebb and Flow of English Public Law' [2000] *Public Law* 240.

[234] The rules were proposed by a research network ReNEUAL (see www.reneual.eu). The issue is considered in detail in Ch. 4 below.

when they act in the scope of EU law then the difference would be that all details of administrative procedure would be regulated directly by the EU rules. There was considerable opposition to the application of the model rules to Member States, more especially from national administrative courts, and UK judges were also opposed. While the rationale for this opposition varied, the general tenor was that it would intrude too greatly on the terrain covered by national acts of administrative procedure or the equivalent. Discretion being the better part of valour, the framers' of the model rules decided not to jeopardize the whole project by pressing the issue, hence the rules were framed to apply to EU institutions, and Member States only insofar as EU legislation stipulated.

(iii) Autochthony and substance

The most visible manifestation of substantive autochthony is the UK Independence Party's desire to leave the EU, and the Tory eurosceptic desire for very significant renegotiation of the terms of UK membership, with repatriation of many powers currently exercised by the EU to the Member States. The general debates about UK membership of the EU are, however, beyond the remit of this work,[235] and will be resolved when the referendum occurs. Those debates do not turn on anything to do with administrative law, by way of

[235] P. Craig, 'The United Kingdom, the European Union and Sovereignty', in R. Rawlings, P. Leyland and A. Young (eds.), *Sovereignty and the Law: Domestic, European and International Perspectives* (Oxford: Oxford University Press, 2013), Ch. 10; P. Craig, 'Responsibility, Voice and Exit: Britain Alone?', forthcoming.

contrast with substantive debates about the UK and the ECHR, which do turn on issues relating to the nature of rights-based adjudication and who should undertake it.

There are, however, important public law issues that have consequences for the substantive dimension of autochthony between Member States and the EU. Article 4(2) TEU was added to the Lisbon Treaty and provides, inter alia, that 'the Union shall respect the equality of Member States before the Treaties as well as their national identities, inherent in their fundamental structures, political and constitutional, inclusive of regional and local self-government'.[236] It lends force to the interpretive precept voiced by Lords Reed, Neuberger and Mance in *HS2* that national courts should, in the spirit of co-operation, read CJEU judgments so as to avoid an interpretation that conflicts with valued national principles, or that places in question the identity of the national constitutional order. This interpretive precept was used when

[236] L. Besselink, 'National and Constitutional Identity before and after Lisbon' (2010) 6 *Utrecht Law Review* 36; A. von Bogdandy and S. Schill, 'Overcoming Absolute Primacy: Respect for National Identity under the Lisbon Treaty' (2011) 48 *Common Market Law Review* 1417; T. Konstadinides, 'Constitutional Identity as a Shield and as a Sword: The European Legal Order within the Framework of National Constitutional Settlement' (2011) 13 *Cambridge Yearbook of European Legal Studies* 195; B. Guastaferro, 'Beyond the Exceptionalism of Constitutional Conflicts: The Ordinary Functions of the Identity Clause' (2012) 31 *Yearbook of European Law* 263; A. Arnaiz and C. Llivina (eds.), *National Constitutional Identity and European Integration* (Antwerp: Intersentia, 2013); E. Cloots, *National Identity and the European Court of Justice* (Oxford: Oxford University Press, 2014).

considering whether EU law should be so construed as to require a national court to undertake the kind of in-depth review of the quality of the legislative process that would be problematic from the perspective of UK constitutional law. Lord Reed held that 'a decision of the Court of Justice should not be read by a national court in a way that places in question the identity of the national constitutional order',[237] and the same sentiment was voiced by Lord Neuberger and Lord Mance.[238]

The debate about supremacy of EU law and what limits, if any, should be placed on this also has implications for the substantive dimension of autochthony. There have been divergent responses from the CJEU and national constitutional courts, with the former consistently asserting the supremacy of all EU law over all national law, while some national courts place 'locks' framed in terms of fundamental rights, vires and identity on the EU's power. This has in turn generated a vibrant debate as to how the relationship between the EU and national legal orders should be conceptualized, whether in monistic or pluralistic terms, and what implications this might have for the supremacy issue.[239]

[237] *R (HS2 Action Alliance Ltd)*, at [111].

[238] *R (HS2 Action Alliance Ltd)*, at [202].

[239] N. MacCormick, *Questioning Sovereignty* (Oxford: Oxford University Press, 1999); M. Kumm, 'Who Is the Final Arbiter of Constitutionality in Europe? Three Conceptions of the Relationship between the German Federal Constitutional Court and the European Court of Justice' (1999) 36 *Common Market Law Review* 351; N. Walker, 'The Idea of Constitutional Pluralism' (2002) 65 *Modern Law Review* 317; N. Walker, 'Late Sovereignty in the European Union', in N. Walker (ed.),

(c) *The UK and the global legal order: status, source and substantive autochthony*

(i) Autochthony and status

There is a wealth of literature concerning the status of international law within domestic law. Suffice it to say for the present that leaving behind the 'glacial uplands of juristic abstraction' of debates between dualism and monism,[240] the UK position in relation to the status of international law within domestic law is relatively clear.

Treaties must be transformed or adopted into national law in order to be enforceable in national courts,[241] and will not generate enforceable rights unless this has been done.[242] This reflects the constitutional imperative that Parliament makes law in the UK, but that the executive negotiates and ratifies treaties. If treaties thus ratified by the executive could become enforceable in the UK without

Sovereignty in Transition (Oxford: Hart, 2003), Ch. 1; M. Maduro, 'Contrapunctual Law: Europe's Constitutional Pluralism in Action', in Walker, *Sovereignty in Transition*, Ch. 21; A. von Bogdandy, 'Pluralism, Direct Effect, and the Ultimate Say: On the Relationship between International and Domestic Constitutional Law' (2008) 6 *I-CON* 397; K. Jaklic, *Constitutional Pluralism in the EU* (Oxford: Oxford University Press, 2014).

240 J. Crawford, *Brownlie's Principles of Public International Law* (Oxford: Oxford University Press, 8th ed., 2012), p. 50; P. Sales and J. Clement, 'International Law in Domestic Courts: The Developing Framework' (2008) 124 *Law Quarterly Review* 388.

241 *JH Rayner (Mincing Lane Ltd)* v. *Department of Trade and Industry* [1990] 2 AC 418; *Thomas* v. *Baptiste* [2000] 2 AC 1, at 23.

242 *JH Rayner (Mincing Lane Ltd)* v. *Department of Trade and Industry* [1990] 2 AC 418; *R* v. *Home Secretary, ex p. Brind* [1991] 1 AC 696.

parliamentary ratification, this would accord the executive the right to legislate in such areas and thereby undermine Parliament. The rule requiring treaties to be transformed into legislation thereby preserves autochthony as conceived in terms of national constitutional tradition. The corollary is that decisions of international courts and tribunals that find the UK in breach of an international obligation flowing from an unimplemented treaty do not have effect in our national court, since this would indirectly undermine the need for Parliament to transform the treaty into domestic law.[243]

The position in relation to customary international law is somewhat different. There is some authority that it is incorporated and considered part of the law of the land,[244] but the better view is that it is a source of national law 'that the courts can draw on as required'.[245] Thus as Lord Bingham stated, following Brierly,[246] 'international law is not a part, but is one of the sources, of English law'.[247] This juridical view, which is 'more nuanced than either the doctrines of incorporation or transformation would suggest',[248] enables national courts to give force to customary international law, while retaining control over the process by which this occurs and the result within our national legal order.

243 *R* v. *Lyons* [2003] 1 AC 976, at 995.

244 *Trendtex Trading Corporation* v. *Central Bank of Nigeria* [1977] QB 529, at 554.

245 *Brownlie's Principles of Public International Law*, p. 68.

246 J. Brierly, 'International Law in England' (1935) 51 *Law Quarterly Review* 24.

247 *R* v. *Jones (Margaret)* [2007] 1 AC 136, at 155.

248 *Brownlie's Principles of Public International Law*, p. 68.

While the preceding picture is relatively clear, there is nonetheless something resembling a black hole that is especially pertinent to the subject matter of this study. The doctrinal rules adumbrated above apply to formal treaties and custom, the foundations of public international law as classically conceived. They do not touch the netherworld of global regulatory rules that are not customary international law or treaties between states. There is a very considerable body of such rules, as the later discussion of global administrative law will reveal.[249]

Suffice it to say for the present that prominent examples include rules made by non-governmental regulatory organizations, such as the the International Organization for Standardization (ISO),[250] the International Electrotechnical Commission (IEC)[251] and the International Accounting Standards Board (IASB).[252] These bodies produce rules and standards that will commonly be applicable to a range of products, and compliance with the relevant criteria will often be required either to secure market access, or because the regulatory requirements are incorporated in national laws, directly or indirectly.[253] In other instances there will be transnational networks and co-ordination arrangements which may be embedded in a treaty, but need not be, and where the principal

[249] See below, Ch. 5. [250] See www.iso.org/iso/home.html.

[251] See www.iec.ch.

[252] See www.iasplus.com/en/resources/ifrsf/iasb-ifrs-ic/iasb.

[253] W. Mattli and T. Büthe, 'Setting International Standards: Technological Rationality or Primacy of Power' (2003) 56 *World Politics* 1; T. Büthe and W. Mattli, *The New Global Rulers, the Privatization of Regulation in the World Economy* (Princeton: Princeton University Press, 2011).

objective is co-operation among state regulators, as exemplified by the Basel Committee on Banking Supervision.[254] In yet other instances there is 'hybrid intergovernmental–private administration', as exemplified by the Codex Alimentarius Commission,[255] where the food standards are adopted through a decision-making process that includes participation by non-governmental actors as well as government representatives, and by ICANN, the Internet Corporation for Assigned Names and Numbers,[256] which, although founded as a non-governmental body, now includes government representatives.

The rules made by such bodies will commonly shape de jure or de facto national regulatory strategies, whether those are run by state agencies, private standardization organizations or an admixture of the two. The rules thus made are not formally subject to the gatekeeping functions performed by legal doctrine that governs the applicability in national law of international treaties *stricto sensu*, or custom. This is so notwithstanding the fact that Parliament may in reality be bypassed by the application of such global rules at national level.[257]

(ii) Autochthony and source

The duality noted in the previous section between treaties and custom, on the one hand, and other global rules, on the other, is also evident when we reflect on autochthony and source.

[254] See www.bis.org/bcbs. [255] See www.codexalimentarius.org.

[256] See www.icann.org.

[257] See below, pp. 569–80, for further discussion.

The prevailing rules relating to the reception of treaties and custom in national law embody safeguards that protect important traditions of the national legal order. Thus it is standard doctrine not only that a treaty must be transformed into national law in order to protect Parliament's legislative authority, but also that once transformed it takes effect within the national legal order like any other statute, with the corollary that a subsequent statute will take precedence over an earlier statute that embodies an international treaty in the event of an inconsistency between the two.[258] The courts will seek to avoid such a clash where possible, as epitomized by the common law presumption that Parliament does not intend to act in breach of international law, including treaty obligations.[259] This does not alter the point made here, which is further reinforced by the fact that while national courts will normally follow the ruling of an international court interpreting a treaty, such rulings are not binding. This point was captured by Lord Hoffmann, who noted that when legislation confirmed a treaty, it was the statute that formed part of UK law, not the treaty, and national courts 'will not (unless the statute expressly so provides) be bound to give effect to interpretations of the treaty by an international court, even though the United Kingdom is bound by international law to do so'.[260]

[258] *IRC* v. *Collco Dealings Ltd* [1962] AC 1; *Woodend (KV Ceylon) Rubber and Tea Co.* v. *IRC* [1971] AC 321.

[259] *Salomon* v. *Commissioners of Customs and Excise* [1967] 2 QB 116, at 143; *R* v. *Home Secretary, ex p. Brind* [1991] 1 AC 696, at 747–8.

[260] *R* v. *Lyons*, at 992.

These doctrinal rules will in principle also be applicable to global rules made by bodies of the kind set out in the preceding section, when those rules are applied at national level. While this may be so 'in principle', the reality may be rather different. Where formal treaty obligations are transformed into national law there is by definition a statute, and the possibility that this might be qualified by a later enactment. Where global rules shape national regulatory strategies de jure or de facto this will often occur through agency rule making or decision making. To be sure, the national regulatory strategy derived from global rules can be changed by statute, but this does not alter the crucial point that the global rules will commonly impact on rule making or decision making by the national regulatory agency, with the consequence that the issue may not appear on Parliament's radar at all. This is a fortiori the case in relation to global norms that have a major impact at the national level, but which take effect through, for example, standardization bodies that are non-governmental. While national regulatory strategies will perforce be subject to judicial review for compliance with the enabling statute, this does not in itself touch the point made here.

(iii) Autochthony and substance

There may well be concerns relating to the substance of measures derived from international law and whether such measures cohere with national constitutional precepts. These concerns play out rather differently in relation to treaties and customary international law. The very fact that treaties must be transformed into national law through statute provides occasion for Parliament to express its approval of the substance of the proposed enactment. The statute, once enacted, will, moreover, then be subject to challenge for compliance with the Human Rights Act 1998. These twin precepts foster legitimate space for autochthony in this domain.

There is greater difficulty in relation to customary international law. This should, as seen above, be regarded as a source for national law obligations, rather than being directly incorporated as such. This still leaves much to be determined as to how it functions as a source, and the limits that should be placed on it in this respect. It is clear from *R* v. *Jones (Margaret)* that a customary rule will not be accepted if it contradicts a national constitutional principle, in the instant case the principle being that only Parliament could create crimes.[261] It is clear also from *Chung Chi Cheung* v. *R* that if a customary rule is transposed into the common law, it will take effect subject to any statute to the contrary.[262]

Philip Sales and Joanne Clement provide forceful arguments as to why courts should be wary about too readily allowing custom to operate as a source of UK law:[263] custom may change quite rapidly; a state may be bound by a new custom without having assented to it; the state-practice component of custom will normally be executive action with scant, if any, legislative involvement, thereby subject to objections, in terms of bypassing Parliament, analogous to those that pertain to treaties; and the

[261] [2007] 1 AC 136. [262] [1938] 4 All ER 786.

[263] Sales and Clement, 'International Law in Domestic Courts', 413–21.

terms of the custom may be unclear. There are analogous concerns about the substance of global rules that impact on national law, even where they do not take the form of treaties or custom. This is a natural bridge to the subsequent discussion concerning regulatory challenges for administrative law.

8 Interaction between legal orders: regulation

There is a vast literature on regulation, the import of which goes far beyond this work.[264] Regulation is nonetheless central to administrative law. The ensuing analysis will focus on the challenges posed for national administrative law by the very fact that regulation will often emanate de jure or de facto from the EU or global level. This issue is considered from the EU and global perspectives in later chapters.[265] What follows should therefore be read in tandem with this.

[264] See, e.g., S. Breyer, *Regulation and Its Reform* (Cambridge, MA: Harvard University Press, 1982); A. Ogus, *Regulation, Legal Form and Economic Theory* (Oxford: Oxford University Press, 1994); T. Prosser, *Law and the Regulators* (Oxford: Oxford University Press, 1997); B. Morgan and K. Yeung, *An Introduction to Law and Regulation, Text and Materials* (Cambridge: Cambridge University Press, 2007); D. Oliver, T. Prosser and R. Rawlings, *The Regulatory State: Constitutional Implications* (Oxford: Oxford University Press, 2010); T. Prosser, *The Regulatory Enterprise: Government, Regulation and Legitimacy* (Oxford: Oxford University Press, 2010); R. Baldwin, M. Cave and M. Lodge, *Understanding Regulation: Theory, Strategy and Practice* (Oxford: Oxford University Press, 2nd ed., 2012).

[265] See below, Chs. 4, 6.

(a) Regulatory competence

National regulatory competence is framed by obligations that flow from EU law, other international treaties, and global rules made by transnational organizations. The nature and extent of the constraint will perforce depend on, for example, the content of the particular treaty obligation.

Thus in relation to the EU, where an issue falls within the EU's exclusive competence Member States lose all independent regulatory capacity. It is only the EU that has power to legislate and adopt binding Acts, subject to the caveat that Member States can do so when empowered by the EU, or for the implementation of EU Acts.[266] It is more common for competence to be shared between the EU and the Member States, with the implication that both have regulatory competence in the relevant area. This is, however, subject to the caveat that the Member State can only exercise its competence to the extent to which the EU has not done so.[267] Whether there is any room for Member State action will depend on whether the EU regulatory initiative was maximal or minimal, and this may not always be evident from the face of the EU regulatory instrument. Even where it is the latter, the Member State will have to comply with the regulatory minimum provided by the EU, with the consequence that national regulatory protection over and beyond this will almost always sit within a regulatory frame provided by EU law. The reality is therefore that in the areas where the EU has competence

[266] Art. 2(1) TFEU. [267] Art. 2(2) TFEU.

it will commonly establish the regulatory schema. This will often be detailed in terms of both the substance of the regulatory obligations, and the procedures through which they are to be put into effect.

The scope of national regulatory competence may also be bounded by rules that emanate from an international treaty. Thus a particular treaty may not itself be the source of further regulatory initiatives, but it may impose binding constraints on national regulatory initiatives. It may, moreover, render these constraints more effective through enforcement mechanisms at national level. This is the common pattern in the World Trade Organization. A particular WTO agreement will establish detailed regulatory criteria, which are applied by national administrative authorities, subject to possible oversight by administrators and adjudicators at the WTO level. This is exemplified by the Anti-dumping Agreement,[268] Article 1 of which provides that an 'anti-dumping measure shall be applied only under the circumstances provided for in Article VI of GATT 1994 and pursuant to investigations initiated and conducted in accordance with the provisions of this Agreement'. Article 5 is concerned with the investigation, which is initiated by complaint from the domestic industry. It is then incumbent on the 'authorities' to 'examine the accuracy and adequacy of the evidence to determine whether there is sufficient

[268] Agreement on Implementation of Article VI of the General Agreement on Tariffs and Trade 1994, www.wto.org/english/docs_e/legal_e/legal_e.htm.

evidence to justify the initiation of an investigation',[269] and, if there is, to make the determination as to whether dumping has occurred. There are detailed rules as to the procedures that must be followed by the authorities when conducting such an investigation,[270] and as to the remedies that can be imposed.[271] The centrality of national authorities to the investigative exercise is further emphasized by the obligation in Article 13 to maintain an effective and independent regime of judicial review.

In both of the preceding examples national regulatory competence is de jure circumscribed by obligations undertaken at the EU or international level. The impact on such competence may, however, be de facto, but real nonetheless. Thus, to take but one example, the International Organization for Standardization is a non-governmental organization, with members from 165 countries.[272] It has produced more than 19,500 standards covering business, food and technology. Its constituent members are national standards agencies that help decide the applicable standards within the ISO, and it is these same national agencies that promote ISO standards in their own countries. Compliance with the standards will often be required either to secure market access, or because the regulatory requirements are incorporated in national laws, directly or indirectly.[273]

[269] Art. 5(3) Anti-dumping Agreement.
[270] Art. 6 Anti-dumping Agreement.
[271] Arts. 7–9 Anti-dumping Agreement.
[272] See www.iso.org/iso/home.html.
[273] Mattli and Büthe, 'Setting International Standards'.

(b) Regulatory object and design

There is an extensive literature on regulatory object and design. Tony Prosser has posited a helpful distinction between regulation as control and regulation as an enterprise, the two models having differing characteristics.[274]

Regulation as control is predicated on regulation being an intrusion into private autonomy, which is justified for reasons of market failure. The principal regulatory objective is efficiency to be achieved through promotion of competition and the correction of externalities. Distributive concerns are regarded as the province of government, not the regulatory agency, and the very fact that such concerns are hived off serves to justify the independence of the regulatory authority. This in turn is said to promote stability of the system, by removing it from the vagaries of day-to-day politics. This stability is then further enhanced through rules to guide the behaviour of those who come within the agency's remit, although this may be in tension with desires to keep public intervention to a minimum through the fostering of social co-ordination.

Regulation as an enterprise conceives regulators as governments in miniature, in 'which efficiency and distributive goals are both legitimate regulatory concerns, and anyway are inseparable'.[275] The regulatory goals may include social

[274] T. Prosser, 'Models of Economic and Social Regulation', in Oliver, Prosser and Rawlings, *The Regulatory State: Constitutional Implications*, pp. 37–9.

[275] Prosser, 'Models of Economic and Social Regulation', p. 38.

cohesion, and this function may be shared with government. Regulatory independence is not regarded as central, because regulation is conceived as a collaborative project between agencies and other organs of government. Regulation in this mould is seen as 'delegation by government of its inherent powers to act in the public interest'.[276] The emphasis is on different actors working towards a common enterprise, with accountability conceived primarily in terms of public law mechanisms such as proceduralization, judicial review and parliamentary scrutiny. For Prosser this model has the virtue of rendering it easier to understand in areas where regulation has a social rationale, and is not driven by considerations of economic efficiency.

These models are helpful in thinking about the ways in which we undertake regulation in distinct areas. The salient point for present purposes is that the freedom to make this choice will be circumscribed where regulatory competence flows from the EU or international level in the ways adumbrated in the previous section. Thus where regulatory competence resides in, for example, the EU, the object and design of the regulatory initiatives will be set by the EU, subject to Member State input through the ordinary legislative process. The detailed specification of such regulation will perforce be established with the needs of twenty-eight Member States in mind, and reform may be driven by the 'weakest link'. EU initiatives may exhibit a similar regulatory duality to that posited by Prosser, but this does not alter the fact that the choice is set elsewhere. This is not a criticism of the EU,

[276] Prosser, 'Models of Economic and Social Regulation', p. 38.

or of other international organizations that shape regulatory design. It is simply an inevitable consequence of membership. Thus Member States join the EU cognizant of the benefits and costs of doing so, the former including access to an enlarged single market, the latter including the circumscription of regulatory autonomy that attends this.

To take but one example, national utilities regulation is set within regulatory objectives framed by the EU. The principal objective of Directive 2009/72 is to complete the internal market in electricity and to expedite market liberalization, albeit subject to certain universal-service obligations.[277] Member States and their national regulatory authorities are given broad powers and duties to effectuate the Union objective. They have responsibilities for matters such as: the substantive criteria for the construction of generating capacity in their territory, subject to guidance in the Directive; application of these criteria; and ensuring network access and non-discriminatory transmission and distribution tariffs. They are given discretionary power as to whether to impose on electricity undertakings public-service obligations in the general economic interest, relating to matters such as security, regularity, quality and price of supplies, and environmental protection. They are obliged to ensure that all household customers, and, where Member States deem it appropriate, small enterprises, enjoy universal service, defined as the right to be supplied with electricity of a

[277] Directive 2009/72/EC of the European Parliament and of the Council of 13 July 2009 concerning common rules for the internal market in electricity and repealing Directive 2003/54/EC, OJ 2009 No L211/55.

specified quality at reasonable prices. They can appoint a supplier of last resort to ensure provision of universal service, and have the power to give compensation or exclusive rights to undertakings for the fulfilment of these obligations. They are obliged to take appropriate measures to protect final customers, in particular those who are vulnerable or who live in remote areas; to ensure high levels of consumer protection; and to enable customers to switch to a new supplier. The overall regime is overseen at national level by regulatory authorities, which are responsible for ensuring non-discrimination, effective competition and the efficient functioning of the market.

(c) Regulatory efficacy and control

Regulatory efficacy and control can take many forms, including parliamentary oversight, judicial review, audit and internal agency checks. The fact that much national regulation emanates from, or is circumscribed by, EU, international or global rules will shape this in a variety of ways.

First, it can shape the incidence of legal controls. Thus it is a cardinal feature of EU law that national courts cannot invalidate an EU regulatory norm that is challenged before them. If the national court believes that there is merit to the challenge it is then obliged to request a preliminary ruling from the CJEU, which will decide on the validity of the challenged regulation.[278] It is an equally cardinal feature of

[278] Case 314/85, *Firma Foto-Frost* v. *Hauptzollamt Lübeck-Ost* [1987] ECR 4199.

EU law that individuals can derive rights from the Treaty and norms made thereunder that enable them to challenge national regulatory measures for compliance with EU law. National courts have the power and duty to apply EU law in such cases and can therefore strike down the national regulation where the challenge is warranted, or send a reference to the CJEU if they are uncertain of what EU law demands in the instant case.[279] Such challenges before national courts will, moreover, be in accord with EU rules of judicial review. The incidence of judicial review can also be shaped by rules flowing from other international treaties. Thus the judicial review pursuant to WTO agreements requires national courts to apply substantive and procedural criteria specified in that agreement.

Second, the very fact that much national regulatory activity occurs within a framework of rules that emanate from the EU, an international treaty or other transnational global rules can pose significant problems for regulatory efficacy, both in terms of its attainment and in terms of its measurement. This is exemplified by the shared administration that is used for delivery of much EU policy. It is predicated on the fact that both EU and national administration have related but distinct tasks for the delivery of the regulatory objectives, which are commonly set out in legal terms in the enabling legislation.[280] Regulatory policy in areas as diverse

[279] Cases 28–30/62, *Da Costa en Schaake NV* v. *Nederlandse Belastingadministratie* [1963] ECR 31; Case 283/81, *Srl CILFIT* v. *Ministry of Health* [1982] ECR 3415.

[280] Craig, *EU Administrative Law*; C. Harlow and R. Rawlings, *Process and Procedure in EU Administration* (Oxford: Hart, 2014).

as agriculture, the Structural Funds, financial regulation, telecommunications and utilities regulation is run in this manner. The challenges in terms of regulatory efficacy have been significant. They flow in part from the fact that the regulatory design may be imperfect, thereby enabling Member States to escape their obligations; they may be the result of insufficient resources to deal with the problem, whether at national or EU level or both; they may also be more horizontal in nature, stemming from the fact that the success of the regulatory initiative is dependent on cross-border co-operation between administrations in Member States.

Third, there can be problems of regulatory legitimacy and control where national rules are shaped by global initiatives that have not received any direct imprimatur from the legislature. This problem will be considered in detail when discussing the challenges posed by global administrative law.[281] Suffice it to say for the present that there are, as Richard Stewart notes, three possible ways of addressing the problem.[282] The first he terms the 'bottom-up' approach, whereby domestic administrative law is applied so as to assert more effective control of the supranational elements of domestic regulation. The second approach is 'top-down', whereby the global regulatory regimes develop more fully the type of administrative law safeguards commonly found

[281] See below, Ch. 6.

[282] R. Stewart, 'The Global Regulatory Challenge to U.S. Administrative Law' (2005) 37 *New York University Journal of International Law and Policy* 695, at 709–11.

in national systems. Stewart's third approach follows an 'integrative' logic 'through substantive principles and regulatory due process requirements applicable to decisions by domestic agencies that affect international trade and investment, aliens, and other extra-national interests'.[283]

9 Conclusion

When I first began to teach in 1976 a senior professor opined that there were not many contentious issues in UK administrative law. This opinion did not in reality convey an accurate impression of the landscape then, much less so now. There are vibrant debates that affect all aspects of the subject, which bear testimony to its importance. This is reflective of the challenges facing administrative law, which have certainly not lessened in the new millennium.

The horizontal challenges that are internal to the UK system speak to endemic problems faced by any system of administrative law, including access to review, the balance between legal and political methods of accountability, the applicability of process rights, and the limits of substantive review. These issues would have been readily understood by the founders of administrative law in the UK – Coke, Holt, Hale, Mansfield and Blackstone – although it is also true that recent developments, such as enactment of the HRA, have cast the problems into higher relief.

[283] Stewart, 'The Global Regulatory Challenge to U.S. Administrative Law', 710–11.

The vertical challenges posed by the inter-relationship between the UK, the EU, the ECHR and international legal orders are more novel. The relationship between national and international law has, of course, been an issue ever since the law of nations became a legal reality. The issues raised by membership of the EU and ECHR are, however, not truly analogous to anything hitherto, and that is also so in relation to increased globalization, which has meant that rules are increasingly made through international and transnational organizations that bind the national legal order de jure or de facto. This very dynamic has led to a paradox that is apparent rather than real, but important nonetheless. The increased profile of judicial doctrine that is grounded in autochthony is not fortuitous. It is the national reaction to an increasingly globalized world, which has prompted legal orders to think hard about their own legal heritage and the 'entry conditions' they place on norms from other legal orders. This issue will not disappear any time soon, and similar themes can be seen in the CJEU's case law. It is to the foundations and challenges of EU administrative law that we now turn.

3

EU administrative law

Foundations

1 Introduction

The previous chapters considered UK administrative law, its foundations and the challenges it faces. It is readily apparent from this discussion that the challenges included the impact of EU law on domestic precepts of constitutional and administrative law. The focus in this chapter and that which follows switches to EU administrative law, the foundations of which are considered in this chapter, and the challenges faced by it in the chapter that follows.

The discussion begins with the formal foundation of EU administrative law. This was less controversial than in the UK, since the European Coal and Steel Community (ECSC) Treaty, from its very inception, contained provisions authorizing judicial review, which were taken over in amended form into the Rome Treaty that established the European Economic Community. There was nonetheless much judicial creativity required to transform this formal foundation into a body of doctrine with precepts of administrative law analogous to those found in the Member States. The development of general principles of law was central in this respect. While much has been written about such principles the story concerning their evolution as precepts of administrative law has not been fully revealed and is told in the section that follows.

The focus then turns to the substantive foundations of EU administrative law, and the way in which the rule of law has informed development of doctrine in this area. There is analysis of the nature of the political order in the emergent Community in the 1960s and 1970s, since this is essential in order to understand the imperatives underlying the development of EU administrative law. This is followed by examination of the more particular ways in which the rule of law informed doctrinal development in this area. There is analysis of judicial review in terms of its availability, its targeting, the grounds of such review, and access. The objective is not to provide detailed analysis of the grounds of review, which would require a book in itself. It is rather to consider how these were elaborated, drawing analogies with the development of principles of judicial review in the UK set out in the first chapter.

The final section of the chapter is concerned with the regulatory foundations of EU administrative law. Its development cannot be understood divorced from the administrative regime that pertains in the EU. It is complex, with an admixture of direct and shared administration, comitology and agencies. The nature of this regime as it relates to single-case decision making and rule making is therefore explicated. The ensuing discussion is directed towards the need for EU administrative law viewed in the light of this administrative landscape, in part in order to imbue the norms made therein with legitimacy, but in part also to provide opportunity for judicial interpretation of the relevant treaty or regulatory provisions in order to ensure that the policy objectives were effectuated. This is followed by critical consideration of a more ambitious thesis, to the effect that EU integration should be seen in administrative rather than constitutional terms.

2 Formal foundations

(a) Treaty foundations: power and intent

(i) Power

The earlier discussion revealed the controversy concerning the foundations of judicial review in the UK. The EU, by way of contrast, has been more secure in this respect, with formal affirmation of the ECJ's right to engage in judicial review dating back to the ECSC Treaty, Article 33 of which was framed as follows:

> The Court shall have jurisdiction in actions brought by a Member State or by the Council to have decisions or recommendations of the High Authority declared void on grounds of lack of competence, infringement of an essential procedural requirement, infringement of this Treaty or of any rule of law relating to its application, or misuse of powers. The Court may not, however, examine the evaluation of the situation, resulting from economic facts or circumstances, in the light of which the High Authority took its decisions or made its recommendations, save where the High Authority is alleged to have misused its powers or to have manifestly failed to observe the provisions of this Treaty or any rule of law relating to its application.

This served as the blueprint for the Rome Treaty. Article 173 EEC borrowed closely from the grounds of review in Article 33 ECSC, albeit without the qualification in the last sentence thereof:

> The Court of Justice shall review the legality of acts of the Council and the Commission other than recommendations or opinions. It shall for this purpose have jurisdiction in actions brought by a Member State, the Council or the Commission on grounds of lack of competence, infringement of an essential procedural requirement, infringement of this Treaty or of any rule of law relating to its application, or misuse of powers.

Article 173 has been amended on numerous occasions, most recently by the Lisbon Treaty, but there has been no change in the grounds of judicial review. The continuity with the past is evident in Article 263 TFEU:

> The Court of Justice of the European Union shall review the legality of legislative acts, of acts of the Council, of the Commission and of the European Central Bank, other than recommendations and opinions, and of acts of the European Parliament and of the European Council intended to produce legal effects *vis-à-vis* third parties. It shall also review the legality of acts of bodies, offices or agencies of the Union intended to produce legal effects *vis-à-vis* third parties.
>
> It shall for this purpose have jurisdiction in actions brought by a Member State, the European Parliament, the Council or the Commission on grounds of lack of competence, infringement of an essential procedural requirement, infringement of the Treaties or of any rule of law relating to their application, or misuse of powers.

(ii) Intent

The very fact that the ECJ had express authorization derived from Article 33 ECSC and Article 173 EEC thereby obviated concerns about the legitimacy of engaging in judicial review of the kind that plagued UK scholarship. The Treaty provisions nonetheless left the ECJ with much to do in giving meaning to the four heads of review mentioned therein.

Lack of competence, infringement of an essential procedural requirement and misuse of power were relatively discrete grounds of judicial review, which limited the need for judicial creativity, but limited also their potential for the development of more wide-ranging principles of judicial review of the kind that existed in national legal systems.

The injunction in Article 33 ECSC and Article 173 EEC that the ECJ shall review for infringement of the 'Treaty or any rule of law relating to its application' was, however, more promising in this respect. It could provide a foundation for what became the general principles of law that fashioned EU judicial review,[1] which were read into the Treaty by the ECJ, in particular during the 1970s. The *travaux préparatoires* for the original Rome Treaty were not available for over thirty years. This is a blessing, since it means that we

[1] A. Arnull, *The General Principles of EEC Law and the Individual* (London: Leicester University Press, 1990); J. Schwarze, *European Administrative Law* (Luxembourg and London: Office for Official Publications of the European Communities and Sweet & Maxwell, rev. ed., 2006); T. Tridimas, *The General Principles of EU Law* (Oxford: Oxford University Press, 2nd ed., 2006); H. Hofmann, G. Rowe and A. Türk, *Administrative Law and Policy of the European Union* (Oxford: Oxford University Press, 2011); P. Craig, *EU Administrative Law* (Oxford: Oxford University Press, 2nd ed., 2012); C. Harlow and R. Rawlings, *Process and Procedure in EU Administration* (Oxford: Hart, 2014); P. Birkinshaw, *European Public Law: The Achievement and the Challenge* (Alphen aan den Rijn: Kluwer Law International, 2nd ed., 2014).

have not been beset with debates about original intent of the kind that have plagued US constitutional scholarship. The very absence of the *travaux préparatoires* meant, however, that the ECJ developed its own interpretation of the scope of Article 33 ECSC and Article 173 EEC.

A broad interpretation of Article 173 might be facilitated by Article 164 EEC, now Article 19 TEU, which provided that the 'Court of Justice shall ensure that in the interpretation and application of this Treaty the law is observed'. This might have been interpreted in a limited manner to connote the idea that, for example, Commission decisions should be made within the limits of the primary Treaty articles and secondary legislation. The word 'law' within this article was, however, open to a broader interpretation that was used by the ECJ to fashion a system of general principles through which the legality of Union and Member State action could be determined.[2]

It is important to view the interpretation of Article 33 ECSC and Article 173 EEC against the backdrop of the more general role perceived for the Court by the Treaty framers. There was tension in this regard between France and Germany. Jean Monnet was initially opposed to a permanent court as an ECSC institution, fearful of a *gouvernement des juges* that would unduly constrain the High Authority. Judicial supervision should in his view be limited

[2] There are instances where the ECJ used language, in the context of applying general principles, that was redolent of that in what is now Art. 19 TFEU; see, e.g., Case 224/82, *Meiko-Konservenfabrik* v. *Federal Republic of Germany* [1983] ECR 2539, at [11]; Case C-325/91, *France* v. *Commission* [1993] ECR I-3283, at [30].

to an ad hoc arbitral tribunal. Germany, by way of contrast, favoured something more akin to a constitutional court, with Walter Hallstein seeking to create 'a Federal Court similar to the new German *Bundesverfassungsgericht* that would ensure the development of a German *Rechtsstaat*'.[3] This vision was given voice by Walter Hallstein to an 'unenthusiastic Monnet in early July 1950',[4] with the Benelux countries more inclined towards the German vision. Monnet enlisted the aid of Maurice Lagrange, a member of the Conseil d'état, who was 'appointed to scale back the Court to resemble the model of the French Administrative Court'.[5] Lagrange played a significant role in shaping the emergent Court, although the 'Germans, whose judicial system did not include a court similar to the Conseil d'Etat, grew exasperated at Lagrange's constant reference to the French experience'.[6] The upshot after three weeks of intense negotiation was a Court that, in the words of Anne Boerger-de Smedt, defied easy categorization: 'more than an international Court, but not quite a constitutional Court either, it was mainly an administrative Court, empowered to ensure that the HA would act within the

[3] M. Rasmussen, 'The Origins of a Legal Revolution: The Early History of the European Court of Justice' (2008) 14 *Journal of European Integration History* 77, at 83.

[4] A. Boerger-de Smedt, 'Negotiating the Foundations of European Law, 1950–57: The Legal History of the Treaties of Paris and Rome' (2012) 21 *Contemporary European History* 339, at 342. See also A. Boerger-de Smedt, 'La Cour de Justice dans les négociations du traité de Paris instituant la CECA' (2008) 14 *Journal of European Integration History* 7.

[5] Boerger-de Smedt, 'Negotiating the Foundations of European Law', 345.

[6] Boerger-de Smedt, 'Negotiating the Foundations of European Law', 346.

powers granted by the treaty',[7] subject to the caveat expressed in Article 33 ECSC precluding the Court from adjudicating on economic evaluation.

There were, in relative terms, fewer tensions in the crafting of the ECJ's powers in the EEC Treaty. Lagrange's position shifted subtly, as he came to perceive the Court's potential constitutional role within the ECSC.[8] The French delegation nonetheless opposed the idea of a permanent Court, with Georges Vedel proposing to remove the Court completely and replace it with something akin to a court of arbitrage staffed by technical experts.[9] This opposition only ended as part of a broader deal struck between France and Germany in November 1956.[10] The important legal work thereafter was done by a jurist committee, known as the Groupe de rédaction, which was established by Henri Spaak to ensure the legal cohesion of the Treaties and to craft the general and institutional provisions. It is clear from Pierre Pescatore, who was a member of the group, that all members except the French favoured strong European institutions.[11] While the text of Article 173 EEC was narrower in certain respects than Article 33 ECSC, this was balanced by the fact that the limitation precluding the ECJ from adjudicating on

[7] Boerger-de Smedt, 'Negotiating the Foundations of European Law', 346.

[8] M. Lagrange, 'La Cour de Justice de la Communauté européenne du charbon et de l'acier' (1954) 2 *Revue du droit public et de la science politique en France et à l'étranger* 417.

[9] Rasmussen, 'The Origins of a Legal Revolution', 87.

[10] Rasmussen, 'The Origins of a Legal Revolution', 87.

[11] P. Pescatore, 'Les travaux du "Groupe juridique" dans la négociation des Traités de Rome' (1981) XXXIV *Studia Diplomatica* 158.

economic evaluation was removed. Furthermore, the crafting of Article 177 EEC to allow preliminary references on the interpretation and validity of EEC law was to prove an especially significant change as compared to Article 41 ECSC, which countenanced preliminary references only in relation to validity. In the words of Morten Rasmussen,

> the negotiations on the Treaty of Paris and the Treaties of Rome were influenced by negotiators and jurists, who wanted to promote the development of a Federal and Constitutional Court and furnish the Treaties with distinct constitutional features. These actors worked under serious political constraints and the progress they made during the above mentioned negotiations often seemed very small indeed. However, in the end they provided sufficient legal basis for the ECJ to revolutionise European law. The early history of the European legal order is thus one of federalist political and legal forces promoting, through different actors at different points in time, a particular constitutional thinking about the Treaties and the ECJ.[12]

The negotiations concerning the role of the Court are the backdrop to more specific inquiry as to the meaning of the key phrase in Article 33 ECSC and Article 173 EEC, viz. infringement of the Treaty or any rule of law relating to its application. The intent might simply have been to ensure that Commission decision making complied not only with the primary Treaty articles, but also with regulations, directives and the like passed pursuant thereto. If this had been the

[12] Rasmussen, 'The Origins of a Legal Revolution', 97–8.

intent it could, however, have been expressed more directly. The intent might alternatively have been to capture not only compliance with secondary legislation, but also with other rules of law relating to the application of the Treaty that might be developed by the courts.[13] This interpretation might be enhanced by the fact that French juristic thought is clearly imprinted on the grounds of review in Article 173 and French doctrine includes *principes généraux du droit*.[14]

The historical record is somewhat equivocal, although certain matters are clear. Thus the words *violation du Traité ou de toute règle de droit relative à son application* were introduced during negotiations between the first and second comprehensive drafts of the ECSC Treaty. They replaced the words *abus du droit* used in the first draft of 9 November 1950. It seems, moreover, from a memorandum by Jean Monnet on 22 December 1950, that the latter part of the Treaty formulation was intended to cover violation of general principles of law, regulations made pursuant to the Treaty and other binding norms.[15] This reading is confirmed by another document that might have been drafted by Lagrange, when the ECSC Treaty was presented to the French parliament. In a draft 'Exposé des motifs' of 17 June 1951, the author provides an interpretation of the wording of Article 33 that

[13] See, e.g., K. Lenaerts, D. Arts, I. Maselis and R. Bray, *Procedural Law of the European Union* (London: Sweet & Maxwell, 2nd ed., 2006), 7–152.

[14] J. Schwarze, *European Administrative Law* (Brussels and London: Office for Official Publications of the European Communities and Sweet & Maxwell, revised ed., 2006), p. 40.

[15] Note sur la competence de la Cour de Justice (Article 33 du projet de Traite), 22 December 1950.

coheres with that in Jean Monnet's memorandum, and it would not be surprising if Lagrange had been the authorial inspiration behind Monnet's document.

It is, however, surprising that it is difficult to find specific chapter and verse in subsequent jurisprudence that locates the Court's case law on general principles in this manner. In most cases nothing is said relating to textual provenance of general principles of law. On the rare occasions when the Court alludes to the issue, the reasoning is brief and ambivalent. Thus in *Lucchini* the Court appeared to accept the way in which the case was argued by the claimant, who distinguished between breach of a rule of law relating to the application of the Treaty to cover violation of formal decisions made pursuant to a Treaty article, and breach of general principles of law, in the instant case legitimate expectations.[16]

It might be contended, by way of contrast, that the concept of general principles of law could exist outside the confines of Article 263, and that the very nature of such principles, fashioned as they are from generally accepted normative precepts, could be said to support this. There are, however, very real difficulties with this view. The fact that a legal principle may owe its origin to normative precepts found in the more general legal order, national and international, does not thereby obviate the need to locate a Treaty foundation through which such principles can be applied within EU law. It is one thing to contend that breach of the Treaty or of any rule of law relating to its application should be read so as

[16] Case 1252/79, *SpA Acciaierie e Ferriere Lucchini* v. *Commission* [1980] ECR 3753.

to include general principles of law, it is another to argue that such principles can be applied independently of this or any other ground of review in Article 263. There is, moreover, the further difficulty that if general principles were conceptualized as subsisting outside the grounds of review in Article 263, then it is difficult to see how the other conditions for judicial review, such as the nature of the acts that can be challenged, the rules on standing and those on time limits, would be applicable to challenges cast in terms of general principles of law. It is, however, clear that claims for judicial review based on general principles are subject to such conditions.

(b) Grounds of review and general principles of law: the double equivocation and its resolution

The very fact that foundation for the judicial exercise of power can be located in what is now Article 19 TEU and Article 263 TFEU should not mask the creativity involved, more especially so given that the ECJ was not unduly forthcoming about the justificatory arguments for the flesh that it read onto the bare bones of Article 33 ECSC and Article 173 EEC. It should not, moreover, mask the fact that the story of the emergence of general principles of law is imperfectly understood. This story was characterized by a double equivocation.

There was uncertainty as to the meaning that the term 'general principles of law' should bear. Thus even accepting the evidence adumbrated above for the framers' intent that the wording of Article 33 ECSC and Article 173

EEC should cover general principles of law, this still left uncertainty as to whether this should mean something akin to the portmanteau of legal concepts now understood as falling within the phrase, or as something more modest and less far-reaching. The answer to this was not preordained, as attested to by the different meanings accorded to the phrase in the Court's early jurisprudence.

There was, in addition, uncertainty as to whether recognition of principles such as proportionality, legitimate expectations and the like should be regarded as truly 'general', in the sense of applicable to all areas of the Treaty. This was reflective of the duality inherent in the adjectival form 'general'. It connoted the idea that a principle was general in the sense that it embodied an important value that was applicable across legal orders, and also that it might be of generalized application within a particular legal order. The latter did not, however, follow a priori from the former. Thus even when the ECJ concluded that general principles of law did connote principles of the type currently regarded as falling within its remit, it was uncertain as to whether the principles thus recognized were truly applicable across the entirety of the Community legal order. This uncertainty was only resolved at the beginning of the 1970s in the manner explicated below.

(i) The equivocation manifest: ECSC case law

The ECSC case law makes interesting reading in this respect. The Franco-German political dominance of the initial six Member States was reflected in the legal domain by Advocates General Lagrange and Roemer. It was they who played the

S.N.U.P.A.T.,[19] where it held that there was a basic principle of law to the effect that a person must have access to documents on which the decision is based in order to be able to formulate an opinion on them. It finds expression once again in *Société des fonderies de Pont-à-Mousson*,[20] where the Court gave express recognition to the idea of general principles of law, in the instant case the principle of non-discrimination, albeit aided in this respect by the fact that this particular principle found expression in Article 4 ECSC.

There were, however, other cases where the concept of general principles of law was used in a manner more akin to that in public international law, to connote the idea that recourse could be had to generally accepted unwritten principles that were normatively significant, which could be used to fill gaps left by other norms, more especially where the latter could not reasonably be interpreted without resort to the former. That the concept should be used in this manner was unsurprising, given the Treaty foundation for the ECSC. It is exemplified by Advocate General Roemer's Opinion in *Mannesmann*.[21] The case concerned an 'invitation' by the High Authority that certain German undertakings, which were scrap consumers, should pay back equalization amounts that had been allegedly wrongly paid to them. The companies resisted, claiming that the High Authority had no legal basis

[19] Cases 42 and 49/59, *Société nouvelle des usines de Pontlieue – Aciéries du Temple (S.N.U.P.A.T.)* v. *High Authority* [1961] ECR Spec. Ed. 53.

[20] Case 14/59, *Société des fonderies de Pont-à-Mousson* v. *High Authority* [1959] ECR Spec. Ed. 215.

[21] Cases 4–13/59, *Mannesmann AG* v. *High Authority* [1960] ECR Spec. Ed. 113.

for the 'demand'. Advocate General Roemer was unmoved by this contention. He opined that an express entitlement was not indispensable in order to assert rights to repayments within the framework of a scrap equalization scheme, and that it sufficed to refer to general legal principles according to which the rights to repayment could subsist. He acknowledged the need to ensure that the High Authority remained within the limits of its assigned powers, but also counselled against an excessively strict method of interpretation, endorsing previous authority to the effect that the rules established by an international treaty or by a law implied the existence of the rules without which the former would be meaningless or incapable of reasonable and useful application.[22] Viewed from this perspective the obligation to repay equalization payments improperly received could be properly conceived as a general principle of law, since it was no more than the indispensable corollary of the right to receive equalization payments. This meaning of general principle of law is important, but less powerful than that set out in the previous paragraph, the difference being that the second meaning does not in itself create any new ground of judicial review. Thus in *Mannesmann* the obligation to repay sums unlawfully received does not create any new head of illegality,

[22] Case 8/55, *Federation Charbonnière de Belgique* v. *High Authority* [1954–6] ECR Spec. Ed. 292. See also Case 25/59, *Netherlands* v. *High Authority* [1960] ECR Spec. Ed. 355, where it was acknowledged that writers and case law were agreed in recognizing that the rules established by a treaty implied the principles without which the rules could not effectively or reasonably be applied.

although it does generate a second order right to repayment where illegality can be proven on some other ground.

There were yet other cases where the concept of general principles of law was used in a sense more akin to importing principles of interpretation commonly found in national legal systems. This is exemplified by *Erzbergbau AG*,[23] where Advocate General Lagrange made reference to general principles of law to capture the idea that a document could be interpreted in a particular manner, viz. that Sunday would not be counted as a day for certain delivery purposes. It finds expression once again in *Plaumann*,[24] where Advocate General Roemer used general principles of law to capture the need for a claimant to be aware of the principles governing civil liability for damages in national legal systems when determining the meaning of non-contractual liability for the EEC, and in *Lachmüller*,[25] where Advocate General Roemer once again used the concept of general principles to connote what Member States did in relation to the salient legal issue in their own legal systems.

(ii) The equivocation manifest: EEC case law, 1960s

The transition from the ECSC to the EEC was significant in many respects, but it did not initially signal any great shift in the way in which general principles of law were conceptualized by the ECJ. There was continuity with the

[23] Cases 3–18, 25–6/58, *Erzbergbau AG* v. *High Authority* [1960] ECR Spec. Ed. 173.

[24] Case 25/62, *Plaumann* v. *Commission* [1963] ECR Spec. Ed. 95.

[25] Cases 43, 45, 48/59, *Lachmüller* v. *Commission* [1960] ECR Spec. Ed. 463.

past, rather than any cognizable change. Thus the 1960s were characterized by reference to general principles of law, but little by way of detailed conceptualization and little done to locate the concept within the formal Treaty provisions of the EEC, either Article 164 or Article 173 EEC. The abiding impression when revisiting this case law is of a concept that is loosely anchored, with the Court unclear as to its boundaries or textual provenance. This sense is then reinforced through the seminal decisions at the beginning of the 1970s, which owe their significance to the breadth of their remit, as opposed to the depth of the Court's analytical conceptualization.

Thus the standard approach in the relatively few cases where the Court addressed general principles of law in the 1960s saw the ECJ accept the concept, but say little about its reach or textual foundation.[26] This is exemplified by *Pistoj*[27] and *Huber*,[28] where the ECJ judgments were framed in terms of infringement of rights of defence, breach of the *audi alteram partem* principle and violation of general principles of law. The precise relationship between these grounds was not spelt out, the ECJ declining to do so in part at least because the applicant lost on the facts, and in part

[26] See, e.g., Case 54/65, *Compagnie des forges de Châtillon, Commentry & Neuves-Maisons* v. *High Authority* [1966] ECR Spec. Ed. 185; Case 57/69, *ACNA SpA* v. *Commission* [1972] ECR 935; Case 19/70, *Almini* v. *Commission* [1971] ECR 632, AG Dutheillet de Lamothe; Case 10/69, *S.A. Portelange* v. *S.A. Smith Corona Marchant International* [1969] ECR 318, AG Roemer.

[27] Case 26/63, *Pistoj* v. *Commission* [1963] ECR Spec. Ed. 341.

[28] Case 78/63, *Huber* v. *Commission* [1964] ECR 367.

because there was, in any event, legal foundation for the rights of defence in particular provisions of the Staff Regulations, thereby obviating the need for more precise conceptual inquiry concerning general principles of law.

There is, however, an explanation for the judicial equivocation and uncertainty about the concept of general principles of law, which is easily overlooked. The rationale for the paucity of reference to the concept is explicable in part at least because the ECJ made relatively little use of the main general principles of law during this period, thereby obviating the need for analytical clarity as to the meaning of the overarching concept and its textual provenance. To put the same point in a different way, if the ECJ used the specific principles that constituted the category of general principles only sparingly, it thereby reduced the need or incentive for close attention to the intellectual foundations of the overarching concept.

This is apparent when consideration is given to the Court's jurisprudence on four important general principles: proportionality, legitimate expectations, fair hearings and equality. The figures make interesting reading in this respect. In the period between 1959 and 1970 prior to the seminal ruling in *Internationale Handelsgesellschaft*,[29] there was only a small handful of cases that dealt with proportionality as a control on Community action. The judgments were equivocal about the status of the concept within EEC law – more especially whether, if it existed, it was limited in application

[29] Case 11/70, *Internationale Handelsgesellschaft mbH* v. *Einfuhr-und Vorratsstelle für Getreide und Futtermittel* [1970] ECR 1125.

to particular Treaty articles.[30] There was but one case in which the ECJ made brief mention of legitimate expectations.[31] The case law on fair hearings developed primarily in the 1970s,[32] although the rights of the defence were litigated in the 1960s.[33] There were more cases on equality, but the numbers were still not large, there being less than twenty. The nature of these claims obviated the need for much weight to be placed on the overarching concept of general principles of law, given that more discrete foundations for the application of equality could be found. Thus some cases concerned equality in relation to the ECSC, and non-discrimination as embodied in Article 4 was central to the ECSC schema;[34] in other cases the equality argument was grounded in a particular Treaty provision concerning free movement,[35] or

[30] See, e.g., Case 73/69, *Firma H. Oehlmann & Co.* v. *Hauptzollamt Münster* [1970] ECR 467, [4]; Case 62/70, *Werner A. Bock* v. *Commission* [1971] ECR 897.

[31] Cases 9 and 12/60, *Société commerciale Antoine Vloeberghs SA* v. *High Authority* [1961] ECR Spec. Ed. 197.

[32] Case 17/74 *Transocean Marine Paint* v. *Commission* [1974] ECR 1063, at [15]; Case 85/76, *Hoffmann-La Roche* v. *Commission* [1979] ECR 461, at [9].

[33] See, e.g., Cases 56 and 58/64, *Établissements Consten S.à.R.L. and Grundig-Verkaufs-GmbH* v. *Commission* [1966] ECR Spec. Ed. 299; Case 35/67, *Van Eick* v. *Commission* [1968] ECR Spec. Ed. 329; Case 12/68, *X.* v. *Audit Board of the European Communities* [1969] ECR 109.

[34] See, e.g., Case 111/63, *Lemmerz-Werke GmbH* v. *High Authority* [1965] ECR Spec. Ed. 677; Case 37/64, *Mannesmann AG* v. *High Authority* [1965] ECR Spec. Ed. 725; Case 39/64, *Société des Aciéries du Temple* v. *High Authority* [1965] ECR Spec. Ed. 761.

[35] Case 15/69, *Württembergische Milchverwertung-Sudmilch-AG* v. *Salvatore Ugliola* [1969] ECR 363.

gender equality;[36] in yet other cases the discrete foundation was the obligation for equal treatment of Community staff.[37]

(iii) The equivocation resolved: Internationale Handelsgesellschaft and Ruckdeschel

It was in the 1970s that the real potential of general principles of law became apparent, and the judgments in *Internationale Handelsgesellschaft* and *Ruckdeschel* were seminal in this respect. While much has been written on the former case from the perspective of fundamental rights, its broader significance for the development of general principles of law and judicial review has not been fully understood, and this is equally true of the latter decision. Their centrality for EU administrative law and for EU law more generally cannot be underestimated. It resided in the ECJ's willingness in both cases to untether general principles from the confines of particular Treaty articles and to treat them as truly general in their application across the Community legal order. It was on this issue that the ECJ had equivocated hitherto.

The nature of the dispute in *Internationale Handelsgesellschaft* is well known.[38] It involved a challenge in the German courts to a deposit scheme made pursuant to the

[36] Case 80/70, *Defrenne* v. *Belgian State* [1971] ECR 445.

[37] Cases 55–76, 86, 87 and 95/71, *Marie-Josée Besnard* v. *Commission* [1972] ECR 543; Cases 63–75/70, *Fritz August Bode* v. *Commission* [1971] ECR 549.

[38] Case 11/70, *Internationale Handelsgesellschaft mbH* v. *Einfuhr-und Vorratsstelle für Getreide und Futtermittel* [1970] ECR 1125; Case 25/70, *Einfuhr-und Vorratsstelle für Getreide und Futtermittel* v. *Köster et Berodt & Co.* [1970] ECR 1161, at [22].

Common Agricultural Policy, in which the German court was asked to set aside an EEC measure concerning forfeiture of an export-licence deposit that was said to conflict with German constitutional rights and principles such as economic liberty and proportionality. The system of deposits was said to be contrary to certain structural principles of German constitutional law, which must be protected within the framework of Community law, with the result that the primacy of supranational law must yield before the principles of the German Basic Law. The obligation to import or export resulting from the issue of the licences, together with the deposit attaching thereto, was said to constitute an excessive intervention in the freedom of disposition in trade, as the objective of the regulations could have been attained by methods of intervention having less serious consequences.

The ECJ's response is equally well known – a blend of stick and carrot. It powerfully reaffirmed the supremacy of Community law over all national law, holding that recourse to national legal rules to judge the validity of measures adopted by the institutions of the Community would have an adverse effect on the uniformity and efficacy of Community law, with the consequence that the validity of a Community measure or its effect within a Member State could not be affected by allegations that it ran counter to either fundamental rights as formulated by the constitution of a Member State, or national constitutional principles. If the ECJ's judgment had stopped there it would likely have signalled a constitutional crisis, but the force of the 'stick' was softened by the 'carrot', whereby the Court affirmed in the very next paragraph of its judgment that fundamental rights formed 'an integral part of the general principles of law protected by the Court of Justice',[39] with the consequence that the ECJ would test whether the deposit system infringed such fundamental rights. The decision became central to the story concerning fundamental rights in the EEC, with the ECJ being forced to react to the threat of revolt from the national court by recognizing fundamental rights as part of Community law in a manner that it had hitherto hinted at, but not unequivocally affirmed in the manner that it did in the instant case.

It was, however, also of broader significance for the evolution of general principles of law within the Community legal order for the following reasons. The national challenge involved allegations that the deposit scheme violated not only fundamental rights in the form of economic liberty, but also proportionality, thereby forcing the Court to confront the latter as well as the former. The ECJ responded to the challenge by denying the capacity of the national legal system to assess an EEC norm for compliance with fundamental rights, but affirming that the ECJ would do so. This strategy might conceivably have been pursued on the basis that the ECJ, when undertaking its review of fundamental rights and proportionality, was merely engaged in the interpretation of a particular Treaty article.

This was indeed the advice proffered by Advocate General Dutheillet de Lamothe, who considered the possible legal sources of proportionality control within EEC law. Having rejected the argument that such control should exist

[39] Case 11/70, *Internationale Handelsgesellschaft mbH* [1970] ECR 1125, at [4].

ipso facto because it was demanded by German constitutional law, he then considered whether it should be legitimated as a general principle of Community law, or whether it should rather be said to flow from the wording of Articles 39 and 40 EEC. While he admitted that either might suffice in this regard, his preference was for the latter:

> I think that it is good judicial technique to apply unwritten law only in cases of obscurity, insufficiency or gaps in the written law and also that since Article 40 of the Treaty refers not to more or less defined aims of general interest but more precisely to the objectives listed in Article 39 it thereby ensures a more precise guarantee of the rights of individuals than the general principles of Community law. In sum, I think therefore that the problem which has been put to the Court in very wide and sometimes even in politico-philosophical terms may be reduced to a simpler question: 'Have the Community authorities, in instituting the disputed system of deposits, infringed Article 40 of the Treaty under which only measures which are required to attain the objectives of the common agricultural market set out in Article 39 may be issued.'[40]

The ECJ adopted much of the advocate general's thinking in terms of the supremacy of the Community legal order, but did not follow his lead in grounding fundamental rights and proportionality review solely in the interpretation of Articles 39 and 40 EEC. The ECJ, by way of contrast, located such

[40] Case 11/70, *Internationale Handelsgesellschaft mbH* [1970] ECR 1125, at 1147.

review squarely within general principles of law, and this encompassed both fundamental rights and proportionality.[41] This choice was clearly considered, given that the advocate general had expressly placed the respective options before the Court. Its choice meant that fundamental-rights and proportionality review, legitimated as instances of general principles of law, could be used in relation to any part of Community law, although the application thereof would perforce be affected by the terms of the particular Treaty provision at stake in a particular case. The judgment thereby imbued the concept of general principles of law with a vigour and impact that it had lacked hitherto, as attested to by the fact that it became the key precedent cited by later cases that developed fundamental-rights and proportionality review.[42]

The ruling in *Ruckdeschel* was less well-known than that in *Internationale Handelsgesellschaft*, but it was nonetheless central to the more robust approach to general principles as a ground of review in the 1970s.[43] The case concerned discrimination in the treatment of *quellmehl* and starch, whereby a production refund was given for maize used in the production of the latter, but not the former. It was

[41] Case 11/70, *Internationale Handelsgesellschaft mbH* [1970] ECR 1125, at [4], [14].

[42] See, e.g., Case 149/77, *Defrenne* v. *Société anonyme belge de navigation aérienne Sabena* [1978] ECR 1365; Case 136/79, *National Panasonic* v. *Commission* [1980] ECR 2035; Case 4/73, *Nold* v. *Commission* [1974] ECR 492.

[43] Cases 117/76 and 16/77, *Ruckdeschel* v. *Hauptzollamt Hamburg-St. Annen* [1977] ECR 1753, at [7]; Case 8/78, *Milac GmbH* v. *Hauptzollamt Freiburg* [1978] ECR 1721, at [18].

pre-eminent role in legal discourse in the early years of the ECSC and EEC. The reality is nonetheless that the concept of general principles of law was interpreted in a plethora of ways in the early ECSC case law, and the linkage with the textual wording of Article 33 ECSC was rarely, if ever, formally made.

Thus there were some cases where the concept of general principles was used in what became its modern paradigm, as a vehicle for the application of more specific principles of good governance such as equality, which could then be used as the ground for seeking judicial review pursuant to Article 33. This is exemplified by Advocate General Lagrange's Opinion in *Groupement des hauts fourneaux et aciéries belges*,[17] where he stated that the principle of equality relied on by the applicants constituted a general principle of law 'of which the Court can and must take account in appropriate cases', drawing on analogies with French and German Law, but furnishing no explicit linkage with the textual foundation for the Court's power in Article 33. Advocate General Roemer's Opinion in *Chambre syndicale de la sidérurgie française* is in the same vein.[18] There is express recognition of general principles of law as a ground of review, capturing in the instant case the need for reasoned decisions and legal certainty, but little by way of connection with the wording of Article 33. This approach was echoed by the Court in

[17] Cases 8–13/57, *Groupement des hauts fourneaux et aciéries belges* v. *High Authority* [1958] ECR Spec. Ed. 265, AG Lagrange.

[18] Cases 3 and 4/64, *Chambre syndicale de la sidérurgie française* v. *High Authority* [1965] ECR Spec. Ed. 441, at 460–1, AG Roemer.

argued that this was contrary to the prohibition on discrimination in Article 40(3) EEC, which provided that the common organization of agricultural markets should exclude any discrimination between producers or consumers within the Community.

The Court noted that while this wording clearly prohibited discrimination between producers of the same product, it did not refer in such clear terms to the relationship between different industrial or trade sectors in the sphere of processed agricultural products. It nonetheless held that the prohibition of discrimination laid down in Article 40(3) EEC was 'merely a specific enunciation of the general principle of equality which is one of the fundamental principles of Community law', so as to demand that similar situations should not be treated differently unless the differentiation was objectively justified.

The Court's judgment evinced a willingness to read particular Treaty references as indicative of a more general principle of equal treatment and non-discrimination that underpinned the legal order. It made fertile use of this juridical technique of generalization from mention in a particular instance, interpreting such specific provisions against the aims and imperatives of the Treaty in order thereby to provide the justification for generalized principles of non-discrimination, proportionality and the like.

The decisions in *Internationale Handelsgesellschaft* and *Ruckdeschel* removed the equivocation about the reach of general principles. The presumption henceforth was that such principles could be applicable across the range of subject matter covered by the constituent treaties. This presumption might be rebutted if it could be shown that there was some reason why a general principle as normally formulated should not be applicable in a particular area, such as where the wording of a Treaty article evinced a clear intent that a narrower, more specific conception of the principle was applicable in that sphere. The application of a general principle could, moreover, be shaped by the substantive area to which it was applied. This did not, however, alter the fact that the style of the Court judgments from the 1970s onwards now took on the modern format of principles that were applicable across the Community legal order.

The significance of these decisions was also apparent from consideration of the number of cases in which particular principles were pleaded. The contrast with the previous decade was marked. There were circa fifty cases in which proportionality, now readily acknowledged as a free-standing principle of Community law, was pleaded.[44] Legitimate-expectations jurisprudence took off during this decade, with upwards of thirty-five decisions in which it was a central part of the cause of action.[45] The 1970s also witnessed the

[44] See, e.g., Case 114/76, *Bela-Mühle Josef Bergmann KG* v. *Grows-Farm GmbH & CO. KG* [1977] ECR 1211; Case 179/78, *Procureur de la République* v. *Michelangelo Rivoira* [1979] ECR 1147; Case 138/79, *SA Roquette Frères* v. *Council* [1980] ECR 3333; Case 139/79, *Maizena GmbH* v. *Council* [1980] ECR 3393; Case 52/79, *Procureur du Roi* v. *Marc J.V.C. Debauve* [1980] ECR 833; Cases 154, 205, 206, 226 to 228, 263 and 264/78, 39, 31, 83 and 85/79, *Valsabbia* v. *Commission* [1980] ECR 911.

[45] See, e.g., Case 74/74, *Comptoir national technique agricole (CNTA) SA* v. *Commission* [1975] ECR 533; Case 2/75, *Einfuhr-und Vorratsstelle für Getreide und Futtermittel* v. *C. Mackprang* [1975] ECR 607; Case 97/76, *Merkur Außenhandel GmbH & Co. KG* v. *Commission* [1977] ECR 1063;

flowering of the case law concerning the right to be heard and rights of the defence, with circa thirty cases being decided on this ground.[46] The case law on discrimination and equality directed against both national and Community action expanded considerably during this period, with circa 250 cases being litigated on this ground, some of which were decided pursuant to discrimination as embodied in a particular Treaty article, others of which were framed in terms of discrimination as a general principle of Community law.[47]

General principles of law continued to develop over the subsequent decades, as attested to by a brief glance at the figures for the first decade of the new millennium, in which

Case 84/78, *Tomadini Snc* v. *Amministrazione delle finanze dello Stato* [1979] ECR 1801; Case 99/78, *Decker KG* v. *Hauptzollamt Landau* [1979] ECR 101; Case 1252/79, *SpA Acciaierie e Ferriere Lucchini* v. *Commission* [1980] ECR 3753; Case 127/80, *Grogan* v. *Commission* [1982] ECR 869.

[46] See, e.g., Case 54/69, *SA française des matières colorantes (Francolor)* v. *Commission* [1972] ECR 851; Case 48/69, *Imperial Chemical Industries Ltd* v. *Commission* [1972] ECR 619; Case 17/74, *Transocean Marine Paint* v. *Commission* [1974] ECR 1063, at [15]; Case 85/76, *Hoffmann-La Roche* v. *Commission* [1979] ECR 461, at [9]; Case 136/79, *National Panasonic* v. *Commission* [1980] ECR 2035; Case 155/79, *AM & S Europe Limited* v. *Commission* [1982] ECR 1575.

[47] See, e.g., Case 152/73, *Sotgiu* v. *Deutsche Bundespost* [1974] ECR 153; Case 43/75, *Defrenne* v. *Société anonyme belge de navigation aérienne Sabena* [1976] ECR 455; Case 127/75, *Bobie Getränkevertrieb GmbH* v. *Hauptzollamt Aachen-Nord* [1976] ECR 1079; Case 116/76, *Granaria BV* v. *Hoofdproduktschap voor Akkerbouwprodukten* [1977] ECR 1247; Case 120/78, *Rewe-Zentral AG* v. *Bundesmonopolverwaltung für Branntwein* [1979] ECR 649; Case 55/79, *Commission* v. *Ireland* [1980] ECR 481; Case 140/79, *Chemial Farmaceutici SpA* v. *DAF SpA* [1981] ECR 1; Case 168/78, *Commission* v. *France* [1980] ECR 347.

proportionality featured in over 1,000 actions, legitimate expectations in nearly 600, and the right to be heard/rights of the defence in roughly 350 cases, while discrimination and equality claims numbered in excess of 1,100.

(iv) General principles and interpretive creativity: selectivity and choice

The discussion concerning general principles and their formal foundation within EU law would be incomplete without elaboration of the Court's interpretive creativity. This was manifest in relation both to the sources from which the Court drew such principles, and to its choice as to whether to elevate a particular precept into a general principle of EU law. These will be considered in turn.

In terms of sources, the ECJ and the Court of First Instance (CFI) drew primarily upon administrative law doctrine from the Member States. To be sure, the structure of what is now Article 263(2) bore a French imprint, in terms of the four generic categories of review. This nonetheless left the ECJ with considerable interpretive discretion when developing general principles of law. It did not regard itself as bound to French doctrine, nor did it systematically trawl through the legal systems of each Member State in order to find common principles. The approach was, rather, to consider principles in the major national legal systems, to use those that were felt to be best developed and to fashion them to suit the EU's needs. Thus as Advocate General Lagrange stated, the ECJ did not seek arithmetical common denominators between the national approaches to a particular problem, but rather chose from 'each of the Member States those solutions which, having regard to the objects of the Treaty, appear to be the best or, if one may use the expression, the most progressive'.[48] German law was most influential in this regard. It was German jurisprudence on proportionality and legitimate expectations that was of principal significance for the development of EU law in these areas.

In terms of interpretive choice as to whether to elevate a norm into a general principle of law, the EU courts have considerable discretion, as exemplified by the reasoning that led to the precautionary principle being accepted as a general principle of law. The judicial building blocks for the new general principle were drawn in part from Treaty articles and in part from prior case law, and it was the CFI in *Pfizer*[49] and *Artegodan*[50] that crafted the seminal judgments in this respect.

The starting point in terms of Treaty foundations was the express mention of the precautionary principle in what is now Article 191(2) TFEU concerning environmental policy. A single mention in relation to a specific area of Union action is scarcely sufficient to ground a new general principle. The CFI therefore looked further for Treaty legitimation. It placed reliance on Article 11 TFEU, which stipulates that environmental protection must be integrated into the definition and implementation of other EU policies. Given this injunction,

[48] Case 14/61, *Hoogovens* v. *High Authority* [1962] ECR 253, at 283–4, AG Lagrange.

[49] Case T-13/99, *Pfizer Animal Health SA* v. *Council* [2002] ECR II-3305, at [113]–[115].

[50] Cases T-74, 76, 83–5, 132, 137 and 141/00, *Artegodan GmbH* v. *Commission* [2002] ECR II-4945, at [181]–[186].

it must follow, said the CFI, that the precautionary principle being a part of environmental protection should also be a factor in other EU policies.[51]

This conclusion was reinforced through interpretation of other, more specific, Treaty articles. Thus the CFI held in *Artegodan*[52] that Article 191 provided that an objective of environmental protection was public health; that Article 168(1) TFEU stated that a high level of human health protection should be secured in the definition and implementation of all EU policies; that a similar injunction to ensure a high level of consumer protection and to integrate such protection into the definition and implementation of other Union policies was to be found in Articles 12 and 169 TFEU; and that the precautionary principle was to be applied in these areas in order to ensure this requisite level of protection.

The CFI buttressed the argument from the Treaty by drawing on prior case law. It relied on the *BSE*[53] and *NFU*[54] decisions for the proposition that the precautionary principle applies where the EU takes measures in the context of the CAP in order to safeguard health.[55] The CFI also followed

[51] Case T-13/99, *Pfizer* [2002] ECR II-3305, at [114]; Cases T-74, 76, 83–5, 132, 137 and 141/00, *Artegodan* [2002] ECR II-4945, at [183].

[52] Cases T-74, 76, 83–5, 132, 137 and 141/00, *Artegodan* [2002] ECR II-4945, at [183].

[53] Case C-180/96, *UK* v. *Commission* [1998] ECR I-2265.

[54] Case C-157/96, *The Queen* v. *Ministry of Agriculture, Fisheries and Food, Commissioners of Customs & Excise, ex p National Farmers' Union* [1998] ECR I-2211, at [62]–[64].

[55] Case T-13/99, *Pfizer* [2002] ECR II-3305, at [114].

well-established techniques of reasoning by analogy, alluding to other cases where the existence of the precautionary principle 'has in essence and at the very least implicitly been recognized by the Court of Justice'.[56] The Treaty articles, combined with prior case law, provided the foundations for the recognition of a new general principle of EU law. The CFI in *Artegodan* expressed its conclusion in the following terms:

> It follows that the precautionary principle can be defined as a general principle of Community law requiring the competent authorities to take appropriate measures to prevent specific potential risks to public health, safety and the environment, by giving precedence to the requirements related to the protection of those interests over economic interests. Since the Community institutions are responsible, in all their spheres of activity, for the protection of public health, safety and the environment, the precautionary principle can be regarded as an autonomous principle stemming from the abovementioned Treaty provisions.[57]

[56] Case T-13/99, *Pfizer* [2002] ECR II-3305, at [115].

[57] Cases T-74, 76, 83–5, 132, 137 and 141/00, *Artegodan* [2002] ECR II-4945, at [184]; Case T-147/00, *Les Laboratoires Servier* v. *Commission* [2003] ECR II-85, at [52]; Case C-504/04, *Agrarproduktion Staebelow GmbH* v. *Landrat des Landkreises Bad Doberan* [2006] ECR I-679, at [38]–[39]; Case 334/07, *Denka International BV* v. *Commission* [2009] ECR II-4205, at [116]; Case T-326/07, *Cheminova A/S* v. *Commission* [2009] ECR II-2685, at [165]–[166]; Case C-333/08, *Commission* v. *France* [2010] ECR I-757, at [92]; Case C-77/09, *Gowan Comércio Internacional e Serviços Lda* v. *Ministero della Salute* [2010] ECR I-13533, at [73]–[75].

(v) General principles of law: the hierarchy of norms

The importance of general principles of law in the world after *Internationale Handelsgesellschaft* and *Ruckdeschel* was further enhanced by their status in the hierarchy of norms. In UK law, the principles of judicial review can be used to invalidate secondary norms and to interpret primary legislation, but they cannot be used to invalidate the latter. In EU law the position is different. The general principles of law sit below the Treaties, but above all else. They can therefore be used to interpret and invalidate EU legislative acts, delegated acts and implementing acts.[58] This status attaches to all general principles of law, not merely to that part dealing with fundamental rights. Thus if a claimant can show that an EU legislative act is contrary to, for example, the principle of legitimate expectations or the precautionary principle, and that it cannot be interpreted to be in conformity with such precepts, then it will be declared void, even if the case has nothing to do with fundamental rights.[59]

The formal rationale for the status accorded to general principles within the hierarchy of norms is disarmingly simple, this being that it flows from the very structure of Article 33 ECSC and Article 173 EEC, now carried over to Article 263 TFEU. Thus once the ECJ was willing to recognize

[58] Arts. 288–91 TFEU.

[59] Where the clash is between a general principle of law and national law, the ECJ does not declare the offending national norm void, but finds it inconsistent with EU law, with the result that national institutions, including courts, have an obligation to remove the inconsistency pursuant to the principle of EU supremacy.

general principles of law within the schema of judicial review, with the magic phrase 'any rule of law relating to their application' being the Treaty location, it was natural to place them above legislative, delegated and implementing acts in the hierarchy of norms, since Article 263(1) TFEU and its predecessors were expressly predicated on such acts being susceptible to judicial review.

The formal status accorded to general principles of law gave the ECJ a very powerful tool to shape the emerging Community legal and political order, since it is the ultimate decider as to whether a regulation, directive or decision is consonant with the ever-expanding list of general principles of EU law. The Commission, the Council and the European Parliament might respond to invalidation of such an act by redrafting it to remove the legal infirmity. This does not alter the fact that the judicial view as to what is demanded by general principles of law will trump any such estimation made by the Community political organs, irrespective of whether the case is concerned with fundamental rights.

It is doubtful whether the Treaty framers were truly cognizant of the above, or of its full implications for the emergent Community, and this is so notwithstanding the evidence presented above concerning the intent of those who framed the ECSC Treaty. It is one thing to provide for invalidation of regulations, directives and decisions on the ground that they are inconsistent with an article of the primary Treaty itself, or because there was no competence to enact the contested norm. It is quite another to provide for such invalidation for non-compliance with very open-textured general principles of the law, the legal existence and application of which are determined by the ECJ.

It might be argued by way of response that the legislative process at the inception of the EEC was imperfectly democratic to say the least. Decision making was dominated by the Commission and Council, and thus the idea that judicial review in accord with general principles of law should sit 'above' norms made in this manner could be accepted with relative equanimity. The structural relationship between Article 263(1) and (2) TFEU has, however, remained unchanged in the subsequent years, notwithstanding the significant development and democratization of the EU legislative process. It could be argued further that the framers of the Lisbon Treaty were fully mindful of review for compliance with general principles of law, which had existed for over forty years, and were content that the new Lisbon category of legislative act should be subject to this same regime. There is force in this view. There is nonetheless scant, if any, evidence from the deliberations that led to the Constitutional Treaty to suggest that thought was given to this issue. There was discussion of the hierarchy of norms, which led to the Lisbon distinctions between legislative, delegated and implementing acts. There is, however, no indication of considered reflection on the status of general principles of law within the hierarchy of norms in a regime where the passage of legislative acts has some real democratic legitimacy.[60]

[60] This point is equally applicable to the post-Maastricht era, given that the co-decision procedure, the precursor to the ordinary legislative procedure, had democratic legitimacy in the areas to which it applied.

It might also be contended that the status of general principles of law was explicable by way of domestic analogy with French law, in which the *principes généraux du droit* sit above legislation but below the Constitution. We have seen that French juristic thought was indeed prominent in the framing of Article 33 ECSC. This analogy is nonetheless imperfect, since the Conseil d'état could not invalidate primary legislation, and the Conseil constitutionnel had not yet undergone its (re)birth. The renaissance of the Conseil constitutionnel in the 1970s facilitated challenge to primary legislation, but only *ex ante*, and there was no possibility for challenge *ex post* prior to the recent constitutional reforms in France.[61]

Whatsoever one's view on the preceding issue, judicial possession is often nine-tenths of legal reality. The Court's emerging jurisprudence ensured that general principles of law were a central part of judicial review and enjoyed a formal status below the Treaties and above all else. The rest is, as they say, history. If justification for this status is sought over and beyond the source-based legitimation flowing from the wording of Article 263 TFEU, then it must ultimately rest on normative argumentation to the effect that it is legitimate for courts to create general principles of law that can lead to legislative invalidation in the above manner.

[61] M. Rogoff, 'Fifty Years of Constitutional Evolution in France: The 2008 Amendments and Beyond' (2011) 6 *Jus Politicum*, at http://juspoliticum.com/Fifty-years-of-constitutional,391.html.

(c) *Grounds of review: judicial review of law, fact and discretion*

General principles of law are best known among the grounds of judicial review. They are also the most high-profile for the reasons considered above. They do not, however, exhaust the grounds of judicial review in EU law. There are very many cases decided via direct review pursuant to Article 263 TFEU, or indirect review via Article 267 TFEU, which do not entail general principles of law. Some may be decided on another ground of review, such as lack of competence, breach of an essential procedural requirement or misuse of power. Many others are decided as claims for violation of a rule of law relating to application of the Treaty, where the allegation relates to non-compliance with a regulation, directive or decision. Yet other cases are concerned with breach of the Treaty itself, or a norm made pursuant thereto, where the allegation is that there was some error of fact, law or discretion. Claims of this kind commonly raise issues concerning the intensity of judicial review, which will be examined in detail in the next chapter. The salient point for present purposes is that application of these key features of judicial review entails interpretive choice by the EU courts, just as much as is the case when they decide on the meaning and application of general principles of law.

This can be briefly exemplified by consideration of the early case law involving review of economic fact and discretion. The issue was addressed directly by Article 33 ECSC, which, after listing the grounds of review, qualified the Court's power by providing that

> the Court may not, however, examine the evaluation of the situation, resulting from economic facts or circumstances, in the light of which the High Authority took its decisions or made its recommendations, save where the High Authority is alleged to have misused its powers or to have manifestly failed to observe the provisions of this Treaty or any rule of law relating to its application.

The ECJ accepted this limitation and held that the word 'manifest' presupposed that 'the failure to observe provisions of the Treaty was of such an extent that it appeared to derive from an obvious error in the assessment, in the light of the provisions of the Treaty, of the situation in respect of which the decision was taken'.[62]

Article 173 EEC contained no analogous express limit on judicial review, but the ECJ in its early case law nonetheless applied judicial review sparingly, mindful of the complex factual and discretionary determinations made by the Commission. This is exemplified by *Westzucker*,[63] which was oft-quoted in later cases. The applicant challenged a Commission regulation that set the denaturing premium for sugar at zero.[64] The regulation provided that intervention agencies 'may' grant denaturing premiums, and also contained criteria indicating how the primary discretion should be exercised. These criteria were laid down by the Council

[62] Cases 129/95, 2 and 97/96, *Neue Maxhütte Stahlwerke GmbH and Lech-Stahlwerke GmbH* v. *Commission* [1999] ECR II-17.

[63] Case 57/72, *Westzucker GmbH* v. *Einfuhr-und Vorratsstelle für Zucker* [1973] ECR 321.

[64] Council Regulation 1009/67EEC of 18 December 1967 on the common organization of the market in sugar [1967] OJ L308/1.

when enacting further rules for the application of the denaturing scheme, and the Commission took these into account when passing the regulation subject to challenge. The criteria were, however, broad and open-textured, including matters such as the level of intervention prices, the foreseeable market prices for animal feeding stuffs that would compete with denatured sugar, the costs of denaturing, the nutritional value of competing animal feeding stuffs and the whole of the sugar surplus available for denaturing in the Community. The applicant's challenge was to the way in which the Commission had exercised this discretion by setting the denaturing premium at zero.

The ECJ was clear that the Commission's significant freedom of evaluation meant that it was not for the courts to substitute their judgement for that of the Commission. Judicial review was limited to deciding whether there was a patent error or misuse of power.[65] This light-touch review was itself applied sparingly. The ECJ devoted but one paragraph to the issue,[66] stating that the applicant's allegations revealed no indication of such an error or misuse of power. The applicant had argued that the sugar market was not being reorganized at the relevant time and that there was a continuing surplus of sugar requiring the maintenance of the denaturing premiums. The ECJ accepted that the existence of a surplus had been proven, but held that that this did not affect the Commission's freedom of evaluation to decide how best to eliminate it. The patent-error test was therefore applied with a light touch.

[65] Case 57/72, *Westzucker* [1973] ECR 321, at [14].
[66] Case 57/72, *Westzucker* [1973] ECR 321, at [15].

3 Substantive foundations

The discussion thus far has focused on the formal foundations of EU administrative law, their location in the Treaty and the way in which the ECJ crafted the precepts of judicial review for the emergent Community. The analysis now shifts to the substantive foundations of EU administrative law.

(a) The rule of law and the political order

The substantive foundations were at the most fundamental level grounded in the rule of law. The Member State legal systems have precepts of administrative law concerning procedural and substantive review. The details vary between legal systems, but there is, not surprisingly, significant overlap, and this is so irrespective of whether the same term or label is used. It is common for the development of these national precepts to be justified by recourse to the rule of law, which is a concept with diverse meanings, both formal and substantive.[67] The idea that administration should be procedurally and substantively accountable before the courts has, however, been central to the rule of law. It was therefore unsurprising that ECJ judges should approach their task with such national traditions in mind and feel the imperative that EEC decision making should be subject to analogous constraints.

The jurisprudence on general principles informed by the background precept of the rule of law was well developed

[67] P. Craig, 'Formal and Substantive Conceptions of the Rule of Law: An Analytical Framework' [1997] *Public Law* 467.

by the time of the Treaty of Amsterdam in 1997. The amendment of the TEU to provide express recognition that the EU was founded, inter alia, on the rule of law was nonetheless supportive of the judicial strategy,[68] and now finds expression in Article 2 TEU. The Commission more recently affirmed that the EU conception of the rule of law was both formal and substantive.[69]

The way in which this vision was conceptualized and realized will be considered in the next section. Before doing so it is, however, necessary to set this development of the rule of law against the political order as it existed at the outset of the Rome Treaty and as it unfolded for the next thirty years. This is necessary to understand the nature of the decisions subject to judicial review and the relationship between legal controls and political controls, both of which are central to the reality of administrative law.

It is therefore important to appreciate the disposition of power in the original Rome Treaty. The Assembly was accorded limited power, and its only role in the legislative process was a right to be consulted where a particular Treaty article so specified. The principal institutional players were the Council and the Commission, but the Rome Treaty placed the Commission in the driving seat in the development of Community policy. The Commission had the right of legislative initiative; it could alter a measure before the Council acted; its measures could only be amended by unanimity in

[68] Art. F TEU.

[69] A New EU Framework to Strengthen the Rule of Law, COM(2014) 158 final, p. 5.

the Council;[70] it devised the overall legislative agenda; and it had a plethora of other executive, administrative and judicial functions. The message was that while the Council had to consent to proposed legislation, it was not easy for it to alter the Commission's proposal. The Commission might therefore have become something akin to a 'government' for the emerging Community.[71] The Commission's power was, however, constrained in various ways in the early years of the Community.

It was in part the result of tensions between an intergovernmental view of the Community, championed initially by President de Gaulle of France, but not necessarily shared by other Member States, and a more supranational perspective espoused initially by Walter Hallstein, the Commission president. De Gaulle objected to the 'federalist logic' of certain Commission proposals,[72] and, after a failure to reach a compromise in the Council, France refused to attend further Council meetings and adopted what became known as the 'emptychair' policy, which was resolved after seven months through the Luxembourg Accords, which were essentially an agreement to disagree over voting methods in the Council.[73]

[70] Art. 250(1) EC.

[71] K. Neunreither, 'Transformation of a Political Role: Reconsidering the Case of the Commission of the European Communities' (1971–2) 10 *Journal of Common Market Studies* 233.

[72] J. Pinder, *The Building of the European Union* (Oxford: Oxford University Press, 3rd ed., 1998), p. 12.

[73] The French asserted that even in cases governed by majority decision making, discussion should continue until unanimity was reached

The Council's power was further enhanced by institutional developments, more particularly the Committee of Permanent Representatives, comitology and the European Council. The Committee of Permanent Representatives (Coreper), is staffed by senior national officials. It cannot take substantive decisions in its own right,[74] but nonetheless evolved 'into a veritable decision-making factory',[75] considering draft legislative proposals from the Commission, and setting the agenda for Council meetings,[76] these functions being especially significant given that Council members were commonly full-time national politicians, who attended Council meetings for the scheduled time, normally one day, and then returned home. Coreper and the working groups that fed into it were therefore necessary if the Council was to take an informed view of the merits of Commission proposals and have considered input into the making of primary regulations and directives.

It also became apparent that the Council sought influence over secondary norms and created an institutional

whenever important national interests were at stake, but the other Member States declared that in such circumstances the Council would 'endeavour, within a reasonable time, to reach solutions which can be adopted by all'. Bull EC 3–1966, p. 9.

[74] Case C-25/94, *Commission* v. *Council* [1996] ECR I-1469.

[75] J. Lewis, 'National Interests: Coreper', in J. Peterson and M. Shackleton (eds.), *The Institutions of the European Union* (Oxford: Oxford University Press, 2nd ed., 2006), Ch. 14.

[76] J. Lewis, 'The Methods of Community in EU Decision-Making and Administrative Rivalry in the Council's Infrastructure' (2000) 7 *Journal of European Public Policy* 261; D. Bostock, 'Coreper Revisited' (2002) 40 *Journal of Common Market Studies* 215.

mechanism to facilitate this. It is common in nation states for primary legislation to be complemented by secondary norms, which flesh out principles contained in the enabling statute. The secondary norms may address issues of principle or political choice that are just as controversial as those dealt with in the primary legislation. This is especially so in the EU, which has been characterized as a regulatory state,[77] where secondary regulations will often deal with matters of principle or political contestation. This serves to explain the birth of the committee system known as comitology.[78] While the disposition of primary legislative power in the Rome Treaty was relatively clear, with the Commission proposing and the Council then voting, it was more ambiguous in relation to the passage of secondary norms. The legal reality was that the Rome Treaty provided little by way of definitive guidance on the making of secondary norms, or the conditions that could be attached to this process. The political reality was that Member States were unwilling to give the Commission a blank cheque over secondary implementing rules, since power

[77] G. Majone, 'The Rise of the Regulatory State in Europe' (1994) 17 *West European Politics* 77; G. Majone, *Regulating Europe* (London: Routledge, 1996); G. Majone, 'Europe's "Democratic Deficit": The Question of Standards' (1998) 4 *European Law Journal* 5.

[78] C. Joerges and E. Vos (eds.), *EU Committees: Social Regulation, Law and Politics* (Oxford: Hart, 1999); E. Vos, *Institutional Frameworks of Community Health and Safety Legislation: Committees, Agencies and Private Bodies* (Oxford: Hart, 1999); M. Andenas and A. Turk (eds.), *Delegated Legislation and the Role of Committees in the EC* (Alphen aan den Rijn: Kluwer Law International, 2000); C. Bergstrom, *Comitology, Delegation of Powers in the European Union and the Committee System* (Oxford: Oxford University Press, 2005).

once delegated without encumbrance generated legally binding rules without the option for further Council oversight. The net result was the creation of the comitology system, whereby national technocratic representatives were involved with the Commission in the deliberations that led to secondary regulations, with the possibility of recourse to the Council if, for example, the Committee voted against the draft. While some see comitology in principal/agent terms,[79] others contend that it is best viewed as a form of deliberative supranationalism.[80] It is nonetheless clear that comitology became an established feature of the political landscape in all areas regulated by the EEC.

Member State influence over decision making was also enhanced by the emergence of the European Council as a political actor.[81] The Rome Treaty gave no institutional role to the heads of state, but meetings between them were common from the early 1960s. The decision to institutionalize such meetings was taken in 1974 at the Paris summit. The conclusion from the summit stated that such meetings would occur three times per year, normally outside the confines of the Council, but where necessary within the Council. These meetings continued to be held during the 1970s and 1980s,

[79] M. Pollack, *The Engines of Integration, Delegation, Agency and Agenda Setting in the EU* (Oxford: Oxford University Press, 2003).

[80] C. Joerges and J. Neyer, 'From Intergovernmental Bargaining to Deliberative Political Processes: The Constitutionalization of Comitology' (1997) 3 *European Law Journal* 273.

[81] S. Bulmer and W. Wessels, *The European Council* (London: Macmillan, 1987); F. Hayes-Renshaw and H. Wallace, *The Council of Ministers* (London: Palgrave, 2nd ed., 2006), Ch. 6.

even though there was no formal remit until the Single European Act 1986. It provided an institutionalized forum for the expression of Member State views at the highest level, which then shaped subsequent Community policy, despite the fact that European Council conclusions were not formally binding. It thus allowed political leaders input into the overall Community agenda, operated as a forum for a Community response to external problems, and facilitated resolution of disagreements between Member States that could not be resolved through ordinary Council mechanisms.

The political tableau depicted above prevailed for almost thirty years between the Rome Treaty and the Single European Act 1986. It constituted the political backdrop against which judicial review was crafted by the ECJ. The Court was fully aware of the political order, and cognizant also of the way in which it functioned in practice, in broad terms at least. It was mindful of the fact that power was effectively divided, such that decision making was captured by the aphorism 'the Commission proposes, the Council disposes', with the Assembly, even after direct elections had been introduced, having scant role in the process, this largely being confined to the right to be consulted where a particular Treaty article so specified. The application of judicial doctrine was affected by the practical operation of this decision-making schema.

It had a marked impact on direct effect, still the single most important judicial creation by the ECJ. The Rome Treaty was structured so as to lay down the principles governing core concepts such as free movement, with the express stipulation that regulations and directives should be enacted to make these principles a reality. The passage of legislative initiatives became increasingly difficult during the 1970s and early part of the 1980s – what has been characterized as the 'dark ages' for the Community.[82] The Council rejected social measures, such as directives on co-determination and worker consultation, and many others were stalled, awaiting a Council decision. There was growing concern that the Community's objectives were not being fulfilled. These difficulties led to what Middlemas termed a 'condition of immobility'.[83] Attainment of Community objectives through the normal political process was therefore difficult, and in this sense 'decisional supranationalism' was at a low ebb during this period. This led, as Joseph Weiler argued,[84] to the growing significance of 'normative supranationalism', whereby the ECJ, through doctrines of direct effect and supremacy, ensured the continued development of Community law, notwithstanding the difficulties of securing legislation through the political process. The ECJ made clear that it was willing to deploy direct effect to enforce important Treaty provisions, notwithstanding the fact that

[82] J. Caporaso and J. Keeler, 'The European Union and Regional Integration Theory', in C. Rhodes and S. Mazey (eds.), *The State of the European Union: Building a European Polity?* (London: Longman, 1995), p. 37.

[83] K. Middlemas, *Orchestrating Europe, The Informal Politics of the European Union 1973–1995* (London: Fontana, 1995), p. 90.

[84] J.H.H. Weiler, 'The Community System: The Dual Character of Supranationalism' (1981) 1 *Yearbook of European Law* 267; J.H.H. Weiler, 'The Transformation of Europe' (1991) 100 *Yale Law Journal* 2403, at 2412–31; P. Craig, 'Once upon a Time in the West: Direct Effect and the Federalization of EEC Law' (1992) 12 *Oxford Journal of Legal Studies* 453.

implementing legislation had not been enacted because of difficulties in the political process.[85] Normative supranationalism also supplemented decisional supranationalism by shaping the very nature of the regulatory process within the Community, as exemplified by *Cassis de Dijon*.[86]

The practical operation of the Community decision-making schema also had a marked impact on judicial review. The need to make the imperative of judicial review effective, as mandated by Article 173 EEC, was given added force by the political concentration of power in the Commission and the Council. It had become readily apparent by the 1970s that the EEC was enacting legislation as judged in substantive terms, even if it did not have that nomenclature, and that it was doing so largely without input or imprimatur from the Assembly. It was equally apparent that the parent regulations and directives would commonly address issues of social and political, as well as economic, choice. The legislative choices would themselves be based on Commission proposals, which could be predicated on contestable interpretation of vaguely worded Treaty articles.

There was a perceived need for some form of legal counterweight in terms of judicial review, through which the procedural and substantive legality of Community regulations, directives and decisions could be rendered accountable.

[85] Case 33/74, *Van Binsbergen* v. *Bestuur van de Bedrijfsvereniging voor de Metaalnijverheid* [1974] ECR 1299; Case 2/74, *Reyners* v. *Belgian State* [1974] ECR 631; Case 43/75, *Defrenne* v. *Société anonyme belge de navigation aérienne* [1976] ECR 455.

[86] Case 120/78, *Rewe-Zentrale AG* v. *Bundesmonopolverwaltung für Branntwein* [1979] ECR 649.

This review also enabled the Court to check the meaning given to Treaty articles and thereby help shape the developing Community, more especially given that there were often rival interpretations not only between the Member States and Community institutions, but also between the Community institutions themselves, as manifested in frequent intra-institutional litigation.

General principles of law proved doubly attractive from this perspective. They could with justification be regarded as enhancing accountability by fleshing out the principles of EEC judicial review through the recognition of principles commonly found in national administrative law, which principles could be used to annul Community regulations, directives and decisions if they could not be read so as to be in compliance with them. They also cemented the Court's own position within the Community legal and political order, by the very fact that although such principles could not be used to annul primary Treaty articles, they could be used as interpretive guides, thereby enabling the Court to exert control over the meaning of the Treaty itself. There was, moreover, the added benefit that such principles could be used against national measures that fell within the scope of EU law, although, as we shall see, the range of measures caught in this manner is not free from doubt.

There were four principal ways in which the rule of law was realized through the ECJ's foundational jurisprudence on judicial review, which does not, of course, mean that it was uncontroversial. There was case law concerning the availability of judicial review, targeting of review, grounds of review and access to judicial review. These will be considered in turn.

(b) *The rule of law and the legal order*

(i) Availability of judicial review

A central feature of any system of judicial review is that bodies making decisions that have legal impact should be susceptible to judicial review. This precept was powerfully endorsed in *Les Verts*, which concerned a legal challenge to certain funding decisions made by the European Parliament (EP). Article 173 EEC did not expressly render the EP subject to judicial review. The ECJ nonetheless held that it must, as a matter of principle, be amenable to review:

> It must first be emphasized in this regard that the European Economic Community is a community based on the rule of law, inasmuch as neither its member states nor its institutions can avoid a review of the question whether the measures adopted by them are in conformity with the basic constitutional charter, the Treaty. In particular, in Articles 173 and 184 on the one hand, and in Article 177 on the other, the Treaty established a complete system of legal remedies and procedures designed to permit the court of justice to review the legality of measures adopted by the institutions.[87]

The ECJ acknowledged that by way of contrast to Article 177 EEC, which referred in general to acts of the institutions, Article 173 EEC was framed more narrowly in terms of acts of the Council and the Commission. It nonetheless drew on previous case law for the proposition that the general scheme

[87] Case 294/83, *Parti Écologiste – 'Les Verts'* v. *Parliament* [1986] ECR 1339, at [23].

of the Treaty was to make a direct action available against all measures adopted by the Community institutions that were intended to have legal effect.[88] It reinforced this reasoning by proffering an explanation as to why the EP had not been included within the bodies amenable to review under Article 173. It opined that this was because at the inception of the EEC the EP merely had powers of consultation and political control, rather than the power to adopt measures intended to have legal effects vis-à-vis third parties. It concluded in the following vein:

> An interpretation of Article 173 of the Treaty which excluded measures adopted by the European Parliament from those which could be contested would lead to a result contrary both to the spirit of the Treaty as expressed in Article 164 and to its system. Measures adopted by the European Parliament in the context of the EEC Treaty could encroach on the powers of the Member States or of the other institutions, or exceed the limits which have been set to the Parliament's powers, without its being possible to refer them for review by the court. It must therefore be concluded that an action for annulment may lie against measures adopted by the European Parliament intended to have legal effects vis-a-vis third parties.[89]

The CFI applied the same reasoning to justify review of EU agencies in *Sogelma*.[90] They are now expressly included in the

[88] Case 22/70, *Commission* v. *Council* [1971] ECR 263.

[89] Case 294/83, *Les Verts* [1986] ECR 1339, at [25].

[90] Case T-411/06, *Sogelma – Societá generale lavori manutenzioni appalti Srl* v. *European Agency for Reconstruction (AER)* [2008] ECR II-2771.

list of bodies amenable to review in Article 263 TFEU, but were not so listed in Article 230 EC. The CFI, however, filled the gap prior to the Lisbon Treaty and did so by drawing on *Les Verts*. The applicant sought judicial review of a decision by the European Agency for Reconstruction (EAR), to cancel a public tender for a public procurement project. The applicant was one of those who had tendered a bid for this project before the tender was withdrawn. The agency claimed that it was not susceptible to review under Article 230, since agencies were not listed therein.

The CFI acknowledged that agencies were not mentioned in Article 230, but held that the European Agency for Reconstruction was nonetheless subject to judicial review by reasoning from the principle in *Les Verts*.[91] The CFI held that 'the general principle to be elicited from that judgment is that any act of a Community body intended to produce legal effects vis-à-vis third parties must be open to judicial review'.[92] It acknowledged that the ruling in *Les Verts* referred only to Community institutions listed in Article 7 EC, which did not include the EAR. The CFI nonetheless concluded that

> the situation of Community bodies endowed with the power to take measures intended to produce legal effects

See also Case T-70/05, *Evropaïki Dynamiki – Proigmena Systimata Tilepikoinonion Pliroforikis kai Tilematikis AE* v. *Agence européenne pour la sécurité maritime (EMSA)* [2010] ECR II-313, at [61]–[75]; Case T-213/12, *Elitaliana SpA v. Eulex Kosovo* EU: T:2013:92, at [34].

91 Case 294/83, *Les Verts* [1986] ECR 1339, at [23].

92 Case T-411/06, *Sogelma* [2008] ECR II-2771, at [37].

> vis-à-vis third parties is identical to the situation which led to the *Les Verts* judgment: it cannot be acceptable, in a community based on the rule of law, that such acts escape judicial review.[93]

In reaching this conclusion the CFI distinguished its earlier ruling in *Keeling*,[94] which concerned the Office for Harmonization in the Internal Market (OHIM). In *Keeling* the CFI held that the OHIM was not amenable to review because it was not among the bodies listed in Article 230(1) EC, nor was it a Community institution for the purposes of Article 7 EC. The CFI in *Sogelma* nonetheless distinguished *Keeling* on the ground that the judgment in the latter case had been premised on the existence of other remedies that were available against the OHIM. The CFI in *Sogelma* therefore concluded that the decision in *Keeling* did not preclude an action under Article 230 EC against a decision of a Community body not mentioned in Article 7.[95]

The decision that Community agencies were subject to judicial review constituted teleological judicial reasoning in anticipation of Treaty amendment. The CFI's conclusion can be supported not only on the ground that it coheres with legal principle and constitutes a natural application of the reasoning in *Les Verts*, but also because, although not mentioned in *Sogelma*, the ECJ has made it clear that the principle in *Les Verts* can be applied to Community bodies endowed

[93] Case T-411/06, *Sogelma* [2008] ECR II-2771, at [37].
[94] Case T-148/97, *Keeling* v. *OHIM* [1998] ECR II-2217.
[95] Case T-411/06, *Sogelma* [2008] ECR II-2771, at [46].

with legal personality, even if they are not formally listed as Community institutions in Article 7 EC.[96]

The principle in *Les Verts* has often been repeated in high-profile cases. Thus in *Kadi* the ECJ stated that 'it is to be borne in mind that the Community is based on the rule of law, inasmuch as neither its Member States nor its institutions can avoid review of the conformity of their acts with the basic constitutional charter, the EC Treaty'.[97] In similar vein the Court held in *UPA* that the EC is a 'community based on the rule of law in which its institutions are subject to judicial review of the compatibility of their acts with the Treaty and with the general principles of law which include fundamental rights'.[98]

(ii) Targeting judicial review

If judicial review is to be effective it must be applied to the institution that made the operative decision. The EU courts have been adept at ensuring that this occurs. This is exemplified by *Sogelma*, where the power to decide upon contract tenders had been lawfully delegated by the Commission to the European Agency for Reconstruction. It followed that 'decisions which the Commission would have taken cannot

[96] Case C-15/00, *Commission* v. *EIB* [2003] ECR I-7281, at [75]; Case C-370/89, *SGEEM and Etroy* v. *EIB* [1992] ECR I-6211, at [15]–[16]; K. Lenaerts, 'Regulating the Regulatory Process: "Delegation of Powers" in the European Community' (1993) 18 *European Law Review* 23, at 46.

[97] Cases 402 and 415/05 P, *Kadi and Al Barakaat International Foundation* v. *Council and Commission* [2008] ECR I-6351, at [281].

[98] Case C-50/00, *Unión de Pequeños Agricultores* v. *Council* [2002] ECR I-6677, at [38].

cease to be acts open to challenge solely because the Commission has delegated powers to the EAR, otherwise there would be a legal vacuum'.[99] The CFI rejected the EAR's argument that the case should have been brought as an indirect action in the national court via what was then Article 234 EC, on the ground that while the contracting authority was the Serbian Ministry of Capital Investments, it was the EAR that cancelled the tender procedure, and the national court did not have jurisdiction to assess the legality of that decision.[100]

The CFI held that 'as a general rule, actions must be directed against the body which enacted the contested measure, in other words, the Community institution or body from which the decision emanated'.[101] This general rule was applied to the instant case: the EAR was a Community body established by regulation and endowed with legal personality; the regulation expressly empowered the Commission to delegate to the EAR the implementation of Community assistance, including invitations to tender and the award of contracts; and it was the EAR that decided to cancel the tender procedure. The Commission played no part in the decision-making process, it was the EAR that enacted the contested measure, and therefore it was the proper defendant in the legal proceedings.

The CFI acknowledged that in certain cases the Community courts had held that acts adopted pursuant to delegated powers were to be imputed to the delegating institution,

[99] Case T-411/06, *Sogelma* [2008] ECR II-2771, at [40].

[100] Case T-411/06, *Sogelma* [2008] ECR II-2771, at [42].

[101] Case T-411/06, *Sogelma* [2008] ECR II-2771, at [49].

which was obliged to defend them in court. It nonetheless distinguished such cases.[102] This was because some such decisions had involved the European Medicines Agency (EMA), which had advisory powers, the formal decision being made by the Commission,[103] whereas, by way of contrast, the powers of the EAR were not advisory in relation to the tender and awarding of contracts. The CFI also distinguished cases where the relationship between the Commission and the relevant agency was such that the Commission had overall responsibility for the programme, and where the conclusion of any contract by the agency was subject to the Commission's prior agreement, with the consequence that decisions on funding were imputable to the Commission.[104] The contrast with *Sogelma* was that decisions taken by the EAR in relation to procurement were not subject to prior approval of the Commission.

The EU courts have also dealt creatively with the converse situation. There may be agencies, such as the EMA, where the formal decision is made by the Commission, but where it is heavily reliant on the views of the agency or one of its committees. The structure of the EMA regulation is premised on the assumption that the Commission will normally adopt the agency's recommendation. If review is to be effective it is therefore necessary for the EU courts to be able

[102] Case T-411/06, *Sogelma* [2008] ECR II-2771, at [55]–[56].

[103] Case T-133/03, *Schering-Plough* v. *Commission and EMEA* EU: T: 2007: 365, at [22]–[23].

[104] Cases T-369/94 and 85/95, *DIR International Film* v. *Commission* [1998] ECR II-357.

to go behind the Commission decision and consider the agency's reasoning, which must be susceptible to review even though it is not the formal author of the decision.

The CFI ensured that this was so in *Artegodan*, which was concerned with withdrawal of authorization to market medicinal products containing 'amphetamine-like' anorectic agents, used in the treatment of obesity by accelerating the feeling of satiety.[105] The Commission had relied on findings made by the Committee for Proprietary Medicinal Products (CPMP), one of two committees that undertake the scientific work for the EMA. While the Commission was not bound by its opinion, the CFI stressed the importance of the mandatory consultation with the CPMP laid down by the relevant directive. Given that the Commission could not assess for itself the safety or efficacy of the product, consultation with the CPMP was necessary to give the Commission the scientific evidence from which it could make a reasoned decision.

The CFI held that the 'Community judicature may be called on to review, first, the formal legality of the CPMP's scientific opinion and, second, the Commission's exercise of its discretion' in deciding whether to accept that opinion.[106] While the CFI acknowledged that it could not substitute its view for that of the CPMP, it could consider the reasons proffered by it and whether there was an understandable link

[105] Cases T-74, 76, 83–5, 132, 137 and 141/00, *Artegodan GmbH* v. *Commission* [2002] ECR II-4945, at [198]. See also Case 212/91, *Angelopharm GmbH* v. *Freie Hansestadt Hamburg* [1994] ECR I-171, at [32]–[38].

[106] Cases T-74, 76, 83–5, 132, 137 and 141/00, *Artegodan* [2002] ECR II-4945, at [199].

between the medical evidence relied on by the CPMP and its conclusions. It was, moreover, incumbent on the CPMP to refer to the main scientific reports on which it had relied and to explain why it disagreed with, for example, divergent scientific opinion presented by the undertakings concerned in the case.[107]

The logic of the CFI's reasoning is unassailable: since the Commission would normally follow the opinion of the scientific committee, and had done so in this case, if judicial review was to be meaningful then the CFI should be able to consider the CPMP's reasoning.[108] The CFI did not state how this fitted with the requirement that for an act to be reviewable it must be binding on and capable of affecting the legal interests of the applicant. The CFI could, however, have held that the mandatory consultation of the CPMP rendered its opinion, which was then adopted by the Commission, an integral part of the legally binding decision made by the Commission, and was therefore reviewable, which was in effect the approach taken by the CFI in *Olivieri*.[109]

(iii) The grounds of review

The rule of law was also furthered through the development of the grounds of review that form the core of

[107] Cases T-74, 76, 83–5, 132, 137 and 141/00, *Artegodan* [2002] ECR II–4945, at [199]–[200].

[108] The CFI's decision was upheld on appeal, but the ECJ did not consider this particular issue. Case C-39/03 P, *Commission* v. *Artegodan GmbH* [2003] ECR I-7885.

[109] Case T-326/99, *Olivieri* v. *Commission and EMEA* [2003] ECR II-6053, at [55].

EU administrative law. While the grounds were listed in Article 33 ECSC and thence taken forward to Article 173 EEC, in Article 230 EC and onwards to Article 263 TFEU, there was much that was left unspecified by the Treaty articles, including general principles of law and the nature of review for law, fact and discretion. This is not the place for detailed analysis of the grounds of review.[110] The creativity of the Court's jurisprudence in relation to general principles and the elaboration of the intensity of review were noted in the previous section, and the important challenges flowing from this doctrine will be discussed in the chapter that follows.

The present analysis focuses on the way in which the EU grounds of review were elaborated, by analogy with the development of principles of judicial review in the UK set out in an earlier chapter.[111] It was argued that the development of common law legal doctrine could be conceptualized as proceeding in three stages. There was the imperative for judicial involvement in an area, followed by the fashioning of particular categories of legal doctrine applicable within the relevant area, and the elaboration of the more detailed meaning of the doctrinal areas established. This pattern of development is incremental and analogical and the relationship between the three levels is symbiotic, with developments at one level impacting on the others. The content of the three levels will, moreover, evolve; it is not static. The very values that

[110] See Tridimas, *The General Principles of EU Law*; Hofmann, Rowe and Türk, *Administrative Law and Policy of the European Union*; Craig, *EU Administrative Law*.

[111] See Ch. 1 above.

underpin a body of law change over time. It is interesting to reflect on the development of EU administrative law in the light of this analysis. This is more especially so given that the EU courts did not have the luxury of having four centuries in which to fashion the tools of judicial review.

Thus judicial review was felt to be warranted at what was termed the first level, because of the twin imperatives of the need to ensure that EU institutions remained within the remit of their allotted power, and that their decision making complied with certain precepts of good governance. It was, as seen above, readily apparent by the 1970s and 1980s that the EEC had considerable power and that a schema of judicial review was required in order to ensure that norms of Community law were subject to proper oversight. The ECJ's jurisprudence could therefore be depicted as legitimate in enhancing the rule of law by ensuring that Community decision making was subject to controls by way of judicial review that were analogous to those in the Member States. The imperfections in the Community legislative process enhanced the legitimacy of judicial review in furtherance of the rule of law. The period from the inception of the Community until the Single European Act 1986 was marked by the dominance of the Commission and Council. It is therefore unsurprising in the light of the decision-making process that the ECJ should feel the need to put flesh on the bare bones of Article 263 TFEU through the development of general principles, and it is equally unsurprising that its jurisprudence was seen as pushing at an open door, being welcomed as a method of rendering technocratic Community decision making more accountable.

The doctrinal categories in EU law, and their more specific meaning, levels two and three, are the result of reasoned analysis that draws on, and gives more concrete expression to, the foundational ideas that underlie EU judicial review, just as they do in the UK. There are doctrinal similarities and differences between the two systems. The latter are reflective of different conclusions concerning the specific implications that should be drawn from the background values that underpin EU judicial review. The relationship between levels one to three, and the similarities and differences between UK and EU law, can be revealed through examples that mirror those discussed in relation to UK law.

Consider in this respect the way in which the ECJ developed doctrinal controls dealing with error of law, error of fact, use of power for improper purposes, and invalidity. Legal doctrine of this kind is necessary in order to fulfil the background purpose of EU administrative law, which is in part to ensure that decision makers remain within the remit of the powers assigned to them. Given this background objective, controls of the kind elaborated here are a necessary part of the doctrinal architecture at level two. They receive less attention than some of the better-known precepts of EU administrative law, such as proportionality or legitimate expectations, but they have nonetheless been an integral part of the doctrinal terrain since its inception. Many cases continue to be decided on grounds of error of law, error of fact and misuse of power.[112]

[112] Craig, *EU Administrative Law*, Ch. 15.

The more particular meaning accorded to these concepts differs in some respects from analogous doctrine in UK law, thereby reflecting different value assumptions that play out at what was termed level three. Thus, to take but one example, the EU courts have from the outset undertaken judicial review of all questions of fact, with intervention grounded on the applicant being able to show a manifest error.[113] This stands in contrast to the difficulties that have plagued UK law in this area. Although the UK courts have clarified the scope of intervention for mistake of fact, uncertainties still remain.[114] The particular differences in legal doctrine can also result from legislation, or from Treaty provisions. Thus UK law on invalidity struggled to balance the principled imperative that an ultra vires act should be retrospectively void with the factual difficulties that unmitigated application of this precept can generate, the result being for many years covert manipulation of the terms 'void' and 'voidable' rather than open discussion of the circumstances in which the invalidity should be prospective rather than retrospective. EU law, by way of contrast, benefited from the fact that the Treaty, at its outset, stipulated in Article 174 EEC[115] that while the prima facie consequence of invalidity was that the act was void, it was nonetheless open to the ECJ to consider which effects of the challenged norm should be held to be definitive. The ECJ used this power to deal with cases

[113] Craig, *EU Administrative Law*, Ch. 15.

[114] P. Craig, *Administrative Law* (London: Sweet & Maxwell, 7th ed., 2012), Ch. 17.

[115] Now Art. 264 TFEU.

where retrospective nullity would lead to very real difficulties for institutions and/or individuals.[116]

Consider as a second example the way in which EU courts rapidly developed within the doctrinal armoury, at what was termed level two, general principles of law that embodied moral precepts designed to enhance good governance. This is exemplified by recognition of fundamental rights within general principles of law. It is true that the ECJ was pressed to take this step by the German and Italian courts, which threatened to test EU regulations for compliance with national constitutional rights in the absence of EU fundamental-rights protection.[117] It is nonetheless likely that the ECJ would have taken this step, even if it had not been pushed to do so by national courts. It was creating general principles of law at this time, and inclusion of fundamental rights was a natural step. The ECJ was fully aware of the

[116] See, e.g., Case 81/72, *Commission* v. *Council* [1973] ECR 575; Case 51/87, *Commission* v. *Council (Generalized Tariff Preferences)* [1988] ECR 5459, at [21]–[22]; Case C-392/95, *European Parliament* v. *Council* [1997] ECR I-3213, at [25]–[27]; Case C-93/00, *European Parliament* v. *Council* [2001] ECR I-10119, at [47]–[48]; Case C-378/00, *Commission and European Parliament* v. *Council* [2003] ECR I-937, at [73]–[77]; Cases C-402 and 415/05 P, *Kadi and Al Barakaat International Foundation* v. *Council and Commission* [2008] ECR I-6351, at [373]–[376].

[117] M. Dauses, 'The Protection of Fundamental Rights in the Community Legal Order' (1985) 10 *European Law Review* 398; A. Cassese, A. Clapham and J. Weiler (eds.), *European Union: The Human Rights Challenge* (Baden-Baden: Nomos, 1991); A. Clapham, 'A Human Rights Policy for the European Community' (1990) 10 *Yearbook of European Law* 309; K. Lenaerts, 'Fundamental Rights to be Included in a Community Catalogue' (1991) 16 *European Law Review* 367.

increasing power wielded by the EEC even in the 1970s, and the fact that the power transcended the purely economic sphere. It was cognizant of the fact that the quid pro quo for increased governmental power within liberal polities was recognition of some form of rights-based limit on its exercise, in order thereby to enhance the legitimacy of the political order.[118]

The judicial development of fundamental rights within EU law bore many of the hallmarks of 'common law' reasoning, being incremental and analogical. Indeed the ECJ's very recognition of fundamental rights as an integral part of Community law prior to the EU Charter of Rights bears analogy with the process whereby the UK courts 'discovered', prior to the Human Rights Act 1998, that such rights were embedded in the common law. The principal difference was that the ECJ, unencumbered by Diceyan impediments to the recognition of rights, reached this solution a whole lot more quickly than its UK counterparts.

Due process is integral to any administrative law regime, and it was conceptualized as part of fundamental rights by the ECJ.[119] The principle had to be respected both where there was no specific legislation, and where legislation existed but did not give sufficient protection to

[118] The relationship between review for fundamental rights and the EU legislative process will be considered more fully below in Ch. 4.

[119] Case C-49/88, *Al-Jubail Fertilizer* v. *Council* [1991] ECR I-3187, at [15]; Case C-458/98 P, *Industrie des Poudres Sphériques* v. *Council and Commission* [2000] ECR I-8147, at [99]; Case C-141/08 P, *Foshan Shunde Yongjian Housewares & Hardware Co. Ltd* v. *Council* [2009] ECR I-9147, at [83].

the principle.[120] While the catalyst for the ECJ's recognition of process rights was in part the common law precepts of natural justice, the ECJ's reasoning was also shaped by civilian conceptions of the rights of the defence. The moral precept of equality of arms that is integrally related to civilian conceptions of rights of the defence helps to explain some of the significant differences of detail between EU and UK law at what was termed level three, which is concerned with the detailed working out of legal doctrine. This is exemplified by recognition of access to the file as an important aspect of EU process rights,[121] and its absence from common law concepts of natural justice.

Consider a third example concerning discretionary power. The EU courts recognized, analogously to their UK counterparts, that the primary decision maker had been given discretionary power pursuant to EU legislation and therefore that they should not substitute judgement on the merits. The ECJ also concluded, in common with courts in the UK, that there should be constraints on the exercise of discretionary power. It considered that even if the primary decision maker,

[120] Case T-260/94, *Air Inter SA* v. *Commission* [1997] ECR II-997, at [60].

[121] Case T-7/89, *SA Hercules Chemicals NV* v. *Commission* [1991] ECR II-1711, at [53]–[54]; Cases T-30–2/91, *Solvay SA* v. *Commission* [1995] ECR II-1775; Cases C-204–5, 211, 213, 217, 219/00 P, *Aalborg Portland* v. *Commission* [2004] ECR I-123; M. Levitt, 'Access to the File: The Commission's Administrative Procedures in Cases under Articles 85 and 86' (1997) 34 *Common Market Law Review* 1413; C.-D. Ehlermann and B. Drijber, 'Legal Protection of Enterprises: Administrative Procedure, in Particular Access to Files and Confidentiality' [1996] *European Competition Law Review* 375; H. Nehl, *Principles of Administrative Procedure in EC Law* (Oxford: Hart, 1999), Ch. 5.

normally but not always the Commission, acted for a proper purpose there should still be some constraint on the way in which the discretionary power was exercised. The particular EU legal solution differed from that chosen by UK courts, thereby reflecting a difference in doctrinal choice at levels two and three. Whereas the UK courts opted for limited rationality review, the EU courts chose to proceed via a general test of proportionality that was applied with varying degrees of intensity.[122] This is not the place to rehearse the arguments for and against proportionality being a general head of review in the UK.[123] Nor is that the purpose of this analysis, which is rather to stress the way in which legal doctrine develops through the instrumentality of the three levels adumbrated above. The doctrinal differences between the two systems are reflective of different conclusions concerning the specific implications that should be drawn from the background values that underpin EU judicial review.

It should, moreover, be noted that the existence of such doctrinal variations does not preclude the existence of similar values informing the application of the legal doctrine, and this is so irrespective of whether it is accorded the same linguistic tag or not. Thus EU courts do not articulate the

[122] G. de Búrca, 'The Principle of Proportionality and Its Application in EC Law' (1993) 13 *Yearbook of European Law* 105; N. Emiliou, *The Principle of Proportionality in European Law* (Alphen aan den Rijn: Kluwer, 1996); G. Gerapetritis, *Proportionality in Administrative Law* (Athens: Sakkoulas, 1997); D.-U. Galetta, *Principio di Proporzionalità e Sindacato Giurisdizionale nel Diritto Amministrativo* (Milan: Giuffrè, 1998); Craig, *EU Administrative Law*, Ch. 19.

[123] See above, pp. 256–60.

varying intensity of proportionality review through language cast in terms of deference to the primary decision maker. It is clear nonetheless that the predominant test for proportionality review of social, political or economic discretionary power, whereby it is for the claimant to show manifest disproportionality,[124] is informed by similar considerations. The very fact that the exercise of such discretionary power entails complex social, political or economic assessment, and that the primary decision maker has been given this responsibility either by the Treaty or by a norm made pursuant to the Treaty, is the reason why intervention is pitched in terms of manifest disproportionality. The very test for review therefore embodies respect accorded to the primary decision maker in the making of such complex assessments.

(iv) Access to judicial review

The final foundational tenet of EU judicial review concerns the rules on standing, which have been controversial from the outset. Any system of administrative law will have access points or gateways, which determine who can get into the system. There will be procedural rules determining who is entitled to be heard before the initial decision is made, or who is entitled to be consulted before a legislative-type norm is enacted. There will also be rules of standing that determine

[124] Case C-491/01, *R* v. *Secretary of State for Health, ex p British American Tobacco (Investments) Ltd and Imperial Tobacco Ltd* [2002] ECR I-11453, at [123]; Case C-210/03, *The Queen, on the application of Swedish Match AB and Swedish Match UK Ltd* v. *Secretary of State for Health* [2004] ECR I-11893, at [48].

who should be able to complain to the court that the initial decision maker overstepped its powers. The rules are crucial. A legal system may have very sophisticated tools for judicial review, but if the access points or gateways are drawn too narrowly the opportunity for an individual to utilize them will necessarily be limited. There have been many critical analyses of the ECJ's jurisprudence.[125] The problematic jurisprudence can therefore be dealt with briefly here, and the issue will be considered again in the following chapter.

Article 230 EC, the predecessor to Article 263 TFEU, provided for direct review of legality. Member States, the EP, the Council and the Commission were regarded as privileged applicants and therefore had standing to challenge the legality of any acts. The Court of Auditors and the European Central Bank (ECB) could bring actions to protect their prerogatives. Non-privileged applicants had to satisfy Article 230(4), which provided,

[125] See, e.g., A. Barav, 'Direct and Individual Concern: An Almost Insurmountable Barrier to the Admissibility of Individual Appeal to the EEC Court' (1974) 11 *Common Market Law Review* 191; H. Rasmussen, 'Why Is Article 173 Interpreted against Private Plaintiffs?' (1980) 5 *European Law Review* 112; P. Craig, 'Legality, Standing and Substantive Review in Community Law' (1994) 14 *Oxford Journal of Legal Studies* 507; A. Arnull, 'Private Applicants and the Action for Annulment under Article 173 of the EC Treaty' (1995) 32 *Common Market Law Review* 7; P. Craig, 'Standing, Rights and the Structure of Legal Argument' (2003) 9 *European Public Law* 493; T. Tridimas and S. Poli, 'Locus Standi under Article 230(4): The Return of Euridice?', in A. Arnull, P. Eeckhout and T. Tridimas (eds.), *Continuity and Change in EU Law: Essays in Honour of Sir Francis Jacobs* (Oxford: Oxford University Press, 2008), Ch. 5.

> Any natural or legal person may, under the same conditions, institute proceedings against a decision addressed to that person or against a decision which, although in the form of a regulation or decision addressed to another person, is of direct and individual concern to the former.

Direct challenge to the legality of EU norms by non-privileged applicants was extremely difficult. It was determined in accord with the *Plaumann* test,[126] which has remained authoritative ever since the early 1960s. Persons other than those to whom a decision was addressed could only claim to be individually concerned if the decision affected them by reason of certain attributes peculiar to them, or by reason of circumstances in which they were differentiated from all other persons, and by virtue of these factors were distinguished individually, just as in the case of the person addressed. The applicant in the instant case failed because it practised a commercial activity that could be carried on by any person at any time. This made little sense pragmatically, since the existing range of firms is established by supply and demand. If there are two or three firms in the industry they can satisfy the current market demand, and thus the number is unlikely to alter significantly, if at all. The ECJ's reasoning also rendered it impossible for an applicant to succeed, except in a very limited category of retrospective cases. The applicant failed because the activity of importing clementines could be carried out by anyone at any time. It was, however, always

[126] Case 25/62, *Plaumann & Co.* v. *Commission* [1963] ECR 95.

open to the Court to contend that others could enter the industry, and hence deny standing to existing firms, and they did so frequently.

The difficulty of directly challenging EU norms in the form of regulations was equally marked. The *Calpak* test required the non-privileged applicant to show that the measure in question was not a real regulation, but that it was in reality a decision of individual concern to him.[127] This was not easy, because of the abstract-terminology test. The ECJ held that a real regulation was a measure that applied to objectively determined situations and produced legal effects with regard to categories of persons described in a generalized and abstract manner. The nature of the measure as a regulation was not called in question by the mere fact that it was possible to determine the number or even identity of those affected. The *Codorniu* case raised hopes that the standing rules for direct challenge were being liberalized, but the decision was of limited impact.[128] The ECJ affirmed the abstract-terminology test as the criterion for whether a regulation was a real regulation, rather than a decision, but held that this did not prevent the regulation from being of individual concern to some applicants. The test for whether an applicant was individually concerned was, however, that laid down in *Plaumann*.[129] It was for the applicant to show that the contested provision affected him by reason of certain attributes

[127] Cases 789 and 790/79, *Calpak SpA and Societa Emiliana Lavorazione Fruita SpA* v. *Commission* [1980] ECR 1949.

[128] Case C-309/89, *Codorniu* v. *Council* [1994] ECR I-1853.

[129] Case 25/62, *Plaumann* [1963] ECR 95.

which were peculiar to him, or by reason of circumstances in which he was differentiated from all other persons; the fact that the applicant operated a trade, which could be engaged in by any other person, served to deny individual concern.

Indirect challenge to contest the legality of EU norms was an imperfect substitute for more liberal standing rules for direct challenge. The narrow rules for standing in cases of direct challenge were often justified judicially by the existence of indirect challenge via Article 234 EC, since the individual could get to the ECJ via the national courts.[130] The limits to this reasoning were, however, noted by Advocate General Jacobs in *Extramet*.[131] He pointed out that Article 230 contained no suggestion that the availability of annulment depended on the absence of an alternative means of redress in the national courts. He listed the disadvantages of the indirect action under Article 234 by comparison with the direct action under Article 230: national courts lacked expertise in the subject; they did not have the benefit of participation of the Council and Commission; proceedings in national courts could involve substantial delays and extra costs; there might be no implementing measures at national level for the claimant to challenge; national courts had no jurisdiction to declare EU regulations invalid; and the claimant's progress to the ECJ was dependent on the willingness of the national court to make a reference. Advocate General Jacobs returned

130 An early formulation of this reasoning is to be found in Case 294/83, *Les Verts* [1986] ECR 1339, at [23].

131 Case C-358/89, *Extramet Industrie SA* v. *Council* [1991] ECR I-2501, AG Jacobs.

to the same theme at greater length in the *UPA* case,[132] arguing that the right to effective judicial protection could not be adequately protected by indirect challenge via Article 234 EC. He was unequivocal, noting the serious difficulties in regarding the preliminary reference as providing full and effective judicial protection against general measures, including the fact that the claimant might have to break the law in order to challenge ensuing sanctions. He concluded that the only way to secure the effective right of judicial protection was to have a test for direct challenge based on substantial adverse impact, which would remove the anomaly under the current case law that the greater the number of persons affected, the less likely it was that there would be effective judicial review.

The ECJ, however, declined the invitation to revisit the case law in this area and reaffirmed the *Plaumann* test.[133] In relation to the indirect action, it reiterated the mantra that the Treaty established a complete system of legal remedies for challenging the legality of EU action,[134] and held that it was for the Member States to ensure that they had a system of legal remedies that ensured respect for the right to effective judicial protection,[135] albeit without addressing the difficulties with the indirect action noted by the advocate general. In relation to the direct action, it held that the advocate general's

[132] Case C-50/00 P, *Unión de Pequeños Agricultores* [2002] ECR I-6677.

[133] Case C-50/00 P, *Unión de Pequeños Agricultores* [2002] ECR I-6677, at [37].

[134] Case C-50/00 P, *Unión de Pequeños Agricultores* [2002] ECR I-6677, at [40].

[135] Case C-50/00 P, *Unión de Pequeños Agricultores* [2002] ECR I-6677, at [41]–[42].

interpretation of individual concern would go beyond what would be allowed by way of Treaty interpretation and thus would require Treaty amendment, albeit without explaining why this was so. An amendment was duly made by the Lisbon Treaty,[136] the effect of which will be considered in the following chapter.

(c) The Janus dimension of judicial review

The discussion concerning the UK revealed what I termed the Janus dimension of judicial review,[137] capturing the idea that it both served to render power accountable in the sense articulated above, and served as the site through which the courts interpreted the regulatory legislation in order to ensure its efficacy. The same duality is apparent in EU administrative law. Claimants frequently lose, and in reaching their conclusions the courts seek to uphold the objectives of the regulatory schema and enhance its effectiveness. That does not always mean that courts get it right. They are, like all institutions, imperfect. It does mean that this is an important dimension of judicial review and that our perception is unbalanced if we are not cognizant of it. Evidence for this can be gleaned from any regulatory sphere where the EU has competence. A couple of examples will serve for present purposes.

The Common Agricultural Policy (CAP) operates under shared management, whereby the Member States and the Commission have formal legal and financial responsibilities. It consumes a considerable portion of the EU budget,

[136] Art. 263(4) TFEU. [137] See above, pp. 62–5.

and it is therefore no small wonder that legal disputes as to the allocation of financial responsibility when things go wrong are common. The general reaction of administrative lawyers is for the eyes to glaze over concerning annulment actions in relation to CAP funding, with the consequence that the Court's contribution to the 'law' that governs the CAP regime is missed. It consistently interpreted the legislation in a teleological manner, with important consequences for the allocation of financial responsibilities between the EU and the Member States.

Thus Member States argued that the relevant regulation meant that losses flowing from an incorrect but bona fide application of an EU rule by a national authority should be borne by the EU, except where there was negligence at the national level. The Court disagreed. It held that the regulation contained 'too many contradictory and ambiguous elements to provide an answer to the question at issue'.[138] The ECJ concluded that only sums paid in accordance with the rules correctly interpreted could be charged to the relevant EU fund. It was for the Member States to bear the burden of other sums paid, since otherwise Member States might give a broad interpretation to the relevant rules, thereby benefiting their traders as compared to those in other states. The Court held in a series of other cases that it was for the Member State to ensure the correct implementation of the CAP, prevent irregularities and recover sums lost due to irregularity or fraud, this being seen as an application of the general duty

[138] Case 11/76, *Netherlands* v. *Commission* [1979] ECR 245, at [6].

of co-operation in what is now Article 4(3) TEU. It was for the Commission to prove an infringement of the CAP rules, and to give reasons explaining the defect in the national procedures, but it was for the state to adduce evidence to show that it had carried out the necessary checks, or that its figures were accurate, and that the Commission's assertions were inaccurate.[139] This judicial reasoning was of real importance for the operation of the CAP, and the procedure concerning the clearance of accounts.

Similar themes are apparent in relation to the Structural Funds, whereby money is disbursed to disadvantaged areas within the EU. It too consumes a considerable portion of the EU budget, and the EU courts have sought to ensure the regulatory efficacy of the schema when adjudicating on judicial review applications. The relevant regulations allowed the Commission to reduce, suspend or cancel assistance in the event of an irregularity.[140] The EU courts interpreted the relevant provisions broadly so as to support the Commission in its endeavour to ensure the probity of the system.

Thus the ECJ accepted that although the regulation did not expressly allow the cancellation of assistance, it would be deprived of its effectiveness if the Commission could not cancel the entirety of the assistance where this was

[139] Case C-235/97, *France* v. *Commission* [1998] ECR I-7555, at [45]; Case C-278/98, *Netherlands* v. *Commission* [2001] ECR I-1501, at [39], [41], [92]; Case C-253/97, *Italy* v. *Commission* [1999] ECR I-7529, at [6].

[140] Council Regulation (EEC) 4253/88, laying down provisions for implementing Regulation (EEC) 2052/88, OJ 1988 No L374/1, Art. 24.

warranted. This was more especially so because reduction of assistance directly in proportion to irregularities detected would encourage fraud, since applicants would risk only the loss of the sums unduly paid.[141] In another case the ECJ held that it was lawful for a Member State to revoke assistance granted to an undertaking from a Community fund. The Court acknowledged that the regulation did not expressly provide for this action by a Member State, but held that it would be deprived of useful effect if a Member State could not adopt such measures, more especially because it had the primary responsibility for monitoring the operation of the project.[142]

The EU courts were equally strident in relation to procedural aspects of the enforcement regime, insisting that proper functioning of the system of controls established to ensure lawful use of EU funds meant that applicants for aid must provide the Commission with information which was reliable and not apt to mislead.[143] The same theme is apparent in case law stipulating that while the Commission had the burden of proving irregularities, it was then for the beneficiary of the assistance to show that expenditure was properly

[141] Case C-500/99 P, *Conserve Italia Soc Coop arl* v. *Commission* [2002] ECR I-867, at [88]; Cases C-383–5/06, *Vereniging Nationaal Overlegorgaan Sociale Werkvoorziening and Gemeente Rotterdam* v. *Minister van Sociale Zaken en Werkgelegenheid* [2008] ECR I-1561.

[142] Case C-271/01, *Ministero delle Politiche Agricole e Forestali* v. *Consorzio Produttori Pompelmo Italiano Soc Coop arl (COPPI)* [2004] ECR I-1029, at [41].

[143] Case C-500/99 P, *Conserve Italia*.

incurred on the particular project, and provide the Commission with all documentation required to dispel its doubts.[144]

4 Regulatory foundations

(a) *The regulatory framework and the need for EU administrative law*

The discussion thus far has been concerned with the formal and substantive foundations for EU administrative law. This picture would, however, be incomplete without an understanding of its regulatory foundations, connoting in this respect the regulatory framework to which the precepts of EU administrative law are applicable. The vision of the EU as a regulatory state commonly captures the idea that the EU has relatively little by way of power to tax and spend in the manner common to nation states, and that, by way of contrast, it relies on regulation to attain its desired goals.[145] There is force in this thesis, although the normative conclusions drawn therefrom can be more contestable, as will be seen in the next chapter. It is nonetheless important to understand the nature of Community regulation and administration in order to appreciate the need for EU administrative law to oversee the relevant bodies, when they undertook single-case decision making and rule making. This task

144 Case T-196/01, *Thessalonikis* v. *Commission* [2003] ECR II-3987, at [47]; Case C-330/01, *Hortiplant SAT* v. *Commission* [2004] ECR I-1763, at [31], [32].

145 Majone, 'The Rise of the Regulatory State in Europe'; Majone, *Regulating Europe*.

is facilitated by the rich body of literature dealing with the nature of EU administration.[146]

It was axiomatic to the framers that Community law had to be implemented, but the Rome Treaty nonetheless contained relatively little detail as to how this was to be done.

[146] See, e.g., S. Cassese, 'Il sistema amministrativo europeo e la sua evoluzione' (1991) *Rivista Trimestrale di Diritto Pubblico* 769; C. Franchini, 'L'impatto dell'integrazione comunitaria sulle relazioni al vertice dell'amministrazione. Poteri governativi e poteri amministrativi' (1991) *Rivista Trimestrale di Diritto Pubblico* 775; E. Schmidt-Aßmann, 'Verwaltungskooperation und Verwaltungskooperationsrecht in der Europäischen Gemeinschaft' (1996) *Europarecht* 270; E. Chiti and C. Franchini, *L'Integrazione Amministrativa Europea* (Bologna: Il Mulino, 2003); S. Cassese, 'European Administrative Proceedings' (2004) 68 *Law and Contemporary Problems* 21; E. Chiti, 'Forms of European Administrative Action' (2004) 68 *Law and Contemporary Problems* 37; G. della Cananea, 'The European Union's Mixed Administrative Proceedings' (2004) 68 *Law and Contemporary Problems* 197; C. Franchini, 'European Principles Governing National Administrative Proceedings' (2004) 68 *Law and Contemporary Problems Law* 83; E. Chiti, 'Administrative Proceedings involving European Agencies' (2004) 68 *Law and Contemporary Problems* 219; M. Egeberg (ed.), *Multilevel Union Administration: The Transformation of Executive Politics in Europe* (London: Palgrave Macmillan, 2006); H. Hofmann and A. Türk, 'The Development of Integrated Administration in the EU and Its Consequences' (2007) 13 *European Law Journal* 253; D. Curtin, *Executive Power of the European Union: Law, Practices and the Living Constitution* (Oxford: Oxford University Press, 2009); E. Schmidt-Aßmann, 'Introduction: European Composite Administration and the Role of European Administrative law', in O. Jansen and B. Schöndorf-Haubold (eds.), *The European Composite Administration* (Mortsel: Intersentia, 2011), Ch. 1; Craig, *EU Administrative Law*, Ch. 1; Harlow and Rawlings, *Process and Procedure in EU Administration*.

The relevant Treaty provision was Article 155 EEC, but like many of the other institutional provisions it was cast in general terms and short on detail. The first indent of Article 155 EEC instructed the Commission to ensure that the provisions of the Treaty and the measures taken by the institutions pursuant thereto were applied, while the third indent accorded the Commission its own power of decision in the manner provided for in the Treaty. Article 155 EEC thus gave the Commission the primary responsibility for implementation of EEC law, while providing little in the way of detail as to how this should be done.

The breadth of Article 155 EEC, more especially the first indent, might have been interpreted by the Commission as authority for direct administration of Community policy within the Member States. It might therefore have established Community agencies in the original six Member States to implement Community regulations. The fact that it did not do so was largely because of practical considerations, rather than any formal limit on its powers. It rapidly became clear that working with and through Member State administrations was the optimal method of implementing EEC policy, more especially given the limited manpower resources within the Commission itself.

Shared administration thus became the paradigm concerning single-case decision making or individualized adjudication, as attested to by its use from the outset in areas such as customs, where Community legislation was applied by national customs authorities,[147] and agriculture, where the

[147] Council Regulation (EEC) 2913/92 of 12 October 1992 establishing the Community Customs Code, OJ 1992 No L302/1; Commission Regulation

Common Agricultural Policy regulations were applied by national intervention agencies. The CAP was an early paradigm for shared administration: the Commission and the Member States had distinct administrative tasks, which were interdependent and set down in legislation, and both had to discharge their respective tasks for the Community policy to be implemented successfully.[148]

The rationale for this form of administration was not difficult to discern. The CAP's principal focus for many years was price support,[149] which required multiple complex payments to farmers throughout the Community. It could not realistically be undertaken by the Commission itself, which therefore operated through national bureaucracies, commonly in the form of a specialist national agency to discharge the duties. The very fact that the Member States' duties were formally enshrined in Community regulations served to sharpen the duality of the responsibility for implementation of the policy.

(EEC) 2454/93 of 2 July 1993 laying down provisions for the implementation of Council Regulation (EEC) 2913/92 establishing the Community Customs Code, OJ 1993 No L253/1. There have been many subsequent amendments.

148 Committee of Independent Experts, Second Report on Reform of the Commission, Analysis of Current Practice and Proposals for Tackling Mismanagement, Irregularities and Fraud (10 September 1999), Vol. 1, at [3.2.2].

149 W. Grant, *The Common Agricultural Policy* (London: MacMillan, 1997); R. Fennell, *The Common Agricultural Policy: Continuity and Change* (Oxford: Clarendon Press, 1997); J. McMahon, *Law of the Common Agricultural Policy* (London: Longman, 2000); M. Cardwell, *The European Model of Agriculture* (Oxford: Oxford University Press, 2004).

The same pattern of shared administration was to be used where the Community became involved in new areas requiring complex interchange with the Member States. It thus became the cornerstone of the Structural Fund regime, which was developed after the Single European Act 1986 (SEA) as an indirect consequence of the drive to complete the internal market. The expansion of this regime was seen as necessary to ensure the acceptability of the market-based initiatives contained in the SEA. There were fears that the wealthier economies would benefit from the completion of the single market, with the consequence that the gap with the less advantaged economies would widen. Reform of the Structural Funds was seen as one way of alleviating these concerns and was based squarely on shared administration.[150] In relation to input, the Member States submitted their regional development plans to the Commission, which then reviewed the plans for conformity with the Regulation. This in turn led to an agreement with the Member State in the form of a Community Support Framework (CSF) for Community structural fund operations, which specified the priorities adopted for Community assistance, the form of the assistance, its duration, and the financing plan. In relation to output, it was the Member States who were accorded initial responsibility for ensuring that Community funds for particular

150 Council Regulation (EEC) 2052/88 of 24 June 1988 on the tasks of the structural funds and their effectiveness and on co-ordination of their activities between themselves and with the operations of the European Investment Bank and the other existing financial instruments, OJ 1988 No L185/9.

projects were properly expended, subject to constraints in Community regulations as to how this should be done, in order to minimize the possibility of fraud and mismanagement. The Commission was also empowered to recover funds that were improperly expended.

The service sector constitutes a third example of the use of shared administration to deliver Community policy. The internal market was not 'literally completed' in 1992. Changes in technology, combined with the development of new products, meant that completion of the internal market should be viewed as an ongoing process, rather than an end to be achieved once and for all. The Commission turned its attention to integration in the services sector, including in this respect telecommunications, gas and electricity, where market integration had lagged behind other areas. It initiated a range of legislative measures to meet this deficiency and shared administration has been the norm throughout.

This can be briefly exemplified by considering the Community directives concerned with telecommunications.[151] Telecommunications liberalization was achieved through a series of directives, consisting of a Framework Directive[152] and a number of other directives dealing with specific issues,

[151] P. Craig, 'Shared Administration, Disbursement of Community Funds and the Regulatory State', in H. Hofmann and A. Türk (eds.), *Legal Challenges in EU Administrative Law: Towards an Integrated Administration* (Cheltenham: Edward Elgar, 2009), Ch. 2.

[152] Directive 2002/21/EC of the European Parliament and of the Council of 7 March 2002 on a common regulatory framework for electronic communications networks and services (Framework Directive), OJ 2002 No L108/33.

such as the Universal Service Directive.[153] The competitive market was regarded as the optimal method for the distribution of these services, but legislative intervention via universal service obligations was thought necessary to correct market failure. The Universal Service Directive specified the particular services that had to be made available to end users, while leaving Member States to determine the best method of implementation, subject to respect for principles of objectivity, transparency, non-discrimination and proportionality. The Universal Service Directive sets out the relevant universal-service obligations, relating to matters such as access to public phone services, directory inquiry service, quality of service and affordability of tariffs. It is the national regulatory authorities that are required to deal with such issues. There are detailed provisions specifying their obligations, combined with further provisions requiring the exercise of discretion by the national agencies, albeit subject to constraints laid down by the directive. The directive contains additional regulatory controls on undertakings with significant market power in specific markets, and once again it is the national regulatory authority that is charged with applying the relevant provisions.

[153] Directive 2002/22 of the European Parliament and the Council of 7 March 2002 on universal service and users' rights relating to electronic communications networks and services (Universal Service Directive), OJ 2002 No L108/51; W. Sauter, 'Universal Service Obligations and the Emergence of Citizens' Rights in European Telecommunications Liberalization', in M. Freedland and S. Sciarra (eds.), *Public Services and Citizenship in European Law: Public and Labour Law Perspectives* (Oxford: Clarendon Press, 1998), Ch. 7.

While shared administration is the dominant mode of service delivery, there are nonetheless important areas where individualized adjudication is done pursuant to what is known as direct or centralized administration by the Commission, the two principal examples from the Rome Treaty being competition policy and state aids. Truth to tell, although the administration of competition law is sometimes regarded as a paradigm of centralized administration, in the sense that the Commission was empowered to determine infringements of Articles 85 and 86 EEC, and more generally to develop the precepts of competition law, the pattern of administration established under Regulation 17[154] was more complex than this,[155] even prior to the reform of competition enforcement at the turn of the new millennium.[156] Viewed from this perspective the administration of state aids was always a 'purer' form of centralized administration, with the Member States being obliged to inform the Commission of proposed state aid, and the Commission being charged with making the relevant binding decisions concerning the compatibility of such aid with the Treaty.[157]

[154] EEC Council Regulation No 17, First Regulation implementing Articles 85 and 86 of the Treaty, OJ 1962 No L13/204.

[155] Craig, *EU Administrative Law*, Ch. 1.

[156] Council Regulation (EC) No 1/2003 of 16 December 2002 on the implementation of the rules on competition laid down in Articles 81 and 82 of the Treaty, OJ 2003 No L1/1.

[157] Arts. 107–9 TFEU; Council Regulation 659/1999 of 22 March 1999 laying down detailed rules for the application of Article 93 of the Treaty, OJ 1999 No L83/1.

The turn of the new millennium has also seen centralized administration used in rather different areas, notably those where the EU is accorded competence to supplement and support action of the Member States, such as health, education and vocational training, research and technological development, and culture. In this context centralized administration captures the idea that the Commission will implement a programme without formal, systematic co-operation with national bureaucracies. It does not mean that the Commission carries out the entirety of the activity itself, 'in-house'. It may do so; it may not. It may choose to use an executive agency, or contract out part of the work. The programmes to which this form of administration applies commonly entail awards in the form of subsidies, grants or contracts to private parties to carry forward the objectives of the programme. The new-style executive agencies will normally manage such programmes, as exemplified by the administrative regime in relation to public health, where the Executive Agency for Health and Consumers manages relations with some 2,200 beneficiaries involved in nearly 200 projects.[158] The same pattern is apparent in relation to education and vocational training, where the programmes are managed by the Education, Audiovisual and Culture Executive Agency;[159] energy, where the programmes were run by the Intelligent Energy

[158] See http://ec.europa.eu/eahc.

[159] Commission Decision 2005/56/EC of 14 January 2005 setting up the Education, Audiovisual and Culture Executive Agency for the management of Community action in the fields of education, audiovisual and culture in application of Council Regulation (EC) 58/2003, OJ 2005 No L24/35.

Executive Agency,[160] now superseded by the Executive Agency for Competitiveness and Innovation (EACI);[161] and the EU's research programme, where the Research Executive Agency plays a central role in assessing and managing multiple research projects in the FP7 programme, ranging from outer space to security, and from social-science projects to research that will benefit small and medium-sized enterprises.[162]

The discussion thus far has focused on the emerging pattern of Community administration relating to single-case decision making or individualized adjudication. Novel institutional solutions were also forthcoming to deal with rule making by the administration.

The disposition of power to make primary regulations and directives in the Rome Treaty was relatively clear. In most areas the maxim 'the Commission proposes, the Council disposes' held true. Legislative authority was carved up between the Commission, exercising the right of legislative initiative, and the Council, voting on the proposals. The Rome Treaty provided, by way of contrast, scant guidance on authority over secondary rule making, connoting in this respect the making of rules pursuant to the primary regulation or directive that fleshed out in more detail an aspect of the subject matter covered by it.

[160] Commission Decision 2004/20/EC of 23 December 2003 setting up an Executive Agency, the 'Intelligent Energy Executive Agency', to manage Community action in the field of energy in application of Council Regulation (EC) 58/2003, OJ 2004 No L5/85.

[161] See http://europa.eu/agencies/executive_agencies/eaci/index_en.htm.

[162] See http://ec.europa.eu/research/rea/index.cfm?pg=home.

The Commission articulated a picture of the 'Community method' in which it characterized itself as the executive, which should have sole or principal responsibility for the making of such secondary rules. The Commission's claim for such power was predicated on the wording of Article 155 EC, which provided that in order to ensure the proper functioning and development of the common market the Commission should 'exercise the powers conferred on it by the Council for the implementation of the rules laid down by the latter'. This did not, however, provide a secure foundation for Commission autonomy over the making of secondary legislative rules. The provision was, as the ECJ noted,[163] optional and only became operative when the Council conferred power on the Commission for the implementation of the primary regulation. The meaning of 'implementation' was, moreover, unclear. It could refer to the 'making' of secondary rules, although this still left open the possibility of attaching conditions by the Council to the delegation of such power. It could alternatively refer to the 'execution' of the primary regulation or directive, connoting the need to take measures, including individual decisions, to ensure that the primary regulation or directive was properly applied.[164]

The reality was that the Rome Treaty provided little by way of definitive guidance on the making of secondary rules, or the conditions that could be attached to this process.

[163] Case 25/70, *Einfuhr-und Vorratsstelle für Getreide und Futtermittel* v. *Koster, Berodt & Co.* [1970] 2 ECR 1161, at [9].

[164] Case 16/88, *Commission* v. *Council* [1989] ECR 3457, at [11]–[13].

The early years of the Community's existence should therefore be regarded as a working out of this issue, not as some upsetting of a carefully contrived institutional balance clearly delineated in the original Treaty.

It was the Common Agricultural Policy that gave birth to comitology.[165] It rapidly became clear that the administration of the CAP required the deployment of detailed rules in ever-changing market circumstances. Recourse to primary regulations or directives was impracticable. It became equally apparent that the Member States were wary of according the Commission a blank cheque over the making of implementing rules, especially given that power once delegated without encumbrance would generate legally binding rules without further possibility of Council oversight. The committee system was also a way of dealing with disagreements between the Member States, which might agree on the general regulatory principles for a particular area, but disagree on the more detailed ramifications thereof. Involvement in the making of the implementing rules served, moreover, to facilitate interaction between national administrators who would be responsible for the application of the rules at national level. This was the foundation for the committees of national technocratic representatives to oversee Community secondary rule making

[165] C. Bertram, 'Decision-Making in the EEC: The Management Committee Procedure' (1967–8) 5 *Common Market Law Review* 246; P. Schindler, 'The Problems of Decision-Making by Way of the Management Committee Procedure in the EEC' (1971) 8 *Common Market Law Review* 184; Bergstrom, *Comitology: Delegation of Powers in the European Union and the Committee System*, Ch. 2.

that became the hallmark of comitology, with the possibility of recourse to the Council in accord with the voting rules applicable to management and regulatory committee procedures, if the committee could not agree with the Commission. What began in the CAP rapidly spread to other areas, such that notwithstanding the continued inter-institutional tensions over comitology in the ensuing years the reality was that primary regulations and directives in all subject matter areas made provision for secondary rule making to be subject to comitology constraints.

A constant in the discussion thus far is that the Commission represents the Community interest, whether this is in the context of single-case decision making through shared or centralized administration, or in the context of rule making. This interest is, however, now commonly mediated by and through an EU agency. There has been increased resort to such agencies in the nation state.[166] They facilitate use of experts who are not part of the normal bureaucratic structure, free up the parent department so that it can concentrate on strategic policy, insulate the resolution of technical regulatory issues from

[166] M. Thatcher and A. Stone Sweet, 'Theory and Practice of Delegation to Non-majoritarian Institutions' (2002) 25 *West European Politics* 1; J. Ziller, 'Organizing the Central Administration: Policy and Instruments', Law Department, EUI, 2006; T. Christensen and P. Lægreid (eds.), *Autonomy and Regulation, Coping with Agencies in the Modern State* (Cheltenham: Edward Elgar, 2006); M. Groenleer, *The Autonomy of European Union Agencies: A Comparative Study of Institutional Development* (Delft: Eburon, 2009).

the vagaries of day to day political change and increase the credibility of the choices thus made.[167]

These factors have also been relevant in the EU. Thus the Commission in its communication on agencies stated that agencies 'would make the executive more effective at European level in highly specialized technical areas requiring advanced expertise and continuity, credibility and visibility of public action'.[168] It continued in the following vein, claiming that 'the main advantage of using the agencies is that their decisions are based on purely technical considerations of very high quality and are not influenced by political or contingent considerations'.[169] The Commission also emphasized the value of agencies in enabling the Commission to focus on its core function of policy formation, with the agencies implementing this policy in specific technical areas.[170]

[167] G. Majone, 'Temporal Consistency and Policy Credibility: Why Democracies Need Non-majoritarian Institutions', Working Paper RSC No 96/57, Florence EUI; F. Gilardi, 'Policy Credibility and Delegation to Independent Regulatory Agencies: A Comparative Empirical Analysis' (2002) 9 *Journal of European Public Policy* 873; M. Busuioc, M. Groenleer and J. Trondal (eds.), *The Agency Phenomenon in the European Union: Emergence, Institutionalisation and Everyday Decision-Making* (Manchester: Manchester University Press, 2012); M. Everson, C. Monda and E. Vos (eds.), *European Agencies in between Institutions and Member States* (Alphen aan den Rijn: Kluwer Law International, 2014).

[168] The Operating Framework for the European Regulatory Agencies, COM(2002) 718 final, 5.

[169] The Operating Framework, 5.

[170] The Operating Framework, 2.

Academics proffered a plethora of rationales for resort to the agency option in the EU. For some the principal rationale was the fostering of administrative integration.[171] For others it was the desire to further integration at a time when increase in the power of the Commission itself was not politically acceptable.[172] For yet others the rationale was best conceived in terms of networking, with agencies conceived as a more permanent institutionalized locus through which this could occur between EU and national officials.[173] A further view emphasized the mismatch between the highly complex regulatory tasks assigned to the EU and the limited administrative, financial and cognitive resources available to the Commission, leading to agencies that could fill the epistemic gap.[174]

Whichever rationale for agency creation is regarded as the most important, it is clear that agencies are now central to the EU's administrative architecture. The agency model was initially used in 1975 when two agencies were established. The second wave in the 1990s saw the creation of ten further agencies, dealing with matters such as the environment,

[171] A. Kreher, 'Agencies in the European Community: A Step towards Administrative Integration in Europe' (1997) 4 *Journal of European Public Policy* 225.

[172] M. Shapiro, 'The Problems of Independent Agencies in the United States and the European Union' (1997) 4 *Journal of European Public Policy* 276.

[173] R. Dehousse, 'Regulation by Networks in the European Community: The Role of European Agencies' (1997) 4 *Journal of European Public Policy* 246.

[174] G. Majone, 'Delegation of Regulatory Powers in a Mixed Polity' (2002) 8 *European Law Journal* 319.

medicines, trademarks, health and safety at work and the monitoring of drug addiction. The new millennium saw further use of the agency model in what can be regarded as a third wave, with agencies established in areas such as food safety, maritime safety, aviation safety, network and information security, chemicals, railways, and fundamental rights. Some of the most powerful agencies are those dealing with securities regulation and banking in the wake of the financial crisis.

This, then, was the regulatory tableau that formed the backdrop to EU administrative law, the development of which was necessary in terms of legitimacy and efficacy. The former is better known than the latter, but both are equally important and will be considered in turn.

Judicial review actions, direct and indirect, were the vehicle through which the courts elaborated the structural, procedural and substantive conditions on which such regulatory power was exercised in order thereby to help legitimate it. There are numerous examples of this, but the following will suffice for present purposes. Thus it was the ECJ that laid the structural foundations for comitology, upholding the new committee system against challenge in the *Koster* case.[175] It rejected the argument that the committee procedure attached to the delegation of power to the Commission was inconsistent with the institutional balance established by the Treaty.

[175] Case 25/70, *Einfuhr-und Vorratsstelle für Getreide und Futtermittel* v. *Koster, Berodt & Co.* [1970] 2 ECR 1161; Case 23/75, *Rey Soda* v. *Cassa Conguaglio Zucchero* [1975] ECR 1279, at [13]; Case 5/77, *Carlo Tedeschi* v. *Denkavit Commerciale S.r.l.* [1977] ECR 1555.

To have acceded to this claim would have led to real problems, given the importance that Member States attached to the new schema. The ECJ held that the Treaty gave the Council discretion to confer on the Commission implementing powers, with the consequence that it could attach conditions to the conferral, more especially because the committees did not have autonomous decision-making power. It was the courts that crafted the procedural conditions attendant upon the exercise of regulatory power, and shaped them to the reality of shared administration that constituted the norm for implementation of Community policy. Process rights had to be adhered to at all stages of the decision-making process, including by national agencies that were integral to the discharge of Community policy in the relevant sphere.[176] The development of substantive judicial review, as manifest through doctrines such as proportionality, legitimate expectations, equality and fundamental rights, sought to reassure Member States that EU regulatory power would be subject to controls analogous to those exercised within the nation state. The application of these same precepts to Member States when they acted within the scope of EU law was the natural response to the reality of shared administration.

Judicial review was equally significant from the perspective of efficacy, connoting in this respect the idea that regulations, directives and decisions should be interpreted

[176] See, e.g., Case C-269/90, *Hauptzollamt München-Mitte* v. *Technische Universität München* [1991] ECR I-5469; Case T-450/93, *Lisrestal* v. *Commission* [1994] ECR II-1177; Case C-32/95 P, *Commission* v. *Lisrestal* [1996] ECR I-5373.

teleologically to ensure that EU legislative objectives were fulfilled. There was thus from the outset, as we have seen above, a duality in judicial review, which served both as the vehicle through which precepts of good governance could be imposed on the administration, and also as the means through which the EU courts could interpret the regulatory norms in order to plug gaps and facilitate their efficacious implementation. The EU courts gave seminal rulings that affected the legality and effectiveness of administration. The tendency is to regard such rulings simply as examples where the claimants lost, or as instances of judicial teleological interpretation that are of no general interest for EU administrative law. This is far too narrow. We should be concerned as administrative lawyers with the overall effectiveness of the administrative systems that exist within the EU. The ECJ's judgments were of seminal importance in this regard and many were given in the context of judicial review actions, direct and indirect. This is exemplified by the ECJ's jurisprudence examined earlier in relation to the Common Agricultural Policy and the Structural Funds, where the rulings were designed to foster financial probity and responsibility in circumstances where the legislative provisions were ambiguous. This does not mean that such decisions should always be accepted with equanimity. Administrative efficacy is no automatic trump that can justify any legal decision given in its name. Nor should we veer in the opposite direction and view such decisions as illegitimate or unwarranted. It is part of the judicial function to effectuate an administrative regime by interpreting the empowering regulations or directives to attain the overall purpose.

(b) The regulatory framework and the sufficiency of the administrative perspective

(i) The administrative governance thesis

The preceding discussion focused on the need for administrative law, judged in terms of legitimacy and efficacy when viewed against the backdrop of the EU's regulatory landscape. There is, however, a more far-reaching thesis advanced by Peter Lindseth that seeks to explain the legitimacy of the EU as a whole in administrative as opposed to constitutional terms:

> To put it bluntly, European governance is *administrative, not constitutional.* The process of European integration has had, without doubt, profound constitutional implications for its constituent states. It has both disciplined certain negative externalities of national democracy and offered market actors a range of transnational rights and duties, all to construct a new market-polity transcending national borders. Nevertheless, this polity has had great difficulty being understood as constitutional in its own right. That is, it has struggled to be seen as the embodiment or expression of a new political community ('Europe') capable of self-rule through institutions historically constituted for that purpose. Rather, in this critical regard, the EU is fundamentally administrative, with a ruling legitimacy still ultimately derived from the historically constituted bodies of representative government on the national level.[177]

[177] P. Lindseth, *Power and Legitimacy: Reconciling Europe and the Nation-State* (Oxford: Oxford University Press, 2010), p. 1. Italics in the original.

Lindseth thus views the EU as a system of 'Europeanized administrative governance' analogous to the national administrative state, which has been constructed in response to demands for increased regulatory capacity in the face of an array of political, social and economic challenges.[178] The institutional strategy for meeting these challenges at both national and supranational levels is to diffuse normative power away from institutions of representative self-government at the national level.[179] For Lindseth, 'integration is best understood as a supranational manifestation of the broader historical process of diffusion and fragmentation of regulatory power that characterizes modern governance',[180] and delegation is the key normative principle underpinning this conception.[181]

It is central to Lindseth's argument that while EU regulatory power has expanded considerably, its democratic and constitutional legitimacy has remained 'stubbornly weak'.[182] Thus while the EU may have legal and technocratic legitimacy, it lacks the classic democratic and constitutional legitimacy enjoyed by the nation state.[183] For Lindseth the academic impulse to 'characterize EU governance in autonomously constitutional terms'[184] is misconceived, with the consequence that EU governance as a whole 'is best understood as an extension of administrative governance on the national

[178] Lindseth, *Power and Legitimacy*, pp. 1–2.
[179] Lindseth, *Power and Legitimacy*, p. 2.
[180] Lindseth, *Power and Legitimacy*, p. 2.
[181] Lindseth, *Power and Legitimacy*, pp. 49–50, 56–7.
[182] Lindseth, *Power and Legitimacy*, p. 6.
[183] Lindseth, *Power and Legitimacy*, pp. 6–10.
[184] Lindseth, *Power and Legitimacy*, p. 15.

level over the course of the twentieth century'.[185] Autonomous regulatory power at the EU level does not demand constitutionalism beyond the state, nor does it require a direct form of legitimation rather than one mediated through the nation state. To the contrary, he maintains that integration should be conceived in administrative, not constitutional, terms, such that all EU institutions 'exercise power that is understood to be derived from national constitutional orders, rather than being autonomously constitutional in itself:[186]

> The persistence and growth of national oversight mechanisms in European public law have worked to 'maintain the connection' between supranational regulatory power and the historically constituted bodies of the nation-state, providing an essential means of legitimation and administrative governance in its now supranational form. In the integration context, just as in the administrative state, the separation of regulatory power from democratic and constitutional legitimacy has been accomplished through transfers of authority that are best understood culturally (if not always functionally) as *delegations* in an administrative sense – that is, as transfers from constitutional principal to administrative agent – *not* as the establishment of a constitutionally original or autonomous level of governance at the supranational level.[187]

185 Lindseth, *Power and Legitimacy*, p. 15.

186 Lindseth, *Power and Legitimacy*, p. 19.

187 Lindseth, *Power and Legitimacy*, p. 23. Italics in the original. See also pp. 48–50.

Peter Lindseth has presented a challenging thesis, but it is nonetheless problematic. This is in part because the thesis leaves untouched a significant dimension of the constitutionalization thesis as it is commonly understood, and in part because the argument as to why integration must be conceptualized in administrative rather than constitutional terms is more difficult to sustain than is apparent from Lindseth's own analysis. These points will be considered in turn.

(ii) The standard constitutionalization thesis

The constitutionalization thesis as commonly understood takes the following form. The Treaty is, in the ECJ's language, regarded as the constitutional charter for the EU.[188] It is not formally a constitution, but judged substantively it performs many of the same functions. Thus constitutions have a horizontal, a territorial and a vertical dimension. The horizontal dimension is concerned with the rules that regulate the main organs of government, their constitution and powers. There are typically both substantive and procedural norms of this nature. Substantive norms demarcate the respective powers of the legislature, executive and courts. Procedural norms are concerned with how legislation is enacted; whether special majorities are required; the extent, if any, to which a court can inquire into the legislative process; and the like. The territorial dimension is relevant in federal states, or where there is some measure of devolution. There will be structural provisions of the constitution that identify the respective powers of the

[188] Case 294/83, *Les Verts* [1986] ECR 1339, at [23]; Cases 402 and 415/05 P, *Kadi* [2008] ECR I-6351, at [281].

federal and state or regional governments. The vertical dimension is concerned with the constitutional rules that regulate the interrelationship between citizen and state, the paradigm example being rights-based constraints on government action contained in a Bill of Rights. The EU treaties have from the outset contained many provisions that speak directly to these horizontal, territorial and vertical dimensions. This is more particularly so after the Lisbon Treaty, given that it contains more explicit provisions on, for example, the division of competence between the EU and Member States than hitherto, and given that the Charter of Rights is rendered formally binding.

The standard constitutionalization thesis does not, however, rest solely on this foundation. It is, in addition, based on constitutionalization through judicial doctrine, which thereby broadened the gap between the EU Treaty and other international treaties. Constitutionalization viewed from this perspective connotes the idea that the EU developed from a legal order binding on states qua states to one which confers rights and obligations on private parties, who exert control on public power similar to that of nation states.[189] The judicial creation of direct effect and supremacy was central in

[189] J. Weiler, 'The Constitution of Europe' (1991) 100 *Yale Law Journal* 2430; A. Stone Sweet, 'Constitutional Dialogues in the European Community', in A.-M. Slaughter, A. Stone Sweet, and J.H.H. Weiler (eds.), *The European Court and National Courts: Doctrine and Jurisprudence* (Oxford: Hart Publishing, 1998), Ch. 11; J.-C. Piris, 'Does the European Union Have a Constitution? Does It Need One?' (1999) 24 *European Law Review* 557; P. Craig, 'Constitutions, Constitutionalism and the European Union' (2001) 7 *European Law Journal* 125.

this regard, and so too was the ECJ's recognition of fundamental rights, coupled with other norms of good governance. The interpretation accorded to what is now Article 267 TFEU had a profound effect on the relationship between the ECJ and national courts, imbuing ECJ decisions with precedential force and transforming national courts into EU courts in their own right, thereby fashioning the judicial architecture for the emergent Community legal order. The very language used by the ECJ was couched in terms of distancing the EEC from paradigm international treaties, in order thereby to justify and facilitate doctrinal developments that did not have a secure footing in international law.[190]

Peter Lindseth gives little attention to this sense of constitutionalization in forging his thesis that EU governance should be viewed as administrative rather than constitutional, and dismisses it on the ground that it does not address the EU's democratic legitimacy,[191] which must, in his view, still be regarded as residing with the Member States, hence justifying his depiction of the EU in administrative rather than constitutional terms. Let it be assumed for the present that the argument concerning the Member States being the ultimate repository of democracy is sound, although it will be contested below. To conclude therefrom that EU integration must be conceived in administrative and not constitutional terms is nonetheless unwarranted. It downplays all

[190] Case 26/62, *N.V. Algemene Transporten Expeditie Onderneming van Gend en Loos* v. *Nederlandse Administratie der Belastingen* [1963] ECR 1, at 12; Case 6/64, *Costa* v. *ENEL* [1964] ECR 585, at 593.

[191] Lindseth, *Power and Legitimacy*, pp. 31–2.

the features of the EU adumbrated above that have been properly regarded as constitutional. It does so by regarding democratic legitimacy as the defining issue, the sine qua non, regarding whether the EU should be conceived of in constitutional terms.

The reality, both normative and practical, is surely to the contrary. Thus even if one accepts the obvious truth that Member States created the EU and set the initial limits for the power conferred thereon, it does not mean that the polity thus created lacks the features that have led scholars and courts to denominate it as a constitutional order, nor does it mean that those features are not worthy of that appellation. These features are of real importance to the very nature of the EU and the way in which it functions, and they are of constitutional import for the reasons set out above. The foundations of EU administrative law subsist within this constitutional frame, in the same way that precepts of administrative law are framed by constitutional principles at national level, even though there may be differences in the precise nature of the respective constitutional schema.

(iii) The administrative governance thesis revisited

The reader might accept the preceding argument, but it does not touch Lindseth's thesis that integration should be conceived in terms of administrative governance, insofar as the thesis is based on the assumption that the EU and its institutions lack democratic legitimacy that flows from national representative institutions, without which the system cannot be truly 'constitutional'. While this claim is oft-repeated, its foundations are not clearly spelt out.

It might be regarded as an a priori claim, to the effect that it is simply not viable for the EU to be conceived as a fully constituent democratic polity. Peter Lindseth makes brief reference to the no-*demos* thesis, but there is little by way of elaboration of this argument, which is highly contestable, as attested to by the existing literature. This form of argument is, moreover, contestable from a different perspective. If democratic pedigree is the sine qua non to regard a national polity in constitutional terms, with the consequence that such states must be conceptualized from an administrative perspective whatsoever this might mean, this would preclude historical usage of the term 'constitutional' in relation to patterns of political ordering that were not democratic, which was pretty much all, and equally preclude use of the term in relation to nation states that are not currently organized on a classic democratic model. This conclusion could only be avoided by accepting that warrant for the appellation 'constitutional' can be justified in some other terms, which then raises the question why this could not also be true in relation to the EU.

It might alternatively be regarded as a contingent claim, to the effect that the present form of political ordering within the EU reveals a democratic deficit, most notably because the inter-institutional distribution of power renders it difficult for the people to vote out those of whom they disapprove.[192] The disjunction between the locus of much power, residing as it does with the Commission and the

[192] J. Weiler, U. Haltern and F. Mayer, 'European Democracy and Its Critique', in J. Hayward (ed.), *The Crisis of Representation in Europe* (London: Frank Cass, 1995), p. 4; A. Follesdal and S. Hix, 'Why There Is

Council, and the direct electoral mandate, residing with the European Parliament, has meant that there is no ready connection between electoral displeasure with existing policy and the ability to change it through the ballot box, since the people voted in do not control the policy agenda. There is force in this argument, although it is unclear to what extent Lindseth regards it as the foundation for his thesis. There are, however, three points to note about the argument that are apposite in this context.

In political terms, the preceding problem is contingent and there are indications that it is being alleviated, most notably as a result of developments during the 2014 elections for the European Parliament, in which rival candidates for the Commission Presidency openly campaigned on behalf of different political groupings in the EP. This thereby bridged the gap, to some extent, between the locus of power in the Commission and the results of the elections, more especially because the European Council felt, despite opposition from some Member States, that the Commission presidency should indeed be accorded to the person who had campaigned openly on behalf of the party that secured the majority of seats, notwithstanding that the European Council had discretion in this respect under the Treaty.[193] This does not cure the problem set out in the preceding paragraph, but it does alleviate it.

a Democratic Deficit in the EU: A Response to Majone and Moravcsik' (2006) 44 *Journal of Common Market Studies* 533.

193 Art. 17(7) TEU.

In conceptual terms, it is by no means self-evident that the premise justifies the conclusion that Lindseth wishes to draw from it. Thus reasoning from the premise of democracy deficit, the conclusion that democracy must be perceived as residing within the nation state and that the EU must be perceived in administrative, not constitutional, terms does not readily follow. It assumes that the democratic infirmity at EU level serves to deny all democratic credentials to the EU institutions, rendering them in Lindseth's terms dependent wholly on legitimation via the nation state. The existence of democratic imperfections in EU decision making does not, however, mean that no democratic legitimation can justifiably be ascribed at the EU level, nor does it mean that EU integration cannot be conceived in constitutional terms, more especially so given the existence of democratic imperfections at national level. It may, by way of contrast, mean that democratic legitimation should be situated at both EU and national levels, in the manner articulated by Kalypso Nicolaïdis in her theory of 'demoicracy', whereby legitimation flows from multiple *demoi*.[194] This was not, however, Peter Lindseth's initial thesis, although he has more recently sought to argue that his argument can be read with it.[195]

In normative terms, Lindseth's argument assumes that the nation states can be the site of democratic and

[194] K. Nicolaïdis, 'European Demoicracy and Its Crisis' (2013) 51 *Journal of Common Market Studies* 351.

[195] P. Lindseth, 'Equilibrium, Demoi-cracy and Delegation: On the "Administrative" not "Constitutional" Legitimacy of European Integration', Jean Monnet Working Paper 7/13.

constitutional legitimation for the EU, this being imbued with practical force through increased political scrutiny by national legislatures and legal scrutiny by national courts.[196] This assumption rests on contestable foundations. The primary treaty may well be conceptualized in terms of conferral of power by Member States, but this provides no basis for the conclusion that the polity thus created cannot be conceived in constitutional terms. To conceive of Member States as the sole or primary site of democratic and constitutional legitimation is even more problematic in relation to legislation made pursuant to the Treaty. The problem is not just that most national parliamentary scrutiny of draft EU legislation is of limited efficacy when framed in terms of subsidiarity controls, or when they stray beyond this to consider the proportionality of the measure. The real problem as judged in normative terms is the very perspective which the national parliaments bring to bear when undertaking such review. If they undertake such review from a truly EU perspective then this raises the question why such assessments should be the sole or primary site of democratic legitimation to the exclusion of such assessments made by the EP and other EU institutions. If, alternatively, they undertake such review from a

[196] The reality is that judicial control through national courts is limited, insofar as checks on the vires of EU action is concerned. Now, to be sure, the EU courts should be more searching in their review in this respect, but the reality is that national courts have exercised little by way of vires control over the many thousands of EU norms that have been enacted, and notwithstanding more strident tones emanating from national courts this picture is unlikely to change significantly in the future.

perspective of national self-interest, which is increasingly likely the more the assessment moves beyond subsidiarity towards the general content of the measure, it raises the question why such views should be thought to be normatively determinative in democratic or constitutional terms. Twenty-eight views each expressed from a perspective of national self-interest is self-evidently not the same as a decision reached from an EU perspective.

5 Conclusion

Analysis of the foundations of EU administrative law provides interesting insight into the evolution of legal doctrine. While the formal basis for judicial review existed in the ECSC Treaty from the outset, and was then carried over into the Rome Treaty, much was left to be done to render the four heads of review serviceable as a regime for administrative law analogous to that existing in Member States. The judicial elaboration of general principles of law, combined with the working out of tests for review of law, fact and discretion, were central to this development. These tasks were informed in substantive terms by rule-of-law considerations that shaped precepts concerning the availability and targeting of review, forged the grounds of such review and determined the rules relating to access. The steps on this road were not uncontroversial, as attested to by enduring critiques of the rules relating to access. At the same time, the very architecture of EU administrative law was shaped by the regulatory regime to which it applied, and in turn shaped that regime, in a symbiotic manner. The focus now turns to the challenges faced by EU administrative law.

4

EU administrative law

Challenges

1 Introduction

The previous chapter considered the foundations of EU administrative law, and this chapter addresses the principal challenges that it faces, some of which are horizontal, in the sense of internal to the regime of EU administrative law, while others are vertical in nature, flowing from the interplay between EU law and national administrative law or global administrative law.

The discussion begins with the caseload problems that beset the EU courts. In the past the discourse on this issue has been directed principally towards the ECJ, with concerns about its capacity to cope with the increase in the number of preliminary references. More recently it has been the General Court that has been most problematic in this regard, which is of particular importance for EU administrative law given that it has jurisdiction over direct actions for judicial review. The sources of the caseload problem are examined, the implications that this has for EU administrative law are explored and the proposed solutions are scrutinized.

The discussion then turns to process and the challenges that EU administrative law faces in this regard. The EU courts have achieved much in this area, especially in relation to process rights that relate to individualized adjudication.

Their jurisprudence crafted on general principles of law and fundamental rights has ensured protection for the right to be heard and the more general rights of the defence. The EU courts have, however, faced difficulties flowing from initiatives to tackle terrorism post-9/11, more especially in the form of legal challenges to asset-freezing orders imposed by the EU pursuant to decisions made by the UN. The infirmities of due process at the UN level prompted legal challenges to the EU regulations. This in turn has forced the courts to articulate how the right to be heard can be balanced against the needs of security. The remainder of the discussion on process considers the possibility of a general law or set of model rules on administrative procedure, which would be applicable not merely to individualized adjudication, but also to rule making, public contracts, mutual assistance between national administrations, and data transfers. It will be argued that model rules of this nature are desirable and that concerns about such a development are misplaced.

The focus then shifts to substantive review, and begins with tensions that have arisen in relation to fundamental rights. The very fact that such rights are protected in the national legal order has inevitably led to boundary problems concerning the respective areas in which EU and national law is applicable. This is an endemic problem in a polity where rights are protected at more than one level. It has, however, been thrown into sharp relief by the EU Charter of Rights becoming legally binding, and has generated disputes between national courts and their EU counterparts as to where the boundary line should be drawn. There have, in addition, been difficult challenges posed by the fact that the interpretations accorded to a particular right by EU law and by national constitutional law do not always cohere. The boundary lines between the EU Treaty and the ECHR have given rise to equally difficult problems. The discussion in this section concludes with analysis of the uncertainties surrounding the intensity of substantive review, and why greater clarity in this respect would be desirable.

The last part of the chapter is concerned with the regulatory challenges broadly conceived that face EU administrative law. The subject matter of all systems of administrative law includes, inter alia, rules and decisions made by the administration pursuant to primary legislation. The EU is no different in this regard. The Lisbon Treaty introduced the distinction between delegated and implementing acts, which has been problematic from the outset, and remains so notwithstanding rulings by the CJEU. The place of agencies within the schema of administration is equally central to systems of administrative law, and so too is the nature of their powers. The EU has grappled with this issue from the outset, and the problem has been further highlighted by the creation of a new breed of agencies with greater powers than hitherto. The judicial response to this development is considered and the relevant options are evaluated. The chapter concludes with consideration more generally of the challenges faced by design of regulatory systems of shared administration to ensure that they are efficient and efficacious, as exemplified through the difficulties encountered with the Common Agricultural Policy, the Structural Funds and utilities regulation.

2 Caseload

(a) *Caseload: the scale of the problem*

The discussion of the challenges faced by UK administrative law revealed the impact of governmental initiatives designed to ease judicial workload, and the dangers this posed for central features of judicial review. Caseload problems are not, however, confined to the UK, and they may indeed be more severe in the EU, where they have cast a shadow over many issues, including those relating to administrative law, such as standing. Discourse on reform of the EU judicial system has been driven principally by such concerns.[1]

[1] C. Turner and R. Munoz, 'Revising the Judicial Architecture of the European Union' (1999–2000) 19 *Yearbook of European Law* 1; A. Arnull, 'Judicial Architecture or Judicial Folly? The Challenge Facing the European Union' (1999) 24 *European Law Review* 516; H. Rasmussen, 'Remedying the Crumbling EC Judicial System' (2000) 37 *Common Market Law Review* 1071; P. Craig, 'The Jurisdiction of the Community Courts Reconsidered', in G. de Búrca and J.H.H. Weiler (eds.), *The European Court of Justice* (Oxford University Press, 2001), Ch. 6; J. H.H. Weiler, 'Epilogue: The Judicial Après Nice', in ibid., p. 215; R. Caranta, 'Diritto comunitario e tutela giuridica di fronte al giudice amministrativo italiano' (2001) *Rivista Trimestrale di Diritto Pubblico* 81; A. Dashwood and A. Johnston (eds.), *The Future of the Judicial System of the European Union* (Oxford: Hart, 2001); N. Forwood, 'The Judicial Architecture of the European Union: The Challenges of Change', in M. Hoskins and W. Robinson (eds.), *A True European: Essays for Judge David Edward* (Oxford: Hart, 2003), p. 81; B. Vesterdorf, 'The Community Court System Ten Years from Now and Beyond: Problems and Possibilities' (2003) 28 *European Law Review* 203; C. Timmermans, 'The European Union's Judicial System' (2004) 41 *Common Market Law Review* 393; I. Pernice, J. Kokott and C. Saunders (eds.), *The Future*

This is readily apparent from the reports discussing such reform at the turn of the millennium.[2] The Courts' paper stressed that the organizational and procedural framework 'must be revised to enable the Court of Justice and the Court of First Instance to shorten existing time limits and deal with further increases in the number of cases brought'.[3] If this did not occur then there would be delays that could not be reconciled with an acceptable level of judicial protection in the Union. The Courts' paper continued in the following vein:

> Furthermore, in the case of the Court of Justice, the extra case-load might well seriously jeopardise the proper accomplishment of its task as a court of last instance which, in addition, has a constitutional role. The Court would then no longer be able to concentrate on its main functions, which are to guarantee respect for the distribution of powers between the Community and its Member States and between the Community institutions, the uniformity and consistency of Community law and to

of the European Judicial System in Comparative Perspective (Berlin: Nomos, 2006); H. Rasmussen, 'Present and Future European Judicial Problems after Enlargement and the Post-2005 Ideological Revolt' (2007) 44 *Common Market Law Review* 1661; N. Forwood, 'The Court of First Instance, Its Development, and Future Role in the Legal Architecture of the European Union', in A. Arnull, P. Eeckhout and T. Tridimas (eds.), *Continuity and Change in EU Law: Essays in Honour of Sir Francis Jacobs* (Oxford: Oxford University Press, 2008), Ch. 3.

[2] The Future of the Judicial System of the European Union (Proposals and Reflections) (May 1999), available at http://europa.eu.int/cj/en/instit/txtdocfr/autrestxts/ave.pdf, p. 8; Report by the Working Party on the Future of the European Communities' Court System (January 2000).

[3] The Future of the Judicial System, p. 8.

> contribute to the harmonious development of the law of the Union. Such a failure on the part of the Court would undermine the rule of law on which, as stated in Article 6(1) EU, the Union is founded.[4]

Four factors led to the increase in the caseload of the Court of Justice and the General Court. The most obvious is EU enlargement, from a Community of six to a Union of twenty-eight Member States, which has naturally generated more business for the EU courts. The second reason is equally evident, this being the expansion of areas over which the EU has competence, which occurred at every major Treaty revision. A further factor placing a strain on EU judicial resources has been the very success of harmonization initiatives. New EU legislation will generate important issues that require judicial clarification, more especially where the legislation is complex, as exemplified by the introduction of the Community trademark, which led to much extra work for the GC. The final rationale for the increase in caseload has been the growing awareness of EU law by lawyers. At the inception of the Community, EEC law remained the preserve of a limited number of specialists. Taking an EEC point was often seen as a matter of last resort. This has now changed markedly, such that while there are EU law specialists, most lawyers will now think about whether there is an EU 'angle' to a case which comes before them.

[4] The Future of the Judicial System, p. 9; Report by the Working Party, pp. 5–8.

The increase in caseload is evident from a brief glance at the statistics. Thus in 2010 the CJEU had 631 new cases brought before it, at that time the highest number in the Court's history, and a significant increase as compared with 562 new cases in 2009. The situation was replicated in relation to preliminary references. The number of references submitted in 2010 was 385, which was the highest ever, and exceeded the number in 2009, 302 references, by 27.4 per cent. There were 484 references pending in 2010.[5] By 2013 the Court had 699 new cases brought before it, which was an increase of 10 per cent compared with 2012 and constituted the highest annual number of cases brought in the Court's history.[6] The increase was primarily attributable to more appeals and references for preliminary rulings, the latter rising to 450, currently the highest ever, although extrapolation from past evidence indicates that the figure is likely to increase next year.

The length of time for a ruling to be given is especially important for the litigants. The CJEU made strident efforts to reduce this, with some success, given that at one stage it was taking close to two years to obtain the results of a preliminary reference. In 2013 the wait for a preliminary reference was 16.3 months, but this was nonetheless an increase compared to 15.6 months in 2012. It should not, moreover, be forgotten that litigants in preliminary-reference

[5] Proceedings of the Court of Justice, Annual Report 2010, available at http://curia.europa.eu/jcms/jcms/Jo2_11035/rapports-annuels.

[6] Proceedings of the Court of Justice, Annual Report 2013, available at http://curia.europa.eu/jcms/upload/docs/application/pdf/2014-06/qdag14001enc.pdf.

cases will already have spent time litigating in national courts, and will have had to endure whatever the wait time is in that legal system. The time to obtain other kinds of ruling from the CJEU has also increased, with appeals now taking 16.6 months and direct actions 24.7 months, whereas the latter figure for 2012 was 19.7 months. These tensions are evident in statements from the president of the Court of Justice, Vassilios Skouris, who, while expressing satisfaction at the increased throughput of cases, also noted that the 'intensification of judicial activity is liable, in the not necessarily distant future, to undermine the efficiency of the European Union's judicial system as a whole', with the consequence that there was a 'continuous need to seek means, in the form of both legislation and working methods, of improving the efficiency of that judicial system'.[7]

The caseload problems that beset the General Court are equally, if not more, serious.[8] This is especially significant for judicial review, since direct actions brought by individuals seeking to contest the legality of EU action under Article 263 TFEU are heard initially by the GC. The scale of the problem is apparent if we take the same two reference years as used in relation to the CJEU, 2010 and 2013. In 2010, 636 new cases were lodged at the GC, at that time the highest number, as compared with 568 in 2009. The GC completed 527 cases in 2010, but there were still 1,300 cases pending in December 2010. By 2013 there were 790 new cases, an increase

[7] Proceedings of the Court of Justice, Annual Report 2013, p. 5.

[8] Proceedings of the Court of Justice, Annual Report 2013.

of 30 per cent over the previous year, 702 completed cases, and 1,325 cases pending.

The time taken for a decision varies significantly depending on the nature of the case before the GC. Competition cases are generally the worst in this respect, with the wait time for a decision being 45.7 months in 2010, and 48.6 months in 2013. State aid cases are nearly as bad, with the respective figures being 32.5 months in 2010, and 48.1 months in 2013. The problem is not as bad for direct actions, which include those seeking annulment via judicial review, but this is merely a relative statement, given that a claimant would still have had to wait 24.9 months in 2013 for the outcome of the case, as compared to 23.9 months in 2010. On the plus side, the GC has improved efficiency as judged by the throughput of cases per annum. Notwithstanding this the president of the General Court, Marc Jaeger, did not view the present situation with equanimity, stating,

> It is apparent upon examination . . . that, whilst the action taken by the Court to improve its efficiency has borne fruit, the Court has control neither over the stability of its composition nor over its workload. More than ever, it is incumbent upon the competent European Union authorities to realise that it is absolutely essential to provide the Court with the means to enable it to perform its fundamental task, namely ensuring the right to effective judicial protection, a right which entails for the European Union judicature requirements both as to quality and intensity of judicial review and of [*sic*] speed.[9]

[9] Proceedings of the Court of Justice, Annual Report 2013, pp. 113–14.

The rationale for the increase in the GC's workload is partly explicable by the same factors that pertain to the CJEU, especially the increase in the size of the EU and the expansion in its sphere of competence. It is also clear from the statistics that a major component of the GC's caseload is intellectual property, accounting for 293 of the 790 new cases in 2013, which is by far the largest category of case defined by subject matter, while general actions for annulment accounted for 319 cases.

The strain on judicial resources is reflected at one stage removed, in changes made to case reporting, more especially given the costs entailed by the need to translate decisions into all official languages.[10] This prompted the CJEU to decide not to publish all of its decisions in the law reports, although they were available online.[11] A more recent manifestation of this has been the decision whereby cases are only published online, with the consequence that the European Court Reports, as hitherto known, cease to exist.[12] Thus from 1 January 2012 the reports of the CJEU and the GC, and from 1 January 2010 the reports of Staff Cases, are published exclusively in digital format on the EUR-Lex site.[13] The criteria for publication in the digital

[10] F. Jacobs, 'Recent and Ongoing Measures to Improve the Efficiency of the European Court of Justice' (2004) 29 *European Law Review* 823, at 827–8.

[11] Proceedings of the Court of Justice, Annual Report 2004, available at http://curia.europa.eu/jcms/jcms/Jo2_11035/rapports-annuels, pp. 11–12.

[12] See http://curia.europa.eu/jcms/jcms/P_106308.

[13] See http://eur-lex.europa.eu/homepage.html?locale=en.

Reports remain unchanged from those of the paper Records for the CJEU and the GC.

It is also important to recognize, when considering the time taken to reach a decision by the EU courts, that the parties may often have already spent time in another judicial forum. This is self-evidently so in relation to preliminary references where the time for the CJEU to reach a decision will be in addition to that spent before national courts. The point is, however, of more general relevance, more especially for administrative law, since direct actions heard by the GC may take the form of appeals from a lower-tier EU judicial organ. Thus the GC's increased workload in intellectual property is largely the result of trademark appeals pursuant to determinations of the Office for Harmonization in the Internal Market,[14] which is the EU agency dealing with this area. The OHIM Boards of Appeal are doing a good job of keeping on top of their caseload, receiving 2,602 appeals and taking 2,568 decisions in 2013.[15] The great majority of decisions, circa 80 per cent, were notified within eight months, and of those taken on appeal the GC affirmed the finding of the Board of Appeal in 86.5 per cent of cases. The bottom line is that from the parties' perspective the aggregate time for the decision is circa 26.7 months, taking account of the eight months plus the time for the GC's decision, which was 18.7 months in 2013.[16]

14 See https://oami.europa.eu/ohimportal/en/contact-us.

15 See http://pmd.oami.europa.eu.edgesuite.net/Annual-Report/FINAL/ohim/en/introduction.html.

16 Proceedings of the Court of Justice, Annual Report 2013, p. 182.

(b) Addressing caseload: judicial techniques

There are judicial mechanisms for dealing with the caseload problem, either by declining to hear certain cases or by expediting the discharge of cases that are heard.

(i) Limiting the cases that are heard

The first strategy, limiting the cases which come before the CJEU and the GC, operates differently for the main heads of the EU courts' jurisdiction. There are, however, 'costs' judged not financially, but rather in terms of the overall effectiveness of legal protection.

In relation to direct actions contesting the validity of EU norms, standing requirements have been the main control device applicable to actions brought by private parties under Article 263 TFEU. The rules have, however, been very tight and it would not be possible to address the workload problem by making them any tighter.

In relation to enforcement actions brought by the Commission before the CJEU under Article 258 TFEU, the main control mechanism relevant to caseload is the Commission's discretion as to whether it should take a case or not.[17] The number of cases brought under Article 258 is, however, not large and the Commission uses its scarce resources to fight those cases it believes to be most significant, and hence there is no real way of alleviating the CJEU's workload by reform in this area.

[17] R. Rawlings, 'Citizen Action and Institutional Attitudes in Commission Enforcement' (2000) 6 *European Law Journal* 4.

In relation to preliminary rulings under Article 267 TFEU, the CJEU can limit the number of such requests pursuant to the *Foglia* jurisprudence,[18] whereby it declined to hear cases that were hypothetical, where the questions raised were not relevant to the substantive action,[19] where the questions were not articulated clearly enough, and where the facts were insufficiently clear for the Court to be able to apply the relevant legal rules.[20] The results of this case law were incorporated in a memorandum providing guidance for national courts.[21] While the CJEU has therefore exerted greater control over the admissibility of references than hitherto, the Court has made it clear that it will only decline to

[18] Case 104/79, *Pasquale Foglia* v. *Mariella Novella* [1980] ECR 745; Case 244/80, *Pasquale Foglia* v. *Mariella Novello (No 2)* [1981] ECR 3045.

[19] See, e.g., Case C-83/91, *Wienand Meilicke* v. *ADV/ORGA F.A. Meyer AG* [1992] ECR I-4871; Case C-18/93, *Corsica Ferries Italia Srl* v. *Corpo dei Piloti del Porto di Genova* [1994] ECR I-1783; Case C-428/93, *Monin Automobiles–Maison du Deux-Roues* [1994] ECR I-1707; Cases C-320, 328, 329, 337, 338 and 339/94, *Reti Televisive Italiane SpA (RTI)* v. *Ministero delle Poste e Telecommunicazione* [1996] ECR I-6471; Case C-313/07, *Kirtruna SL and Elisa Vigano* v. *Red Elite de Electrodomésticos SA* [2008] ECR I-7907.

[20] See, e.g., Cases C-320–2/90, *Telemarsicabruzzo SpA* v. *Circostel, Ministero delle Poste e Telecommunicazioni and Ministerio della Difesa* [1993] ECR I-393; Case C-157/92, *Banchero* [1993] ECR I-1085; Case C-2/96, *Criminal Proceedings against Sunino and Data* [1996] ECR I-1543; Case C-257/95, *Bresle* v. *Préfet de la Région Auvergne and Préfet du Puy-de-Dome* [1996] ECR I-233; Case C-293/03, *Gregorio My* v. *ONP* [2004] ECR I-12013; Case C-152/03, *Ritter-Coulais* v. *Finanzamt Gemersheim* [2006] ECR I-1711.

[21] Information Note on References from National Courts for a Preliminary Ruling, OJ 2005 No C143/1, OJ 2009 No C297/01.

give a ruling if the issue of EU law on which an interpretation is sought is manifestly inapplicable to the dispute before the national court, or bears no relation to the subject matter of that action.[22] The *Foglia* principle therefore only excludes a limited number of references, and because national courts have learned to frame their references better there will therefore be fewer cases that can be excluded on this ground.

(ii) Expediting the throughput of cases

There are also techniques for expediting the throughput of cases that reach the EU courts. Thus there is a simplified procedure where a question referred for a preliminary ruling is identical to one on which the Court has already ruled, or where the answer to the question admits of no reasonable doubt or may be clearly deduced from existing case law. In such circumstances, the CJEU may, after hearing the advocate general, give its decision by reasoned order, citing the relevant case law. The procedure was used thirty-three times in 2013.[23] There is also an expedited procedure, which enables the Court to give its rulings quickly in very urgent cases by reducing the time limits and giving such cases priority. Use of this procedure is, however, conditional on approval by the president of

[22] See, e.g., Case C-85/95, *Reisdorf* v. *Finanzamt Köln-West* [1996] ECR I-6257; Case C-138/05, *Stichting Zuid-Hollandse Milieufederatie* v. *Minister van Landbouw, Natuur en Voedselkwaliktiet* [2006] ECR I-8339; Case C-484/08, *Caja de Ahorros y Monte de Piedad de Madrid* v. *Asociación de Usuarios de Servicios Bancarios (Ausbanc)* [2010] ECR I-4785, at [19]; Case C-440/08, *Gielen* v. *Staatssecretaris van Financiën* [2010] ECR I-2323, at [29].

[23] Proceedings of the Court of Justice, Annual Report 2013, p. 10.

the Court, and of the fourteen applications made in 2013, none were accepted.[24] There has, however, been increased use of the option of deciding a case without an Opinion of the advocate general in cases that do not raise a new point of law, this being used in 48 per cent of the judgments delivered in 2013.[25]

(c) Addressing caseload: legislative reform

Concerns over caseload have prompted legislative reform, the catalyst being initiatives from the CJEU. It began in earnest with a letter from the president of the CJEU to the president of the European Parliament, in which he stated the case for amendments to the Statute of the Court of Justice to tackle the workload problem.[26] These included changes to the composition of the Grand Chamber and appointment of a vice president for both the Court of Justice and the General Court to ease the workload of the respective presidents. These measures have been enacted.[27]

[24] Proceedings of the Court of Justice, Annual Report 2013, p. 10.

[25] Proceedings of the Court of Justice, Annual Report 2013, p. 10.

[26] 28 March 2011.

[27] Regulation (EU, Euratom) 741/2012 of the European Parliament and of the Council of 11 August 2012 amending the Protocol of the Statute of the Court of Justice of the European Union and Annex I thereto, OJ 2012 No L228/1; Decision 2012/671/EU of the Court of Justice of 23 October 2012 concerning the judicial functions of the vice-president of the Court, OJ 2012 No L300/47; Protocol (No 3) On the Statute of the Court of Justice of the European Union, Consolidated Version, 1 July 2013.

The initial proposal from the CJEU president also addressed the severe workload problems facing the GC, proposing an increase of twelve judges. This can be done under the Treaty, which provides that there should be at least one judge from each Member State on the GC, and thus clearly allows for more.[28] This was preferred to the option of creating more specialized courts,[29] since it was felt that this would be a less efficient way of dealing with the problem, and could, moreover, create a further tier of appeal in the subject matter area assigned to the specialized court. The Commission[30] and European Parliament[31] favoured appointment of more judges to the GC, but this proposal was nonetheless taken separately from those set out above, because there was controversy as to the manner of appointment of the extra judges.

If the extra appointments were based on nationality, there would have to be a rotation system, since there are fewer additional positions than the number of Member States. There would then be further questions as to the nature of the rotation criterion, whether it would be based on formal state equality, or whether there should be differentiation based on the size of the state. The Legal Affairs Committee of the European Parliament was, however, against this

[28] Art. 19(2) TEU. [29] Art. 257 TFEU.

[30] On the requests for the amendment of the Statute of the Court of Justice of the European Union, presented by the Court, COM(2011) 596 final.

[31] On the draft regulation of the European Parliament and of the Council amending the Protocol on the Statute of the Court of Justice of the European Union by increasing the number of judges at the General Court, Committee on Legal Affairs, A7–0252/2013, 10 July 2013, Rapporteur A. Thein.

criterion. It felt that the nationality principle was already fully represented in the application of the existing criterion for membership of the GC, since there was one judge from each Member State. The criteria for selection of the twelve additional judges should therefore be based on merit, subject to the caveat that there should be no more than two judges from a Member State at any one time.[32] This position was endorsed by the plenary of the EP,[33] and it remained of this view in its first reading of the proposed regulation.[34]

There is much to be said for the EP's position, which is based on sound principle. The outcome of the legislative deliberations nonetheless remains to be seen. The Council, although inclined to the nationality criterion, has agreed to a three-stage phased increase of GC judges, beginning with an extra twelve in 2015, culminating in 2019 with a total of fifty-six judges, which includes seven posts from the Civil Service Tribunal, which would be merged with the GC. It is vital that the increase in the number of GC judges is secured. An increase in the number of advocates general from six to nine

32 Committee on Legal Affairs, A7-0252/2013, Rapporteur A. Thein.

33 Amendments adopted by the European Parliament on 12 December 2013 on the draft regulation of the European Parliament and of the Council amending the Protocol on the Statute of the Court of Justice of the European Union by increasing the number of Judges at the General Court, P7-TA(2013)0581, 12 December 2013.

34 European Parliament legislative resolution of 15 April 2014 on the draft regulation of the European Parliament and of the Council amending the Protocol on the Statute of the Court of Justice of the European Union by increasing the number of Judges at the General Court, P7-TA(2014) 0358, 15 April 2014.

in July 2013, followed by a further addition to eleven in October 2015, has already become law.[35]

This, together with the extra judges for the GC, will go some way to alleviate the severe caseload problems. It will, in any event, take some considerable time to bring the backlog of cases down. It is regrettable that the present malaise has had to reach these proportions before action is taken, assuming that the increase does occur, given that the caseload problem has been developing for years.

This is in part because the delay in gaining judgment can lead to significant difficulties for the parties to a case, including those engaged in direct actions that are the foundation of judicial review. When such delays lead the CJEU to condemn the GC for breach of Article 6 of the European Convention of Human Rights, for failing to reach a decision within a reasonable time in a case that had taken in excess of five years, there is something seriously amiss.[36] From an administrative law perspective, it is scant comfort to litigants to be presented with an impressive array of judicial protections if the time to secure relief renders such protection chimerical. If, moreover, the system is structured such that litigants find it necessary to fight their way through multiple courts before reaching a forum that is capable of resolving the matter, then this will dissuade many who do not have the resources for such a 'journey'.

[35] Council Decision of 25 June 2013 increasing the number of advocates-general of the European Union, OJ 2013 No L179/92.

[36] Case C-385/07 P, *Der grüne Punkt–Duales System Deutschland GmbH* v. *Commission* [2009] ECR I-6155.

The present malaise is also regrettable for the less obvious but equally important reason that the caseload problem has prevented serious consideration of the rational division of authority between the CJEU and the GC. The jurisdictional remit of the GC has grown in an ad hoc manner. It was given heads of jurisdiction primarily to relieve the ECJ's workload, hence the assignment of staff cases and competition cases to the GC. The transfer of all direct actions brought by non-privileged applicants was fuelled by similar concerns. Coherence has not been at the forefront of the jurisdictional division between the CJEU and the GC. This is reflected in the piecemeal summation of that division on the official website.[37] It is apparent yet again in the absence of fit between nomenclature and sphere of jurisdiction, since the Court of First Instance was never a first-instance court across all areas, and the General Court is not in reality a court of general jurisdiction. Detailed analysis of what would be a rational division of jurisdiction between the CJEU and the GC is beyond the remit of the present study.[38] Suffice it to say

[37] See http://curia.europa.eu/jcms/jcms/j_6.

[38] See, e.g., J. Azizi, 'Opportunities and Limits for the Transfer of Preliminary Reference Proceedings to the Court of First Instance', in Pernice, Kokott and Saunders, *The Future of the European Judicial System*, pp. 241–56; S. Prechal, 'Who Should Do What?', in *La Cour de Justice des Communautés européennes, 1952–2002: Bilan et Perspectives* (Brussels: Bruylant, 2004), pp. 63–85; U. Everling, 'The Future of the European Judiciary within the Enlarged European Union', in *Mélanges en hommage à Michel Waelbroeck* (Brussels: Bruylant, 1999), pp. 333–54; P. Dyrberg, 'What Should the Court of Justice Be Doing?' (2001) 26 *European Law Review* 291; P. Craig, *EU Administrative Law* (Oxford: Oxford University Press, 2nd ed., 2012), Ch. 10.

for the present that the answer depends in part on the reform objectives. Studies in the past have emphasized the need to secure the unity of Union law by means of a supreme court; the need to ensure that the judicial system is transparent, comprehensible and accessible to the public; and the need to dispense justice without unacceptable delay.[39] A further factor must surely be that the system should be structured such that the most important points of law are decided by the CJEU, and that it is not troubled by less important cases.[40] This is not assured by the existing jurisdictional regime. What form the jurisdictional division would take as judged by these criteria may well be contestable. The salient point for present purposes is that the caseload crisis in the GC as it has unfolded over the last decade has stifled such strategic thinking, with those on the front line preoccupied with a constant daily battle to prevent the situation becoming worse.

3 Process and access

Any system of administrative law has access points or gateways, which determine who can get into the system. There are two crucial access points in any legal regime. There will be procedural rules determining who is entitled to be heard or to intervene before the initial decision is made, or who is entitled

[39] The Future of the Judicial System, p. 18; Report by the Working Party, p. 10.

[40] Forwood, 'The Court of First Instance', p. 36; B. Vesterdorf, 'A Constitutional Court for the EU' in I. Pernice, J. Kokott, and C. Saunders (eds.), *The Future of the European Judicial System in Comparative Perspective* (Baden-Baden: Nomos, 2006), p. 87.

to be consulted before a legislative-type norm is enacted. There will also be rules of standing that determine who should be able to complain to the court that the initial decision maker overstepped its powers. The judicial and legislative stance on these matters is crucial. The EU courts make real connections concerning the ambit of these two access points, as do courts in other legal systems.[41] A legal system may have very sophisticated tools for substantive judicial review, but if the access points or gateways are drawn too narrowly the opportunity for an individual to utilize such tools will perforce be limited. The challenges for EU administrative law concerning process and access are considered in this section.

(a) The status quo: the building blocks of process

The sources of EU administrative law are eclectic, and this is especially marked in relation to procedural norms, which are found in the Treaty, the Charter of Fundamental Rights, EU legislation, the case law of the EU courts and decisions made by the European Ombudsman. Thus the Treaty contains articles mandating the provision of reasons and access to information.[42] The right to be heard before an adverse individual measure is taken is included within the Charter of Fundamental Rights.[43] EU legislation embodies sector-specific

[41] R. Stewart, 'The Reformation of American Administrative Law' (1975) 88 *Harvard Law Review* 1667.

[42] Arts. 296, 15 TFEU.

[43] Charter of Fundamental Rights of the European Union, Art. 41(2), OJ 2010 No C83/2.

procedural codes for particular areas. The EU Ombudsman has reinforced the procedural precepts of judicial review through decisions on cases that fall within his jurisdiction.

The major work on the construction of EU process-based norms has, nonetheless, been done by the CJEU and the GC, which treat such norms as part of the general principles of law read into the Treaty. They have been activist in protecting process in relation to individual decisions, imposing a right to be heard as a general rule of Union law, irrespective of whether this requirement was found in the relevant Treaty article, regulation, directive or decision. These norms also bind Member States when they act within the scope of EU law. These principles were developed relatively early in the Court's jurisprudence. They are exemplified by recent rulings in which it held that observance of the rights of the defence was a general principle of EU law, which was applicable where the authorities were minded to adopt a measure that would adversely affect an individual. The authorities of the Member States were bound to observe these rights when they took decisions within the scope of EU law, even though the EU legislation applicable did not expressly provide for such a procedural requirement.[44] The story of this development has been told elsewhere[45] and there is no intent to repeat it here.

[44] Case C-276/12, *Sabou* v. *Finanční ředitelství pro hlavní město Prahu* EU:C:2013:678, at [38]; Case C-349/07, *Sopropé–Organizações de Calçado Lda* v. *Fazenda Pública* [2008] ECR I-10369, at [37]; Case C-383/13 PPU, *M.G. and N.R.* v. *Staatssecretaris van Veiligheid en Justitie* EU:C:2013:533, at [35].

[45] D. Curtin, 'Constitutionalism in the European Community: The Right to Fair Procedures in Administrative Law', in J. O'Reilly (ed.), *Human*

The ensuing discussion will rather focus on the strains on process rights flowing from the measures taken to fight terrorism post-9/11, and on more general proposals for a set of model rules on process in EU law.

(b) *Strains on process: security and equality of arms*

The challenges faced by UK law in relation to process included, as we have seen,[46] those flowing from legislation to deal with the threat posed by terrorism post-9/11. The EU has, not surprisingly, faced similar challenges.[47] In the famous *Kadi* case the ECJ struck down the EU's implementation of UN Security Council anti-terrorist asset-freezing resolutions,

Rights and Constitutional Law: Essays in Honour of Brian Walsh (Dublin: Round Hall Press, 1992), p. 293; J. Schwarze, 'Developing Principles of European Administrative Law' [1993] *Public Law* 229; G. Nolte, 'General Principles of German and European Administrative Law: A Comparison in Historical Perspective' (1994) 57 *Modern Law Review* 191; J. Schwarze, 'Towards a Common European Public Law' (1995) 1 *European Public Law* 227; K. Lenaerts and J. Vanhamme, 'Procedural Rights of Private Parties in the Community Administrative Process' (1997) 34 *Common Market Law Review* 531; H. Nehl, *Principles of Administrative Procedure in EC Law* (Oxford: Hart, 1999), pp. 70–99; H. Hofmann, G. Rowe and A. Türk, *Administrative Law and Policy of the European Union* (Oxford: Oxford University Press, 2011), pp. 204–21; Craig, *EU Administrative Law*, Chs. 11–12.

46 See above, pp. 199–209.

47 C. Eckes, 'Decision-Making in the Dark: Autonomous EU Sanctions and National Classification', in I. Cameron (ed.), *EU Sanctions: Law and Policy Issues Concerning Restrictive Measures* (Cambridge: Intersentia, 2013), pp. 177–98.

for violation of fundamental rights.[48] It held that the Community was based on the rule of law and that fundamental rights formed an integral part of the general principles of law, compliance with which was a condition precedent for the lawfulness of Community acts. Obligations imposed by an international agreement could not prejudice the constitutional principles of the EC Treaty, including respect for fundamental rights. The ECJ concluded that the applicants' right to be heard was violated by the EC Regulation giving effect to the asset-freezing regime emanating from the Security Council, because they could not contest the grounds on which they were included in the Security Council list.

The ECJ decided that the relevant regulation could, however, remain in force for three months, to allow time for the EU institutions to cure the procedural error and re-list the applicants if they wished to do so, which they duly did. Following the publication and communication to the applicants of summary reasons provided by the UN Sanctions Committee, and having allowed them a brief opportunity to respond to the allegations, the Commission adopted a new

[48] Cases C-402 and 415/05 P, *Kadi & Al Barakaat International Foundation* v. *Council and Commission* [2008] ECR I-6351; M. Nettesheim, 'U.N. Sanctions against Individuals: A Challenge to the Architecture of European Union Governance' (2007) 44 *Common Market Law Review* 567; G. de Búrca, 'The European Court of Justice and the International Legal Order after *Kadi*' (2010) 51 *Harvard International Law Journal* 1; T. Tridimas and J. Guitierrez-Fons, 'EU Law, International Law, and Economic Sanctions against Terrorism: The Judiciary in Distress?' (2009) 32 *Fordham International Law Journal* 660; M. Cremona, F. Francioni and S. Poli (eds.), 'Challenging the EU Counter-terrorism Measures through the Courts', *EUI Working Paper* 2009/10.

regulation maintaining the sanctions against Kadi. This was then challenged by the applicant in *Kadi II*.[49] The General Court held that the contested regulation must be subject to 'full review' in terms of the adequacy of the evidence offered to justify the sanctions, and observation of the rights of the defence. It concluded that there were serious failings, and that the protection afforded to the applicant's rights of defence was superficial and inadequate.

The CJEU on appeal fleshed out the process requirements incumbent on the EU institutions in cases of this kind.[50] The Commission, and a number of Member States, vigorously contested the intensity of review applied by the GC. The CJEU nonetheless affirmed that the EU courts should undertake a full review of the lawfulness of the contested measure in the light of EU fundamental rights, although its interpretation of 'full review' did not accord in all respects with that of the GC.

It held that the rights of the defence included the right to be heard and the right of access to the file, the latter being subject to issues of confidentiality. The right to effective judicial protection required that the person concerned must be able to ascertain the reasons for the decision, either by reading it or by obtaining disclosure of those reasons.[51]

[49] Case T-85/09, *Kadi* v. *Commission* [2010] ECR II-5177, at [171]–[188].

[50] Cases C-584, 593, 595/10 P, *Commission* v. *Kadi* EU:C:2013:518, at [97]–[141].

[51] Cases C-584, 593, 595/10 P, *Commission* v. *Kadi* EU:C:2013:518, at [101]. The CJEU recognized in accord with Art. 52(1) of the EU Charter of Rights that the rights could be limited, provided that the limitation was proportionate and that the essence of the right was still protected.

Respect for these rights demanded that the EU authorities disclose the evidence against the individual concerned,[52] and allow the person to make known his views on the case against him. These responses should be carefully evaluated by the EU authorities, which should give 'individual, specific and concrete reasons'[53] why they believed that the individual should be subject to restrictive measures.

It was for the EU courts via judicial review to police compliance with these procedural precepts and to ensure that the decision was taken on a sufficiently solid factual basis. This entailed verification of the factual allegations in the summary of reasons, to make sure that the decision could be factually substantiated. The EU courts could request the relevant EU authority to produce information or evidence, confidential or not, relevant to such an examination. It was not necessary to produce all the information or evidence that underpinned the reasons alleged in the summary provided by the UN Sanctions Committee, but it was necessary that the information or evidence supported the reasons relied on against the person concerned. If the EU authority was unable to comply with the request this did not per se constitute a violation of the individual's rights, but it did mean that the EU courts would base their decision solely on the material that had been disclosed to them, such that if the material did not suffice to substantiate a finding that a reason was well

[52] In this case it meant the summary of reasons provided by the UN Sanctions Committee.

[53] Cases C-584, 593, 595/10 P, *Commission* v. *Kadi*, at [116].

founded, the EU courts would disregard that reason as a basis for the contested decision. If the EU authority provided the information or evidence, the EU courts would assess its probative value.

The CJEU then gave guidance on the process that should pertain where security considerations might affect disclosure of evidence to the person concerned. If the EU courts decided that the security considerations did not merit non-disclosure, in whole or in part, the EU authority would be given the opportunity to disclose the evidence to the person concerned. If it failed to do so the EU courts would assess the lawfulness of the contested measure solely on the basis of the material that had been disclosed. If, however, there were valid reasons for non-disclosure a balance had to be struck between the security needs and the rights of the individual, and consideration should be given to disclosure of a summary of the evidence. The EU courts would assess how far failure to disclose evidence to the person concerned and his consequential inability to respond affected the probative value of the evidence. Such judicial review was especially important given the persistence of procedural shortcomings in the sanctions' listing process at the UN level.

The CJEU then applied the preceding principles to the facts of the case. It concluded, contrary to the GC's decision, that some of the allegations against Kadi in the summary findings of the UN Sanctions Committee were sufficiently specific and reasoned, but that the evidence to substantiate the reasons was lacking, given the rebuttals submitted by Kadi.

The principles enunciated by the CJEU in *Kadi II* have been applied in subsequent case law.[54] They constitute a measured response to the endemic problems posed by the need to balance process rights and security in cases of this nature. The Court's willingness to assess whether the reasons given to the person affected are sufficiently specific, whether retention of evidence or information is warranted and whether the reasons can be substantiated in the light of the available evidence is to be welcomed. The Rules of Procedure of the General Court have been amended by the addition of new provisions that reflect the CJEU's jurisprudence and create for the first time something akin to a closed-material procedure for the EU, albeit with safeguards for its use.[55]

(c) Looking to the future: model rules/general law on administrative procedure

(i) Emerging proposals

An important issue concerning process is whether we continue much as we have done thus far, or whether we make efforts to construct more general norms of administrative procedure, which can nonetheless be supplemented by sector-specific provisions. The desirability of a general law

[54] See, e.g., Case C-348/12 P, *Council* v. *Manufacturing Support & Procurement Kala Naft Co., Tehran* EU:C:2013:776; Case C 280/12 P, *Council* v. *Fulmen* EU:C:2013:775; Case T-306/10, *Yusef* v. *European Commission* EU:T:2014:141.

[55] Rules of Procedure of the General Court, OJ 2015 No. L105/1.

to regulate administrative procedure has been debated in the academic literature.[56]

The detailed contours of such model rules or general law remain to be determined. The Committee on Legal Affairs of the European Parliament passed a resolution in favour of such a law, which would apply to all EU institutions, agencies, offices and bodies in relation to direct administration and individual administrative decisions,[57] and this was affirmed by resolution of the European Parliament.[58] The proposed EU law would establish default principles of administrative procedure where no sector-specific rule existed, but such sectoral rules should not provide less protection than the general procedural law. The proposal is for a set of principles such

[56] European Ombudsman, European Code of Good Administrative Behaviour (2005), available at www.ombudsman.europa.eu/resources/code.faces; C. Harlow, 'Codification of EC Administrative Procedures? Fitting the Foot to the Shoe or the Shoe to the Foot' (1996) 2 *European Law Journal* 3; M. Shapiro, 'Codification of Administrative Law: The US and the Union' (1996) 2 *European Law Journal* 26; J. Ziller, 'Is a Law of Administrative Procedure for the Union Institutions Necessary? Introductory Remarks and Prospects', European Parliament, DG for Internal Policies, 2010; Oriol Mir-Puigpelat, 'Arguments in Favour of a General Codification of the Procedure Applicable to EU Administration', European Parliament, DG for Internal Policies, 2011, www.europarl.europa.eu/activities/committees/studies.do?language=EN; www.reneual.eu.

[57] Committee on Legal Affairs, Draft Report with Recommendations to the Commission on a Law on Administrative Procedure of the European Union, 2012/2024, 21 June 2012, Rapporteur Luigi Berlinguer.

[58] European Parliament Resolution of 15 January 2013 with recommendations to the Commission for a Law on Administrative Procedure, 2012/2024 INI, P7-TAPROV(2013)0004.

as legality, proportionality, non-discrimination and legitimate expectations to be set out at a high level of generality, with more detailed specification of the process rights for hearings. The Committee returned to the topic in 2015, consideration being given to a law on process rights in adjudication.

The proposals advanced by ReNEUAL, a research network on EU administrative law, are more far-reaching.[59] They went live online on 1 September 2014 and are contained in six 'books'. Book 1 contains an introduction to the project and deals with general definitional issues that affect the scope of the rules. The subsequent books deal with procedures relating to rule making, single-case decision making, contracts, mutual assistance between national administrations and information management. The overall package of rules is regarded in methodological terms as 'innovative codification'.[60] This captures the idea that a new law can take over principles found in current laws, modify existing principles where this is felt to be desirable and add new principles or rules where necessary. This should be seen in contrast to the more rigid *codification à droit constant*, where the objective is to produce a consolidated version of existing legislation.

The ReNEUAL proposals were the result of comparative study of existing national procedural regimes. They should not be regarded as the imposition of some 'EU' solution fashioned in disregard of national procedural norms.

[59] ReNEUAL is a network of over 100 scholars, academics and practitioners interested in the field of European administrative and regulatory law; see www.reneual.eu.

[60] ReNEUAL, Book 1, at [17] (www.reneual.eu).

To the contrary, the model rules draw on existing national procedural rules by way of learning and inspiration when crafting provisions for the EU. ReNEUAL draws its academic membership from across the EU, and the steering committee responsible for drafting the proposals contains members from France, Germany, Holland, Ireland, Italy, Luxembourg, Poland, Portugal, Spain and the United Kingdom.

(ii) Competence

We shall consider below the arguments for and against development of a set of model rules. Before doing so we should consider whether the EU has competence to enact a formal law on administrative procedure, albeit being mindful that such rules can still be of real value even if not embodied in formal legislation. This raises complex issues that have been examined elsewhere,[61] the essentials of which are as follows.

It is generally accepted that the EU can stipulate norms of administrative procedure that apply to EU institutions and national agencies pursuant to specific Treaty articles dealing with different subject matter areas.[62] The sector-specific

[61] P. Craig, 'A General Law on Administrative Procedure, Legislative Competence and Judicial Competence' (2013) 19 *European Public Law* 503; O. Mir, 'Die Kodifikation des Verwaltungsverfahrensrechts im Europäischen Verwaltungsverbund', in J.-P. Schneider and F. Velasco Cabrera (eds.), *Strukturen des europäischen Verwaltungsverbunds* (Berlin: Duncker and Humblot, 2009), pp. 206–9.

[62] See, e.g., Council Regulation 1/2003/EC of 16 December 2002 on the implementation of the rules on competition laid down in Articles 81 and 82 of the Treaty, OJ 2003 No L1/1; Report on the functioning of Regulation 1/2003, COM(2009) 206 final; Council Directive 96/61/EC of

legislation is often very detailed and mandatory. It is also generally accepted that such sector-specific legislation applicable to Member States is not dependent on any express power to make regulations or directives relating to administrative procedure applicable at national level. The relevant Treaty articles simply contain an explicit competence to make regulations or directives to govern the area, and this has been interpreted to include rules relating to national administrative procedure. It cannot therefore plausibly be argued that express Treaty authorization is a condition precedent for competence to make norms regulating national administrative procedure. The underlying principle is that such norms can be made pursuant to a power to make regulations or directives in the relevant area, and will be regarded as legitimate if they are integral to that regulatory regime.

A general law on administrative procedure might be grounded in Article 298 TFEU, which was a new addition to the Lisbon Treaty. It provides,

24 September concerning integrated pollution prevention and control, OJ 1996 No L257/26; Directive 2008/1/EC of the European Parliament and of the Council of 15 January 2008 concerning integrated pollution prevention and control (codified version), OJ 2008 No L24/8; Directive of the European Parliament and of the Council 2002/21/EC of 7 March 2002 on a common regulatory framework for electronic communications networks and services (Framework Directive), OJ 2002 No L108/33, 24 April 2002, as amended by Directive 2009/140, OJ 2009 No L337/37.

1. In carrying out their missions, the institutions, bodies, offices and agencies of the Union shall have the support of an open, efficient and independent European administration.
2. In compliance with the Staff Regulations and the Conditions of Employment adopted on the basis of Article 336, the European Parliament and the Council, acting by means of regulations in accordance with the ordinary legislative procedure, shall establish provisions to that end.

Its origins can be traced, like much else in the Lisbon Treaty, to the Convention on the Future of Europe and the final report of Working Group v on complementary competences,[63] which recommended inclusion of such a clause.[64] These recommendations must be seen in the light of two earlier working documents that shaped the conclusions.[65] Analysis of the final report and the working documents reveals that there were two dimensions to Article 298, which was in that sense Janus-faced.

It was concerned in part with the internal workings of EU administration, the efficiency dimension, and in part with the external impact of EU administration on those affected by it, the procedural-rights dimension.[66] The internal dimension found expression in the final report of Working Group v, which spoke of the need to safeguard 'good administrative

[63] Final Report of Working Group v on Complementary Competencies, CONV 375/1/02, Brussels 4 November 2002, pp. 17–18.

[64] It became Art. iii-398 in the Constitutional Treaty.

[65] Working Group v, Working Document 13, Brussels, 30 July 2002; Working Group v, Working Document 21, Brussels, 4 September 2002.

[66] Craig, 'A General Law on Administrative Procedure', 509–11.

culture in the EU administration to increase efficiency and legitimacy'.[67] The external dimension was equally prominent in the documentation that led to Article 298. Thus the final report of the Working Group stated that a Treaty article should highlight 'basic principles for good administration of the work of the EU institutions, e.g. service obligations, objectivity and impartiality, increased openness, consultations, and improved anticorruption measures',[68] which would involve analysis of the legal situation 'with respect to general principles of law concerning good administration as interpreted by the Court of Justice'.[69] There are three possible interpretations of Article 298, as determined by its wording and the *travaux préparatoires*.

The first and narrowest interpretation would be that Article 298 only empowers the making of regulations relating to the internal workings of the EU institutions, bodies, offices and agencies, and does not authorize regulations specifying process rights for those affected by decisions made by such institutions. The foundation for this view is that Article 298(2) states that the regulations should achieve the end specified in Article 298(1), this being an 'open, efficient and independent administration'. There are, however, difficulties with this narrow reading: it does not fit with the historical documentation, which clearly provides for an external as well as an internal dimension to Article 298; if Article 298 is limited in this manner then it would be redundant, since the objectives

[67] Final Report of Working Group v, p. 17.
[68] Final Report of Working Group v, p. 17.
[69] Final Report of Working Group v, p. 18.

can be attained through Article 336 TFEU, which is the legal foundation for the Staff Regulations;[70] and institutional reforms to improve accountability and efficiency after the resignation of the Santer Commission were achieved when Article 298 TFEU did not exist, the conclusion being that the EU had competence to introduce such measures prior to the creation of Article 298.[71]

The second interpretation of Article 298 TFEU would be that it provides the foundation for a law of administrative procedure, but it would only be applicable to EU institutions, bodies, offices and agencies, and not to Member State administration when it acts in the context of shared administration. The second interpretation appears to be that of the European Parliament and is premised on Article 298 having an external as well as an internal dimension.

The third interpretation builds on the second, but extends it to cover national administration when it acts within the scope of EU law. The textual support for this argument focuses on the wording of Article 298(1), which provides that 'the institutions, bodies, offices and agencies of the Union shall have the *support* of an open, efficient and independent *European* administration'.[72] This wording can accommodate national administration when it operates within the sphere of EU law, more especially because the latter part of the sentence is couched in terms of European, not EU, administration. It is not strained to read this to mean that the EU institutions

[70] See http://ec.europa.eu/civil_service/docs/toc100_en.pdf; http://europa.eu/epso/discover/careers/staff_regulations/index_en.htm.

[71] See http://ec.europa.eu/reform/index_en.htm. [72] Italics added.

must have support from an open, efficient and independent European administration, connoting both EU bureaucrats *stricto sensu* and also national bureaucrats when they operate in the sphere of EU law.[73] This textual reading coheres with reality, which is that in very many areas of shared administration national administration has formal legal duties pursuant to EU policy, which cannot successfully be delivered unless the national administration is open, efficient and independent. However, for the reasons set out below, it will be seen that most of the ReNEUAL proposals are confined to EU administration and do not cover Member States, unless sector-specific EU legislation so provides, or unless the state chooses to adopt the model rules.

Article 352 TFEU is the alternative foundation for a general law on administrative procedure. It provides that if action by the EU should prove necessary, within the framework of the policies defined in the Treaties, to attain one of the objectives set out in the Treaties, and the Treaties have not provided the necessary powers, then the Council acting unanimously on a Commission proposal can take the appropriate measures, after obtaining the consent of the European Parliament.

The conditions in Article 352(1) could be met without difficulty in this context. The Treaty values, which include the

[73] This interpretation is not precluded by Art. 298(2) TFEU. The fact that any regulations must comply with the Staff Regulations does not entail the conclusion that the regulations can only apply to EU staff. It merely means that insofar as the regulations made to achieve the ends in Art. 298(1) do apply to EU staff they must also comply with the Staff Regulations.

rule of law, are specified in Article 2 TEU and the Treaty objectives are delineated in Article 3 TEU. The two Treaty provisions are intimately connected. Principles of administrative procedure are central to the rule of law, and therefore satisfy this condition within Article 352. The articulation of such principles through model rules can be regarded as necessary within the framework of EU policies in general, not just in a specific substantive area. It can be forcefully argued that the objectives in Article 3 TEU could not be adequately achieved without such principles, the content, clarity and transparency of which would be enhanced through promulgation of a general law.

(iii) Arguments in favour

The principal arguments in favour of such model rules have been advanced by Jacques Ziller and Oriol Mir-Puigpelat and developed in the ReNEUAL project:[74] they can enhance the clarity of, and facilitate access to, the law; increase the coherence of principles and procedures; set up default procedures to fill gaps in existing law; and establish the functions of administrative procedure.

The model rules are drafted so that they can be enshrined in a formal, general law, or they can alternatively, as noted above, serve as detailed guides to best practice even if formal legislation is not favoured. The rules can, in either eventuality, function as a boilerplate, which can be

[74] Ziller, 'Is a Law of Administrative Procedure for the Union Institutions Necessary?'; Mir-Puigpelat, 'Arguments in Favour of a General Codification of the Procedure Applicable to EU Administration'; ReNEUAL, Book 1, www.reneual.eu.

supplemented by more sector-specific norms that address the needs of particular subject matter areas. They do not preclude more experimental procedural developments in particular policy areas, subject to the general caveat that sector-specific procedural rules should be interpreted to be in coherence with the model rules. The model rules can, moreover, supplement sector-specific provisions.[75]

We should resist the temptation to regard EU rules of administrative procedure as merely technical issues. This is quite wrong. They embody and reflect constitutional values, which are intrinsically important, and can have a marked impact on outcomes.[76] This is reflected in the very starting point of the ReNEUAL project, which was to determine how EU constitutional values broadly conceived could be translated into administrative procedure.[77] The model rules on administrative procedure can enhance legal certainty, reduce the costs of designing procedural principles for different sectoral areas, and lower litigation costs where they flow from uncertainty as to the nature of the requisite procedural obligations.

This is more especially so given the prevalence of shared or composite administration in the delivery of EU policy, where there is often uncertainty as to the procedural obligations imposed on national and EU administration

[75] ReNEUAL, Art. I-2.

[76] D. Curtin, H. Hofmann and J. Mendes, 'Constitutionalising EU Executive Rule-Making Procedures: A Research Agenda' (2013) 19 *European Law Journal* 1.

[77] ReNEUAL, Book I, at [1], [12], [14], [20].

respectively, in circumstances where both play a role in the final determination. Clarity as to the rules of administrative procedure is necessary in order to ensure that the rights and interests of affected parties do not fall into a 'black hole' between review and accountability in accord with EU precepts, and analogous national mechanisms.

The current rules on EU administrative law are the result of an admixture of case law combined with sector-specific legislation, with the result that there is often significant fragmentation between sectors. This is to be lauded if it is the result of considered thought as to the procedural requisites tailored for particular areas. While this is sometimes so, the reality in many instances is that it is the fortuitous result of what hard-pressed legislative drafters from a particular Commission Directorate-General chose to include in the legislative proposal, with the result being complexity as to the applicable rules and principles.

This is evident in relation to matters such as how an application should be made for a benefit under EU law, the nature of the hearing that should be provided, and the relative responsibilities in this regard of the EU and the national administrations in those instances governed by shared administration. The conceptual reality is that most procedural issues are not specific to a single policy area, but the practical reality is that few issues of EU administrative procedure law are subject to a systematic approach across policy areas, with the consequence that most transversal issues are not addressed in a transversal manner.[78]

[78] ReNEUAL, Book 1, at [14], [22].

If a set of model rules were to be enacted it would, moreover, give the Member States the opportunity for 'voice' on the content of the particular provisions in a way that has been lacking hitherto. At present, Member States can use the ordinary legislative procedure to voice their views on sector-specific legislation dealing with administrative procedure. They also have some opportunity for input into general principles of law through participation in legal actions before the CJEU, but this gives little possibility for input concerning the overall shape of administrative procedure. It is for this very reason that enactment of model rules on EU administrative procedure would provide an opening for discourse on its particular provisions.

(iv) Arguments against: unnecessary

The arguments against a set of model rules or a general law on administrative procedure vary, but two principal strands can be discerned: it is not necessary, and would have detrimental effect on pluralism in administrative procedure in the Member States. The former will be considered in this subsection, the latter in the subsection that follows.

The contention that such a law is not needed is predicated in its more aggressive form on the argument 'If it ain't broke why fix it?' and in its softer form on the assumption that adequate provision is made by the existing admixture of norms derived from Treaty provisions, sector-specific rules and case law.

The aggressive version of the argument only has force in a reductionist sense. There is no doubt that the EU can continue to function with the current system of administrative procedure. If the EU as an entity is endangered it is surely not going to founder for the lack of reform in this area. This argument, however, proves too much. The aggressive form of the argument could be applied to negate pretty much every reform initiative that one could imagine, in just about any area, whether at national or EU level.

The softer version is, by way of contrast, premised on unspoken assumptions as to what constitutes 'adequate provision'. It is clear on closer inquiry that the conception of adequacy is premised on two related assumptions, viz. that the rules of administrative procedure are fine in relation to the types of decision making to which they are applicable, and that they should not be extended beyond those areas. These assumptions are, however, far less secure the closer we test their conceptual and empirical foundations.

The legal status quo is that the precepts of administrative procedure apply to administrative decisions that affect an individual or a small number of individuals, through withdrawal of a benefit, imposition of a penalty and the like. The EU courts have done a good job in this area. Their activist jurisprudence has provided the requisites of due process, and they have supplied the omission of the legislature when the latter has failed to provide for such hearings, or where the standards of procedural rectitude have been insufficiently demanding.[79] Sector-specific rules have drawn on the case law

[79] See, e.g., Case C-49/88, *Al-Jubail Fertilizer* v. *Council* [1991] ECR I-3187, at [15]; Case C-291/89, *Interhotel* v. *Commission* [1991] ECR I-2257, at [14]; Case T-260/94, *Air Inter SA* v. *Commission* [1997] ECR II-997, at [60]; Case C-367/95 P, *Commission* v. *Sytraval and Brink's France* [1998]

and advanced beyond it through provision of more detailed regulatory precepts for different sectoral areas. There is, nonetheless, much room for further improvement in this area.

Most EU lawyers, even specialists in this area, would be hard-pressed to articulate in detail the applicable rules on a range of issues that are central to single-case decision making. These include the procedural norms that regulate the way in which applications should be made, the duties of the administration when in receipt of an application, the way in which complaints should be made, the duties of the administration when managing an administrative procedure, the administration's powers of investigation and inspection, the rules that govern who can be a party to a hearing, the nature of the hearing that must be afforded, and the due-process rules that pertain respectively to the EU and to the national administration when both play a central role in the final decision.[80]

Now, to be sure, the well-trained EU lawyer will, given sufficient time, be able to work out the answers to at least some of these issues. But that, of course, does not suffice to show that the current system is adequate in the preceding sense, more especially if the EU lawyer is charging for his or

ECR I-1719, at [67]; Case C-458/98 P, *Industrie des Poudres Sphériques* v. *Council and Commission* [2000] ECR I-8147, at [99]; Case C-141/08 P, *Foshan Shunde Yongjian Housewares & Hardware Co. Ltd* v. *Council* [2009] ECR I-9147, at [83].

80 See, e.g., Case T-260/94, *Air Inter SA* [1997] ECR II-997; Case T-450/93, *Lisrestal* v. *Commission* [1994] ECR II-1177; Case C-32/95 P, *Commission* v. *Lisrestal* [1996] ECR I-5373; Case T-50/96, *Primex Produkte Import-Export GmbH & Co. KG* v. *Commission* [1998] ECR II-3773; Case T-290/97, *Mehibas Dordtselaan BV* v. *Commission* [2000] ECR II-15.

her services and the 'meter' is running while the research is being undertaken. We should not rest content with a system in which lawyers have to fathom out the answers to such basic issues afresh each time, even if, or perhaps more especially if, they are academics, or practitioners working pro bono. Nor should we rest content with a system in which hard-pressed administrators and draft legislators have to patch together a package of procedural rules, even assuming that they draw on what are perceived to be relevant rules from analogous areas. There is little doubt that the existing regime could be significantly improved for legal advisers, those devising legislation and those applying it if there were some boilerplate model rules of the kind devised by ReNEUAL, which address the preceding issues in a clear and systematic manner.[81]

The second strand of the adequacy argument, to the effect that there is no need for procedural rules beyond their present confines, is equally contestable. Thus the ReNEUAL project on administrative procedure covers rule making, public contracts, procedures of mutual assistance between the EU and national administration as well as between national administrations when they act in the scope of EU law, and information management, in addition to single-case decision making. Rule making is not covered by the CJEU's existing law of procedural due process;[82] the procedural

[81] ReNEUAL, Book III.

[82] Case C-104/97 P, *Atlanta AG* v. *Commission* [1999] ECR I-6983; Case C-258/02 P, *Bactria Industriehygiene-Service Verwaltungs GmbH* v. *Commission* [2003] ECR I-15105, at [43]; Case C-221/09, *AJD Tuna Ltd* v. *Direttur tal-Agrikoltura u s-Sajd and Avukat Generali* [2011] ECR I-1655, at [49].

norms that should govern public contracts are relatively well developed in relation to public procurement, but outside this area they are still being forged by academics; procedures for mutual assistance exist, but there has been little considered thought as to the general principles that should underlie this area; and the rules on information management are highly complex and difficult to discern, even though information exchange is increasingly common between national administrations and between them and the EU administration, and even though it can have significant implications for privacy rights of the individuals concerned. There may be differences of opinion as to the content of procedural norms in these areas, but we should not proceed on the basis of some complacent assumption that the status quo is adequate.

Thus, to take but one example, there has been vibrant debate as to whether there should be greater procedural protection for rule making.[83] The EU courts' jurisprudence embodies a normative choice. The right to be heard in relation to individual determinations is regarded as fundamental; it is not dependent on a foundation in a Treaty article, regulation or directive; Union norms will be read subject to the right; and the courts can raise the right of their own motion. The courts' stance on participation or consultation in relation to norms of a legislative nature is markedly different. Such rights only exist where there is foundation in a

[83] See, e.g., Craig, *EU Administrative Law*, Ch. 11; J. Mendes, *Participation in EU Rulemaking: A Rights-Based Approach* (Oxford: Oxford University Press, 2011).

Treaty article, regulation, directive or decision; the courts will not lightly interpret these norms as giving rise to such rights; and the fact of participation in their making will not increase the applicant's chance of being accorded standing to seek judicial review. This distinction is contestable, since it may be fortuitous whether a person is affected through an individualized determination, or through a rule. The individualized determination may in any event have precedential impact and establish a rule or principle for a category of cases that impact on a broad range of people: policy can be developed by ad hoc adjudication as well as through rules. Furthermore, the twin rationales used to justify procedural rights in individual adjudication, instrumental and non-instrumental or dignitarian, are equally applicable in the context of rule making. According hearing rights in adjudication does not make up for the absence of participation rights when a norm of a legislative nature is made, since while it enables the individual to be heard as to the application of the rule, it does not allow for any input into the content of the rule itself. It should, in any event, be noted that the EU courts' jurisprudence, even if contestable, is only authority for the proposition that such process rights must be found in Treaty provisions or in EU legislation, and that it will not be judicially developed through general principles of law. The ReNEUAL proposal is, however, cast in just such terms, in the form of procedural norms that could be enshrined in EU legislation, subject to possible modification through sector-specific provisions.

The procedure to govern mutual assistance provides a further example of an area that will benefit from enhanced procedural clarity. Networks abound in the EU.[84] The Commission will use national networks in policy making, provided that it has a firm hand on the reins of power.[85] It is in the sphere of enforcement that such networks are most prevalent. It is not fortuitous that the most formal networks exist where there is the strongest incentive for effective enforcement of EU law across national borders.[86] The Commission is normally in the driving seat and presses for measures that enhance the enforcement capacities of the relevant national agencies to render the Union regulatory regime more effective. A network of national enforcement agencies may be created as a result of EU legislation, or the EU may use existing agencies. The national agencies are willing to surrender some enforcement autonomy on their own territory, since they gain reciprocal powers of cross-border enforcement in other Member States. This is exemplified by the regimes in customs and agriculture, where problems of cross-border fraud have been especially prevalent.[87] Such legislation

[84] P. Craig, 'Shared Administration and Networks: Global and EU Perspectives', in G. Anthony, J.-B. Auby, J. Morison and T. Zwart (eds.), *Values in Global Administrative Law: Essays in Honour of Spyridon Flogaitis and Gerard Timsit* (Oxford: Hart, 2011), Ch. 4.

[85] See, e.g., on policy making in relation to customs, http://ec.europa.eu/taxation_customs/customs/index_en.htm.

[86] The policy incentive may well differ; prominent examples include tax issues (Case C-276/12, *Sabou*, EU:C:2013:678), consumer protection and tracking of cross-border crime.

[87] Council Regulation (EC) 515/97 of 13 March 1997 on mutual assistance between the administrative authorities of the Member States and co-operation between the latter and the Commission to ensure the correct application of the law on customs and agricultural matters, OJ 1997 No L82/1, replacing earlier provisions dating from 1981.

will commonly include provisions concerning request for assistance between such authorities, and obligations to make information available to another authority and to conduct administrative enquiries concerning operations that constitute breach of the relevant regulatory scheme. EU legislation of this kind will, in addition, often make provision not only for the horizontal dimension of network co-operation, but also for the vertical dimension concerning relations between the national authorities and the Commission. While some networks have a legislative foundation, others do not. In either instance the rules developed by ReNEUAL will assist in the crafting of the process norms that should apply in such areas, subject to the caveat that sector-specific legislation may modify them.

(v) Arguments against: diversity and pluralism

Let us, then, turn to the second argument raised against a general EU law on administrative procedure, which is that it can stifle national diversity and plurality of value. The proposal from the European Parliament is limited to direct administration by EU institutions, bodies, offices and agencies. The ReNEUAL proposal applies to all EU administration, whether direct or shared/composite, but Books I–IV only apply to Member States if sector-specific legislation so stipulates, or if the Member State chooses to accept them.[88] A little drafting history is required in order to understand this decision as to the reach of the model rules.

Member States are already bound by general principles of EU law when they act within the sphere of EU law,

[88] ReNEUAL, Arts. I-1, I-3.

and this includes the requirements of procedural fairness as they pertain to the making of individualized decisions. It follows that a national agency operating within a regime of shared administration is already obliged to comply with the principles of fair procedure enunciated by the EU courts, as well as with sector-specific legislation. Decisions made by such agencies can be challenged via Article 267 TFEU if they do not comply with such precepts.

There is, nonetheless, a difference between the status quo and what this would become if the model rules were rendered applicable to Member States. Under the present regime, Member States are bound by general principles of law when they act in the scope of EU law, but the applicable rules remain the national administrative procedure acts or the equivalent, supplemented as needs be to ensure that the rules comply with the demands flowing from EU general principles of law. If the model rules were applicable to Member States when they act in the scope of EU law then the difference would be that all details of administrative procedure would be regulated directly by the EU rules. Thus under the current regime a Member State can meet the process requirements of general principles of EU law through application of national administrative law norms, whereas the alternative would require it to comply with the process requirements in the model rules.

There would be advantages if the model rules were applicable to Member States when they act in the sphere of EU law. It would provide those affected by such national decisions with a clear set of procedural rights and render it easier for national administrations to understand the procedural obligations incumbent on them. They would not have to determine afresh on each occasion whether procedural rules in national-court decisions, national codes of procedure or an admixture of the two sufficed to meet the requirements of EU law. The exclusion of national administration from the reach of such rules will make life more complex for claimants, national administrations and EU administration, more especially when they act in the context of shared administration. They will have to piece together the appropriate procedural obligations from the model rules as they apply to the EU administration, with the addition of national procedural norms, insofar as they are consonant with EU general principles of law, being applicable to the national element of the determination. If decisions are made to which EU and national administrations contribute via shared administration, then to confine the procedural rules to one part of the shared schema is not optimal, since it presumes that their respective contributions to the decision can be hermetically sealed or differentiated in a way that is often belied by the legal and administrative structure of such schema. The rationale for inclusion of a Member State administration when it acts in the sphere of EU law is therefore grounded on the legal and political reality of shared administration, a reality repeatedly sanctioned by and through EU legislation agreed to by the Member States.

There were, nonetheless, reasons why the model rules were confined to EU administration, subject to the caveat that sector-specific legislation could render them applicable to Member States, or that the Member State might choose to adopt them. It was in part because of doubts as to EU competence to enact such model rules. The competence issue was considered above, and while a plausible argument for application of such rules to Member States can be made, it is contestable, as recognized by the ReNEUAL steering committee. The choice as to the scope of application of the model rules was also in part the result of consultation exercises undertaken during the drafting of the model rules. The steering committee received much valuable assistance from meetings with judges, practitioners and academics knowledgeable with regard to administrative procedure. It became apparent that there was considerable opposition to the application of the model rules to Member States, more especially from national administrative courts. The rationale for this opposition varied, but the general tenor was that it would intrude too greatly on the terrain covered by national administrative procedure acts or the equivalent. The soundness of this concern may be debated, but the bottom line was that the issue threatened to derail the project as a whole. The existence of EU legal competence and political acceptance of a legislative initiative drafted pursuant to such competence are self-evidently distinct. Thus even if it was decided that there was competence to enact a set of model rules, the writing on the wall was clear, viz. that national judicial opposition would translate into political rejection in the Council. The steering committee therefore decided to limit the scope of application of the model rules in the manner adumbrated above.

The rest, as they say, is history, for the present at least, if that is not an oxymoron. The objection that the rules would intrude too greatly on Member State action and therefore diminish desirable plurality of view is therefore moot.

I do not, however, believe that this concern was warranted, in relation to the core proposals concerning single-case decision making. There was nothing in the content of the proposals that should have caused alarm in this respect. The rules were drafted fully cognizant of the analogous provisions on applications, complaints, inspections, hearings and the like contained in existing EU legislation and in national procedural codes. Now, to be sure, there may well be particular detailed provisions that differ from those in relevant national legislation. But while national diversity is an important value, it should surely be kept in perspective. In an EU of twenty-eight Member States, it is commonly the case that there have to be compromises in relation to substantive issues related to trade, goods, services and the like. There is no a priori reason to place national rules of administrative procedure on a higher plane in this regard.[89]

(d) Access: standing

The discussion thus far has been concerned with access in terms of the right to be heard when the initial determination

[89] The situation is somewhat different in relation to contacts made by public authorities. There are deeper differences between Member States as to whether general contract law applies to public contracts, or whether a specific administrative contract law is applicable. However, this difference should not be over-exaggerated. Thus, even where 'general' contract law applies to contracts made by public bodies, it is commonly modified, judicially or administratively, such that the result is not that different from systems that use a 'distinctive' public contract law. R. Noguellou and U. Stelkens (eds.), *Comparative Law on Public Contracts* (Brussels: Bruylant, 2010).

is made. The focus now shifts to access to judicial review where a party seeks to challenge such norms. The problems concerning standing to seek judicial review for non-privileged applicants are well known, as attested to by the extensive literature.[90]

Direct challenge to the legality of EU norms required non-privileged applicants to show that they were directly and individually concerned by the measure, pursuant to Article 230(4) EC. This was extremely difficult. The *Plaumann* test demanded that persons other than those to whom a decision was addressed could only claim to be individually concerned if the decision affected them by reason of certain attributes peculiar to them, or by reason of circumstances in which they were differentiated from all other persons, and by virtue of these factors were distinguished individually, just as in the case of the person addressed.[91] The applicant failed because the activity of importing clementines could be carried out by anyone at any time, but it was always open to the Court to contend that others could enter the industry, and hence to deny standing to existing firms, even if this made no sense

[90] See, e.g., H. Rasmussen, 'Why Is Article 173 Interpreted against Private Plaintiffs?' (1980) 5 *European Law Review* 112; A. Arnull, 'Private Applicants and the Action for Annulment under Article 173 of the EC Treaty' (1995) 32 *Common Market Law Review* 7; A. Ward, *Judicial Review and the Rights of Private Parties in EC Law* (Oxford: Oxford University Press, 2nd ed., 2007); A. Arnull, 'Private Applicants and the Action for Annulment since *Codorniu*' (2001) 38 *Common Market Law Review* 7; P. Craig, 'Standing, Rights and the Structure of Legal Argument' (2003) 9 *European Public Law* 493.

[91] Case 25/62, *Plaumann & Co.* v. *Commission* [1963] ECR 95.

in terms of supply and demand. It thus became well-nigh impossible for individuals to challenge decisions that were not directly addressed to them, save in a limited number of retrospective cases. The difficulty of directly challenging EU norms in the form of regulations was equally marked, since the ECJ would only countenance this if a regulation was not a real regulation, but was in reality a decision of individual concern to the applicant. This was not easy to prove, because the Court held that a real regulation was a measure that applied to objectively determined situations and produced legal effects with regard to categories of persons described in a generalized and abstract manner, and that this was not called in question by the mere fact that it was possible to determine the number or even identity of those affected.[92]

Indirect challenge to contest the legality of EU norms was an imperfect substitute for more liberal standing rules for direct challenge. The narrow rules for standing in cases of direct challenge were often justified judicially by the existence of indirect challenge via Article 234 EC, since the individual could get to the ECJ via the national courts. Advocate General Jacobs in *Extramet*[93] and *UPA*[94] pointed out the serious limitations of this reasoning: national courts lacked expertise in the subject matter and did not have the benefit of participation of the Council and Commission;

[92] Case 789 and 790/79, *Calpak SpA and Societa Emiliana Lavorazione Fruita SpA* v. *Commission* [1980] ECR 1949.

[93] Case C-358/89, *Extramet Industrie SA* v. *Council* [1991] ECR I-2501, AG Jacobs.

[94] Case C-50/00 P, *Union de Pequenos Agricultores* v. *Council* [2002] ECR I-6677, AG Jacobs.

indirect actions could involve substantial delays and costs, because of the need to contest the case through national courts before getting to the ECJ; the applicant had no right under the preliminary-ruling procedure to decide whether a reference was made, which measures were referred for review or what grounds of invalidity were raised, and thus had no right of access to the ECJ; there could be cases where it was difficult or impossible for an applicant to challenge a general measure indirectly where there were no challengeable implementing measures or where the applicant would have to break the law in order to be able to challenge ensuing sanctions; and national courts had no jurisdiction to declare EU regulations invalid. Advocate General Jacobs therefore concluded that the only way to secure the effective right of judicial protection was to have a test for direct challenge based on substantial adverse impact.

The ECJ in *UPA* was, however, unmoved by such considerations and declined to follow the advocate general. It reiterated the *Plaumann* test, and held that if the conditions therein were not fulfilled then a natural or legal person could not seek the annulment of a regulation under any circumstances.[95] It also reiterated its view that the Treaty established a complete system of legal remedies for challenging the legality of EU action. While the meaning of individual concern must be interpreted in the light of the right of effective judicial protection, this could only be in the context of defining the circumstances that could distinguish an applicant individually. An interpretation of individual concern in the light

[95] Case C-50/00 P, *Union de Pequenos Agricultores*, at [37].

of the right to effective judicial protection could not have the effect of setting aside that condition, which was expressly laid down in the Treaty. This would, said the ECJ, go beyond the jurisdiction of the EU courts, and would require a Treaty amendment.

There were significant difficulties with the ECJ's reasoning in *UPA*. These difficulties concerned the assumption that the Treaty provides a complete system of legal protection through direct and indirect review, its interpretation of the right to effective legal protection and its reasoning as to what could be a legitimate judicial interpretation of Article 230(4) EC.[96] The ruling was, however, followed in later cases, with the result that change could only be forthcoming through Treaty amendment. This duly occurred when Article 263(4) TFEU was recast, following suggestions in the Constitutional Treaty:

> Any natural or legal person may, under the conditions laid down in the first and second paragraphs, institute proceedings against an act addressed to that person or which is of direct and individual concern to them, and against a regulatory act which is of direct concern to them and does not entail implementing measures.[97]

The term 'regulatory act' did not fit easily with the Lisbon classification of legal acts. It could be construed broadly to cover any legally binding act, whether legislative, delegated or implementing, provided that it does not entail implementing measures. It could be interpreted more narrowly to cover any

[96] Craig, *EU Administrative Law*, Ch. 11.

[97] Art III-365(4) CT.

legislative, delegated or implementing act, provided that it takes the form of a regulation or decision that does not entail implementing measures. It could cover only delegated and implementing acts, in the form of regulations or decisions, which do not entail implementing measures, or only delegated acts subject to the same condition.

The CJEU held in *Inuit* that the term 'regulatory act' does not cover legislative acts.[98] In reaching this conclusion it drew on the drafting history of the analogous provision in the Constitutional Treaty, which was said to indicate that the reform was not intended to touch the standing requirements for legislative acts. It felt also that the contrary conclusion would render the distinction drawn between 'acts' and 'regulatory acts' in Article 263(4) TFEU illusory. The advocate general had, moreover, argued that regulatory acts should not cover legislative acts, because the latter possessed greater legitimacy through enactment via the ordinary legislature. The novel aspect of Article 263(4) whereby individual concern is dispensed with does not, therefore, apply to legislative acts.

The liberalized standing rule will, moreover, only be applicable to a regulatory act that is of direct concern and does not entail implementing measures. It follows that the broader the meaning given to the concept of implementing act, the narrower is the scope of the exception in Article 263(4). Thus even if there is a regulatory act, the exception will not apply if there are deemed to be implementing

[98] Case C-583/11 P, *Inuit Tapiriit Kanatami* v. *Parliament and Council*, EU:C:2013:625.

measures, and it will be for the claimant to show individual concern in the *Plaumann* sense in order to maintain a direct action.

Telefónica gave a broad interpretation to the concept of implementing measure, thereby limiting the circumstances in which the liberalized rule can apply.[99] The applicant challenged a Commission decision declaring a Spanish tax provision to be incompatible with the state aid rules. The Court rejected the applicant's argument that the challenged measure was a regulatory act that did not entail implementing measures. It held that the Commission decision concerning the legality of the tax scheme was addressed solely to Spain and did not bind other persons. When Spain gave effect to that decision there would then be tax consequences for the applicant, and these constituted implementing measures 'entailed' by the Commission decision that could be challenged indirectly in national courts via Article 267.

There are two respects in which the new status quo is unsatisfactory. This is in part because the liberalization has been a good deal less liberalizing than some might have hoped. The exclusion of legislative acts from the ambit of the reformed Article 263(4) has received most comment in this respect. It is, however, the interpretation accorded to 'implementing measure' that has an equally dramatic impact on the scope of the reform. There is force in the applicant's contention in *Telefónica* that if any measure that

[99] Case C-274/12 P, *Telefónica SA* v. *Commission*, EU:C:2013:852; Case C-132/12 P, *Stichting Woonpunt* v. *European Commission*, EU:C:2014:100.

a Member State is required to adopt in order to give effect to an EU act constitutes an implementing measure, however minor it may be, then a very wide variety of regulatory acts will be automatically excluded from the scope of the revised Article 263(4). The CJEU's ruling de facto endorses that broad view by regarding the measures taken by Spain as a consequence of the illegality of the aid scheme to be implementing measures for these purposes. If the applicant cannot take advantage of the exception for regulatory acts that do not entail implementing measures, it must then prove *Plaumann* in order to bring a direct action under Article 263, or challenge the national measures indirectly via an indirect action under Article 267. The former route leads to all the difficulties of proving individual concern in accord with the *Plaumann* reasoning. The latter remains beset by the difficulties with indirect actions pointed out cogently by Advocate General Jacobs, which remain unanswered by the CJEU.

The second reason why the new status quo is unsatisfactory is because the chosen reform was itself questionable. It was beset from the outset with studied ambivalence as to whether the object was to make the standing rules for direct actions more liberal and thereby render the difficulties of indirect actions less problematic, or whether the *raison d'être* was simply to prevent an individual from having to break a law in order to challenge it. This ambiguity was present in the deliberations during the Constitutional Treaty. We should, however, be wary of drawing too heavily on that drafting history, given that the Discussion Circle concerning the EU courts had very limited time for deliberation and consultation.[100] The CJEU placed its considerable weight behind the latter, narrow reading of the reform, which is unsurprising.[101] I, like many others, favour more liberal standing rules, and thus prefer the former reading of the reform. Truth to tell, however, if the real objective were to liberalize standing then the new addition to Article 263(4) is not how it should be done. This is because it makes little sense in normative terms to deny the need for any individual concern in relation to some species of act, while insisting on some very strict showing of such concern for other types of act. If principled liberalization was the objective then Advocate General Jacobs's criterion of substantial adverse impact would undoubtedly be the preferred choice.

4 Substance, intensity and variation

In every system of administrative law the courts exercise some control over factual and discretionary determinations made by the administration. This commonality is matched by debate, academic and judicial, as to the intensity of such review, how far it should vary depending on the nature of the subject matter, how transparent the courts should be about the factors that drive the choices that they make and how far process considerations should inform the resulting test for substantive review. The debate ebbs and flows in and across legal systems, with claims that the courts are

[100] CONV 543/03, Discussion Circle on the Court of Justice, Brussels, 7 February 2003.

[101] Case C-274/12 P, *Telefónica SA*, at [27].

trespassing too far beyond their proper remit and intervening on the merits of decisions made by the political branch of government, met by counterclaims that if substantive review becomes too exiguous then it ceases to exist as any form of meaningful judicial oversight. It is therefore unsurprising that these issues are salient in the EU.

The judicial approach has not changed since the inception of the EEC. The general legal mantra is that the court should not substitute its judgment for that of the initial decision maker on issues of fact and discretion. The applicant must show some manifest error, misuse of power or clear excess in the bounds of discretion in order for the court to intervene. However, although the 'formal test' has remained constant its interpretation has altered over time. It has been used in three different ways, with the crucial variant being the intensity of review.[102]

In the early case law, the ECJ applied the test for review of fact and discretion, especially that of manifest error, with a very light touch, such that it was difficult for the applicant to succeed. The ECJ would characteristically deal with the allegation of manifest error within a few brief paragraphs and dismiss the claim unless there was some flagrant or egregious error on the face of the decision. This reflected the duality inherent in the very idea of manifest error, where the adjective 'manifest' can connote the seriousness of the error and the degree to which it is apparent on the face of the challenged decision. The reality was that the ECJ required the applicant to prove both in order to succeed and it was

[102] Craig, *EU Administrative Law*, Ch. 15.

reluctant to delve into the reasoning that led to the contested determination. It was common for the ECJ to devote but one or two brief paragraphs of its judgment to the issue, stating that the applicant's allegations revealed no indication of such an error or misuse of power.[103] Judicial review for manifest error was therefore light-touch during these early years. This was unsurprising given that prior to the creation of the Court of First Instance in 1986 the ECJ was the only judicial body that could determine the validity of Community regulations, and given also that the ECJ would have been mindful of the political compromises made when balancing the broad discretionary Treaty criteria that informed regulations in areas such as agriculture.

The early case law lasted in effect until the 1990s, and thus was the norm for the initial thirty years of the Community's existence. While the formal test remained the same thereafter, the legal reality, judged by the manner in which it was applied, was different, in some areas at the least, as evidenced by a willingness to review the factual findings and reasoning process far more closely in order to determine whether the requisite manifest error existed. This was especially evident in the CFI's jurisprudence. The shift in intensity of review was apparent in certain subject matter areas, which

[103] See, e.g., Case 57/72, *Westzucker GmbH* v. *Einfuhr-und Vorratsstelle für Zucker* [1973] ECR 321; Case 74/74, *Comptoir National Technique Agricole (CNTA) SA* v. *Commission* [1975] ECR 533; Case 78/74, *Deuka, Deutsche Kraftfutter GmbH, B J Stolp* v. *Einfuhr-und Vorratsstelle für Getreide und Futtermittel* [1975] ECR 421; Case 98/78, *Firma A. Racke* v. *Hauptzollamt Mainz* [1979] ECR 69; Case 730/79, *Philip Morris Holland BV* v. *Commission* [1980] ECR 2671.

were characterized by long CFI judgments, often in excess of 100 pages, in which considerable space was devoted to consideration of the pleas relating to factual and discretionary error. Prominent examples of this could be seen in risk-regulation cases, as exemplified by *Pfizer*,[104] where the CFI spent 125 paragraphs of its judgment examining the claims of manifest error relating to fact, and ninety-two paragraphs to manifest error relating to discretion, which contrasted markedly with the one or two paragraphs to be found in the earlier jurisprudence. High-intensity review was also evident in relation to judicial review of competition, where the CFI annulled several merger decisions for manifest error,[105] and the same intensity of review was carried over to other competition disputes.[106] The EU courts also deployed high-intensity review for manifest error in some cases concerned with fundamental rights, most notably those concerning the freezing of assets of suspected terrorists pursuant to the placing of such people on the relevant list by the UN Sanctions Committee.[107]

[104] See, e.g., Case T-13/99, *Pfizer Animal Health SA* v. *Council* [2002] ECR II-3303; Case T-70/99, *Alpharma Inc.* v. *Council* [2002] ECR II-3495.

[105] See, e.g., Case T-342/99, *Airtours plc* v. *Commission* [2002] ECR II-2585; Case T-5/02, *Tetra Laval BV* v. *Commission* [2002] ECR II-4381.

[106] See, e.g., Case 201/04, *Microsoft Corp.* v. *Commission* [2007] ECR II-3601; Case T-427/08, *Confédération européenne des associations d'horlogers-réparateurs (CEAHR)* v. *European Commission* [2010] ECR II-5865.

[107] Case T-85/09, *Kadi* v. *European Commission* [2010] ECR II-5177; Cases C-584, 493, 595 P, *European Commission* v. *Yassin Abdullah Kadi*, EU:C:2013:518.

It would, nonetheless, be mistaken to assume that this intensity of review has characterized all case law from the 1990s onwards. The reality is that there is much jurisprudence in which the test for review has been used differently from the previous two modes of interpretation depicted above. The hallmark of these cases is that the interpretation of the manifest-error test is more searching than the first mode of interpretation, but less than the second. The EU courts examine the claim that the decision was vitiated by manifest error in greater depth and detail compared to the early case law, although it is not easy for applicants to succeed in these cases, but will not engage in the very searching review of the kind evident in cases of risk regulation, competition and fundamental rights. This third approach is evident in much of the case law concerning common policies, Structural Funds and state aids.[108]

The relative intensity of review produced debate and contestation in the EU as it has elsewhere. Thus the Commission was surprised and 'stung' by the CFI's rulings that overturned its merger decisions. A measure of the 'heat'

[108] See, e.g., Case C-120/99, *Italy* v. *Council* [2001] ECR I-7997; Case C-390/95, P *Antillean Rice Mills NV* v. *Commission* [1999] ECR I-769; Case C-289/97, *Eridania SpA* v. *Azienda Agricola San Luca di Rumagnoli Viannj* [2000] ECR I-5409; Cases C-27 and 122/00, *R* v. *Secretary of State for the Environment, Transport and the Regions, ex p Omega Air Ltd* [2002] ECR I-2569; Case T-81/00, *Associacao Comercial de Aveiro* v. *Commission* [2002] ECR II-2509; Cases C-57 and 61/00 P, *Fresistaat Sachsen and Volkswagen AG and Volkswagen Sachsen GmbH* v. *Commission* [2003] ECR I-9975; Case T-75/06, *Bayer CropScience AG* v. *Commission* [2008] ECR II-2081; Case C-176/09, *Luxemburg* v. *European Parliament and Council* [2011] ECR I-3727.

generated by this issue was apparent from the Commission's appeal, in which it stated that the CFI had distorted the content of the contested decision, and misconstrued the concept of manifest error so as to render it tantamount to substitution of judgment.[109] Its argument proved to little avail before the ECJ, which upheld the CFI's decision.[110] The ECJ, while reiterating the test for manifest error in relation to fact, imbued that concept with a rigour and scope it had lacked hitherto:

> Whilst the Court recognizes that the Commission has a margin of discretion with regard to economic matters, that does not mean that the Community courts must refrain from reviewing the Commission's interpretation of information of an economic nature. Not only must the Community courts, *inter alia*, establish whether the evidence relied on is factually accurate, reliable and consistent but also whether that evidence contains all the information which must be taken into account in order to assess a complex situation and whether it is capable of substantiating the conclusions drawn from it. Such a review is all the more necessary in the case of a prospective analysis required when examining a planned merger with conglomerate effect.[111]

There were reasons that could be divined for the increased intensity of review, although the Court did not voice these

[109] Case 12/03 P, Appeal brought by the Commission against the judgment delivered by the CFI in Case T-5/02, OJ 2003 No C70/7.

[110] Case C-12/03 P, *Commission* v. *Tetra Laval* [2005] ECR I-987.

[111] Case C-12/03 P, *Commission* v. *Tetra Laval*, at [39].

explicitly. Thus risk regulation coupled with the attendant precautionary principle has been controversial, more especially in EU–USA legal relations.[112] Heightened judicial review can be seen as one way to lend legitimacy to administrative decisions concerning risk and precaution by subjecting the reasoning to closer judicial scrutiny. There were concerns in relation to competition, the most prominent being that the Commission was acting as prosecutor, judge and jury. More intense judicial review of fact and discretion was once again viewed as part of the solution, coupled with institutional reform as to the way in which such decisions were made by the Commission. The increased judicial oversight was designed to allay fears that Commission decisions with important legal and financial consequences for the parties were not subject to external scrutiny. This sentiment was not expressed in the CFI's decisions, but it was given voice extra-judicially by the president of the CFI.[113] The greater intensity of review in cases of human rights has been justified squarely on the basis of the importance of the right, although the Court has not always been consistent in the intensity of judicial scrutiny even in cases of this kind.

[112] See, e.g., C. Sunstein, *Risk and Reason: Safety, Law, and the Environment* (Cambridge: Cambridge University Press, 2002); C. Sunstein, 'Beyond the Precautionary Principle' (2003) 151 *University of Pennsylvania Law Review* 1003; G. Marchant and K. Mossman, *Arbitrary and Capricious: The Precautionary Principle in the European Union Courts* (Cambridge, MA: AEI Press, 2004).

[113] Judge B. Vesterdorf, 'Certain Reflections on Recent Judgments Reviewing Commission Merger Control Decisions', in Hoskins and Robinson, *A True European*, pp. 118, 143.

It might be felt at this juncture that substantive review of fact and discretion is in good shape in the EU. The test for review is applied with varying intensity depending on the nature of the subject matter. If courts wish to expand the scope of substantive review they can do so in one of two ways. They might choose to add new heads of substantive review to those currently available within that system. They might also expand the reach of substantive review by taking existing heads of review and giving them a more expansive interpretation than hitherto. The techniques can be used in tandem, but the latter, however, has 'attractions' for the judiciary. It is easier for courts minded to expand substantive review to preserve the impression of continuity with existing doctrine if they continue to use well-recognized heads of review, while at the same time imbuing them with greater force than hitherto. This approach obviates the need for judicial self-inquiry that attends the decision as to whether to introduce a new head of review to the existing armoury. Investing existing heads of review with more vigour will, moreover, only be apparent when the task has been judicially accomplished. Reflection on the new status quo, whether by academics or by courts, will therefore take place against the backdrop of an already developed jurisprudence that embodies the modified meaning given to the 'classic' head of review. So, on this view, what we have is as good as it gets. The pattern of varied intensity of review can be discerned by academic scrutiny. The EU courts do not generally give voice to this, but that is often the case in legal systems, and we should not expect it to be different in the EU.

This view is certainly possible, but we should nonetheless pause before accepting it with equanimity. There is something foundational and fundamental captured by the precept 'Say what you mean and do what you say'. It is especially telling in this context. Courts spend much of their time in administrative law cases admonishing administrators to provide reasons that adequately and accurately explain their action. This is as it should be, given the centrality of reason-giving to accountability. It is therefore somewhat paradoxical that we do not demand the same of EU courts when they fashion and apply the tools of review. They are disinclined to move beyond the repetition of the standard formula of manifest error, misuse of power or clear excess in the bounds of discretion. The pretence is that this has remained unchanged since the inception of the EEC, but it has clearly been used in very different ways as the preceding analysis has shown. It does not, therefore, seem too much to ask the courts to give explicit voice to the factors that drive the differential application of the test for review, so that they can be known and assessed. To put the same point in a different way, the EU courts would not rest content with repetition of a standard formula by administrators to explain their action when it was apparent that it was being interpreted in very different ways, and what is good practice in terms of administrative accountability should also pertain to judicial accountability. Judicial reticence in this regard may be explicable for a number of reasons, including a reluctance to give voice to factors on which the judiciary might be divided, the disinclination in some civilian legal systems to articulate the policy factors that drive judicial determinations, and in more basic terms the fact that no one can force courts to do it.

The argument for greater transparency in this regard does not, however, rest solely on the principled argument adumbrated above. The pretence that it is a uniform test for review that is being applied leads to the consequence that there is little judicial self-inquiry as to its application in particular types of case. Thus we need, for example, to think hard about whether the test for review of fact in *Tetra Laval* as applied therein and in subsequent cases is pitched at the right level,[114] or whether it is too intrusive, leading de facto to substitution of judgment by the reviewing court for the Commission, more especially so given that the case law wrongly elides issues that are distinct, these being the standard of proof that the administrator is required to meet and the standard of judicial review.[115] We also need to think hard about the application of the test by the GC and the CJEU. It is the GC that has given the very lengthy rulings pursuant to its jurisdiction over direct actions, reflecting the view expressed by Advocate General Vesterdorf that the creation of the CFI as a court of both first and last instance for the examination of facts in the cases brought before it was 'an invitation to undertake an intensive review in order to ascertain whether the evidence on which the Commission relies in adopting a contested decision is sound'.[116]

[114] Case C-12/03 P, *Commission* v. *Tetra Laval*, at [39].

[115] Craig, *EU Administrative Law*, Ch. 15.

[116] Case T-7/89, *Hercules* v. *Commission* [1991] ECR II-867, I.B.1; Case C-344/98, *Masterfoods Ltd* v. *HB Ice Cream Ltd* [2000] ECR I-11369, at [54], AG Cosmas.

Crafting very long and detailed judgments is, however, time-consuming and there are questions whether it is sustainable in the light of the caseload problems faced by the GC charted above. There are, in addition, pressing issues about the parity of treatment of cases brought via direct action before the GC, and by indirect action before the CJEU, where the latter rules on the validity of an EU measure pursuant to a preliminary ruling from a national court. Insofar as the test for manifest error is subject to less detailed scrutiny by the CJEU as compared to the GC, it calls into question the oft-repeated assertion that the EU has a complete set of legal protection, which is predicated on the assumption that the degree of judicial oversight should not differ depending on the fortuity of whether review is direct or indirect.

5 Substance and the interaction between legal orders

The EU interacts with national and international legal orders. This vertical dimension has implications that go beyond administrative law, and there has been considerable discussion about the relationship between the EU and international legal orders arising from the *Kadi* litigation, which has been considered above in the context of process review.[117] This section will therefore focus on high-profile disputes concerning substantive review for compliance with fundamental rights and the way in which these affect the interaction between national legal orders and the EU, and between the

[117] See above, pp. 441–6.

ECHR and the EU. There will be further consideration of the vertical problems concerning the relationship between the EU and the global legal order in a later chapter.[118]

(a) *Fundamental rights and Member States: contentious issues*

(i) Scope of application

We saw from discussion of UK administrative law that there was some national judicial disquiet concerning the extent to which EU conceptions of fundamental rights bind the Member States. This exemplifies the challenge posed by the interplay between legal orders.

It is regulated by the EU Charter of Fundamental Rights,[119] Article 51(1) of which states that the Charter provisions are addressed to the Member States only when they are implementing Union law, the meaning of which was debated in the academic literature. The narrow interpretation was that Member States were only bound by the Charter when acting as agents in the application of EU law and where implementing an EU directive, and not in other instances where EU courts had held that the fundamental-rights jurisprudence bound the Member States.[120] The broader construction was

[118] See below, pp. 765–806. [119] OJ 2010 No C83/389.

[120] See, e.g., L. Besselink, 'The Member States, the National Constitutions and the Scope of the Charter' (2001) 8 *Maastricht Journal of European and Comparative Law* 68; D. Thym, 'Charter of Fundamental Rights: Competition or Consistency of Human Rights Protection in Europe?' [2002] *Finnish Yearbook of International Law* 11.

that Member States were bound by the Charter whenever they acted within the scope of EU law,[121] although there was attendant debate as to what, more specifically, this connoted.[122] This was supported by the fact that the CJEU had in its prior jurisprudence used the phrase 'implementing Community rules' as synonymous with Member State action that fell within the scope of Community law, and by the Charter explanatory memorandum,[123] which must be given due regard when interpreting Charter rights.[124] The narrow view would, in addition, have led to formalistic distinctions between situations where Member States were bound by the Charter and those where they were not. The broader

[121] See, e.g., R. Alonso Garcia, 'The General Provisions of the Charter of Fundamental Rights' (2002) 8 *European Law Journal* 492, at 495–6; P. Eeckhout, 'The EU Charter of Fundamental Rights and the Federal Question' (2002) 39 *Common Market Law Review* 945; P. Craig, *The Lisbon Treaty: Law, Politics and Treaty Reform* (Oxford: Oxford University Press, 2010), Ch. 6.

[122] See, e.g., K. Lenaerts, 'Exploring the Limits of the EU Charter of Fundamental Rights' (2012) 8 *European Constitutional Law Review* 375; M. Safjan, 'Areas of Application of the Charter of Fundamental Rights of the European Union: Fields of Conflict?', EUI Working Paper No 2012/22; T. von Danwitz and K. Paraschas, 'A Fresh Start for the Charter: Fundamental Questions on the Application of the European Charter of Fundamental Rights' (2012) 35 *Fordham International Law Journal* 1396.

[123] Charte 4473/00, Convent 49, 11 October 2000, 46; CONV 828/03, Updated Explanations Relating to the Text of the Charter of Fundamental Rights, 9 July 2003, p. 45; Explanations Relating to the Charter, OJ 2007 No C303/17, p. 16. The EP took the same view; see www.europarl.eu.int/comparl/libe/elsj/charter/art51/default_en.htm.

[124] Art. 6(1) TEU.

interpretation of Article 51 was, moreover, assumed to be correct by UK courts.[125]

The scope of application of Article 51 has now been confirmed in favour of the wider view in *Åkerberg Fransson*.[126] The case concerned the applicability of Article 50 of the Charter, which provides that 'no one shall be liable to be tried or punished again in criminal proceedings for an offence for which he or she has already been finally acquitted or convicted within the Union in accordance with the law'. The Swedish Court asked whether national enforcement mechanisms for an EU VAT directive were compatible with Article 50. The directive allowed Member States to impose obligations they deemed necessary for the correct collection of the tax and for prevention of evasion. Sweden adopted a system of tax and criminal penalties which allowed judges to impose criminal sanctions on persons who had already been sanctioned by the tax authorities, albeit the judge in the criminal proceedings could deduct the administrative penalty from the criminal sanction. Sweden argued that the case did not fall within Article 51(1), because the national law was not directly implementing a provision of EU law.

The CJEU rejected the argument. It held that Article 51 confirmed the Court's case law relating to the extent to which Member State action had to comply with EU fundamental rights. This was 'in all situations governed

[125] *RFU* v. *Consolidated Information Services* [2012] UKSC 55, at [28]; *R (Zagorski)* v. *Secretary of State for Business, Innovation and Skills* [2011] HRLR 6 140, at [66]–[71].

[126] Case C-617/10, *Åklagaren* v. *Hans Åkerberg Fransson* EU:C:2013:105.

by European Union law, but not outside such situations',[127] this being borne out by the Explanations attached to the Charter:

> Since the fundamental rights guaranteed by the Charter must therefore be complied with where national legislation falls within the scope of European Union law, situations cannot exist which are covered in that way by European Union law without those fundamental rights being applicable. The applicability of European Union law entails applicability of the fundamental rights guaranteed by the Charter.[128]

The CJEU further held that Sweden was acting in the scope of EU law in the instant case, because the tax and criminal penalties were imposed, in part at least, for non-payment of VAT, which was governed by EU law. The fact that the national legislation upon which those tax and criminal penalties are founded was not adopted to transpose the EU directive did not alter this conclusion, because it was designed to penalize an infringement of the directive and was therefore intended to implement the obligation imposed on the Member States by the Treaty to maintain effective penalties for conduct prejudicial to the financial interests of the European Union.[129]

The CJEU was, however, willing to accord the national court some latitude in the application of fundamental rights. It held that where the case is not determined

[127] Case C-617/10, *Åkerberg Fransson* EU:C:2013:105, at [19].
[128] Case C-617/10, *Åkerberg Fransson* EU:C:2013:105, at [21].
[129] Case C-617/10, *Åkerberg Fransson* EU:C:2013:105, at [28].

entirely by EU law national courts can apply national standards of protection on fundamental rights, subject to the twin caveats that the level of protection provided for by the Charter and the primacy, unity and effectiveness of EU law are not undermined.[130] It held, moreover, that the mere co-existence of tax penalties and criminal sanctions would only infringe Article 50 if the tax penalty could itself be regarded as criminal in nature, and this was a matter to be decided by the national court in the light of criteria laid down by the CJEU.

The decision in *Åkerberg Fransson* was welcomed by some academics,[131] and criticized by others.[132] It also prompted extra-judicial criticism from the president of the German Constitutional Court,[133] and led the First Senate to state in a decided case that just because a provision has some connection with the abstract scope of EU law, or incidentally interacts with EU law, is not sufficient to trigger the application of the Charter.[134] The criticism has been echoed

[130] Case C-617/10, *Åkerberg Fransson* EU:C:2013:105, at [29].

[131] See, e.g., D. Sarmiento, 'Who's Afraid of the Charter? The Court of Justice, National Courts and the New Framework of Fundamental Rights Protection in Europe' (2013) 50 *Common Market Law Review* 1267.

[132] See, e.g., F. Fontanelli, 'The Implementation of European Union Law by Member States under Article 51 of the Charter of Fundamental Rights' (2014) 20 *Columbia Journal of European Law* 193.

[133] President A. Voßkuhle, 'European Integration and the Bundesverfassungsgericht', Sir Thomas More Lecture, Lincoln's Inn, 31 October 2013.

[134] 1 BvR 1215/07, Judgment of 24 April 2013.

extra-judicially by Lord Mance,[135] and been voiced by the House of Commons European Scrutiny Committee.[136]

The critique is based on arguments by Advocate General Cruz Villalón, viz. that the relevant Swedish law was not enacted to implement the 2006 VAT directive. The Advocate General, while cognizant of the legal fact that the directive had to be adequately enforced, felt that this was insufficient to regard the case as coming within 'implementation' for the purposes of Article 51 of the Charter, given that the relevant Swedish rules on administrative and criminal enforcement for tax evasion were general in scope.

The Charter provisions are only applicable where the Member State is acting within the scope of EU law, and there must therefore be some 'lock on' to EU law before a claimant can make use of the Charter. The CJEU has in the past rejected claims because the link is too tenuous.[137] There will inevitably be differences of view as to whether a Member State can be regarded as acting in the scope of EU law so as to trigger application of the Charter. The CJEU's reasoning can nonetheless be defended on principled grounds.[138]

[135] Lord Mance, 'Destruction or Metamorphosis of the Legal Order?', World Policy Conference, Monaco, 14 December 2013, pp. 9–10.

[136] House of Commons, European Scrutiny Committee, 'The Application of the UK Charter of Fundamental Rights in the UK: A State of Confusion' (2014, HC 979).

[137] See, e.g., Case C-299/95, *Kremzow* v. *Austria* [1997] ECR I-2629; Case C-291/96, *Criminal Proceedings against Grado and Bashir* [1997] ECR I-5531; Case C-309/96, *Annibaldi* v. *Sindaco del Commune di Guidoma* [1997] ECR I-7493; Case C-333/09, *Noël* v. *SCP Brouard Daude* [2009] ECR I-205.

[138] Case C-617/10, *Åkerberg Fransson* EU:C:2013:105, at [24]–[28].

Article 51 renders the Charter applicable to Member States when they are implementing Union law, which includes the directive itself and other obligations held by the CJEU to flow from it. Directives impose obligations on Member States, and accord them choice as to the form and methods of implementation, provided that the objectives of the directive are attained within the time specified for implementation. A Member State may choose among any of the following non-exhaustive list of methods to implement the obligations in a directive. It might simply copy out the entirety of the directive into national law; it might enact a short law adopting the directive; it might use existing national legal rules and apply them to all or certain parts of the directive; it might use an admixture of primary and secondary law to implement different parts of the directive. It would be wrong in principle, generate considerable uncertainty and lead to formalism for the application of the Charter to Member States to turn on the precise method of implementation chosen.

The VAT directive in *Åkerberg Fransson* dated from 2006, but was the culmination of earlier directives dating back more than thirty years. The prior case law was clear that the VAT directives imposed an obligation on Member States to take all legislative and administrative measures appropriate for ensuring collection of VAT due on their territory and for preventing evasion.[139] It follows that correct implementation of the Directive requires Member States to have some regime for penalizing those who evade VAT. A national legal system

[139] Case C-132/06, *Commission* v. *Italy* [2008] ECR I-5457, at [37], [46]; Case C-367/09, *SGS Belgium* [2010] ECR I-10761, at [40]–[42].

may choose to fulfil this obligation in a number of ways: it might include such provisions in the national primary law through which the directive is implemented into national law; it might do so through an additional primary law; it might use secondary law; it might draw on existing national law and apply it to fulfil the obligation from the directive. These options are open to the Member State precisely because a directive allows Member States choice as to methods of implementation. The fact that Sweden chose to use an existing national law to fulfil the obligation flowing from the directive was therefore perfectly legitimate.

It would, however, be contrary to principle if the application of the Charter to the Member State were to turn on the method chosen for fulfilling the obligations flowing from the directive. The determinative issue is therefore not whether the Swedish law in *Åkerberg Fransson* was enacted to implement the VAT directive, but whether it was being used to implement the obligations flowing from the directive, which it clearly was.[140] The contrary conclusion is untenable, since it would mean that the Charter would be triggered if a Member State chose to implement the relevant obligations by, for example, enacting discrete legal provisions on enforcement solely in relation to the EU VAT directive, but it would not be applicable if the Member State chose to meet the obligations through application of existing enforcement rules to EU VAT, even though the content of the rules is the same. The interaction between national law and EU law was, moreover, not merely incidental in *Åkerberg Fransson*. VAT is a

[140] Case C-617/10, *Åkerberg Fransson* EU:C:2013:105, at [28].

primary source of EU revenue, and the penalty regime for evasion is therefore central to that revenue base. Statements to the effect that *Åkerberg Fransson* was wrong because the applicability of the double jeopardy principle in that case did not bear on implementation of an EU obligation are not explained and do not withstand examination.[141] I do not therefore believe that this criticism of the judgment is sound, nor does it answer the reasoning in the Court's judgment or the preceding analysis.

The ruling in *Åkerberg Fransson* must, in any event, be seen in the light of the subsequent case law. The CJEU has reaffirmed the principle in that case, to the effect that the Charter is applicable to Member State action that falls within the scope of EU law.[142] It has, however, in accord with its earlier jurisprudence, rejected numerous claims where there was no sufficient connection to EU law to justify application of the Charter to national measures.[143]

[141] The European Scrutiny Committee (2014, HC 979), at [167].

[142] Case C-258/13, *Sociedade Agrícola e Imobiliária da Quinta de S. Paio Lda* v. *Instituto da Segurança Social IP* EU:C:2013:810, at [18]–[20]; Case C-390/12, *Proceedings Brought by Robert Pfleger*, 30 April 2014, at [31]–[35]; Case C-206/13, *Siragusa* v. *Regione Sicilia – Soprintendenza Beni Culturali e Ambientali di Palermo* EU:C:2014:126, at [21]–[22].

[143] See, e.g., Case C-498/12, *Pedone* v. *N* EU:C:2013:76; Case C-14/13, *Cholakova* v. *Osmo rayonno upravlenie pri Stolichna direktsia na vatreshnite rab* EU:C:2013:374; Case C-258/13, *Sociedade Agrícola e Imobiliária da Quinta* EU:C:2013: 810; Case C-56/13, *Érsekcsanádi Mezőgazdasági Zrt* v. *Bács-Kiskun Megyei Kormányhivatal*, 22 May 2014; Case C-265/13, *Marcos* v. *Korota SA and Fondo de Garantía Salarial*, 27 March 2014; Cases C-614/12 and 10/13, *Dutka* v. *Mezőgazdasági és Vidékfejlesztési Hivatal*, 16 January 2014.

It has also provided more guidance as to the meaning of acting within the scope of EU law.

This was exemplified by the ruling in *Siragusa*,[144] where the reference concerned the legality of an Italian order requiring the claimant to dismantle work carried out in breach of a law protecting the cultural heritage and the landscape. There was some connection with EU law, since the national legislation sought to protect the landscape, which was an aspect of EU environmental protection. The CJEU nonetheless held that the concept of 'implementing Union law' in Article 51 required a degree of connection above and beyond the fact that the matters covered were closely related, or that one such matter had an indirect impact on the other. Its reasoning in this respect was informed by reference to the objectives of protecting fundamental rights in EU law, which was to ensure that those rights were not infringed in areas of EU activity, whether through action at EU level or through national implementation of EU law. The latter coverage was necessary in order to avoid a situation in which the level of protection of fundamental rights varied according to the national law involved, such as to undermine the unity, primacy and effectiveness of EU law.

In order to determine, in the light of these principles, whether national legislation involved implementation of EU law for the purposes of the Charter, the CJEU held that a number of factors should be considered: whether the national

144 Case C-206/13, *Siragusa* EU:C:2014:126, at [23]–[33]. See also Case C-198/13, *Hernández* v. *Reino de España (Subdelegación del Gobierno de España en Alicante)*, EU:C:2014:2055, at [34]–[37].

legislation was intended to implement a provision of EU law; the nature of that legislation and whether it pursued objectives other than those covered by EU law, even if it was capable of indirectly affecting EU law; and whether there were specific rules of EU law on the matter or capable of affecting it. It was also necessary to consider the nature of the relevant EU provisions, such that if they did not impose any obligation on the Member State with regard to the situation in the proceedings at national level, then the Charter would not be applicable to the national legislation.

Applying these principles to the instant case, the CJEU concluded that the Charter was not applicable to the Italian legislation. Neither the Lisbon Treaty, nor the relevant directives, contained specific obligations to protect the landscape akin to those found in Italian law. Furthermore, the objectives of the EU legislation were not the same as those in the Italian law, notwithstanding the fact that landscape was a factor to be taken into consideration in assessing the impact of a project on the environment under the directives. The Italian law was not therefore implementing rules of EU law and the Charter was inapplicable.

The fears expressed in some quarters that *Åkerberg Fransson* would lead to application of the Charter in relation to national action in an ever-widening array of cases have not, therefore, been borne out by the subsequent jurisprudence. The Court has rejected peremptorily numerous such actions by way of order, without recourse to a full hearing, on the ground that there was no connection with EU law. They have also given more indication as to the meaning that the term 'implementing EU law' should bear in this context.

It should, moreover, not be forgotten that the ruling in *Åkerberg Fransson* left latitude to the national courts in deciding on the application of fundamental rights where EU law did not cover the entire terrain, subject to the caveat that the level of protection provided for by the Charter and the primacy, unity and effectiveness of EU law were not undermined. This may well not satisfy some who feel that EU law is still too far-reaching in this respect. It is then necessary to provide a reasoned justification why the fortuitous decision as to how a Member State chooses to implement EU law should be determinative of whether the EU Charter is applicable or not.

(ii) National constitutional rights

The relationship between EU law and national constitutional law has long been a fertile source of case law and commentary. The tension between judicial claims voiced by the CJEU to the effect that all EU law was supreme over all national law, whatsoever the relative status of the respective norms, and the response of many national constitutional courts that were unwilling to accept such far-reaching assertions, has been ever-present in the EU legal order. It has been a staple part of the discourse on the supremacy of EU law and its limits. Instances where there is a clash between EU law and national constitutional rights have been regarded by national courts as one such limit to the supremacy of EU law.[145]

[145] P. Craig and G. de Búrca, *EU Law: Text, Cases and Materials* (Oxford: Oxford University Press, 6th ed., 2015), Ch. 11.

The issue came before the CJEU in *Melloni*,[146] which was decided by the Grand Chamber and the judgment handed down the same day as *Åkerberg Fransson*. The case concerned the European Arrest Warrant (EAW), and the circumstances in which a state could refuse to execute a warrant issued by another state. The circumstances in which the latter state could refuse to execute the EAW were amended in 2009, through what became Article 4a(1) of Framework Decision 2002/584.[147] The 2009 amendment provided that if a person convicted in absentia was aware, in due time, of the scheduled trial and was informed that a decision could be handed down if he did not appear for the trial, or, being aware of the scheduled trial, gave a mandate to a lawyer to defend him at the trial, the executing judicial authority was required to surrender that person, and could not make the surrender subject to there being an opportunity for a retrial of the case at which he was present in the issuing Member State.

This was problematic from the perspective of the executing state, Spain, since its Constitutional Tribunal had held that the Spanish Constitution required that there should be some opportunity for retrial of the case in the issuing state, which was Italy, where the original conviction was given in absentia, even if the accused was represented by a lawyer when that initial conviction occurred. The reason why Melloni was absent from the trial in Italy is that he had been

[146] Case C-399/11, *Stefano Melloni* v. *Ministerio Fiscal* EU:C:2013:107.

[147] Council Framework Decision of 13 June 2002 on the European Arrest Warrant and the surrender procedures between Member States (2002/584/JHA), OJ 2002 No L190/1.

arrested and was on bail before being sent to Italy for trial, but broke his bail conditions and absconded.

The CJEU held that Article 4a(1) of the Framework Decision was compatible with the right to an effective judicial remedy and a fair trial, and with the rights of the defence, protected respectively by Article 47 and Article 48(2) of the Charter. This interpretation of Charter rights was, said the CJEU, consistent with the case law of the European Court of Human Rights, pursuant to Article 6 ECHR.[148]

The CJEU then considered the most difficult aspect of the case, which concerned the fact that the Spanish Constitutional Tribunal had held that Article 4a(1) was contrary to Spanish conceptions of fundamental rights. Article 53 of the Charter provides that nothing therein should be interpreted as restricting or adversely affecting human rights as recognized, in their respective fields of application, by, inter alia, Member States' constitutions. The national court asked whether Article 53 must be interpreted as allowing the executing Member State to make the surrender of a person convicted in absentia conditional upon the conviction being open to review in the issuing Member State, in order to avoid an adverse effect on the right to a fair trial and the rights of the defence guaranteed by the executing state's constitution.

The CJEU rejected the argument. It held that Article 53 could not allow the Spanish authorities to make execution of the EAW contingent upon conditions other than those laid down in Article 4a(1), even though the extra condition stemmed from an interpretation of the Spanish Constitution

[148] Case C-399/11, *Stefano Melloni* EU:C:2013:107, at [49]–[50].

by the Spanish Constitutional Tribunal.[149] The national court had, said the CJEU, interpreted Article 53 as a general authorization to a Member State to apply the standard of protection of fundamental rights guaranteed by its constitution when it was higher than that in the Charter and, where necessary, to give it priority over EU law.

This interpretation of Article 53 could not, said the CJEU, be accepted, since it would 'undermine the principle of the primacy of EU law inasmuch as it would allow a Member State to disapply EU legal rules which are fully in compliance with the Charter where they infringe the fundamental rights guaranteed by that State's constitution'.[150] What Article 53 countenanced was rather that national conceptions of fundamental rights could be applied when a Member State implemented EU law, provided that the level of protection provided for by the Charter, as interpreted by the CJEU, and the primacy, unity and effectiveness of EU law were not thereby compromised.

The CJEU reiterated its settled view that the primacy of EU law applied against all national law, including its constitutional law.[151] It sought to justify application of this precept in the instant case by adverting to the purpose of the EU amending legislation. It was intended to remedy difficulties with the mutual recognition of decisions given in the absence of the person concerned at his trial, which arose from differences between the Member States in the protection of fundamental

[149] Case C-399/11, *Stefano Melloni* EU:C:2013:107, at [56]–[64].
[150] Case C-399/11, *Stefano Melloni* EU:C:2013:107, at [58].
[151] Case C-399/11, *Stefano Melloni* EU:C:2013:107, at [59].

rights. The amending legislation thus constituted harmonization of the conditions for execution of an EAW where a conviction was given in absentia, 'which reflects the consensus reached by all the Member States regarding the scope to be given under EU law to the procedural rights enjoyed by persons convicted in absentia who are the subject of a European arrest warrant'.[152] It was not therefore open to a particular Member State to make surrender of a person convicted in absentia dependent on a condition not contained in the amending legislation, even where it felt that this was required to safeguard its constitutional conception of the right to a fair trial.

The *Melloni* judgment was controversial, which was unsurprising. This was reflected in the starkly different academic assessments of the case. The positive reading of the decision was proffered by Daniel Sarmiento, who argued that *Melloni*, together with *Åkerberg Fransson*, represented a principled reading of the Charter, and embodied a normatively defensible division of authority between the CJEU and national constitutional courts in relation to the application of fundamental rights.[153] There were, however, many negative reactions to *Melloni*, exemplified by that of Leonard Besselink, who criticized the ruling for jeopardizing national protections of fundamental rights, for misreading Article 53 of the Charter and for placing concerns about EU primacy above those about fundamental-rights protection.[154] There is, therefore,

[152] Case C-399/11, *Stefano Melloni* EU:C:2013:107, at [62].

[153] Sarmiento, 'Who's Afraid of the Charter?'.

[154] L. Besselink, 'The Parameters of Constitutional Conflict after *Melloni*' (2014) 39 *European Law Review* 531.

no doubt that *Melloni* threw into sharp relief the tension between EU law and national constitutional rights. It generated questions about the vertical relationship of the respective legal orders. It invited inquiry as to the limits of EU norms when they clashed with national constitutional and administrative precepts.

An answer to such inquiry is disarmingly simple, viz. that the judgment was wrong and that the primacy of EU law is indeed bounded by national conceptions of constitutional rights. This response is certainly possible, but does not do justice to the normative complexity of the scenario in the *Melloni* case. This was not a simple case where fundamental rights were protected by the national constitutional order, and undermined by the EU, which lacked such protections.

The factual reality in *Melloni* was very different, since the Spanish government supported enactment of the contested EU amendment to the EAW, and there was, moreover, disagreement between the Spanish courts as to what the right to a fair trial demanded when the trial was held in absentia.

The conceptual reality was also very different. This was a case where there was contestation, within a regime of mutual recognition of arrest warrants, as to what should be the protection for the right to a fair trial and rights of the defence where a trial was held in absentia. The meaning of a right can be contestable within a particular legal system. This is a fortiori the case where legislation that impacts on rights is enacted for the twenty-eight Member States that constitute the EU. It is axiomatic that Member States might differ in this regard, since the answer necessarily entails complex balancing of the rights of the accused, the rights of the victim, and the respective interests of the issuing and executing states. The 2009 amendment to the EAW system was the considered EU legislative response to this problem. It had been discussed and voted on by the Member States, was consistent with ECHR jurisprudence and was susceptible to judicial review.

To contend that national constitutional rights of the kind posited in *Melloni* should per se be accorded priority would therefore mean that there would be twenty-eight national constitutional veto points. It would mean, moreover, that any such veto could be exercised, even if it was inconsistent with, for example, the constitutional conception of a right to a fair trial held by another Member State, such as that which issued the arrest warrant. It would, by parity of reasoning, mean that the veto could also be exercised if a particular state took a different view as to the balance between, for example, liberty and equality, or liberty and security, from that taken by other states that was embodied in EU legislation, even if exercise of that veto could have important consequences for nationals from other Member States.

This does not mean that it would never be justified for a Member State to rely on national conceptions of constitutional rights when challenging EU legislation. There may be cases where it is indeed legitimate to question the sufficiency of the rights-based safeguards in the EU legislation as compared to those embodied in the national constitution. The mere fact that the rights-based protections differ should not, however, suffice in this respect, for the very reason set out above, viz. that the EU legislation will embody the considered views of twenty-eight Member States that might have differing views that are legitimate on the meaning of, for example, free speech or the right to a fair trial. It would have to be shown that there was some more structural or systemic infirmity in the EU measure to warrant reliance on the particular conception of a right embodied in a national constitution, or that the national interpretation accorded to that right really was reflective of national identity in that particular state.

It should, moreover, be emphasized that legislation of the kind contested in *Melloni* is not immune from rights-based challenge. It is open to judicial review via a direct action, or an indirect challenge emanating from a national court through a preliminary ruling. It will be subject to scrutiny for compliance with the Charter in the same way as any other EU legal norm. In reaching its conclusion as to whether the contested measure is compliant with the Charter, the CJEU will properly take account of the fact that the measure constitutes the considered view of the EU political institution or institutions that were involved with its passage. These views will not be determinative of whether the measure is in accord with the Charter right, but they are deserving of respect when the Court reaches its decision.

(b) Fundamental rights and the ECHR: contentious issues

Debate about the relationship between the EU and the ECHR is, as Jean-Paul Jacqué rightly notes,[155] as old as the

[155] J.-P. Jacqué, 'The Accession of the European Union to the European Convention on Human Rights and Fundamental Freedoms' (2011) 48 *CMLRev* 995.

Community itself. Suffice it to say for the present that prior to the Lisbon Treaty the ECtHR jurisprudence was the most formative influence on the ECJ's fundamental-rights case law, but the EU was not formally bound by the ECHR, and there were doubts over its competence to accede.[156] The Lisbon Treaty resolved the status of the EU's Charter of Rights by rendering it legally binding, with the same legal status as the constituent treaties.[157] The Lisbon Treaty also stipulated that the EU should accede to the ECHR.[158] Negotiations began in July 2010 and a draft text was concluded in April 2013, which had to be accepted by the EU and the Council of Europe.[159] The EU sought an opinion from the CJEU.

The Commission concluded that the draft Agreement between the ECHR and the EU was compatible with EU law, and this view was shared by the twenty-four Member States that submitted opinions, and by the Council and the European Parliament. The CJEU disagreed, and held that the draft Agreement could not be accepted in its present form.[160] The EU's obligation to accede to the ECHR was, said the CJEU, subject to conditions: it must not affect the Union's competences as defined in the Treaties;[161] the accession agreement must

[156] Opinion 2/94, *On Accession by the Community to the ECHR* [1996] ECR I-1759.

[157] Art. 6(1) TEU. [158] Art. 6(2) TEU.

[159] See http://hub.coe.int/web/coe-portal/what-we-do/human-rights/eu-accession-to-the-convention; www.coe.int/t/dghl/standardsetting/hrpolicy/Accession/Working_documents_en.asp.

[160] Opinion 2/13, *Accession of the European Union to the European Convention for the Protection of Human Rights*, EU:C:2014:2454.

[161] Art. 6(2) TEU.

preserve the specific characteristics of the EU and EU law, and must not affect Article 344 TFEU;[162] and accession must be arranged so as to preserve the specific features of EU law.

These conditions were intended, said the CJEU, to 'ensure that accession does not affect the specific characteristics of the EU and EU law'.[163] The characteristics included those arising from the very nature of EU law: the fact that EU law stems from an independent source of law, the Treaties; its primacy over national law; and the direct effect of many of its provisions. They also included certain substantive and institutional features of the EU.[164] It followed that 'the autonomy enjoyed by EU law in relation to the laws of the Member States and in relation to international law requires that the interpretation of [EU] fundamental rights be ensured within the framework of the structure and objectives of the EU'.[165] The CJEU concluded against this backdrop that the draft Agreement could not be accepted for five reasons. The judgment is complex and contains much that is designed to protect the autochthony of EU law, as perceived by the CJEU, from outside influence.

(i) 'The specific characteristics and the autonomy of EU law'

The CJEU acknowledged, albeit somewhat reluctantly, that it was acceptable for an external judicial organ to have the

162 Lisbon Treaty, Protocol No 8.

163 Opinion 2/13, *Accession of the European Union*, EU:C:2014:2454, at [164].

164 Opinion 2/13, *Accession of the European Union*, EU:C:2014:2454, at [171]–[177].

165 Opinion 2/13, *Accession of the European Union*, EU:C:2014:2454, at [170].

authority to control EU institutions, including the CJEU, since this is what EU membership of the ECHR would entail.[166] There were, however, three respects in which the CJEU found that the draft Agreement offended the specific characteristics and autonomy of EU law.

First, it should not, said the CJEU, be possible for the ECtHR to call into question the Court's findings in relation to the scope *ratione materiae* of EU law, for the purposes, in particular, of determining whether a Member State is bound by fundamental rights of the EU. The CJEU had interpreted Article 53 of the Charter to mean that application of national protection of fundamental rights must not compromise the level of protection provided for by the Charter or the primacy, unity and effectiveness of EU law. By way of contrast, the Court said that Article 53 ECHR essentially reserved the power of the contracting parties to lay down higher standards of protection of fundamental rights than those guaranteed by the ECHR.[167] The power accorded to Member States via Article 53 ECHR had therefore to be limited with respect to Charter rights that corresponded to those guaranteed by the ECHR to that necessary to ensure that the level of protection provided for by the Charter and the primacy, unity and effectiveness of EU law were not compromised.

Second, the CJEU also found the draft Agreement to be problematic in terms of the autonomy of EU law because of related ideas of mutual trust and mutual recognition. Mutual trust between the Member States was, said the CJEU,

[166] Opinion 2/13, *Accession of the European Union*, EU:C:2014:2454, at [185].
[167] Opinion 2/13, *Accession of the European Union*, EU:C:2014:2454, at [189].

fundamental in the EU, and required each Member State, save for limited exceptions, to consider all the other Member States to be complying with fundamental rights recognized by EU law. A Member State could not, therefore, demand 'a higher level of national protection of fundamental rights from another Member State than that provided by EU law'.[168] This had, said the CJEU, been ignored in the Accession Agreement, with the consequence that Member States that were contracting states of the ECHR would have to check that another Member State had observed fundamental rights, even though EU law imposed an obligation of mutual trust between those Member States.

Third, the draft Agreement was said to be deficient from the perspective of the autonomy of EU law because of the relationship between preliminary rulings under EU law and the new Protocol 16 ECHR. The latter provided for the highest national courts to request the ECtHR to give advisory opinions on questions of principle relating to the interpretation or application of ECHR rights, which was problematic because the same national courts might be obliged to refer under Article 267 TFEU.

(ii) 'Article 344 TFEU'

An international agreement cannot, said the CJEU, affect the allocation of powers fixed by the Treaties or the autonomy of the EU legal system. This principle is enshrined in Article 344 TFEU, such that Member States undertake not to submit a dispute concerning the interpretation or

[168] Opinion 2/13, *Accession of the European Union*, EU:C:2014:2454, at [192].

application of the Treaties to any method of settlement other than those provided for therein.

The result of accession would mean that the ECHR would form an integral part of EU law, with the consequence that 'where EU law is at issue, the Court of Justice has exclusive jurisdiction in any dispute between the Member States and between those Member States and the EU regarding compliance with the ECHR'.[169] However, the procedure in Article 33 ECHR whereby any contracting party can refer to the ECtHR any breach of the ECHR by any other contracting party could, said the CJEU, apply to disputes between the Member States, or between those Member States and the EU, even though it is EU law that is in issue.

The CJEU held that Article 5 of the draft Accession Agreement, whereby proceedings before the Court of Justice would not be regarded as a means of dispute settlement that the Contracting Parties had to forgo in accordance with Article 55 ECHR, was insufficient to preserve the exclusive jurisdiction of the Court of Justice, since a Member State might still submit an application to the ECtHR under Article 33 ECHR, concerning an alleged violation by a Member State or the EU in conjunction with EU law. The 'very existence of such a possibility undermines the requirement set out in Article 344 TFEU',[170] the consequence being that only the express exclusion of the ECtHR's jurisdiction

[169] Opinion 2/13, *Accession of the European Union*, EU:C:2014:2454, at [204].

[170] Opinion 2/13, *Accession of the European Union*, EU:C:2014:2454, at [208].

under Article 33 ECHR over disputes between Member States or between Member States and the EU in relation to the application of the ECHR within the scope *ratione materiae* of EU law would be compatible with Article 344 TFEU.[171]

(iii) 'The co-respondent mechanism'

The third reason why the CJEU felt that the draft Agreement was problematic related to the co-respondent mechanism. This was a new type of procedure designed to provide a mechanism whereby both the EU and a Member State could be parties to an ECtHR case, even where only one had been initially named as a party to the action. The CJEU held that this was incompatible with EU law because it would enable the ECtHR to interpret EU law when assessing requests to apply this process; because a ruling by the ECtHR on the joint responsibility of the EU and its Member States could impinge on Member State reservations to the Convention; and because the CJEU held that the ECtHR could not allocate responsibility for breach of the ECHR between the EU and Member States, given that only the CJEU itself could rule on EU law.[172]

(iv) 'The procedure for the prior involvement of the CJEU'

The negotiating team had spent considerable time devising provisions to ensure that the ECtHR did not rule on an issue

[171] Opinion 2/13, *Accession of the European Union*, EU:C:2014:2454, at [213].

[172] Opinion 2/13, *Accession of the European Union*, EU:C:2014:2454, at [215]–[235].

before the CJEU had had time to consider it. The CJEU nonetheless found the provisions to be problematic for two reasons.

First, the issue of whether the CJEU had already given a ruling on the same question of law as that at issue in the proceedings could only be resolved by the competent EU institution, this being the CJEU, whose decision should bind the ECtHR. It could not be made by the ECtHR, since this would be tantamount to conferring on it jurisdiction to interpret the case law of the Court of Justice, but this possibility was not excluded by Article 3(6) of the draft Accession Agreement.

Second, the CJEU also found the procedure in Article 3(6) of the draft Agreement to be problematic because it was too limited. The object of Article 3(6) was to enable the CJEU to rule on an issue where it had 'not yet assessed the compatibility' of the relevant provision with ECHR rights. The CJEU objected that the circumstances in which it would be accorded such time were too limited, because the explanatory report attached to the draft Agreement interpreted Article 3(6) to mean the ability to rule on the *validity* of a secondary law or on the *interpretation* of a provision of primary law. This was problematic, said the CJEU, because it might also wish to rule on the *interpretation* of secondary law.

(v) 'The specific characteristics of EU law as regards judicial review in CFSP matters'

The fifth and final ground on which the CJEU held the draft Agreement to be problematic concerned the Common Foreign and Security Policy (CFSP). The CJEU's argument here was relatively straightforward. The Lisbon Treaty only accords the CJEU limited jurisdiction over CFSP matters. However, the draft Agreement would mean that the ECtHR would be empowered to rule on the compatibility with the ECHR of certain CFSP acts that lay beyond the CJEU's jurisdiction. The CJEU said that the EU could not accede to a Treaty whereby another court would have review powers of a kind and scope not possessed by the CJEU.

(vi) Autonomy, autochthony and choice

Opinion 2/13 did not in general receive a 'good press' from the academic community, and the advent of blogs meant that critical voices were aired almost contemporaneously with publication of the CJEU's judgment.[173] The issues raised by the judgment are complex, and cannot be examined in detail here.[174] The discussion in this and subsequent sections will, however, raise points of more general significance that shape responses to particular aspects of the Court's Opinion.

It should be made clear at the outset that the very definition of the 'specific characteristics of the Union and Union law' that are to be preserved requires creative judgement.[175] It is not self-evident. It could be defined 'thinly'

[173] A collection of the blog references can be found in D. Halberstam, '"It's the Autonomy Stupid!" A Modest Defense of Opinion 2/13 on Accession to the ECHR, and the Way Forward', University of Michigan, Public Law and Legal Theory Paper No 432, 2015, fn 3. P. Eeckhout, 'Opinion 2/13 on EU Accession to the ECHR and Judicial Dialogue: Autonomy or Autarky?', Jean Monnet Working Paper 01/15.

[174] See Halberstam, 'It's the Autonomy Stupid!', for detailed treatment.

[175] Protocol No 8, Art. 1.

or 'thickly', with important consequences either way. Thus, other things being equal, the thicker the definition of this ambiguous phrase, the more substantial is the notion of the autonomy of EU law, and the more difficult it will be for the EU to accede to the ECHR. To put the same point in another way, the thicker the definition of the specific characteristics of the EU and its law, the deeper the sense of EU autochthony, which raises the barriers to ECHR membership. The CJEU adopted a very thick definition of the specific characteristics of the Union and Union law in Opinion 2/13, embracing a wide range of constitutional, institutional, doctrinal and substantive features of EU law,[176] which shaped much of its subsequent reasoning.

(vii) Jurisdictional autonomy, interpretation and constraint

The thickness of this definition shaped the CJEU's opinion and is the explanation for the strong sense of jurisdictional autonomy that pervades the ruling, as manifest in its approach to Article 344. This article is a *lex generalis*, which captures an important point of principle, viz. that Member States undertake not to submit a dispute concerning the Treaties to any method of settlement other than those provided therein.

The injunction in Protocol 8 that this should be respected when drafting the Accession Agreement was said by the CJEU to mean that post-accession the ECHR would become part of EU law, with the consequence that the CJEU

[176] Opinion 2/13, *Accession of the European Union*, EU:C:2014:2454, at [160]–[175].

would have exclusive jurisdiction in any dispute between the Member States and between those Member States and the EU regarding compliance with the ECHR, which could not then be heard before Strasbourg.[177] This reasoning is regarded as unexceptionable by most commentators, the only live issue being the remedy for the drafting infirmity revealed by the CJEU.[178]

This is not, however, self-evident. Consider its implications. A Member State contests the legality of an EU act on a number of grounds, including compliance with fundamental rights. The CJEU upholds the legality of the contested measure. The Member State believes that its conclusions as to fundamental rights are wrong in principle and that they do not comport with ECHR jurisprudence. It cannot take the case to the ECtHR, because the CJEU has exclusive jurisdiction, based on the preceding interpretation of Article 344. It is not, however, clear why it must be interpreted in this manner. There is assuredly good reason based on Article 344 for saying that such a case should be heard initially by the CJEU, but the Court is unequivocal that Article 344 'precludes any prior or subsequent external control'.[179] It is not, however, clear why that article must be read so as to prevent onward challenge to the ECHR, more particularly in the context of the injunction in Article 6(2) TEU, which is the *lex specialis* for these purposes, that the EU should join the ECHR and be subject to the

[177] Opinion 2/13, *Accession of the European Union*, EU:C:2014:2454, at [204], [213].

[178] See, e.g. Halberstam, 'It's the Autonomy Stupid!', 13.

[179] Opinion 2/13, *Accession of the European Union*, EU:C:2014:2454, at [210].

external control that flows from acceptance of this obligation. Accession to the ECHR is predicated on the belief that there should be some external control over the EU by the ECtHR, which the CJEU interpretation of Article 344 prevents when EU action for compliance with rights is challenged by a Member State.

The CJEU's interpretation of Article 344 would, moreover, have the following implication. There may be an action challenging an EU norm that is brought both by a Member State and by an individual, or there may be a separate action raising the same issue brought by a private individual. The Court rejects both claims. The Member State cannot then proceed onwards to the ECHR, but the individual is able to do so. It makes scant sense in normative terms that the possibility of such challenge is dependent on such fortuitous factors.

(viii) Substantive autonomy, interpretation and constraint

The thickness of the CJEU's definition of the 'specific characteristics of the EU and EU law' also shaped its conception of substantive autonomy in the following manner, with important consequences for key elements within the ruling.

The fault lines between legal systems may be clear, and they may be fudged. The latter may occur for good reason, as exemplified by the interplay between the CJEU and national courts over the possible limits to the supremacy of EU law, whereby the two sides have maintained their respective positions, neither spoiling for the ultimate fight. There may, however, be costs to, or consequences of, fudging.

The reality is that an important fault line between the ECHR and the EU has been fudged from the outset, with consequences that are evident in Opinion 2/13. The fudge was present in the draft Accession Agreement, which stated that, as a result of accession, EU acts would be subject to external control by the ECtHR, but that the competence of the Strasbourg Court to 'assess the conformity of EU law with the provisions of the Convention will not prejudice the principle of the autonomous interpretation of EU law'.[180]

There are indeed some senses of autonomy in relation to which this is true.[181] Thus the concept of an autonomous legal order may connote the idea of a separate legal system, with its own rule of recognition, which has relationships with other legal orders. EU accession to the ECHR does not jeopardize the autonomy of EU law in this sense, since the mere fact that a legal order chooses to become party to an international treaty that entails some subjection to its norms does not thereby entail the conclusion that the legal order ceases to be autonomous, since otherwise no legal order could be so regarded. The concept of autonomy might also be used to connote the idea that a particular legal order has features that might be regarded as distinctive from other legal orders, with the consequence that it should be interpreted differently in certain respects, this being the foundation for the ECJ's

[180] Steering Committee for Human Rights, Fifth Negotiation Meeting between the CDDH Ad Hoc Negotiation Group and the European Commission on Accession of the European Union to the European Convention on Human Rights (2013), Appendix v, at [5].

[181] P. Craig, 'EU Accession to the ECHR: Competence, Procedure and Substance' (2013) 36 *Fordham International Law Journal* 1115, at 1142–5.

reasoning concerning direct effect. There is, once again, no reason why EU accession to the ECHR should undermine the claim that the EU Treaty is autonomous in the sense of distinctive, since the claim for novelty or distinction never rested on the idea that the EU was immune from external obligations.

There is, however, a sense of 'the autonomous interpretation of EU law' that is markedly affected by external control by the ECtHR, and it is this that really matters. The normal default position is that the CJEU exercises a 'hermeneutic monopoly'[182] over the interpretation of EU law. It is the ultimate repository of its meaning, and the meaning it accords is autonomous, in the sense that it is not bound by how analogous terms are used in national law. The bottom line is that this hermeneutic monopoly is affected by EU accession to the ECHR, with implications for the autonomy of EU law as hitherto perceived, since the meaning of Convention rights is ultimately determined by the ECtHR, as is the balance between such rights and the pursuit of other goals as mediated through a proportionality test, albeit leavened by a margin of appreciation.

Fudges can, as noted above, have costs, and the cost of the pretence that ECHR membership would not affect the autonomous interpretation of EU law was evident in Opinion

[182] F. Mancini, 'The Free Movement of Workers in the Case-Law of the European Court of Justice', in D. Curtin, T.F. O'Higgins, and D. O'Keeffe (eds.), *Constitutional Adjudication in European Community and National Law: Essays for the Hon. Mr Justice T.F. O'Higgins* (Dublin: Butterworths, 1992), p. 67.

2/13, where the CJEU sought to make the pretence a reality, by limiting as far as possible the ECtHR's substantive authority in relation to the EU. This is apparent in the CJEU's identification of the first two 'problems' in the draft Accession Agreement, viz. that contracting states could provide more extensive protection than stipulated by the ECHR, and that contracting states did not have to furnish the mutual trust required of Member States in EU law. There is much that can be and has been said in relation to the detail of both arguments,[183] but it is the conceptual premise that I wish to emphasize here.

The very identification of these as problems relating to 'the specific characteristics and the autonomy of EU law' must be unpacked.[184] It is noteworthy that the relevant Treaty provisions, Article 6(2) TEU and Protocol 8, do not use the word 'autonomy' at all. It is read in by the CJEU as a specific characteristic of EU law, and becomes part of the heading for the first set of infirmities identified in the draft Accession Agreement. The meaning ascribed to autonomy within the CJEU's subsequent discourse is eclectic. The dominant interpretation throughout is, however, autonomy as reflective of the CJEU's pre-existing hermeneutic monopoly.

Thus the CJEU states that it must inquire whether the draft Agreement would adversely affect the thick set of specific characteristics of EU law it had identified, and the 'autonomy of EU law in the interpretation and application

[183] Halberstam, 'It's the Autonomy Stupid!'; Eeckhout, 'Opinion 2/13 on EU Accession'.

[184] Opinion 2/13, *Accession of the European Union*, EU:C:2014:2454, at [179].

of fundamental rights, as recognized by EU law and notably by the Charter'.[185] The same theme is at work in the CJEU's reasoning concerning mutual trust. The fact that the ECHR did not work on the basis of such mutual trust 'was liable to upset the underlying balance of the EU and undermine the autonomy of EU law'.[186] The theme is apparent yet again in the injunction that a condition precedent to signature of an international agreement is that the essential character of the CJEU's powers is respected and 'consequently there is no adverse effect on the autonomy of the EU legal order'.[187]

The force of the CJEU's reasoning can now be appreciated. It acknowledged that the EU could be bound by decisions from another international court, more especially where provision for conclusion of such an agreement was made in the Lisbon Treaty.[188] It accepted also that ECtHR judgments would have effect on the EU as on other contracting parties, but any such effect was limited by the need to comply with the thick sense of autonomy that conditioned the EU's acceptance of any accession agreement. The CJEU's argument concerning contracting parties not undertaking higher standards than those prescribed by the ECHR, and that concerning mutual trust, were the visible manifestations of the CJEU's desire to ensure that the EU's vision of rights would structure and confine the terms of its membership of the ECHR, even if this did not conform to the normal status quo therein.

[185] Opinion 2/13, *Accession of the European Union*, EU:C:2014:2454, at [178].
[186] Opinion 2/13, *Accession of the European Union*, EU:C:2014:2454, at [194].
[187] Opinion 2/13, *Accession of the European Union*, EU:C:2014:2454, at [183].
[188] Opinion 2/13, *Accession of the European Union*, EU:C:2014:2454, at [182].

6 Regulation, acts, institutions and efficacy

EU administrative law faces a number of regulatory challenges in addition to those concerned with caseload, process and substance discussed above. Exigencies of space mean that the discussion must perforce be selective. The ensuing analysis considers the challenges posed by the divide between delegated and implementing acts, the degree of regulatory autonomy that is and should be given to agencies, and the more general problems of designing efficacious systems of shared administration.

(a) Delegated and implementing acts: the nature of the divide

A central concern of administrative law is the way in which norms other than primary legislation are made. The norms may take the form of individualized decisions, addressed to a particular person or persons. They may take the form of secondary rules that flesh out the detailed meaning of an issue dealt with at a higher level of abstraction in the primary legislation. There will be concerns to ensure that the provisions thus made are subject to an appropriate regime of legal and political accountability. Much of the preceding discussion, and that in the previous chapter, has considered the procedural and substantive constraints developed by courts and legislatures to ensure such accountability.

There are, however, also issues concerning the structural integrity of the schema. This may be established by the Treaty, or by legislation made pursuant thereto. In either eventuality, it is common for courts to play a role in resolving controversial structural issues concerning the nature of the regime thus established. This is readily apparent in relation to the pre-Lisbon comitology regime, since as we saw in the previous chapter the Court's imprimatur was crucial for acceptance of that regime.[189] The CJEU has inevitably been called on to deal with important structural regulatory issues in the post-Lisbon world. The Lisbon Treaty created the divide between delegated and implementing acts in Articles 290 and 291 TFEU,[190] which was predicated on differential procedures in the way in which such norms should be made.

Thus, in relation to delegated acts, old-style comitology committees were replaced by the *ex ante* and *ex post* controls specified in Article 290. The *ex ante* control requires that the legislative act should specify the essential elements of the area, and that the objectives, content, scope and duration

[189] Case 25/70, *Einfuhr-und Vorratsstelle für Getreide und Futtermittel* v. *Koster, Berodt & Co.* [1970] 2 ECR 1161; Case 23/75, *Rey Soda* v. *Cassa Conguaglio Zucchero* [1975] ECR 1279, at [13]; Case 5/77, *Carlo Tedeschi* v. *Denkavit Commerciale S.r.l.* [1977] ECR 1555.

[190] P. Craig, 'Delegated Acts, Implementing Acts and the New Comitology Regulation' (2011) 36 *European Law Review* 671; S. Peers and M. Costa, 'Accountability for Delegated and Implementing Acts after the Treaty of Lisbon' (2012) 18 *European Law Journal* 427; J. Bast, 'New Categories of Acts after the Lisbon Reform: Dynamics of Parliamentarization in EU law' (2012) 49 *Common Market Law Review* 885; J. Mendes, 'Delegated and Implementing Rule Making: Proceduralisation and Constitutional Design' (2013) 19 *European Law Journal* 22; T. Christiansen and M. Dobbels, 'Non-legislative Rule Making after the Lisbon Treaty: Implementing the New System of Comitology and Delegated Acts' (2013) 19 *European Law Journal* 42.

of the delegation of power must be explicitly defined in the legislative acts. The *ex post* control is either the nuclear option, which is to revoke the delegation, or the less extreme response by Council or the European Parliament, whereby either institution can veto the particular delegated act. While old-style management and regulatory committees cease to exist in this area, there are advisory committees that operate in an informal world structured by a Common Understanding between the major institutional players.[191]

The defining features of implementing acts were very different. Article 291 TFEU ensures the survival of comitology in relation to implementing acts, as regulated by the new Comitology Regulation.[192] The conceptual assumptions in this area are that these committees are representatives directly of the Member States, with the consequence that there is no formal recourse to the Council in the event that the committee disagrees with the Commission proposal; there is a very limited role for the Council and the EP in formal terms; and the emphasis is squarely on national technocrats as representatives of the Member States.

The constitutional implications of the regimes for delegated and implementing acts were noted by Advocate General Jääskinen. He stated that the TFEU had introduced a 'sharp conceptual distinction between delegated acts and

[191] Common Understanding on Delegated Acts, Council 8753/1/11, Brussels 14 April 2011.

[192] Regulation (EU) No 182/2011 of the European Parliament and of the Council of 16 February 2011 laying down the rules and general principles concerning mechanisms for control by Member States of the Commission's exercise of implementing powers, OJ 2011 No L55/13.

implementing acts'.[193] Article 290 delegated acts were non-legislative (regulatory) acts of general application adopted by the Commission to amend or supplement non-essential elements of a legislative act. Article 291 TFEU implementing acts could be either regulatory acts or individual administrative decisions, and were adopted by the Commission or the Council to secure uniform implementation of legally binding EU measures. The principal concern in relation to delegated acts pertained, said the Advocate General, to democratic accountability, viz. how much legislative power could be delegated and how could the exercise of such power be controlled by the legislature.[194] By way of contrast, the main constitutional focus in relation to implementing acts related to 'respect for the primary competence of the Member States with respect to implementation of EU law, and the institutional balance between the Council and the Commission when they assume implementing roles'.[195]

The distinction between the two kinds of secondary measure generated very considerable tensions, which cannot be explored here.[196] Suffice it to say that the analytical problem from the outset was that the divide between delegated and implementing acts was fraught with difficulty. The very fact

[193] Case C-270/12, *United Kingdom* v. *Council and Parliament* EU:C:2013:562, at [81].

[194] Case C-270/12, *United Kingdom* v. *Council and Parliament*, at [83].

[195] Case C-270/12, *United Kingdom* v. *Council and Parliament*, at [83].

[196] P. Craig, 'Comitology, Rulemaking and the Lisbon Settlement: Tensions and Strains', in C.-F. Bergstrom and D. Ritleng (eds.), *Rulemaking by the Commission: The New System* (Oxford: Oxford University Press, forthcoming 2015).

that the dichotomy embodied the important constitutional implications set out above merely served to exacerbate the problem. Article 290 TFEU stipulates that an act that amends or supplements a legislative act must be a delegated act. It is the application of this criterion that has proven problematic, more especially that part concerning supplementation of a legislative act, since it is very difficult to conceive of any act made pursuant to a legislative act that does not in some manner supplement that legislative act. If a secondary measure does so it must be a delegated act. If it does not, then it can be an implementing act. All secondary measures, however, involve some addition to the basic or primary act. The Lisbon regime therefore necessitated the drawing of the following line.

It might be considered that the article in the legislative act sufficiently resolved the relevant issues, the conclusion being that the secondary measure, while obviously imbuing the article of the legislative act with greater detail, and hence 'adding something', did not supplement it by adding any 'new' non-essential element so as to trigger recourse to Article 290, and therefore Article 291 could be used. It might in other instances be considered that the relevant article in the legislative act is less definitive, the conclusion being that while the legislative act provided sufficient guide concerning essential principles as to be lawful under Article 290, the secondary measure nonetheless 'supplemented' it by the addition of 'new' non-essential elements, and therefore Article 290 had to be used.

The problematic distinction has inevitably come before the EU courts. Advocate General Jääskinen felt that implementing acts were different from delegated acts because the former enabled 'the promulgation of the normative content of the act that is being implemented, in a more detailed manner, in order to facilitate its application', while the latter obviated the EU legislature from the need to amend or supplement non-essential elements of a legal act. This distinction does not, with respect, withstand examination.[197] The reality is that both delegated and implementing acts imbue the normative content of the relevant measure with greater specificity, as is apparent from consideration of the contested delegated regulation in the instant case, which imbued the relevant article of the legislative act with greater normative specificity.

The leading decision on the divide between delegated and implementing acts thus far is *Commission* v. *European Parliament and Council*.[198] A legislative act had been enacted concerning biocidal products, and empowered the Commission to make implementing regulations pursuant to Article 291. The Commission contended that Article 290 should rather be used, because the regulation supplemented the legislative act and thus should be regarded as a delegated act.

The Commission argued that the power conferred by Article 291 TFEU was purely implementing in nature, whereas that contained in Article 290 was a quasi-legislative power.

[197] Case C-270/12, *United Kingdom* v. *Council and Parliament*, at [77]. The CJEU did not advert to this issue when giving judgment. Case C-270/12, *United Kingdom* v. *Council and Parliament* EU:C:2014:18.

[198] Case C-427/12, *Commission* v. *European Parliament and Council* EU: C:2014:170.

It contended that the choice between a delegated and an implementing act should be based on objective and clear factors that were amenable to judicial review. Articles 290 and 291 TFEU were mutually exclusive and implementing acts could not affect the content of the legislative act. If the purpose was to adopt non-essential rules of general application, which completed the normative framework of the legislative act, then those rules supplemented the legislative act and had to be made via Article 290. If, however, the purpose was merely to give effect to the rules already laid down in the basic act while ensuring uniform conditions of application within the EU then Article 291 could be used.

The CJEU provided little guidance as to the divide between the two species of act, saying merely that delegated acts supplemented or amended non-essential elements of the legislative act, whereas implementing acts enabled the Commission to provide further detail in relation to the content of a legislative act, in order to ensure that it was implemented under uniform conditions in all Member States.[199] The CJEU did not sharpen the nature of the analytical divide, but chose rather to leave considerable choice to the EU legislature:

> It must be noted that the EU legislature has discretion when it decides to confer a delegated power on the Commission pursuant to Article 290(1) TFEU or an implementing power pursuant to Article 291(2) TFEU. Consequently, judicial review is limited to manifest errors of assessment as to whether the EU legislature could

[199] Case C-427/12, *Commission* v. *European Parliament and Council*, at [37]–[39].

> reasonably have taken the view, first, that, in order to be implemented, the legal framework which it laid down regarding the system of fees referred to in Article 80(1) of Regulation No 528/2012 needs only the addition of further detail, without its non-essential elements having to be amended or supplemented and, secondly, that the provisions of Regulation No 528/2012 relating to that system require uniform conditions for implementation.[200]

This approach obviated the need for the Court to give clear guidance on the nature of the dichotomy between delegated and implementing acts, but it is problematic. The difficulty resides in the very premise in the extract, viz. that the EU legislature has discretion as to whether to confer a delegated or an implementing power on the Commission. This proposition elides two distinct issues, these being the legislature's power to use both delegated and implementing acts, and whether the conditions for the application of the respective types of act have been met.

Thus it is true that the legislature has 'discretion' as to the former issue, but only in the reductionist sense that the Lisbon Treaty makes provision for both delegated and implementing acts, with the consequence that it is open to the EU legislature in the legislative act to choose whether further rules should be made pursuant to Article 290 or Article 291.

This provides, however, no foundation for the conclusion that the EU legislature has 'discretion' as to the latter issue, which is whether the conditions for the application of

[200] Case C-427/12, *Commission* v. *European Parliament and Council*, at [40].

Article 290 or Article 291 have been met in any particular instance. Thus the fact that the EU legislature may take the view that, for example, an implementing act will suffice for rules made pursuant to a particular article of the legislative act because it only adds some further detail that does not thereby amend or supplement its non-essential elements does not 'make it so'. This is more especially so given that the analytical problem is compounded by a temporal one. The EU legislature will stipulate the type of secondary act to be used pursuant to different articles of the legislative act. However, the particular delegated or implementing act has by definition not been made at this point. It is only when it is made that it can be determined whether it does in reality conform to the definition of a delegated or implementing act provided in the Treaty. This problem is further compounded by the fact that different procedures are used for the two kinds of act, with the consequence being that once an act is prima facie regarded as being a delegated rather than an implementing act, or vice versa, the institutions will be reluctant to accept that it should be reclassified since it would render the procedure for its enactment ultra vires.

It can be accepted that when reviewing the choice made by the legislature the Court should consider the reasons why it chose to proceed via a delegated act rather than an implementing act, or vice versa. This is, however, to say no more than that when exercising judicial review a Court should be properly informed as to the reasoning that underpinned the decision of the body being reviewed. It provides no foundation for the conclusion that the body subject to review has 'discretion' as to whether the conditions for the application of delegated or implementing acts are met, with the consequence that the Court uses only light-touch review for manifest error.

The real lesson from this case is that the analytical divide between delegated and implementing acts is fragile and difficult. The CJEU was faced with a choice. It could choose to give guidance as to the nature of this divide, but this would lead to the analytical criterion set out above, or something analogous thereto, as suggested by the Commission in the instant case. This would then invite frequent challenges as to whether an act fell on the right or the wrong side of this analytical divide, a scenario that the Court would not welcome. The Court therefore chose the alternative route, which was to avoid close analytical scrutiny of the dichotomy between the two types of act through recourse to the intensity of review, manifest error being said to be warranted because of the 'discretion' possessed by the legislature. This will discourage claimants from challenging the correctness of the use of delegated or implementing acts, because of the difficulty of proving manifest error.

This cannot, however, conceal the paradox that besets this area. The distinction between delegated and implementing acts was adopted because it was felt to be important constitutionally and pragmatically. The paradox is that it is the very problematic nature of this divide which led the Court to back away from addressing the substantive distinction between the two types of act, and to sidestep the issue by assigning 'discretion' as to its application to the EU legislature, to be policed only through light-touch review for manifest error.

(b) EU agencies: power and authority

The emergence of EU agencies was charted in the previous chapter, as was the increased resort to this institutional option for the delivery of EU policy.[201] The ECJ has, as in the case of comitology, played a key role in determining the structural regulatory parameters within which agencies operate.

These were laid down at the inception of European integration in the *Meroni* case,[202] which involved a challenge by the applicant company to a decision requiring it to pay money to the Imported Ferrous Scrap Equalization Fund (IFSEF). The applicant argued that there had been an unlawful delegation of power from the ECSC institutions to the IFSEF, which was administering part of the ECSC scheme. The ECJ held, inter alia, that it was not possible to delegate power involving a wide margin of discretion. The Court accepted that it was possible for the High Authority to delegate certain power under the ECSC, but imposed limits:

> The consequences resulting from a delegation of powers are very different depending on whether it involves clearly defined executive powers the exercise of which can, therefore, be subject to strict review in the light of objective criteria determined by the delegating authority, or whether

[201] E. Chiti, 'The Emergence of a Community Administration: The Case of European Agencies' (2000) 37 *Common Market Law Review* 309; E. Chiti, 'Decentralisation and Integration into the Community Administrations: A New Perspective on European Agencies' (2004) 10 *European Law Journal* 402.

[202] Case 9/56, *Meroni & Co., Industrie Metallurgiche SpA* v. *High Authority* [1958] ECR 133.

> it involves a discretionary power, implying a wide margin of discretion which may, according to the use which is made of it, make possible the execution of actual economic policy.
>
> A delegation of the first kind cannot appreciably alter the consequences involved in the exercise of the powers concerned, whereas a delegation of the second kind, since it replaces the choices of the delegator by the choices of the delegate, brings about an actual transfer of responsibility.[203]

The ECJ concluded that the power delegated to the agencies in the instant case contained significant discretionary power that was not bounded by objective criteria and hence was not compatible with the Treaty. The *Meroni* principle remained the constitutional limit to delegation.[204] The EU courts have been willing to uphold delegations of power when they were felt to be warranted, but they have done so from within the framework of the *Meroni* reasoning, rather than straying outside it.[205]

The legal view served to shape the political perspective. The Commission, while content to use agencies, was also

[203] Case 9/56, *Meroni* [1958] ECR 133, at 152.

[204] See, e.g., Cases C-154–5/04, *The Queen, on the application of Alliance for Natural Health and Nutri-link Ltd* v. *Secretary of State for Health* [2005] ECR I-6451, at [90].

[205] Case C-301/02 P, *Tralli* v. *ECB* [2005] ECR I-4071, at [42]–[52]; Cases T-369/94 and 85/95, *DIR International Film Srl* v. *Commission* [1998] ECR II-357, at [52]–[53], reversed on appeal on different grounds, Case C-164/98 P, *DIR International Film Srl* v. *Commission* [2000] ECR I-447.

eager to preserve the limits to their authority as laid down in *Meroni* and resisted any shift whereby agencies would have autonomous regulatory power. This was apparent in its 2002 communication on regulatory agencies,[206] which was premised on the judicial status quo, as was later documentation.[207] The Commission acknowledged the rationale for agency creation cast in terms of independence, credibility and expertise, but this was balanced by repeated references to the need to preserve and reinforce 'the unity and integrity of the executive function' to ensure 'that it continues to be vested in the chief of the Commission if the latter is to have the required responsibility vis-à-vis Europe's citizens, the Member States and the other institutions'.[208] The participation of agencies should therefore be 'organised in a way which is consistent and in balance with the unity and integrity of the executive function and the Commission's ensuing responsibilities'.[209]

The Commission could therefore accept agencies with individual decision-making power in discrete fields. It could embrace information and co-ordination agencies, where it continued to have the final say. It was reluctant to create real regulatory agencies exercising discretionary power through adjudication and rule making, since if such power could be delegated then the Commission's sense of the unity and integrity of the executive function vested in it would

[206] The Operating Framework for the European Regulatory Agencies, COM(2002) 718 final.

[207] Draft Interinstitutional Agreement on the Operating Framework for the European Regulatory Agencies, COM(2005) 59 final, Art. 5(1).

[208] Operating Framework, p. 3.

[209] Operating Framework, p. 2.

be undermined. This was more especially so given that the agencies would have a degree of independence and that Member States would continue to exert considerable influence through membership of the administrative boards. The Commission reiterated its view once again in 2008, stating that there are 'clear and strict limits to the autonomous power of regulatory agencies in the current Community legal order' and that they cannot be given 'power to adopt general regulatory measures'.[210]

Political imperatives, however, led to institutional developments that placed the orthodox interpretation of agency power under strain. The financial crisis generated numerous responses, including new agencies to deal with banking and financial services to replace the pre-existing regime.[211] These EU supervisory authorities (ESAs) are accorded power to enact draft delegated acts, and the strong assumption, both legally and politically, is that these norms will be accepted by the Commission. It is the agency that drafts the regulatory standards. Thus where the primary regulation delegates power to the Commission to make

[210] European Agencies: The Way Forward, COM(2008) 135 final, p. 5.

[211] Regulation (EU) No 1095/2010 of the European Parliament and of the Council of 24 November 2010 establishing a European Supervisory Authority (European Securities and Markets Authority), OJ 2010 No L331/84; Regulation (EU) No 1093/2010 of the European Parliament and of the Council of 24 November 2010 establishing a European Supervisory Authority (European Banking Authority), OJ 2010 No L331/12; Regulation (EU) No 1094/2010 of the European Parliament and of the Council of 24 November 2010 establishing a European Supervisory Authority (European Insurance and Occupational Pensions Authority), OJ 2010 No L331/48.

delegated acts pursuant to Article 290 TFEU, it is the agency that drafts these acts, which are then endorsed by the Commission, subject to the possibility of veto by the Council or the European Parliament in accordance with Article 290 TFEU. It is, moreover, the agency that drafts the implementing technical standards pursuant to Article 291 TFEU. The regulations make it clear that the Commission should amend the draft regulations only in very limited circumstances, the rationale being that the agency has expertise within the area. The Commission is, moreover, only able to adopt a draft delegated act itself if the agency has failed to do so within the time specified. It must also give a reasoned explanation for departure from an agency draft rule and cannot make any such change without discussion with the agency. The legal as well as political reality is therefore that these EU agencies are run by the Member States through top-level national officials in a manner that is at the very least different in degree and arguably in kind compared with other agencies.

It was therefore inevitable that the CJEU would be called on to decide whether these agencies were compatible with the *Meroni* principle, and whether that principle should still be regarded as a constitutional limit to agency power. The issue came before the CJEU in the *Short Selling* case,[212] and the Court was therefore called on once again to determine the

[212] Case C-270/12, *United Kingdom* v. *Council and Parliament* EU:C:2014:18; M. Chamon, 'EU Agencies between *Meroni* and *Romano* or the Devil and the Deep Blue Sea' (2011) 48 *Common Market Law Review* 1055; M. Everson and E. Vos, 'European Agencies: What about the Institutional Balance?', Maastricht Faculty of Law Working Paper 2014/4.

structural regulatory framework within which EU institutions operated. The European Securities and Markets Authority (ESMA) was empowered to prohibit temporarily, or restrict, certain financial activities that threatened the orderly functioning and integrity of financial markets, or the stability of the EU financial system.[213] Article 28 of Regulation 236/2012 set out in more detail the circumstances in which ESMA could intervene,[214] which included restriction or prohibition of short selling, the rationale being that this had in the past seriously destabilized EU financial markets.

The UK contended that Article 28 violated the *Meroni* principle. This was because it accorded ESMA a large measure of discretion in deciding whether the conditions for intervention were met, since Article 28(2) required ESMA to decide whether there was a threat to the orderly functioning and integrity of financial markets, or to the stability of the whole or part of the financial system, and also to determine whether national authorities had taken measures to address such a threat. The UK argued further that ESMA had considerable discretion as to how to meet such threats, and that in deciding on this it had to make complex assessments concerning a range of factors set out in Article 28(3). The EU institutions, by way of contrast, contended that the contested provision was consistent with *Meroni*. They took the view that ESMA was merely exercising technical assessments in

[213] Reg. 1095/2010, OJ 2010 No L331/84, Art. 9(5).

[214] Regulation (EU) No 236/2012 of the European Parliament and of the Council of 14 March 2012 on short selling and certain aspects of credit default swaps, OJ 2012 No L86/1, Art. 28.

its field of expertise. Delegation of clearly defined executive decision-making powers to a distinct body was lawful, since it did not constitute actual transfer of responsibility by which the choices of the delegator were replaced by the choices of the delegate.

The CJEU, not surprisingly, rejected the UK claim. The Court noted that the bodies in question in *Meroni* were entities governed by private law, whereas ESMA was an EU agency. It held that Article 28 did not confer any autonomous power on ESMA that went beyond the bounds of the regulatory framework established by the ESMA regulation. It concluded that the exercise of power pursuant to Article 28 was circumscribed by various conditions which limited ESMA's discretion.[215] Thus the CJEU placed emphasis on the conditions that ESMA had to satisfy before it could intervene, which were set out in Article 28(2) and Article 28(3). It also took cognizance of the fact that the key criterion in Article 28 (2), which conditioned intervention on proof that it was necessary for the orderly functioning of financial markets, or for the integrity of the EU financial system, had itself been further specified by a delegated regulation.[216]

Courts not infrequently are faced with choices as to how to deal with legal principles enunciated in prior jurisprudence where circumstances have changed. They can formally

[215] Case C-270/12, *United Kingdom* v. *Council and Parliament*, at [46]–[55].

[216] Commission Delegated Regulation (EU) No 918/2012 of 5 July 2012 supplementing Regulation (EU) No 236/2012 of the European Parliament and of the Council on short selling and certain aspects of credit default swaps, OJ 2012 No L274/1.

discard the pre-existing principle, on the ground that the conditions that underpinned it no longer prevail. They can create exceptions to the principle, fine-tuning it so as better to accord with changed circumstance. They can retain the principle, but loosen it so as to render it more flexible. This is less dramatic than the previous options, and ensures that the court retains maximal discretion as to the application of the principle for the future, without thereby committing it to the sharper choices resulting from the first two options. A court will, moreover, be minded to choose this third option where the circumstances of the case do not compel it to confront the more dramatic first option.

This was the strategy in the instant case, as is readily apparent by juxtaposing the mode of argument used respectively by the CJEU and the UK. The CJEU reached the conclusion that Article 28 was consistent with *Meroni* primarily by pointing to the conditions that had to be satisfied before the power could be used, these being listed in Article 28(2)–(3). This did not, however, really touch the nub of the UK argument, which was that those very conditions entailed difficult discretionary choices. The CJEU's response was to point to the need for consultation before such measures were imposed, and to the fact that the delegated regulation gave further guidance as to the factors that should inform the application of Article 28. Whether this really sufficed to meet the UK arguments, or whether it merely added a further layer of discretion, is contestable.

This does not mean that the Court's decision was wrong. It does mean that we should recognize it for what it was – a decision that formally preserved a principle, but imbued it with greater flexibility by loosening it in order to render it compatible with the new reality of agency power. The legal reality is that the ESAs have been accorded power greater than other agencies, and come closest to having regulatory autonomy in their assigned fields. The political reality is that the Member States were unwilling to accept the reformed agency regime in this area, unless it was structured in this manner, with the agency making the choices subject to limited oversight by the Commission. The CJEU would have been mindful of this disposition of power, and it would not readily interpret *Meroni* to upset this schema.

The judicial strategy in the *Short Selling* case sufficed to resolve the instant dispute, but there continues to be vibrant debate as to whether the Court should have gone further and overruled *Meroni*. For some, *Meroni* embodies the important principle that discretionary decision making should be legitimated through democratic organs, which should retain control over the choices thus made, the implication being that while the *Meroni* principle might be loosened to accommodate the ESAs it should not be discarded.[217] The need for the positive imprimatur of the principal EU institutions, and/or their capacity to veto the choice made by the agency, is regarded as crucial. For others, *Meroni* is seen as the block to the creation of true regulatory agencies

[217] S. Griller and A. Orator, 'Everything under Control? The "Way Forward" for European Agencies in the Footsteps of the Meroni Doctrine' (2010) 35 *European Law Review* 3; J.-P. Schneider, 'A Common Framework for Decentralized EU Agencies and the *Meroni* Doctrine' (2009) 61 *Administrative Law Review* 29.

that would be beneficial for decision making in the EU, the implication being that it should be discarded, or further loosened, with alternative safeguards being put in place to ensure agency accountability.[218] The loosening of *Meroni* does not suffice, because it is regarded as conceptually muddled, preserving the form of democratic oversight while stripping away much of its substance, and because this solution, as reflected in the ESA empowering regulations, creates uncertainty within the agencies as to the real scope of their power. We should, on this view, recognize the new reality for what it is, and not act on the pretence that it can be accommodated within a pre-existing schema.

This debate raises important issues concerning the role of agencies within the schema of EU decision making. This has hitherto been justified in terms of their expertise, the enhanced credibility they bring to decision making by preserving technical regulatory issues from the vagaries of day-to-day political change, and the fact that they enable the Commission to concentrate on its core tasks of policy formation. The granting of real discretionary power to agencies, requiring them to balance competing public interests when

[218] M. Everson, 'Independent Agencies: Hierarchy Beaters?' (1995) 1 *European Law Journal* 180; E. Vos, 'Reforming the European Commission: What Role to Play for EU Agencies?' (2000) 37 *Common Market Law Review* 1113; G. Majone, 'Delegation of Regulatory Powers in a Mixed Polity'·(2002) 8 *European Law Journal* 319; E. Chiti, 'Decentralisation and Integration into the Community Administrations: A New Perspective on European Agencies' (2004) 10 *European Law Journal* 402.

making binding formal rules or individual decisions, requires re-evaluation of this rationale.

Justifications cast in terms of expertise become weaker, since the agency accorded such new powers has no special claim to expertise when it comes to balancing broad, competing public interests, or when deciding on, for example, the level of risk that is acceptable within society. Agency technical expertise does not translate into specialist skills in balancing broad public interests, and is not the same as democratic legitimacy.[219] Justifications cast in terms of the credibility argument must also be reconsidered. If agencies are accorded broad discretionary powers requiring them to balance competing public interests then it is by no means self-evident that such decisions should be insulated from political change expressed by and through the ordinary political process. Nor is it self-evident that EU agencies exercising such enhanced power would be viewed as more credible than majoritarian decision-making institutions.

It follows that if *Meroni* were to be discarded this would have to be based on an argument that transcends that made hitherto. Giandomenico Majone advanced such an argument that embraced expertise and credibility, but moved beyond them.[220] It was not possible, he argued, in areas such as risk regulation to distinguish between the technical issues dealt with by an agency and the policy matters residing in

[219] Case T-13/99, *Pfizer Animal Health SA* v. *Council* [2002] ECR II-3303, at [201].

[220] G. Majone, *Regulating Europe* (London: Routledge, 1996); Majone, 'Delegation of Regulatory Powers in a Mixed Polity'.

majoritarian institutions, more especially given the fact that complex regulatory tasks faced by the EU could not be adequately handled by the Commission, with its limited administrative, financial and cognitive resources. Recourse to stronger and more autonomous regulatory institutions at European level was therefore the best response, provided that this 'regulatory estate' was subject to controls to ensure accountability and legitimacy.

Whether we should retain the *Meroni* principle in its loosened form, or whether we should discard it or loosen it even further, is an issue that will continue to divide commentators. The accountability controls for agencies are important if *Meroni* is retained in its loosened form, and they assume even greater significance if *Meroni* is discarded. This requires consideration of procedural and substantive legal controls, and also political controls cast in terms of legislative specification of agency tasks in the enabling regulation, agency composition, reporting requirement, audit, impact assessment and legislative veto.[221]

The choice between retention of *Meroni* in its more loosened form and discarding it should not, however, be overstated. The reality is that the powers accorded to agencies have increased and been legitimized by the CJEU in the *Short Selling* case. What this means in practical terms is that while *Meroni* remains a constitutional principle within EU law it is consistent with an agency structure in which very

[221] Craig, *EU Administrative Law*, Ch. 6; Joint Statement of the European Parliament, the Council of the EU and the European Commission on decentralised agencies, Council 11450/12, Brussels, 18 June 2012.

considerable substantive authority is accorded to the agency, including authority for the making of complex regulatory choices, in circumstances where the Commission's capacity for altering the norms thus made is closely circumscribed by the enabling regulation.

(c) Regulatory design: the continuing challenge

(i) The centrality of shared administration

The discussion in the previous chapter revealed the centrality of shared administration to the discharge of EU policy. The scale of this undertaking is noteworthy in itself. To devise regulatory regimes that entail close collaboration between the EU institutions and twenty-eight Member States with different linguistic, cultural and administrative traditions is an ambitious undertaking, and considerably more problematic than interaction between different levels of government within classic federal systems. The success of such regulatory regimes is dependent on the Commission and national administrations discharging the respective tasks assigned to them by EU legislation, and dependent also on interaction between the national administrations in the Member States. The regulatory structures thus created exemplify multi-level governance in action. The design of such structures continues to be one of the principal challenges for the EU, and for EU administrative law.

The rationale for and prevalence of shared administration is readily explicable. The most obvious rationale is simply workload. The Commission does not possess anything like sufficient resources to administer directly the complex regimes that apply in relation to agriculture, regional aid, customs, utility regulation and the like. Using national administrations was therefore the obvious choice. A related reason is that it facilitates the expression of Member State preferences and drawing on Member State expertise in the application of EU policy, as exemplified by the Structural Fund regime, where the nature of the projects that should be funded will be shaped by Member State preferences concerning the types of project to which it accords priority. A third rationale is that shared administration may be required because the very nature of the EU rules requires application that is Member State-specific, as exemplified by the universal-service obligations applicable to network industries, which require that certain services should be available to consumers at 'affordable' prices, this determination being left to the national regulatory authority since it will vary between Member States.

It is, then, unsurprising that shared administration has been used for EU regimes that entail disbursement of EU funds, such as the Common Agricultural Policy and Structural Funds, and for the discharge of other policies through classic regulatory means even where there is no EU funding involved, such as regulation of telecommunications, energy and the application of competition policy. The application of shared administration within the latter category will impact on the overall economic health of the EU, but this does not alter the fact that the successful design and implementation of shared administration will be affected by whether the objective is the disbursement of EU funds, or the attainment of some other EU regulatory goal.

There are, nonetheless, significant commonalities in this regard. The success of any scheme of shared administration is crucially dependent on the specification of legislative objectives that the EU and national administrators are instructed to attain, and on the design of the regime whereby this is implemented at EU and national level, in order to ensure that the objectives are effectively achieved. Legislative choice will therefore shape administrative effectiveness, and so too will the design of service delivery at national level. The interplay between these issues is evident in areas subject to shared administration.

(ii) The CAP, specification of legislative objective and national implementation

The legislative objective underpinning the CAP until the end of the last millennium was cast in terms of price support,[222] with the Council establishing common prices for most agricultural goods. There was a target price, this being the price that it was hoped farmers would be able to obtain on the open market. There was an intervention price, which was the price at which the Commission would buy up produce from the market. There was also a threshold price, this being the price to which imports were raised when world prices were less than those prevailing in the EU. The price support system was

[222] J. Usher, *Legal Aspects of Agriculture in the European Community* (Oxford: Oxford University Press, 1988); R. Fennell, *The Common Agricultural Policy: Continuity and Change* (Oxford: Clarendon Press, 1997); J. McMahon, *Law of the Common Agricultural Policy* (London: Longman, 2000); M. Cardwell, *The European Model of Agriculture* (Oxford: Oxford University Press, 2004).

very costly for the EU, consuming the largest share of the budget, and was eventually replaced by a system of income support. The price support regime proved resilient to reform, hence its survival for nearly forty years, since it created vested interests that benefited from the status quo, which were then able to put pressure on their Member States in the Council to resist change.

The problems flowing from specification of legislative objective were compounded by design of the implementation regime, which reflected a tension between the collective interests of the Member States in the Council, and the interests of individual Member States as recipients of CAP funds. The Member States in their collective capacity had an interest in the correct allocation of the EU budget, and the proper use of funds. There was, however, a tension between this objective, and the accountability of individual Member States for the correct disbursement of CAP funds. Individual states sought to minimize their liability for incorrect CAP allocations, this being of considerable importance given that the price support regime entailed multiple payments to multiple recipients. This tension was reflected in the EU legislation, which contained procedural and substantive conditions for eligibility for funds, and specified rules as to liability when things went wrong. These matters were crucial to the way in which shared management operated.[223]

Thus, to take but one example, the successful implementation of EU policy was dependent on systems for accreditation and certification of accounts. The Commission

[223] Craig, *EU Administrative Law*, Ch. 4.

argued that it should be responsible for the accreditation of paying agencies, and for approval of the national certifying bodies, but these suggestions were rejected by the Council. The Member States were empowered to accredit agencies,[224] and specify the certifying bodies.[225] This was problematic, with bodies being accredited that did not fulfil the relevant criteria.[226] The problem was compounded by the fact that Member States were obliged from the outset to submit to the Commission details of the paying agencies, and the accounting conditions for payment.[227] However, prior to 1996 there were 'hundreds of un-notified small de facto agencies making EAGGF [European Agricultural Guidance and Guarantee Fund] Guarantee payments in the Member States without any structured procedures for checking on their activities or accounts'.[228] This illegality was practised by the Member States and tolerated by the Commission, which

[224] Council Regulation (EC) 1258/1999 of 17 May 1999 on the financing of the Common Agricultural Policy, OJ 1999 No L160/103, Art. 4.

[225] Commission Regulation (EC) 1663/95 of 7 July 1995 laying down detailed rules for the application of Council Regulation (EEC) 729/70 regarding the clearance of accounts of the EAGGF Guarantee Section, OJ 1995 No L158/6, Art. 3.

[226] Court of Auditors, Special Report 21/98, Concerning the Accreditation and Certification Procedures as Applied to the 1996 Clearance of Accounts for EAGGF-Guarantee Expenditure, OJ 1998 No C389/1, at [2.11].

[227] Council Regulation 729/70/EEC on the financing of the common agricultural policy, OJ 1970 No L94/13, Art. 4.

[228] Committee of Independent Experts, Second Report on Reform of the Commission, Analysis of Current Practice and Proposals for Tackling Mismanagement, Irregularities and Fraud (10 Sept 1999), Vol. 1, at [3.9.6].

could do little in practice to stop it. In this context 'shared administration amounted to not much more than shared acceptance that the Regulation could be flouted'.[229]

A second example of the tension between the collective and individual interest and the way in which this impacted on implementation of the regulatory regime was the system of responsibility for financial irregularity.[230] Member States had an obligation to prevent irregularities, and to recover sums lost as a result of irregularities or negligence. However, in the absence of total recovery, the financial consequences of irregularities or negligence were borne by the Community, with the exception of losses attributable to irregularities or negligence by administrative bodies of the Member States. This created, as the Committee of Independent Experts noted, a perverse pattern of incentives:

> It is difficult to believe that the administrative authorities . . . in the Member States are always inclined to highlight for the Commission instances of irregularity or negligence on their part which would result in them bearing the resulting financial consequences. It is also difficult to believe that they are never negligent. In other words the arrangements which this basic Regulation established and which still pertain do not provide the immediate disbursers of 48% (at one time as high as 70%) of the Community's budget, the EAGGF paying agencies in the Member States, with any immediate incentive

[229] Committee of Independent Experts, Second Report, Vol. 1, at [3.9.6].
[230] Council Regulation 729/70/EEC, Art. 8.

> for rigour and tight control of what is in effect someone else's, that is the Community's, money.[231]

The ECJ used its best efforts to interpret the enabling legislation teleologically so as to minimize the opportunity for evasion of responsibility, and to close gaps that had become apparent in the legislative regime.[232] It could, however, only do so much through adjudication, as evidenced by the fact that the Court of Auditors routinely refused to sign off the Community accounts because of systemic problems with the CAP.

The specification of legislative objectives and the implementation regime has now changed markedly, although the CAP still operates within a framework of shared administration. The financial burden of the price support regime could not be sustained, more especially in the light of impending enlargement, and pressures from the WTO. This was the catalyst for the shift from price support to income support proposed by the Commission,[233] which was introduced in 2003. The legislative objective of the reformed CAP was a single farm payment for EU farmers, which was largely decoupled from production, this payment being linked to respect for standards concerning the environment, food

[231] Committee of Independent Experts, Second Report, Vol. 1, at [3.7.5].

[232] Case 11/76, *Netherlands* v. *Commission* [1979] ECR 245; Case C-235/97, *France* v. *Commission* [1998] ECR I-7555; Case C-54/95, *Germany* v. *Commission* [1999] ECR I-35; Case C-278/98, *Netherlands* v. *Commission* [2001] ECR I-1501.

[233] Agenda 2000: For a Stronger and Wider Union (1997).

safety, animal and plant health and animal welfare.[234] The shift in legislative objective was significant in addressing the malaise of the previous price support system, the very complexity of which, with its multiplicity of rules relating to quotas, subsidies and the like, invited fraud.

The Commission has always been willing to learn from the regulatory lessons of the past. The implementation package that was enacted made considerable headway in this regard. The rules relating to accreditation of national paying agencies were reinforced;[235] so too were those relating to national bodies that would certify the accounts of the paying agencies. These provisions were complemented by those that reinforced Member States' obligation to take all necessary measures to protect the EU's financial interests, including the prevention of irregularities and the recovery of sums lost through irregularity or negligence.[236] There were, in addition, provisions that empowered the Commission to reduce or suspend payments if information indicated that funds had not been used in compliance with EU rules,[237] and the enabling regulation also imposed financial obligations on Member

[234] Council Regulation (EC) No 73/2009 of 19 January 2009 establishing common rules for direct-support schemes for farmers under the Common Agricultural Policy and establishing certain support schemes for farmers, amending Regulations (EC) No 1290/2005 (EC) No 247/2006 (EC) No 378/2007 and repealing Regulation (EC) No 1782/2003, OJ 2009 No L30/16.

[235] Council Regulation (EC) 1290/2005 of 21 June 2005 on the financing of the Common Agricultural Policy, OJ 2005 No L209/1, Art. 6.

[236] Council Regulation (EC) 1290/2005, Art. 9.

[237] Council Regulation (EC) 1290/2005, Arts. 17, 27.

States that failed to clear their accounts within a stipulated time.[238] This does not mean that the reformed regime has been unproblematic. The Court of Auditors attested to ongoing difficulties with the income support system and its implementation.[239] It is nonetheless a significant improvement on the price support regime that it superseded.

The income support regime has now been further modified through four regulations that lay the framework for the CAP until the year 2020.[240] This builds on the existing regime and places particular emphasis on enhancing the competitiveness of EU agriculture, rendering it more sustainable and environmentally friendly and targeting support payments in a more equitable manner.[241]

(iii) The Structural Funds, specification of legislative objective and national implementation

The Structural Funds account for the second-largest disbursement of EU funds after the CAP, currently one-third of

[238] Council Regulation (EC) 1290/2005, Art. 32(4)(a).

[239] Court of Auditors, Special Report 5/2011, 'Single Payment Scheme (SPS): Issues to be Addressed to Improve Its Sound Financial Management', http://eca.europa.eu/portal/pls/portal/docs/1/8322724.PDF; Court of Auditors, Special Report 7/2011, 'Is Agri-environment Support Well Designed and Managed?', http://eca.europa.eu/portal/pls/portal/docs/1/8772726.PDF; Court of Auditors, Special Report 7/2010, 'Audit of the Clearance of Accounts Procedure', http://eca.europa.eu/portal/pls/portal/docs/1/7912724.PDF.

[240] 'The CAP towards 2020: Meeting the Food, Natural Resources and Territorial Challenges of the Future', COM(2010) 672 final.

[241] 'Overview of CAP Reform 2014–2020', available at http://ec.europa.eu/agriculture/cap-post-2013/index_en.htm.

the budget.[242] The objective of Structural Fund policy has been to provide assistance to disadvantaged regions.[243] The policy can be traced back to the late 1960s, and was established in 1972. It was expanded after 1986, since it was seen as necessary to ensure the acceptability of the market-based initiatives in the Single European Act. There were fears that the wealthier economies would benefit from completion of the single market, and that the gap between these and the less advantaged economies would widen. Reform of the Structural Funds was intended to alleviate these concerns. The 1988 reforms identified four principal objectives for the Structural Funds: development of disadvantaged regions, conversion of regions seriously affected by industrial decline, combating long-term unemployment and assisting in the occupational integration of young people.[244]

[242] The governing Treaty provision is now Art. 174 TFEU. The relevant funds are the European Agricultural Guidance and Guarantee Fund, Guidance Section, EAGGF; the European Social Fund (ESF); the European Regional Development Fund (ERDF); and the Cohesion Fund (CF). Arts. 175, 177 TFEU.

[243] J. Scott, *Development Dilemmas in the European Community: Rethinking Regional Development Policy* (Buckingham: Open University Press, 1995); L. Hooghe (ed.), *Cohesion Policy and European Integration* (Oxford: Oxford University Press, 1996); I. Bache, *The Politics of European Union Regional Policy: Multi-level Governance or Flexible Gatekeeping?* (Sheffield: Sheffield Academic Press, 1998); J. Scott, 'Regional Policy: An Evolutionary Perspective', in P. Craig and G. de Búrca (eds.), *The Evolution of EU Law* (Oxford: Oxford University Press, 1999), Ch. 17; A. Evans, *The EU Structural Funds* (Oxford: Oxford University Press, 1999).

[244] Council Regulation (EEC) 2052/88 of 24 June 1988 on the tasks of the Structural Funds and their effectiveness and on co-ordination of their

A number of principles ran through the 1988 scheme: 'concentration' connoted the idea that funding should be allocated to the areas in greatest need; 'additionality' captured the precept that Community funding should genuinely add to regional assistance, and not replace that hitherto provided by Member State financing; 'partnership' meant close co-operation between the Commission and Member States in the preparation, financing, monitoring and assessment of the operations; and 'programming' meant the grant of funding for a certain period, after which it would be reviewed. There were further reforms to Structural Fund policy in 1993, 1999 and 2007,[245] which recast the objectives in terms of convergence for those areas that were economically lagging behind, regional competitiveness and employment, and territorial co-operation. The principles that guided structural policy hitherto were preserved, albeit with some modification.

The tension between the collective EU interest and the interests of individual Member States that was evident in relation to the CAP was also present in this area, albeit in different ways. It was manifest in relation to the criteria for access to the Funds, and the supervision of funded projects in order to prevent fraud.

activities between themselves and with the operations of the European Investment Bank and the other existing financial instruments, OJ 1988 No L185/9, Arts. 1–2.

245 Council Regulation (EC) No 1083/2006 of 11 July 2006 laying down general provisions on the European Regional Development Fund, the European Social Fund and the Cohesion Fund and repealing Regulation (EC) No 1260/1999, OJ 2006 No L210/25.

In terms of the criteria for access, the successive Structural Fund regulations embodied commitment to concentration, additionality, partnership and programming as ideals that shaped the collective interest in a rational EU regional policy. The legislation, however, accorded the individual Member States significant discretion concerning the application of these ideals in the context of project selection, and the legislation was amended as a result of Member State pressure, thereby weakening the peremptory force of the collective commitment to additionality.

In relation to the supervision of funded projects, the collective interest favours the proper deployment of EU resources to attain the goals of EU regional policy. This requires machinery to ensure that projects and programmes selected are properly monitored, that there is effective machinery to detect financial irregularity through audit and the like, and that the rules provide a meaningful regime for compliance by the relevant players. Individual Member States may, however, have an incentive to avoid these consequences in relation to projects on their territory, more especially where the consequences will be financial penalties imposed on the state, or the withholding of further disbursements to particular projects. This issue assumed greater significance post-1999, where the strategy was to devolve more responsibility for monitoring and the like to the Member States, since the Commission lacked the resources to do the job. Successive legislative amendments sought to ratchet up the rules relating to financial oversight, monitoring, auditing and the like,[246] but effective implementation of the rules was not easy.

[246] Craig, *EU Administrative Law*, Ch. 4.

These tensions were recognized in the Second Report of the Committee of Independent Experts.[247] Thus the committee was critical of certain aspects of the legislative design embodied in the Structural Fund regulations even after 1999. It concluded that the balance of decision-making power had shifted to the Member States, but that a number of factors tended to divest them of responsibility: the criterion for additionality was weak; the Commission had little control over individual projects; and the ceiling for national expenditure was in effect also a target, with implications for project selection, evaluation and control. The issue concerning Commission resources surfaced again in relation to Member State management and control systems, the Committee noting that while the legislation imposed obligations in this regard the resources for control were 'woefully inadequate to ensure proper implementation of the new Regulation'.[248] The paucity of claims for recovery in cases of national financial irregularity was also a cause for concern, not because of inadequacies in the legislation per se, but because of inadequate implementation by the Commission combined with resistance by the Member States.[249]

A major overhaul of the Structural Funds took place in 2013, with the legislation designed to regulate this area

[247] Committee of Independent Experts, Second Report, Vol. 1, at [3.15]–[3.22].

[248] Committee of Independent Experts, Second Report, Vol. 1, at [3.17.3].

[249] Committee of Independent Experts, Second Report, Vol. 1, at [3.17.4–3.17.6].

until 2020.[250] The reform links what are now termed the European Structural and Investment Funds (ESIs) more closely with the overall Europe 2020 programme designed to foster growth, employment and innovation,[251] and also with macro-economic planning in the wake of the EU financial crisis.[252] This is reflected in the broadened list of legislative objectives for the ESIs,[253] which are then given more specific meaning in the regulations dealing with each particular fund.[254] The principles that underpinned earlier regulations, such as concentration, additionality, partnership and programming, are still present, albeit modified to fit with the broadened list of objectives. The recitals emphasize the need to ensure that the regime of shared administration and national disbursement of funds operates in a legal and

[250] Regulation (EU) No 1303/2013 of the European Parliament and of the Council of 17 December 2013 laying down common provisions on the European Regional Development Fund, the European Social Fund, the Cohesion Fund, the European Agricultural Fund for Rural Development and the European Maritime and Fisheries Fund and laying down general provisions on the European Regional Development Fund, the European Social Fund, the Cohesion Fund and the European Maritime and Fisheries Fund and repealing Council Regulation (EC) No 1083/2006, OJ 2013 No L347/320.

[251] See http://ec.europa.eu/regional_policy/what/europe2020/index_en.cfm.

[252] See http://ec.europa.eu/regional_policy/what/crisis/index_en.cfm.

[253] Regulation (EU) No 1303/2013, Art. 9.

[254] See, e.g., Regulation (EU) No 1301/2013 of the European Parliament and of the Council of 17 December 2013 on the European Regional Development Fund and on specific provisions concerning the investment for growth and jobs goal and repealing Regulation (EC) No 1080/2006, OJ 2013 No L347/289, Art. 5.

regular manner and in accord with more general EU rules on financial probity,[255] and the new Regulation contains detailed provisions on performance review, monitoring, programme oversight, management and control, audit, financial recovery and the like.

It remains to be seen how the new regime works. The bottom line is that sharing the administration of complex activities is difficult across twenty-eight Member States with diverse bureaucratic traditions, more especially at the level of operational detail concerning certification, audit and the like. It is clear that legislative design is a necessary condition for successful policy delivery, whether with regard to the criteria for access to the ESIs or with respect to management, oversight, audit and the correction of irregularity. The rules contained in the EU legislation embody incentives for compliance, which may be more or less effective depending upon their content. While legislative design is a necessary condition for successful policy delivery, it is not sufficient. There are instances where the failings flowed not from inadequate rules, but from inadequacy in their implementation, whether this was due to failures of management systems, insufficient personnel or personal shortcomings. We should nonetheless be careful about the ascription of blame when things go wrong. The tendency has to been to lay the fault at the door of the EU, and more especially the Commission. This suits the Member States, and anti-European commentators. The Commission has been at fault on occasion, but to suggest that the entire malaise should be laid at the Commission's door is a

[255] Regulation (EU) No 1303/2013, rec. 10.

gross oversimplification. The existing regime is also the result of Member State preferences, expressed in the relevant legislation and manifest in the way in which it is applied at national level.

(iv) Utilities regulation, specification of legislative objective and national implementation

The application of shared administration in relation to the CAP and the Structural Funds has received most attention because of the sums involved, and because of the reports from the Committee of Independent Experts and the Court of Auditors. It is, however, important to press further and understand the framework of shared administration that is applicable in areas where the EU functions in its 'classic mode' as regulatory state,[256] as exemplified by utility regulation.

The objective of EU policy in this area, as apparent from the Treaty and attendant legislation, is the enhancement of cross-border competition as part of the single-market strategy, coupled with ensuring continuity of energy supply. This was embodied in the directives at the turn of the millennium designed to complete the internal energy market and expedite the process of liberalization, as qualified by detailed provisions setting out public-service obligations to protect

[256] G. Majone, 'The Rise of the Regulatory State in Europe' (1994) 17 *West European Politics* 77; G. Majone, *Regulating Europe* (London: Routledge, 1996); G. Majone, 'From the Positive to the Regulatory State: Causes and Consequences of Changes in the Mode of Governance' (1997) 17 *Journal of Public Policy* 139.

the customer.[257] There were, however, substantive and institutional difficulties with realization of the 2003 schema.

In substantive terms, there were tensions between the collective Union interest and the interests of some Member States. The legislative scheme was simply not tough enough in certain crucial respects, thereby enabling established states and firms to avoid the full rigours of cross-border competition. The Commission noted the 'lack of integration between national markets', and the fact that with few exceptions 'electricity and gas markets in the EU remain national in economic scope'.[258] There was much evidence that energy suppliers from other Member States could not compete equally with existing companies in certain states.

Thus while the 2003 legislation required that network operations should be separated from supply and generation or production activities, some Member States had 'complied' with this requirement by creating a legal entity within an integrated company. This was felt to be unsatisfactory, since the transmission system operator could treat its affiliated companies better than competing third parties in ways that

[257] See, e.g., Directive 2003/54/EC of the European Parliament and of the Council of 26 June 2003 concerning common rules for the internal market in electricity and repealing Directive 96/ 92, OJ 2003 No L176/37; Directive 2005/89/EC of the European Parliament and of the Council of 18 January 2006 concerning measures to safeguard security of electricity supply and infrastructure investment, OJ 2005 No L33/22; Directive 2003/55/EC of the European Parliament and of the Council of 26 June 2003 concerning common rules for the internal market in natural gas and repealing Directive 98/30, OJ 2003 No L176/57.

[258] Report on Progress in Creating the Internal Gas and Electricity Market, COM(2005) 568 final, p. 2.

were difficult to detect. The 2009 legislative reforms were therefore directed to 'ownership unbundling', so as to ensure that the same person could not exercise control over a supply undertaking and hold an interest in a transmission system.[259]

In institutional terms, there were weaknesses in relation to national regulatory agencies that administered the 2003 energy regime, and co-ordination problems between such authorities. This was especially significant given the centrality of their role in ensuring that the directive was fulfilled, in relation both to market liberalization and to compliance with universal-service obligations. Thus while the national authorities did a reasonable job of protecting universal-service obligations, there were concerns that in some Member States the regulatory authority was relatively weak, while in others regulatory authority was dispersed, whereas what was required for a properly functioning internal market was strong and independent regulators.[260]

The 2009 legislative reform therefore required each Member State to designate a single national regulatory authority, guarantee its independence and ensure that it exercised its powers impartially and transparently. The Member State was

[259] Directive 2009/72/EC of the European Parliament and of the Council of 13 July 2009 concerning common rules for the internal market in electricity and repealing Directive 2003/54/EC, OJ 2009 No L211/55; Directive 2009/73/EC of the European Parliament and of the Council of 13 July 2009 concerning common rules for the internal market in natural gas and repealing Directive 2003/55/EC, OJ 2009 No L211/94.

[260] Proposal for a Directive of the European Parliament and of the Council amending Directive 2003/54/EC concerning common rules for the internal market in electricity, COM(2007) 528 final, p. 8.

required to make sure that the regulatory authority had legal personality, budgetary autonomy and adequate human and financial resources to carry out its duties.[261] The centrality of the national regulatory authorities to the energy regime is apparent in the strengthening of their duties, which include ensuring compliance by undertakings with the obligations in the directive, such as those on unbundling and public-service obligations, fixing or approving tariffs, as well as a host of monitoring obligations.[262] These duties are to be exercised so as to attain more general regulatory objectives, such as a competitive energy market, consumer choice and enhanced efficiency.[263] The emphasis placed on having strong regulatory authorities is apparent once again in provisions stipulating that Member States must ensure that their regulatory authorities have the requisite powers to enable them to carry out their newly expanded range of duties 'in an efficient and expeditious manner'.[264] Thus they must have the power to, inter alia, issue binding decisions, carry out investigations into the functioning of energy markets and request information from undertakings relevant for its tasks, and the power to impose 'effective, appropriate and dissuasive sanctions' on undertakings for non-compliance with their obligations under the directive or any decision made thereunder,[265] or to propose that a court should impose such a penalty.[266]

[261] See, e.g., Directive 2009/72/EC, Art. 35.

[262] See, e.g., Directive 2009/72/EC, Art. 37.

[263] See, e.g., Directive 2009/72/EC, Art. 36.

[264] See, e.g., Directive 2009/72/EC, Art. 37(4).

[265] See, e.g., Directive 2009/72/EC, Art. 37(4)(d).

[266] See, further, Commission Staff Working Document, 'The Regulatory Authorities', 22 January 2010.

The 2009 legislative reforms also sought to improve interaction between national regulatory authorities. This had existed prior to 2009, but it was felt that it could be improved, this being the catalyst for the creation of the Agency for Cooperation of Energy Regulators.[267] It provides a framework for national regulators to co-operate in order to improve the handling of cross-border situations, and to increase the exchange of information and the apportionment of competence where more than one Member State is involved.

The Third Energy Package embodied in the 2009 legislation became operative in 2011, when the date for the transposition of the directives expired.[268] There is no doubt that it is an improvement on the pre-existing regime. It exemplifies a positive feature of EU regulation more generally, which is the willingness to confront problems with the status quo, and make efforts to meet them through considered reform. The Third Energy Package did that, addressing the difficulties with the 2003 schema through legislative change directed at the pre-existing substantive and institutional problems. This is certainly a necessary step towards securing a competitive energy market and security of supply.

It is not, however, sufficient, since it is dependent on timely implementation of the legislative imperatives at national level. This is an endemic problem, even in relation to national legislation applicable to a single state. It is,

[267] Regulation (EC) No 713/2009 of the European Parliament and of the Council of 13 July 2009 establishing an Agency for the Cooperation of Energy Regulators, OJ 2009 No L211/1.

[268] See http://ec.europa.eu/energy/gas_electricity/index_en.htm.

however, exacerbated when the legislation seeks to attain objectives across twenty-eight states. This is evident from the Commission's 2012 report. It concluded that the internal energy market would not be completed by 2014, which was the stipulated date. This was because Member States were slow in adjusting national legislation and creating fully competitive markets, and were still too often wedded to inward-looking or nationally inspired policies.[269] There was, moreover, considerable divergence in energy market development in different parts of the EU, and attainment of competitive cross-border trade was hampered by national price regulation.

7 Conclusion

It is important in concluding this chapter to maintain a sense of perspective. All systems of administrative law, whether national, regional or global, face challenges. Some are perennial, as exemplified by debates as to the desirable intensity of substantive review, others change with the effluxion of time, as epitomized by novel regulatory responsibilities flowing from technological change. The fact that the EU should have its share of such challenges should therefore come as no surprise. This is more especially so because EU administrative law is applicable across twenty-eight Member States with diverse administrative, legal and cultural traditions. The difficulties that beset the subject should not be denied. The legal and political solutions adopted should properly be subject to critical scrutiny. We should therefore not be complacent, but

[269] 'Making the Internal Energy Market Work', COM(2012) 663 final.

we should also be balanced in our assessment. This means recognizing the positive dimension of EU administrative law and the way in which it has enhanced accountability. It means recognizing also that the best is sometimes the enemy of the good, which in this context connotes the need to appreciate the political or pragmatic difficulties of securing the outcome felt to be most desirable. It means finally recognizing the challenges posed more generally by systemic deficiencies in some Member States that undermine the rule of law.[270]

[270] 'A New EU Framework to Strengthen the Rule of Law,' COM(2014) 158 final; A. von Bogdandy, M. Kottmann, C. Antpohler, J. Dickschen, S. Hentrei and M. Smrkolj, 'Reverse Solange: Protecting the Essence of Rights against Member States' (2012) 49 *Common Market Law Review* 489; A. von Bogdandy and M. Ioannidis, 'Systemic Deficiency in the Rule of Law: What It Is, What Has Been Done, What Can Be Done' (2014) 51 *Common Market Law Review* 59.

5

Global administrative law

Foundations

1 Introduction

The discussion thus far has focused primarily on national and EU administrative law, although the challenges posed by global administrative law have been raised in the earlier analysis. This chapter and that which follows focus directly on global administrative law. The field has developed very considerably in the new millennium, and there is much valuable scholarship.[1] Neil Walker has astutely observed that to

[1] There is a large and growing literature. A bibliography can be found at www.iilj.org/gal/default.asp. There have been a number of symposia devoted to the topic: *Law and Contemporary Problems* (2005); *New York University Journal of International Law and Policy* (2005); *European Journal of International Law* (2006); *German Law Journal* (2008); *International Organizations Law Review* (2009). The following provide valuable analyses of the field: S. Shapiro, 'International Trade Agreements, Regulatory Protection and Public Accountability' (2002) 54 *Administrative Law Review* 415; G. della Cananea, 'Beyond the State: The Europeanization and Globalization of Procedural Administrative Law' (2003) 9 *European Public Law* 563; R. Stewart, 'Administrative Law in the Twenty-First Century' (2003) 78 *New York University Law Review* 437; A. Aman, 'Globalization, Democracy and the Need for a New Administrative Law' (2003) 10 *Indiana Journal of Global Legal Studies* 125; S. Cassese, 'Administrative Law without the State? The Challenge of Global Regulation' (2005) 37 *New York University Journal of International Law and Policy* 663; B. Kingsbury, N. Krisch and R. Stewart, 'The Emergence of Global Administrative Law' (2005) 68 *Law and Contemporary Problems* 15; R. Stewart, 'US Administrative Law: A Model

subscribe to phrases such as 'postnational constitutionalism' and 'postnational public law' is itself to take a normative position in relation to postnational sceptics,[2] who deny that conceptions of constitutionalism or public law can flourish

for Global Administrative Law?' (2005) 68 *Law and Contemporary Problems* 63; S. Cassese, 'Global Standards for National Administrative Procedure' (2005) 68 *Law and Contemporary Problems* 109; D. Esty, 'Good Governance at the Supranational Scale: Globalizing Administrative Law' (2006) 115 *Yale Law Journal* 1490; N. Krisch and B. Kingsbury, 'Introduction: Global Governance and Global Administrative Law in the International Legal Order' (2006) 17 *European Journal of International Law* 1; A. von Bogdandy, P. Dann and M. Goldmann, 'Developing the Publicness of Public International Law: Towards a Legal Framework for Global Governance Activities' (2008) 9 *German Law Journal* 1375; A. von Bogdandy and P. Dann, 'International Composite Administration: Conceptualizing Multi-level and Network Aspects in the Exercise of International Public Authority' (2008) 9 *German Law Journal* 2013; B. Kingsbury and L. Casini, 'Global Administrative Law Dimensions of International Organizations Law' (2009) 6 *International Organizations Law Review* 319; N. Krisch, *Beyond Constitutionalism: The Pluralist Structure of Postnational Law* (Oxford: Oxford University Press, 2010); S. Cassese, B. Carotti, L. Casini, E. Cavalieri and E. MacDonald, with the collaboration of M. Macchia and M. Savino, *Global Administrative Law: The Casebook* (IRPA/IILJ, 3rd ed., 2012); S. Cassese, *The Global Polity: Global Dimensions of Democracy and the Rule of Law* (Sevilla: Global Law Press, 2012); R. Stewart, 'Remedying Disregard in Global Regulatory Governance: Accountability, Participation, and Responsiveness' (2014) 108 *American Journal of International Law* 211; G. della Cananea, *Due Process of Law beyond the State* (Oxford: Oxford University Press, 2015); S. Cassese (ed.), *Global Administrative Law: A Research Handbook* (Cheltenham: Elgar, 2015).

2 See, e.g., G. Anthony, J.-B. Auby, J. Morrison and T. Zwart (eds.), *Values in Global Administrative Law* (Oxford: Hart, 2011); A. Peters, 'The Merits of Global Constitutionalism' (2009) 16 *Indiana Journal of Global Legal Studies* 367; J. Klabbers, A. Peters and G. Ulfstein,

beyond the traditional Westphalian state.[3] The literature on global administrative law is predicated on the assumption that discourse concerning the application of public law principles beyond the nation state is meaningful, an assumption that I share.

This chapter begins with an overview of the regulatory foundations of global administrative law that maps the landscape, followed by an explanation of the rise in global governance and increased regulatory activity at the global level. This is complemented by consideration of the judicial foundations of global administrative law. The material is rich, complex and diverse, and thus consideration of these foundational issues is essential for understanding the subsequent discussion in this chapter and the chapter that follows. The focus then shifts to legal issues that are central to the foundations of global administrative law, which are contestable and still contested. Four such issues are discussed in the course of the chapter.

The first concerns the very way in which we conceptualize legal involvement in this area. The dominant view, as reflected in the title to this chapter, is to think of it in terms of global administrative law. This view has not, however, gone unchallenged. It has been argued that to conceptualize legal

The Constitutionalization of International Law (Oxford: Oxford University Press, 2009).

[3] N. Walker, 'Postnational Constitutionalism and Postnational Public Law: A Tale of Two Neologisms', University of Edinburgh, School of Law, Research Paper 2012/20.

intervention in these terms is problematic in various respects, and that it is preferable to think in terms of the control of international public authority based on international institutional law. The focus then shifts to the second foundational issue, which concerns the very claim that global administrative law is 'law', and the sense of law that is being deployed for these purposes. This raises interesting and difficult points concerning the extent to which global administrative law can be conceptualized in traditional positivist terms, and the extent to which it is expressive of a non-positivist conception of law.

The third and fourth issues both concern the relationship between pluralism and global administrative law, albeit from different perspectives. Thus there is the claim that global administrative law is problematic because it imposes a certain set of largely traditional Western values on the rest of the global polity and thereby undermines an important plurality of value that would otherwise have prevailed. This claim is assessed; so too is the related, but distinct, pluralist claim to the effect that national and global regimes of administrative law are based on very different foundations, the former being conceived as resting on unitary, hierarchical foundations, whereas the latter is regarded as heterarchical and pluralistic.

2 Regulatory foundations: mapping the global terrain

A very considerable literature on global administration and global administrative law has emerged in the new millennium, and this is so notwithstanding the fact that there was earlier scholarship. These valuable contributions have helped to map the terrain, and have come from numerous disciplines. Thus Anne-Marie Slaughter, working from an international-relations perspective, considers the way in which networks have transformed the global political order:

> Terrorists, arms dealers, money launderers, drug dealers, traffickers in women and children, and the modern pirates of intellectual property all operate through global networks. So, increasingly, do governments. Networks of government officials – police investigators, financial regulators, even judges and legislators – increasingly exchange information and coordinate activity to combat global crime and address common problems on a global scale. These government networks are a key feature of world order in the twenty-first century, but they are underappreciated, undersupported and underused to address the central problems of global governance.[4]

She explains how networks are a prevalent feature of the global order, ranging from the environment to security, from financial regulation to international trade and from policing to macro-economic policy. The networks are normally horizontal in nature, in the sense that the relevant players are commonly bankers, trade officials or environmental activists from different countries. Networks can, however, be vertical, existing between players at different levels within

[4] Anne-Marie Slaughter, *A New World Order* (Princeton: Princeton University Press, 2004), p. 1. See also K. Raustiala, 'The Architecture of International Cooperation: Transgovernmental Networks and the Future of International Law' (2002) 43 *Virginia Journal of International Law* 1.

a supranational organization. The networks may be free-standing, external to any international organization, but they commonly also feature within such organizations. Slaughter adopts a broad view of network, using it to capture 'all the different ways that individual government institutions are interacting with their counterparts either abroad or above them'.[5] She defines a network as a 'pattern of regular and purposive relations among like government units working across the borders that divide countries from one another and that demarcate the "domestic" from the "international" sphere'.[6] The networks perform different functions, although some networks may have more than one role.[7]

There are enforcement networks, designed to render enforcement more efficacious across international boundaries, thereby rendering compliance with international rules more efficacious. There are information networks, aimed at the exchange of information between governmental agencies or the like, on matters as diverse as security, the environment, policing, health, and fundamental rights, thereby facilitating international co-operation. The third category is the harmonization network, designed to foster closer uniformity in regulatory standards, which can thereby facilitate convergence on an issue, or help to ensure that divergence of view is informed by reasoned dialogue based on understanding of the other side's perspective.

[5] Slaughter, *A New World Order*, p. 14.

[6] Slaughter, *A New World Order*, p. 14.

[7] Slaughter, *A New World Order*.

Tim Büthe and Walter Mattli, writing from the perspective of international political economy, focus on regulatory output, distinguishing between four types of global rule making.[8] The distinctions take account of whether the rule making is developed in public or private settings, and also whether the standard-setters compete, or whether there is a dominant body that is 'the focal point for developing international standards in a given issue area'.[9] This typology yields the four species of global rule making.

The first is public/governmental non-market standard-setting, whereby traditional intergovernmental organizations function as the non-market standard-setting body, as exemplified by bodies such as the Universal Postal Union,[10] which dates from 1874; the International Labour Organization,[11] founded in 1919; and the International Monetary Fund,[12] created in 1944. The second strand of the typology assumes the form of public standard-setting bodies that operate in market competition, such that the standard is the result of competition between 'legislatures or regulatory agencies of individual states and regional or minilateral standard-setting bodies'.[13] This is exemplified by the competition that prevails between standards established by the

[8] T. Büthe and W. Mattli, *The New Global Rulers: The Privatization of Regulation in the World Economy* (Princeton: Princeton University Press, 2011).

[9] Büthe and Mattli, *The New Global Rulers*, p. 18.

[10] See www.upu.int/en.html.

[11] See www.ilo.org/global/lang–en/index.htm.

[12] See www.imf.org/external/index.htm.

[13] Büthe and Mattli, *The New Global Rulers*, p. 23.

US and the EU in relation to matters such as product safety, the environment and the like.

Market-based private international standard-setting constitutes the third mode of global rule making, the spur often being the slow pace of public initiatives, combined with the lack of technical expertise, more especially in fields where the pace of technological change is rapid. In these areas the rules are made by 'firms or other non-governmental bodies, competing individually or in small groups to establish their preferred technical solutions as the de facto standard',[14] as exemplified by the information and technology sector, where Microsoft established the Windows operating system as the de facto global standard. Non-market private international standard-setting completes the typology, and is characterized by an international non-governmental organization that is regarded as the focal institution for that type of rule making. Prominent examples include the International Organization for Standardization (ISO);[15] the International Electrotechnical Commission (IEC);[16] and the International Accounting Standards Board (IASB).[17] This type of rule making is increasingly important judged in terms of the number of products covered and the impact of the rules that are made. Thus the standards will often be applicable to a range of products and compliance with the relevant criteria will often be required either to secure market access or because the regulatory requirements are incorporated in national laws, directly

[14] Büthe and Mattli, *The New Global Rulers*, p. 26.

[15] See www.iso.org/iso/home.html. [16] See www.iec.ch.

[17] See www.iasplus.com/en/resources/ifrsf/iasb-ifrs-ic/iasb.

or indirectly.[18] The significance of such standards is thrown into sharp relief by the output of the ISO and the IEC:

> Jointly, they account for about 85 per cent of all international product standards. ISO's standards include standards for freight containers, paints and varnishes, screw heads, corrosion protection, thermal performance and air quality measurement, as well as the "ISO 9000" series management standards. IEC standards specify, for instance, safe and effective radiation dosages for x-ray machines, the standard dimensions and other characteristics of audio CDs and battery sizes, as well as methods to measure electromagnetic interference and thresholds to safeguard against it, so that the operation of one piece of electric equipment, such as a vacuum cleaner or microwave, does not interfere with the operation of other crucial equipment such as pacemakers or computerized security systems. For most industries, either ISO or IEC is clearly the focal point for setting international product standards, and where their areas of expertise overlap they collaborate closely.[19]

Lawyers have also made important contributions to this mapping exercise. Benedict Kingsbury, Nico Krisch and Richard Stewart stressed that underlying the emergence of global administrative law was the 'vast increase in the reach and form of transgovernmental regulation and administration

[18] W. Mattli and T. Büthe, 'Setting International Standards: Technological Rationality or Primacy of Power' (2003) 56 *World Politics* 1.

[19] Büthe and Mattli, *The New Global Rulers*, pp. 29–30.

designed to address the consequences of global administration'.[20] They note that global administrative bodies can assume a plethora of forms, which include 'formal intergovernmental regulatory bodies, informal intergovernmental regulatory networks and coordination arrangements, national regulatory bodies operating with reference to an international intergovernmental regime, hybrid public–private regulatory bodies, and some regulatory bodies exercising transnational governance functions of particular public significance'.[21] They propose the following taxonomy, while accepting that there can be some instances of overlap between them:

> (1) administration by formal international organizations; (2) administration based on collective action by transnational networks of cooperative arrangements between national regulatory officials; (3) distributed administration conducted by national regulators under treaty, network, or other cooperative regimes; (4) administration by hybrid intergovernmental–private arrangements; and (5) administration by private institutions with regulatory functions.[22]

Thus in some instances global administration will take the form of 'international administration', where formal inter-governmental organizations established through treaty are the principal administrative actors. In other instances there will be 'transnational networks and coordination

[20] Kingsbury, Krisch and Stewart, 'Global Administrative Law', 17.
[21] Kingsbury, Krisch and Stewart, 'Global Administrative Law', 17.
[22] Kingsbury, Krisch and Stewart, 'Global Administrative Law', 20.

arrangements', which may be, but need not be, embedded in a treaty, and where the principal objective is co-operation among state regulators, as exemplified by the Basel Committee on Banking Supervision. In instances of 'distributed administration', domestic regulatory agencies play a prominent role, while in other areas there is 'hybrid intergovernmental–private administration'. This is exemplified by the Codex Alimentarius Commission, where the food standards are adopted through a decision-making process that includes participation by non-governmental actors as well as government representatives, and by ICANN, which, although founded as a non-governmental body, now includes government representatives. Regulatory functions at the global level may also be undertaken by 'private bodies', such as the ISO, although its decisions may well have significant impact because they are adopted at national level, and because they are used in the decision-making process of the WTO. For Kingsbury, Krisch and Stewart, the challenge is to consider how far administrative law precepts concerning matters such as procedural participation, transparency, reasoned decision making and judicial review, including substantive rationality or proportionality scrutiny, can be applied to the different forms of trans-governmental regulation.

Sabino Cassese points to the significant differences between regulatory regimes at the global level: some merely provide a framework for state action, while others generate guidelines for domestic agencies; some have their own enforcement mechanisms, while others use national or regional authorities for implementation; some use judicial bodies to resolve disputes, while others have recourse to negotiation, conciliation or mediation.[23] Cassese also emphasizes the prevalence of such bodies across virtually all areas of human activity:

> Such global regulatory regimes operate in so many areas that it can now be said that almost every human activity is subject to some form of global regulation. Global regulatory regimes cover fields as diverse as forest preservation, the control of fishing, water regulation, environmental protection, standardization and food safety, financial and accounting standards, internet governance, pharmaceuticals regulation, intellectual property protection, refugee protection, coffee and cocoa standards, labour standards, antitrust regulation, regulation and finance of public works, trade standards, regulation of finance, insurance, foreign investments, international terrorism, war and arms control, air and maritime navigation, postal services, telecommunications, nuclear energy and nuclear waste, money laundering, education, migration, law enforcement, sport, and health.[24]

Similar themes are evident in Daniel Esty's work.[25] He acknowledges that while governance can mean different things in different contexts, it generally relates to group decision making to address shared problems:

> Supranational governance might therefore refer to any number of policymaking processes and institutions that help to manage international interdependence, including

[23] Cassese, *The Global Polity*, p. 20. [24] Cassese, *The Global Polity*, p. 20.
[25] Esty, 'Good Governance at the Supranational Scale'.

> (1) negotiation by nation-states leading to a treaty; (2) dispute settlement within an international organization; (3) rulemaking by international bodies in support of treaty implementation; (4) development of government-backed codes of conduct, guidelines, and norms; (5) pre-negotiation agenda-setting and issue analysis in support of treaty making; (6) technical standard-setting to facilitate trade; (7) networking and policy coordination by regulators; (8) structured public–private efforts at norm creation; (9) informal workshops at which policymakers, NGOs, business leaders, and academics exchange ideas; and (10) private sector policymaking activities.[26]

It is, moreover, important to recognize, as Kenneth Abbott notes, that in many instances international regulatory co-operation is at work in a particular area, in the sense that the relevant rules or guidelines are the result of interchange between a number of international and transnational organizations. This is, for example, the common pattern in relation to matters such as financial regulation, climate change and health.[27]

It would be impractical within the confines of the present study to list all of the approximately 2,000 regulatory

[26] Esty, 'Good Governance at the Supranational Scale', 1497–8.

[27] K. Abbott, 'International Organizations and International Regulatory Co-operation: Exploring the Links', in OECD, *International Organizations and International Regulatory Co-operation: The Cases of the OECD and the IMO* (Paris: OECD Publishing, 2014), Ch. 1. See also OECD, *International Regulatory Co-operation: Addressing Global Challenges* (Paris: OECD Publishing, 2013).

regimes that constitute what Cassese has termed this neo-medieval system.[28] Some sense of the types of body that inhabit this world is nonetheless important. They include international organizations established by states, such as the United Nations,[29] the World Trade Organization,[30] the World Health Organization,[31] the Financial Action Task Force,[32] the World Bank,[33] the Organization for Economic Cooperation and Development[34] and the Codex Alimentarius Commission.[35]

There are, however, also a range of important transnational regulatory networks, the membership of which varies. The following are but examples. Thus the Basel Committee on Banking Supervision,[36] which has the primary responsibility for global banking standards, is composed of representatives from national central banks and national financial regulatory authorities. ICANN, the Internet Corporation for Assigned Names and Numbers, is, as the nomenclature would suggest, the body that assigns Internet names, and is a not-for-profit company that was incorporated in California.[37] The International Organization for

[28] Cassese, *The Global Polity*, p. 16. [29] See www.un.org/en.

[30] See www.wto.org. [31] See www.who.int/en.

[32] See www.fatf-gafi.org. [33] See www.worldbank.org.

[34] See www.oecd.org.

[35] See www.codexalimentarius.org. It promulgates international food standards, guidelines and codes of practice designed to foster international food safety. The basic membership of the Commission is drawn from all Member Nations and Associate Members of the Food and Agriculture Organization of the UN and the WHO, and the EU is also a member.

[36] See www.bis.org/bcbs/about.htm. [37] See www.icann.org.

Standardization (ISO),[38] is a network of national standardization bodies which seeks to facilitate agreement on the co-ordination and unification of industrial standards in different countries. It has, since its creation in 1947, fostered agreement on 19,500 such standards that relate to many areas of technology and manufacturing. The International Labour Organization (ILO) is a specialized agency of the UN, charged with the protection of employment rights broadly conceived, and works through dialogue between representatives of workers, employers and government.[39] The International Union for Conservation of Nature (IUCN) is a global environmental organization with a hybrid membership composed of governmental and non-governmental organizations.[40] The International Chamber of Commerce (ICC) is, by way of contrast, a private global regulator, which brings together private bodies with the objective of fostering international trade and investment.[41]

3 Regulatory foundations: rationale

The range and variety of bodies that constitute the global administrative landscape naturally prompt inquiry as to the rationale for the development. This must be seen against the more general literature on the forces that drive regulation at the national level, on which there has been long-standing debate.

[38] See www.iso.org/iso/home.html.

[39] See www.ilo.org/global/lang–en/index.htm.

[40] See www.iucn.org/about.

[41] See www.iccwbo.org.

Public-interest theories regard regulation in a positive light as a cure for market failure.[42] While the ordinary competitive process determines supply and demand in most instances, regulation is required where the market fails. This may arise in relation to 'public goods',[43] where consumption by one person does not leave less for others to consume, and it is impossible or too costly for the supplier to exclude those who do not pay for the service, national defence being the oft-cited example. A further classic example of market failure is natural monopoly, where it is less costly for production to be carried out by one firm rather than by many, and thus price regulation of the monopoly may be required. As Breyer has stated:

> The most traditional and persistent rationale for governmental regulation of a firm's prices and profits is the existence of a 'natural monopoly'. Some industries, it is claimed, cannot efficiently support more than one firm. Electricity producers or local telephone companies find it progressively cheaper (up to a point) to supply extra units of electricity or telephone service. These 'economies of scale' are sufficiently great so that unit costs of service would rise significantly if more than one firm supplied service in a particular area. Rather than have three

[42] A. Ogus, *Regulation: Legal Form and Economic Theory* (Oxford: Oxford University Press, 1994), Ch. 3; R. Baldwin and M. Cave, *Understanding Regulation: Theory, Strategy and Practice* (Oxford: Oxford University Press, 1999), Ch. 2; B. Morgan and K. Yeung, *An Introduction to Law and Regulation: Text and Materials* (Cambridge: Cambridge University Press, 2007), Ch. 2.

[43] Ogus, *Regulation*, p. 33.

> connecting phone companies laying separate cables where one would do, it may be more efficient to grant one firm a monopoly subject to governmental regulation of its prices and profits.[44]

A further public-interest rationale for regulatory intervention is where an activity creates externalities for others, the classic example being the firm that pollutes a river when making its product, the object of the regulation being to ensure that the firm internalizes the full costs of its operation, including the harm caused to the river. Regulatory intervention may also be required to correct information deficits, or to address circumstances where there is a strong asymmetry in information. This idea is captured by Ogus:

> The market system of allocation is fuelled by an infinite number of expressions of . . . preferences. However, the assertion that observed market behaviour in the form of expressed preferences leads to allocative efficiency depends crucially on two fundamental assumptions: that decision-makers have adequate information on the set of alternatives available, including the consequences to them of exercising choice in different ways; and that they are capable of processing that information and of 'rationally' behaving in a way that maximizes their expected utility. A significant failure of either assumption may set up a prima facie case for regulatory intervention.[45]

[44] S. Breyer, *Regulation and Its Reform* (Cambridge, MA: Harvard University Press, 1982), p. 15.

[45] Ogus, *Regulation*, p. 38.

The idea that regulation is intended to serve the public interest has, however, been contested.[46] It has been argued by those within the public-choice literature that much regulation is designed to serve the private interests of certain groups within society. The intellectual ancestors of public choice were pluralists, who emphasized the group nature of politics and stressed that the public interest was nothing more than the outcome of the current group exchange.[47] Public-choice theorists brought more finely tuned tools of economic analysis to the political forum to explain the behaviour of political markets, but agreed, on many points, with the conclusions reached by earlier pluralist writers.[48] The public-choice theorists based their analysis on methodological individualism, and while they were willing to accept that individuals could have selfish or altruistic preferences, they were also of the

[46] Ogus, *Regulation*, Ch. 4.

[47] A. Bentley, *The Process of Government: A Study of Social Pressures* (Chicago: The University of Chicago Press, 1908); D. Truman, *The Governmental Process: Political Interests and Public Opinion* (New York: A. Knopf, 1951).

[48] J. Buchanan and G. Tullock, *The Calculus of Consent. Logical foundations of Constitutional Democracy* (Ann Arbor: University of Michigan Press, 1962); J. Buchanan, *The Limits of Liberty: Between Anarchy and Leviathan* (Chicago: The University of Chicago Press, 1975); J. Buchanan, *Freedom in Constitutional Contract: Perspectives of a Political Economist* (College Station: Texas A & M, 1978); J. Buchanan, *Liberty, Market and State: Political Economy in the 1980s* (Brighton: Wheatsheaf Books, 1986); G. Brennan and J. Buchnanan, *The Reason of Rules* (Cambridge: Cambridge University Press, 1985); I. McLean, *Public Choice: An Introduction* (Oxford: Basil Blackwell, 1987); D. Mueller, *Public Choice* (Cambridge: Cambridge University Press, 1979).

view that there was no conception of the public interest separate from the results of individual choice.[49] Collective action was a means of reducing the costs of purely private or voluntary action. Individuals would engage in such action where the costs thereby saved outweighed the transaction costs, combined with the costs of loss of autonomy, in the sense of the consequential risk that the individual might have to accept a decision which he or she disliked. The fact that collective political decisions took place over time generated vote-trading, with each individual's vote possessing an economic value for which a market would develop in the same way as with any other commodity.

Regulation was seen as a function of the demands of interest groups which would benefit from the measure, coupled with the responses of those, normally politicians, who had power to deliver the measure. Proponents of this thesis argued that producer groups would normally be stronger, more coherent and better financed than other groups, and that therefore most regulation could be expected to benefit industry directly or indirectly.[50] Public-choice theorists believed that the role of the state should be narrowly confined. They felt that private markets were better at reaching optimal decisions than political markets. They argued

[49] Buchanan and Tullock, *The Calculus of Consent*, pp. 32, 122–4, 125–30, 209.

[50] G. Stigler, 'The Theory of Economic Regulation' (1971) 2 *Bell Journal of Economics and Management Science* 137; R. Posner, 'Theories of Economic Regulation' (1974) 5 *Bell Journal of Economics and Management Science* 335; S. Peltzman, 'Towards a More General Theory of Regulation?' (1976) 19 *Journal of Law & Economics* 211.

that much regulatory legislation was a front to mask wealth transfer and rent-seeking behaviour by particular interest groups. Competition would normally eliminate such rent, but it was argued that regulation, such as that limiting entry into a profession, was often designed to protect the existing incumbents from competition, allowing them to retain monopoly rents rather than passing them on to the consumer. Public-choice theorists also disapproved of regulation because they felt that governmental intervention via redistributive policies was illegitimate, since it offended against individual entitlements.[51]

The descriptive and normative assumptions that underlie public choice have been contested. In descriptive terms, it has been argued that the equation between individual behaviour in the marketplace and the political arena is not self-evidently correct. Even if the assumption is accepted it still leaves open the issue of how marketplace behaviour itself should be perceived. At one extreme is the view that elected officials and individuals seek to maximize a specific wealth function. At the other is the non-falsifiable view that seeks to incorporate all ideological and other variables within an individual's utility function. On this latter view, behaviour and motivation are flattened and reduced to an economic calculus, which often amounts to little more than the tautological observation that people who understand the consequences of their actions 'will do things that make them as well off as

[51] Brennan and Buchanan, *The Reason of Rules*, Chs. 6–8; Buchanan, *Liberty, Market and State*, Chs. 12, 13, 15, 22, 23; Buchanan, *The Limits of Liberty*.

they can be'.[52] The normative aspect of public choice has proven equally contentious.[53] The methodology is self-avowedly contractarian, but there are crucial differences in the use of this methodology when compared to the work of, for example, Rawls. It is highly debatable whether a vision of politics that seeks to legitimate legislation on the basis of group bargain is consistent in normative terms with the theory of justice postulated by public-choice theorists. The norms which public-choice theorists regard as emerging from their contractarian foundations are questionable, and their arguments for the restriction of wealth transfers on the ground that they offend entitlements are weak.

It is unsurprising in the light of the contestation between public- and private-interest theories of regulation at national level that similar themes should be apparent in the rationales for global regulation. Thus public-interest rationales for regulation are articulated by commentators who perceive bodies such as the WTO and the ISO as primarily driven by the desire to enhance efficiency, while organizations such as the ILO are designed to promote justice in the workplace. The need to address externalities and spillover is evident at the global level in the fact that national policy can impact on neighbouring states, thereby generating the need for global regulation to manage this interdependence. Viewed from this

[52] M. Kelman, 'On Democracy Bashing: A Skeptical Look at the Theoretical and Empirical Practice of the Public Choice Movement' (1988) 74 *Virginia Law Review* 199, at 206.

[53] P. Craig, *Public Law and Democracy in the United Kingdom and the United States of America* (Oxford: Oxford University Press, 1990), pp. 84–90.

perspective the argument for global administration can be seen, as Esty notes, as an extension of the logic of international law, such that 'without a commitment to structured cooperation international relations remain in a Hobbesian state of nature':

> While a power-dominated world may seem attractive to a hegemon, like the United States in the early twenty-first century, a lawless international realm is ultimately costly and potentially unstable. In such a world, order must be imposed on an ad hoc and issue-by-issue basis and will therefore be of limited effectiveness. Thus, even those most committed to a world order based on realism find some value in having structures in place to facilitate international policymaking.[54]

In a related vein, Lorenzo Casini contends that one force driving global regulation is the need to protect global public goods, such as the environment, another being the inability of any state adequately to regulate issues that have a trans-border dimension.[55] Cassese strikes a similar chord when noting that the spread of global administration is a response to issues that cannot readily be resolved by any individual government, irrespective of whether they relate directly to public goods:

> Global regulatory regimes are established because a growing number of issues and problems cannot be addressed or resolved by national governments alone.

54 Esty, 'Good Governance at the Supranational Scale', 1501.

55 L. Casini, 'The Expansion in the Material Scope of Global Law', in Cassese, *Global Administrative Law: A Research Handbook*, Ch. 1.

> These issues themselves are global in nature, and as such are beyond the power of individual governments to regulate: internet governance, environmental control, the Olympic Games, and the recent economic crisis provide examples.[56]

More private-interest rationales for regulation also feature at the global level, although they do not necessarily share all the assumptions of the private-interest approach as explicated above. The regulatory standards may have distributional implications, which can lead to conflict over the particular standard adopted. The standards will inevitably reflect cultural and social traditions that may vary between states. The interests that drive the regulatory outcomes will, moreover, be affected by the institutional forum or fora through which the rules are developed. Thus it can be expected that state power, as articulated in the realist school of international relations, will exercise a decisive influence, where the rules result from public non-market standard-setting within international organizations, enabling the more powerful states to secure the support of those with less power, through promises of side payments and the like.[57] By way of contrast, where the rules emanate from public market-based standards, the

[56] Cassese, *The Global Polity*, p. 21. See also F. Cafaggi, 'Transnational Private Regulation and the Production of Global Public Goods and Private "Bads"' (2012) 23 *European Journal of International Law* 695; G. Shaffer, 'International Law and Global Public Goods in a Legal Pluralist World' (2012) 23 *European Journal of International Law* 669.

[57] R. Cox and H. Jacobson, *The Anatomy of Influence: Decision-Making in International Organizations* (New Haven: Yale University Press, 1974).

respective countries' market size is likely to be an important factor when such standards compete, since the national standard may determine access to the relevant national market. Thus, as Büthe and Mattli note,

> From the 1960s through the 1980s, for instance, manufacturers from Europe and Asia often ended up implementing the stringent U.S. consumer and environmental protection standards for their entire production, because the U.S. (and sometimes just Californian) market was too important for them, and producing to a different standard for each market would have forced them to forgo valuable economies of scale.[58]

The politics of regulatory standard-setting may be different yet again when the rules are made by a private-focal-point institution, which operates in non-market conditions in the sense explicated above. In such circumstances, Büthe and Mattli argue that institutional complementarity theory best explains the degree of influence that other actors can bring to bear on the regulatory output. This theory posits that

> [w]hen one international organization is the clear focal point for setting global rules, the ability of firms and others to influence the specific outcomes of private rule-making is a function of the fit between these stakeholders' domestic institutions and the international organization – as well as their technical expertise and economic resources. Specifically, given common features of the private

[58] Büthe and Mattli, *The New Global Rulers*, p. 37.

> rule-making organization at the international level, domestic institutions need to provide timely information to allow those who have a stake in the content of the standard to influence that content in the early stages of standards development. Further, domestic institutions need to enable effective, uncontested representation of these stakeholders at the international level.[59]

Thus countries that have hierarchical domestic standardization institutions are said to be better placed to exert influence because this entails procedures for aggregating preferences, which renders it more likely that that 'a single national technical standard exists prior to the globalization of standard-setting, and that the preferences of the country's stakeholders are closely aligned',[60] thereby ensuring that the country's representative can present a clear choice at the international level. Where, by way of contrast, a country has a non-hierarchical system of standardization, with the result that there may be diverse national positions on the same issue, it is all the more difficult for that country to present a common position at the international level, the corollary being that its influence will thereby be lessened.[61]

The incidence of global regulation can more generally be posited in terms of supply and demand. Thus as Walter Mattli and Ngaire Woods note, 'the institutional context of regulation describes the locus where the rules are drafted,

[59] Büthe and Mattli, *The New Global Rulers*, p. 43.

[60] Büthe and Mattli, *The New Global Rulers*, p. 54.

[61] Büthe and Mattli, *The New Global Rulers*, pp. 54–5.

implemented, monitored, and enforced'.[62] The institutional contexts may be limited or extensive, which affects the supply of regulation:

> An extensive institutional context signifies open forums, proper due process, multiple access points, and oversight mechanisms. A limited institutional context indicates that the few regulatory forums are club-like, that is, exclusive, closed, and secretive. In some instances, the drafting of regulation takes place in an open forum, the implementation is delegated to a more exclusive and secretive agency, while the enforcement is left decentralized or unspecified.[63]

The demand for regulation will perforce be affected by a number of factors. Global regulation by definition entails some change from the *status quo ante*, and there must be something to trigger the demand for such change. This may take the form of a disaster, what Mattli and Woods term a demonstration effect,[64] whereby circumstances such as a Chernobyl nuclear leak, or a Bhopal chemical catastrophe, act as the catalyst for regulatory intervention. Such incidents render it more likely that the regulatory initiatives are directed towards the common interest, rather than being reflective of purely private interests, since 'the negative

[62] W. Mattli and N. Woods, 'In Whose Benefit? Explaining Regulatory Change in Global Politics', in W. Mattli and N. Woods, *The Politics of Global Regulation* (Princeton: Princeton University Press, 2009), p. 17.

[63] Mattli and Woods, 'In Whose Benefit?', p. 17.

[64] Mattli and Woods, 'In Whose Benefit?', p. 22.

consequences of capture are revealed to the wider public'.[65] The externalities flowing from such events increase the demand for change, but the 'public needs resourceful, expert, well-organized, and committed allies at each stage of the regulatory process to ensure that defenders of the status quo do not succeed in distorting or hijacking the process of change'.[66]

4 Judicial foundations: institutions and adjudication

The discussion thus far has considered the regulatory foundations of global administrative law, and the rationale for this development. The focus now shifts to the judicial foundations that underpin the subject, in terms of both institutions and doctrine.

(a) International adjudication: the expanding terrain

A generation ago discourse concerning legal institutions at the international level focused primarily on the International Court of Justice, with some attention given to the European Court of Human Rights and the European Court of Justice, these latter two being regarded as instances where the judicial imperative was less voluntarist and more compulsory than in the context of the ICJ. Thus it was when I was taught public

[65] Mattli and Woods, 'In Whose Benefit?', p. 25.
[66] Mattli and Woods, 'In Whose Benefit?', p. 27.

international law in 1972, and it remained so for some considerable time thereafter. Matters have changed considerably since then, although the realization of how much international adjudication is 'out there' continues to elude many lawyers, let alone others.

The sea change taking place was, however, recognized by Robert Keohane, Andrew Moravcsik and Anne-Marie Slaughter, writing at the turn of the new millennium, who numbered international courts and tribunals between seventeen and forty, depending on the precise definition used.[67] They distinguished inter-state and transnational dispute resolution. The former reflected the traditional view of international law, in which states were the principal actors. They controlled access to courts, and were in the driving seat so far as implementation was concerned. States thus acted as 'gatekeepers both to the international legal process and from that process back to the domestic level'.[68] The latter, transnational dispute resolution, was characterized by more open rules of access to court by private parties as well as governments, thereby attenuating at the very least the gatekeeping capacities of governments.

Keohane, Moravcsik and Slaughter conceptualize the extent of access in terms of a spectrum. Near the restrictive end there are inter-state tribunals, such as the GATT and

[67] R. Keohane, A. Moravcsik and A.-M. Slaughter, 'Legalized Dispute Resolution: Interstate and Transnational' (2000) 54 *International Organization* 457.

[68] Keohane, Moravcsik and Slaughter, 'Legalized Dispute Resolution: Interstate and Transnational', 457.

WTO panels and the ICJ, where only participating states may bring an action against another state, although powerful industrial interests can exert pressure on their state to pursue an action. Towards the other end of the spectrum there are courts such as the CJEU, where inter-state actions and public enforcement by the Commission have been powerfully reinforced through private enforcement made possible by direct effect. It is therefore to be expected that, as the authors conjecture, the broader the access to the international court or tribunal, the greater the number of cases it will receive, and these cases will involve challenge to national as well as international action.

The distinction between inter-state and transnational dispute resolution also plays out in terms of their respective 'embeddedness', which denotes for the authors the extent to which dispute resolution decisions can be implemented without governments having to take action to do so. Thus in some instances, such as the previous GATT regime, panel decisions had to be affirmed by consensus, thereby according litigants an *ex post* veto. At the other end of this spectrum are systems such as the EU, where national courts have a duty to enforce CJEU rulings against Member States, and must ensure that there are adequate remedies for breach of the EU law.

Karen Alter, writing in 2014, helps to place reality in perspective in terms of the number and type of international courts (ICs);

> ICs today review the validity of administrative decisions, assess state compliance with international law, and speak to constitutional issues affecting both international and

> domestic politics. There are now at least twenty-four permanent international courts.
>
> Eighty percent of operational ICs have a broad compulsory jurisdiction and eighty-four percent authorize non-state actors – supranational commissions, prosecutors, and/or private actors – to initiate litigation. These ICs have collectively issued over thirty-seven thousand binding rulings in individual contentious cases, ninety-one percent of which were issued since the fall of the Berlin Wall. Since few of these ICs and cases are about inter-state dispute adjudication, we need to update our understandings about international courts.[69]

Alter's figures include regional as well as global legal bodies, and ad hoc as well as more permanent institutions, but the numbers are significant nonetheless. She draws on themes from earlier work, noting that whereas 'old-style international courts lack compulsory jurisdiction so that cases can only proceed with the consent of the defendant-state', the 'new-style ICs have compulsory jurisdiction, and they allow non-state actors – international commissions, prosecutors, institutional actors, and private litigants – to initiate litigation'.[70] These different visions of international adjudication reflect, at one stage

[69] K. Alter, *New Terrain of International Law: Courts, Politics, Rights* (Princeton: Princeton University Press, 2014), pp. 3–4. See also K. Alter, 'The Multiple Roles of International Courts and Tribunals: Enforcement, Dispute Settlement, Constitutional and Administrative Review', in J. Dunoff and M. Pollack (eds.), *International Perspectives on International Law and International Relations: The State of the Art* (Cambridge: Cambridge University Press, 2013), pp. 175–96.

[70] Alter, *New Terrain of International Law*, p. 5.

removed, contrasting conceptions of international law, such that the former envisions it in terms of a contract between states, whereas the latter embodies more a rule-of-law perspective.

Alter, in common with others writing in the field, regards the fact that non-state actors can access many of these courts as especially important, given the fact that inter-state litigation is relatively rare, since governments are normally reluctant to resort to legal action, preferring other modes of dispute resolution, in part at least because of fears of retaliatory suits. Private parties, by way of contrast, are less likely to be dissuaded by such considerations.

This is indeed part of the explanation for the European Court of Justice's creation of direct effect.[71] It complemented inter-state enforcement of EU law and public enforcement by the Commission,[72] with private enforcement whereby individuals could, subject to certain conditions, bring actions in their own name in national courts to enforce EU law against Member States, EU institutions and other private parties. Inter-state enforcement was of limited utility for the reason given above. Public enforcement was limited given the Commission's institutional capacity, which was nowhere near sufficient to prosecute all possible violations of EU law, even if it knew about them, which was a separate constraint in its own right. Private actions, rendered possible

[71] J. Weiler, 'The Community System: The Dual Character of Supranationalism' (1981) 1 *Yearbook of European Law* 267; P. Craig, 'Once Upon a Time in the West: Direct Effect and the Federalization of EEC Law' (1992) 12 *Oxford Journal of Legal Studies* 453.

[72] Art. 258 TFEU.

by direct effect, complemented the enforcement role of the Commission by sanctioning claims brought by individuals in their own capacity. An individual who believed that a Member State had acted contrary to EU law was, moreover, in the optimal position to know the facts to which the alleged violation related, and had a strong incentive to take steps to have the matter tested.

The supplementation of public enforcement with private enforcement was particularly significant given that the Commission, which was vested with the enforcement powers, possessed a wide array of other powers, legislative as well as judicial. This could lead to tension, whereby a decision whether to use such powers against a recalcitrant state could be affected by the Commission's desire to ensure that legislation on some other matter was enacted, leading to wariness about bringing such an action lest the Member State should manifest its displeasure by rendering the passage of the legislation more protracted. A system which relies exclusively on public enforcement, where the 'prosecutor' also exercises legislative powers, will be prone to this tension. Direct effect eased this tension dramatically, since the individual was not subject to the same pressures as the Commission.

The growth in international judicial institutions has been matched by expansion of their functions. Thus whereas old-style international courts were primarily concerned with dispute settlement, many of the newer such bodies have, in addition, the power to engage in administrative review, enforcement and constitutional review.[73] The administrative

[73] Alter, *New Terrain of International Law*, Ch. 1.

review jurisdiction is especially apposite for present purposes, since it enables parties to contest the validity of administrative determinations and rules made by the relevant body. Alter identified thirteen international courts with such jurisdiction, eleven of which have authority to review acts of supranational administration, and eight of which have power to review national implementation of international rules:[74]

> All ICs with designated administrative review roles have compulsory jurisdiction associated with this role, and allow private actors to initiate litigation so that the subjects of administrative decision-making can pursue a legal remedy. Twelve ICs also allow national judges to refer to the IC cases where community rules are at issue. ICs' key compliance partners in this role are administrators themselves who seek help in interpreting legal lacunae and in coordinating interpretation across actors and borders, and who deflect criticism and benefit from judicial validation of their rulings via administrative review.[75]

The rationale for the expansion in international adjudication lies beyond the scope of this work,[76] but it is generally accepted that part of the answer in relation to administrative review is that it enhances the credibility of the rules of the organization vis-à-vis other players, and provides a

[74] Alter, *New Terrain of International Law*, Ch. 6.

[75] Alter, *New Terrain of International Law*, pp. 13–14.

[76] See, e.g., E. Posner and J. Yoo, 'A Theory of International Adjudication' (2005) 93 *California Law Review* 1; L. Helfer and A.-M. Slaughter, 'Why States Create International Tribunals: A Response to Professors Posner and Yoo' (2005) 93 *California Law Review* 899.

mechanism for contesting the legality of the norms made by the organization pursuant to delegated authority.[77] While there may be obstacles to the enforceability of international judgments, the nature and extent of which will vary depending on the particular adjudicative body in question, it is nonetheless the case that other things being equal the existence of an international legal remedy will empower those who have international law on their side, and thereby increase 'their out-of-court political leverage'.[78]

The authoritative nature of an international court's ruling can itself vary. Karen Alter, Laurence Helfer and Mikael Madsen explore this issue,[79] seeking to explain why some formally constituted courts receive few cases even if legal violations are widespread, or issue decisions that are largely ignored, while other international courts succeed in transforming formal legal authority into de facto authority, which has two components: recognition or acceptance of an obligation to comply with court rulings, and engaging in meaningful practices that give full effect to those rulings:

> Many scholars analyze ICs either by evaluating particular qualities of courts and their decisions, or by measuring state compliance with their judgments. In contrast, we assess the *de facto* authority of international judges

[77] A. Stone Sweet, *The Judicial Construction of Europe* (Oxford: Oxford University Press, 2004).

[78] Alter, *New Terrain of International Law*, p. 19.

[79] K. Alter, L. Helfer and M. Madsen, 'How Context Shapes the Authority of International Courts', University of Copenhagen, Faculty of Law, iCourts Working Paper Series, No 18, 2015.

> by examining the practices of key audiences. ICs control neither the sword nor the purse. They cannot coerce litigants or other actors to behave in particular ways. Instead, ICs issue decisions that identify violations of international rules and create a legally binding obligation to comply with the court's judgments and its interpretation of those rules. Whether such compliance actually occurs, however, depends upon the responses of the different audiences . . .[80]

They distinguish between five levels of authority in this respect.[81] There may be some courts that lack de facto authority, such that while they possess formal jurisdiction flowing from the initial act of delegation, litigants do not generally use them, and when they do the judgments are often ignored. A ruling may have what they term narrow legal authority when the parties to a dispute acknowledge that they are bound by a legal obligation flowing from the court's judgment, and seek to comply with it. Intermediate authority connotes the situation in which a similar group of parties recognize the ruling as authoritative, taking it into account as a guide to their own action, and so do government officials with responsibility for implementing the international rules, such as members of the executive, administrative agencies and national judges. Karen Alter has termed this audience 'compliance partners', connoting those national actors with power

[80] Alter, Helfer and Madsen, 'How Context Shapes the Authority of International Courts', p. 9.

[81] Alter, Helfer and Madsen, 'How Context Shapes the Authority of International Courts', pp. 13–15.

to decide whether to comply with international law.[82] There is extensive legal authority when a larger group of players, which would normally include academics, government officials, legal professionals and members of civil society, accept the relevant rulings as being authoritative. International courts with such authority are able to shape law and politics in the relevant area. The final level is what the authors term popular authority, which covers those instances where acceptance of the court's rulings extends beyond the legal field to include the general public. The authors acknowledge that the degree of power wielded by any particular international court will, however, vary depending on the breadth of its subject matter jurisdiction and the number of states that are party to the treaty according the court its formal authority.[83]

Alter, Helfer and Madsen proffer interesting insights as to the contextual factors that shape the authority of international courts.[84] They distinguish between the institution-specific context, which captures features distinctive to a particular international court; the constituency context, connoting the interlocutors, such as government officials, judges, lawyers and civil society, with which the court will relate; and the geopolitical context, which factors in the way in which politics broadly conceived at the global, regional and national levels affects the authority of an international court.

82 Alter, *New Terrain of International Law*, p. 53.

83 Alter, Helfer and Madsen, 'How Context Shapes the Authority of International Courts' (Pt IV).

84 Alter, Helfer and Madsen, 'How Context Shapes the Authority of International Courts' (Pt III).

Thus, to take institution-specific factors by way of example, these will include matters such as rules concerning access, alternatives to international litigation and variations in the subject matter mandate. In terms of access, traditional international courts are the preserve of states. It is only states that can invoke such jurisdiction, and the court only has authority to adjudicate when states signal their consent by submitting a particular case to it, or by agreeing in advance to the court's having jurisdiction over a particular class of case.[85] Since the Second World War it has been increasingly common for submission to the court's authority to be required as a condition for membership of a particular treaty.[86] Where this is so it is self-evidently more difficult to block litigation, and inter-state negotiation will often occur against the backdrop of formal adjudication, thereby increasing the bargaining power of the party that believes that its view is best supported by the positive law.

The ability to block litigation is further diminished where there are multiple access points to the court, as exemplified by the EU system where public enforcement through inter-state suits and actions by the Commission has been complemented by private enforcement by individuals, made possible through direct effect. The force of this regime is further enhanced by the fact that claimants can initiate their

[85] See, e.g., Statute of the International Court of Justice, Arts. 34–6, www.icj-cij.org/documents/index.php?p1=4&p2=2&p3=0#CHAPTER_II.

[86] C. Romano, 'From the Consensual to the Compulsory Paradigm in International Adjudication: Elements for a Theory of Consent' (2007) 39 *New York University Journal of International Law and Politics* 791.

claim in a national court, which can then make a preliminary reference to the CJEU, or decide the matter itself in the light of existing CJEU case law.[87]

The other institution-specific factors, alternatives to litigation and subject matter, will further determine the authority of any particular international court. Thus to the extent that there are attractive alternatives to international litigation, such as conciliation, mediation and arbitration, this will reduce the number of cases taken to court. The breadth of the subject matter jurisdiction will be of major significance, as attested to by bodies such as the European Court of Justice, the European Court of Human Rights, and the Appellate Body of the World Trade Organization.

It is important, notwithstanding the above, to keep the range and number of judicial institutions in perspective. We can distinguish between five institutional settings. There are some organizations that possess adjudicative bodies dealing primarily with staff cases. There are other organizations where the judicial institution has a broader remit, including the authority to undertake administrative review of the organization's decisions. There are treaties that mandate formal court or tribunal procedures at national level. There are, however, also many bodies listed earlier in this chapter that have no internal judicial organ, with the consequence that administrative law precepts must be judicially applied, if at all,

[87] P. Craig and G. de Búrca, *EU Law: Text, Cases and Materials* (Oxford: Oxford University Press, 6th ed., 2015), Chs. 7, 13; A. Stone Sweet, 'Judicialization and the Construction of Governance' (1999) 32 *Comparative Political Studies* 147.

by an external judicial organ at national or international level. Whether this is feasible will depend on the nature of the subject matter, and the way in which it impacts on parties at national or international level. There is finally the option of arbitration, which has assumed greater importance in recent years.

(b) *Staff cases: international administrative tribunals*

There is a judicial tradition of what is termed international administrative law, which began in earnest after the creation of the League of Nations in the 1920s. The nomenclature can, however, be misleading in the light of the more modern terminology of global administrative law. The reality is, as Yarik Kryvoi notes, that 'this branch of international public law determines the rights and obligations of international civil servants in their dealings with public bodies, primarily intergovernmental organizations enjoying immunity'.[88] International administrative law thus imposes restraints on the exercise of powers by international organizations in relation to those who work for it, and in that respect enhances accountability and legitimacy, but such organs do not exercise broader powers of administrative review over rules or decisions made by the relevant organization. There are several prominent examples of this kind of tribunal.

[88] Y. Kryvoi, 'The Law Applied by International Administrative Tribunals: From Autonomy to Hierarchy' (2015) 47 *George Washington International Law Review* 267, at 271–2.

The Administrative Tribunal of the International Labour Organization has the longest history,[89] being heir to the Administrative Tribunal of the League of Nations, which was competent from 1927 to 1946 to hear complaints against the Secretariat of the League of Nations and against the International Labour Office. The Tribunal has since 1947 heard complaints from current and former officials of the International Labour Office, and of other international organizations that have recognized its jurisdiction. It is currently open to approximately 46,000 international civil servants from roughly sixty organizations, including the World Health Organization. The Tribunal is composed of seven judges of different nationalities, and its case law comprises nearly 3,000 judgments.

The UN Dispute Tribunal (UNDT) was established by the UN General Assembly, and became operational on 1 July 2009.[90] It is staffed by judges, and replaced the UN Administrative Tribunal, which had existed since 1949. The UNDT operates as the first-instance court, which decides cases concerning current and former staff members who appeal administrative decisions that are alleged not to be in compliance with their terms of appointment or contract of employment. The Tribunal conducts hearings, issues orders, and renders binding judgments. Its jurisdictional remit includes all departments and offices of the UN Secretariat, peacekeeping and political missions, UN regional commissions, and a host of other UN programmes. The judgments of

[89] See www.ilo.org/public/english/tribunal.

[90] See www.un.org/en/oaj/dispute.

the UNDT can be appealed to the United Nations Appeals Tribunal, which also has jurisdiction over appeals from decisions concerning pensions.[91]

The World Bank Administrative Tribunal has similar features.[92] It was established in 1980, and is the independent judicial forum of last resort for the resolution of cases submitted by staff members of the Bank who allege non-observance of their contracts of employment or terms of appointment. The Tribunal's decisions are final and binding, and it, like the UNDT, is staffed by judges drawn from nationals of different Member States of the Bank.

The International Monetary Fund Administrative Tribunal (IMFAT) is analogous in terms of its jurisdictional remit,[93] although it has distinctive features. Thus IMFAT serves as an independent judicial forum for the resolution of employment disputes arising between the IMF and its staff members. An applicant can, however, challenge the legality of an 'individual' or 'regulatory' decision of the IMF that 'adversely affects' him. Challenges to individual decisions are, however, only possible when the applicant has exhausted all available channels of administrative review. The judgments of IMFAT are, once again, final and without appeal.

There is much commonality in the statutes of such organizations. The relevant rules will normally provide for the right of staff members to appear before the tribunals and the

[91] See www.un.org/en/oaj/appeals.

[92] See http://web.worldbank.org/external/default/main?pagePK=7333373&contentMDK=22956391.

[93] See www.imf.org/external/imfat.

rules will stipulate issues such as the composition of the tribunals, the time limits for the making of an application, the way in which the judges are appointed and the fact that the tribunal's determinations are final and conclusive. Most such statutes furnish relatively little guidance as to the law that will be applied to decide the dispute. The formulation in Article 2a of the UN Dispute Tribunal Statute is common, stating that the tribunal will decide disputes concerning non-compliance with the terms of appointment or with the contract of employment, and that these terms 'include all pertinent regulations and rules and all relevant administrative issuances in force at the time of alleged non-compliance'.[94]

The IMF Administrative Tribunal Statute and its commentary are noteworthy for the guidance they provide as to the applicable law. Article III states that in deciding on an application, 'the Tribunal shall apply the internal law of the Fund, including generally recognized principles of international administrative law concerning judicial review of administrative acts'. The commentary gives interesting insight as to the meaning of the latter phrase. Thus we are told that Article III requires the Tribunal to 'adhere to such principles concerning judicial review as elaborated in the

[94] Statute of the United Nations Dispute Tribunal, Art. 2a, www.un.org/en/oaj/dispute. See, to like effect, Art. 11 of the Statute of the World Bank Administrative Tribunal, http://web.worldbank.org/external/default/main?pagePK=7333373&contentMDK=22956367; Art. 11 of the Statute of the Administrative Tribunal of the International Labour Organization, www.ilo.org/public/english/tribunal/about/statute.htm.

case law of both international administrative tribunals and domestic judicial systems, particularly with respect to review of decisions taken under discretionary powers'.[95]

It is clear that the reference to such principles serves as a resource of applicable principles of review, as exemplified by the fact that certain principles, such as the right to be heard, 'are so widely accepted and well-established in different legal systems that they are regarded as generally applicable to all decisions taken by international organizations, including the Fund'.[96] It is, however, equally clear that the reference to such principles of review is also interpreted as imposing limits on the degree of the Tribunal's legitimate intrusiveness, as determined by the standard of review. Thus the commentary provides that the reference to recognized principles of international administrative law is intended to limit the powers of the tribunal by making clear that the standards of review applied by the tribunal should not go beyond those applied by other tribunals, and the tribunal 'will not substitute their judgment for that of the competent organs and will respect the broad, although not unlimited, power of the organization to amend the terms and conditions of employment'.[97] In a similar vein, the commentary emphasizes that

[95] Commentary on the Statute of the Administrative Tribunal of the IMF, p. 17, www.imf.org/external/imfat/report.htm.

[96] Commentary on the Statute of the Administrative Tribunal of the IMF, p. 18, www.imf.org/external/imfat/report.htm.

[97] Commentary on the Statute of the Administrative Tribunal of the IMF, p. 17, www.imf.org/external/imfat/report.htm.

> with respect to review of individual decisions involving the exercise of managerial discretion, the case law has emphasized that discretionary decisions cannot be overturned unless they are shown to be arbitrary, capricious, discriminatory, improperly motivated, based on an error of law or fact, or carried out in violation of fair and reasonable procedures.[98]

Analogous limits on judicial review can be found in the jurisprudence of other administrative tribunals.[99]

The trend appears to be to accord greater weight to general principles of law than hitherto,[100] as attested to by inclusion of reference to such principles in the statutes of some international administrative tribunals explicitly, and the increased use made of them even where there is no explicit mention in the governing instrument.[101]

98 Commentary on the Statute of the Administrative Tribunal of the IMF, p. 19, www.imf.org/external/imfat/report.htm. See, e.g., *Ms J* v. *International Monetary Fund*, IMFAT Judgment 2003-1; *Ms W* v. *International Monetary Fund*, IMFAT Judgment 2005-2; *Ms BB* v. *International Monetary Fund*, IMFAT Judgment 2007-4; *Ms JJ* v. *International Monetary Fund*, IMFAT Judgment 2014-1.

99 See the following decisions of the World Bank Administrative Tribunal, *de Merode*, Decision No 1 [1981]; *Bertrand*, Decision No 81 [1989]; *Nunberg*, Decision No 245 [2001]; *Moussavi*, Decision No 360 [2007]; *Denis*, Decision No 458 [2011]; *L.T. Mpoy-Kamulayi (No 5)*, Decision No 463 [2012].

100 Kryvoi, 'The Law Applied by International Administrative Tribunals' (fn 104).

101 See, e.g., in relation to the World Bank Administrative Tribunal, *de Merode*, Decision No 1 [1981], at para. 25; *Bertrand*, Decision No 81 [1989]; *Marshall*, Decision No 226 [2000]; *Nunberg*, Decision No 245 [2001]; *Desthuis-Francis*, Decision No 315 [2004]; *Moussavi*, Decision No

The internal law of international organizations nonetheless has its own hierarchy:

> Constituent instruments (primary law), often adopted in the form of international treaties, prevail over staff regulations and staff rules, which in turn trump manuals, circulars and similar documents (secondary law). It must be noted that for secondary law to be regarded as a source of law, it must have a general effect. In other words, legislative enactments have the force of general law for other cases while administrative decisions are only applicable to those whom they address.[102]

There is nonetheless much to recommend Kryvoi's suggestion that it would be advantageous if there were a clear normative hierarchy between international law, including general principles of law, and the internal law of international organizations, with the former prevailing over the latter.[103]

(c) *Judicial review of decision making: variations on a theme*

Judicial review of a global actor's decision making may occur in a number of different ways. This section considers judicial review by a legal body that is internal to the particular

360 [2007]; *Denis*, Decision No 458 [2011]; *L.T. Mpoy-Kamulayi (No 5)*, Decision No 463 [2012].

[102] Kryvoi, 'The Law Applied by International Administrative Tribunals', 282.

[103] Kryvoi, 'The Law Applied by International Administrative Tribunals', 270–1.

institution. These are what Alter terms new-style international courts, where judicial review can be initiated by private actors, and where the defendant will normally be either a contracting state or the international institution itself.[104] The EU and the role of the CJEU and General Court therein have been the model for much judicial development elsewhere.[105] This review has been facilitated by direct effect, allowing cases to begin and end in national courts, thereby enhancing access to court and implementation of EU law. Alter identifies, as noted earlier, thirteen international courts with jurisdiction to review the validity of acts of the international institution, and/or national implementation of supranational decisions/rules.[106] The jurisdiction of such courts is compulsory, although a number of these bodies are not very active, this being reflective of the fact that in such instances there is often a relative paucity of international rules for the relevant international court to apply.

[104] Alter, *New Terrain of International Law*, p. 202.

[105] D. Kelemen, *Eurolegalism: The Transformation of Law and Regulation in the European Union* (Cambridge, MA: Harvard University Press, 2011).

[106] Alter, *New Terrain of International Law*, pp. 208–9. These are: the ECJ 1952; Benelux 1974; Andean Tribunal of Justice 1984; European Free Trade Area Court 1992; Central American Court of Justice 1992; International Tribunal for the Law of the Sea – Seabed Chamber 1996; West African Economic and Monetary Union 1995; Court of Justice of the Common Market of Eastern and Southern Africa 1998; Central African Monetary Community 2000; Caribbean Court of Justice 2001; East African Court of Justice 2001; Economic Community of West African States Court of Justice 2001; South African Development Community 2005.

There are, however, certain judicial bodies not included in Alter's list because private actors cannot initiate proceedings, which nonetheless exercise important review functions, the legal panels and Appellate Body of the WTO being the prime example in this respect.[107] The GATT 1947 regime was characterized primarily by 'diplomatic negotiation and the pursuit of consensus',[108] but this was changed through the Understanding on Rules and Procedures Governing the Settlement of Disputes (DSU), introduced by the Uruguay reforms,[109] which established a permanent Dispute Settlement Body (DSB). The DSB was authorized to establish panels and adopt panel and Appellate Body reports. It is central to the DSU schema that contracting parties do not make unilateral determinations of violations or suspend concessions, but utilize the DSU dispute settlement rules and procedures.[110] A panel report is deemed to be adopted unless either party files an appeal, or the DSB votes unanimously for non-adoption.[111] A report from the Appellate Body of the WTO is adopted by the DSB, unless it decides within thirty days by consensus that the report should not be adopted.[112]

When the panel report or the Appellate Body report is adopted, the party concerned must notify its intentions with respect to implementation of adopted recommendations. If it is impracticable to comply immediately, the party

[107] P. Mavroidis, *Trade in Goods* (Oxford: Oxford University Press, 2nd ed., 2012).

[108] M. Herdegen, *Principles of International Economic Law* (Oxford: Oxford University Press, 2013), p. 256.

[109] See www.wto.org/english/docs_e/legal_e/legal_e.htm.

[110] Art. 23 DSU. [111] Art. 16.4 DSU. [112] Art. 17.14 DSU.

concerned must be given a reasonable period of time, this being decided either by agreement of the parties and approval by the DSB within forty-five days of adoption of the report, or through arbitration within ninety days of adoption. The DSB keeps implementation under regular surveillance until the issue is resolved. There are provisions concerning compensation, or the suspension of concessions in the event of non-implementation.[113] The DSB will grant such authorization within thirty days of the expiry of the agreed time frame for implementation.

Disputes must be initiated by a Member of the WTO, the corollary being that private parties do not have standing in this respect. The panels and Appellate Body would therefore, on Keohane, Moravcsik and Slaughter's schema, be regarded as coming within inter-state dispute resolution, rather than transnational dispute resolution. The authors nonetheless acknowledge the reality that the WTO judicial regime falls betwixt and between the preceding ideal types. While states remain the formal gatekeepers of the WTO legal process, they often act at the behest of powerful industry interests.

> In the GATT/WTO proceedings the principal actors from civil society are firms or industry groups, which are typically wealthy enough to afford extensive litigation and often have substantial political constituencies. Industry groups and firms have been quick to complain about allegedly unfair and discriminatory actions by

[113] Art. 22.3 DSU.

their competitors abroad, and governments have often been willing to take up their complaints. Indeed, it has often been convenient for governments to do so, since the best defense against others' complaints in a system governed by reciprocity is often the threat or reality of bringing one's own case against their discriminatory measures. In a 'tit-for-tat' game, it is useful to have an army of well-documented complaints 'up one's sleeve' to deter others from filing complaints or as retaliatory responses to such complaints. Consequently, although states retain formal gatekeeping authority in the GATT/WTO system, they often have incentives to open the gates, letting actors in civil society set much of the agenda. The result of this political situation is that the evolution of the GATT dispute-settlement procedure looks quite different from that of the ICJ: indeed, it seems intermediate between the ideal types of interstate and transnational dispute resolution. Dispute-resolution activity levels have increased substantially over time, as the process has become more legalized.[114]

(d) Judicial review of decision making: treaty-mandated national adjudication

International treaties may, in addition, or as an alternative, to adjudication in the preceding sense, contain concrete provisions mandating adjudication at national level, as

[114] Keohane, Moravcsik and Slaughter, 'Legalized Dispute Resolution: Interstate and Transnational', 486.

exemplified by the WTO regime. Thus, as Greg Shaffer notes, 'multiple WTO agreements require mechanisms of judicial review, in particular for customs, import relief, and intellectual property law'.[115]

This is evident in the context of anti-dumping,[116] where Article 11 stipulates that an anti-dumping duty shall remain in force only as long as, and to the extent, necessary to counteract dumping which is causing injury. It is incumbent on the relevant authorities to review the need for the continued imposition of the duty. This is then reinforced through Article 13, which provides that each Member whose national legislation contains provisions on anti-dumping measures must maintain 'judicial, arbitral or administrative tribunals or procedures for the purpose, *inter alia*, of the prompt review of administrative actions relating to final determinations and reviews of determinations within the meaning of Article 11'. These tribunals or procedures shall be independent of the authorities responsible for the determination or review in question.

The same theme is evident in the Trade-Related Aspects of Intellectual Property Rights (TRIPS) Agreement.[117] Articles 41–2 impose obligations concerning domestic enforcement of the provisions of the TRIPS Agreement.

[115] G. Shaffer, 'How the WTO Shapes Regulatory Governance', University of California, School of Irvine, Legal Studies Research Paper Series, No 2014–53, p. 12.

[116] Agreement on Article VI of the General Agreement on Tariffs and Trade, www.wto.org/english/docs_e/legal_e/legal_e.htm#antidump.

[117] See www.wto.org/english/docs_e/legal_e/27-trips_01_e.htm.

Thus Article 41 stipulates that Members of the WTO must ensure that enforcement procedures are available under their law so as to permit effective action against any act of infringement of intellectual property rights covered by the TRIPS Agreement, including expeditious remedies to prevent infringements and remedies which constitute a deterrent to further infringements. The procedures must be applied so as to avoid the creation of barriers to legitimate trade and to provide for safeguards against their abuse. Procedures concerning enforcement of intellectual property rights must be fair and equitable, meaning in this context that they should not be unnecessarily complicated or costly, or entail unreasonable time limits or unwarranted delays. Decisions must preferably be in writing and be reasoned, and must be based only on evidence in respect of which parties were offered the opportunity to be heard. Parties to a proceeding must have an opportunity for review by a judicial authority of final administrative decisions and, subject to jurisdictional provisions in a Member's law concerning the importance of a case, of at least the legal aspects of initial judicial decisions on the merits of a case.

Article 41 is complemented by Article 42, which provides that Members shall make available to right holders civil judicial procedures concerning the enforcement of any intellectual property right covered by this Agreement. Defendants have the right to written notice which is timely and contains sufficient detail, including the basis of the claims. Parties must be allowed to be represented by independent legal counsel, and all parties are entitled to substantiate their claims and to present all relevant evidence.

(e) *No legal forum attached to the particular treaty: alternative legal recourse*

The expansion of international adjudication broadly conceived must, as stated above, be kept within perspective. There are many instances where there is no legal forum attached to the particular international treaty or transnational regulatory schema. There are, in addition, many areas where the relevant treaty or transnational regulatory scheme contains nothing that directly mandates legal recourse at national level.

It was just such circumstances that gave rise to the well-known *Kadi* case. Thus while the UN has a tribunal for resolving staff disputes there is no court within the UN system with general jurisdiction to review the legality of its actions, and this is so notwithstanding possible recourse to an advisory opinion from the International Court of Justice. This was the backdrop to the ECJ decision in *Kadi*, where it struck down the EC's implementation of UN Security Council anti-terrorist asset-freezing resolutions for violation of fundamental rights.[118] It held that the Community was based on the rule

[118] Cases C-402 and 415/05 P, *Kadi & Al Barakaat International Foundation* v. *Council and Commission* [2008] ECR 1-6351; M. Nettesheim, 'U.N. Sanctions against Individuals: A Challenge to the Architecture of European Union Governance' (2007) 44 *Common Market Law Review* 567; G. de Búrca, 'The European Court of Justice and the International Legal Order after *Kadi*' (2010) 51 *Harvard International Law Journal* 1; T. Tridimas and J. Guitierrez-Fons, 'EU Law, International Law, and Economic Sanctions against Terrorism: The Judiciary in Distress?' (2009) 32 *Fordham International Law Journal* 660; M. Cremona, F. Francioni and S. Poli (eds.),

of law and that fundamental rights formed an integral part of the general principles of law, compliance with which was a condition precedent for the lawfulness of Community acts. Obligations imposed by an international agreement could not prejudice the constitutional principles of the EC Treaty, including respect for fundamental rights. The ECJ concluded that the applicants' right to be heard was violated by the EC Regulation giving effect to the asset-freezing regime emanating from the Security Council, because they could not contest the grounds on which they were included in the Security Council list.

Whether an individual can take advantage of such protections at national or regional level depends on first principles relating to jurisdiction and choice of law. Thus the initial inquiry will be whether the national or regional court has jurisdiction over the matter brought before it. This was relatively straightforward in *Kadi* because the claimant was challenging an EC regulation that gave effect to a Security Council determination. There was considerable discussion in the case as to the way in which the EU courts should regard determinations of the UN Security Council, with disagreement between the ECJ and the CFI in this respect. There was, however, no doubt as to the jurisdiction of the Community courts to consider the legality of the contested EC regulation. In other cases matters will not be so straightforward. It will be for the particular national court to decide whether it has international jurisdiction over the case at hand. Its rules

'Challenging the EU Counter-terrorism Measures through the Courts', EUI Working Paper 2009/10.

must conform with international law, which will commonly demand some legitimate nexus to the particular state.[119] The link may take the form of nationality of the parties, domicile, the locus of a tort, or the place of performance of a contract. It is also open to the parties by agreement to choose a particular jurisdiction.[120] The rules concerning international jurisdiction in the EU have been regularized through the Brussels regime, and the Brussels Convention was incorporated into EC law in 2001.[121]

(f) Private dispute settlement: arbitration

While parties may seek to litigate disputes through national or regional courts, it is common to use arbitration as a dispute settlement mechanism, particularly in disputes relating to international economic law. The arbitral tribunal may be established ad hoc by agreement between the parties, or it may operate pursuant to an institutionalized schema dealing with arbitration.

[119] F. Mann, 'The Doctrine of Jurisdiction in International Law' (1964-I) 111 *Receuil des cours de l'Académie de droit international de la Haye* 1; F. Mann, 'The Doctrine of International Jurisdiction Revisited after Twenty Years' (1984-III) 186 *Receuil des cours de l'Académie de droit international de la Haye* 9; C. Ryngaet, *Jurisdiction in International Law* (Oxford: Oxford University Press, 2008).

[120] A. Briggs, *Agreements on Jurisdiction and Choice of Law* (Oxford: Oxford University Press, 2008).

[121] Council Regulation (EC) No 44/2001 of 22 December 2000 on jurisdiction and the recognition and enforcement of judgments in civil and commercial matters, OJ 2001 No L12/1.

The latter is exemplified by the ICSID, which is an autonomous international institution established under the Convention on the Settlement of Investment Disputes between States and Nationals of Other States, or the Washington Convention, which has in excess of 140 Member States.[122] The primary purpose of ICSID is to provide facilities for conciliation and arbitration of international investment disputes. The multilateral treaty was formulated by the International Bank for Reconstruction and Development (the World Bank), and entered into force in 1966. The rationale underlying the Convention is to remove impediments to private investment that flow from the absence of specialized international methods for investment dispute settlement. ICSID thus operates as an impartial international forum for resolution of legal disputes between eligible parties, through conciliation or arbitration procedures.

The International Chamber of Commerce (ICC) is a further prominent example of an institutionalized forum for arbitration. The International Court of Arbitration was established in 1923 as the ICC's arbitration body.[123] The Court developed resolution mechanisms for business disputes in an international context. While the dispute itself is resolved by independent arbitrators, the Court supervises the process.

[122] Convention on the Settlement of Investment Disputes between States and Nationals of other States, www.sloarbitration.eu/Portals/0/Arbitrazno-pravo/CRR_English-final.pdf.

[123] See www.iccwbo.org/products-and-services/arbitration-and-adr/arbitration.

There are no restrictions as to who can use ICC arbitration, or who can act as arbitrators. Since its inception, the Court has administered more than 20,000 cases, involving parties and arbitrators from some 180 countries. The force of arbitral awards is enhanced by the fact that they can, subject to certain conditions, enjoy international recognition pursuant to the 1958 New York Convention on the Recognition and Enforcement of Foreign Arbitral Awards, the principal objective of which is to ensure that foreign and non-domestic arbitral awards will not be discriminated against.[124]

There are now major centres of arbitration around the globe. Thus in addition to the ICC there are prominent venues in London (the London Court of International Arbitration),[125] Stockholm (the Arbitration Institute of the Stockholm Chamber of Commerce),[126] Singapore (the Singapore International Arbitration Centre),[127] and New York (the International Center for Dispute Resolution of the American Arbitration Association).[128]

While study of arbitration has been largely practitioner-oriented, there has been increased academic interest in the role played by arbitration in global governance. Walter Mattli and Thomas Dietz draw four models from the set of essays they edited, which provide different explanations concerning the nature of international arbitration: the economic-rationalist model, the cultural-sociological

[124] See www.uncitral.org/uncitral/en/uncitral_texts/arbitration/NYConvention.html.

[125] See www.lcia.org.

[126] See www.sccinstitute.com.

[127] See www.siac.org.sg.

[128] See www.icdr.org/icdr/faces/home?.

model, the power-based model and the constitutionalization model.[129] We shall return to this issue in the next chapter. Suffice it to note the following important point of contact between this material and that charted earlier in this chapter:

> It has been widely noted that the transformation of modern statehood involves partial transfer of authority to international organizations, such as the United Nations, the World Trade Organization, or the European Union. These organizations are based on international treaties among nation states. Their governance power and legitimacy derive to a large extent from the central role played by representatives of national governments in these inter- and supranational organizations. States are the architects and responsible masters of these institutions. By contrast, arbitration courts do not involve governmental representatives. The powers exercised by arbitrators are not directly linked to nation states. Unlike international governmental organizations, international commercial arbitration courts present a form of transnational private authority.[130]

[129] W. Mattli and T. Dietz, 'Mapping and Assessing the Rise of International Commercial Arbitration in the Globalization Era: An Introduction', in W. Mattli and T. Dietz (eds.), *International Arbitration and Global Governance: Contending Theories and Evidence* (Oxford: Oxford University Press, 2014), Ch. 1.

[130] Mattli and Dietz, 'Mapping and Assessing the Rise of International Commercial Arbitration', p. 5.

5 Contestable legal issues: conceptual basis of intervention

The preceding discussion considered the causes for and expansion of global administration. There is, however, contestation as to how the role of law in this area should be conceptualized, with the principal divide coming between those who articulate that in terms of global administrative law, and those who contend that it should be seen as a branch of international institutional law dealing with international public authority. The former camp includes Kingsbury, Krisch and Stewart, Esty and Cassese, who conceptualize legal intervention in terms of global administrative law. The latter is represented most prominently by Von Bogdandy and co-authors, who reject this in preference for international institutional law and international public authority.

Armin von Bogdandy, Philipp Dann and Matthias Goldmann advocate an approach based on international institutional law that seeks to 'reconstruct the exercise of international public authority by using comparative perspectives on administrative scholarship',[131] while at the same time developing a constitutionalist framework that would provide the foundation for the critique of 'the procedures, instruments and accountability of international institutions when engaging in the exercise of public authority',[132] and reflecting on the

[131] Von Bogdandy, Dann and Goldmann, 'Developing the Publicness of Public International Law', 1395.

[132] Von Bogdandy, Dann and Goldmann, 'Developing the Publicness of Public International Law', 1395.

interrelations between international and domestic institutions. They regard this combination of constitutionalist, administrative and institutionalist thinking as a public law approach:

> In sum, constitutional, administrative and international institutional law approaches to global governance (and, thus, international institutions) share the aim of understanding, framing and taming the exercise of international public authority in the post-national constellation. None of these approaches laments the decline of the Westphalian order. They rather aim at rendering the exercise of international public authority more efficient and legitimate. We therefore hold that these three internal approaches can be combined, using international institutional law as the basis for a framework of the exercise of public authority. We believe that the *law* of international institutions can place the analysis of the exercise of international public authority on a firm disciplinary basis. This assumption also rests on a degree of skepticism towards establishing an entirely new field of global or international administrative law.[133]

We need, however, to press further to understand their scepticism towards global administrative law. This is premised on a number of interconnected lines of argument. Three such arguments can be discerned.

The first is that global administrative law is 'too global' and implies a fusion between domestic administrative law and international law. This is apparent in the following quotation:

[133] Von Bogdandy, Dann and Goldmann, 'Developing the Publicness of Public International Law', 1394. Italics in the original.

> this does not advocate drawing all too simple 'domestic analogies': the differences between domestic institutions and international institutions are too important. Precisely for that reason, our approach differs from that of *global administrative law* approach as we conceive it as too 'global': it risks to efface or to blur distinctions essential to the construction, evaluation and application of norms concerning public authority. Put differently, we wonder what would be the overarching legal basis of a global administrative law. Would it be general principles? Or would it have a status of its own, above positive law? The notion of *global administrative law* implies a fusion of domestic administrative and international law that does not give consideration to the fact that international legal norms and internal norms possess a categorically different 'input legitimacy': state consent versus popular sovereignty, according to the classical understanding. A global approach thus glosses over and threatens to obscure this fundamental difference.[134]

A second line of argument is that 'if global administrative law is in some respects too broad, it is too narrow in others', and hence 'appears of little use',[135] since its only use is to investigate principles that deal 'exclusively with administrative activity'.[136] The argument appears to be that this thereby ignores more general principles of public law, such as concern

[134] Von Bogdandy, Dann and Goldmann, 'Developing the Publicness of Public International Law', 1393. Italics in the original.

[135] A. von Bogdandy, 'General Principles of International Public Authority: Sketching a Research Field' [2008] *German Law Journal* 1909, at 1920.

[136] Von Bogdandy, 'Sketching a Research Field', 1920.

for human rights, which can be taken cognizance of within a theory couched more generally in terms of public law and international public authority.[137]

The third line of argument is that global administrative law has federal or quasi-federal leanings, which seems to connote a separate space for administrative law distinct from international law and domestic law, and also the emergence of principles that can apply to both international and domestic public authorities. This line of argument is apparent in the following extract:

> The proto-federal global administrative law rests on assumptions which appear to me even more problematic than the constitutional understanding of international law which is not, by necessity, federal. Similarly, the proponents of a global administrative law assert the advent of a 'single, if multifaceted global administrative space distinct from the domains of international law and domestic law', built by overarching principles. The term 'space' is revealing: *space* or *area* have become the proxy for *federal* in *Eurospeak:* the EU is an *area* of freedom, security and justice, a research *area*, not least an *area* of free movement, each with its administrative dimension. In my understanding, there is little ground for a global doctrine of principles encompassing international and domestic public authorities.[138]

Thus while von Bogdandy agrees with the proponents of a global administrative law that there should be a 'theoretical

[137] Von Bogdandy, 'Sketching a Research Field', 1920.

[138] Von Bogdandy, 'Sketching a Research Field', 1919. Italics in original.

and doctrinal framework for international, supranational and national public law which conceptualizes their linkages', he finds 'neither the theory nor the doctrine of administrative law convincing at this point in time in this respect',[139] and contends moreover that 'this approach blurs categories which are indispensable for attributing political and legal responsibility'.[140]

It is important for there to be searching inquiry as to the foundation of an emerging body of law, more especially when, as here, it is applicable to a broad range of bodies. The critique of global administrative law voiced by von Bogdandy, Dann and Goldmann should therefore be taken seriously. It is by parity of reasoning important to subject the critique itself to close scrutiny. The following points may therefore be made by way of rejoinder.

I do not believe that the criticism of global administrative law as being 'too global', and implying a fusion between domestic administrative law and international law, thereby ignoring the fact that international law and domestic law have different input legitimacy, is warranted. The academics who have written prominently in terms of global administrative law have all stated repeatedly that there cannot be any simple cut and paste between the domestic and global arenas.[141] They have all taken cognizance of the different input legitimacy that pertains to global administration in its

139 Von Bogdandy, 'Sketching a Research Field', 1921.

140 Von Bogdandy, 'Sketching a Research Field', 1921.

141 See, e.g., B. Kingsbury, 'The Concept of "Law" in Global Administrative Law' (2009) 20 *European Journal of International Law* 23, at 27.

divergent administrative forms, and to domestic administration in a traditional national state, given that in the latter power is commonly delegated to the administration by a democratically elected legislature in order to 'execute' programmes agreed by the legislature.

The reason why the nomenclature of global administrative law has nonetheless been adopted by many working in the field is that while the differences between the domestic and global arenas are acknowledged, it nonetheless remains the case that the precepts of accountability developed in domestic administrative law are regarded as a resource that can properly be drawn on when thinking about accountability at the global level. To put the same point in a different way, precepts of administrative law couched in terms of rights to be heard, participation in rule making, transparency and judicial review are felt to be apposite to exercise of public power at the global level, even if careful thought has to be given concerning the precise way in which these and other principles are applied to any particular global administrative activity. This appears to be accepted by von Bogdandy, who, while stressing that there cannot be strict equivalence between principles applied at the global and domestic levels, nonetheless also acknowledges that 'the more an international authority impacts an individual, the stronger the assumption is that international principles require legal arrangements which are functionally equivalent to what is to be expected in the domestic realm'.[142]

[142] Von Bogdandy, 'Sketching a Research Field', 1918.

The second critique, to the effect that global administrative law is too narrow and hence of little use as an organizing precept at the global level, rests on differences in the way that common lawyers and civil lawyers conceptualize the realm of administrative law. The criticism is predicated on the assumption that administrative law, and hence global administrative law, cannot accommodate concerns with the constitutional dimension of administrative organization on the one hand, nor with concerns for human rights on the other, both of which von Bogdandy believes to be important and both of which he includes within his conception of international public authority built on international institutional law. Administrative lawyers schooled in a common law tradition would agree that both of these issues are important, but they would also contend that they can properly be considered as part of administrative law.

Thus, as David Dyzenhaus has rightly noted, the elements of domestic administrative law include what he terms constitutive administrative law, this being the law that constitutes the authority of administrative bodies. For Dyzenhaus this captures the important issue of whether the body has a warrant for its action, since it must be able to trace its authority to a delegation by the state.[143] The constitutive dimension of administrative law is, however, broader than this. It also commonly encompasses issues of institutional design, denoting thereby the suitability of this type of body to perform the task assigned to it. This inquiry is commonly

[143] D. Dyzenhaus, 'Accountability and the Concept of (Global) Administrative Law' (2009) *Acta Juridica* 3, at 3–4.

undertaken by administrative lawyers and has both a normative and functional dimension. The former captures the issue of whether, for example, certain types of task hitherto undertaken by the state should be privatized or contracted out.[144] The latter captures the issue of the choice as to the administrative form for delivery of administrative tasks, with much literature addressing, for example, the pros and cons of agencies as opposed to more traditional administration by and though parent departments, and the way in which such administrative organization should be designed so as to maximize accountability and functional efficacy.[145] The relevant point for present purposes is that study of domestic administrative law is not confined to procedural and substantive principles of judicial review, but includes this broader remit, the corollary being that there is no reason why this should not also be so at the global level.

[144] C. Graham and T. Prosser, *Privatizing Public Enterprises: Constitutions, the State, and Regulation in Comparative Perspective* (Oxford: Oxford University Press, 1991); T. Prosser, *Law and the Regulators* (Oxford: Oxford University Press, 1997); A.C.L. Davies, *Accountability: A Public Law Analysis of Government by Contract* (Oxford: Oxford University Press, 2001); P. Vincent-Jones, *The New Public Contracting: Regulation, Responsiveness, Relationality* (Oxford: Oxford University Press, 2006); A.C.L. Davies, *The Public Laws of Government Contracts* (Oxford: Oxford University Press, 2008).

[145] T. Christensen and P. Laegreid (eds.), *Autonomy and Regulation: Coping with Agencies in the Modern State* (Cheltenham: Elgar, 2006); M. Flinders, *Delegated Governance and the British State: Walking without Order* (Oxford: Oxford University Press, 2008); P. Craig, *Administrative Law* (London: Sweet & Maxwell, 7th ed., 2012), Chs. 4–5.

This is equally true for the other important dimension noted by von Bogdandy, which is concern for human rights. Protection of human rights is a core element of constitutional law, with much case law and commentary focusing on rights-based protection against state action, and in some legal systems against private action too. Human rights is not, however, the exclusive preserve of constitutional law, and features importantly as part of domestic systems of administrative law within common law regimes. Thus discourse as to the extent to which standards of review should vary depending on the nature of the individual interest affected by administrative action is a commonplace of judicial doctrine[146] and academic commentary,[147] with the courts undertaking more intensive judicial review where a human right is involved in a case against the administration. There is therefore no reason why global administrative law should be perceived as 'too narrow' in this respect, and there is indeed already good evidence in the form of the *Kadi* litigation to show

[146] See, e.g., in the UK, *R* v. *Secretary of State for the Home Department, ex p Brind* [1991] 1 AC 696; *R* v. *Ministry of Defence, ex p Smith* [1996] QB 517; *R* v. *Secretary of State for the Home Department, ex p McQuillan* [1995] 4 All ER 400; *Derbyshire County Council* v. *Times Newspapers Ltd* [1993] AC 534; *R* v. *Secretary of State for the Home Department, ex p Leech* [1994] QB 198.

[147] See, e.g., in the UK, Sir John Laws, 'The Infiltration of a Bill of Rights' [1992] *Public Law* 397; Sir Stephen Sedley, 'Human Rights: A Twenty-First Century Agenda' [1995] *Public Law* 386; M. Hunt, *Using Human Rights Law in English Courts* (Oxford: Hart, 1997).

that where the interest affected at the global level is a fundamental right then this will generate calls for increased oversight.[148]

Let us turn, then, to the third critique of global administrative law, which, it will be recalled, is that it has federal or quasi-federal connotations. Armin von Bogdandy argues that proponents of global administrative law conceive of it as occupying a space distinct from international law and domestic law, and as being applicable to both international and domestic public authorities. Now there is undoubtedly an issue here, which is, at its most fundamental, the fact that the range of institutions that exercise authority at the global level is very heterogeneous, the consequence being that many of the bodies do not fall neatly into the traditional dichotomy of international–domestic. How to regard such bodies, and which norms they should be subject to, are precisely what commentators are trying to determine. When proponents of global administrative law speak of it occupying a space distinct from international law and domestic law they do so in recognition of the preceding fact. It is not an attempt

[148] Cases C-402 and 415/05 P, *Kadi & Al Barakaat International Foundation* v. *Council and Commission* [2008] ECR I-6351; Cases C-584, 593, 595/10 P, *Commission* v. *Kadi* EU:C:2013:518; Nettesheim, 'U.N. Sanctions against Individuals'; G. de Búrca, 'The European Court of Justice and the International Legal Order after *Kadi*' (2010) 51 *Harvard International Law Journal* 1; Tridimas and Guitierrez-Fons, 'EU Law, International Law, and Economic Sanctions against Terrorism'; Cremona, Francioni and Poli, 'Challenging the EU Counter-terrorism Measures through the Courts'.

to cast global administrative law in federal garb. Kingsbury captures the point well:

> Instead of neatly separated levels of regulation (private, local, national, inter-state), a congeries of different actors and different layers together form a variegated 'global administrative space' that includes international institutions and transnational networks, as well as domestic administrative bodies that operate within international regimes or cause transboundary regulatory effects. The idea of a 'global administrative space' marks a departure from those orthodox understandings of international law in which the international is largely inter-governmental, and there is a reasonably sharp separation of the domestic and the international. In the practice of global governance, transnational networks of rule-generators, interpreters and appliers cause such strict barriers to break down. This global administrative space is increasingly occupied by transnational private regulators, hybrid bodies such as public–private partnerships involving states or inter-state organizations, national public regulators whose actions have external effects but may not be controlled by the central executive authority, informal inter-state bodies with no treaty basis (including 'coalitions of the willing'), and formal inter-state institutions (such as those of the United Nations) affecting third parties through administrative-type actions.[149]

There is, to be sure, a further issue, which is the relationship between norms of administrative law at the global level, and

[149] Kingsbury, 'The Concept of "Law"', 25.

analogous precepts in domestic law. This too is complex and will be considered more fully below. Suffice it to say for the present, however, that insofar as proponents of global administrative law think in terms of the precepts applying to international and domestic public authorities, this is normally in relation to administration at the global level, where domestic regulatory authorities are integral to that regulatory schema. There is once again no covert federal agenda, but rather an attempt to fashion appropriate principles for this kind of integrated or mixed administration.

It might be argued that the very attempt to craft principles of global administrative law for such bodies that do not fit into the traditional international–domestic dichotomy lacks legitimacy. We shall return to this issue in the following section. Suffice it to say for the present that the same claim could be made against those who wish to ground intervention in terms of international institutional law. It is true that the concept of international institutional law is established, but equally true that it has to be given an expansive reading to cope with the challenges posed by the range of bodies considered earlier in this chapter. Thus, as von Bogdandy, Dann and Goldmann state,

> In order to be commensurate to the challenge of global governance, international institutional law should encompass not only the activities of international organizations *sensu stricto* but also that of institutions with a different legal status, such as treaty regimes and informal regimes.[150]

[150] Von Bogdandy, Dann and Goldmann, 'Developing the Publicness of Public International Law', 1394.

The reality is that the same normative imperatives to develop appropriate principles are present irrespective of whether one frames intervention in terms of global administrative law or international institutional law.

6 Contestable legal issues: the nature of global administrative 'law'

The discussion thus far has been predicated implicitly on the assumption that even though there is debate concerning the conceptual foundation for involvement in the realm of global administration this can nonetheless be thought of in terms of 'legal involvement'. This, however, raises the issue of what we mean by 'law' in this context.

Benedict Kingsbury has shed helpful light on this issue.[151] He argues that global administrative law, conceived in terms of the legal mechanisms, principles and practices that promote accountability among global administrative bodies, is conceived as 'global' rather than 'international' 'to avoid implying that this is part of the recognized *lex lata* or indeed *lex ferenda*',[152] thereby including bodies and practices not normally encompassed within the rubric of international law. Kingsbury is open about the task at hand, acknowledging that if a claim to 'law' is made in relation to many of the situations covered by global administrative law 'it is a claim that diverges from, and can be sharply in tension with the

[151] Kingsbury, 'The Concept of "Law"'.
[152] Kingsbury, 'The Concept of "Law"', 25–6.

classical models of consent-based inter-state international law and most models of national law'.[153] The very fact that global administrative law is conceived in this way renders it all the more important to identify the sense of 'law' that underpins the emerging discipline.

Kingsbury rejects command theories of law that are predicated on a command issued by a single determinate sovereign, since they do not fit the empirical reality of global administrative law. He nonetheless focuses on the positivist conception of law made famous by Hart, who conceived of law in terms of a system of primary norms, combined with secondary rules of change, adjudication and recognition. The authoritative source of the law, combined with the internal sense of obligation to obey the relevant norms, was central to this concept of law.[154]

Kingsbury notes that positivist as opposed to non-positivist, or content-based, conceptions of law have been preferred by international lawyers, and argues for an 'extended positivist conception of law' to underpin global administrative law.[155] Thus law is conceived in terms of social fact, there must be an internal sense of obligation for a norm to be regarded as a rule of 'law', and there must be some agreement among the key officials as to what sources can be regarded as authoritative in terms of law generation. Kingsbury argues that the authoritative

[153] Kingsbury, 'The Concept of "Law"', 26.

[154] H.L.A Hart, *The Concept of Law* (Oxford: Oxford University Press, 1961).

[155] Kingsbury, 'The Concept of "Law"', 29.

sources of law include the classic foundations of international law, such as customary international law, *jus cogens*, general principles of law and treaties, but contends that a concept of law based on such sources alone is not adequate.[156] He also acknowledges that insofar as global administrative law goes beyond classic international law, it cannot yet claim to have an overarching rule of recognition,[157] institutionalized secondary rules of change are not generally present, and those of adjudication may or may not exist. This positivist approach is, however, qualified substantially by Kingsbury's recourse to what he terms the qualities immanent in public law:

> The key idea is that in choosing to claim to be law, or in pursuing law-like practices dependent on law-like reasoning and attractions . . . a particular global governance entity or regime embraces or is assessed by reference to the attributes, constraints and normative commitments that are immanent in public law. These norms have multiple specific sources, but they are discernible from the practices of public law in different national systems and in transnational and public-international law arenas. They are not simply choices that could have been made or not made in each venue, although in many cases they may have started to obtain prevalence and purchase that way. Rather, as the layers of common normative practice thicken,

156 Kingsbury, 'The Concept of "Law"', 29.

157 Kingsbury, 'The Concept of "Law"', 29–30, although recognition rules may pertain within particular sectoral areas.

> they come to be argued for and adopted through a mixture of comparative study and a sense that they are (or are becoming) obligatory. Where they have not been adopted by a great political decision (that is, where they are not directly applicable by treaty or a decisive resolution of the relevant international organization, etc), the usual case for them is that they are justified (and perhaps required) by what is intrinsic to public law as generally understood.[158]

Kingsbury acknowledges that this looks a lot closer to Fuller's conception of law than to Hart's.[159] Kingsbury builds on these Fuller-type foundations, and draws on Jeremy Waldron's work to develop the idea of publicness as a necessary element of the concept of law in a democratic society,[160] this capturing the claim 'made for law that it has been wrought by the whole society'.[161] The more particular aspects of publicness include principles of legality, transparency, due process, rationality, proportionality, the rule of law and human rights.[162]

I do not disagree with the resulting depiction of 'law' within global administrative law. It is nonetheless necessary to look more closely at the reasoning process, more especially the extent to which the result can be justified in positivist as

[158] Kingsbury, 'The Concept of "Law"', 30.

[159] Kingsbury, 'The Concept of "Law"', 30, 40; L. Fuller, *The Morality of Law* (New Haven: Yale University Press, 1964).

[160] J. Waldron, 'Can There Be a Democratic Jurisprudence?', NYU PILT Research Paper, 08–35 SSRN.

[161] Kingsbury, 'The Concept of "Law"', 31.

[162] Kingsbury, 'The Concept of "Law"', 32–3.

opposed to non-positivist terms. A preliminary word is in order concerning positivism in national and international law before returning to the blend of positivist and non-positivist elements in Kingsbury's thesis. There is, of course, a wealth of literature at the national level concerning legal positivism, with numerous debates about its more precise implications and about whether positivist theory is to be preferred to non-positivist alternatives.[163] There is a similar wealth of literature at the international level, where rival theories of international law are fiercely contested.[164] The object of the present inquiry is, however, more narrowly circumscribed. It is to understand the positivist approach in order to determine the extent to which 'law' within global administrative law can be said to rest on positivist as opposed to non-positivist foundations.

The allure of Hartian positivism is not hard to discern.[165] Law is conceived in terms of social fact, coupled

[163] See, e.g., L. Green, 'Legal Positivism', Stanford Encyclopaedia of Jurisprudence, http://plato.stanford.edu/entries/legal-positivism.

[164] See, e.g., S. Ratner and A.-M. Slaughter, 'Symposium on Method in International Law, Appraising the Methods of International Law: A Prospectus for Readers' (1999) 93 *American Journal of International Law* 291, at 293–4, where the authors list seven approaches: positivism, the New Haven policy-oriented approach, international legal process, critical legal studies, international law and international relations, feminist jurisprudence, and law and economics; J. d'Aspremont and J. Kammerhofer (eds.), *International Legal Positivism in a Post-modern World* (Cambridge: Cambridge University Press, 2014).

[165] J. Gardner, 'Legal Positivism: 5½ Myths' (2001) 46 *American Journal of Jurisprudence* 199.

with an internal sense of obligation in relation to the relevant norms and some consensus among key players as to what is to count as an authoritative source. Particular laws can be identified irrespective of their content, their merit or the values that underpin them, and that is so irrespective of the fact that some values will inevitably underlie societal acceptance of what is to count as an authoritative source. The essence of positivism is captured by Leslie Green:

> The positivist thesis does not say that law's merits are unintelligible, unimportant, or peripheral to the philosophy of law. It says that they do not determine whether laws or legal systems *exist*. Whether a society has a legal system depends on the presence of certain structures of governance, not on the extent to which it satisfies ideals of justice, democracy, or the rule of law. What laws are in force in that system depends on what social standards its officials recognize as authoritative; for example, legislative enactments, judicial decisions, or social customs. The fact that a policy would be just, wise, efficient, or prudent is never sufficient reason for thinking that it is actually the law, and the fact that it is unjust, unwise, inefficient or imprudent is never sufficient reason for doubting it. According to positivism, law is a matter of what has been posited (ordered, decided, practiced, tolerated, etc.); as we might say in a more modern idiom, positivism is the view that law is a social construction.[166]

[166] Green, 'Legal Positivism', 1. Italics in the original.

This vision of law has considerable pedigree within national legal orders.[167] There is, then, little surprise that it should be appealing at the international level, given that international law grounded on state consent can provide the foundation for a set of legally binding norms in circumstances where it may be difficult for such norms to develop in a non-positivist manner. Thus, in the words of Bruno Simma and Andreas Paulus, 'it is precisely this need to get our legal message through to other people, especially representatives of states who might not share our individual moral or religious sensibilities, that constitutes one of the main reasons for the adoption of a positivist view of international law'.[168] They regard the principal characteristic of the classic view of positivism as the association of law with an emanation of state will. This voluntarism requires that all norms should be deduced from acts of state will, the corollary being that

[167] The relationship between positivism and classic rule-of-law values, such as that the law should be clear, consistent, prospective and the like, cannot be examined here. It may be true that law could not guide behaviour without possessing these attributes to a minimal degree. It is, however, important to be mindful of the point made by Green, 'Legal Positivism', 8: 'It suffices to note that this is perfectly consistent with law being source-based. Even if moral properties were identical with, or supervened upon, these rule-of-law properties, they do so in virtue of their rule-like character, and not their law-like character. Whatever virtues inhere in or follow from clear, consistent, prospective, and open practices can be found not only in law but in all other social practices with those features, including custom and positive morality.'

[168] B. Simma and A. Paulus, 'The Responsibility of Individuals for Human Rights Abuses in Internal Conflicts: A Positivist View' (1999) 93 *American Journal of International Law* 302.

the lawyer's role was limited to interpreting the will of the states concerned.[169] For Simma and Paulus, drawing on Kelsen and Hart, positivism also connoted 'the strict separation of the law in force, as derived from formal sources that are part of a unified system of law, from non-legal factors such as natural reason, moral principles and political ideologies'.[170] They summarize the positivist perspective as follows:

> Law is regarded as a unified system of rules that, according to most variants, emanate from state will. This system of rules is an 'objective' reality and needs to be distinguished from law 'as it should be'. Classic positivism demands rigorous tests for legal validity. Extralegal arguments, e.g., arguments that have no textual, systemic or historical basis, are deemed irrelevant to legal analysis; there is only hard law, no soft law. For some, the unity of the legal system will provide one correct answer for any legal problem; for others, even if law is 'open-textured', it still provides determinate guidance for officials and individuals.[171]

This summation is echoed by Steven Ratner and Anne-Marie Slaughter, who stress the positivist attachment to law predicated on formal criteria independent of moral or ethical

[169] Simma and Paulus, 'The Responsibility of Individuals for Human Rights Abuses', 303–4.

[170] Simma and Paulus, 'The Responsibility of Individuals for Human Rights Abuses', 304.

[171] Simma and Paulus, 'The Responsibility of Individuals for Human Rights Abuses', 304.

considerations.[172] This positivist vision explains the centrality of treaties and custom as traditional sources of international law, since the former embody the express consent of states, while the latter is validated through tacit consent, as moderated by the requirements of state practice and *opinio juris*. It follows also for proponents of the positivist view that treaties, even those that create new rules, are binding only on the contracting parties.[173] Thus for positivists 'international law is no more or less than the rules to which states have agreed through treaties, custom, and perhaps other forms of consent',[174] the corollary being that where such expression of consent is lacking the positivist assumption is that states retain their freedom of action.

For traditional positivists, state actors were, not surprisingly, the central players, and for some they were the only subjects of international law. More modern positivists recognize the increased importance of 'intergovernmental organizations, as well as nongovernmental organizations, global economic players and the global media'.[175] They acknowledge also some change in the traditional sources of international law,[176] including broadening of the concept of state practice in the context of custom, and greater weight

[172] Ratner and Slaughter, 'Symposium on Method' 293.

[173] Simma and Paulus, 'The Responsibility of Individuals for Human Rights Abuses', 305.

[174] Ratner and Slaughter, 'Symposium on Method', 293.

[175] Simma and Paulus, 'The Responsibility of Individuals for Human Rights Abuses', 306.

[176] Simma and Paulus, 'The Responsibility of Individuals for Human Rights Abuses', 306–7.

being accorded to general principles of law[177] and international adjudication[178] than hitherto.

We can now return to Benedict Kingsbury's thesis and consider the extent to which the sense of 'law' within global administrative law is driven by positivist and non-positivist reasoning. The reality is that it is the latter that is really driving the analysis, not the former, and this is, as will be seen, equally true for others working in this area. I do not have a problem with this, but we should nonetheless be cognizant about the nature of the legal enterprise that we are engaged in.

We have to be realistic as to how much is actually 'posited', from which to construct a positivist foundation for global administrative law. If positivism is to be regarded as the foundation, albeit in part, for the 'law' in global administrative law, then we have to inquire more closely as to what precisely we are getting from law conceived in this manner. There is no doubt that we can get something from this legal perspective.

177 B. Cheng, *General Principles of Law as Applied by International Courts and Tribunals* (Cambridge: Cambridge University Press, 1953); M. Cherif Bassiouni, 'A Functional Approach to "General Principles of Law"' (1989–90) 11 *Michigan Journal of International Law* 768; B. Simma and P. Alston, 'The Sources of Human Rights Law: Custom, Jus Cogens, and General Principles' (1992) 12 *Australian Yearbook of International Law* 82; C. Voigt, 'The Role of General Principles in International Law and Their Relationship to Treaty Law', RETFÆRD ÅRGANG 31 2008 NR. 2/121.

178 See, e.g., R. Keohane, A.-M. Slaughter, J. Goldstein and M. Kahler (eds.), *Legalization and World Politics* (Cambridge, MA: MIT Press, 2001); A. von Bogdandy and I. Venzke, 'Beyond Dispute: International Judicial Institutions as Lawmakers' (2011) 12 *German Law Journal* 979.

It is, for example, clear from the scholarship in this area that some bodies that act in the global administrative arena adhere to norms of process, rationality, review and the like that comprise what is termed global administrative law. To the extent that the key players and officials within such regimes recognize such standards and treat them as authoritative, there is a foundation for treating them as law judged by positivist precepts. It is, however, equally clear that practice is uneven.[179] It is also accepted that there are no coherent rules of recognition, change and adjudication that cover the world of global administrative law,[180] the reality being that particular organizations operate within their own structures, and this is so notwithstanding the fact that there might be some learning or connection between some such bodies.

The temptation is to attempt to square the circle and remain in positivist garb by stretching positivist precepts, but in doing so the risk is always that of undermining the very core of positivism. Kingsbury is alive to this danger, but still succumbs. Thus, for example, while acknowledging that his conception of principles immanent in public law does not sit naturally with Hartian reasoning, Kingsbury nonetheless opines that the fit will be much closer if 'the rule of recognition is understood as including a stipulation that only rules and institutions meeting these publicness requirements

[179] See, e.g., Cassese, *The Global Polity*; D. Dyzenhaus, 'The Rule of (Administrative) Law in International Law' (2005) 68 *Law and Contemporary Problems* 127.

[180] Kingsbury, 'The Concept of "Law"', 30–1.

immanent in public law (and evidenced through comparative materials) can be regarded as law'.[181]

This reasoning is, however, doubly problematic from a positivist perspective. It undermines the central precept of positivism that what is to count as law depends on what social standards are regarded as authoritative by officials within *that* system, which are then reflected in that system's rule of recognition. It also undermines the precept that is even more central to positivism that the merits or content of a law do not determine its existence. Kingsbury's immanent principles of public law include, inter alia, precepts such as rationality, proportionality, and protection for human rights. These may well be desirable. It is, however, very difficult to maintain that respect for such precepts should by definition be stipulated as a condition precedent to what is to count as a law, while at the same purporting to bring this within a positivist frame that is predicated on the assumption that the merits or content of the law do not determine its existence.

The reality is that much of the imperative underlying the ascription of 'law' to the set of precepts that comprise global administrative law is merit- or content-driven, rather than the result of source-based positivist choices made by the particular legal system. The normative commitments immanent in public law are drawn primarily from national legal systems, and some transnational arenas. They are seen by Kingsbury as 'not simply choices that could have been made

[181] Kingsbury, 'The Concept of "Law"', 30.

or not made in each venue',[182] but as the layers of 'common normative practice thicken' they are argued for through an admixture of comparative study combined with a sense that they are becoming obligatory.[183]

This is reinforced by elaboration of the particular components that comprise the immanent principles of public law, such as legality, rationality, transparency, reason-giving, proportionality, the rule of law and human rights. They are thus regarded because it is felt that they express normative ideals that should be respected, in particular when exercising public power. They have been developed primarily within national legal systems, and applied, to varying degrees, within some international/transnational organizations, and are thus seen as 'intrinsic to public law as generally understood'.[184] The field of global administrative law is predicated on the assumption that such norms should be generally applicable at the global level, more especially as regulatory power in certain areas has moved upwards from the nation state.

Similar normative reasoning is evident in other literature. Thus Armin von Bogdandy argues that any 'domestic principle applicable to domestic public authority provides for a perspective to juridically examine international public authority'.[185] There is therefore 'a presumption that an established principle of domestic public authority raises an issue to

[182] Kingsbury, 'The Concept of "Law"', 30, even though they may have gained their original purchase in this manner.

[183] Kingsbury, 'The Concept of "Law"', 30.

[184] Kingsbury, 'The Concept of "Law"', 30.

[185] Von Bogdandy, 'Sketching a Research Field', 1917.

which the law of an international institution should provide a principled answer'.[186] This may differ from that given in domestic legal orders, but 'the more an international authority impacts an individual, the stronger the assumption is that international principles require legal arrangements which are functionally equivalent to what is to be expected in the domestic realm'.[187] For von Bogdandy, most constituent instruments offer a basis 'from which to argue the applicability of general normative considerations':[188]

> I see much potential for a framing and taming of international institutions based on general principles. I do not know of an international institution today that would simply repudiate the demand for an embedding of its activity in the *rule of law* or in *good governance*; this can be interpreted as an acknowledgement of principles. It is obvious that otherwise the institution would lose legitimacy and endanger its existence.[189]

We see analogous themes in Sabino Cassese's work. He contends that the body of public law developing at the global level requiring, for example, that public authorities provide information to private parties, hearings, reasons and the like draws its inspiration 'from some core principles of administrative law, common to many national legal orders: transparency, the duty to inform and to hear, and judicial review'.[190] He notes

[186] Von Bogdandy, 'Sketching a Research Field', 1917–18.
[187] Von Bogdandy, 'Sketching a Research Field', 1918.
[188] Von Bogdandy, 'Sketching a Research Field', 1926.
[189] Von Bogdandy, 'Sketching a Research Field', 1926. Italics in the original.
[190] Cassese, *The Global Polity*, p. 43.

that an ever-increasing range of powers are transferred from domestic agencies to global authorities, and asks whether those authorities can 'avoid granting private individuals the same rights that they otherwise enjoy in their national legal orders (e.g. to transparency and disclosure of information, to consultation, to a hearing, to receive a reasoned decision, and to judicial review)?'[191]

David Dyzenhaus, writing from a non-positivist perspective, notes that national judges working in a common law frame have not only recognized the legal nature of international law, but have considered it to be 'constitutive of their understanding of the rule of law or legality, so that public officials must comply with international law if they are to abide by the rule of law'.[192] It was therefore incumbent on international bodies that made decisions affecting the interests of individuals to repay the compliment, and put in place 'mechanisms that will help to ensure that their officials comply with the package of rule-of-law controls'.[193]

The realization that a good part of the intellectual justification for the ascription of 'law' within global administrative law is merit- or content-driven, rather than the result of source-based positivist choice, prompts further inquiry as to the perceived legal consequences for non-compliance with law thus conceived. The literature provides no definitive answer to this inquiry, or, put more accurately, one can discern a range of responses.

[191] Cassese, *The Global Polity*, p. 48.
[192] Dyzenhaus, 'The Rule of (Administrative) Law', 128.
[193] Dyzenhaus, 'The Rule of (Administrative) Law', 128.

At one end of the spectrum is the argument made by Kingsbury that compliance with the immanent principles that constitute publicness could be regarded as a condition precedent for a norm to be regarded as law, such that if an international organization wishes or purports to act by and through law it can only do so if it complies with such publicness requirements.[194]

At the other end of the spectrum is the view proffered by Dyzenhaus that if there is non-compliance with norms associated with the rule of law at national level, then 'domestic courts should consider decisions of international bodies suspect, though not necessarily invalid, to the extent that these decisions do not comply with such controls'.[195]

There is a range of intermediate options, which include a liberal reading of such rule-of-law precepts into the constituent documents of the international organization, and encouraging adjudicative bodies of whatever persuasion at the international level to impose and enforce such requirements as a condition for the legality of decisions or rules made by the relevant organization.[196]

We should be mindful, when reflecting on such choices, of the normative connection between the precepts driving global administrative law and the concept of *jus cogens*.[197] The latter captures the idea that certain norms of

[194] Kingsbury, 'The Concept of "Law"', 30–1.

[195] Dyzenhaus, 'The Rule of (Administrative) Law', 128.

[196] Von Bogdandy, 'Sketching a Research Field'; Cassese, *The Global Polity*; Cassese, 'Global Standards'.

[197] A. Verdross, 'Jus Dispositivum and Jus Cogens in International Law' (1966) 60 *American Journal of International Law* 55; L. Hannikainen,

international law are so important that states should not be able to derogate from them by treaty or the like. The very category is expressive of the principle that these norms are so significant that the normal voluntarist principle of international law whereby states are free to make whatever choices they wish on the international plane by treaty is qualified. It finds expression in Article 53 of the Vienna Convention on the Law of Treaties, which states,

> A treaty is void if, at the time of its conclusion, it conflicts with a peremptory norm of general international law. For the purposes of the present Convention, a peremptory norm of general international law is a norm accepted and recognized by the international community of States as a whole as a norm from which no derogation is permitted and which can be modified only by a subsequent norm of general international law having the same character.

There is considerable debate in the literature as to what should count as *jus cogens*, and this uncertainty has been a source of concern from the outset.[198] Article 53 stipulates that the norm must be a norm of general international law, and

Peremptory Norms (Jus Cogens) in International Law: Historical Development, Criteria, Present Status (Helsinki: Lakimiesliiton Kustannus, 1988), A. D'Amato, 'It's a Bird, It's a Plane, It's Jus Cogens' (1990) 6 *Connecticut Journal of International Law* 1; R. Nieto-Navia, 'International Peremptory Norms (*Jus Cogens*) and International Humanitarian Law', available at www.iccnow.org/documents/WritingColombiaEng.pdf, P. Stephan, 'The Political Economy of Jus Cogens' (2011) 44 *Vanderbilt Journal of Transnational Law* 2073.

[198] Nieto-Navia, 'International Peremptory Norms', 9; D'Amato, 'It's a Bird, It's a Plane, It's Jus Cogens'.

be recognized by the international community of states as a whole. Article 53 is complemented by Article 64 of the Vienna Convention, which provides that if a new peremptory norm of international law emerges then any existing treaty that conflicts with this norm becomes void and terminates. The difficult issue is to identify precisely which norms that have this character should be regarded as peremptory, with the consequence that they can only be modified by a subsequent norm of general international law having the same character.

This is exemplified by the *Kadi* litigation. The Court of First Instance held that it could exceptionally engage in indirect review of the Security Council's compliance with *jus cogens* when the Security Council seized the claimant's assets for suspicion of involvement in terrorist activity where the claimant was not afforded an opportunity to be heard prior to the seizure.[199] The ECJ reversed this part of the CFI's judgment, concluding that it was not open to the ECJ to review the Security Council resolution, even on grounds of *jus cogens*, with the consequence that it focused on the validity of the Community measure giving effect to the SC resolution.[200] The ECJ did not, therefore, have to take any view as to whether the right to be heard did or did not fall within *jus cogens* for the purpose of international law. This was a contentious issue. The existence of international

[199] Case T-315/01, *Kadi* v. *Council and Commission* [2005] ECR II-3649, at [230]–[231].

[200] Cases C-402 and 415/05 P, *Yassin Abdullah Kadi and Al Barakaat International Foundation* v. *Council and Commission* [2008] ECR I-6351, at [287]–[288].

human rights law is well established, but which rights fall within *jus cogens*, and the interpretation of any such right on the facts of the case, can be considerably more contentious. Thus the CFI in its indirect review of the Security Council resolution assumed that the right to be heard was in principle within the category of *jus cogens*, although it provided scant detailed analysis to justify this, in part because it concluded that there was no breach of this right on the facts of the case as judged by the precepts of international law.[201] By way of contrast, France, the Netherlands and the UK argued that the right to a hearing and the right to property did not in any event fall within the category of *jus cogens*.[202]

There is undoubtedly some linkage between the arguments underlying global administrative law and those that underpin *jus cogens*, since both partially qualify the normal positivist and voluntarist underpinnings of international law and do so because of the normative importance of the principles at stake. There is, in addition, a more discrete connection insofar as certain of the principles that inform global administrative law concerning human rights are also candidates for inclusion in the category of *jus cogens*, although, as the *Kadi* litigation shows, there can be disagreement as to which rights should be included and as to how they should be interpreted for this purpose.

The linkage between global administrative law and *jus cogens* should nonetheless cause us to be wary before ascribing the peremptory force to the former that Kingsbury

[201] Case T-315/01, *Kadi*, at [259], [261], [268].

[202] Cases C-402 and 415/05 P, *Yassin Abdullah Kadi*, at [265]–[266].

adverts to. The effect of *jus cogens* is to prevent an established norm of international law from being subverted by treaty. The effect of Kingsbury's proposal is more dramatic, since the immanent principles of publicness would operate as a condition precedent for something to be regarded as law at the international level, even though those principles were not embedded in customary international law.

7 Contestable legal issues: global administrative law, pluralism and values

The development of global administrative law has, not surprisingly, generated concerns that this will elevate certain Western principles to prominence at the 'global' level, with a detrimental effect on value-pluralism.

These concerns have been voiced by Carol Harlow, who discerns four sources from which principles of global administrative law might be drawn: ideas of legality and due process developed by national legal systems; values promoted by those attached to ideals of free trade and economic liberalism; good-governance values such as transparency, participation and accountability promoted by bodies such as the World Bank and the IMF; and human rights as a source of administrative law values such as due process.[203] Harlow's analysis is important in pointing to the values and normative choices at stake when deciding what should constitute administrative law.

[203] C. Harlow, 'Global Administrative Law: The Quest for Principles and Values' (2006) 17 *European Journal of International Law* 187.

She poses a serious challenge to the global administrative law project, arguing that it will lead to excessive juridification and the imposition of Western-style principles, with the consequence of unwarranted uniformity and the sacrifice of pluralism. Her thoughts in this respect are captured in the following quotation:

> The underlying argument of this paper has been that a universal set of administrative law principles, difficult in any event to identify, is neither welcome nor particularly desirable; diversity and pluralism are greatly to be preferred. Administrative law is largely a Western construct, taking its shape during the late 19th century as an instrument for the control of public power. Dominated by a philosophy of control, administrative law has played an important part in the struggle for limited government, its core value being conformity to the rule of law.[204]

Similar themes are evident in the work of Daphne Barak-Erez and Oren Perez.[205] They express concern that the norms of global administrative law are not ideologically neutral, but 'are driven by certain perceptions regarding the nature of a good and just society, more specifically by a neo-liberal, capitalist vision'.[206] This ideological dimension is said to be problematic 'because it remains concealed behind a discourse

[204] C. Harlow, 'Global Administrative Law', 207.

[205] D. Barak-Erez and O. Perez, 'Whose Administrative Law Is It Anyway? How Global Norms Reshape the Administrative State' (2013) 46 *Cornell International Law Journal* 455.

[206] Barak-Erez and Perez, 'Whose Administrative Law is it Anyway?', 483.

of rationality and objectivity', with the consequence that this 'ideological bias undermines any attempt to ground the legitimacy of global administrative law on some universal rationality'.[207] Barak-Erez and Perez contend that this neo-liberal, capitalist vision is particularly dominant in the regulatory regimes of the WTO and international investment law, which assumes greater prominence because of the institutional links between the WTO and global standardization regimes:

> Exposing the capitalist undercurrents of the universal administrative law norms highlights the need to develop new institutional venues in which the ideological presuppositions of this new body of law could be subject to public contestation. What is needed, in other words, are institutionalized mechanisms that could support reflexive deliberation regarding these rule-making processes, in a way that will enable the public to unveil and criticize their underlying presuppositions. One way to promote this goal is to create a new global alliance (or alliances) of transnational institutions that pursue non-economic objectives.[208]

These are powerful arguments. There are, however, six related points that should be borne in mind when assessing this pluralist challenge to global administrative law.

First, while it is surely correct that principles of administrative law are not value-free, and that we should be wary about giving canonical status to any particular 'list'

[207] Barak-Erez and Perez, 'Whose Administrative Law is it Anyway?', 483.
[208] Barak-Erez and Perez, 'Whose Administrative Law is it Anyway?', 484.

thereof, we should be equally wary of the opposite assumption, viz. that because certain such principles have been developed in Western legal systems they would not therefore be accepted by those from other cultures. The distinction between historical provenance and current acceptance is important. The fact that ideas of, for example, due process and legality were developed from the seventeenth century in certain Western countries does not mean that they do not now resonate with people from other cultures that have not hitherto shared this development. Thus while we should be duly mindful of difference, we should also be mindful of the too-ready assumption that 'others' do not wish to benefit from the same principles that we take for granted. The latter smacks of colonialism just as much as does the former. My own sense is that the great majority of individuals from whatever society would, for example, value the opportunity to be heard before state action is taken against them, for the same type of instrumental and non-instrumental reasons that led to the recognition of this principle within Western legal regimes.[209]

Second, global regulation is not going to disappear, since the very reasons that have driven its emergence

[209] Hart, *Concept of Law*, pp. 156, 202; J. Rawls, *A Theory of Justice* (Oxford: Oxford University Press, 1973), p. 235; J. Resnick, 'Due Process and Procedural Justice', in J. Pennock and J. Chapman (eds.), *Due Process* (Baden-Baden: Nomos, 1977), p. 217; F. Michelman, 'Formal and Associational Aims in Procedural Due Process', in ibid., Ch. 4; J. Mashaw, *Due Process in the Administrative State* (New Haven: Yale University Press, 1985); D. Galligan, *Due Process and Fair Procedures* (Oxford: Oxford University Press, 1996).

continue to have purchase. Some choice must therefore be made concerning the principles that should be applied to rule making and decision making in the global arena, and inaction in this respect entails a choice just as much as does action. The nature of these choices will be explored more fully in the following chapter, but it is clear that the principles can in any event vary in the manner explicated below. The inevitability of values underlying the principles that should pertain in this area can be acknowledged. There is, in that sense, no neutrality to be had. The world of global rule making and decision making is nonetheless a practical reality. We either make our best efforts to craft a set of principles of administrative law for this reality, or we walk away.

Third, the recognition of global principles of administrative law does not necessitate rigid universality in application across different sites of global governance. It leaves room for pluralism and diversity. We are accustomed to such diversity within national administrative law systems, where the application of the relevant principles is influenced by functional considerations concerning the nature of the subject matter and the type of administrative regime. There is no reason why matters should be different at the global level. A similar point can be made about the danger of juridification. Carol Harlow is right to warn us of this. The existence of this danger underlies debates in national legal systems about the optimal balance of legal and political methods of holding government to account. These debates should be undertaken openly in relation to the global level. It should not be assumed that formal law is always the best in this respect, but the global administrative law project is not predicated on that assumption.

Fourth, we need to tread carefully when thinking about the alleged ideological bias of global administrative law. The substantive regulatory regimes that exist at the global level will be devised to serve certain goals, whether those are free trade, health protection, Internet management, environmental protection or banking security. It is therefore inevitable that every regulatory regime will embody certain values, and this is as true at the national or regional level as at the global. It follows that the substantive tools of administrative law, such as rationality or proportionality review, will necessarily be interpreted in the context of the values of that particular regulatory regime. This does not in itself betoken any bias built into the tools of global administrative law, or in the way in which they are applied. To the contrary, it reflects the fact that the rationality or proportionality of administrative action must necessarily be determined taking into account the constituent documents of that organization and the objectives specified therein. Those values will shape any evaluation of the administration's reasoning process, and the manner in which it weighed the relevant considerations, in order to determine whether the resulting decision was rational or proportionate. To apply these substantive controls without taking cognizance of such objectives and values would render the resultant judicial decision illegitimate.

Fifth, talk of ideological bias might mean a critique to the effect that global regulatory regimes are predicated too greatly on liberal capitalist values, at the expense of non-economic objectives. This is clearly a concern voiced by Barak-Erez and Perez. Analogous concerns have been voiced by others. Richard Stewart addresses the problem of disregard that pertains within global regulation, whereby weaker interests, including non-economic interests, can be disregarded in the global regulatory process.[210] Eyal Benvenisti and George Downs have argued that the relative dominance of national executives at the global regulatory level, and the relative exclusion of national legislatures, has exacerbated the tendency of well-organized interests to dominate, to the disadvantage of more diffuse interests.[211] They are perfectly right to raise such concerns, and debate should properly be had about the background values underlying regulatory intervention at the global level, just as much as at the national level, or the regional level.[212] The extent of the causal connection between the very fact of regulation at the global level and the increased prevalence of a neo-liberal capitalist vision of a good society raises issues that cannot be explored here. Whatsoever the answer is, it is difficult to argue that we would be better off if the precepts of global administrative law were not applicable to bodies at the global level, including those that are driven by

[210] Stewart, 'Remedying Disregard'.

[211] E. Benvenisti and G. Downs, 'The Empire's New Clothes: Political Economy and the Fragmentation of International Law' (2007) 60 *Stanford Law Review* 595.

[212] See, e.g., Slaughter, *A New World Order*, pp. 248–9, who argues for a concept of 'legitimate difference', which entails the idea that difference of view 'reflects a desirable diversity of ideas about how to order an economy or society', with willingness to reconsider how an issue is dealt with at home, and respect different choices made by other societies. Thus legitimate difference 'enshrines pluralism as a basis for, rather than a bar to regulatory cooperation, leaving open the possibility of further convergence between legal systems in the form of mutual recognition or even harmonization, but not requiring it'.

a neo-liberal agenda. The fact that a commentator might prefer a different set of values to underlie a particular regulatory regime is surely no reason to conclude against the application of controls designed to enhance the accountability of that body as presently configured, more especially if those precepts include measures designed to alleviate the problem of disregard of disadvantaged interests.[213]

Sixth and finally, the alternative sense of ideological bias might mean that the adjudicatory arm of a global organization is interpreting the rationality or proportionality constraints on discretionary power too heavily in favour of, for example, a free-market agenda, in circumstances where this is not necessitated by the constituent documents, which could, properly construed, allow greater balance between pursuit of economic and non-economic factors. This is certainly possible. We should be alive to the danger. We should scrutinize decisions with care in order to determine whether it has occurred. This problem is, however, endemic within all regimes of administrative law, whether at national, regional or global level. There is no reason why it is more likely to occur at the global level, nor is there any reason why it is inherent in the idea of global administrative law.

8 Contestable legal issues: global administrative law, pluralism and hierarchy

Pluralism plays a different role in the insightful work of Nico Krisch, who argues for a pluralist conception of postnational

[213] Stewart, 'Remedying Disregard'.

administrative law.[214] He regards the issue of to whom global governance should be accountable as contestable, and contrasts this with the unitary, hierarchical foundations of national administrative law. By way of contrast, global regulation is faced by challenges from domestic courts, international civil society, and competing international regimes, all of which are relatively independent.[215] For Krisch this pluralist dimension distinguishes it from national administrative law and is something to be lauded. It allows room for legitimate diversity and is to be preferred to attempts to constitutionalize the global political order 'by forcing it into a coherent unified framework'.[216] In national administrative law, accountability is perceived ultimately in relation to the people, thereby reflecting 'the aspiration to coherence, unity and normative hierarchy characteristic of modern constitutionalism'.[217]

At the global level the issue is more contested and Krisch identifies three possible accountability constituencies in this regard: the national, the international and the cosmopolitan. He regards this contestation as 'written into the institutional structures of global governance and global administrative law',[218] and exemplifies it through various

[214] Krisch, *Beyond Constitutionalism*; N. Krisch, 'The Pluralism of Global Administrative Law' (2006) 17 *European Journal of International Law* 247; N. Krisch, 'The Case for Pluralism in Postnational Law', LSE, Law, Society and Economy Working Papers 12/2009.

[215] Krisch, 'The Pluralism of Global Administrative Law', 248.

[216] Krisch, 'The Pluralism of Global Administrative Law', 248, 256.

[217] Krisch, 'The Pluralism of Global Administrative Law', 253.

[218] Krisch, 'The Pluralism of Global Administrative Law', 256.

case studies.[219] Thus in the case study of regulation of genetically modified organisms (GMOs) there is substantive disagreement concerning the optimal approach to the regulation of GMOs, and this then plays out in conflict between the principal institutional actors, these being the EU and the WTO, with the Codex Alimentarius Commission and the Cartagena Protocol on Biosafety also playing a significant role.

The resultant regulatory landscape is shaped by the interaction between such bodies, and their mutual accommodation, rather than by claims to hierarchical superiority. This pluralist interplay is regarded as preferable to other forms of accommodation, such as consociationalism, and Krisch finds the normative foundations of pluralism in ideas of associations and associational democracy, drawing on the work of those such as Maitland, Figgis and Laski, and more recent scholarship by writers such as Hirst, Galston and Kukathas.[220]

[219] Krisch, *Beyond Constitutionalism*, Chs. 3–6.

[220] *The Collected Papers of William Maitland* (ed. H.A.L. Fisher) (Cambridge: Cambridge University Press, 1911); J.N. Figgis, *Churches in the Modern State* (London: Longmans, 1913); D. Nicholls, *The Pluralist State: The Political Ideas of J.N. Figgis and His Contemporaries* (London: MacMillan, 2nd ed., 1994); H.J. Laski, *Studies in the Problem of Sovereignty* (New Haven: Yale University Press, 1917); H.J. Laski, *Authority in the Modern State* (New Haven: Yale University Press, 1919); P.Q. Hirst (ed.), *The Pluralist Theory of the State: Political Writings of G.D.H. Cole, J.N. Figgis and H.J. Laski* (London: Routledge, 1989); W.A. Galston, *Liberal Pluralism: The Implications of Value Pluralism for Political Theory and Practice* (Cambridge: Cambridge University Press, 2002); C. Kukathas, *The Liberal Archipelago: A Theory of Diversity and Freedom* (Oxford: Oxford University Press, 2003).

This is an interesting thesis, but it is nonetheless contestable in terms of the contrast drawn between national and global administrative law, and how we perceive of legitimacy within the latter, which will be considered in turn. The contrast drawn by Krisch between the unitary, hierarchical conception of national administrative law, as compared with the pluralist conception of its global cousin, is too stark.[221] The national accountability constituency may in some ultimate sense be the people, but this conceals as much as it reveals. It underplays the contestation within national administrative law systems concerning the plurality of ways in which this might be conceived and realized. Note, in this respect, the diverse ways in which this can be manifest.

It may play out institutionally, as exemplified by the not infrequent instances in which more than one domestic agency has authority over a particular problem – whether that be genetically modified organisms, environmental standards or banking supervision – and the respective agencies differ markedly as to how the issue should be resolved.[222] There may be scant, if any, formal guidance or hierarchy between them, and the outcome will be determined by the normal admixture of power, law and political status, not very

[221] For related arguments, see A. Stone Sweet, 'The Structure of Constitutional Pluralism: Review of Nico Krisch, 'Beyond Constitutionalism: The Pluralist Structure of Post-national Law' (2013) 11 *International Journal of Constitutional Law* 491; G. Shaffer, 'A Transnational Take on Krisch's Postnational Pluralist Order' (2012) 23 *European Journal of International Law* 565.

[222] See, e.g., P.-H. Verdier, 'Transnational Regulatory Networks and Their Limits' (2009) 34 *Yale Journal of International Law* 113, at 128–9.

different from that which Krisch describes in the global sphere. The pluralist dimension within national administrative law may play out in contestation as to the optimal mix of political and legal techniques through which to secure the ultimate accountability to the 'people', which is one reading of the debate between legal and political constitutionalists in the UK.[223]

The pluralist dimension within administrative law is manifest yet again in the very literature on which Krisch draws concerning associations. The objective of writers such as Laski, Figgis and Cole was to challenge the unitary conception of the state and the people that informed much prior writing, such as that of Austin and Dicey,[224] and to proffer in its place argument for a pluralist vision of society, which denied that that there was some single hierarchical conception of the good for the people as a whole. The pluralists revealed the historical foundations of the unitary view of the state. The idea that sovereignty was indivisible appeared initially in the writings of, among others, Hobbes as a defence against anarchy.[225] The state must be all-powerful in order to prevent a breakdown in society. This political justification for the unitary state was unsurprising given the turmoil that occurred in the English Civil War. This reasoning was

[223] See above, Ch. 2.

[224] J. Austin, *The Province of Jurisprudence Determined* (ed. W. Rumble) (Cambridge: Cambridge University Press, 1995); A.V. Dicey, *An Introduction to the Study of the Law of the Constitution* (ed. E.C.S. Wade) (London: MacMillan, 1959).

[225] T. Hobbes, *Leviathan* (ed. R. Tuck) (Cambridge: Cambridge University Press, 1991).

reinforced in the nineteenth century by jurists like Austin who argued that it was simply not possible to have a sovereign whose power was limited. Dicey built on Austin. In a democracy where the people elected MPs who represented their views and controlled the executive, it was 'right' that this central power should be all-embracing. The pluralists challenged the unitary view in descriptive and prescriptive terms. In descriptive terms, they contested the idea that all public power was wielded by the state, pointing to pressure groups that shaped state action, and religious, economic and social associations that exercised authority. In prescriptive terms, group power was applauded rather than condemned. The all-powerful unitary state was dangerous. Liberty was best preserved by the presence of groups within the state to which the individual could owe allegiance. Decentralization and the preservation of group autonomy were to be valued. This vision of political pluralism was complemented by a concern with the social and economic conditions within the state. There was a strong belief that political liberty was closely linked with social and economic equality.

The contrast drawn by Krisch between national and global administrative law is therefore too stark. His thesis also raises intriguing issues as to how we think about legitimacy in the context of global administrative law. The implications for output are clear, those for input less so.

By output I mean the conclusions that flow from an attachment to the pluralist vision. This entails for Krisch heterarchy rather than hierarchy, mutual accommodation rather than supremacy of a single vision, contestation rather than the inexorable triumph of an established order, and multiple voices rather than a single locus of representation. Krisch makes a plausible empirical case for this vision of the global order through the case studies. Indeed, in certain respects the positive dimension to the thesis could be presented more forcefully. We do not have the structures through which a hierarchical, top-down regime could operate in the global sphere. Given that this is so, some form of mutual accommodation broadly conceived between the respective institutional players with differing agendas in order to determine the regulatory outcome in a particular area should be expected. It should not come as a surprise. Krisch also advances normative arguments in favour of this outcome,[226] which cannot be examined here.

By input I mean the implications of the thesis for the way in which we think about and apply the tenets of global administrative law. We have already seen that these are concepts such as transparency, participation, reasoned decision, legality and effective review of the rules and decisions thus made.[227] Now it is true that the 'output' dimension to the thesis may, for example, help to explain judicial inclination to craft judgments that take account of the views of players in other institutions, as evidenced by decisions of the respective adjudicative organs in the EU and the WTO.[228] The pluralist

[226] Krisch, *Beyond Constitutionalism*, Chs. 2–3, 7–8.

[227] See, e.g., Kingsbury, Krisch and Stewart, 'Global Administrative Law', 17, 28, 34–8.

[228] G. Shaffer, *Defending Interests: Public–Private Partnerships in WTO Litigation* (Washington, DC: Brookings Institution Press, 2003); M. Pollack and G. Shaffer, *Transatlantic Governance in the Global Economy* (Oxford: Rowman and Littlefield, 2001).

thesis can 'recognize' this when it has occurred. It provides, however, little *ex ante* guidance as to whether it will occur, or more importantly the extent to which it should occur. Thus in the context of differing perspectives on GMOs, and more generally about the precautionary principle,[229] the overall regulatory landscape still reveals significant differences of view, which have not been transcended by the mutual accommodation that has taken place. There are, moreover, plenty of instances in relation to EU decision making where such accommodation is scant or non-existent. The positive and normative reality is that mutual accommodation of differing views is a prima facie, not an absolute, good. The pluralist thesis gives little by way of *ex ante* guidance as to whether and how far it should be taken into account by judicial organs exercising their role of judicial review within the schema of global administrative law.

[229] E. Fisher, 'Precaution, Precaution Everywhere: Developing a "Common Understanding" of the Precautionary Principle in the European Community' (2002) 9 *Maastricht Journal of European and Comparative Law* 7; C. Sunstein, *Risk and Reason: Safety, Law, and the Environment* (Cambridge: Cambridge University Press, 2002); G. Majone, 'What Price Safety? The Precautionary Principle and Its Policy Implications' (2002) 40 *Journal of Common Market Studies* 89; C. Sunstein, 'Beyond the Precautionary Principle' (2003) 151 *University of Pennsylvania Law Rev* 1003; I. Forrester, 'The Dangers of Too Much Precaution', in M. Hoskins and W. Robinson (eds.), *A True European: Essays for Judge David Edward* (Oxford: Hart, 2003), Ch. 16; Jose Luis da Cruz Vilaca, 'The Precautionary Principle in EC Law' (2004) 10 *European Public Law* 369; G. Marchant and K. Mossman, *Arbitrary and Capricious: The Precautionary Principle in the European Union Courts* (Washington, DC: AEI Press, 2004).

This is a fortiori the case in relation to other tenets of global administrative law, such as transparency and participation. Consider the example of rule making in relation to GMOs. We wish to ensure that such rules as made by the EU are legitimate. We must perforce begin with the principles concerning transparency, legislative scrutiny, comitology and the like that are extant at any point in time. We may then ask whether those principles could be improved by, for example, provision of greater transparency or legally enforceable participation rights, and we make this determination in relation to the particular institutional attributes of the EU. We may also ask how such principles should be applied and question the desired content of the resulting rules on GMOs. Pluralism contains scant guidance as to whether, and if so to what extent, this decision-making process and outcome should be 'other-regarding', in the sense of taking into account or accommodating diverse views from institutional players outside the EU. We may be able to recognize this when it has occurred, but it furnishes little to indicate whether it will or should occur, more especially given that there will inevitably be a plethora of differing views within the EU that jostle for influence on the outcome.

9 Conclusion

The scholarship on global administrative law has developed very considerably in the new millennium, notwithstanding earlier literature that touched on the area. The discussion has been enriched with insights drawn from related disciplines such as political science and international relations, more especially since scholars from these disciplines have explored the causes and consequences of global governance. It is not surprising that increased legal attention to global regulation broadly conceived should have generated differences concerning issues that constitute the very foundations of the subject. This chapter has explored four such issues, and debate on such matters will doubtless continue. The discussion in the next chapter turns to the challenges faced by global administrative law.

6

Global administrative law

Challenges

1 Introduction

The previous chapter considered the foundations of global administrative law;[1] the present chapter addresses the

[1] There is a large and growing literature. A bibliography can be found at www.iilj.org/gal/default.asp. There have been a number of symposia devoted to the topic: *Law and Contemporary Problems* (2005), *New York University Journal of International Law and Policy* (2005), *European Journal of International Law* (2006), *German Law Journal* (2008) and *International Organizations Law Review* (2009). The following provide valuable analyses of the field: S. Shapiro, 'International Trade Agreements, Regulatory Protection and Public Accountability' (2002) 54 *Administrative Law Review* 415; G. della Cananea, 'Beyond the State: The Europeanization and Globalization of Procedural Administrative Law' (2003) 9 *European Public Law* 563; R. Stewart, 'Administrative Law in the Twenty-First Century' (2003) 78 *New York University Law Review* 437; A. Aman, 'Globalization, Democracy and the Need for a New Administrative Law' (2003) 10 *Indiana Journal of Global Legal Studies* 125; S. Cassese, 'Administrative Law without the State? The Challenge of Global Regulation' (2005) 37 *New York University Journal of International Law and Policy* 663; B. Kingsbury, N. Krisch, R. Stewart, 'The Emergence of Global Administrative Law' (2005) 68 *Law and Contemporary Problems* 15; R. Stewart, 'US Administrative Law: A Model for Global Administrative Law?' (2005) 68 *Law and Contemporary Problems* 63; S. Cassese, 'Global Standards for National Administrative Procedure' (2005) 68 *Law and Contemporary Problems* 109; D. Esty, 'Good Governance at the Supranational Scale: Globalizing Administrative Law' (2006) 115 *Yale Law Journal* 1490; N. Krisch and B. Kingsbury, 'Introduction: Global Governance and Global Administrative Law

challenges posed by this development, distinguishing between challenges of a horizontal and a vertical nature.

The horizontal challenge builds on existing scholarship by examining the more particular doctrinal features that are commonly said to comprise global administrative law, and the difficulties of applying these at the global level. Benedict Kingsbury, Nico Krisch and Richard Stewart defined these essential features as

> the mechanisms, principles, practices, and supporting social understandings that promote or otherwise affect the

in the International Legal Order' (2006) 17 *European Journal of International Law* 1; A. von Bogdandy, P. Dann and M. Goldmann, 'Developing the Publicness of Public International Law: Towards a Legal Framework for Global Governance Activities' (2008) 9 *German Law Journal* 1375; A. von Bogdandy and P. Dann, 'International Composite Administration: Conceptualizing Multi-level and Network Aspects in the Exercise of International Public Authority' (2008) 9 *German Law Journal* 2013; B. Kingsbury and L. Casini, 'Global Administrative Law Dimensions of International Organizations Law' (2009) 6 *International Organizations Law Review* 319; Anthony et al., *Values in Global Administrative Law*; S. Cassese, B. Carotti, L. Casini, E. Cavalieri and E. MacDonald, with the collaboration of M. Macchia and M. Savino, *Global Administrative Law: The Casebook* (IRPA/IILJ, 3rd ed., 2012); S. Cassese, *The Global Polity: Global Dimensions of Democracy and the Rule of Law* (Sevilla: Global Law Press, 2012); R. Stewart, 'Remedying Disregard in Global Regulatory Governance: Accountability, Participation, and Responsiveness' (2014) 108 *American Journal of International Law* 211; G. della Cananea, *Due Process of Law beyond the State* (Oxford: Oxford University Press, 2015); S. Cassese (ed.), *Global Administrative Law, A Research Handbook* (Cheltenham: Elgar, 2015).

> accountability of global administrative bodies,[2] in particular by ensuring they meet adequate standards of transparency, participation, reasoned decision, and legality, and by providing effective review of the rules and decisions they make.[3]

Similar doctrinal features are found in the work of other authors, notwithstanding differences of nuance and degree.[4] Commentators generally agree that the intellectual origin of these doctrinal principles lies in national administrative law, while at the same time stressing that their application to global governance poses particular problems, with the consequence that domestic public law precepts cannot simply be cut and pasted onto the global level. We need, however, to press further to understand more precisely how administrative decision making and rule making are legitimated at national level, and the difficulties of transposing such techniques to the global sphere. This will in turn shed light on how these difficulties may be surmounted, or how they may be alleviated in other ways.

[2] Kingsbury, Krisch and Stewart, 'Global Administrative Law', 17, define these to include 'formal intergovernmental regulatory bodies, informal intergovernmental regulatory networks and coordination arrangements, national regulatory bodies operating with reference to an international intergovernmental regime, hybrid public–private regulatory bodies, and some private regulatory bodies exercising transnational governance functions of particular public significance.'

[3] Kingsbury, Krisch and Stewart, 'Global Administrative Law', 17.

[4] See, e.g., Cassese, *The Global Polity*; Esty, 'Good Governance at the Supranational Scale'; A.-M. Slaughter, *A New World Order* (Princeton: Princeton University Press, 2004); von Bogdandy, Dann and Goldmann, 'Developing the Publicness of Public International Law'.

This is followed by discussion of the vertical challenges, which take the form of interaction between legal orders. This is evident in relation to individual decisions made at the global level, which are felt to be deficient when judged in terms of administrative law precepts that pertain at the national and regional levels. The relationship between legal orders also covers the broader impact of the transfer of regulatory power to the global level, and the impact that this has on regulatory regimes and administrative law at the national and EU levels.

2 Horizontal challenge: fashioning doctrine for the global level

The challenge is to develop principles of public law for the global level. The principles commonly listed in this respect have, not surprisingly, been drawn from national traditions of administrative law, although there is no reason why entirely new concepts could not be fashioned. However, insofar as the principles of global administrative law are drawn from national legal systems, we need to understand their conceptual and political foundations, in order thereby to comprehend the difficulties of applying them at the global level, and the ways in which they might be alleviated.

Administration in nation states is rendered accountable and legitimated in three principal ways: through legislative oversight/imprimatur from the top, through legislative imprimatur combined with executive authority and technocratic expertise, or through participation from the bottom by input from those affected. A national system may use more than one such technique. The ensuing discussion considers the rationale, the mode of delivery and the role of the courts in relation to each method of securing accountability, and examines the difficulties of applying such concepts at the global level.

(a) *National legitimation from the top: democracy, legislation and delegation*

(i) Rationale

There are inevitably differences in conceptions of administration across nation states, but there are nonetheless common precepts. Thus there is commonly a hierarchy of norms, with the constitution at the apex, followed by primary legislation and a third tier comprising administrative norms, which may be either individualized decisions or rules of a legislative nature. It is axiomatic that there is a distinction to be drawn between primary legislation and secondary norms, whether the latter take the form of administrative decisions or rules. It is also axiomatic to this schema in democratic states that the legislature, legitimated by the vote in accord with regular elections under a democratic franchise, will enact the primary legislation and decide what power should be given to the administration. The executive may, in certain national systems, also have certain inherent powers, including powers of an administrative nature.[5]

[5] P. Craig and A. Tomkins (eds.), *The Executive and Public Law: Power and Accountability in Comparative Perspective* (Oxford: Oxford University Press, 2005).

The normal picture is nonetheless one in which most administrative power in the modern day is accorded by statute. The legislature will decide that there should, for example, be a licensing regime for access to a certain profession, that provision should be made for various kinds of social assistance, that markets should be liberalized subject to regulatory oversight, that planning controls should be exercised at local level and that corporate behaviour should be controlled so as to prevent anti-competitive practices. This is the familiar terrain within which administrative determinations are made, often pursuant to discretionary power set out in the primary legislation. The very existence of the administrative power is therefore normally legitimated by the democratic process, through which the legislature delegates such power to an administrative body to carry out the tasks assigned to it.

The administrative power may be exercised through individualized decision or through rules made by the administration, or an admixture of the two. The factors that affect this choice are well known.[6] Thus rule making may be

[6] D. Shapiro, 'The Choice of Rulemaking or Adjudication in the Development of Administrative Policy' (1965) 78 *Harvard Law Review* 921; K.C. Davis, *Discretionary Justice: A Preliminary Inquiry* (Baton Rouge: Louisiana State University Press, 1969); G. Robinson, 'The Making of Administrative Policy: Another Look at Rule-Making and Adjudication and Administrative Procedures Reform' (1970) 118 *University of Pennsylvania Law Review* 485; J. Jowell, *Law and Bureaucracy: Administrative Discretion and the Limits of Legal Action* (New York: Dunellen, 1975); D. Galligan, 'The Nature and Function of Policy within Discretionary Power' [1976] *Public Law* 332; R. Baldwin and K. Hawkins, 'Discretionary Justice: Davis Reconsidered' [1984] *Public Law* 570.

preferred in circumstances of mass administrative justice. In such cases, justice, in terms of like cases being treated alike, combines with efficiency, in terms of not wishing each administrator to rethink the wheel, and favours rules over individualized determinations. Rules may also be favoured where there is a high premium on certainty and on sending a clear message to affected parties as to what constitutes allowable behaviour. Individualized determinations may, by way of contrast, be preferred where the administration is still feeling its way and is not yet confident enough to embody its strategy within rules, or where the subject matter is inherently ill-suited to rule-like formulation.

It is generally accepted that there has to be some delegation of rule-making power to the administration. The legislature may not be able to foresee all ramifications of the legislation when the initial statute is made. It may have neither the time nor the expertise to address all the issues in the original legislation. The measures consequential to the original statute may have to be passed expeditiously, which precludes the use of primary legislation.

It is, however, also accepted that such rule-making power must be subject to control in order to validate 'the exercise of essentially legislative powers that do not enjoy the formal legitimation of one-person one-vote election'.[7] The same theme is evident in the Report of the European Parliament on the power of legislative delegation, where the premise throughout was that delegation was a delicate

[7] R. Stewart, 'The Reformation of American Administrative Law' (1975) 88 *Harvard Law Review* 1667, at 1668.

operation in which the Commission was instructed to exercise a power, which was intrinsic to the legislator's own role.[8] Rules made by the administration were legislative in nature and warranted oversight by the parent legislature.

The need for legislative oversight is heightened because there is no simple divide between primary legislation, which deals with all points of principle, and secondary rules that address insignificant points of detail. There is no simple dichotomy between principle and detail. There is no ready equation between detail and absence of political controversy. This is so even if a legal system uses a non-delegation doctrine to ensure that the essential principles are laid down in the primary statute to guide the framing of the rules made by the executive or administration. It does not mean that the rules made pursuant to the primary legislation will thereby be self-executing, politically uncontroversial or merely technical.

The preceding rationale for legislative oversight is not shared by all national legal systems. Thus in some systems the constitution may accord a separate rule-making competence to the executive in its own right and protect this from encroachment by the legislature. In other systems the courts may interpret the constitution so as to preclude such control being exercised by one constituent branch of the legislature.[9]

[8] Committee on Legal Affairs, On the Power of Legislative Delegation, A-7 0110/2010, Rapporteur J. Sjazer, at pp. 3, 11–12.

[9] *Immigration and Naturalization Service* v. *Chadha* 462 US 919 (1983).

(ii) Legal and political control

There is considerable choice as to the form of legislative oversight for those systems that regard this as integral to control over rule making. There is a spectrum in this respect.

At one end of the spectrum there may be legal systems where the principal focus is on legislative specification of the principles governing regulation. The non-delegation doctrine is accorded pride of place, the assumption being that if it is complied with there should be little by way of legislative scrutiny of particular rules made by an agency or the administration.

As we move along the spectrum we encounter legal regimes in which deployment of the non-delegation doctrine is accompanied by an explicit power of legislative veto over agency rules, this being exercised by the constituent bodies of the legislature. There may, however, be no explicit power to amend the contested rule.[10] Political reality may nevertheless play out such that the legislature arrogates to itself a de facto power of amendment through threat of the veto, or the legislature may alternatively remain limited to its de jure veto power.

At the other end of the spectrum the legislature may possess, in addition to the power/obligation flowing from the non-delegation doctrine, and in addition to a legislative veto, an explicit power to amend the rule placed before it. In such a regime the legislative power will be further enhanced if the

[10] See, e.g., in relation to the EU, Art. 290 TFEU; in relation to the UK, P. Craig, *Administrative Law* (London: Sweet & Maxwell, 7th ed., 2012), Ch. 15.

rule has to be laid in draft and is subject to legislative approval before it becomes law. The alternative, which places the legislature in a relatively weaker position, is for the rule to become law unless the legislature decides to take action.[11] Some legal systems may use both techniques, the choice between them depending on the importance of the rule.[12]

(iii) Courts

The courts have a role to play in relation to each mode of legitimation. Four distinct, albeit related, roles can be identified in relation to legitimation from the top, although, as will be evident, some are applicable to individualized decision making and rule making, and some only to the latter.

First, it will be for the courts to decide whether the agency has remained within the confines of the power that it has been delegated. Thus the law reports are replete with challenges to exercise of agency power, where the allegation is that the agency has overstepped the legal bounds of the power delegated to it, and this is so irrespective of whether the power was exercised through an individual decision or through the making of a rule. The courts will, in addition, commonly exercise some control over the factual basis on which the challenged norm was made, and will be zealous to ensure that due process was observed, at least in relation to individualized adjudication. They will, moreover, exercise control over the substance of the decision reached, whether

[11] See, e.g., Art. 290 TFEU.

[12] See, e.g., Craig, *Administrative Law*, Ch. 15.

this takes the form of a decision or a rule, with controls cast in terms of rationality or proportionality commonly employed as a check on discretionary power.

Second, the courts will police application of the non-delegation doctrine, where compliance is a condition precedent for the legality of rule-making power. How intensively they do this is a matter of judicial choice. The US courts have, for example, shown little appetite for vigorous enforcement of the US non-delegation doctrine.[13] The same disinclination is evident in the ECJ's approach, which in the years prior to the Lisbon Treaty deployed what was in effect a non-delegation doctrine with a very light touch.[14] It remains to be seen whether this changes in the post-Lisbon world of Article 290 TFEU.

Third, the courts will decide whether the constitution mandates legislative scrutiny of rules made by the administration, or alternatively whether it allows scrutiny, and if so the terms on which it should be exercised. Much turns in this respect on the particular national constitution, and on the approach to constitutional interpretation adopted by the national supreme or constitutional court.[15]

Finally, the courts will adjudicate on disputes concerning the details of any system of legislative oversight that is laid down in the constitution or founding treaty. Thus it will,

[13] A. Aman and W. Mayton, *Administrative Law* (St Paul, MN: West Publishing, 3rd ed., 2014).

[14] Case C-156/93, *European Parliament* v. *Commission* [1995] ECR I-2019; Case C-417/93, *European Parliament* v. *Council* [1995] ECR I-1185.

[15] See, e.g., *Immigration and Naturalization Service* v. *Chadha* 462 US 919 (1983).

for example, be for the ECJ to settle disputes concerning the system of legislative oversight laid down in Article 290 TFEU, and to decide on the boundaries between delegated and implementing acts in Articles 290 and 291 TFEU.

(b) *Global legitimation from the top: norms, consent and delegation*

(i) The problem

The preceding discussion has articulated some central features of legitimation of administrative norms from the top in nation states through democracy, legislation and delegation. We now consider how far such ideas can be applied to the world of global governance. The bodies that operate at the global level vary significantly, in terms of institutional structure, degree of formality, legal status and the like. This can be accepted, but it would nonetheless be regrettable if the justified concern for heterogeneity were to confine analysis to single instances and preclude more general observations. Thus, with the preceding cautionary notes in mind, we can consider how far the precepts concerning legitimation by legislative scrutiny can apply to the world of global governance.

The difficulties in this respect are significant, since most sites of governance beyond the state have no established legislature that is legitimated by democratic vote. There are some exceptional instances, the EU being an example in this regard. Most international or transnational organizations do not have a legislature directly elected by popular franchise, and this is a fortiori the case for the norms that emerge from horizontal interchange between different entities at the international level.

The preceding difficulty is compounded by the fact that there will often be no divide between legislative and executive power of the kind commonly found in national systems. If there is no elected legislature the divide between legislative and executive power is more difficult to maintain, and even if a body can be identified as the legislature, irrespective of whether it is elected by the people, there is no reason why the divide between its power and that of a body that might be regarded as the executive should replicate with exactitude that with which we are familiar in national law. The significance of these differences between the national and global levels cannot be underestimated when considering the legitimation of administrative power from the top. There are, however, two ways forward.

(ii) Delegation and consensual validation

It would be too hasty to conclude that validation from the top has no relevance to the global arena, simply because the relevant organization has no democratically elected legislature. Such legitimation is predicated at the most basic level on the assumption that power to make decisions or rules should receive the imprimatur of the institution within the overall organization that has the requisite authority to make the delegation. It is important, therefore, to disaggregate two features of legitimation from the top: delegation and the fact that the delegation is made by a democratically elected body. The absence of the latter does not remove the importance of the former, although it modifies its application.

In the simplest, and what may still be the paradigm, case at the global level, the foundation for the making of further administrative decisions or rules will come from, or can be traced back to, the treaty that provides the foundation for that international institution. State consent in the classic international law sense will therefore underpin the treaty and the delegation of power made pursuant to it.[16] That is equally true where the parties are not states, but national regulatory institutions. The agreement between such bodies will provide the conceptual foundation for the exercise of power. The preceding point can be put in another way. Notwithstanding the fact that most international organizations do not have a democratically elected legislature, we would still expect that power to make decisions or rules of an administrative nature can be traced back to some valid source, the foundation for the delegation of power, and this will often reside in the primary treaty or agreement validated by consent of the signatory parties.

It may be that delegation validated in this manner is more general or open-textured by way of comparison with that in nation states when administrative power is exercised pursuant to specific legislation. Such primary legislation will commonly set out the regulatory schema applicable to, for example, banking, utilities, or telecommunications. It will

[16] See J.H.H. Weiler, 'The Geology of International Law: Governance, Democracy and Legitimacy' (2004) 64 *Zeitschrift für ausländisches öffentliches Recht und Völkerrecht* 547, at 548, for the linkage between state consent and sovereign equality, and the difference between such precepts and that of democracy.

stipulate the administrative body to implement the schema and its powers to make decisions and/or rules. In the global arena, by way of contrast, the empowering treaty may be a good deal less specific as to the contours of power that can be exercised by a body pursuant to the treaty, with the consequence that any delegation will be less specific. Much will, however, depend on the nature of the particular treaty, and how detailed it is concerning the regulatory objectives that it is designed to achieve.

It may also be the case that even where there is a valid delegation at the global level there is a power imbalance between the 'agent' to which power is delegated and the 'principal' that is responsible for the formal delegation. Other things being equal, the stronger the 'agent', and the more diffuse the 'principal' from which the authority emanates, the more difficult will it be for the latter to exert meaningful control over the former, more especially if the constituent treaty rules say little about the controls that can be exercised. The difficulty of the principal securing sufficient control over the agent is not, however, confined to the global arena. To the contrary, there is a voluminous literature about such principal–agent relations at national and regional levels,[17]

[17] See, e.g, M. Thatcher and A. Stone Sweet (eds.), *The Politics of Delegation: Non-majoritarian Institutions in Europe* (London: Frank Cass, 2003); M. Pollack, *The Engines of European Integration: Delegation, Agency and Agenda-Setting in the EU* (Oxford: Oxford University Press, 2003); D. Hawkins, D. Lake, D. Nielsen and M. Tierney (eds.), *Delegation and Agency in International Organizations* (Cambridge: Cambridge University Press, 2006); C. Donnelly, *Delegation of Governmental Power*

and there is no reason to conclude that these problems are necessarily more serious at the global level.

Delegation as conceived above is not a sufficient condition for the accountability or legitimacy of administrative decisions or rules, which is why the preceding discussion has been cast in terms of validation rather than legitimation. Space precludes detailed discussion of legitimacy as it pertains to global governance institutions.[18] Suffice it to say for the present that, as Daniel Bodansky notes,[19] legitimate authority in this context normally connotes justified authority, with the requisite justification being sought on grounds such as democracy, legality or rationality. The legitimacy is, moreover, normally conceived as operating independently of content, in the sense that authority can be perceived to be legitimate even if one disagrees with a particular rule made in exercise of that legitimate authority.[20] Allen Buchanan and Robert Keohane have, however, forcefully argued that while state consent

to Private Parties: A Comparative Perspective (Oxford: Oxford University Press, 2007).

[18] See, e.g., D. Bodansky, 'The Legitimacy of International Governance: A Coming Challenge for International Environmental Law' (1999) 93 *American Journal of International Law* 596; A. Buchanan and R. Keohane, 'The Legitimacy of Global Governance Institutions' (2006) 20 *Ethics and International Affairs* 405. See, more generally, R. Wolfrum and V. Roeben (eds.), *Legitimacy in International Law* (Berlin: Springer, 2008). J. Brunnée and S. Toope, *Legitimacy and Legality in International Law: An Interactional Account* (Cambridge: Cambridge University Press, 2010).

[19] Bodansky, 'Legitimacy of International Governance', 601.

[20] Bodansky, 'Legitimacy of International Governance', 602; Buchanan and Keohane, 'Legitimacy of Global Governance Institutions', 411.

may be a requirement of formal legality, it is difficult to regard it as the foundation for substantive legitimacy:

> it is hard to see how state consent could render global governance institutions legitimate, given that many states are non-democratic and systematically violate the human rights of their citizens and are for that reason themselves illegitimate. State consent cannot in these cases transfer legitimacy for the simple reason that there is no legitimacy to transfer. To assert that state consent, regardless of the character of the state, is sufficient for the legitimacy of global governance institutions is to regress to a conception of international order that fails to impose even the most minimal normative requirements on states.[21]

The need for formal legality nonetheless remains important. We need to ensure that the authority exercised by an official or organ within an international institution can be traced back to a valid source within the constituent document, and that the body to whom the power has been delegated remains within the scope of its authority. This is so whether one chooses to term this formal legitimacy, legality or, in the words of Bodansky, legal legitimacy:

> To the extent that authority is exercised at the international level by institutions rather than by international rules directly, then, in addition to general consent, we also need a concept of "legal legitimacy" – "the condition of

[21] Buchanan and Keohane, 'Legitimacy of Global Governance Institutions', 413. See also Bodansky, 'Legitimacy of International Governance', 611.

> being in accordance with law or principle," as the *Oxford English Dictionary* puts it. Legal legitimacy is what connects an institution's continuing authority to its original basis in state consent. The authority of the International Court of Justice, for example, derives from its Statute, to which UN member states consented. And the Court's continuing authority depends on its acting in accordance with the Statute. If it went outside or against the Statute, then its actions would lack legitimacy. The same would be true of decisions by the Security Council that exceeded its legal mandate under the UN Charter.[22]

(iii) Delegation and democratic validation

The preceding sense of validation is a necessary but not sufficient condition for the legitimacy of norms made at the global level. It might be regarded as 'thin', but this is reflective of the fact, acknowledged in much of the literature, that it is not possible to replicate the mechanisms of national representative democracy at the global level. Consider in this respect Joseph Weiler, who regards the existence of a *demos* as an ontological requirement for the existence of democracy:

> At the international level, we do not have the branches of government or the institutions of government we are accustomed to from statal settings. This is trite but crucial. When there is governance it should be legitimated democratically. But democracy presumes demos and presumes the existence of government.

[22] Bodansky, 'Legitimacy of International Governance', 605.

> Whatever democratic model one may adopt it will always have the elements of accountability, representation and some deliberation. There is always a presumption that all notions of representation, accountability, deliberation can be grafted on to the classical institutions of government. Likewise, whatever justification one gives to the democratic discipline of majority rule, it always presumes that majority and minority are situated within a polity the definition of which is shared by most of its subjects. The international system of governance with government and without demos means there is no purchase, no handle whereby we can graft democracy as we understand it from statal settings on to the international arena.[23]

Analogous views have been advanced by other writers. Sabino Cassese acknowledges that there is no representative democracy at the global level, with the consequence that 'surrogate, deliberative democracy emerges through participation in the decision making processes', a theme that will be explored in the next section.[24] For Cassese, democracy in the context of the nation state cannot be equated to democracy at the cosmopolitan level.[25] This view is echoed by Benedict Kingsbury, Nico Krisch and Richard Stewart, who state that the idea of a democratic role for global administrative law 'faces a number of serious problems of definition and implementation',[26] including doubts as to whether there is

[23] Weiler, 'The Geology of International Law', 560.

[24] Cassese, *The Global Polity*, p. 27.

[25] Cassese, *The Global Polity*, pp. 60, 61–2.

[26] Kingsbury, Krisch and Stewart, 'Global Administrative Law', 48.

sufficient agreement in international society on democratic standards such as to be able to use them as the foundation for global administration, and the difficulty of replicating the domestic model of administrative law, which is predicated on law-making by a democratic legislature, at the global level.[27] They conclude that 'if electoral or other models of direct representation fail, most of what is left is recommendations for different forms of participatory or deliberative democracy',[28] and they are, moreover, sceptical as to the applicability of ideas of democratic experimentalism. Daniel Esty notes that there is no 'representative global public to hold power-wielders in the international domain accountable',[29] while Ruth Grant and Robert Keohane make clear that the mechanisms for accountability that are required at the global level cannot 'simply replicate, on a larger scale, the familiar procedures and practices of democratic states'.[30]

27 Kingsbury, Krisch and Stewart, 'Global Administrative Law', 48–9.

28 Kingsbury, Krisch and Stewart, 'Global Administrative Law', 49.

29 Esty, 'Good Governance at the Supranational Scale', 1507.

30 R. Grant and R. Keohane, 'Accountability and Abuses of Power in World Politics' (2009) 99 *American Political Science Review* 29, at 29. See also R.L. Howse, 'Transatlantic Regulatory Co-operation and the Problem of Democracy', in G. Bermann, M. Herdegen and P. Lindseth (eds.), *Transatlantic Regulatory Cooperation: Legal Problems and Political Prospects* (Oxford: Oxford University Press, 2000), pp. 478–80; C. Scott, F. Cafaggi and L. Senden, 'The Conceptual and Constitutional Challenge of Transnational Private Regulation' (2011) 38 *Journal of Law and Society* 1; D. Curtin and L. Senden, 'Public Accountability of Transnational Private Regulation: Myth or Reality?' (2011) 38 *Journal of Law and Society* 163.

This dominant view in the literature has not gone unchallenged. Gráinne de Búrca has urged that democracy should continue to be regarded as of principal importance within global governance.[31] She acknowledges that there are significant problems with the transposition of national democratic models to the global or transnational context,[32] but maintains that 'we should not jettison democratic values when we attempt to shape more legitimate governance structures beyond the state'.[33] De Búrca argues for a 'democratic-striving approach', in preference to what she terms 'compensatory approaches' to democracy and transnational governance.

Compensatory approaches are predicated on the assumptions inherent in the literature cited above, viz. that democratic transnational governance is not feasible because representative democracy cannot work beyond a certain scale, and requires a *demos* that does not exist at the global level. The absence of democracy as conceived at national level is said to be compensated by attention given to other broadly liberal democratic values such as openness, accountability, fundamental rights, responsiveness, deliberation and reason-giving.[34]

The democratic-striving approach recognizes the difficulty of democratizing transnational governance 'yet insists on its necessity, and identifies the act of continuous striving

[31] G. de Búrca, 'Developing Democracy beyond the State' (2007–8) 46 *Columbia Journal of Transnational Law* 221.

[32] De Búrca, 'Developing Democracy beyond the State', 226, 253.

[33] De Búrca, 'Developing Democracy beyond the State', 227.

[34] De Búrca, 'Developing Democracy beyond the State', 244–5.

itself as the source of legitimation and accountability'.[35] For de Búrca the 'democratic-striving approach proposed would translate the principle of political equality into a requirement of fullest possible participation in effective processes of decision-making by those concerned',[36] with the aim of ensuring that the policies were public-regarding. The approach is said to tread a path between mere functional participation and universal participation, with the emphasis on ensuring that the circle of participants remains continuously open, and subject to revision, coupled with incentives to generate the fullest degree of participation possible.[37] The contrast drawn between compensatory approaches and the preferred democratic-striving approach is evident in the following:

> Compensatory approaches differ from the democratic-striving approach that I am advocating in a number of ways. In abstract terms, compensatory approaches do not view democracy as a concept that can be transposed from the state to the transnational level. In concrete terms, they do not try to design mechanisms of participation or representation in transnational governance that would have the same function, in normative and practical terms, as representation and participation do within national democratic systems – in particular, the function of ensuring that adopted policies are public-oriented or public-regarding.[38]

[35] De Búrca, 'Developing Democracy beyond the State', 237.
[36] De Búrca, 'Developing Democracy beyond the State', 253.
[37] De Búrca, 'Developing Democracy beyond the State', 251.
[38] De Búrca, 'Developing Democracy beyond the State', 247.

Gráinne de Búrca's argument is thoughtful and thought-provoking. The contrast drawn between the compensatory and democratic-striving approaches is nonetheless too sharp. An adherent to the democratic-striving approach would necessarily have regard to the range of other liberal-democratic considerations that are considered by those attached to broadly compensatory approaches. Thus even assuming that participation was accorded the meaning that de Búrca gives to it, legitimate global governance would still require attention to values such as openness, accountability, fundamental rights, responsiveness, deliberation and reason-giving. The same point can be put in another way. Public lawyers who focus on national law, whether from a common law or a civilian tradition, do not think of these values as 'compensation' for the relative paucity of democratic controls over delegation within the nation state. To the contrary, they regard them as integral to a developed system of public law, and the fact that delegation of administrative power is made in accord with foundational precepts of representative democracy does not alter this. Such delegation may be regarded as necessary for legitimate administration, but it is not sufficient, which is why controls cast in terms of reason-giving, fundamental rights, openness, legality, process and the like are seen as central to accountable and legitimate administration. It may be that Gráinne de Búrca merely meant that controls of this nature have to carry extra weight where the delegation has not been validated through democratic precepts. This may be so, but it does not alter the fact that they would still play a central role even if a democratic-striving approach worked successfully.

The distinction between the compensatory and the democratic-striving approach is, then, dependent on their respective conceptions of participation. It is accepted by adherents to both approaches that national conceptions of representative democracy cannot be cut and pasted to the global level. For Gráinne de Búrca the crucial distinction appears to be that advocates of a compensatory approach regard participation in unduly attenuated terms, conceiving of it as merely functional participation akin to corporatist or neo-corporatist approaches[39] that seek to privilege certain groups within the decision-making process.[40] There may be some adherents of a compensatory approach that conceive of participation in this manner, but it is not the dominant approach. The differences of view between commentators who adopt the compensatory approach concerning the breadth of participation turn primarily on the nature of the organization, its regulatory subject matter and the like. They may also have differing views of the importance of participation relative to other techniques for ensuring accountability at the global level. This does not alter the fact that participation is conceived by many such commentators as going considerably beyond narrow conceptions of functional

39 P. Schmitter and G. Lehmbruch (eds.), *Trends toward Corporatist Intermediation* (London: Sage, 1979); P. Schmitter and G. Lehmbruch (eds.), *Patterns of Corporatist Policymaking* (London: Sage, 1982); A. Cawson, *Corporatism and Welfare* (London: Heinemann, 1982); R. Harrison (ed.), *Corporatism and the Welfare State* (London: Allen & Unwin, 1984); P. Birkinshaw, I. Harden and N. Lewis, *Government by Moonlight: The Hybrid Parts of the State* (London: Unwin Hyman, 1990).

40 De Búrca, 'Developing Democracy beyond the State', 242–3, 251–2, 253.

participation,[41] and is more akin to the conception of participation that Gráinne de Búrca espouses.

(iv) Courts

Courts are central to administrative law controls in nation states. They are not the only method of securing administrative justice, and will co-exist with political safeguards, internal agency procedures, ombudsmen and the like. Courts nonetheless play a key role in this respect and that is so notwithstanding continued discourse as to the optimal balance between judicial and political controls, or the standards of review that should pertain when the courts intervene. Thus courts will, for example, commonly decide whether agencies have strayed beyond their defined remit, committed an error of law, made findings unsustainable on the facts, violated due process, acted for improper purposes or made decisions that are felt to be irrational or disproportionate.

This is all standard fare at national level, but it is interesting to reflect on the judicial role within the body of emerging global administrative law. Certain facts are clear, as is evident from the discussion in the preceding chapter.[42] Thus some global governance institutions come with an in-built judicial organ; others do not. Some have transparent and open procedures; others do not. Some will exercise

[41] See, e.g., Cassese, *The Global Polity*, pp. 109–76; Cananea, *Due Process of Law beyond the State*; Kingsbury, Krisch and Stewart, 'Global Administrative Law', 17, 29, 33, 35, 38, 48–9; Stewart, 'A Model for Global Administrative Law?'.

[42] See above, pp. 592–610.

sophisticated controls akin to those applied by national courts; others will be more rudimentary.

There is, however, an important difference between the national and global levels that is not revealed by these contrasts. When we think of courts at the national level we commonly have in mind judicial organs external to the primary administrative decision maker that subject the contested decision or rule to judicial review. This is so irrespective of whether the contested decision or rule has been made by, or reviewed by, a judicial organ or a body that applies judicial precepts that is internal to the administrative body. The standard of judicial review applied by the ordinary courts external to the administration may differ depending on whether the contested decision was made by a judicial organ from within the administration. This does not, however, alter the point of principle being made here, which is that some discourse concerning judicial organs at the global level in the context of global administrative law refers to judicial-type bodies operating as part of the particular organization.

Insofar as this is so, they are not in that sense akin to courts external to the organization exercising the principles of judicial review. This is not intended as pejorative to judicial organs that make decisions within such bodies. It is simply by way of descriptive and normative clarification of what we mean when we talk of courts or judicial organs in the global arena. The point is neatly captured by Steve Charnovitz, when referring to the World Trade Organization, which has judicial panels that adjudicate on WTO disputes, but no external judicial control:

> The traditional administrative law model fits the WTO in some respects, yet fails to fit when it comes to judicial review of WTO actions. What fits is that principals at the national level can demand that WTO-level rulemaking and adjudications be appropriately transparent and adhere to accepted norms of due process. Where a gap exists is that there is no international judicial control on the WTO as an administrative agency, and so that central dimension of administrative law is absent.[43]

This does not preclude the existence of judicial control. There might be instances in which recourse could be had to the International Court of Justice. There might be instances in which national or regional courts can play some external judicial oversight role, albeit indirect, by, for example, refusing to apply a decision made by an international organization that did not comply with principles of due process, as exemplified by the *Kadi* litigation considered below.[44]

It does mean that such external judicial control will be infrequent and partial. The principles of administrative law might be applied of their own volition by the judicial organs internal to the international organization, or they might be rendered applicable through decisions reached at the political level of the relevant organization. This does not alter the fact that there is no external, institutionalized judicial oversight to check on the application and development of such principles across the diverse areas that constitute global governance.

[43] S. Charnovitz, 'Transparency and Participation in the World Trade Organization' (2004) 56 *Rutgers Law Review* 927, at 947.

[44] See below, pp. 766–8.

(c) *National legitimation from the top: legislation, executive authority and expertise*

(i) Rationale

The discussion thus far has focused on legitimation of administrative action from the top, which in the case of nation states commonly entails democratic legitimation through statute that authorizes the delegation of such power to ministers, agencies and the like. This form of legitimation will commonly be supplemented by recourse to arguments concerning executive authority and expertise, which are predicated on an admixture of normative and functional considerations.

The most forceful version of the normative argument is that the nature of the executive entails authority over decisions or rules other than primary legislation. On this view, the legislature legislates, and the executive executes, and the latter encompasses everything that is not the former. If it is not primary legislation then it is made pursuant to primary legislation and authority should reside in the executive, whether this is for the making of secondary rules or individual discretionary determinations. The boldest version of this thesis goes a step further by asseverating that not only should the executive be regarded as having authority for such determinations, but that also in making them it should only be constrained by limited external forces, for the very reason that this thereby circumscribes the normatively justified executive autonomy.[45]

[45] The normative argument presented in the text should be distinguished from that which is applicable to constitutional systems in which an

This normative argument is contestable, but gains currency from the fact that legal systems are notoriously indecisive when it comes to defining the boundaries of executive power. Constitutions in common and civil law countries are imprecise as to the scope of executive power, and the constitutional specifications concerning such power are frequently partial and incomplete.[46] This is reflective of the endemic and enduring difficulties in defining what executive power connotes. This difficulty has been exacerbated as a result of institutional developments in the last thirty to forty years, such as the spread of agencies, the use of contracting out and the like, with the result that the very locus of executive power has become more diffuse.

The normative argument is, nonetheless, contestable. It can be accepted that the executive should presumptively have authority to draft secondary rules pursuant to primary legislation. The primary legislation will indeed often specify this, and even where it does not do so the default assumption is that the executive is empowered to execute the primary legislation, including, where necessary, the framing of secondary rules, as well as individual discretionary determinations. This does not, however, make the case for the executive to have conclusive authority over the rules thus made. The secondary rules remain legislative in nature, and this is so even if the legal system makes use of a non-delegation doctrine. The idea

executive authority such as the president is given constitutional authority over certain subject matter, which is accompanied by rule-making authority in relation to that subject matter.

[46] Craig and Tomkins, *The Executive and Public Law*.

that such rules can be regarded as purely technical, fleshing out points of detail where all essentials have been laid down in primary law, is simply fanciful and misrepresents reality. Take any instance where there has been a shift in policy effectuated through a legislative act. The secondary rules enacted thereafter will regularly deal with practical and normative issues of real importance, the solution to which may be guided, but rarely determined, by the legislative act. It is precisely for this reason that many legal systems insist on some degree of legislative oversight of the kind considered above.

It is, however, at this point that the functional rationale for executive authority supplements the normative argument. It does so by furnishing an argument that any legislative or judicial oversight should be limited, because the executive has expertise in the making of the secondary rules or individual determinations that cannot be matched in either the legislative or judicial arenas. The justification is cast primarily in terms of output legitimation: the executive should be the body that devises such rules and the constraints thereon should be tempered so as not to allow those with less expertise to damage the rules that it creates.

Note the diverse ways in which this argument can be manifest. It can be used as the rationale for limiting legislative scrutiny to the veto power, with no right to amend, the reason being that while the legislature should be able to say an overall yes or no to the measure, it has insufficient expertise to modify the rule and may well render it less efficacious in doing so. It can be used also as the rationale for limiting judicial review, such that the rule or decision will only be invalidated if it is manifestly arbitrary.

Note also the very duality that exists in the expertise argument, which is manifest in the elision of bureaucratic and technocratic expertise. The terms are often used synonymously, but while this may be warranted there is no reason why it will always be so. Thus if we take language seriously, bureaucratic expertise captures the idea that the full-time official will for that reason have the requisite expertise over the relevant area. Whether this is so depends on variables such as the length of time served in that department, the nature of the work and other such factors. However, the fact an official 'scores' well on such factors and thus has bureaucratic expertise does not necessarily mean that she has technical expertise. An official may have spent twenty years in the ministry of agriculture. It does not mean that her bureaucratic expertise will translate into technical expertise when it comes to drafting a secondary rule on genetically modified foods.

The functional dimension of the argument for executive authority, whether cast in terms of bureaucratic or technocratic expertise, has in any event been subject to criticism in recent years.[47] There is less trust in technocracy than there

[47] See, e.g., M. Shapiro, 'The Problems of Independent Agencies in the United States and the European Union' (1997) 4 *Journal of European Public Policy* 276; P. Alston, 'The Myopia of Handmaidens: International Lawyers and Globalization' (1997) 8 *European Journal of International Law* 441; M. Shapiro, 'Administrative Law Unbounded: Reflections on Government and Governance' (2001) 8 *Indiana Journal of Global Legal Studies* 369; M. Shapiro, '"Deliberative", "Independent" Technocracy v. Democratic Politics: Will the Globe Echo the EU?' (2005) 68 *Law and Contemporary Problems* 341.

was a generation ago. The idea that we should trust in those who know best, and that those with technical expertise should be regarded as *primus inter pares* in this respect, is now viewed with greater scepticism. The related idea that science provides 'objective' answers to certain problems that have to be dealt with has likewise come under strain. It has been recognized that the 'answer' may be contentious in scientific terms, and that any one version of the scientific solution may embody value judgements of a social, moral or political nature, even if such factors are not immediately apparent on the face of the decision.[48] Both concerns have been voiced by Martin Shapiro:

> For some high-tech states that purport to be democratic, one central issue has been democracy versus technocracy. Precisely because what is being regulated is technologically complex and rapidly changing, regulators must have high technical skills themselves. One cannot regulate what one does not understand. It has become widely recognized, however, that by virtue of the very specialization of knowledge required for the achievement of high technological skills, experts are themselves special interest groups whose perspectives and self-interests render them non-representative of the demos as a whole.[49]

[48] See, e.g., C. Sunstein, *Risk and Reason: Safety, Law, and the Environment* (Cambridge: Cambridge University Press, 2002); E. Fisher, *Risk Regulation and Administrative Constitutionalism* (Oxford: Hart, 2007).

[49] Shapiro, '"Deliberative", "Independent" Technocracy v. Democratic Politics', 342–3.

(ii) Legal and political control

The legal and political controls may be configured in various ways that reflect attachment to the idea of executive authority and expertise, notwithstanding that there is less attachment to it than hitherto.

First, this can be done through the constitution. It might take the form of separate subject matter jurisdiction for the executive branch of government, coupled with empowerment to make rules for those areas within its remit.[50] This approach could also be secured even where there is no formal subject matter divide between executive and legislative authority in the constitution. There could, nonetheless, be express constitutional provisions enabling the executive to make rules of a secondary nature, which stipulate limits to legislative control. This is in effect the regime in the European Union. Article 290 TFEU empowers the executive to make delegated acts where so specified in a legislative act, and limits the controls that can be exercised by the legislature. It can revoke the delegation and it can veto the particular delegated act, but it cannot in formal terms amend the delegated act and there cannot be limits on executive authority other than those in Article 290.

Second, it is possible for executive expertise to be secured through statutory means. There can, for example, be legislation in specific areas, which is predicated on giving a high profile to executive expertise, the consequence being significant limits placed on interference with those executive

[50] See, e.g., S. Boyron, *The Constitution of France: A Contextual Analysis* (Oxford: Hart, 2013).

choices, even by other branches of the executive that are perceived to have less expertise. This is exemplified by the EU schema for agencies dealing with banking, financial services and the like, where the legislation is expressly crafted so as to curtail severely the Commission's ability to modify the draft rule proposed by the agency.[51]

Third, belief in executive authority and expertise can be reflected in non-statutory conventional rules. This is exemplified by the UK schema of legislative scrutiny over delegated legislation contained in the Statutory Instruments Act 1946, which provides for legislative scrutiny of different degrees for certain secondary rules. There is, however, much not dealt with by the legislation, including the details of the committee system put in place to scrutinize these rules. Parliament decided to distinguish between consideration of the vires and the merits of the secondary rules. The committee established to deal with the latter cannot amend the rule, but is limited to recommending to the House of Commons that the rule should be approved or rejected.[52]

(iii) Courts

There are two kinds of judicial control that are especially pertinent to legitimation via executive authority and expertise.

It will be for the courts to determine the meaning and ambit of any relevant provisions that are contained in the

[51] See, e.g., Regulation (EU) No 1093/2010 of the European Parliament and of the Council of 24 November 2010 establishing a European Supervisory Authority (European Banking Authority) OJ 2010 No L331/12, 15 December 2010.

[52] Craig, *Administrative Law*, Ch. 15.

constitution or in statute. Thus, for example, it will be for the courts to decide whether provisions that specify certain controls by the legislature over rule making by the executive should be regarded as the only constraints that can be imposed. This will entail judicial evaluation in the light of the court's overall perception of the constitutional or statutory schema. The courts possess well-tested interpretive tools that enable them to reach either conclusion. They could reason that if the constitution or a statute stipulates certain controls then it must have intended these to be the sole lawful constraints. There are, however, numerous instances where courts reason in a contrary manner, stating that the mere fact that the constitution or statute sets out one type of control should not be taken to mean that other constraints are thereby precluded.[53]

It will also be for the courts to decide on the intensity of review brought to bear on decisions or rules made by the executive. Individual discretionary decisions are subject to judicial review, and so too is rule making. The precepts of judicial review can be used with varying degrees of intensity, and this is so whether they are expressed in terms of rationality, proportionality or arbitrariness. The courts can express their belief in executive expertise by applying such principles of review with low intensity, thereby making it far more difficult for claimants to succeed. This is, for example, what occurred in the USA when the courts required the claimant to

[53] See, e.g., Case 26/62, *NV Algemene Transporten Expeditie Onderneming van Gend en Loos* v. *Nederlandse Administratie der Belastingen* [1963] ECR 1.

show that an agency rule really was manifestly arbitrary and capricious before they would intervene. This approach was predicated on trust in administrative expertise and reluctance to become judicially involved in the complex topics regulated by such agencies. The shift away from this minimalist reading of the arbitrary and capricious test to what became known as hard-look judicial review reflected a decline in the weight that the court was willing to accord to executive expertise, combined with an increased willingness to test the assumptions underlying agency policy choices through requirements for reasoned analysis, scrutiny of the evidentiary foundations of agency choices, relevancy and the like.[54]

(d) Global legitimation from the top: consent, executive authority and expertise

(i) Rationale

We have already considered the difficulties of applying legislative legitimation in the global arena, and the limits of legitimation cast in terms of consent. The reality is that legitimation through executive authority and expertise may have 'greater purchase' in the global arena. The reasons are not hard to divine, since notwithstanding changes over the last half a century, it remains the case that many international organizations are executive-dominated in a double sense.

It is, on the one hand, national executives who created many such bodies with limited input from national

[54] See, e.g., M. Shapiro, 'Codification of Administrative Law: The US and the Union' (1996) 2 *European Law Journal* 26, at 28–33.

legislatures. It is national executives who commonly appoint statal representatives to them. The responsibility for national participation in such organizations is regarded as falling within the executive domain as an integral aspect of foreign policy. It can be accepted that the world of global regulation is increasingly complex, such that some organizations are created by industry and are not 'sponsored' by national executives, but the salient point for present purposes is that nor are these organizations 'sponsored' by national legislatures.

It is, on the other hand, also the case that many such organizations have been regarded as executive institutions. There may well be within the organization a body that is representative of all participants, and a smaller executive authority that is responsible for day-to-day operations, and/or the more important decisions. The fact remains that the organization as a whole will commonly see itself, and be seen, as an executive entity. There has traditionally been little, if any imperative to invest the more representative body within such institutions with any direct or indirect electoral credentials, through votes cast by people from states that are party to the organization. The international/transnational institutions have traditionally been predicated on the assumption of executive authority to take decisions and make rules, which either flows from express provisions in the empowering treaty, or is seen as implicit in the existence of authority to regulate the specified area. The very fact that the divide between legislative acts and secondary rules commonly found in statal systems is absent or less marked in many international organizations merely served to fuel this conclusion.

The EU provides an interesting case study in this respect. The initial vision for integration was premised on executive authority, technocratic expertise and output legitimacy. Monnet's conception of Europe was strongly influenced by the role of technocrats trained in the French *grands écoles*. This explained the structure of the ECSC, with the centrality of the High Authority being expressive of the technocratic approach. Integration was based on the combination of benevolent technocrats and economic interest groups, which would build transnational coalitions for European policy.[55] Monnet's strategy was thus for what has been termed elite-led gradualism.[56] The Assembly's powers within the ECSC were very limited.

The same general institutional structure was carried over to the EEC: 'enlightened administration on behalf of uninformed publics, in cooperation with affected interests and subject to the approval of national governments, was therefore the compromise again struck in the Treaties of Rome'.[57] For Monnet and kindred spirits, the legitimacy of the Community was to be secured through outcomes, peace and prosperity. The ECSC was established in part to prevent a third European war. The EEC was created in

[55] W. Wallace, 'European Governance in Turbulent Times' (1993) 31 *Journal of Common Market Studies* 300.

[56] W. Wallace and J. Smith, 'Democracy or Technocracy? European Integration and the Problem of Popular Consent', in J. Hayward (ed.), *The Crisis of Representation in Europe* (London: Frank Cass, 1995), p. 140.

[57] Wallace and Smith, 'Democracy or Technocracy', 143.

large part for the direct economic benefits of a common market. Peace and prosperity were potent benefits for people in the 1950s. Democracy was, by way of contrast, a secondary consideration, since it was felt that the best way to secure peace and prosperity was by technocratic elite-led guidance.

This approach was challenged and there was increased emphasis on democratic input into the making of EU norms.[58] The EP's initial focus was on securing some say in the primary legislative process. The seminal change came with the creation of the co-operation procedure in the SEA. Having gained this foothold, the story in subsequent years was the EP building on this foothold to win the upgrade to co-decision in the Maastricht Treaty, and the further strengthening and expansion of this power in the Amsterdam and Nice Treaties. It was not, however, fortuitous that this period also saw the EP press for greater control over secondary rule making. It saw its success in relation to the primary legislative process undermined by its minimal role in the comitology system that generated secondary rules. Its dissatisfaction with this regime led to the inter-institutional battles that began in the late 1980s,[59] with an uneasy truce flowing from the

[58] P. Craig, 'Competence and Member State Autonomy: Causality, Consequence and Legitimacy', in H.-W. Micklitz and B. de Witte (eds.), *The European Court of Justice and the Autonomy of the Member States* (Intersentia, 2012), pp. 11–34.

[59] C.-F. Bergstrom, *Comitology: Delegation of Powers in the European Union and the Committee System* (Oxford: Oxford University Press, 2005).

2006 modifications to the second comitology decision,[60] and further accommodation coming with the Lisbon reforms in Articles 290–1 TFEU.

Legitimacy was thus initially conceived in terms of executive authority, expertise and output. This still has some force, as exemplified by the limits placed on legislative oversight. It does not, however, hold centre stage in the way that it did fifty years ago. It is now accepted that there should be some focus on input through legislative legitimation, and there has been much discussion of legitimation through participation.

It remains to be seen how far the discourse on global administrative law leads to changes in the dominant legitimating model that pertains to other international organizations that engage in rule making. We need to be balanced in this respect. The EU is an imperfect analogy for other international institutions, because its institutional structure is sui generis. This should not, however, lead us to conclude that developments in the EU have no relevance for debates about legitimacy in relation to a broader group of organizations.

It is, nonetheless, important to note that the concerns expressed earlier relating to tensions between democracy and technocracy may be more pronounced at the international than at the national level for the reasons noted by Martin Shapiro:

[60] Council Decision 2006/512/EC of 17 July 2006 amending Decision 1999/468/EC laying down the procedures for the exercise of implementing powers by the Commission, OJ 2006 No L200/11, 22 July 2006.

> Transnational regulation is more likely than national regulation to be dominated by technocratic decision-making for another related reason: transnational regimes are likely to involve the standard logic of cartels. Each member of the cartel becomes and remains a member because each sees the joint cartel rules and practices as more advantageous to it individually than uncoordinated action by all members. Yet each member is under the constant temptation to seek to initiate rules and practices most advantageous to itself. In a nation-state setting, intervention by elected politicians against technocrats might appear democratic. In a transnational setting, however, attempts at political intervention in 'technical' regulatory decisions largely will be attempts by politicians representing particular nation-states. They will be seen not as democratic interventions against technocracy but as national interventions intended to gain national advantage at the expense of other members of the transnational regime. Therefore, in a transnational regulatory regime, politics and politicians tend to be identified with bad national self-interest, and international technicians with the common good.[61]

(ii) Legal controls and courts: introduction

Discourse concerning global administrative law has not surprisingly focused at a relatively abstract level on the types of administrative law control that should be applicable to international and transnational organizations. This leaves open a

[61] Shapiro, '"Deliberative", "Independent" Technocracy v. Democratic Politics', 349.

plethora of issues concerning the more detailed meaning to be accorded to the precepts of procedural and substantive review.

In some instances there is little data on which to base any such estimation. Thus if the governing instrument of the relevant body provides no guidance on such matters, and if there is no judicial organ to shape the pertinent principles, then it will perforce be left to reasoned conjecture as to how the particular administrative law principles should be interpreted in detail. As Stewart notes, 'specialized regime-specific reviewing bodies that afford review as a right are slowly growing in number but are far from ubiquitous'.[62]

There are, by way of contrast, international organizations where we find guidance as to the detailed meaning of the principles of review in the governing instrument and its interpretation by the judicial organ. This is exemplified by the Administrative Tribunal of the IMF and by the adjudicatory bodies under the WTO. It is important to consider such material, which provides a window onto the challenges faced by global regimes in delineating the appropriate contours of judicial review.

It is inherent in the ensuing analysis that the results of the inquiry will not necessarily be immediately transferable to other global regimes where the governing instrument, players and context may be different. Leaving aside the obvious rejoinder, which is that the same might be said in relation to different administrative regimes within a nation state, the inquiry is nonetheless important if we are to move beyond

[62] Stewart, 'Remedying Disregard', 266.

generalities concerning grounds of review for global organizations viewed merely at an abstract level.

(iii) Legal controls and courts: the administrative tribunal of the IMF

Article III of the Statute of the Administrative Tribunal of the IMF states that in deciding on an application, 'the Tribunal shall apply the internal law of the Fund, including generally recognized principles of international administrative law concerning judicial review of administrative acts'. The commentary accompanying the Statute provides that Article III requires the Tribunal to 'adhere to such principles concerning judicial review as elaborated in the case law of both international administrative tribunals and domestic judicial systems, particularly with respect to review of decisions taken under discretionary powers'.[63]

This has been taken to justify procedural principles of review, such as the right to be heard, which 'are so widely accepted and well-established in different legal systems that they are regarded as generally applicable to all decisions taken by international organizations, including the Fund'.[64] It has also been taken as the foundation for building appropriate principles of substantive review. Thus while the IMF Administrative Tribunal engages in substantive review, this is bounded by what it regards as general precepts of administrative law, such that it 'will not substitute its judgment for

[63] Commentary on the Statute of the Administrative Tribunal of the IMF, www.imf.org/external/imfat/report.htm, p. 17.

[64] Commentary on the Statute of the Administrative Tribunal of the IMF, www.imf.org/external/imfat/report.htm, p. 18.

that of the competent organs and will respect the broad, although not unlimited, power of the organization to amend the terms and conditions of employment'.[65] In a similar vein the commentary emphasizes that

> with respect to review of individual decisions involving the exercise of managerial discretion, the case law has emphasized that discretionary decisions cannot be overturned unless they are shown to be arbitrary, capricious, discriminatory, improperly motivated, based on an error of law or fact, or carried out in violation of fair and reasonable procedures.[66]

Analogous limits on judicial review can be found in the jurisprudence of other administrative tribunals.[67]

(iv) Legal controls and courts: the WTO and due process

The challenges of crafting administrative law precepts for a global organization are thrown into sharp relief by the rulings

[65] Commentary on the Statute of the Administrative Tribunal of the IMF, www.imf.org/external/imfat/report.htm, p. 17.

[66] Commentary on the Statute of the Administrative Tribunal of the IMF, www.imf.org/external/imfat/report.htm, p. 19. See, e.g., *Ms J* v. *International Monetary Fund*, IMFAT Judgment 2003–1; *Ms W* v. *International Monetary Fund*, IMFAT Judgment 2005–2; *Ms BB* v. *International Monetary Fund*, IMFAT Judgment 2007–4; *Ms JJ* v. *International Monetary Fund*, IMFAT Judgment 2014–1.

[67] See the following decisions of the World Bank Administrative Tribunal, *de Merode*, Decision No 1 [1981]; *Bertrand*, Decision No 81 [1989]; *Nunberg*, Decision No 245 [2001]; *Moussavi*, Decision No 360 [2007]; *Denis*, Decision No 458 [2011]; *L.T. Mpoy-Kamulayi (No 5)*, Decision No 463 [2012].

from the WTO Appellate Body and the WTO panels, even if they are not technically 'courts'. It will be recalled that the GATT 1947 regime was characterized primarily by 'diplomatic negotiation and the pursuit of consensus',[68] but this was changed through the Understanding on Rules and Procedures Governing the Settlement of Disputes (DSU), introduced by the Uruguay reforms,[69] which established a permanent Dispute Settlement Body (DSB). The DSB was authorized to establish panels and adopt panel and Appellate Body reports. The panel reports and those of the Appellate Body reveal creativity in crafting, and applying to the complex system that is the WTO, core principles of administrative law, which comprise a number of separate agreements dealing with different aspects of the regime.

This is reflected in the fact that there are general provisions that affect judicial review and also separate agreements that govern different parts of the WTO system, with distinctive provisions that impact on particular precepts of judicial review. The general provisions are contained in Article 11 of the DSU:[70]

> The function of panels is to assist the DSB in discharging its responsibilities under this Understanding and the covered agreements. Accordingly, a panel should make an objective assessment of the matter before it, including an objective assessment of the facts of the case

[68] M. Herdegen, *Principles of International Economic Law* (Oxford: Oxford University Press, 2013), p. 256.

[69] See www.wto.org/english/docs_e/legal_e/legal_e.htm.

[70] See www.wto.org/english/docs_e/legal_e/legal_e.htm.

> and the applicability of and conformity with the relevant covered agreements, and make such other findings as will assist the DSB in making the recommendations or in giving the rulings provided for in the covered agreements. Panels should consult regularly with the parties to the dispute and give them adequate opportunity to develop a mutually satisfactory solution.

Article 11 is applicable to the WTO agreements listed in Appendix 1 of the DSU,[71] the principal agreements being the Agreement Establishing the World Trade Association, Multilateral Agreements on Trade in Goods, the General Agreement on Trade in Services and the Agreement on Trade-Related Aspects of Intellectual Property Rights. There are, however, additional provisions in other agreements that impact on judicial review, such as the Agreement on Anti-dumping, and the default position is that in the event of a clash between the provisions of the DSU and those contained in other agreements the latter prevail.[72]

It is fitting to begin with the fundamentals of due process. In *Chile – Price Band System* the Appellate Body held that Article 11 required that in making an 'objective assessment' a panel must ensure that due process is respected, this being an 'obligation inherent in the WTO dispute settlement system'.[73] In *Shrimp – Turtle* the Appellate Body confirmed that an appellee from a panel ruling was, 'of course, always

[71] Art. 1.1 DSU. [72] Art. 1.2 DSU.

[73] Report of the Appellate Body, *Chile – Price Band System and Safeguard Measures Relating to Certain Agricultural Products*, WT/DS207/AB/R, 23 September 2002, para. 176.

entitled to its full measure of due process', when the case was taken on appeal.[74] The inherent nature of due process was further stressed in *Canada – Continued Suspension*, where the Appellate Body reiterated that it was fundamental to ensuring a fair and orderly conduct of dispute settlement proceedings, and that due process was an 'essential feature of a rules-based system of adjudication, such as that established under the DSU'.[75] To similar effect was the ruling in *Thailand – Cigarettes (Philippines)*, where the Appellate Body stated that 'due process is a fundamental principle of WTO dispute settlement', which 'informs and finds reflection in the provisions of the DSU',[76] and the panel must ensure that it is protected. The Appellate Body continued as follows:

> Due process is intrinsically connected to notions of fairness, impartiality, and the rights of parties to be heard and to be afforded an adequate opportunity to pursue their claims, make out their defences, and establish the facts in the context of proceedings conducted in a balanced and orderly manner, according to established rules. The protection of due process is thus a crucial means of guaranteeing the legitimacy and efficacy of a rules-based system of adjudication.[77]

[74] Report of Appellate Body, *United States – Import Prohibition of Certain Shrimp and Shrimp Products*, WT/DS58/AB/R, 12 October 1998, para. 87.

[75] Report of the Appellate Body, *Canada – Continued Suspension of Obligations in the EC – Hormones Dispute*, WT/DS321/AB/R, 16 October 2008, para. 433.

[76] Report of Appellate Body, *Thailand – Customs and Fiscal Measures on Cigarettes from the Philippines*, WT/DS371/AB/R, 17 June 2011, para. 147.

[77] *Thailand – Cigarettes (Philippines)*, para. 147.

The more detailed application of due process is evident in particular rulings. Thus in *Chile – Price Band* the Appellate Body held that there was a failure to respect due process if a panel made a finding on a matter that was not before it, since it would thereby deprive a party of the right to respond.[78] In *Thailand – H-Beams*, due process was said to demand sufficient clarity with respect to the legal basis of the complaint, since the defending party was 'entitled to know what case it has to answer, and what violations have been alleged so that it can begin preparing its defence'.[79] Analogous process rights were to be afforded to third parties that participated in the proceedings. In *Thailand – Cigarettes (Philippines)* the Appellate Body reiterated the centrality to due process of a meaningful opportunity to respond to the opposing arguments, while emphasizing that due process also required the panel to ensure 'an aggrieved party's right to have recourse to an adjudicative process in which it can seek redress in a timely manner',[80] a corollary being that parties should bring alleged procedural deficiencies to the attention of a panel at the earliest possible opportunity. In *Shrimp – Turtle* the Appellate Body concluded that the certification procedure used by the US in granting export certificates appeared to be 'singularly informal and casual', with the consequence that exporting

[78] *Chile – Price Band System*, para. 164. See also Report of the Appellate Body, *Australia – Measures Affecting Importation of Salmon*, WT/DS18/AB/R, 20 October 1998, paras. 272, 278.

[79] Report of the Appellate Body, *Thailand – Anti-dumping Duties on Angles, Shapes and Sections of Iron or Non-alloy Steel and H-beams from Poland*, WT/DS122/AB/R, 12 March 2001, para. 88.

[80] *Thailand – Cigarettes (Philippines)*, para. 150.

Members applying for certification whose applications were rejected 'are denied basic fairness and due process'.[81] The Appellate Body held, moreover, that

> rigorous compliance with the fundamental requirements of due process should be required in the application and administration of a measure which purports to be an exception to the treaty obligations of the Member imposing the measure and which effectively results in a suspension *pro hac vice* of the treaty rights of other Members.[82]

It is clear, moreover, that due process operates in a more structural manner to inform the way in which the panels function. This is apparent from *Thailand – Cigarettes (Philippines)*, where the Appellate Body stated that 'panel working procedures should both embody and reinforce due process', and that 'the use by panels of detailed, standardized working procedures promotes fairness and the protection of due process'.[83] More specifically, the Appellate Body stressed that due process can best be served by working procedures that provide for appropriate factual discovery at an early stage in panel proceedings, and that due process could be of particular concern where a party raised new facts at a late stage of the panel proceedings.[84]

While due process is thus regarded as inherent in the overall WTO system, there is more explicit foundation

[81] *Shrimp – Turtle*, para. 181. [82] *Shrimp – Turtle*, para. 182.

[83] *Thailand – Cigarettes (Philippines)*, para. 148.

[84] *Thailand – Cigarettes (Philippines)*, para. 149.

in some WTO agreements, as exemplified by that on anti-dumping,[85] Article 6 of which provides,

> 6.1 All interested parties in an anti-dumping investigation shall be given notice of the information which the authorities require and ample opportunity to present in writing all evidence which they consider relevant in respect of the investigation in question.
>
> 6.2 Throughout the anti-dumping investigation all interested parties shall have a full opportunity for the defence of their interests. To this end, the authorities shall, on request, provide opportunities for all interested parties to meet those parties with adverse interests, so that opposing views may be presented and rebuttal arguments offered. Provision of such opportunities must take account of the need to preserve confidentiality and of the convenience to the parties. There shall be no obligation on any party to attend a meeting, and failure to do so shall not be prejudicial to that party's case. Interested parties shall also have the right, on justification, to present other information orally.

Article 6 contains a wealth of detail as to the application of due process in such cases, including provisions on confidential information, time limits, timely opportunities for interested parties to see all non-confidential information relevant to the presentation of their cases, and an obligation on the

[85] Agreement on Implementation of Article VI of the General Agreement on Tariffs and Trade 1994, www.wto.org/english/docs_e/legal_e/legal_e.htm.

authorities imposing the duty, before a final determination is made, to inform all interested parties of the essential facts that form the basis for the decision whether to apply definitive measures. In *US – Oil Country Tubular Goods Sunset Reviews* the Appellate Body interpreted the key provisions of Article 6.1 and 6.2 as follows:

> These provisions set out the fundamental due process rights to which interested parties are entitled in anti-dumping investigations and reviews. Articles 6.1 and 6.2 require that the opportunities afforded interested parties for presentation of evidence and defence of their interests be 'ample' and 'full', respectively. In the context of these provisions, these two adjectives suggest there should be liberal opportunities for respondents to defend their interests. Nevertheless, we agree with the United States that Articles 6.1 and 6.2 do not provide for 'indefinite' rights, so as to enable respondents to submit relevant evidence, attend hearings, or participate in the inquiry as and when they choose. Such an approach would 'prevent the authorities of a Member from proceeding expeditiously' in their reviews, contrary to Article 6.14. It would also affect the rights of other interested parties. In this regard, we recall that the Appellate Body has previously recognized the importance for investigating authorities of establishing deadlines and controlling the conduct of their investigations.[86]

[86] Report of Appellate Body, *United States – Sunset Reviews of Anti-dumping Measures on Oil Country Tubular Goods from Argentina*, WT/DS268/AB/R, 29 November 2004, para. 241.

(v) Legal controls and courts: the WTO and review of law

The appropriate standard of review is a key issue in the jurisprudence of the WTO panels and Appellate Body. Indeed, as Steven Croley and John Jackson note, 'in the waning months of the Uruguay Round, the standard-of-review issue assumed such importance to some negotiators that it reached a place on the short list of problems called "deal breakers" – problems that could have caused the entire negotiations to fail'.[87] The discourse concerning the appropriate standard of review resonates strongly with the considerations that shape debates on such matters at national and regional levels. This is readily apparent from the way in which Claus-Dieter Ehlermann and Nicolas Lockhart frame the inquiry:

> In any legal system, including both EU and WTO law, standard of review is one of the mechanisms used to guarantee the separation of powers. Standard of review refers to the nature and intensity of a court's scrutiny of the legal validity of a legislative or administrative decision. It provides answers to the questions we posed at the outset about the degree of deference judges should accord legislators and regulators. Essentially, standard of review defines the parameters within which judges work, and correspondingly, within which legislators and regulators work. It establishes 'no go' areas for judges, requiring them

[87] S. Croley and J. Jackson, 'WTO Procedures, Standard of Review, and Deference to National Governments' (1996) 90 *American Journal of International Law* 193, at 194.

> to respect choices made by legislators or regulators. Within these 'no go' areas, the first decision-maker has discretion to make choices that the judge cannot reconsider. Beyond the 'no go' areas, the judge has the authority to verify the legal – but not political – validity of the decision. Standard of review is, therefore, an important part of the system of checks and balances in government, helping to ensure the accountability of decision-makers. It should also function to allocate decision-making authority and resources in an efficient manner among the different branches of government.[88]

The detailed elaboration of the WTO standard of review emerges from the wording of the WTO governing instruments, as read together with the Vienna Convention on the Law of Treaties,[89] and as shaped by more general precepts of administrative law derived from national and regional legal systems. The way in which the standard of review plays out in the WTO is particularly interesting, although the reality is that Article 11 DSU provides relatively scant guidance as to the applicable standard of review.[90]

The injunction in that Article that a panel should make an 'objective assessment of the matter before it' is not, as Ehlermann and Lockhart rightly note,[91] determinative, but

[88] C.-D. Ehlermann and N. Lockhart, 'Standard of Review in WTO Law' (2004) 7 *Journal of International Economic Law* 491, at 493.

[89] Vienna, 23 May 1969, 1155 U.N.T.S. 331.

[90] For consideration of the ambiguities in the earlier GATT Panel jurisprudence, see Croley and Jackson, 'WTO Procedures, Standard of Review, and Deference to National Governments', 195–8.

[91] Ehlermann and Lockhart, 'Standard of Review in WTO Law', 495.

must be read in conjunction with an underlying standard of review. This is because the imperative to make an 'objective assessment' is compatible with various standards of review, including substitution of judgment by the panel, or some lesser-intensity review couched in terms of reasonableness. Moreover, although Article 11 DSU appears to be equally applicable to all aspects of a dispute, the reality is that the 'scope and intensity of the panel's assessment is not the same for every issue, in every dispute'.[92]

The Appellate Body of the WTO gave early guidance on the meaning of Article 11 in *EC – Hormones*,[93] where it stated that the 'applicable standard is neither *de novo* review as such, nor "total deference"',[94] but the particular standard will nonetheless depend on whether the issue before the panel is one of law, fact or mixed fact and law.[95] Indeed, the preceding quote from the Appellate Body was framed in relation to review of fact.

In relation to questions of law, the standard is more akin to *de novo* review, in the sense that the panel will substitute its judgement on the meaning of the disputed legal term for that of the primary decision maker. This is in accord with Articles 31 and 32 of the Vienna Convention, which requires the treaty interpreter to seek out the ordinary meaning of the text. It is also in accord with the schema of

[92] Ehlermann and Lockhart, 'Standard of Review in WTO Law', 496.

[93] Report of the Appellate Body, *European Measures Concerning Meat and Meat Products ('EC – Hormones')*, WT/DS26/AB/R, WT/DS48/AB/R, 16 January 1998.

[94] *EC – Hormones*, para. 117.

[95] Ehlermann and Lockhart, 'Standard of Review in WTO Law', 496.

the WTO, and the regime of checks and balances that it embodies. Thus, as Ehlermann and Lockhart point out, the WTO system is intended to guarantee predictability and security to the global trading system. WTO adjudicative bodies contribute to this by providing uniform interpretation of WTO law:

> If individual WTO Members were afforded discretion to interpret WTO law, the uniform interpretation would be lost. It would lead to what Palmeter and Spak describe as a 'Tower of Legal Babel'. The obligations assumed by WTO Members, and the rights acquired, would differ from Member to Member, undermining the core objectives of the rule-based system. There is, therefore, considerable justification for requiring panels and the Appellate Body to conduct an original, *de novo* review of a national authority's legal determinations, using the rules of the Vienna Convention.[96]

The application of Article 11 DSU, interpreted in the preceding manner, is qualified in certain areas, such as anti-dumping, where specific provisions accord weight to permissible interpretations of the Anti-dumping Agreement. Thus Article 17.6(ii) provides,

> The panel shall interpret the relevant provisions of the Agreement in accordance with customary rules of interpretation of public international law. Where the panel finds that a relevant provision of the Agreement admits of more than one permissible interpretation, the panel

[96] Ehlermann and Lockhart, 'Standard of Review in WTO Law', 498.

> shall find the authorities' measure to be in conformity with the Agreement if it rests upon one of those permissible interpretations.[97]

Croley and Jackson examined the genesis of this provision, explaining that some 'government representatives thought it would be wise to have language constraining the standard of review by a GATT or WTO panel, and believed that U.S. administrative law jurisprudence provided a useful model for this constraint', but that this was opposed by 'many nations that felt such a rule would overly constrain panels while giving too much leeway to national governments to act in a manner inconsistent with the purposes of the WTO Agreements'.[98]

They note the analogies between the wording of Article 17.6(ii) and the test for review of questions of law in the US administrative law jurisprudence, as embodied in the *Chevron* test.[99] Croley and Jackson nonetheless rightly point out that the rationales for according deference to agencies in the US pursuant to the *Chevron* test are not readily transferable to the WTO context.[100] Thus insofar as such deference is warranted at national level on grounds of agency expertise,

[97] Agreement on Implementation of Article VI of the General Agreement on Tariffs and Trade 1994, www.wto.org/english/docs_e/legal_e/legal_e.htm.

[98] Croley and Jackson, 'WTO Procedures, Standard of Review, and Deference to National Governments', 199.

[99] *Chevron U.S.A., Inc.* v. *Natural Resources Defense Council, Inc.*, 467 U.S. 837 (1984).

[100] Croley and Jackson, 'WTO Procedures, Standard of Review, and Deference to National Governments', 208–12.

this does not translate to the WTO context, since individual WTO members have no particular claim to such expertise in the interpretation of the legal provisions of the WTO agreements. Nor does the democratic rationale for according deference to agencies at national level play out in the WTO context, since WTO members are not charged with responsibility for implementing the WTO agreements in the same way that a national agency is charged by Congress with implementing a statute, nor are individual WTO members readily accountable to the WTO membership at large. Croley and Jackson moreover foreshadow the danger of affording significant deference over legal issues to WTO members that was subsequently pointed out by Ehlermann and Lockhart, viz. the concern over multiple interpretations of the same legal provision. While Croley and Jackson are therefore rightly sceptical of the *Chevron* analogy, they nevertheless conclude that there is 'an important policy value in recognizing the need for some deference to national government decisions' pursuant to Article 17.6(ii).[101] The subsequent jurisprudence has largely borne out this cautious view.

In *US – Hot-Rolled Steel* the Appellate Body held that Article 17.6(ii) '*presupposes* that application of the rules of treaty interpretation in Articles 31 and 32 of the *Vienna Convention* could give rise to, at least, two interpretations of some provisions of the *Anti-Dumping Agreement*, which, under that Convention, would both be "*permissible*

[101] Croley and Jackson, 'WTO Procedures, Standard of Review, and Deference to National Governments', 212.

interpretations"',[102] with the consequence that a measure would be deemed to be in conformity with the Anti-dumping Agreement if it rested on one of those permissible interpretations. A permissible interpretation was one which was found to be appropriate '*after* application of the pertinent rules' of the Vienna Convention.[103] It was a matter for interpretation which provisions of the Anti-dumping Agreement admitted of more than one permissible interpretation.[104] Article 17.6(ii) did not, moreover, rule out application of Article 11 DSU, insofar as the latter required that the determination should be an 'objective assessment', with the consequence that the Appellate Body would make such an assessment as to the legal provisions at issue, their applicability to the dispute, and the conformity of the measures at issue with the covered agreements.[105] This approach to Article 17.6(ii) has been followed in subsequent rulings, which have made clear that a particular legal provision of the Anti-dumping Agreement may not be susceptible to more than one interpretation.[106]

[102] Report of the Appellate Body, *United States Anti-dumping Measures on Certain Hot-Rolled Steel Products from Japan ('US – Hot-Rolled Steel')*, WT/DS184/AB/R, 21 August 2001, para. 59. Italics in the original.

[103] *US – Hot-Rolled Steel*, para. 60. Italics in the original.

[104] *US – Hot-Rolled Steel*, para. 61. [105] *US – Hot-Rolled Steel*, para. 62.

[106] Report of the Panel, *United States – Investigation of the International Trade Commission in Softwood Lumber from Canada*, WT/DS277/R, 22 March 2004, paras. 7.21–7.22; Report of the Appellate Body, *United States – Final Determination on Softwood Lumber from Canada*, WT/DS264/AB/RW, 15 August 2006, para. 123; Report of the Appellate Body, *United States – Measures Relating to Zeroing and Sunset Reviews*, WT/DS322/AB/R, 9 January 2007, para. 189; Report of the Appellate

The Appellate Body built on the preceding jurisprudence in *United States – Zeroing Methodology*.[107] It held that the second sentence of Article 17.6(ii) contemplated a sequential analysis, the first step of which required a panel to apply the customary rules of interpretation to the Treaty to determine what was yielded by their application, including those codified in the Vienna Convention. It was only after this was done that a panel should decide whether the second sentence of Article 17.6(ii) was applicable. The interpretation of the second sentence of Article 17.6(ii) must, moreover, be consistent with the rules and principles in the Vienna Convention, which precluded an interpretation that would render it redundant, or that derogated from customary rules of interpretation of public international law. This nonetheless left open the possibility that application of the Vienna Convention might give rise to an interpretive range, and if it did then an interpretation falling within that range was permissible. The Appellate Body opined that multiple meanings of a word or term did not automatically equate with 'permissible' interpretations for the purposes of Article 17.6(ii). It was necessary to have recourse to context, object and purpose to elucidate the relevant meaning of the word or term.

Body, *United States – Final Anti-dumping Measures on Stainless Steel from Mexico*, WT/DS344/AB/R, 30 April 2008, paras. 76, 136.

[107] Report of the Appellate Body, *United States – Continued Existence and Application of Zeroing Methodology*, WT/DS350/AB/R, 4 February 2009, paras. 269–73.

(vi) Legal controls and courts: the WTO and review of fact

In relation to review of factual determinations, it will be recalled that the Appellate Body in *EC – Hormones* rejected *de novo* review and total deference to the primary decision maker as standards of review under Article 11 DSU. The *de novo* standard connoted the idea that a panel would have complete freedom to reach a different factual determination from the competent authority of the Member whose act was being reviewed, the corollary being that the panel would verify for itself whether the determination was correct factually and procedurally.[108] WTO panels were, said the Appellate Body, 'poorly suited to engage in such review'.[109] The deference standard connoted the idea that the panel would consider only whether the procedure required by WTO rules had been followed,[110] but total deference to the factual findings of the national authorities was not felt to be compatible with Article 11 DSU.[111]

While it is clear, as Ehlermann and Lockhart note, that panels should afford considerable discretion to national authorities in relation to the finding of facts,[112] the limits to

[108] *EC – Hormones*, para. 111. [109] *EC – Hormones*, para. 117.
[110] *EC – Hormones*, para. 111. [111] *EC – Hormones*, para. 117.
[112] Ehlermann and Lockhart, 'Standard of Review in WTO Law', 502–3. Their conclusion in this respect is, however, rightly predicated on the assumption that the national authority has carried out a proper investigation, which may be required in relation to some agreements that fall within the WTO schema, but not in relation to others. This will perforce have implications for the intensity of factual review in the two types of situation. Ibid., 513–15.

this discretion will depend, inter alia, on the nature of the obligations under the specific WTO agreement, as emphasized by the Appellate Body in *US – Lamb*.[113] It reaffirmed that panels should not undertake *de novo* review of the evidence, nor substitute their own conclusion for that of the competent authorities, and then continued as follows:

> this does *not* mean that panels must simply *accept* the conclusions of the competent authorities. To the contrary, in our view, in examining a claim under Article 4.2(a),[114] a panel can assess whether the competent authorities' explanation for its determination is reasoned and adequate *only* if the panel critically examines that explanation, in depth, and in the light of the facts before the panel. Panels must, therefore, review whether the competent authorities' explanation fully addresses the nature, and, especially, the complexities, of the data, and responds to other plausible interpretations of that data. A panel must find, in particular, that an explanation is not reasoned, or is not adequate, if some *alternative explanation* of the facts is plausible, and if the competent authorities' explanation does not seem adequate in the light of that alternative explanation.[115]

If a panel concluded that the competent authorities had not provided a reasoned or adequate explanation for their

[113] Report of Appellate Body, *United States – Safeguard Measures on Imports of Fresh, Chilled or Frozen Lamb Meat from New Zealand and Australia*, WT/DS177/AB/R, WT/DS178/AB/R, 1 May 2001, paras. 106–7.

[114] Agreement on Safeguards, www.wto.org/english/docs_e/legal_e/legal_e.htm.

[115] *US – Lamb*, para. 106. Italics in the original.

determination, that panel was not thereby undertaking *de novo* review, or substituting its conclusion for that of the competent authorities. Rather, the panel has, 'consistent with its obligations under the DSU, simply reached a conclusion that the determination made by the competent authorities is inconsistent with the specific requirements of Article 4.2 of the Agreement on Safeguards'.[116]

It is common in regimes of administrative law for appeal courts to respect factual determinations made by lower judicial organs, and it is therefore unsurprising to find that the WTO Appellate Body respects rulings on factual matters made by panels. In *United States – Wheat Gluten*,[117] the Appellate Body affirmed that whether a panel had made an 'objective assessment' of the facts was itself an issue of law that could be subject to appeal, but that nonetheless the panel's appreciation of the evidence fell within the scope of the panel's discretion as the trier of facts.[118] It followed that the Appellate Body could not base a finding of inconsistency under Article 11 DSU simply on the conclusion that it might have reached a different factual finding from that reached by the panel. It was for the claimant to show that the panel had exceeded the bounds of its discretion, as the trier of facts, in its appreciation of the evidence, and the

[116] *US – Lamb*, para. 107.

[117] Report of the Appellate Body, *United States – Definitive Safeguard Measures on Imports of Wheat Gluten from the European Communities*, WT/DS166/AB/R, 22 December 2000.

[118] Report of the Appellate Body, *Korea – Taxes on Alcoholic Beverages ('Korea – Alcoholic Beverages')*, WT/DS75/AB/R, WT/DS84/AB/R, 17 February 1999, paras. 161 and 162.

Appellate Body would 'not interfere lightly with the panel's exercise of its discretion'.[119]

The intensity of factual review will be affected by the existence of more specific Treaty provisions dealing with the issue, as exemplified by the Anti-dumping Agreement. Article 17.6(i) contains the pertinent provision:

> In its assessment of the facts of the matter, the panel shall determine whether the authorities' establishment of the facts was proper and whether their evaluation of those facts was unbiased and objective. If the establishment of the facts was proper and the evaluation was unbiased and objective, even though the panel might have reached a different conclusion, the evaluation shall not be overturned.

It provides twofold guidance for the panel, which must ensure that the 'establishment' of the facts was proper and that the 'evaluation' was unbiased and objective. If these twin conditions are met it is not then for the panel to overturn the evaluation merely because it would have reached a different conclusion. This accords with the overall structure of the Anti-dumping Agreement, 'which gives national authorities the responsibility for investigating the facts and making an initial determination', the corollary being that 'the Agreement requires panels to show deference to the national investigative process'.[120]

[119] *US – Wheat Gluten*, para. 151.

[120] Ehlermann and Lockhart, 'Standard of Review in WTO Law', 507.

This has been affirmed in decisions of the WTO Appellate Body and panels. Thus in *Thailand – H-Beams*,[121] the Appellate Body said that the aim of Article 17.6(i) was 'to prevent a panel from "second-guessing" a determination of a national authority when the establishment of the facts is proper and the evaluation of those facts is unbiased and objective'. This was reinforced by the panel in *Guatemala – Cement II*, which decided that Article 17.6(i) did not mandate *de novo* review of the evidence that was before the investigating authority.[122] The panel's duty was rather to review the determination made by the investigating authorities, in accord with the twin criteria laid down in Article 17.6(i) to determine 'whether an unbiased and objective investigating authority evaluating the evidence before it at the time of the investigation could properly have made the determinations made by Guatemala in this case'.[123] This review was to be conducted in accord with Article 17.5(ii), which meant that it was limited to the facts before the investigating authority, with the consequence that it precluded examination of new evidence that was not part of the record of the investigation.

[121] Report of the Appellate Body, *Thailand – Anti-dumping Duties on Angles, Shapes and Sections of Iron or Non-alloy Steel and H-beams from Poland*, WT/DS122/AB/R, 12 March 2001, para. 117.

[122] Report of the Panel, *Guatemala – Definitive Anti-dumping Measures on Grey Portland Cement from Mexico*, WT/DS156/R, 24 October 2000, para. 8.19.

[123] *Guatemala – Cement II*, para. 8.19.

The reasoning in *Guatemala – Cement 1* was to like effect.[124] The panel's role was not to evaluate anew the evidence before the Ministry when it decided to initiate the anti-dumping investigation, but to examine whether the evidence relied on by the Ministry was sufficient – that is, 'whether an unbiased and objective investigating authority evaluating that evidence could properly have determined that sufficient evidence of dumping, injury, and causal link existed to justify initiating the investigation'[125] – the quantum and quality of such evidence required for initiation of the inquiry being less than for the final determination. The panel duly scrutinized 'all the information which was on the record before the Ministry at the time of initiation in examining whether an unbiased and objective investigating authority could properly have made the determination that was reached by the Ministry'.[126]

It is nonetheless clear that the WTO adjudicative bodies take seriously the twin imperatives in Article 17.6(i). Thus in *US – Stainless Steel Korea* it was held that a panel must check 'not merely whether the national authorities have properly established the relevant facts but also the value or

[124] Report of the Panel, *Guatemala – Anti-dumping Investigation Regarding Portland Cement from Mexico*, WT/DS60/R, 19 June 1998.

[125] *Guatemala – Cement 1*, para. 7.57.

[126] *Guatemala – Cement 1*, para. 7.60. See also Report of the Panel, *European Communities – Anti-dumping on Imports of Cotton-Type Bed Linen from India*, WT/DS141/R, 30 October 2000, para. 6.45; Report of the Panel, *Argentina – Definitive Anti-dumping Measures on Ceramic Floor Tiles from Italy*, WT/DS189/R, 28 September 2001, para. 6.27.

weight attached to those facts and whether this was done in an unbiased and objective manner'.[127] It is equally clear from *Argentina – Ceramic Tiles* that the factual arguments are assessed in the light of the evidence as considered by the Member at the relevant time, with the consequence that the panel should not take 'into consideration any arguments and reasons that did not form part of the evaluation process of the investigating authority, but instead are *ex post facto* justifications which were not provided at the time the determination was made'.[128]

(vii) Legal controls and courts: the WTO and rationality/proportionality review

Closely related but distinct from review for law and fact is rationality/proportionality review. The conceptual foundation for such review is derived from an admixture of particular WTO Treaty provisions combined with reasoning from more general precepts of administrative legality.

There are several provisions in WTO agreements that demand or invite review in terms of rationality or proportionality.[129] Thus Article 46 of the TRIPS Agreement,[130] which deals with judicial remedies for violation of intellectual property rights, provides that when considering requests for relief the judicial authorities should take account of 'the need for

[127] Report of Panel, *United States – Anti-dumping Measures on Stainless Steel Plate in Coils and Stainless Steel Sheet and Strip from Korea*, WT/DS179/R, 22 December 2000, para. 6.18.

[128] *Argentina – Ceramic Tiles*, para. 6.27.

[129] See www.wto.org/english/docs_e/legal_e/27-trips.pdf.

[130] Agreement on Trade-Related Aspects of Intellectual Property Rights.

proportionality between the seriousness of the infringement and the remedies ordered', and Article 47, which is concerned with forcing the infringer to reveal third parties involved in the infringement, is subject to the qualification that this should not be out of proportion to the seriousness of the infringement. Article 5 of the Agreement on Safeguards stipulates that a Member shall apply safeguard measures 'only to the extent necessary to prevent or remedy serious injury and to facilitate adjustment'.[131] In a similar vein, Article 2.2 of the Agreement on the Application of Sanitary and Phytosanitary Measures states that Members 'shall ensure that any sanitary or phytosanitary measure is applied only to the extent necessary to protect human, animal or plant life or health, is based on scientific principles and is not maintained without sufficient scientific evidence'. There are analogous provisions in Article 2.2 of the Agreement on Technical Barriers to Trade, which provides that 'technical regulations shall not be more trade-restrictive than necessary to fulfil a legitimate objective, taking account of the risks non-fulfilment would create'.

The Appellate Body has built rationality/proportionality review on these Treaty foundations, and in doing so has drawn on more general principles of review derived from national and international law. Thus in *US – Cotton Yarn (Pakistan)* the Appellate Body held in a dispute about countervailing measures that 'the part of the total serious damage attributed to an exporting Member must be proportionate

[131] See www.wto.org/english/docs_e/legal_e/legal_e.htm#goods.

to the damage caused by the imports from that Member'.[132] It reached this conclusion in part on the basis of Article 6.4 of the relevant agreement, and in part on rules of general international law on state responsibility, 'which require that countermeasures in response to breaches by states of their international obligations be commensurate with the injury suffered'.[133]

Similar reasoning is apparent in the *Shrimp – Turtle* ruling, where the US had imposed an import ban on shrimp harvested with commercial fishing technology that could adversely affect sea turtles. The Appellate Body concluded that 'an alternative course of action was reasonably open to the United States for securing the legitimate policy goal of its measure, a course of action other than the unilateral and non-consensual procedures of the import prohibition', more particularly given that an import prohibition was the 'heaviest "weapon" in a Member's armoury of trade measures'.[134]

The Appellate Body adopted similar reasoning in *Japan – Agricultural Products*, concluding that the obligation in Article 2.2 of the SPS Agreement[135] that an SPS measure not be maintained without sufficient scientific evidence 'requires

[132] Report of the Appellate Body, *United States – Transitional Safeguard Measure on Combed Cotton Yarn from Pakistan*, WT/DS192/AB/R, 21 October 2011, para. 119.

[133] *US – Cotton Yarn (Pakistan)*, para. 120. See also Report of the Appellate Body, *United States – Definitive Safeguard Measures on Imports of Circular Welded Carbon Quality Line Pipe from Korea*, WT/DS202/AB/R, 15 February 2002, para. 257.

[134] *Shrimp – Turtle*, para. 171.

[135] Agreement on the Application of Sanitary and Phytosanitary Measures.

that there be a rational or objective relationship between the SPS measure and the scientific evidence', which would depend on 'the characteristics of the measure at issue and the quality and quantity of the scientific evidence'.[136]

(viii) Legal controls and courts: reflections on the WTO and the challenges of global administrative law

The preceding analysis has shown the significant strides taken by the Appellate Body and panels in the development of administrative law precepts for the WTO.[137] The success in building their judicial authority is, as Greg Shaffer, Manfred Elsig and Sergio Puig relate, a 'combination of actor agency with institutional design and geopolitical context'.[138] While only governments have formal access to the WTO, 'export-oriented businesses and private lawyers quickly found that they had a material interest in taking advantage of the WTO's automatic dispute settlement system, and a stake in building its authority',[139] and thus put pressure on governments to

[136] Report of the Appellate Body, *Japan – Measures Affecting Agricultural Products*, WT/DS76/AB/R, 22 February 1999, para. 84.

[137] For consideration of the extent to which precedent operates de facto within the WTO regime, see, J. Pauwelyn, 'Minority Rules: Precedent and Participation before the WTO Appellate Body', in J. Jemielniak, L. Nielsen and H. Palmer Olsen (eds.), *Judicial Authority in International Economic Law* (forthcoming 2015).

[138] G. Shaffer, M. Elsig and S. Puig, 'The Extensive (but Fragile) Authority of the WTO Appellate Body', School of Law, University of California, Irvine, Legal Studies Research Paper Series, No 2014-54, p. 11.

[139] Shaffer, Elsig and Puig, 'The Extensive (but Fragile) Authority of the WTO Appellate Body', 11.

litigate claims. Multinational companies with complementary interests with small countries helped the latter to litigate a claim where they might not otherwise have recognized the violation.

It would nonetheless be mistaken to regard the development of global administrative law in the WTO context as uncontentious. There are two kinds of problem faced by the system, which have implications more generally for the development of such adjudicative capacity at the global level.

First, there has been criticism voiced as to judicial activism by the Appellate Body.[140] It has been argued that the Appellate Body has overstepped its remit as laid down by Articles 3.2 and 19.2 DSU, which state respectively that the dispute settlement system is intended to preserve the rights and obligations of the Members under the covered agreements, and that the Appellate Body cannot add to or diminish the rights and obligations contained in such agreements. The limit of the judicial role is an endemic issue in all polities, and it should therefore come as no surprise that it is contentious within the WTO. This does not mean that all such critiques are correct, more particularly when they are predicated on assumptions concerning adjudication freed from contestable choice, or devoid of judicial discretion, which are unrealistic in general terms and in the light of the specific WTO texts.

140 See, e.g., M. Cartland, G. Depayre, and J. Woznowski, 'Is Something Going Wrong in the WTO Dispute Settlement?' (2012) 46 *Journal of World Trade* 979; T. Stewart, P. McDonough, J. Smith and S. Jorgensen, 'The Increasing Recognition of Problems with WTO Appellate Body Decision-Making: Will the Message Be Heard?' (2013) 8 *Global Trade and Customs Journal* 390.

There is, nevertheless, no doubting the controversial nature of some Appellate Body rulings, such as that in *Shrimp – Tuna* that allowed amicus briefs,[141] and the rulings concerning the interpretation of the standard of review in Article 17.6(ii) of the Anti-dumping Agreement,[142] as well as particular substantive rulings.[143] It is concerns of this kind that have led commentators to question whether the Appellate Body's extensive authority is 'fragile', in particular when taken in conjunction with related issues, such as non-compliance, delay and what has been termed 'uncompliance', connoting formal compliance with a ruling followed by measures of equivalent effect that nullify the ruling's impact.[144]

The second problem is distinct, albeit related, and concerns accountability writ large within the WTO regime. The interplay between the legal and political is but one part of this discourse. Thus the concerns as to judicial activism by the Appellate Body are heightened by the fact that it is extremely difficult to overturn its rulings legislatively, in part because the existence of such a forum within the WTO is questionable, and in part because 'winning parties can block legislative

[141] General Council, Minutes of the Meeting of 22 Nov. 2000, WT/GC/M/60 (Jan. 23, 2001).

[142] Cartland, Depayre, and Woznowski, 'Is Something Going Wrong in the WTO Dispute Settlement?'

[143] See, e.g., R. Alford, 'Reflections on U.S. – Zeroing: A Study in Judicial Overreaching by the WTO Appellate Body' (2006–7) 45 *Columbia Journal of Transnational Law* 196; Stewart, McDonough, Smith and Jorgensen, 'The Increasing Recognition of Problems with WTO Appellate Body Decision-Making'.

[144] Shaffer, Elsig and Puig, 'The Extensive (but Fragile) Authority of the WTO Appellate Body', 28.

responses to dispute settlement decisions'.[145] There are, in addition, a plethora of accountability issues that have generated extensive discourse within the WTO literature, which is unsurprising given that such issues are debated at national or regional level, even if they may be resolved differently because of differing constitutional and administrative regimes in the different systems. Thus there has been discussion on the meaning of good governance within the WTO schema;[146] there is extensive literature on whether the WTO should be perceived in constitutional terms and, if so, what that should mean in this context;[147] and there is contestation concerning the nature of rights that should be protected within the regime.[148] It is beyond the scope of this work to consider the

[145] Stewart, McDonough, Smith and Jorgensen, 'The Increasing Recognition of Problems with WTO Appellate Body Decision-Making', 397.

[146] D. Esty, 'Good Governance at the World Trade Organization: Building a Foundation of Administrative Law' (2007) 10 *Journal of International Economic Law* 509.

[147] See, e.g., J. McGinnis and M. Movsesian, 'The World Trade Constitution' (2000) 114 *Harvard Law Review* 511; D. Cass, 'The "Constitutionalization" of International Trade Law: Judicial Norm Creation as the Engine of Constitutional Development in International Trade' (2001) 12 *European Journal of International Law* 39; P. Gerhart, 'The Two Constitutional Visions of the World Trade Organisation' (2003) 24 *University of Pennsylvania Journal of International Economic Law* 1; J. Dunoff, 'Constitutional Conceits: The WTO's "Constitution" and the Discipline of International Law' (2006) 17 *European Journal of International Law* 647; J. Trachtman, 'The Constitutions of the WTO' (2006) 17 *European Journal of International Law* 623.

[148] See, e.g., E.-U. Petersmann, 'Time for a United Nations "Global Compact" for Integrating Human Rights into the Law of Worldwide

issues raised by this literature. What is apposite for present purposes is the realization that discussion of global administrative law as it pertains to any particular global or transnational organization cannot be hermetically sealed from broader public law concerns, indeed the line betwixt the two may be contentious. This constitutes in itself one of the challenges when thinking about global administrative law.

(ix) Administrative/legal controls: the WTO committees

The preceding discussion has focused on the development of the precepts of administrative law by the WTO panels and Appellate Body. Andrew Lang and Joanne Scott have, however, rightly noted the important role played by committees within the WTO system, which perform a plethora of functions, including information exchange,

Organizations: Lessons from European Integration' (2002) 13 *European Journal of International Law* 621; R. Howse, 'Human Rights in the WTO: Whose Rights, What Humanity? Comment on Petersmann' (2002) 13 *European Journal of International Law* 651; P. Alston, 'Resisting the Merger and Acquisition of Human Rights by Trade Law' (2002) 13 *European Journal of International Law* 815; E.-U. Petersmann, 'Taking Human Dignity, Poverty and Empowerment more Seriously: Rejoinder to Alston' (2002) 13 *European Journal of International Law* 845; E.-U. Petersmann, 'Multilevel Judicial Governance of International Trade Requires a Common Conception of Rule of Law and Justice' (2007) 10 *Journal of International Economic Law* 529; L. Wallach, 'Accountable Government in the Era of Globalization: The WTO, NAFTA and the International Harmonization of Standards' (2002) 50 *University of Kansas Law Review* 823; H. Hestermeyer, 'Economic, Social and Cultural Rights in the World trade Organization: Legal Aspects and Practice', forthcoming.

norm elaboration, negotiated dispute resolution and the fostering of international harmonization.

Thus Lang and Scott argue that the SPS Committee 'may be viewed as an engine for the generation of global administrative law and as an agent for its enforcement',[149] through establishment of processes designed to enhance accountability of WTO Members.[150] This is exemplified by the SPS Committee complaints procedure, which enables states to raise specific trade concerns. This may be 'thought to represent an institutional expression of the transparency principle, and the instantiation of a reason-giving requirement', whereby the committee's activities 'serve to render visible the transboundary effects of "domestic" regulation, and require that regulating Member States explain and justify their decisions in the light of these'.[151]

(e) National legitimation from the bottom: process, participation and deliberation

(i) Rationale

In national systems, the basic rationale for fostering participation is well known.[152] It may be fortuitous whether a

[149] A. Lang and J. Scott, 'The Hidden World of WTO Governance' (2009) 20 *European Journal of International Law* 575, at 607.

[150] Art. 12 SPS.

[151] Lang and Scott, 'The Hidden World of WTO Governance', 608.

[152] See, e.g., Stewart, 'Reformation of Administrative Law'; C. Pateman, *Participation and Democratic Theory* (Cambridge: Cambridge University Press, 1970); J. Mashaw, *Due Process in the Administrative State* (New Haven: Yale University Press, 1985); R. Baldwin, *Rules and*

person is affected through an individualized determination, or through a rule. Participation enables views to be taken into account before an administrative policy has hardened into a draft rule; it can assist the legislature with technical scrutiny; it can improve the quality of rules by input from interested parties with knowledge of the area being regulated; and it allows those outside government to play some role in the shaping of policy. Participation thus has an instrumental and a non-instrumental aim.

In instrumental terms it is hoped that a better rule will emerge by enabling those with knowledge of the subject matter to proffer their views before the rule is made. This does not mean that the views of such parties are determinative of the content of the rule, but that they should be taken into account before the rule is made. If, for example, the government is making rules to combat the spread of infectious disease in animals it is sensible to allow interested parties, such as farmers and animal welfare groups, to proffer their views as to the most efficacious manner to attain this goal.

In non-instrumental terms, participation fosters citizen involvement in the process of government broadly conceived, which can be regarded as valuable in itself. We are accustomed in modern states to the reality that most decision-making occurs through representative democracy, this being

Government (Oxford: Oxford University Press, 1995); D. Galligan, *Due Process and Fair Procedures* (Oxford: Oxford University Press, 1996); J. Cohen, *Constitution, Democracy and State Power: The Institutions of Justice* (Cheltenham: Edward Elgar, 1996); T. Ziamou, *Rulemaking, Participation and the Limits of Public Law in the USA and Europe* (Aldershot: Ashgate, 2001).

necessitated by the size of nation states and the range of problems they have to deal with. Direct democracy in which all participate in all major decisions is not feasible. The very range of problems dealt with by modern states means, however, that the normal organs of representative democracy struggle in terms of time and expertise to cope with the subject matter placed before them. Thus even if a legal system subscribes to legitimation of rules from the top through legislative oversight, the effectiveness of such constraints will normally be limited. Viewed from this perspective, participation enables the normal mechanisms of representative democracy to be supplemented by recourse to direct democracy, whereby interested parties are enabled to put their opinions and take part in the process of government.

This rationale is not shared by all national regimes. In some systems it is felt wrong to accord legal rights to participate to those who press the claims of a particular group, as opposed to the general public interest. On this view, it is only the parent legislature that speaks for the general interest, the corollary being that it is thought to be mistaken to give legal status to secondary rules legitimated through participation, where they have not been sanctioned by the legislature. This argument should be respected, but is nonetheless based on contestable assumptions.

It is assumed that parties in the legislature represent the 'objective public interest', while groups seeking to participate outside the legislature press 'narrow factional interests'. This is overly simplistic, and fails to capture the reality from both perspectives: legislatures contain groups that are aligned with particular interests, and participation in rule making external to the legislature does not have to entail narrow interest-group representation. It is true that group power in the participation process is often unequal, but it is difficult to believe that less advantaged groups fare better where there are no participatory rights. The more powerful groups exert influence even where there are no formal rights, through the very fact of their power. The introduction of a more structured system of participatory rights policed by courts at least gives the less advantaged groups a chance to air their views. It should, moreover, be emphasized that the final decision is not 'dictated' by the views of those who are consulted. The obligation is to give adequate consideration to those who proffer such views.

(ii) Legal and political control

If a legal system is minded to accord participation rights there are a variety of ways in which this can be delivered. Limits of space preclude detailed elaboration, but the options can be sketched here.

It may be decided to constitutionalize participation rights. This is one reading of what the EU has done in Article 11 TEU, although the precise legal implications remain to be seen.[153] Article 10 TEU enshrines the principle of representative democracy, while Article 11 TEU embodies the principle of direct or participatory democracy. The latter provides that EU institutions must, by appropriate means, give citizens and representative associations the opportunity to make known,

[153] J. Mendes, 'Participation and the Role of Law after Lisbon: A Legal View on Article 11 TEU' (2011) 48 *Common Market Law Review* 1849.

and to publicly exchange, their views in all areas of EU action. They must also maintain an open, transparent and regular dialogue with representative associations and civil society. The European Commission is charged with carrying out broad consultations with parties concerned, in order to ensure that the EU's actions are coherent and transparent.[154] Constitutionalization is the most forceful protection of participatory rights, but much depends on the terms on which such rights are constitutionalized and the way in which these are interpreted by the courts.

A second technique is to enshrine participation rights in a statute. The statute may be particular, governing a specific subject matter area, and most, if not all, legal systems give participation rights this degree of force. The statute may, alternatively, be general in scope, protecting participation rights across a broad range of areas, albeit subject to limited exceptions for rules of particular types. The US Administrative Procedure Act 1946 is the best-known example of this genre. It also exemplifies the scope for variation in the type of participation right, ranging from limited use of full adjudicatory hearings directly analogous to an ordinary trial to the notice-and-comment procedure that constitutes the norm for most rule making.[155]

[154] There is, in addition, provision for a citizens' initiative, whereby one million citizens who are nationals of a significant number of Member States can invite the European Commission, within the framework of its powers, to submit any appropriate proposal on matters where citizens consider that a legal act of the Union is required to implement the Treaties. Art. 11(4).

[155] Aman and Mayton, *Administrative Law*.

A third method for enhancing participation is to eschew law and legal rights to participation in favour of political, non-binding codes, which are intended nonetheless to provide strong guidance for those government departments or agencies that come within their remit. This approach is evident in, for example, both the UK and the EU. The UK has had a code on participation since the beginning of the new millennium. It is repeatedly stated to be non-binding, but nevertheless contains detailed principles on the participatory process that mirror those found in systems that have legal rights to participate.[156] This has also been the general approach of the EU, with the Commission being markedly reluctant to imbue its guidance on consultation with legal force.[157]

There can be difficulties if a legal system seeks to foster participation and to combine this with legitimation through legislative oversight, since it requires careful thought as to how the two legitimation processes link together. The two systems could operate in parallel, such that any draft rule would have to negotiate both hurdles independently.[158] This is not, however, unproblematic, and there could well be difficulties with a system in which rules approved by

[156] See www.berr.gov.uk/files/file47158.pdf; P. Craig, 'Perspectives on Process: Common Law, Statutory and Political' [2010] *Public Law* 275.

[157] Towards a Reinforced Culture of Consultation and Dialogue: General Principles and Minimum Standards for Consultation of Interested Parties by the Commission, COM(2002) 704 final.

[158] This is, in effect, the position in the UK for secondary rules in the form of statutory instruments, if Parliament also imposes a duty to consult interested parties. Craig, *Administrative Law*, Ch. 15.

the legislature were invalidated pursuant to the participatory process. There are, moreover, the practical dangers of putting in place too many process-based constraints, which make effective rule making excessively difficult.

The two systems might, alternatively, be woven together, although the precise way in which this would occur could only be decided in light of the type of legislative oversight prescribed. It is, however, possible, as exemplified by the new EU financial supervisory authorities (ESAs), the European Securities and Markets Authority (ESMA),[159] the European Banking Authority (EBA)[160] and the European Insurance and Occupational Pensions Authority (EIOPA).[161] The ESAs are empowered to draft regulatory and implementing technical standards. The schema is that where, for example, the primary regulation delegates power to the Commission to make delegated acts pursuant to Article 290 TFEU, it is the agency that drafts these acts, which are then endorsed by the Commission, subject to the possibility of veto by the Council or the European Parliament in accordance

[159] Regulation (EU) No 1095/2010 of the European Parliament and of the Council of 24 November 2010 establishing a European Supervisory Authority (European Securities and Markets Authority), OJ 2010 No L331/84.

[160] Regulation (EU) No 1093/2010 of the European Parliament and of the Council of 24 November 2010 establishing a European Supervisory Authority (European Banking Authority), OJ 2010 No L331/12.

[161] Regulation (EU) No 1094/2010 of the European Parliament and of the Council of 24 November 2010 establishing a European Supervisory Authority (European Insurance and Occupational Pensions Authority), OJ 2010 No L331/48.

with Article 290.[162] The recitals to the Regulation make it clear that the Commission should amend the draft produced by, for example, the EBA only in 'very restricted and extraordinary circumstances', the rationale being that the EBA has expertise within this area.[163] The apposite point for present purposes is that this schema of legislative oversight is complemented by legitimation from the bottom in the form of an obligation to consult. Thus the Regulation provides that the ESA, before submitting the draft standard to the Commission, shall conduct open public consultations and analyse the potential related costs and benefits, unless such consultations and analyses are disproportionate in relation to the scope and impact of the draft regulatory technical standards concerned or in relation to the particular urgency of the matter.[164]

(iii) Courts

The courts play two major roles in relation to the development and application of participatory rights. These roles

[162] See, e.g, Regulation (EU) No 1093/2010 of the European Parliament and of the Council of 24 November 2010 establishing a European Supervisory Authority (European Banking Authority), Arts. 10, 13.

[163] See, e.g., Regulation (EU) No 1093/2010 of the European Parliament and of the Council of 24 November 2010 establishing a European Supervisory Authority (European Banking Authority), Rec. 23, although the recital also states that a draft regulatory standard can be amended if it is not compatible with EU law, does not respect proportionality, or runs counter to the fundamental principles of the *acquis* of Union financial-services legislation.

[164] See, e.g., Regulation (EU) No 1093/2010 of the European Parliament and of the Council of 24 November 2010 establishing a European Supervisory Authority (European Banking Authority), Arts. 10(1), 15(1).

are not value-free, and both entail significant choices concerning the reach of legal rules.

It will be for the courts to decide whether to recognize legal participatory rights in the absence of any specific mention thereof in that system's constituent document, or in legislation enacted by that system. The judicial choice is normally made when deciding on the scope of the right to due process/fair procedure. The answer in many legal regimes is that the right to be heard in relation to individual determinations is regarded as fundamental, and is not dependent on foundation in a Treaty article or legislation. The courts' stance on participation in relation to norms of a legislative nature is markedly different. They often conclude that such rights only exist where there is foundation in a constitution, in a Treaty article, or in legislation, and they will not lightly interpret these norms as giving rise to such rights. The premise is that there is a real distinction between provisions that impact on a person in the form of an individualized determination, and those that impact through rules of a more generalized character. This choice is contestable on a variety of grounds,[165] but it informs judicial thinking in many legal systems.

It will also be for the courts to decide on the legal implications of constitutional or statutory provisions that do enshrine participatory rights. This requires judicial choice in circumstances where the relevant statute may provide scant guidance as to the consequences that should follow from the

[165] J. Mendes, *Participation in EU Rulemaking: A Rights-Based Approach* (Oxford: Oxford University Press, 2011); P. Craig, *EU Administrative Law* (Oxford: Oxford University Press, 2nd ed., 2012), Ch. 11.

administration's legal obligation to allow participation. It is common for courts to interpret this so as to require that there should be adequate notice of the right to be consulted, adequate time within which the consultation should take place, access to information in order to make the consultation process a reality, and the need for a reasoned decision by the administration that reveals the way in which it has taken the views proffered into account.[166] The judicial task is therefore to protect the principle of participation and to make it a practical reality, thereby ensuring that the administration does not merely go through the formal motions when allowing participation.

There can, moreover, be 'tension' between the two judicial roles set out above. This is neatly exemplified by the EU, where the ECJ, prior to the Lisbon Treaty, consistently held that the general principle of law protecting process rights was inapplicable to rule making.[167] The Lisbon Treaty introduced Article 11 TEU, which enshrines the principle of direct democracy and contains provisions mandating consultation with the EU citizenry. The ECJ is therefore faced by a stark choice. It could preserve the legal status quo by interpreting Article 11 so as to require de facto consultation in the rule-making process, while

[166] See, e.g., *R* v. *Brent London Borough Council, ex p. Gunning* (1985) 84 LGR 168; R *(East Devon DC)* v. *Electoral Commission Boundary Committee for England* [2009] EWCA Civ 239; *R (Brynmawr Foundation School Governors)* v. *Welsh Ministers* [2011] EWHC 519 (Admin).

[167] Mendes, *Participation in EU Rulemaking*; Craig, *EU Administrative Law*, Ch. 11.

refusing to read it as generating legal rights. It could achieve the same end by interpreting Article 11 so as to leave the EU institutions discretion as to how the consultation should be conducted, making clear that any judicial review of such determinations would be 'light-touch', requiring proof of manifest error. The ECJ could alternatively regard the Lisbon Treaty and Article 11 as a watershed that warrants the rethinking of its previous case law. This view would be reinforced by the fact that Article 11 is expressed in mandatory language and by the fact that a conservative reading of this Article of the kind set out above would send very negative messages about the EU's oft-repeated commitment to engage more closely with its citizens.

(f) Global legitimation from the bottom: process, participation and contestation

(i) Rationale

In national legal systems participation in rule making and the like is seen as an adjunct to the more direct form of legitimation from the top via the ordinary democratic process. In the global arena participation has greater significance, given that national democratic models do not generally apply.

Consider in this respect Buchanan and Keohane's exposition of legitimacy in global governance. They argue that such legitimacy should be judged against three substantive criteria. Global institutions must meet minimal standards of moral acceptability, couched primarily in terms of human rights; they must have comparative benefit, through provision of benefits that could not otherwise be easily attained; and they must exhibit institutional integrity, such that their practice matches their avowed goals.[168]

Buchanan and Keohane accept that there can be factual problems of determining whether an institution has met these criteria, and also difficulties flowing from the persistence of moral disagreement and uncertainty at the global level.[169] The response is to focus on what they term the epistemic–deliberative quality of the institution, which connotes the 'extent to which the institution provides reliable information needed for grappling with normative disagreement and uncertainty concerning its proper functions'.[170] Transparency and participation play important roles in this regard.

Transparency cast in terms of information as to how the institution works is required in order to ensure a minimal level of accountability, and this includes provision of such information not only to those who are the current 'accountability holders', but also to those who may 'contest the terms of accountability'.[171] This thereby enables those external to the institution, such as non-governmental organizations, to proffer suggestions and criticism of the institution's goals and achievements. Transparency also serves the important aim of enabling such external players

[168] Buchanan and Keohane, 'Legitimacy of Global Governance Institutions', 419–23.

[169] Buchanan and Keohane, 'Legitimacy of Global Governance Institutions', 425.

[170] Buchanan and Keohane, 'Legitimacy of Global Governance Institutions', 426.

[171] Buchanan and Keohane, 'Legitimacy of Global Governance Institutions', 427.

to determine whether the public justification for action proffered by the institution is cogent.

Participation enables actors that are not formally part of the institution to play a role in formulation and revision of policy, thereby fostering inclusion and contestation, which Buchanan and Keohane regard as essential for legitimacy. They regard such 'epistemic external actors' as central to a transnational civil-society conception of accountability, this being especially significant in the absence of global democracy and given the implausibility of replicating the national model on the global plane:

> We have argued that the legitimacy of global governance institutions depends on whether there is ongoing, informed, principled contestation of their goals and terms of accountability. This process of contestation and revision depends on activities of actors outside the institution. It is not enough to make information available. Other agents, whose interests and commitments do not coincide too closely with those of the institution, must provide a check on the reliability of the information, integrate it and make it available in understandable, usable form, to all those who have a legitimate interest in the operation of the institution. Such activities can produce positive feedback, in which appeal to standards of legitimacy by the external epistemic actors not only increases compliance with existing standards, but also leads to improvement in the quality of these standards themselves.[172]

[172] Buchanan and Keohane, 'Legitimacy of Global Governance Institutions', 432.

Related themes are apparent in Gráinne de Búrca's work, as is apparent from the centrality accorded to participation. Her democratic-striving approach demands that the principle of political equality should be realized by the fullest possible participation of those concerned. This participation is to be structured such that the circle of participants remains open, combined with incentives to 'generate the fullest degree of participation possible',[173] the intention being to prevent it from degenerating into participation merely by an elite group. A key element in this strategy is that the participatory process is revised at the end of a regulatory cycle, 'so as to include any new actors or interests who identify themselves as concerned stakeholders, or who have otherwise been identified in the course of the process as having a potential claim to be included'.[174]

Anne-Marie Slaughter advances similar arguments. Her principle of 'global deliberative equality' is designed to counter the elitism/exclusion that can attend networks. The process of global governance is seen as a collective deliberation about common problems and hence 'all affected individuals, or their representatives, are entitled to participate'.[175] She contends that all government networks should therefore adopt clear criteria for participation that will be fairly applied. This is linked to her concept of 'legitimate difference', which entails the idea that difference of view 'reflects a desirable diversity of ideas about how to order an

[173] De Búrca, 'Developing Democracy beyond the State', 253.

[174] De Búrca, 'Developing Democracy beyond the State', 253.

[175] Slaughter, *A New World Order*, p. 246.

economy or society',[176] with willingness to reconsider how an issue is dealt with at home and to respect different choices made by other societies. Thus legitimate difference 'enshrines pluralism as a basis for, rather than a bar to regulatory cooperation, leaving open the possibility of further convergence between legal systems in the form of mutual recognition or even harmonization, but not requiring it'.[177]

Armin von Bogdandy strikes a related chord.[178] He notes that the increased role played by international organizations has led to search for legitimation over and beyond state consent. Conceptions of democracy in which deliberation and participation are central assume greater prominence.[179] To this end, 'enabling the participation of nongovernmental organizations (NGOs) as exponents of international civil society is often advanced as possible compensation for the detachment of international processes from national parliamentary control'.[180] Thus von Bogdandy, drawing on Article 11 TEU, which enshrines precepts of participatory democracy, considers how 'the idea of representation of affected interests of individuals in or *vis-à-vis* international institutions through NGOs has become an important strand in conceptualizing more legitimate rule-making and enforcement at the international level'.[181]

[176] Slaughter, *A New World Order*, p. 248.

[177] Slaughter, *A New World Order*, p. 249.

[178] A. von Bogdandy, 'The European Lessons for International Democracy: The Significance of Articles 9–12 EU for International Organizations' (2012) 23 *European Journal of International Law* 315.

[179] Von Bogdandy, 'European Lessons', 320, 325–6.

[180] Von Bogdandy, 'European Lessons', 326.

[181] Von Bogdandy, 'European Lessons', 332.

Richard Stewart distinguishes between decisional and non-decisional participation, both of which can, albeit in different ways, be mechanisms for alleviating the problem of disregard for interests that are often excluded from global regulatory processes. The former connotes participation in the making of the decisions, but it is limited by 'the reluctance by dominant members, especially powerful governments, to share authority; the need for efficient specialization; and the problems in providing effective representation for disregarded interests'.[182] Much participation is therefore non-decisional, including consultation processes in the making of norms or standards, and the ability to submit an amicus brief in adjudication.[183]

(ii) Realization

The emerging consensus on the importance of participation still leaves open its realization. This is necessarily more complex than in national systems given that there is no global legislator or global court that can impose the requirement across the plethora of bodies that inhabit the global arena. Sabino Cassese has, however, provided a valuable taxonomy of five different types of participation that exist, and their incidence.[184]

Three such categories entail state or global entities. Thus global rules can grant participatory rights to national governments in relation to the global decision-making

[182] Stewart, 'Remedying Disregard', 243.

[183] Stewart, 'Remedying Disregard', 261.

[184] Cassese, *The Global Polity*, pp. 114–56.

process. The existence of this type of participatory right is unsurprising given the power of national governments, and Cassese provides numerous examples of its incidence.[185] It provides national governments with an explicit and institutionalized mechanism for involvement with policy formulation, standard-setting and the like, and in addition facilitates collaboration between national agencies and the global institution. Global rules may also accord participatory rights to states in relation to other states, and can make provision for participatory rights of one global organization vis-à-vis another.

The instances where participatory rights are accorded to non-state entities are especially relevant, and can take two principal forms. Global rules may grant participatory rights to private actors in relation to domestic administrations. Such rules will co-exist with any national provisions concerning participation and the global rules may benefit foreigners as well as citizens of that state. The Aarhus Convention is the best-known example,[186] requiring the parties to guarantee rights of access to information, public participation in decision making and access to justice in environmental matters. However, many other treaties grant analogous rights,[187] although their detailed nature, and the fora in which they can be used, differ.[188] They are, in broad terms, designed to

[185] Cassese, *The Global Polity*, pp. 128–33.

[186] Convention on Access to Information, Public Participation in Decision-Making and Access to Justice in Environmental Matters, Aarhus, Denmark, 25 June 1998, www.unece.org/env/pp/introduction.html.

[187] Cassese, *The Global Polity*, pp. 114–24.

[188] Cassese, *The Global Polity*, pp. 124–6.

enhance the involvement of civil society in the decision-making process, and thus promote civic trust, and also to ensure, as in the case of WTO anti-dumping rules, that the accused is accorded due process.

Global rules may also grant participatory rights directly to private actors vis-à-vis global institutions. Cassese provides numerous examples where some species of participatory right are provided to private actors in relation to global institutions,[189] although the focus may vary:

> It may be exercised in policy formulation proceedings (as in the cases of NGO participation before the WTO,[[190]] ICANN,[[191]] or the NAALC[[192]]), in regulatory procedures (as in the BCBS[[193]] and the fisheries cases), in standard setting proceedings (as is the case for accounting standards), in procedures aimed at enforcing global standards in domestic jurisdictions (like in the context of the North American environmental standards), in adjudication proceedings (as in the cases of patents, labour standards and anti-doping). In the case of the CEC,[[194]] consultation is provided for in policy formulation, the preparation of programmes and also in specific projects and issues.[[195]]

[189] Cassese, *The Global Polity*, pp. 147–53. [190] See www.wto.org.

[191] Internet Corporation for Assigned Names and Numbers, www.icann.org.

[192] North American Agreement for Labor Cooperation, www.naalc.org/index.cfm?page=147.

[193] Basel Committee on Banking Supervision, www.bis.org/bcbs.

[194] Commission for Environmental Cooperation, www.cec.org.

[195] Cassese, *The Global Polity*, p. 154.

The efficacy of such participatory rights also varies, but has been enhanced by the Internet.[196] It is no longer necessary to access a physical source to see a draft rule and the documentation underlying it. It is often no longer necessary to ask for the relevant form, write the relevant comment and post it to the relevant address. It is no longer necessary to have access to a written source to see all comments received from others, or to view changes from the original draft rule. These issues can be dealt with online. To be sure, this is dependent on access to the Internet, and on websites being well designed to facilitate participation, but the former is improving all the time, and so, on the whole, is the latter.[197]

The incidence of such participatory rights is nonetheless still dependent on the political will of those who wield power in the particular global institution. The limits imposed on public participation in the context of, for example, the WTO have been well documented. Thus while WTO law imposes some obligations of transparency and participation on national governments, the position is different in relation to decision making at WTO level, where there has been considerable resistance to such initiatives.[198] Charnovitz has argued cogently for increase in participation at the WTO level. The idea that citizen views should be channelled only

[196] S. Coleman and P. Shane (eds.), *Connecting Democracy: Online Consultation and the Flow of Political Communication* (Cambridge, MA: MIT Press, 2012).

[197] O. Perez, 'E-democracy, Transnational Organizations, and the Challenge of New Techno-intermediation', in Coleman and Shane, *Connecting Democracy*, p. 291.

[198] Charnovitz, 'Transparency and Participation', 938.

through their own government disadvantages those who live in non-democratic countries; it disenfranchises individuals from countries that have not yet been allowed to join the WTO; it disables individuals from non-powerful countries, whose governments may lack voice within the WTO; it reinforces a sense of economic nationalism, by framing the debate as one that takes place within national units; it is predicated on the assumption that views will necessarily be national, thereby precluding contribution from transnational groupings; and it reduces the competition between ideas, thereby reinforcing the tendency to status quo thinking.[199]

The incidence of such participatory rights will depend on both 'supply-side' and 'demand-side' factors. It is more likely that something akin to participation rights will emerge where there is an incentive for those making the rules to foster participation. This supply-side incentive may stem from the fact that the rule makers seek the enhanced legitimacy that comes from fostering participation. It may be that they have taken to heart the instrumental value that can be served by participation. They seriously believe that the quality of the rules will be enhanced by taking account of the views of interested parties. The rule makers are more likely to feel such sentiments where they have something to learn from those affected by the rules that are made. This may occur where the subject matter is technical. The rule-making authority may

[199] Charnovitz, 'Transparency and Participation', 948–52. See also D. Esty, 'Non-governmental Organizations at the World Trade Organization: Cooperation, Competition, or Exclusion' (1998) 1 *Journal of International Economic Law* 123.

well be composed of those with some expertise in the relevant area, but it may nevertheless feel that it can benefit from input from a wider constituency of those affected by the rules, where such input will primarily be from those with detailed technical expertise that might exceed its own in certain respects.

Further, the stronger the constituency affected by the rule making, the more likely it is that structured participation will emerge. This demand-side incentive for the development of participation rights is likely to be present where the affected parties are strong and diverse.[200] The very strength of the affected parties, whether they are nation states, banks or multinational corporations, will enable them to use this power to ensure that they are involved in the global rule-making process. A non-transparent, unstructured participation regime will enable any single player to exert influence hidden from others, but this will be equally true for all other players. This is likely to increase demand for some structured medium to ensure that the views of individual players are not lost in the rule-making process, and to ensure that each player has some visibility of the detailed expression of preferences by other players with different interests to their own.

It is therefore less likely for participation to assume prominence where there is neither a supply-side incentive for its development from those who make the rules, nor a

200 See, e.g., M. Barr and G. Miller, 'Global Administrative Law: The View from Basel' (2006) 17 *European Journal of International Law* 15; D. Zaring, 'Finding Legal Principle in Global Financial Regulation' (2012) 52 *Virginia Journal of International Law* 683.

demand-side incentive that can be forcefully voiced by those affected by the rules. Thus, where the rule makers have a strong belief in their own bureaucratic/technocratic expertise, and the constituency affected by the rules is heterogeneous, weak and impermanent, it is unlikely that participation will flourish.[201] This is more especially so where there are external factors pressing for rapid resolution of the problem dealt with by the particular international organization.

It will also be more difficult to fashion a system of binding participatory rights in the absence of a court. The argument is not that courts are essential before a norm can be regarded as a legal norm, since this will not withstand jurisprudential scrutiny. The argument is rather that if an international institution chooses to develop legal participatory rights then their efficacy is likely to be enhanced where courts can spell out the legal consequences of according such rights, in relation to matters such as notice, information and the like, and can also help to ensure that the decision maker gives adequate consideration to the views proffered, rather than just going through the motions of consultation.

3 Vertical challenges: interaction between legal orders

The discussion thus far has considered the challenges faced by the creation of global principles of administrative law.

[201] See, e.g., B. Morgan, 'Turning off the Tap: Urban Water Service Delivery and the Social Construction of Global Administrative Law' (2006) 17 *European Journal of International Law* 215.

The focus now shifts to the vertical plane, which is concerned with the interaction between legal orders. This is analysed in relation to individual decisions, norms of a regulatory nature and judicial interaction.

(a) Individual decisions and the interaction between legal orders

The most obvious vertical challenge concerning the interrelation of the global, regional and national domains has already been considered in earlier chapters.[202] Mention here can therefore be brief. Global bodies may exercise power directly over individuals, or where there are direct consequences at national or regional level for the exercise of such power. This has not surprisingly heightened calls for the development of due process at the global level.

This is powerfully exemplified by the whole saga of the *Kadi* litigation.[203] The root cause of the EU litigation was the absence of procedural safeguards for those brought within the ambit of the Security Council rule concerning the freezing of assets. This schema then formed the foundation for the EU regulations on asset freezing, which were challenged in the EU courts for violation of fundamental rights, thereby raising the complex legal issues as to the relationship between EU law and international law.

[202] See above, Chs. 2 and 4.

[203] Cases C-402 and 415/05 P, *Yassin Abdullah Kadi and Al Barakaat International Foundation* v. *Council and Commission* [2008] ECR I-6351.

The Grand Chamber of the CJEU revisited and clarified certain aspects of the earlier ruling in *Kadi II*.[204]

The first *Kadi* case has been analysed in depth in the academic literature,[205] there is a literature emerging on the second decision,[206] and the issue has been analysed earlier in this work. Suffice it, therefore, to say the following that is relevant to the assessment of global administrative law. You can regard this saga in terms of the cup being either half-full or half-empty. The former, more positive, take on the story would highlight the way in which legal regimes at national and regional levels put pressure on a global institution, to which the latter responded by improving its process requirements, thereby revealing its readiness to embrace precepts of administrative justice developed in other legal systems. The latter, more negative, take on the story would emphasize the fact that something as basic as an individual hearing right was not accorded by the global institution before being pressured

[204] Cases C-584, 593 and 595/10 P, *Commission and United Kingdom* v. *Yassin Abdullah Kadi (No 2)* EU:C:2013:518.

[205] See, e.g., G. de Búrca, 'The European Court of Justice and the International Legal Order after *Kadi*', Jean Monnet Working Paper, No 1/09; T. Tridimas and J. Guitierrez-Fons, 'EU Law, International Law, and Economic Sanctions against Terrorism: The Judiciary in Distress?' (2009) 32 *Fordham International Law Journal* 660; J.-P. Jacqué, 'Primauté du droit international versus protection des droits fondamentaux' (2009) 45 *Revue trimestrielle de droit européen* 161; J. Kokott and C. Sobotta, 'The Kadi Case: Constitutional Core Values and International Law – Finding the Balance?' (2012) 23 *European Journal of International Law* 1015.

[206] H. Hooper, 'An Unsteady Middle Ground' (2014) 20 *European Public Law* 409.

into reform by litigation elsewhere, thereby revealing the relative lack of development of fundamental administrative precepts by that institution at the global level.

There might be an inclination to subscribe to the more positive take on the story, but the reality is surely that there is some truth in both versions. The latter, more negative, take on the events serves as a check on unrealistic empirical assumptions as to how far we have progressed towards global administrative law. Insofar as this is grounded in positivist conceptions of law it should give pause for thought as to how far the social facts that underpin this conception of law really exist,[207] more especially given that this must be shown for each legal regime that constitutes the global legal order.

(b) *Regulatory norms and the interaction between legal orders: two dimensions of accountability*

The vertical relationship between the global, regional and national levels is also manifest in relation to norms of a more regulatory nature. It is readily apparent from discussion in this and the preceding chapters that global institutions play an important role in areas as diverse as health, trade, financial regulation and the environment. This has a significant impact on national regulatory authority, and on application of the precepts of national administrative law. We need, nonetheless, to tread carefully in elaborating the existence and

[207] See above, pp. 635–42.

extent of this impact, which varies between different international and transnational institutions.

The existence of this impact is evident in the way that global norms shape and constrain national administrative action. It is increasingly common for national administrative discretion to be constrained by global standards developed by bodies such as the WTO, created pursuant to a classic international treaty, and also by norms fashioned by transnational regulatory networks, or international standardization organizations.[208] In some instances, national administrative authorities directly adopt standards developed by international organizations, in others this is done voluntarily by private firms. The impact of regulatory initiatives from international organizations may also be felt through instructions to member countries as to the methodology that they should employ when promulgating national regulations, as exemplified by the requirement from the WTO that member countries must take account of its techniques of risk assessment when undertaking their domestic regulatory processes. There are, moreover, issues raised by the disjunction between transfer of regulatory responsibility and responsibility for enforcement, as captured by Daphne Barak-Erez and Oren Perez:

> The accountability challenge focuses on the tension between the processes of regulatory harmonization and transference of enforcement responsibilities . . . and the primarily domestic regimes of accountability (tort law,

[208] D. Barak-Erez and O. Perez, 'Whose Administrative Law Is It Anyway? How Global Norms Reshape the Administrative State' (2013) 46 *Cornell International Law Journal* 455.

> criminal law, and administrative forms of accountability), which are still highly fragmented. In other words, while globalization has triggered a process which requires domestic regulators to exercise their discretion according to globally determined decision-frameworks and to rely on the discretion of external bodies (laboratories and accreditation bodies) in the implementation of local (or global) standards – decisions on liability for the same actions are still governed by domestic systems of accountability.[209]

While the existence of the regulatory impact is clear, there is greater debate as to its extent, which is difficult to measure.[210] Thus, for example, Pierre-Hugues Verdier has questioned the relative balance of power between transnational regulatory networks and the national regulators that combine to create them. He contends that the latter will be anchored by the demands of domestic constituencies, and that domestic preferences will shape the positions taken by national regulators on specific issues.[211] This national regulatory perspective is further heightened when domestic politicians intervene 'to prevent or override the adoption of international standards

[209] Barak-Erez and Perez, 'Whose Administrative Law Is It Anyway?', 486. See, more generally, H. Buxbaum, 'Transnational Regulatory Litigation' (2005) 46 *Virginia Journal of International Law* 251.

[210] K. Abbott, 'International Organizations and International Regulatory Co-operation: Exploring the Links', in *International Organizations and International Regulatory Co-operation: The Cases of the OECD and the IMO* (Paris: OECD, 2014), Ch. 1.

[211] P.-H. Verdier, 'Transnational Regulatory Networks and Their Limits' (2009) 34 *Yale Journal of International Law* 113, at 121.

that would threaten their re-election prospects or other political objectives', or where they 'steer the international regulatory agenda toward politically salient issues that regulators would not otherwise treat as priorities'.[212] National regulatory discretion will, as a consequence, often be exercised in the shadow of the interests of the legislature and the executive. The national regulatory authorities that participate in transnational regulatory networks will, moreover, be subject to domestic legal constraints, in terms of their subject matter jurisdiction and the considerations that they should take into account, which they will not normally be able to modify by agreement with foreign regulators. This is so notwithstanding the discretion that resides in such national administrative authorities.[213] National regulators may be especially likely to promote domestic preferences where the global regulatory standard involves distributive issues.

The concept of shared administration has, as will be seen in subsequent sections, something distinctive to tell us about the existence and extent of this impact. It is only by paying closer attention than is customarily given to the type of shared administration that pertains in any particular instance that we can fully understand the interaction between the global, regional and national orders, and the regimes of administrative law that pertain at each level.

It is important when pursuing such inquiry to dispel any idea that, insofar as there are problems concerning regulatory interaction between the global, regional and national

[212] Verdier, 'Transnational Regulatory Networks', 127.
[213] Verdier, 'Transnational Regulatory Networks', 128.

orders, 'blame' should be placed solely at the door of the global order. This will not withstand examination. The reality is more complex, there being issues of accountability that relate to the national/regional level, and to the global level.

From the national perspective, regulators are more limited in what they can achieve, since they can only regulate conduct that falls within their jurisdiction, but there is also a disjunction between what Joanne Scott has aptly termed 'regulatory jurisdiction and regulatory impact',[214] in the sense that states are not accountable to other states that are affected by their domestic regulation, thereby creating a horizontal accountability gap, since the affected states have no voice in such measures. In similar vein Fred Aman notes that a democracy deficit can arise from the fact that individuals may be affected by decisions that have significant adverse impact, which are made by jurisdictions beyond the reach of those affected.[215] Viewed from this perspective, global regulatory regimes can help to reduce this accountability gap in national regulation, by encouraging horizontal and vertical integration of domestic regulatory systems, and by requiring national regulators to take into account all affected interests, including those of other states.[216]

[214] J. Scott, 'Cooperative Regulation in the WTO: The SPS Committee', Global Law Working Paper, 3/06, Hauser Global Law School Program, NYU School of Law.

[215] A. Aman, *The Democracy Deficit: Taming Globalization through Law Reform* (New York: New York University Press, 2004), p. 3.

[216] S. Battini, 'The Proliferation of Global Regulatory Regimes', in Cassese, *Global Administrative Law*, Ch. 2.

From the global perspective, there are, however, accountability problems that pertain to the very global regulatory regimes established to ameliorate the effect of domestic regulation. This has indeed been the story of the first part of this chapter, and we shall return to these concerns in the ensuing discussion. Thus while some such regimes are accountable to national governments through national representatives on such bodies, this is indirect and of limited efficacy. It is, moreover, only applicable to certain global regulatory regimes, and 'reconnects each member of the global bodies only to its own national community'.[217] The development of precepts of global administrative law is one way of alleviating the accountability problem at global level, but, as will be seen below, this must be complemented by recourse to, and reform of, domestic administrative law.

The preceding duality has been succinctly captured by Richard Stewart, who notes that global administrative law must ensure that 'domestic interests are properly considered in global regulatory decisions and their domestic implementation, and ... that global interests are likewise properly considered in domestic administrative decisions'.[218]

It is important, moreover, to recognize the legal and administrative reality, which is that in many instances global administration operates by and through shared administration with authorities at national or regional level. Indeed, as

[217] Battini, 'The Proliferation of Global Regulatory Regimes'.

[218] R. Stewart, 'The Global Regulatory Challenge to U.S. Administrative Law' (2005) 37 *New York University Journal of International Law and Policy* 695, at 750.

Stewart notes it is mistaken to conceive of global regulation as operating on two distinct levels, international and domestic, since it functions rather 'through a web of interactions and influences, horizontal, vertical, and diagonal, among a diverse multiplicity of different regimes and actors, resembling nothing so much as a Jackson Pollock painting'.[219] This is reflected in the plethora of meanings that the concept of shared administration can bear, and a chapter-length discussion could be devoted to this diversity as it plays out in distinct institutional settings. Space precludes such analysis, which will be restricted to two prominent examples of shared administration as it applies to the WTO and the ISO.

(c) Regulatory norms and the interaction between legal orders: formal shared administration and the WTO

(i) The WTO schema of shared administration

Shared administration as employed in relation to the WTO carries the strong connotation developed in the EU, viz. two or more authorities operating at different levels that have distinct administrative tasks enshrined in legislation, and both must discharge their respective tasks for the relevant policy to be implemented successfully.[220]

219 Stewart, 'The Global Regulatory Challenge to U.S. Administrative Law', 703.

220 Committee of Independent Experts, Second Report on Reform of the Commission, Analysis of Current Practice and Proposals for Tackling Mismanagement, Irregularities and Fraud (10 September 1999), Vol. 1, at [3.2.2].

This can be exemplified by the WTO schema. A common pattern in the WTO is that the particular agreement establishes detailed regulatory criteria, which are triggered and applied by national administrative authorities, and in that sense the agreements operate from the 'bottom up',[221] subject to possible oversight by administrators and adjudicators at the WTO level. This form of shared administrative arrangement is driven in part by political considerations, since a WTO Member would not view with equanimity a WTO official having the initial responsibility for application of the regulatory criteria within its state. It is also driven by more practical considerations, viz. that the WTO does not possess the bureaucracy necessary to undertake such work across all WTO Members, or in relation to all WTO agreements.

This pattern of administration is evident in the Anti-dumping Agreement,[222] Article 1 of which provides that an 'anti-dumping measure shall be applied only under the circumstances provided for in Article VI of GATT 1994 and pursuant to investigations initiated and conducted in accordance with the provisions of this Agreement'. Articles 2–4 deal respectively with the meaning of dumping, the determination of injury and the definition of the domestic industry.

[221] G. della Cananea, 'The European Union's Mixed Administrative Proceedings' (2004) 68 *Law and Contemporary Problems* 197.

[222] Agreement on Implementation of Article VI of the General Agreement on Tariffs and Trade 1994, www.wto.org/english/docs_e/legal_e/legal_e.htm.

Article 5 is concerned with the investigation, which is initiated by complaint from the domestic industry. It is then incumbent on the 'authorities' to 'examine the accuracy and adequacy of the evidence to determine whether there is sufficient evidence to justify the initiation of an investigation',[223] and, if there is, to make the determination as to whether dumping has occurred. There are detailed rules as to the procedures that must be followed by the authorities when conducting such an investigation,[224] followed by equally detailed provisions as to the remedies that can be imposed, including provisional measures, price undertakings and anti-dumping duties.[225] The centrality of national authorities to the investigative exercise is further emphasized by the obligation in Article 13 to maintain an effective and independent regime of judicial review.

The shared administrative input from the WTO takes the form of the Committee on Anti-dumping Practices, composed of representatives from each Member, which meets not less than twice per year. It serves, inter alia, as a forum for the negotiated resolution of disputes between Members concerning the imposition of anti-dumping duties.[226] The emphasis is on consultative solution, but with recourse to the WTO Dispute Settlement Body and the establishment of an adjudicative panel should negotiation fail.[227]

[223] Art. 5(3) Anti-dumping Agreement.

[224] Art. 6 Anti-dumping Agreement.

[225] Arts. 7–9 Anti-dumping Agreement.

[226] Arts. 16–17 Anti-dumping Agreement.

[227] Art. 17 Anti-dumping Agreement.

The same pattern of shared administration is evident in the Agreement on the Application of Sanitary and Phytosanitary Measures, although in this instance the vertical shared administration between national authorities and the WTO is complemented by a horizontal dimension, insofar as the SPS Agreement forges explicit links with other international organizations. The SPS Agreement gives Members the right to take sanitary and phytosanitary measures necessary for the protection of human, animal or plant life or health, provided that such measures are not inconsistent with the provisions of the SPS Agreement.[228] The measures must not impose restrictions greater than necessary, and must not discriminate arbitrarily or unjustifiably between Members.[229]

The SPS Agreement goes to considerable lengths to foster harmonization in the application of such measures, by requiring Members to base such measures on international standards, with special emphasis on those made by the Codex Alimentarius Commission.[230] It also mandates mutual recognition, requiring acceptance of SPS measures from other Members as equivalent, even if they differ from the state of import, provided that the exporting Member demonstrates that its measures achieve the importing Member's appropriate level of sanitary or phytosanitary protection.[231] There are provisions requiring that the SPS measures imposed by a Member are subject to risk assessment, the nature of

[228] Art. 2.1 SPS. [229] Art. 2.2–2.3 SPS. [230] Art. 3 SPS.
[231] Art. 4 SPS.

which is set out in detail.[232] So too are the control, inspection and approval procedures.[233]

It is the importing state Members that are charged with the primary administration of the SPS regime, which is unsurprising given that it is their measures that are at issue. This is subject to the injunction that such 'Members are fully responsible under this Agreement for the observance of all obligations set forth herein', and 'Members shall formulate and implement positive measures and mechanisms in support of the observance of the provisions of this Agreement by other than central government bodies'.[234]

The administrative schema at WTO level is analogous to that seen in the context of the Anti-Dumping Agreement. Thus there is a Committee on SPS Measures, which is designed to facilitate consultation between Members concerning contentious SPS measures, and also foster harmonization initiatives. The Committee is charged with maintaining close contact with relevant international organizations in the field of sanitary and phytosanitary protection, especially with the Codex Alimentarius Commission, the International Office of Epizootics, and the Secretariat of the International Plant Protection Convention.[235] Dispute resolution through consultation mediated by the Committee is complemented by possible recourse to the WTO dispute settlement regime of panels and the Appellate Body, as regulated by the Dispute Settlement Understanding.[236]

[232] Art. 5 SPS. [233] Annex C SPS. [234] Art. 13 SPS.
[235] Art. 12 SPS. [236] Art. 11 SPS.

(ii) The practical and normative consequences for administrative law

The WTO regime has several important implications for the interaction between the global and national legal orders insofar as administrative law is concerned.

In terms of input legitimacy, a powerful network such as the WTO has the legitimacy that flows from the fact that it has been duly established by Treaty, which specifies in detail the powers and duties of its members. There are contentious issues relating to the adequacy of the traditional mechanisms for treaty making, concerning matters such as the balance between legislative and executive power in the negotiation and ratification of such agreements.[237] There are, moreover, highly charged issues that relate more specifically to the WTO, such as the influence of industry representatives during negotiations leading to the conclusion of the 1986–94 Uruguay Round of reforms, and the balance between economic and non-economic concerns embodied in the resulting agreements.[238]

In terms of transparency, this is enhanced by the fact that the WTO regime is enshrined in a series of formal agreements, which are readily available for those interested or affected. There are, to be sure, difficult issues of interpretation in particular WTO agreements, but the prevalence of

[237] See, e.g., Weiler, 'The Geology of International Law'.

[238] See, e.g., Wallach, 'Accountable Government in the Era of Globalization: The WTO, NAFTA and the International Harmonization of Standards'.

such difficulties is not noticeably greater than when analogous matters are regulated at national or regional level. In the WTO context, but certainly not in all other areas of global regulation, a quid pro quo of the limitation of national regulatory autonomy is that Members know their obligations and that affected firms can lock onto the regulatory obligations imposed on Members at national level.

There are, nonetheless, transparency concerns that relate to, for example, the dispute settlement process. The fact that panel deliberations are confidential is not in itself unusual,[239] since this is the norm for most adjudicative bodies. Nor is the fact that the opinions of individual panellists expressed in the panel report are anonymous,[240] since this is the norm in the majority of civil law regimes. The instructions for panel hearings provide, however, that it 'shall meet in closed session' and that the parties only attend when invited to do so,[241] although they are guaranteed presence for the entirety of the argument.[242] The hearing is, moreover, largely confined to the parties to the dispute, with provision for other WTO Members with a 'substantial interest' in a matter before a panel to have an opportunity to be heard and to make submissions.[243] Citizens and citizen groups do not have the right to participate, but they may submit an amicus brief that can be accepted at the discretion of a panel.[244] It seems, however, that the Appellate Body will not

[239] Art. 14.1 DSU. [240] Art. 14.3 DSU. [241] Appendix 3, para. 3 DSU.
[242] Appendix 3, para. 10 DSU. [243] Art. 10.2 DSU.
[244] *United States – Import Prohibitions of Certain Shrimp and Shrimp Products*, 12 Oct. 1998, WT/DS58/AB/R.

accept such briefs unless they are appended to the submissions of a formal party to the dispute.[245]

In terms of judicial review, the WTO commonly makes provision for such oversight at two levels, the national and the global, although the precise admixture will depend on the particular WTO agreement that is at issue. Thus particular WTO agreements impose a requirement of independent judicial review at national level, the efficacy of which will perforce depend on more general considerations concerning the effectiveness of such review in that state. The approach in other WTO agreements – such as TRIPS, dealing with intellectual property – is to mandate that national judicial authorities hear complaints from private parties concerning violation of the TRIPS Agreement.[246]

The agreements will in any event commonly mandate due process at national level, and circumscribe the exercise of substantive discretionary choice by national authorities through requirements relating, inter alia, to mutual recognition, non-discrimination, proportionality, risk assessment and the like. If a Member is dissatisfied with the outcome at national level then it can seek a negotiated solution via the WTO, or trigger the dispute settlement mechanism and attendant judicial review by WTO panels and the Appellate Body. The WTO dispute settlement system is 'tilted toward market liberalization in that it creates opportunities to challenge government measures as trade

[245] Dunoff, 'Constitutional Conceits: The WTO's "Constitution" and the Discipline of International Law', 659–60.

[246] Arts. 41–2, 51–2 TRIPS.

barriers, but not to challenge them for providing insufficient regulatory protection'.[247]

In regulatory terms, the effect of the WTO schema is complex. It closely circumscribes the options available to Members, and narrows representative democratic choice at national level. It thereby prevents the legislature opting for protectionism, and limits legislative choice more generally by providing, for example, that measures restrictive of trade on sanitary grounds are not more trade-restrictive than required.[248] This is subject to the obvious caveat that the national legislature will have approved membership of the WTO in accord with whatever constitutional arrangements pertain in that state. The circumscription of such legislative choice is designed, inter alia, to foster accountability by ensuring that the economic choices of a Member take account of the interests of other Members in the areas covered by the WTO agreements. The national executive's role in relation to the legislature is enhanced because the executive will represent the Member at WTO level, whereas the legislature has no seat at the WTO. The global regulatory package is difficult to amend for the reasons set out above.

While the WTO regime entails trade liberalization it would be mistaken to conceive of this simply in terms of deregulation. The reality is that it involves 'not so much deregulation but re-regulation to facilitate, oversee, and check

247 G. Shaffer, 'How the WTO Shapes Regulatory Governance', University of California, Irvine, Legal Studies Research Paper Series, No 2014–53, p. 5.

248 Art. 5.6. SPS.

capitalism, involving both public and private actors', with the result that 'regulatory governance, quintessentially seen in nation-state terms, has become transnationalized'.[249] The assumption that trade liberalization will lead to a regulatory race to the bottom must also be qualified. This is in part because some WTO agreements allow a Member to maintain standards higher than the international norm.[250] This is in part because the WTO can contribute to a 'race to the top', since producers 'may comply with the standards of the most important trading partner which may in fact be quite high, which, in the WTO context, will likely be either a U.S. or an E.U. standard (known as the "California effect" or the "Brussels effect")'.[251] It is also in part because the WTO regime itself mandates new agencies and bureaucracies at national level to implement WTO regulatory norms. The consequence, as Greg Shaffer points out, is that

> the WTO forms part of broader processes of transnational legal ordering that shapes the boundary between the market and the state. On the one hand, WTO tariff bindings and non-discrimination norms enlarge markets by catalyzing product competition across borders. On the other hand, WTO norms directly and indirectly spur new international and transnational standard-setting initiatives by international organizations, nation states, and private actors. As a result, WTO processes both expand markets and spur regulation to

[249] Shaffer, 'How the WTO Shapes Regulatory Governance', 3.
[250] Art. 3.3 SPS.
[251] Shaffer, 'How the WTO Shapes Regulatory Governance', 8.

become more transnational in scope, in the process arguably expanding regulatory governance more than constraining it.[252]

(d) *Regulatory norms and the interaction between legal orders: shared administration and the ISO*

(i) The ISO schema of shared administration

The discussion in the preceding chapter[253] revealed the importance of bodies such as the ISO.[254] The sense of shared administration that pertains in the International Organization for Standardization is very different from that in the WTO, but it is real nonetheless, notwithstanding the fact that it is not embodied in formal legal rules. ISO administration is shared in a double sense: its constituent members are national standards agencies that help decide the applicable standards within the ISO, and it is these same national agencies that promote ISO standards in their own country. Compliance with the standards will often be required either to secure market access, or because the regulatory requirements are incorporated in national laws, directly or indirectly.[255]

The ISO was officially born in 1947, following a meeting of delegates from twenty-five countries to discuss the future of international standardization. It is a non-governmental organization, with members from 165 countries

[252] Shaffer, 'How the WTO Shapes Regulatory Governance', 10.

[253] See above, pp. 569–80. [254] See www.iso.org/iso/home.html.

[255] W. Mattli and T. Büthe, 'Setting International Standards: Technological Rationality or Primacy of Power' (2003) 56 *World Politics* 1.

and a Central Secretariat that now employs circa 150 people, as compared with five in the early 1950s. It has produced in excess of 19,500 standards, which cover pretty much all aspects of business, food and technology.

The national standards bodies constitute the ISO membership and they represent the ISO in their country. The ISO Statute stipulates that 'the member bodies shall be those national standards bodies most broadly representative of standardization in their respective countries and which have been admitted into the Organization in accordance with procedures defined by Council'.[256] It is the full members that influence ISO standards development and strategy by participating and voting in ISO technical and policy meetings. It is the full members that also sell and adopt ISO standards nationally. There are correspondent members that attend ISO meetings as observers, and can also sell such standards nationally,[257] whereas subscriber members merely keep up to date with ISO business.

The ISO General Assembly decides on strategic objectives, but meets only once per year. The real work of the ISO is done at the executive level by the Central Secretariat and the ISO Council, assisted by a number of committees, and at the technical level by technical committees, which devise the standards, overseen by a technical management board. There are in excess of 250 such committees, composed of technical experts, as well as representatives of industry, NGOs and governments.[258] ISO full members decide whether

[256] Art. 3.1.1 ISO Statute. [257] Art. 3.1.2 ISO Statute.

[258] See www.iso.org/iso/home/standards_development/list_of_iso_technical_committees.htm.

they would like to be a participating member of a particular committee, or merely an observer.[259] Consumer interests are taken into account in standard setting through consumer representatives of national members in the technical committees; the ISO Committee on Consumer Policy;[260] and through Consumers International, a federation of consumer groups from around the world.[261]

(ii) The practical and normative consequences for administrative law

The schema of private standard setting embodied in the ISO is very different from the state-dominated form of global regulation in the WTO, and this is reflected in different senses of shared administration that prevail in the two settings. These differences have important practical and normative consequences for administrative law.

In terms of input legitimacy, the private standard setting undertaken by the ISO is predicated on consensual agreement formally embodied in the ISO Statute, reflective of the simple legal precept that it is open to individuals or private organizations to create a legal entity operating at the global level, which will be formally registered in a particular country. This is, of course, only part of input legitimacy, albeit the most formal part. Input legitimacy in this context also connotes the idea that those who wish to partake in the standard-setting process must come to the table with

[259] See www.iso.org/iso/home/about/iso_members.htm.

[260] See www.iso.org/iso/home/about/iso-and-the-consumer/copolco.htm.

[261] See www.consumersinternational.org/who-we-are/about-us.

the requisite technical and scientific expertise. This 'reinforces the transnational standard-setting body's legitimacy, which is based on technical expertise', and, by 'rendering other (political or economic) arguments impermissible and illegitimate, safeguards the transnational body against overt and political and especially government interference'.[262]

There is a further dimension to input legitimacy in the ISO context, which is the most controversial. The ISO is private in formal terms, in the sense that it is non-governmental, but compliance with the relevant standards will often be required either to secure market access or because the regulatory requirements are incorporated in national or EU laws, directly or indirectly. We will explore this more fully below, when discussing the regulatory dimension of the ISO, and its linkage with national and EU standardization bodies. Suffice it to say for the present that the fact that these 'private' standards are then transformed into 'public' obligations or options perforce raises legitimacy concerns. Thus while bodies such as the ISO emphasize the technical, scientific nature of the inquiry, the reality is that standard setting inevitably entails matters of risk assessment and cost–benefit analysis, which are not and cannot be value-free.

In terms of transparency, the ISO fares well when judged by the transparency of the results. Its standards are readily available to view, which is unsurprising given that the

[262] T. Büthe and W. Mattli, *The New Global Rulers: The Privatization of Regulation in the World Economy* (Princeton: Princeton University Press, 2011), p. 45.

ISO seeks to sell the standards thus promulgated.[263] The formal process by which such standards are adopted is also clear, the lead being taken by a panel of experts, within a technical committee. When the need for a standard is established, the experts negotiate a draft standard, which is then shared with ISO members, who comment and vote on it. It may be sent back to the technical committee if consensus is not forthcoming.[264] The catalyst for development of a new standard normally comes from industry or a stakeholder group, rather than from within the ISO.

While the standard-making process is transparent in the preceding sense it is nonetheless evident that those proposing the standard, together with those stakeholders best informed and organized, have a very considerable influence on the draft that emerges from the technical committee and hence on the resulting standard.[265] Moreover, the preceding concerns as to the value-laden nature of standardization in turn generate concern as to who has 'voice' in the standard-setting process, and the extent to which consumer interests and those of the developing world are adequately represented. This explains the ISO's efforts to portray the way in which such interests are taken into account,[266] although the extent and efficacy of such input have been doubted. Thus Sidney

[263] See www.iso.org/iso/home/store.htm; www.iso.org/iso/home/store/catalogue_ics.htm.

[264] See www.iso.org/iso/home/standards_development.htm.

[265] Büthe and Mattli, *The New Global Rulers*, pp. 162–86.

[266] See www.iso.org/iso/home/standards_development/who-develops-iso-standards.htm; www.iso.org/iso/home/about/iso-and-the-consumer/copolco.htm.

Shapiro notes that while the Codex Alimentarius and the ISO provide for some public representation, 'the vast majority of standards established by these organizations were drafted behind closed doors, typically only with governmental and private industry at the table'.[267] It is also important to recognize that interested parties may have scant information that a standard is being developed and hence are unable to contribute to the process,[268] an issue that will be returned to below.

In terms of judicial review, we need to tread carefully. There is no judicial organ within the ISO that subjects its work to review, either procedurally or substantively. This does not mean that the ISO fails to comply with procedural precepts such as due process, or substantive precepts such as rationality. It does mean that there is no judicial body within the ISO to which appeal can be made by a party affected by a standard who seeks to argue that it is infirm in such respects. If judicial recourse is to be had it must then be via a court at national or regional level. Whether this is feasible will depend on the principles of review that pertain within that system, more particularly those that determine

[267] S. Shapiro, 'International Trade Agreements, Regulatory Protection, and Public Accountability' (2002) 54 *Administrative Law Review* 435, at 451. See also Wallach, 'Accountable Government in the Era of Globalization: The WTO, NAFTA and the International Harmonization of Standards', 839; P. Delimatsis, '"Relevant International Standards" and "Recognized Standardization Bodies under the TBT Agreement"', TILEC Discussion Paper, DP 2014–31.

[268] Shapiro, 'International Trade Agreements, Regulatory Protection, and Public Accountability'.

the type of norms that are susceptible to judicial review. There will, of course, be differences in this respect between different systems.

The potential claimant is nonetheless likely to face similar difficulties within many legal systems, being caught between a rock and a hard place. If the contested standard is not formally embodied in national or EU legislation, then a court may well simply decide that it is not sufficiently 'public' for the purposes of judicial review, even if compliance with the standard is de facto required for entry to a particular market. If, by way of contrast, it is incorporated in national or EU legislation then the court may find either that it is unreviewable in legal systems where primary legislation is not subject to judicial review save on limited constitutional grounds, or, even if the court is willing to review because the standard is embodied in a secondary national norm, it may well do so with a light touch, mindful of the ISO's technical expertise.[269]

[269] Thus, in relation to EU law, there would be considerable difficulties for a non-privileged party in establishing standing to seek direct judicial review, given that the standard by its very nature would constitute a general act applicable to a broad number of operators in the relevant area. If this hurdle were overcome, there would then be issues concerning the nature and intensity of any such review. A claimant would have to show some manifest error in relation to fact or discretion in relation to the contested standard. Craig, *EU Administrative Law*, Chs. 11, 15; P. Craig, 'Legal Control over Regulatory Bodies: Principle, Policy and Teleology', in P. Birkinshaw and M. Varney (eds.), *The European Legal Order after Lisbon* (Alphen aan den Rijn: Kluwer Law International, 2010), Ch. 5.

The latter is particularly likely to occur in a legal regime such as the EU, where many of the standards are based on ISO standards, and where the Commission has persistently emphasized that it does not determine the detailed content of the standards. It accepts that it does not have the requisite expertise to influence the content of standards, while stressing the 'governmental role' in establishing the objectives and targets, leaving it to the standardization bodies to decide on the content of the standards and the best way of meeting governmental objectives. Thus the Commission has stated that 'the technical contents of such harmonised standards are under the entire responsibility of the European standardisation organisations', and that EU harmonization legislation does not 'foresee a procedure under which public authorities would systematically verify or approve either at Union or national level the contents of harmonised standards, which have been adopted by European standardisation organisations'.[270]

In regulatory terms, ISO standardization is a quintessential example of shared administration operating between the global, regional and national levels. We have already touched on this when describing the ISO regime and the fact that the full members are the principal national standardization bodies, which help shape the standards and sell them. The regulatory interaction is, however, more far-reaching than this. There is a symbiotic link between ISO and EU

[270] The 'Blue Guide' on the Implementation of EU Product Rules 2014, para. 4.1.2.2, http://ec.europa.eu/enterprise/policies/european-standards/links/index_en.htm.

standardization,[271] such that 'European standards, including harmonised standards, are often based fully or partially on international ISO or IEC standards'.[272] The resulting EU standards have a real impact on the national level, since they are the most direct way of showing conformity to the essential safety objectives specified in EU legislation.[273] This symbiotic connection is further formalized through the Vienna and Dresden Agreements made between the ISO and the EU standardization bodies.[274] Thus the Vienna Agreement recognizes the primacy of international standards, but recognizes also that the EU may have particular needs in relation to standardization. The agreement therefore provides for the ISO to take the lead in relation to some standards, while the European Committee for Standardization (CEN) takes the

[271] The principal bodies responsible for EU standardization are the European Committee for Standardization (CEN) the European Committee for Electrotechnical Standardization (CENELEC), and the European Telecommunications Standards Institute (ETSI). These bodies are private organizations, with CEN and CENELEC being non-profit technical organizations established under Belgian law in 1961 and 1973 respectively, and ETSI being a non-profit organization set up under French law in 1986.

[272] The 'Blue Guide' on the Implementation of EU Product Rules 2014, para. 4.1.2.4.

[273] Enhancing the Implementation of New Approach Directives, COM (2003) 240; The 'Blue Guide' on the Implementation of EU Product Rules 2014.

[274] Agreement on Technical Co-operation between ISO and CEN (Vienna Agreement), www.cencenelec.eu/intcoop/StandardizationOrg/Pages/default.aspx; IEC–CENELEC Agreement on Common Planning of New Work and Parallel Voting (Dresden Agreement), www.cenelec.eu/aboutcenelec/whoweare/globalpartners/iec.html.

lead on others, with documentation developed by one body being notified for the simultaneous approval by the other.

There is, however, more to this linkage between standardization organizations than symbiotic interaction. There is the all-important issue of whose standard becomes the ISO accepted norm, with the competition commonly between Europe and the US. Büthe and Mattli argue convincingly that Europe has the edge in this respect, with the consequence that it is US firms that more often must bear the costs of modification to comply with the new ISO standard. This is because countries or systems with greater domestic co-ordination and institutional hierarchy in standard-setting benefit from greater complementarity, such that they have greater influence on ISO standard-setting 'because such domestic institutions facilitate effective interest aggregation and information flows'.[275]

(e) *Regulatory norms and the interaction between legal orders: shared administration and the role of national administrative law*

The discussion thus far has considered the different variants of shared administration that characterize the interplay between the global, regional and national legal orders. The development of precepts of administrative law at the global level has been fostered as a way of alleviating concerns about the accountability and legitimacy of global governance regimes. It is nonetheless important to shift

[275] Büthe and Mattli, *The New Global Rulers*, p. 162.

the focus to the contribution that national administrative law might make in this respect.

This is in part because certain global regimes, such as the WTO, have provisions mandating judicial review at national level, and it is therefore central to the success of such regimes that this operates efficaciously to ensure, for example, that national authorities comply with their obligations under the respective WTO agreements. It is the national judicial forum through which state accountability is initially secured, in the sense of checking that the state does not seek to, for example, impose anti-dumping duties when they are not warranted, or attempt to engage in covert protectionism through imposition of sanitary constraints on foreign goods for which there is no objective need. National courts should, where the system operates properly, function as the first point of redress, with disputes only going to the WTO settlement mechanism if they cannot be otherwise resolved legally or politically.

There is, however, a different rationale for paying attention to the potential contribution of national administrative law. This is because even if precepts of global administrative law are developed, there will continue to be accountability gaps that can only be filled lower down, whether at the regional or national level or both.[276]

[276] D. Barak-Erez and O. Perez, 'The Administrative State Goes Global', in M. Helfand (ed.), *Negotiating State and Non-state Law: The Challenge of Global and Local Legal Pluralism* (Cambridge: Cambridge University Press, 2015), Ch. 6.

Thus Stewart, in his seminal study, notes the dramatic shift of regulatory authority from the nation state to a 'dizzying variety of global regulatory regimes', the result being that 'domestic systems of administrative accountability through law are being increasingly sidestepped' by regulatory norms produced by global regimes that are not subject to such disciplines, which are then implemented through domestic regulation.[277] This in turn can exacerbate the danger that the global regulatory process will be captured by powerful, well-organized interests, to the detriment of consumer groups, environmentalists and the like.[278] The problem is exemplified by the fact that a

> government agency that determines capital adequacy requirements for banks, runs a pollution credit trading system, or freezes the assets of suspected terrorists would typically be subject to some form of administrative law procedures for decision-making that would afford the right to present evidence and argument by those affected, and to review by a court. These rights do not exist for the Basel Committee, the Kyoto Protocol Clean Development Mechanism Executive Board, and the Security Council's 1267 Al Qaeda Sanctions Committee respectively.[279]

[277] Stewart, 'The Global Regulatory Challenge to U.S. Administrative Law', 695.

[278] Stewart, 'The Global Regulatory Challenge to U.S. Administrative Law', 706.

[279] Stewart, 'The Global Regulatory Challenge to U.S. Administrative Law', 702, although there have been some improvements in these areas since the article was written in 2005.

Shapiro also considers the effect of international standardization, WTO adjudication and equivalency obligations on the normal regime for accountability of regulation in the US. He argues that compliance with the Administrative Procedure Act 1946 (APA) notice and comment requirements may be ineffective in achieving citizen participation in the development of an international harmonized regulation, since the APA does not require an agency to seek public input in advance of agreeing to a harmonized standard, and when the agreement has been made, 'there is an international commitment by the United States to adopt the harmonized regulation, which creates a substantial disincentive to change or amend the international standard during rulemaking'.[280] In relation to the WTO, Shapiro contends that public participation in the US may be frustrated because any amended rule that an agency proposes to comply with a WTO result may effectively be a fait accompli, coupled with the lack of public participation in the WTO dispute resolution process.[281]

Wallach voices analogous concerns that 'harmonization moves decision making away from accessible, accountable state and national governance fora to international bodies that are largely inaccessible to citizens and generally operate without accountability to those who must live with their decisions', more especially given that 'standard-setting requires not only scientific knowledge, but also subjective

[280] Shapiro, 'International Trade Agreements, Regulatory Protection, and Public Accountability', 441.

[281] Shapiro, 'International Trade Agreements, Regulatory Protection, and Public Accountability', 449.

policy decisions about the level of risk a society is willing to accept'.[282] In similar vein, Aman notes that 'the democratic processes used to conform domestic law to an international ruling may, in reality, be substantially less than those used to create these rules or laws in the first place',[283] as exemplified by the fact that although amendment to domestic law to comply with WTO imperatives will be undertaken through a process that appears democratic, 'the outcomes usually are a foregone conclusion' given the prior Treaty commitments.[284]

There are various possible responses to such concerns. It might be argued that there is no such accountability gap, provided that the precepts of global administrative law really are properly developed and applied at the international or transnational level, although such an argument would be difficult to sustain in empirical and normative terms. The preceding critiques might alternatively be accepted, subject to the caveat that the negative effect on domestic regulatory processes is inevitable, to some degree, in any sphere where international law broadly conceived impacts on national law. It might, by way of contrast, be contended that the negative impact on domestic regulatory mechanisms is regrettable, but no more so than the converse accountability gap that exists when domestic regulations are made without taking cognizance of their effect on outsiders – the disjunction between regulatory jurisdiction and regulatory impact noted earlier.

282 Wallach, 'Accountable Government in the Era of Globalization: The WTO, NAFTA and the International Harmonization of Standards', 863.

283 Aman, *The Democracy Deficit*, p. 4.

284 Aman, *The Democracy Deficit*, p. 4.

A further possibility is to acknowledge the problem, but attempt to 'do something' about it, albeit being mindful of the difficulties involved.

It is worth dwelling on this latter strategy, which coheres with the very idea of shared administration adumbrated above. Given that global regulatory initiatives will commonly entail some form of shared administration with the regional or national level, it is unsurprising that administrative law mechanisms to enhance accountability might have to be fashioned for the global level *and* adjusted at the regional and/or national level.

Of relevance in this respect is Barack Obama's executive order made in 2012 designed to foster international regulatory co-operation.[285] The general policy underlying the order is to promote such co-operation and encourage compromise between US regulatory agencies and their foreign counterparts, in order to prevent, reduce or eliminate unnecessary differences in regulatory requirements. To this end, agencies are charged with ensuring that regulations that have significant international impacts are designated as such, and the agencies must consider eradication of unnecessary regulatory differences when pointed out by stakeholders.

A decade earlier, the American Bar Association was cognizant of the need for adjustment of national administrative law, recommending in 2001 that the president should seek to ensure effective public participation by encouraging federal agencies to list at an appropriate time significant harmonization activities in their annual regulatory agendas

[285] Exec. Order No 13,609, 77 Fed. Reg. 26,413 (1 May 2012).

or some analogous medium. The ABA recommended that agencies should invite the public to comment on new and ongoing significant harmonization activities, including attendance at meetings concerning such activities; should refer significant harmonization issues to advisory committees, where appropriate and feasible; and should make available, under the Freedom of Information Act (FOIA), documents relating to each significant harmonization activity.[286]

From an academic perspective it is Stewart who has worked through the implications of increased global regulation for national administrative law in most detail.[287] He articulates three possible models of interaction.[288] The first he terms the 'bottom-up' approach, whereby domestic administrative law is applied in order to assert more effective control over the supranational elements of domestic regulation by, for example, extending national administrative law process requirements and judicial review to decisions and norms of global regimes implemented by US agencies, or by insisting that the agency address the global elements in its decision, and include them in its review. The second model is 'top-down', whereby the global regulatory regimes develop more fully the type of administrative law safeguards commonly found in national systems, in the manner considered in the first half of this chapter. Stewart's third model of global

[286] Shapiro, 'International Trade Agreements, Regulatory Protection, and Public Accountability', 444–5.

[287] See also J. Marisam, 'The Internationalization of Agency Actions' (2015) 83 *Fordham Law Review* 1909.

[288] Stewart, 'The Global Regulatory Challenge to U.S. Administrative Law', 709–11. See also Stewart, 'Remedying Disregard', 231–3.

administrative law follows an 'integrative' logic 'through substantive principles and regulatory due process requirements applicable to decisions by domestic agencies that affect international trade and investment, aliens, and other extra-national interests'.[289]

Aman has also made valuable suggestions in this respect, which seek to address both dimensions of accountability set out earlier.[290] Thus he urges that 'administrative rule-making processes should include an explicit direction to consider seriously the global implications of proposed rules',[291] which would 'not only encourage participants to indicate the transboundary effects of a rule but also provide a domestic forum to raise the issue'.[292] Aman, in accord with the ABA's approach, also seeks to shift the focus from *post hoc* compliance with the demands of standardization or WTO rulings, to 'the much earlier stages in the decision-making processes when a dialogue on how best to mesh domestic law with likely WTO requirements can take place within domestic political institutions'.[293]

Space precludes detailed discussion of such initiatives. Suffice it to say that this is not a zero-sum game, and these initiatives should therefore be regarded as operating in

[289] Stewart, 'The Global Regulatory Challenge to U.S. Administrative Law', 710–11.

[290] See above, pp. 768–74.

[291] Aman, *The Democracy Deficit*, p. 150. See also A. Aman, 'Globalization, Democracy, and the Need for a New Administrative Law' (2002) 49 *University of California Los Angeles Law Review* 1687.

[292] Aman, *The Democracy Deficit*, p. 151.

[293] Aman, *The Democracy Deficit*, pp. 161–2.

tandem with developments to enhance at the global level accountability of the kind analysed in the first half of this chapter. There are perforce limits as to the transferability of such specific proposals to other states, which have very different domestic mechanisms for securing rule-making accountability. This does not, however, undermine the underlying thrust of this approach, drawing as it does on national and global administrative law.

(f) Individual decision making and regulatory norms: courts and the interaction between legal orders

The vertical dimension will also be markedly affected by the interrelationship between global, regional and national courts. This can arise in a variety of contexts,[294] and is exemplified by the EU jurisprudence on the enforceability of WTO decisions, which in turn raises issues concerning the effect of international agreements within the EU legal order. The ensuing discussion reveals that problems concerning the vertical dimension are not merely 'one-way', with the global having an impact on the regional or national, but the stance taken by regional or national courts may impact in contestable ways on the applicability of global norms at regional or national level.

[294] See, generally, Y. Shany, *The Competing Jurisdictions of International Courts and Tribunals* (Oxford: Oxford University Press, 2004); Y. Shany, *Regulating Jurisdictional Relations between National and International Courts* (Oxford: Oxford University Press, 2007).

The general principle is that international agreements made by the EU are regarded as an integral part of the EU legal order,[295] and are binding on the EU pursuant to Article 216(2) TFEU. The key issue in relation to GATT and the successor WTO is whether they have direct effect, such as to give rise to rights that can be invoked by individuals if they are sufficiently precise and certain. While the ECJ accepted that international agreements can be directly effective under certain circumstances,[296] it has nonetheless been markedly reluctant to find that such conditions are satisfied in relation to GATT and the WTO.

The issue arose in *International Fruit*[297] in terms of the possible incompatibility of a Community regulation with GATT, the General Agreement on Tariffs and Trade. The ECJ held that while the EEC was bound by GATT, the provisions thereof were not directly effective so as to generate rights that individuals could rely on in their national courts to contest the validity of the Community regulation. The ECJ reached this conclusion having considered the purpose, spirit, and general scheme of GATT. It found that the flexibility of its

[295] Case 181/73, *Haegeman* [1974] ECR 449, at [5]; *Opinion 1/91 (EEA Agreement 1)* [1991] ECR 6079, at [37].

[296] Case 104/81, *Hauptzollamt Mainz* v. *CA Kupferberg & Cie KG* [1982] ECR 3641; Case 9/73, *Schluter* v. *Hauptzollamt Lörrach* [1973] ECR 1135; Case C-469/93, *Amministrazione delle Finanze dello Stato Chiquita Italia* [1995] ECR 1-4533; G. Bebr, 'Agreements Concluded by the Community and their Possible Direct Effect: From International Fruit Company to Kupferberg' (1983) 20 *Common Market Law Review* 35.

[297] Cases 21–4/72, *International Fruit Company* v. *Produktschap voor Groenten en Fruit* [1972] ECR 1219.

provisions, combined with the possibility of derogation, and the power of unilateral withdrawal from its obligations, meant that it was not capable of conferring rights that individuals could invoke before national courts. This conclusion was influenced in some degree at least by the fact that the international obligations derived from GATT were commonly used to challenge the legality of EU legislation.

It remained to be seen whether the ECJ would change its stance following the establishment of the WTO and the adoption of the new GATT in 1994, given the more effective means of dispute settlement and enforcement under the new system. Those who hoped that the ECJ would modify its previous position were,[298] however, to be disappointed by the decision in *Portugal* v. *Council*.[299] Portugal brought an action for annulment of a 1996 Council decision, arguing that it was in breach of WTO rules. The ECJ, while noting the differences between the WTO regime and the pre-existing GATT schema, nonetheless held that the former still gave considerable importance to negotiation between the parties. The ECJ noted further that some of the contracting parties to the WTO had concluded from its subject matter and purpose

[298] E.-U. Petersmann, 'The Dispute Settlement System of the World Trade Organization and the Evolution of the GATT Dispute Settlement System since 1948' (1994) 31 *Common Market Law Review* 1157; and E.-U. Petersmann, 'Proposals for a New Constitution for the European Union: Building Blocks for a Constitutional Theory and Constitutional Law of the EU' (1995) 32 *Common Market Law Review* 1123.

[299] Case C-149/96, *Portugal* v. *Council* [1999] ECR I-8395.

that it was not among the rules applicable by their judicial organs when reviewing the legality of their rules of domestic law. This lack of reciprocity by the Community's trading partners could lead to lack of uniformity in application of WTO rules. It would, moreover, deprive the Community legislative or executive organs of the scope for manoeuvre enjoyed by their counterparts in the Community's trading partners. The ECJ therefore concluded that the WTO agreements were not in principle among the rules in the light of which the Court reviewed the legality of measures adopted by the Community institutions. The judgment provoked considerable academic commentary,[300] but the ECJ and the General Court have proved resistant to attempts to limit it,[301] confirming the application of the *Portugal* ruling to other WTO agreements.[302]

[300] G. de Búrca and J. Scott (eds.), *The EU and the WTO: Legal and Constitutional Issues* (Oxford: Hart, 2001); G. Zonnekeyn, 'The Status of WTO Law in the Community Legal Order: Some Comments in the Light of the Portuguese Textiles Case' (2000) 25 *European Law Review* 293; S. Griller, 'Judicial Enforceability of WTO Law in the EU' (2000) 3 *Journal of International Economic Law* 441; A. Rosas, *Portugal* v. *Council* (2000) 37 *Common Market Law Review* 797.

[301] Case C-307/99, *OGT* v. *Hauptzollamt Hamburg-St. Annen* [2001] ECR I-3159.

[302] Case C-89/99, *Schieving-Nijstad* v. *Groeneveld* [2001] ECR I-5851; Case T-279/03, *Galileo International Technology LLC* v. *Commission* [2006] ECR II-1291; Cases C-27 and 122/00, *The Queen* v. *Secretary of State for the Environment, Transport and the Regions, ex parte Omega Air Ltd and Others* [2002] ECR I-2569; Case C-351/04, *Ikea Wholesale* [2007] ECR I-7723; Cases C-120 and 121/06, *FIAMM and Fedon* v. *Council and Commission* [2008] ECR I-6513.

The ECJ has, by way of contrast, been more willing to recognize the enforceability of some other international agreements, even where they did not involve special integration relations with the EU.[303] It has, a fortiori, been willing to accept the direct effect of provisions of association or cooperation agreements with third countries,[304] as well as secondary decisions adopted by association councils or bodies set up under those agreements,[305] since these are regarded as establishing 'special relations of integration'.[306]

It remains, however, to be seen whether the ruling in *Intertanko* heralds some change in this respect, given that the ECJ applied the restrictive reasoning from the GATT/WTO case law to a different international agreement.[307] It refused to assess the validity of EU legislation in the light of the UN Convention on the Law of the Sea (UNCLOS), or the related MARPOL (marine pollution) Convention, holding

303 Case C-162/96, *Racke GmbH & Co.* v. *Hauptzollamt Mainz* [1998] ECR I-3655; Case C-377/98, *Netherlands* v. *Council* [2001] ECR I-7079; Case C-213/03, *Syndicat professionnel coordination des pêcheurs de l'étang de Berre et de la région* v. *EDF* [2004] ECR I-7357.

304 See, e.g., Case C-18/90, *Onem v. Kziber* [1991] ECR I-199; Case C-103/94, *Krid* v. *WAVTS* [1995] ECR I-719; Case C-37/98, *Savas* [2000] ECR I-2927.

305 See, e.g., Case 12/86, *Demirel* v. *Stadt Schwäbisch Gmünd* [1987] ECR 3719; Case C-192/89, *Sevince* [1990] ECR I-3461; Case C-337/07, *Altun* [2008] ECR I-10323.

306 Case C-149/96, *Portugal* v. *Council*, at [42].

307 Case C-308/06, *Intertanko and Others* [2008] ECR I-4057. Similar reasoning is evident in Case C-366/10, *ATAA* v. *Secretary of State for Energy and Climate Change*, EU:C:2011:864; Case C-363/12, *Z.* v. *A Government Department*, EU:C:2014:159.

that UNCLOS did not grant independent rights and freedoms to individuals, and that the nature of UNCLOS prevented the Court from being able to assess the validity of a Community measure in the light of that Convention.

4 Conclusion

The development of global governance institutions, whether pursuant to traditional international treaties, or more informal transnational regulatory networks, raises numerous concerns, including the fear of domination of decision making by unelected experts, the lack of transparency, and the circumvention of the normal rules of representative democracy, allowing policy to be developed without the imprimatur of the elected legislature. There is considerable debate as to how far the increase in global regulatory governance undermines ordinary democratic precepts, or whether it may in certain circumstances enhance them, by, for example, ensuring that the interests of other states are taken into account in national decision making, or by pressing democratic precepts on states that do not adhere to them.[308] There is, moreover, the related but distinct issue concerning the degree of scrutiny that international treaties receive and the values that they embody, as captured by Joseph Weiler:

[308] See, e.g., R. Keohane, S. Macedo and A. Moravcsik, 'Democracy-Enhancing Multilateralism' (2009) 63 *International Organization* 1; Cassese, *The Global Polity*, pp. 77–101; A. von Bogdandy, 'Globalization and Europe: How to Square Democracy and Globalization' (2004) 15 *European Journal of International Law* 885.

> There may be some continued currency to national interest in matters of, say, war and peace and consequently in their reflection in things like mutual defense pacts and the like. But no one can today credibly argue that bilateral treaties of the 'Friendship, Navigation and Commerce' type of which, say, the United States continues to have a plethora, or the bilateral 'free trade areas' which the European Union has with more than half the countries of the world are a non-contested manifestation of the 'national interest'. They are agreements rooted in a certain worldview, which vindicate certain internal socio-economic interests. This, in turn, presents two delicate issues: One is the measure of democratic scrutiny, which treaties such as these receive, in developed democracies such as the USA or the EU. They often receive far less democratic scrutiny than domestic legislation with the same socio-economic redistributive impact. This is certainly quite commonly the case in Europe and not at all infrequent in the USA. The second problem is that economic giants such as the USA and the EU can impose such Treaties on lesser states not only leaving them with little or no margin of negotiation, but with even less concern to their (the would be partner's) internal democratic scrutiny.[309]

The development of principles of global administrative law is not a panacea that can resolve all such issues, some of which go considerably beyond the scope of this work. The reality is that global governance, whether through international organizations or transnational regulatory networks,

[309] Weiler, 'The Geology of International Law', 555–6.

is not going to disappear, and global replication of national electoral models is empirically unlikely and normatively problematic. The development of principles of global administrative law can, however, contribute to the development of more accountable global governance, the value of which should not be underestimated.

INDEX

For EU product safety concerns, contact us at Calle de José Abascal, 56–1°,
28003 Madrid, Spain or eugpsr@cambridge.org.

www.ingramcontent.com/pod-product-compliance
Lightning Source LLC
LaVergne TN
LVHW020325220926
848484LV00001BB/7
* 9 7 8 1 1 0 7 1 2 5 1 2 4 *